DOMESDAY

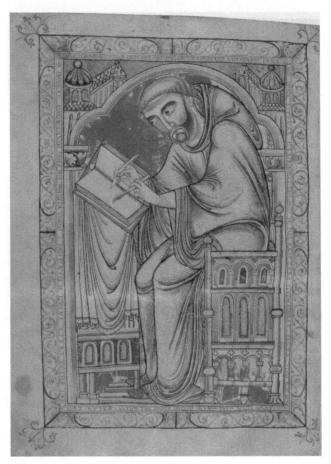

Figure 1. Eadwine the Scribe from the Canterbury Psalter mid twelfth century. Cambridge Trinity College, MS R.17.1, f.283v. By permission of the Master and Fellows of Trinity College, Cambridge.

Domesday

Book of Judgement

SALLY HARVEY

OXFORD

UNIVERSITY PRESS

OXFORD

UNIVERSITY PRESS

Great Clarendon Street, Oxford, OX2 6DP,
United Kingdom

Oxford University Press is a department of the University of Oxford.
It furthers the University's objective of excellence in research, scholarship,
and education by publishing worldwide. Oxford is a registered trade mark of
Oxford University Press in the UK and in certain other countries

First Edition published in 2014

Impression: 1

Published in the United States of America by Oxford University Press
198 Madison Avenue, New York, NY 10016, United States of America

British Library Cataloguing in Publication Data
Data available

Library of Congress Control Number: 2013953480

ISBN 978–0–19–966978–3

As printed and bound by
CPI Group (UK) Ltd, Croydon, CR0 4YY

For L. F.

Preface

I am very grateful to Jean Birrell, Roy Bridge, and my husband, Leslie Fielding, who have read this work in entirety at some point, contributing immeasurably to its readability, and to my Oxford readers for their contributions. I am also grateful to Martin Allen, the late Nicholas Brooks, Howard Clarke, Christopher Dyer, Rosamond Faith, George Garnett, John Grassi, Emma Mason, Michael Metcalf, and Ann Williams who have commented knowledgeably upon drafts of individual chapters—although I have by no means always followed their counsel! And the late Caroline Thorn and Frank Thorn have commented upon various chapter drafts, furnished me with material, and taken time to agree and disagree with scholarship and enthusiasm. Julia Barrow, Judith Green, Pamela Nightingale, David Roffe, and Pamela Taylor have also kindly provided material. Errors of fact and judgement, of course, remain my responsibility. I thank Clare Hall, Cambridge, for a term's fellowship and the University of Birmingham, where I was a student, for giving me an honorary fellowship and access to its Library, whose staff have been unfailingly sympathetic.

Contents

II. THE PURPOSES OF THE INQUIRY AND THE BOOK

List of Figures

Cover Image. The Durham sanctuary door-knocker (*c.*1130) offered the prospect of
sanctuary for fugitives to the protection of St Cuthbert at Durham Cathedral.
Bishop Rannulf (1099–1128) both venerated and feared St Cuthbert, whose
sanctuary, as with the nave of Durham Cathedral, he re-built. Yet, William of
Malmesbury asserted that Bishop Rannulf removed 'without hesitation any
criminal who took refuge in the saint's church'; and, as royal clerk and as
bishop, Rannulf actively pursued fleeing peasants with royal writs. Thus the
knocker may stand as representative of the paradox–the piety and the
ruthlessness–of Norman rule. The original remained on the North door until
recently, when it was removed to the museum.

Table

List of Abbreviations

Acta	*Regesta Regum Anglo-Normannorum: The Acta of William I 1066–1087*, ed. D. Bates (Oxford, 1998), cited by number
Alecto	*Domesday Book*, ed. R. W. H. Erskine, A. Williams, and G. H. Martin (London: Alecto Historical Editions, 1986–2000)
Ann Winton	*Annales Monastici*, ed. H. R. Luard, vol. 2, Rolls Series (RS) 36 (London, 1864–9)
ANS	*Anglo-Norman Studies*
Anselmi Opera 4	*Sancti Anselmi Opera Omnia*, vol. 4, ed. F. S. Schmitt (Edinburgh, 1949), *Epistolae*, by number
ASC	*The Anglo-Saxon Chronicle*, ed. D. Whitelock with D. C. Douglas and S. I. Tucker (London, 1961), under edited year
ASE	*Anglo-Saxon England*
Barlow, *Anglo-Norman Church*	F. Barlow, *The English Church, 1066–1154: A History of the Anglo-Norman Church* (London, 1979)
Barlow, *Confessor*	F. Barlow, *Edward the Confessor* (London, 1970)
Barlow, *English Church*	F. Barlow, *The English Church: A Constitutional History, 1000–1066* (London, 1963)
Barlow, *Rufus*	F. Barlow, *William Rufus* (London, 1983)
Bartlett	R. Bartlett, *England under the Norman and Angevin Kings 1075–1225* (Oxford, 2000)
Bartlett, *Ordeal*	R. Bartlett, *Trial by Fire and Water: The Medieval Judicial Ordeal* (Oxford, 1986)
BJRL	*Bulletin of the John Rylands Library*
BNJ	*British Numismatic Journal*
BT	F. Stenton, Simone Bertrand, et al. (eds), *The Bayeux Tapestry: A Comprehensive Survey* (London, 1957)
Caen, Chibnall	*Charters and Customals of the Abbey of Holy Trinity, Caen*, ed. M. Chibnall, British Academy Records of Social and Economic History, NS 5, Oxford Medieval Texts (Oxford, 1982)
Cam	H. M. Cam, *The Hundred and the Hundred Rolls*, 2nd edn (London, 1963)
Charters	*Anglo-Saxon Charters*, ed. A. J. Robertson, (Cambridge, 1939)
ChronAbing	*Chronicon Monasterii de Abingdon*, ed. J. Stevenson, 2 vols, RS 2 (London, 1858)
DB: Gloucestershire	*Domesday Book 15: Gloucestershire*, ed. J. S. Moore (Chichester, 1982)
DB: Worcestershire	*Domesday Book 16: Worcestershire*, ed. F. and C. Thorn (Chichester, 1982)

DB4	Domesday Book Record Commission (London, 1816), cited by folio of original [see *Exon*]
Dialogus	*Dialogus de Scaccario* [The Dialogue of the Exchequer], ed. C. Johnson (London, 1950)
Dispute Settlement	W. Davies and P. Fouracre (eds), *The Settlement of Disputes in Early Medieval Europe* (Cambridge, 1986)
DMon	*Domesday Monachorum of Christ Church, Canterbury*, ed. D. C. Douglas, Royal Historical Society (RHS) (London, 1944)
Douglas, *Conqueror*	D. C. Douglas, *William the Conqueror* (London, 1964)
Eadmer	*Eadmeri Historia Novorum in Anglia*, ed. M. Rule, RS 81 (London, 1884), with translations from *Eadmer's History of Recent Events in England*, tr. G. Bosanquet (London, 1964)
ECHR	*Economic History Review*
EHD1	English Historical Documents, vol. 1, ed. D. Whitelock, 2nd edn (London, 1979)
EHD2	English Historical Documents, vol. 2: 1142–1189, ed. D. C. Douglas and G. W. Greenaway, 2nd edn (London, 1981)
EHD3	English Historical Documents, vol. 3: 1189–1327, ed. H. Rothwell (London, 1975)
EHR	*English Historical Review*
Erskine and Williams	R. W. H. Erskine and A. Williams (eds), *The Story of Domesday* (Chichester, 2003)
Evesham A	'Evesham A: a Domesday text', ed. P. H. Sawyer, in *Miscellany*, vol. 1, Worcestershire Historical Society, (Worcester, 1960), commentary, 3–21, text 22–36
Exon	Domesday Book Record Commission, vol. 4 (London, 1816), cited by folio [see DB4]
Feudal Documents	*Feudal Documents from the Abbey of Bury St Edmunds*, ed. D. C. Douglas, British Academy, Records of Social and Economic History, vol. 8 (London, 1932)
Finn, *LExon*	R. W. Finn, *Domesday Studies: The Liber Exoniensis* (London, 1964)
Fleming, *Law*	R. Fleming, *Domesday Book and the Law: Society and Legal Custom in Early Medieval England* (Cambridge, 1998)
Galbraith	V. H. Galbraith, *The Making of Domesday Book* (Oxford, 1961)
Garnett	G. Garnett, *Conquered England, Kingship, Succession and Tenure, 1066–1166* (Oxford, 2007)
GDB	Domesday Book Record Commission, vol. 1, ed. A. Farley, (London, 1783), cited by folio and column, a–d
GND	*Gesta Normannorum Ducum of William of Jumièges, Orderic Vitalis, and Robert of Torigni*, ed. E. M. C. van Houts, 3 vols (Oxford, 1992–5)

GP   William of Malmesbury, *De gestis pontificum anglorum*, ed. N. E. S. A. Hamilton, RS 52 (London, 1870; Oxford, 2007)

GRA 1/ GRA 2   William of Malmesbury, *Gesta Regum Anglorum*, ed. and tr. R. A. B. Mynors, R. M. Thomson, and M. Winterbottom, 2 vols, Oxford Medieval Texts (Oxford, 1998–9), cited by page

Green, *Sheriffs*   J. Green, *English Sheriffs to 1154* (London, 1990)

Hallam   E. M. Hallam, *Domesday Book through Nine Centuries* (London, 1986)

Hallam and Bates   *Domesday Book*, ed. E. Hallam and D. Bates (Stroud, 2001)

Harvey 1967   S. Harvey, 'Royal revenue and Domesday terminology', *ECHR*, 2nd ser., 20 (1967), 221–128

Harvey 1970   S. Harvey, 'The knight and the knight's fee', *Past & Present (P&P)*, 49/1 (1970), 3–43

Harvey 1971   S. Harvey, 'Domesday Book and its predecessors', *EHR*, 86, (1971), 753–73

Harvey 1975   S. P. J. Harvey, 'Domesday Book and Anglo-Norman governance', *TRHS*, 5th ser., 25 (1975), 175–93

Harvey 1983   S. P. J. Harvey, 'The extent and profitability of demesne agriculture in England in the later eleventh century', in T. H. Aston, P. R. Coss, Christopher Dyer, and Joan Thirsk (eds), *Social Relations and Ideas: Essays in Honour of R. H. Hilton*, Past & Present Society (Cambridge, 1983), 45–72

Harvey 1985   S. Harvey, 'Taxation and the ploughland', in P. Sawyer (ed.), *Domesday Book: A Reassessment* (London, 1985), 86–103

Harvey 1987   S. P. J. Harvey, 'Taxation and the economy', in J. C. Holt (ed.), *Domesday Studies*, RHS, (Woodbridge, 1987), 249–64

Harvey 1988   S. Harvey, 'Domesday England', in H. E. Hallam (ed.), *The Agrarian History of England and Wales*, vol. 2 (Cambridge, 1988), 45–136

Heirs   *Widows, Heirs, and Heiresses in the late Twelfth Century: The Rotuli de Dominabus et Pueris et Puellis*, ed. and tr. J. Walmsley, Arizona Centre for Medieval and Renaissance Studies, 308 (Tempe, AZ, 2006)

Hemming   *Hemingi Chartularium Ecclesiae Wigorniensis*, ed. T. Hearne (Oxford, 1723), 2 vols but paginated continuously

Herefordshire Domesday   *Herefordshire Domesday*, ed. V. H. Galbraith and J. Tait, Pipe Roll Society (PRS), 63 (1947–8; NS 25, 1950)

HH   Henry, archdeacon of Huntingdon, *Historia Anglorum*, ed. D. Greenway, Oxford Medieval Texts (Oxford, 1996)

HistAbbend 1/2   *Historia Abbendoniensis: History of the Church of Abingdon*, ed. and tr. J. Hudson, 2 vols (Oxford, 2002; 2007)

Holt, *Studies*   J. C. Holt (ed.), *Domesday Studies*, RHS (Woodbridge, 1987)

Hugh Chantor   *Hugh the Chantor: History of the Church of York, 1066–1127*, ed. C. Johnson (London, 1961)

ICC   *Inquisitio Comitatus Cantabrigiensis* [Inquest of the County of Cambridge], *Subjicitur Inquisitio Eliensis*, ed. N. E. S. A. Hamilton (London, 1876), 1–96

IE   *Inquisitio Comitatus Cantabrigiensis, Subjicitur Inquisitio Eliensis*
                                [Inquest of Ely], ed. N.E.S.A. Hamilton (London, 1876),
                                97–195

JW 2/3   *The Chronicle of John of Worcester*, vol. 2, ed. R. R. Darlington
                                and P. McGurk, Oxford Medieval Texts (Oxford, 1995), to
                                1066; vol. 3, ed. P. McGurk, Oxford Medieval Texts (Oxford,
                                1998)

Kalendar, Abbot   *Kalendar of Abbot Samson of Bury St. Edmunds*, ed.
Samson   R. H. C. Davis, Camden Society, 3rd ser., 84 (1954)
Keats-Rohan   K. S. B. Keats-Rohan, *Domesday People, a Prosopography of Persons
                                Occurring in English Documents 1066–1166: I Domesday Book*
                                (Woodbridge, 1999)
Keynes, 'Giso'   S. Keynes, 'Giso, Bishop of Wells (1061–88)', *ANS*, 19 (1996),
                                203–71

Laws are cited by ruler   *The Laws of the Kings of England from Edmund to Henry I*, ed.
and number from: A. J. Robertson (Cambridge, 1925)
LDB   Domesday Book Record Commission, vol. 2, ed. A. Farley,
                                (London, 1783), cited by folio, a–b
LE   *Liber Eliensis*, ed. E. O. Blake, Camden Society, 3rd ser., 92,
                                (1962), Books I–III, cited by *cap.*
LegesHP   *Leges Henrici Primi*, ed. L. J. Downer (Oxford: The Clarendon
                                Press, 1972)
Lennard   R. Lennard, *Rural England, 1086–1135* (Oxford, 1959)
Liber Vitae   *Liber Vitae of the New Minster and Hyde Abbey*, ed. S. Keynes,
                                Early English Manuscripts in Facsimile, 26 (Copenhagen, 1996)
Liebermann   F. Liebermann, *Die Gesetze der Angelsachsen*, vol. 1 (Halle, 1903)
Lanfranc's Letters   *The Letters of Lanfranc, Archbishop of Canterbury*, ed. H. M.
                                Clover and M. T. Gibson (Oxford, 1979)

Maitland   F. W. Maitland, *Domesday Book and Beyond*, 2nd edn (Cam-
                                bridge, 1987)
McDonald   J. McDonald, *Production Efficiency in Domesday England, 1086*
                                (London, 1998)
McDonald and Snooks   J. McDonald and G. D. Snooks, *Domesday Economy: A New
                                Approach to Anglo-Norman History* (Oxford, 1986)
Metcalf, *Atlas*   D. M. Metcalf, *An Atlas of Anglo-Saxon and Norman Coin Finds,
                                c.973–1086*, Royal Numismatic Society Special Publication, 32
                                (London and Oxford, 1998)
Mint Documents   *The De Moneta of Nicholas Oresme and English Mint Documents*,
                                ed. C. Johnson (London, 1956)

NCMH 3   *New Cambridge Medieval History*, vol. 3, ed. T. Reuter (Cam-
                                bridge, 1999)

OV   Orderic Vitalis, *Historica Ecclesiastica*, ed. M. Chibnall, 6 vols,
                                Oxford Medieval Texts (Oxford, 1969–80)

P&P	*Past & Present*
PRS	Pipe Roll Society
PRS Henry I, 2012	*The Great Roll of the Pipe for the Thirty-First Year of the Reign of Henry I, Michaelmas, 1130*, ed. J. Green, PRS, NS 57 (2012)
Raban	S. Raban, *A Second Domesday? The Hundred Rolls of 1279–80* (Oxford, 2004)
Rankin	*The Winchester Troper*, facs. edn with introduction by S. Rankin, Early English Church Music, 50, British Academy (London, 2007)
Reassessment	P. Sawyer (ed.), *Domesday Book: A Reassessment* (London, 1985)
Regesta 1/2/3	*Regesta Regum Anglo-Normannorum*, vol. 1, *1066–1100*, ed. H. W. C. Davis (Oxford, 1913); vol. 2, *1100–1135*, ed. C. Johnson and H. A. Cronne (Oxford, 1956); vol. 3, *1135–54*, ed. H. A. Cronne and R. H. C. Davis (Oxford, 1968)
Roffe, *Decoding*	D. Roffe, *Decoding Domesday* (Woodbridge, 2007)
Roffe, *Inquest*	D. Roffe, *Domesday: The Inquest and the Book* (Oxford, 2000)
Round, 'Danegeld'	J. H. Round, 'Danegeld and the Finance of Domesday', in P. E. Dove (ed.), *Domesday Studies*, vol. 1 (London, 1888), 77–142
RS	Rolls Series
S.	P. H. Sawyer (ed.), *Anglo-Saxon Charters: An Annotated List and Bibliography*, RHS Guides and Handbooks, 8 (1968), now updated and online as *Electronic Sawyer*. <http://www.esawyer.org.uk/about/index.html> (accessed 18 November 2013)
Southern 1933	R. W. Southern, 'Ranulf Flambard and early Anglo-Norman administration', *TRHS*, 4th ser., 16 (1933), 95–128
Southern, *Humanism*	R. W. Southern, *Medieval Humanism and Other Studies* (Oxford, 1970)
Stubbs, *Charters*	W. Stubbs, *Select Charters*, 9th edn (Oxford, 1962)
Symeon	*Symeon of Durham, Libellus de Exordio*, ed. and tr. D. Rollason, Oxford Medieval Texts (Oxford, 2000)
TRE	*tempore regis Eadwardi*, 'in King Edward's time', before 1066
TRHS	*Transactions of the Royal Historical Society*
TRW	*tempore regis Willelmi*, 'in King William's time', before 1086
Van Caenegem, *Lawsuits*	*English Lawsuits from William I to Richard I*, vol. 1, ed. R. C. van Caenegem, Selden Society, 106 (London, 1990)
Van Caenegem, *Writs*	*Royal Writs in England from the Conquest to Glanvill*, ed. R. C. van Caenegem, Selden Society, 77 (London, 1959)
VCH	Victoria County History, Institute of Historical Research, University of London (Oxford and Woodbridge, 1933–)
VitaÆdw	*Vita Ædwardi Regis, The Life of King Edward the Confessor*, ed. F. Barlow, Nelson's Medieval Texts (London, 1962)
Waltham Chronicle	*The Waltham Chronicle*, ed. L. Watkiss and M. Chibnall, Oxford Medieval Texts (Oxford, 1994)

Webber	T. Webber, 'Salisbury and the Exon Domesday: Some Observations Concerning the Origins of Exeter Cathedral MS 3500', in *English Manuscript Studies 1100–1700*, vol. 1 (1989), 1–18
WM Bishops	*Gesta Pontificum Anglorum, William of Malmesbury: The History of the English Bishops*, ed. M. Winterbottom with R. M. Thomson, Oxford Medieval Texts (Oxford, 2008)
WM, *Saints' Lives*	William of Malmesbury, *Saints' Lives*, ed. M. Winterbottom and R. M. Thomson, Oxford Medieval Texts (Oxford, 2002)
Williams, *The English*	A. Williams, *The English and the Norman Conquest* (Woodbridge, 1995; repr. 1997)
Winchester	F. Barlow, M. Biddle, O. von Feilitzen, and D. J. Keene, in M. Biddle (eds), *Winchester in the Early Middle Ages*, Winchester Studies, vol. 1 (Oxford, 1976)
Wills	*Anglo-Saxon Wills*, ed. D. Whitelock (Cambridge, 1930)
Wormald	P. Wormald, 'Domesday Lawsuits: A Provisional List', in C. Hicks (ed.), *England in the Eleventh Century*, Harlaxton Medieval Studies, vol. 2 (Stamford, 1992), 61–102
WP	*The Gesta Guillelmi of William of Poitiers*, ed. and tr. R. H. C. Davis and M. Chibnall, Oxford Medieval Texts (Oxford, 1998), cited by page
Writs	*Anglo-Saxon Writs*, ed. F. E. Harmer (Manchester, 1952)

Bibliographical Note

On Domesday Book: the 1783 edition has accompanied me for forty-five years on my travels and it is on that I rely chiefly. Accordingly, although I have spent several days with the original Domesday at various times, on hand-writing I rely on the expertise of others. I cite Great Domesday by folio and column, a–d; and Little Domesday by folio a–b, and also the entry number and county abbreviation for all individual entries as in the Phillimore CD-ROM text.

BDF	Bedfordshire
BRK	Berkshire
BUK (BKM)	Buckinghamshire
CAM	Cambridgeshire
CHS	Cheshire
CON	Cornwall
DBY	Derbyshire
DEV	Devonshire
DOR	Dorset
ESS	Essex
GLS	Gloucestershire
HAM	Hampshire
HEF	Herefordshire
HRT	Hertfordshire
HUN	Huntingdonshire
KEN	Kent
LEC	Leicestershire
LIN	Lincolnshire
MDX	Middlesex
NFK	Norfolk
NTH	Northamptonshire
NTT	Nottinghamshire
OXF	Oxfordshire
RUT	Rutland
SHR	Shropshire
SOM	Somerset
STS	Staffordshire
SUF (SFK)	Suffolk
SUR (SRY)	Surrey
SUS (SSX)	Sussex
WAR	Warwickshire
WIL	Wiltshire
WOR	Worcestershire
YKS	Yorkshire

I have confined my references to my direct obligations, and to some recent studies which extend the discussion but whose views I have not necessarily adopted. The List of Abbreviations gives an indication of some of the central primary sources and secondary literature central to this work. I have quoted the pagination of whole articles when relevant to the point under discussion, specific pages for the source of specific information.

The vast literature on Domesday Book and its interpretation before 1985 is catalogued by D. Bates, *A Bibliography of Domesday Book* (Woodbridge, 1986). Extensive bibliographies are now to be found in D. Roffe, *The Inquest and the Book* (Oxford, 2000), 252–64, and D. Roffe, *Decoding Domesday* (Woodbridge, 2007), 322–47. The historians of the late nineteenth century, particularly F. W. Maitland, *Domesday Book and Beyond*, and P. Vingradoff, *English Society in the Eleventh Century*, remain unsurpassed. Many of the relevant volumes of the Victoria County Histories contain work of value in their county commentaries, as well as translation. A. Williams and R. W. H. Erskine have produced the *Domesday Book: County Edition* (London, 1986–92), in which a translation of each Domesday county text is preceded by a new introductory commentary written by specialist historians of this period. These are also available in several CD editions of the Digital Domesday, which reproduce the original text, the 1783 transcription, and a translation, and include bibliographies. The 1783 transcription with a new translation is available, county by county, by various scholars, under the original inspiration of John Morris (Chichester, 1974–86); some volumes include appendices with contemporary Domesday texts; its publishers have also developed analytical material and a text on CD. The University of Essex and the University of Hull and The National Archives offer Domesday material online.

Note on Terminology

The terms *villani* and *servi* in Domesday Book create difficulties even for medievalists, as they were sometimes used interchangeably later in the middle ages.[1] But in eleventh-century England, the categories were completely distinct: the *villanus* was an inhabitant of a vill, or manor, and its environs, probably possessing a recognized portion of local assets, and himself a recognized contributor towards rental and fiscal burdens; later connotations of bondage were not necessarily, perhaps not normally, attached to him. The Domesday *servus* was slave rather than semi-free, and could be bought and sold. Here I adopt the term 'villeins' or 'men of the vill' simply to reflect the Domesday text, in which the term covers peasants of a wide range of economic standing: from those, rare, individuals who possessed two plough-teams,[2] and therefore a couple of hundred acres (roughly eighty hectares), to those who were smallholders—Domesday's bordars or cottars—with but a few acres of ground: these were usually differentiated; but they might also be classed as 'villeins'.[3] However, Domesday evidence indicates that groups of villeins whose assets averaged between a quarter and half a plough-team, 2–4 oxen apiece, were the most numerous.[4]

---

[1] R. H. Hilton, *Bondmen Made Free: Medieval Peasant Movements and the English Rising of 1381* (London, 2003), 56.

[2] GDB:73c (WIL:66,5) Gillingham; 80c (DOR:33,1) Gillingham; 21c (SUS:10,51) Hawkridge; 317a (YKS:9,80) Barnsley.

[3] e.g. Stepney, GDB:127c (MDX:3,4).

[4] R. Lennard, 'The economic position of the Domesday *villani*', *The Economic Journal*, 56 (1946), 244–64.

Introduction

There are three times . . . the present of past things is the memory; the present of present things is direct perception; and the present of future things is expectation.

St Augustine, *Confessions*

At a practical level, Domesday Book offers us a gazetteer of English place-names, and a country-wide mine of information on the agrarian assets—in some regions even beehives and pigs—of eleventh-century England before and after the Norman Conquest. More enigmatically, it survives as an exemplar of the processes of the Norman Conquest and Norman rule. Its very achievement epitomizes the strengths—and weaknesses—of William the Conqueror's position at the end of his twenty-year rule. The strengths lay obviously in the economy, and in the capable administration he had taken over and harnessed to maximum effect. But historians nowadays also give due recognition to the peril William and his followers faced from the Danish king: and of the high seriousness with which William confronted it.[1] Not that the jeopardy was openly admitted in this remarkable text, except in the speed and thoroughness with which it was launched and carried through: nor is any apprehension apparent in the Survey's confident encyclopaedic format.

The text that best mirrors the Inquiry's terms of reference survives in the preface to a detailed version of a Domesday text known as the Inquest of Ely:

What is the name of the manor?
Who held it in the time of King Edward? Who holds it now?
How many hides?
How many plough in demesne—of the tenants?
How many villeins—cottars—slaves?
How many freemen—sokemen? How much wood—meadow—pasture?
How many mills—fisheries?
How much has been added or taken away?
How much was the whole worth? How much now?
How much had or has each freeman, sokeman?
All this to be given thrice: that is, in the time of King Edward, and when King
    William gave it, and at the present time.
And, if more can be had than is now had.[2]

---

[1] e.g. Harvey 1975, 181–2; Roffe, *Inquest*, 69–70; J. R. Maddicott, 'Responses to the threat of invasion, 1085', *EHR*, 122 (2007), 986–97.
[2] *IE*, 97.

Such questions produced an assemblage of data that almost echoed the knowledge of the King of Kings, who 'controls in marvellous order those things which are recorded among men under the dome of heaven', as Worcester charters tradition-ally put it.[3] Not so long after its name was first recorded in the late twelfth century the designation 'Domesday' became a byword for official collections of economic data,[4] its range being so wide that now virtually every general book on western Europe in the middle ages contains some reference to its data.

This encyclopaedia, seemingly dispassionate compared with the contemporary narratives of Norman, French, Lorrainer and English chroniclers, remains never-theless the most political of documents, the more dangerously so because its factual character seems to belie this. In that it registered legal claims, it was at best an agreement grounded on force that endeavoured to set a final seal on what was still an unpopular conquest: a minutely ordered bureaucratic enterprise designed to give an authoritative legal framework and some permanence to the subjugation of a peace-hungry and productive society.

Study of the text usually confirms an enhanced respect for the data therein, all the more impressive in that it was collected by a French-speaking elite and recorded in Latin, directly or indirectly from a largely English-speaking and disheartened population. How any administration, let alone an eleventh-century government functioning under duress, could bring such a project to a successful conclusion has inspired historians, both of governance and of Domesday, to seek to unravel the respective contributions of officials, landholders, and men of the localities that were woven together in the complex undertaking that resulted in the Survey and the Book. The verdict usually returned on the data supplied is that what is there is in the main reliable, but not completely so; and that the gaps and eccentricities in the data of Domesday are undeniable—yet they are also instructive.

In my initial encounters with Domesday, the sheer amount of information on the agrarian society excited me—in the late 1960s, Domesday's data was so massive that a great university's computer could only process it at night during the summer vacation—and I surmised that even more on the economy could be gleaned from it, particularly from the study of plough-teams and values. It could indeed; but, to make the maximum use of the great geographical encyclopaedia, it seemed best to start with analysis of its sources and construction that might reveal any distortion inherent in its data.

Fifty years ago, when I started work on Domesday Book, most senior medieval-ists thought it to be a subject that had been largely 'done' by the great Victorians—

---

[3] Charters, nos 21, 64; Hemming, 180.

[4] e.g. G. H. Martin, *Early Court Rolls of the Borough of Ipswich*, Leicester Occasional Paper 5 (Leicester, 1954), 9. The nineteenth century published *The Domesday of St. Paul's*, (ed.) W. H. Hale, *Camden Soc.*, 69 (1858) and *The Domesday of Inclosures, 1517–18*, (ed.) I. S. Leadam, 2 vols, RHS (London, 1897). The tradition continues.

Freeman, Maitland, Round, Tait, and Vinogradoff—and finalized recently by V. H. Galbraith, backed up by R. Welldon Finn, and by H. C. Darby's multi-volume Domesday Geographies. Moreover, fifty years ago, the Book itself was widely deemed to be the extraordinary final pirouette of a successful, if bloody enterprise, the crowning achievement of a dynamic new Establishment that had reinvigorated decadent Anglo-Saxon culture with an injection of the 'new feudalism', whose mechanisms of government were not reliant on memory, but now written down in regulated fashion: a view not entirely relinquished even now.

Yet the great Domesday initiative is now seen also as a response to a regime-threatening crisis. That the harvests of England's economy were so easily targeted and tapped by a well-established and effective taxation system had long made England a tempting prize for would-be conquerors—first Danish and then Norman (with a Norwegian aspirant besides). In 1084, yet another invasion threatened, and the Conqueror's fear that his sovereignty might be all-too short-lived added urgency and scale to the Survey. The Danes, England's previous conquerors, with extensive racial and linguistic links with much of England, were ready and waiting to launch their invasion fleet which, jointly with that of Count Robert of Flanders, was thought to consist of a thousand ships.[5] The impetus for the Inquiry was not merely William's immediate need to obtain cash for military reinforcements, and to tap manpower and traction-power for defensive works. It was vital to appearances, and to his relations with churchmen, who were the lawyers in his council as well as the spiritual advisers, that he should not appear as a conqueror, but as the legal successor to his kinsman King Edward, for although King William's chroniclers had long claimed that his victory at Hastings demonstrated that God was on his side, this circular argument was in danger of going into reverse.

Further, despite, or perhaps because of, the intense and generalized revival in Domesday studies, provoked by the ninth centenary in 1986 and the completion of three widely available editions, in translation and online, no historian of those times would now claim that further study was redundant: yet these excellent editorial contributions also mean that the task of producing an overview has now become almost herculean. Recent work has demonstrated, inter alia, how the Book's minutiae and inconsistencies as well as its central data can contribute to our knowledge of its construction. Computer studies, too, should produce another leap forward, once their programmes take account of nuanced categorization of the data. These revolutionary techniques need, however, to be adopted with an awareness of historical context. Only then will standard tenets be questioned, or dislodged in favour of, one hopes, entirely new viewpoints. Before this second revolution is successfully completed, perhaps it is worthwhile noting down some of the coherent themes that I found, unexpectedly, emerging from my work—which had concentrated initially only on translating the information in Domesday into a realistic picture of the eleventh-century economy and of the ways in which the government set out to oversee and exploit it.

---

[5] *GRA* 1.481.

The Domesday Survey remains the largest single source for the Norman Conquest and on eleventh-century administration; yet the task of separating the day-to-day administration from the extra-ordinary project, and the pre-Conquest from the post-Conquest, remains challenging. So the subjects of my first chapters are the pre-Domesday resources and the men that helped to make the project feasible, from local level to Lotharingian expertise, and who had the vision to contribute to the execution of the project; the first half concludes with a hunt for the Domesday mastermind. The second half of the book is devoted largely to the matters central to the enterprise's objectives: money, the value of landed estates, taxation, and tenure. Domesday's evidence, in the context of other contemporary sources, can also shed a flicker more light on the development of the Treasury, the organization of the coinage, and taxation—as well as on that perennial subject of debate: the real purpose of the Inquiry and its records.

The complex, tiered, process of co-ordinating information remains an enigmatic source of debate, but I have long argued that the task was not quite as impossible as it might seem and certainly did not start from a blank parchment but, like taxation and coinage, stemmed from a structure of Anglo-Saxon records and practices. Well before the Norman Conquest, England had been a much-taxed country; and the people's expectations, as formulated and urged upon its rulers by Church leaders, were that, in return, those rulers should provide security from invaders and peace at home: a peace upheld by the king and defined with the aid of local custom and assent.[6] In general, I have sought to deploy what is known about eleventh-century government to throw light on the still-contentious questions that beset the identification of Domesday's central aims and ambitions; and, conversely, to draw on the Domesday text to contribute to what we know of eleventh-century governance.

Domesday Book was the Conqueror's charter, the king's rent book and, in a more complicated way, the king's tax book. Always in the background are those extraordinarily long-lived institutions, the Treasury, and in effect, the Exchequer—without the chequer board. Strands of procedures well known in the twelfth century are already discernible in Domesday, whose format indeed shaped the long-term purview of the Exchequer, which was also a court of tenure. Beyond this, Domesday's importance in English history lies in the enduring part it played both in ensuring the permanence of the newly-formed great estates, and also in placing that settlement firmly within the surveillance of royal officials. Nevertheless, throughout this attempt to understand the nature of this administrative endeavour, I have tried to think as much in terms of the people who had the competence to act, as with the institutions and labels which cloaked them, because it was a combination of their vision, flexibility, and ability to work on their own, or alongside others, that—against the odds—produced a result.

Whereas for all involved—peasant or king, poor burgess or rich moneyer—the subject-matter remains practical and material—a matter of pounds, shillings, and pence, man- and ox-power, and administration—my theme here is judgement. The Inquiry itself constituted, again for all classes, a judgement on the largest scale:

---

[6] 'Conclusion', *Dispute Settlement*, 226.

indeed, a series of many judgements, some not completed. In the course of the Inquiry, each sector of society, servile apart, had to 'render its account': many literally, others literally and metaphorically. It was no accident that the identical term was used for both a fiscal report to the Treasury and the soul's report to Christ at the Last Judgement. Some native landholders were allowed to 'buy back', to 'redeem' (*redemptio*) their land from the conquerors by gold, silver, or service. At the Treasury, debtors were 'pardoned', *in perdona*, or paid up, *et quietus est*. The assaying of silver for its purity, and of weighing it, as William was accused of doing needlessly, also served as a contemporary metaphor for the assessing of souls at the final Day of Judgement. In 1086–7, neither the royal officials, nor the bishops, nor, indeed, I argue, the king himself, escaped. Herein lies the origin of the Book's final name, and of my final chapter; this deals with William's tenurial revolution from a certain perspective—the light that Domesday's name sheds upon its character.

In recent years, my respect for the weight of the material inscribed has been over-laid by the realization that the fearsome military conqueror was not simply concerned to complement his conquest by a scrupulous record of 'how it was occupied or with what sort of people', but to establish his bureaucratic control to a dictatorial degree.[7] As the Domesday project neared completion, his loyal officials were beginning to appreciate that force, too. For two decades they, as obedient executors of the Conqueror's will, with the ruler more often absent than present, had transferred the possession of hundreds of thousands of acres of land, more or less within the framework of a recognized process. Now, great as these officials had become, they were publicly exposed in open court, accused of putting three acres here (about enough to support one horse, roughly one hectare), or fifteen acres there, into the wrong hands, or of grabbing them for themselves.[8] I argue here, from the clues given when dissent is not only evidently expressed but clearly recorded, that an Inquest of Officials followed on from the Domesday Inquiry and was, indeed, in part included in the Domesday digest. These officials rendered account, not just for royal revenues, but for their actions. The king's own adjutants were adjudged. In Domesday, William sought to control, and manifestly con-trolled, the supervision of his officials: every detail of the assets that they had received and to whom they had redistributed them. These men were not, could not be, always at heel; but he made sure they knew they were on a check-chain. The Survey and its objectives form essential elements in the interpretation of the reigns of William and his sons. The Survey and its follow-up Inquest, I argue, even provoked a serious revolt against William's successor by some of his closest aides.

From the English viewpoint, the harshness of the Conqueror's rule is the stuff of childhood history: wholesale reallocation of land, castle-building, and finally the unprecedented Domesday Survey. Even from the Norman perspective, however, William's raised expectations were extraordinary. The newly great landowners now

---

[7] *ASC*, 1085; e.g. LDB:17b–18a (ESS:9,5; 9,7).
[8] e.g. GDB:193b (CAM:13,2).

found themselves obliged to submit accounts of the silver that they collected annually from their lands; these were inscribed in detail, ready to be employed against the day their estates might become confiscate, their heirs minors, their widows and lands vulnerable, or the headships of religious houses vacant. On those occasions, the product of their lands, saving only sustenance for their resident households, were to be channelled into the king's hands. With feudal dues, and using Domesday data, the royal revenues from the lord–vassal relationship were to be more assiduously documented and collected in the new country than in the old duchy. If, arguably, 'a failed state' is one that lacks a public authority and legal process with the power to enforce its judgements, it was the successful completion of this great enquiry that legitimated the Conqueror's claim to rule. The best that could be said for it was that it conducted a process of legal 'disclosure' in the one-sided dispute over land between conquerors and conquered.

What did the Danish challenge imply about God's judgement of William's stewardship? The king was coming to the end of his fighting life and was seeking to stave off any popular support for the Danes. If he could establish his parcelling-out of English land and English rent-payers on a more convincing legal basis, while holding his officials in tight check, perhaps the men of England would stand by him after all, despite the treatment they had received at his hands, and perhaps God would judge his stewardship charitably and assist his cause. Though there were rebellions after Domesday Book, the interesting fact is that they arose from discontent among the Norman elite: high taxes and rents did not provoke open enmity from the English on a large scale. Indeed, later in the middle ages, and somewhat falsely, Domesday was to provide peasants with precedents for claiming concessions on taxes and services.

This book will explore the rather subtle documentation, and justification, inherent in this supreme document of power and military conquest. Although a conqueror, yet advised and cautioned by his churchmen and with the reign of Cnut offering a precedent, William was acutely conscious of the importance of legality. That much is evident from his advance planning, his coronation, his early insistence on the legality of his rule, and his use of the local Domesday courts to ratify, if under duress, his assignment of the greater part of the land and its riches to an alien elite.

Perhaps too little and too late, the policies exemplified in the Book's record give some hint of William's heeding the precepts of the Church on the need for rulers to observe good and legal lordship over the conquered, if only to save his regime by fostering an expectation, albeit short-lived, that the royal administration might develop a more realistic approach to taxation. Archbishop Lanfranc may well have encouraged such expectations. His reply to an over-assiduous contemporary, an officer who was evidently in charge of organizing a Domesday regional return, concluded with a cautious blessing: 'May God, who alone can know and remember all things . . . at all times defend you from all evil in your work.'[9] Many officiating in the Domesday Inquiry could have done with both the reminder and the blessing: as could this writer.

---

[9] F. Barlow, 'Domesday Book: A letter of Lanfranc', *EHR*, 78 (1963), 284–9; cf. Lanfranc's Letters, no. 56.

1

The English Context: The 'Book of Winchester' and the *Domus Dei*

A book was a treasure in every sense: its production costly of time and resources, and the literate intelligence needed to produce it not readily sourced. Yet all books, however great their value, were made to be used as well as treasured.[1] Great Domesday, the larger of the two encyclopaedic volumes later called 'Domesday Book', drew upon up to 200 sheep-skins, all carefully selected and prepared with expertise; many more would have been expended in the voluminous preparatory work.[2] But despite their traditional and awe-inspiring name, neither volume has a title page, preface, or known editor; and their objectives remain disputed.

Yet in the century before the name 'Domesday' was officially adopted, contemporaries' varied references to the work supply signposts to its historical context. The earliest proper name given to the text was 'the Book of Winchester' and this chapter proposes to explore its import. It makes its appearance within Great Domesday itself, in a heading for the fief of Robert de Brus that was granted and inscribed 'after the Book of Winchester was made';[3] the entry was added to previously blank folios after the description of Yorkshire, possibly between 1114 and 1124, although the change of tenure was made in 1103.[4] In fact, the two volumes eventually designated Domesday Book were held for much of the first century of their life at Winchester, home of the king's treasury and of royal officials. Given that 'Book of Winchester' was Domesday's earliest name, it was reasonable to assume that the bulk of the returns from the circuits of English counties came to Winchester to be condensed and the majority of the counties made up into the single volume of Great Domesday. The returns from the economically advanced and socially complex areas of East Anglia and Essex—conserved in the second volume known as Little Domesday—remained, however, less condensed, probably because of the number of small landholders who complicated the tenurial lay-out. Paradoxically, a description of the borough of Winchester itself is, along with London, the most

---

[1] See the excellent discussion in R. McKitterick, *The Carolingians and the Written Word* (Cambridge, 1989), esp. 164.

[2] M. Gullick, 'The Great and Little Domesday manuscripts', in Erskine and Williams, 144–73, 145–6. Calfskins may also have been used.

[3] GDB:332c.

[4] *Regesta* 2, no. 648; G. Fellows Jensen, 'The Domesday account of the Bruce fief', *Journal of the English Place-Name Society*, 2 (1969–70), 8–17; *PRS Henry I, 2012*, xxii.

glaring omission in the vast compendium of country-wide data that is Domesday. Yet the likely explanation is that separate documentation on the dues and privileges within the city was already safely conserved, since a Winchester survey that was compiled *c.*1110 to re-establish the royal rights of Edward the Confessor's reign still survives, being 'essentially a modernization of an Edwardian list of tenements' paying customary dues, the source of which may now be datable through the names of moneyers to either *c.*1047 or *c.*1057.[5]

Whilst Domesday's first proper name was 'Book of Winchester', the earliest generic name, *descriptio*, preceded it. Both Great and Little Domesday refer to themselves as a *descriptio*, literally 'a writing down'; the term covered all the labour of compiling, ordering, and rewriting; most notably, it was adopted again in the formal conclusion, the colophon, of Little Domesday.[6] *Descriptio* did not, however, have our present-day general connotation: rather, it was functional and particular. It echoed Carolingian imperial records of revenues from royal lands and fiscal rights that, once written, were difficult to gainsay: the term was variously associated with surveys of *mansi*, with customary dues, with rents, with tribute, and with heavy new impositions. *Descriptio* also implied a proper disposition, order, or arrangement, which might be of legal cases, as in a *descriptio causarum,* glossed as 'an index or book in which judicial cases were arranged in order'.[7] Its meaning was fused with *discriptio*: a 'distribution', or 'apportionment';[8] a *discriptor* in Frankish texts was one who recorded men by position and by hundred.[9] The *Dialogue of the Exchequer,* completed in the 1180s, the only official text that attempts to explain Domesday Book, put apportionment of land at the centre of the Survey. In that decade, too, the punctilious abbot, Samson, ordered a *descriptio generalis* to record the hidages, dues, and revenues in each hundred held by Bury St Edmunds, and had them 'set down in writing'.[10] Each of these common usages aligned with particular functions of the Domesday Inquiry and of the resulting text.

Although the main Domesday volume is made up of 382 folios of a shorthand presentation of largely numerical data from fuller regional versions, there is remarkable consistency in its abbreviation, and the handwriting is so uniform that expert opinion agrees that a single official, one of great method, transcribed the final copy, with a small amount of supplementary material from two or more other hands.[11] To

---

[5] F. Barlow, 'The Winton Domesday', in *Winchester*, 9–10.

[6] GDB:3a, (KEN:2,2); 164b (GLS:1,63); *descriptus est,* 247b (STS:2,22); 252a (SHR:C12): 269b (CHS:FT2,19); LDB:450a, quoted in Ch. 4 in this volume, p. 97.

[7] *index seu libellus in quo causae iudicandae ex ordine recensentur,* Dom. du Cange, *Glossarium mediae et infimae Latinatis cum supplementis integris monachorum ordinis S. Benedicti,* vol. 2 (Paris, 1842), 815–16.

[8] *A Latin Dictionary: Founded on Andrews' edition of Freund's Latin Dictionary,* Ethan Allen Andrews, 1787–1858; William Freund, 1806–94; Charlton Thomas Lewis, 1834–1904; Charles Short, 1821–86 (Oxford, 1966), known as Lewis and Short, 555, 589.

[9] Du Cange, 815–16.

[10] *The Chronicle of Jocelin of Brakelond,* ed. H. E. Butler (London, 1962), 29; *Kalendar, Abbot Samson*; also *The Chronicle of Battle Abbey,* ed. E. Searle (1980), esp. 33.

[11] Galbraith, 189–203, and V. H. Galbraith, *Domesday Book: Its place in Administrative History* (Oxford, 1974), 51; A. Rumble, 'The palaeography of the Domesday manuscripts', in *Reassessment,* 49; F. and C. Thorn, 'The writing of Great Domesday', in Hallam and Bates, 48–51.

what extent the Domesday project drew upon a team of scribes of common training reared in royal service remains a fundamental question, important for Domesday itself and for its evidence on eleventh-century administration. For a single scribe, the task demanded assured expertise. Winchester, by the year 1000 a walled enclave of just over 58 hectares (143 acres) already extending into the suburbs beyond its gates, was well placed to supply the established skills demanded.[12] And, wherever it was written up, Domesday was kept there and the title 'Book of Winchester' puts it into its proper context within eleventh-century administration.

THE WINCHESTER HERITAGE

Winchester had long been at the heart of the West Saxon monarchy. Originally a Roman site, it had been an ecclesiastical centre under royal direction from the seventh century; it was laid out anew, probably in the late ninth century, to provide a regular street plan, with wide main streets. In the centuries following, it came to foster a truly civic range of skills—from minters of coin, goldsmiths, and silver-smiths to soap-makers and hosiers.[13] Its immediate hinterland provided for periods of royal sustenance; and amongst those manors furnishing provisions for the king's household, King's Worthy and Andover probably provided royal residences.[14]

In the second half of the tenth century, a dramatic building programme in Winchester had created a complex comparing favourably with any in Europe north of the Alps. The foundations of the civic nucleus created by the tenth-century monarchy have survived to be precisely confirmed in outstanding large-scale excavations by Martin Biddle. The two main minsters were so close to each other that a man could scarcely pass between the two buildings, and the singers and bells of the one minster confused and rivalled the singing and ringers of the other.[15] Following the extension of Old Minster westwards to include St Swithin's grave, the eastern part was remodelled after 980 to create a church no less than 76 metres (*c*.250 feet) in length with a dramatic 'westwork', the base of which was 25 square metres (*c*.30 square yards), to provide for an edifice of presumably 40 to 50 metres (*c*.150 feet) in height.[16] In the same period, New Minster, too, was reconstructed, along with claustral buildings appropriate to the newly imposed monastic rule, and a great tower of 20 metres (*c*.65 feet) added by King Æthelred.[17] A third, less prominent, member of this precinct was Nonnaminster, or St Mary's Abbey: according to later tradition, it too was rebuilt in the tenth century by Bishop Æthelwold. All three minsters benefited from the bishop's redefinition of the site,

---

[12] M. Biddle and D. J. Keene, 'Winchester in the eleventh and twelfth centuries', in *Winchester*, 273; H. Gneuss, 'The origin of standard Old English and Æthelwold's school at Winchester', *ASE*, 1 (1972), 63–83, 70–1.

[13] Biddle and Keene, in *Winchester*, 272–82, 396–422, 427–39.

[14] Biddle and Keene, 465–7.   [15] Biddle and Keene, 317; *GP*, 173–4.

[16] Biddle and Keene, 307.   [17] Biddle and Keene, 315.

when he created a single walled enclosure separating the three communities from 'the tumult of the city'.[18] Adjacent was the bishop's hall, founded on a complex of buildings again datable to the later tenth century.[19] What was possibly a royal palace was sited close to the western towers of both minsters, and extended northwards when the Conqueror's hall was constructed about 1070.[20] The whole made an impressive enclave and the intensive use of the site suggests the pressures put on space by the activity of the adjacent developing town.

This *cité* offered a base unequalled for the exercise of royal and episcopal authority. Together, king and bishop—Edgar, widely recognized as overlord of other kings and peoples in Britain, and Æthelwold, Winchester's bishop from 963 to 983—launched a religious revival based on a more regulated way of life. A code of monastic observance, *Regularis Concordia*, promulgated at the synod of Winchester *c*.970, reconstituted religious life in diocesan centres—henceforth to be staffed by communities composed of Benedictine monks rather than secular clergy—and the revival created its own momentum: peculiar to England was the important part it gave to daily intercession for the king and queen; and to the role of the king in the elections of bishops and abbots.[21] Winchester's ecclesiastical literacy and learning took their part in developing the recognition of royal authority and, in turn, the literature, learning, and artistic endeavour of the Winchester minsters was extended to monastic houses in other regions of England via royal authority. Bishops were the literate advisers to kings; monasteries provided stable, educated, and organized enclaves in otherwise highly mobile and volatile societies. In England, these two mainstays of authority were welded unusually closely together when monastic communities became at this time attached to some bishoprics—Winchester, Canterbury, Worcester, and Sherborne—in contrast to the secular clergy who staffed the bishoprics of western Europe.

The creative scholarship in Winchester in the last century of the Anglo-Saxon kingdom is well recognized. Its monasteries produced original illuminated volumes, drawings, and books in Old English and Latin, and transcribed and translated existing classics. The knowledgeable productions at Winchester were impressive in their scope, embracing musical composition; translations into the vernacular of herbal and medicinal treatises, illustrated and supplemented; Anglo-Latin poems; and Anglo-Latin works abounding in Graecisms.[22] Both Old and New Minster studied and produced advanced computistical and astronomical texts as well the more conventional decorated Psalters.[23]

[18] S.807; Biddle and Keene, in *Winchester*, 321–2, Fig. 9.
[19] Biddle and Keene, 323.   [20] Biddle and Keene, 289–97.
[21] *Regularis Concordia*, ed. T. Symons (London, 1953), 13–14, 16; 6; Dom. T. Symons, 'Regularis Concordia: history and derivation', in D. Parsons (ed.), *Tenth Century Studies* (Chichester, 1975), 44.
[22] M. Lapidge, *Anglo-Latin Literature, 900–1066* (London, 1993), 36–46, 123–8, 183–211, 225–77.
[23] *Liber Vitae*, 66–9; P. Lendinara, 'Instructional manuscripts in England: the tenth- and eleventh-century codices and the early Norman ones', in P. Lendinara, L. Lazzari, and M. A. D'Aronco (eds),

Much probably originated in Bishop Æthelwold's own work, such as the translation of the Benedictine Rule into Old English; and the achievement of his school is beyond question. In the late tenth century, Winchester reared top scholars to spare for teaching purposes, and their high standards spread literary activity when they moved on to other houses. Æthelwold, his biographers relate, 'always took great pleasure in instructing the young men and boys, in explaining Latin to them in the English language, in teaching them the rules of grammar and metre, and exhorting them gently to strive for greater things. And so it was that many of his pupils became abbots, bishops, and even archbishops in England.'[24] Ælfric, a distinguished scholar, the most accomplished writer of the period, entrusted to take charge of teaching at the refounded Abbey of Cerne in Dorset, was one such pupil who had been a monk of Old Minster.

The literature emanating from the Winchester monastic houses had a determining influence on language, deliberately inculcating a standard literary vocabulary. By the first half of the eleventh century, a standard written English was known and used in all regions of the country, whereas no standard language was known for other Germanic dialects of the time, and this dominant standard was the late West Saxon form.[25] That it appears in surviving works from the east and the north of England shows the influence of Winchester schools—influence widely diffused in yet another sphere when an early eleventh-century Winchester Calendar of Saints acquired almost the status of a standard calendar in central and southern England.[26]

Music, too, was composed and copied at Winchester. The *Regularis Concordia* included directions for an Easter enactment of the risen Christ's meeting with the women at the tomb, and the Winchester volumes of church music provided a musical setting for just such a festival drama.[27] The earlier of two surviving manuscripts, probably dating from the 1020s or 1030s, contains 174 pieces of 'the only extant European repertory of liturgical polyphony notated before the twelfth century'.[28] The two volumes offered music for Mass, Divine Office, and also Tropes—that is embellishments—for chants for the Proper and Ordinary of the Mass on major feasts. Polyphonic singing had been described by theorists by the late ninth century; Winchester's great contribution was to codify and record its own extempore enhancements of the older Roman chant, enhancements rich in technical expertise and musical quality.

The feat of the Troper evinces the innovatory spirit and technical mastery with which Winchester was capable of tackling challenging projects, perhaps bearing some

---

Form and Content of Instruction in Anglo-Saxon England in the Light of Contemporary Manuscript Evidence, Fédération Internationale des Instituts d'Études Médiévales (FIDEM), Textes et Études du Moyen Âge, 39 (Turnhout, 2007), 91. I thank Joyce Hill for this reference.

[24] Quoted by Gneuss from the biography ascribed to Wulfstan, in 'Origin of standard Old English', 73.

[25] Gneuss, 63–83.

[26] D. Rollason, *Saints and Relics in Anglo-Saxon England* (Oxford, 1989), 227–8.

[27] Rankin, 10.   [28] Rankin, xi; the works are considered, 3–74.

comparison with Domesday. A volume of 199 ruled folios, the earlier Winchester Troper was, like Domesday, mainly in the English Caroline script of the eleventh century: all the hands writing before the late eleventh century were clearly English. The work of two scribes forms the main body: one scribe primarily concerned with text; the other, possessed of impressive technical knowledge of musical notation, showing 'care for the accuracy (and intelligibility) of every sign that he wrote'.[29] Like Domesday, the enterprise was probably in book form within boards soon after work on it ceased. However, whatever was envisaged, it remained unfinished—the blank pages being used up by groups of scribes working in the late eleventh century. Up to fifty scribes made additions and many stages of musical notation are distinguishable, with Norman techniques apparent in the later stages of the work.[30] A surviving sister book contains a different range of work, containing chants for the Proper of the Mass, but no polyphony; it too drew upon many scribal hands.[31] Both may have survived because they were treasured and kept apart from the main set of chant books.[32] Their musical qualities certainly delighted those concerned, their own rubrics styling pieces 'elegant' or 'sublime'.[33] The new repertories doubtless enchanted the laity also, as wider audiences were present at episcopal consecrations and kingly coronations. New Minster, too, built up close relations with the lay nobility, indicated by its vigilant intercessions for royal souls, lay benefactors, patrons, and those with influence, all enrolled within its eleventh-century *Book of Life*, a work intended to be a forerunner for the final Book of Life at the Last Judgement.[34]

Anglo-Saxon literature in the vernacular, poetry as well as prose, secular history and treatises as well as religious homilies, is known to be of the highest quality. This abundant native tradition stands in contrast to a literary background in Normandy that was sparse by comparison. Documentary materials for early Norman history are few, with no sign of written laws comparable with those issued by the English kings and by Cnut. In England, even in William's reign, charters to the English, such as the Charter to London, were at the start written in Anglo-Saxon or in both Anglo-Saxon and Latin. After the first five years of Norman rule, however, few official documents were issued in Anglo-Saxon and creative literature in that language languished.[35] By the twelfth century, the ascendancy of Wessex English had also disappeared: various dialects once more flourished, suggesting that the peak of Winchester's cultural influence was then over.[36]

The associations between the West Saxon royal house and the Winchester minsters were long and well established. Alfred's body was translated from its original grave in Old Minster to join his wife's in New Minster, which his successors considered the proper burial site for their house: Edward the Elder,

---

[29] Rankin, xi.   [30] Rankin, 3–5, 19–21.
[31] Oxford, Bodleian Library, Bodley 775. I thank Susan Rankin for her assistance.
[32] Rankin, 9.   [33] Rankin, 63.   [34] *Liber Vitae*, ff. 28v–29r.
[35] But see D. A. E. Pelteret, *Catalogue of English Post-Conquest Documents* (Woodbridge, 1990) and M. Swan and E. M. Treharne (eds), *Rewriting Old English in the Twelfth Century* (Cambridge, 2000).
[36] Gneuss, 'Origin of standard Old English', 64.

Eadred, and his nephew Eadwig were all buried there. Edmund Ironside (d.1016), Cnut (d.1035) and Harthacnut (d.1042) all found their last resting place in Winchester.[37] These links held firm until the last decade before the Norman Conquest, when political forces separated the king from royal tradition.

Edward the Confessor and Winchester

Winchester had every claim to be regarded as the capital of the Wessex-based kingdom. Yet during Edward the Confessor's reign, the king's personal investment in it declined, as had his father's before him.[38] The recent strength of Winchester's association with the ruling house of King Cnut, with the Anglo-Danish Earl Godwine and with Archbishop Stigand soon became for the Confessor its greatest limitation. Edward had little cause to venerate the tomb of Cnut, and there is only one hint of a visit after 1053 when, at some point after 1057, the enrolment of their names in the *Liber Vitae* suggests that Edward, Edith, and the young Edgar Aetheling visited New Minster.[39] Instead, in his last years, Edward the Confessor focused his attention on his own constructions at Westminster.

It is not difficult to understand how the religious and kingly associations that Winchester had for his ancestors were cruelly destroyed for Edward. After the death of Edward's father, King Æthelred, Cnut and a Danish aristocracy had fought Edward's half-brother Edmund and, later, executed Edmund's brother Eadwig. Once Cnut had extended his ascendancy over the Danelaw and Mercia to Wessex, he had taken Edward's own mother, Queen Emma, in marriage, an act that completed Edward's exclusion, and led to his exile.[40] Not Edward, but two of Cnut's sons in succession succeeded to the throne on Cnut's death. Only after the murder of Edward's full brother, Alfred, and after the death of Cnut's son, Harold and the accession of Harthacnut, was Edward finally accepted as heir.[41] Queen Emma had formed close ties with Winchester since her initial arrival from Normandy to marry Æthelred II, receiving borough revenues as her traditional 'morning-gift': a gift she retained upon her second marriage.[42] Together with her second husband, Cnut, she had been a munificent benefactor of the New Minster and is thus portrayed in a drawing in its *Book of Life*.[43] She had buried her second husband and their son, King Harthacnut, in Old Minster and given relics to New Minster in Cnut's memory.[44] Yet even as king, Edward was confronted by the over-powerful Anglo-Danish earl of Wessex and his clan who acted first as king-makers, and then

[37] Biddle and Keene, in *Winchester*, 314, 290.
[38] On Edward's father's close relations with London see S. Keynes, 'The burial of King Æthelred the Unready at St Paul's', in D. Roffe (ed.), *The English and their Legacy, 900–1200: Essays in Honour of Ann Williams* (Woodbridge, 2012), 129–48.
[39] *LibVitae*, f.29r. The entries are undated and in the same hand, 97.
[40] Barlow, *Confessor*, 35–6.   [41] Barlow, *Confessor*, 42–50; *ASC*, 1041, C.
[42] S.925; *Writs*, no. 111, S.1153.
[43] *Liber Vitae*, f.6r; reproduced, Barlow, *Confessor*, facing 36.   [44] *ASC*, 1042, E.

conspired to undermine his rule. With all these opponents, past and present, Winchester was peculiarly associated.

Edward the Confessor was consecrated king at Winchester on Easter Day, 1043, some nine months after he was recognized as king. The time lapse suggests a deliberate postponement in order to celebrate the event in Winchester at the high point of the Christian year, and the unusually elaborate music for the Easter feast in Winchester's Troper was possibly intended for this long-planned coronation.[45] Before the year was out, Edward returned 'unexpectedly' to Winchester and seized both his mother's lands and her treasure of gold and silver 'beyond counting'; soon after this Bishop Stigand, who was later to become bishop of Winchester, 'was deprived of his bishopric of East Anglia and all that he owned was placed in the king's control'. The pair seemed to be under suspicion of using their respective positions to take some of the contents of the royal treasury into Emma's own keeping.[46] Whatever the truth, she was still powerful enough, on her death some nine years later, to gain burial in Old Minster, near Cnut.

The revenues of Winchester had been handed over to Edward's own wife, Edith, daughter of Earl Godwine, as her morning-gift in her turn. But this brought the place no closer to Edward in spirit. The marriage had probably been forced upon Edward by the political ambitions of her father, and accepted to retain his crucial support: Godwine was a force to be reckoned with, being generally held responsible for the blinding and death of Edward's brother, Alfred.[47] In all likelihood, the marriage was never consummated. During his later years and after his death, it was claimed that Edward, although married, had remained celibate; and, despite his twentieth-century biographer's doubts,[48] this would seem understandable given Edward's personal history. His date of birth is uncertain, but it seems that he was in his forties when he married and those years of exile, rejection, and political brinkmanship would have aged him further. Age, his relations with his mother, and his dependence on his wife's relatives for his very throne, make it unsurprising if abstinence came easily to him. His biographer, a foreign but contemporary source, said 'the excellent queen served him as a daughter'.[49] Anyway, it became a moot point later whether to attribute the king's abstinence to his love of chastity or to his prudently concealed hatred of his father-in-law, Earl Godwine.[50] Certainly, action against the father-in-law included action against the daughter: when Edward temporarily gained the ascendancy over Godwine in 1051, he confiscated his wife's land and treasure and confined her to a convent. But Godwine not only staged a powerful comeback on his own return from exile in 1052: with the popular endorsement of his anti-Norman stance, he achieved the banishment of several of Edward's Norman nominees. Moreover, Stigand, the mediator who achieved his restoration,

---

[45] Rankin, xi.   [46] *ASC*, 1043, C.
[47] *ASC*, 1036, C.   [48] Barlow, *Confessor*, 81–4.
[49] *Vita Ædw*, 15. This may have been added later when making the case for Edward's canonization.
[50] *GRA* 1.352–5.

added the archbishopric of Canterbury to his bishopric of Winchester, being nominated while Edward's appointee, Robert of Jumièges, was still living.

Following the king's confrontation with the Godwine party and its return to influence, numismatic evidence suggests the extent of Winchester's loss of centrality. Winchester's production of coins declined—relative to London—and the swing of trade was to the mints of the eastern ports and their trade across the North Sea,[51] trading probably fostered by the Godwine family's links with prosperous Flanders, and its comital house. Stigand, albeit now also archbishop, was to remain based in Winchester until the end of Edward's reign. The queen's brother, Harold, became earl of Wessex on Godwine's death in 1053 (later to become powerful enough to take the throne). In all, Edward had come to find Winchester politically claustrophobic: he looked to create a different power base, in Westminster, near London, formerly in Mercia, where his new abbey was dedicated just before his own death in January 1066.

THE IMPORT OF WINCHESTER

Godwine's son, Earl Harold of Wessex, went to Westminster to be at Edward's death-bed, there to be promptly crowned as king; yet in the eleventh and early twelfth century, the first thoughts of potential rulers of England were still directed to Winchester. Although it had lost some of its ceremonial associations, in practical terms it was the site of the chief royal treasury. On Cnut's death 'all his best valuables' there had been promptly safe-guarded by Queen Emma, only to be taken from her by Cnut's son, Harold, when he took the throne.[52] She apparently did the same after Harthacnut's death, since Edward seized the treasure at Winchester in 1043 'because she had withheld it too firmly from him'.[53] William the Conqueror followed in the footsteps of the power-hungry in the Anglo-Saxon state: after first securing Sandwich, the chief naval port of the Anglo-Saxon kingdom and vulnerable to Godwineson allies, he then proceeded via Canterbury to Winchester. His aspirant sons in their turn were each concerned to secure Winchester. William Rufus, in succeeding his father in England—notwithstanding any claim from his eldest brother Robert—went straight from his coronation at Westminster to Winchester, where he 'scrutinized the Treasury and the treasure that his father had accumulated', 'by the power of which he subjugated all England to his will'.[54] Monasteries were then given gold, churches given silver, and every county received £100 'to be distributed among poor men for his [father's] soul'.[55] Henry I, to

[51] D. M. Metcalf, 'The premises of early medieval mints: the case of Winchester', in *I Luoghi della Moneta: Le sedi della zecche dall'antichità all'età moderna* (Milan, 2001), 59–67, at 61, and *Atlas*, tables, 294–301.

[52] *ASC*, 1035, C.   [53] *ASC*, 1043, C, E.

[54] *ASC*, 1087, *GRA* 1.542–3; 'in haste', *JW* 3.46–7.

[55] *ASC*, 1087; considered in detail, Barlow, *Rufus*, 63–4.

procure the succession, rode directly to Winchester to secure the Treasury before all else. And when King Henry's elder brother, Duke Robert, attempted to claim England by invasion, it was towards Winchester that Rannulf Flambard led the duke's army in 1101. Again, after Henry I's death, both contenders for the crown, first Stephen and later Matilda, rode to Winchester to secure the Treasury before attempting to gain acceptance by the Londoners, whose support was also crucial.

Whilst the surrender of London was vital in 1066, and the acclamation in Westminster given to William on Christmas Day a fitting symbol of the completion of the Conquest, yet as an invader himself William showed his awareness of the city's vulnerability, building Baynard's Castle to the west of the City, just outside St Paul's, and the Tower site to the east, as well as other fortifications. London's importance was primarily as England's premier port and commercial centre; it was a production centre for coin-dies, which were returned after use.[56] The City had hithes, and Southwark, on the other bank, extensive harbours, but its very moorings and wharves made it open to sea-borne raids. Moreover, in 1066 the mint at Southwark had probably been destroyed by fire along with the manor, its activity appearing thin and sporadic until late in William's reign.[57] The seaboard access to the Thames estuary also meant vulnerability to Eustace of Boulogne, William's erstwhile rival, intermittently an ally or actively hostile, which was true also of the comital house of Flanders. Both houses were well known for their sea-borne expertise; moreover, the strength of the following of the dead king, Harold, and of course, the Danes, was on the sea.

Sea-transport and the movements of a sea-borne force were, throughout the medieval ages, much more effective and speedy than movements over land, and all coasts were susceptible to surprise raiding parties. However, shipping and trade between England and the continent in the eleventh century was normally conducted between ports facing each other across the Channel,[58] so Winchester and its south-coast outports, well protected by Porchester and the Isle of Wight, looked accessibly across the channel to Rouen and, after 1066 until well beyond the eleventh century, the Treasury operated chiefly from the Wessex capital. Under William, in the 'real economy', as well as at the Treasury, the coin evidence indicates a reversal of the trend under the Godwinesons, and a concomitant severing of contacts between the Danelaw and its trading partners across the North Sea.[59]

Winchester being of prime concern, the Conqueror began a castle there between Christmas 1066 and the following February.[60] It extended over five and a half acres (roughly two hectares), demanding the destruction of streets within and beyond the

---

[56] M. M. Archibald, J. R. S. Lang, and G. Milne, 'Four medieval coin dies from the London waterfront', *Numismatic Chronicle*, 155 (1995), 165–200; M. Allen, 'Mints and money in Norman England', *ANS*, 34 (2011), 12.

[57] Metcalf, *Atlas*, 188, 297.

[58] M. Gardiner, 'Shipping and trade between England and the Continent during the eleventh century', *ANS*, 22 (1999), 72–93.

[59] Metcalf, *Atlas*, 88.   [60] OV 2.194–6.

borough walls. In 1072, William was able to hold his Easter Council 'in the king's chapel sited in the castle', and the outline of an apsidal building, datable to the late 1060s, made of quality masonry with internal wall-paintings and coloured window glass, has been uncovered.[61] By c.1111, perhaps earlier, the Treasury seems to have moved into the Norman castle, for the king's court sat on matters fiscal in 'the castle at Winchester', 'in the treasury at Winchester'.[62] William's reign witnessed the transformation of the enclave, at enormous expense. The royal works consumed no less than twelve houses, five moneyers' workshops, part of a street, and the cemetery of New Minster,[63] the last eventually receiving land and tithes in exchange.[64] Documented mint-sites of early twelfth-century Winchester were, nevertheless, also located just outside the royal enclave, and indeed some royal officials may also have been moneyers.[65] Royal patronage was likely to be important to both moneyers and goldsmiths: one mid eleventh-century Winchester goldsmith was probably a moneyer; another goldsmith boasted a moneyer in the family.[66]

The construction of the Norman cathedral was still more revolutionary; it meant the demolition of Old and New Minster, both less than a century old. Work began on the cathedral in 1079; and the demolition of Old Minster followed upon the translation in 1093 of St Swithin's feretory to the new cathedral.[67] Part of the western end of Old Minster remained under the nave of the Norman cathedral, which was probably not completed until the second decade of the twelfth century. The unique scale of the new cathedral bears witness to the centrality of Winchester in the thinking of the new Norman rulers: its length of 162 metres (c.530 feet) was unequalled by any other ecclesiastical building in western Christendom north of the Alps, apart from St Hugh's great church at Cluny of 1086–1109.[68] In the most extravagant manner—and the most destructive—the Normans superimposed their cultural power onto the royal holy site.

DOMUS DEI

The scale of that extraordinary group of buildings is of great relevance to Domesday. At this period, church towers commonly held records and valuables and were constructed to be defensible, and those of both Old Minster and New Minster at Winchester were grandiose in scale. An analysis of its Book of Life suggests that New Minster's tower contained some six storeys each embellished with external sculpture, perhaps reflecting the dedication of the space inside to a

---

[61] *Acta*, no. 68; Biddle and Keene, in *Winchester*, 303–4.

[62] *Hist.Abbend* 2, nos 168, 169.   [63] *Winchester*, Survey I, nos 57–60, 80–1.

[64] GDB:43a (HAM:6,1); *Acta*, no. 344, 1072 × 1085.

[65] P. Nightingale, 'Some London moneyers and reflections on the organization of the English mints in the eleventh and twelfth centuries', *Numismatic Chronicle*, 142 (1982), 35–50.

[66] Biddle and Keene, in *Winchester*, 421.

[67] *AnnWinton*, 32, 37.   [68] Biddle and Keene, in *Winchester*, 308–10.

particular saint.[69] In Germany—whose imperial links with the Anglo-Saxon royal house were by no means distant—the first or second floors of great church towers have been connected with imperial affairs or ceremonies.[70] Elsewhere in England, in 1072, the upper floor of the nunnery church at Wilton supplied a suitable meeting-place for a major land transaction between important people, presided over by Queen Edith.[71] The two Winchester towers, one around 20 metres (65 feet) high, the other at least 40 metres (130 feet), offered secure sites for conserving documents and valuables. It may even be that one of these havens supplied the very origin of Domesday's name.

The Winchester minsters were the House of God par excellence, with the authority of the royal house welded to that of the spiritual. Between 995 and 1053, copies of wills and charters—royal, monastic, and private—were placed *aet thaes kinges haligdom*, literally 'at the king's sanctuary', implying the safekeeping of documents with the royal collection of sacred treasures and relics.[72] Relics were reverentially preserved within the Minsters and, together with crosses, works of devotion, and key volumes such as the *Book of Life*, they related the laity as well as the religious to eternal life. Some of the wills and charters conserved at Old Minster were transcribed into a cartulary compiled in the first half of the twelfth century at Winchester Cathedral Priory—its institutional successor—thereby preserving a considerable number of the Anglo-Saxon kings' charters and diplomas.

Relics were usually conserved in a chapel; and as priests were the only persons qualified to supervise oaths, relics aided the verification of oaths and assisted the safekeeping of archives, lending fearful authority to documents and witness. Relics reposed in vessels of silver and gold, enamelled and jewelled, of the finest artistry and craftsmanship. Many superb reliquaries survive because of their portable nature, because the minute workmanship exceeded even the value of their materials, and because of their strong representative associations. They survive because they were treasured. They and their contents were, moreover, of commercial as well as religious value, making the religious institutions where they were housed not merely into revered centres of pilgrimage, but the recipients of numerous donations.

Whereas the vicissitudes affecting lay and royal dynasties militated against the preservation of records, ecclesiastical institutions were undying corporations. In contrast to the wooden halls of many royal residences, great churches and their towers were often of stone and became obvious depositories for valuables and documents, especially before the era of stone castles, the patronal saint and his relics conferring an aura of inviolability. Possibly the great ecclesiastical buildings

---

[69] R. N. Quirk, 'Winchester New Minster and its tenth-century tower', *Journal of the British Archaeological Association*, 3rd ser., 24 (1961), 16–54, at 33–5. Biddle and Keene, in *Winchester*, 315.

[70] Discussed by E. Fernie, *The Architecture of the Anglo-Saxons from Alfred to the Monastic Revival* (London 1983), 98–101.

[71] Keynes, 'Giso', App. III, 264–6.

[72] S.939; EHD1, no. 121; Charters, no. 115; S.1478; S.1521, 1035 × 1044. S. Keynes, *The Diplomas of King Æthelred II 'The Unready', 978–1016* (Cambridge, 1980), 148–9 and 'Regenbald, the Chancellor (sic)', *ANS*, 10 (1987), 185–222, at 189–91.

where records and relics were conserved encouraged the confusion, or even fostered the pun—the English were fond of word-games—between the Latin *Domus Dei*, the House of God (there are certainly many *mansiones* in Domesday) and the English *Domes daeg*, Day of Judgement. A later thirteenth-century Glastonbury historian who transcribed the Domesday account for his monastery's lands referred to his source as *Domus Dei*.[73] Domesday's first location on the Winchester ecclesiastical site, before its removal to the castle there (thence to the London Temple Church and the Tower in the late twelfth century and to the precincts of Westminster Abbey in the early thirteenth), was a once-recognized explanation of the name's origin;[74] perhaps legendary, it preserved a tradition.

A ROYAL WRITING OFFICE?

The character and scope of an archive at Winchester—whether indeed an established royal writing office existed at all in the late Anglo-Saxon period—is the subject of on-going discussion by specialists.[75] A minimalist view is that memory and live witness were of greater import than documents; the documents of the *haligdom* were kept for religious sentiment, not for secular reference.[76] The sporadic survival of royal charters in monastic collections did not demonstrate anything more than the appetite of great ecclesiastical houses for defending their possessions, frequently by forgery; albeit some charters were originals, made by the scribes of the monastery concerned, at the royal behest.[77] But they were not the products of a royal chancery.

In considering the nature of central written records, three known elements need to be reconciled: the itinerant nature of kingship; the evident production as well as conservation of royal charters in leading monasteries; and, most relevant to Domesday, the ability of the ruler to grant land with or without fiscal privileges and to levy taxes. Tenth-century texts, surviving via the Winchester cartulary already mentioned, suggested to one scholar the early functioning of a royal writing office based at Winchester.[78] Yet, this interpretation has received little support.[79]

---

[73] *In libro saccarii Londoniae, qui dicitur Domus Dei, quem conponi fecit rex Willelmus primus, subacto sibi et pacificato regno angliae,* Adam of Domerham, *Historia de Rebus Gestis Glastoniensibus,* ed. T. Hearne (Oxford, 1727), 627. The Burton Cartulary and its Penarth version each use the spelling *Domusday*: J. F. R. Walmsley, 'Another Domesday text', *Medieval Studies,* 29 (1977), 109–20, at 112.

[74] See the sixteenth- and seventeenth-century antiquarians, John Stow and Richard Baker, Hallam, 34.

[75] Barlow, *English Church,* 119–37; P. Chaplais, 'The Anglo-Saxon chancery: from the diploma to the writ', *Journal of the Society of Archivists,* 3 (1966), 160–76; Keynes, *Diplomas,* 140, 137, 152–3.

[76] M. T. Clanchy, *From Memory to Written Record* (London, 1979), 14–19.

[77] Clanchy, 248–50.

[78] C. Hart, 'The Codex Wintoniensis and the King's *Haligdom*', in J. Thirsk (ed.), *Land, Church and People: Essays presented to Professor H. P. R. Finberg, Agricultural History Review,* 18, Supplement (1970), 7–38; cf. the Merovingian kings' special relationship with Saint-Denis, D. Ganz, 'Bureaucratic shorthand and Merovingian learning', in P. Wormald, D. A. Bullough, and R. Collins (eds), *Ideal and Reality in Frankish and Anglo-Saxon Society: Studies presented to J. M. Wallace-Hadrill* (Oxford, 1983), 58–73.

[79] N. Brooks, 'Anglo-Saxon charters', in *Anglo-Saxon Myths: State and Church, 400–1066* (London, 2000), esp. 199–200; A. R. Rumble, 'The purposes of the Codex Wintoniensis', *ANS,* 4 (1981), 153–66, 224–32.

Rather bishops present at the king's general council—the witan—and a few favoured abbots drafted and wrote documents or supervised their writing: perhaps Winchester dominated royal output early in the tenth century, with Abingdon becoming a base during Edgar's reign.[80] Further, the similarities of hand and style evident in surviving documents do not represent the common practice of a royal writing office, but of monastic-based resources. Certainly, monastic centres of excellence had regional, and even national, influence and their 'house-styles', visible in survivals, are not disputed; great houses, as was Abingdon Abbey, might 'on occasion' serve others and 'undertake to draw up diplomas for local laymen and other ecclesiastics'.[81] However, the study of royal diplomas of the late tenth and early eleventh century indicates that the facility to produce texts was in demand wherever the witan met, and for this no static ecclesiastical scriptorium was suitable. Rather, they were produced in an itinerant writing office centred upon the king's household.[82]

Before the coming of the Conqueror, the evidence broadens enough for us to see that kingship availed itself of several means of conveying instructions. Domesday shows us that towns were obliged to assist the king's messengers.[83] An ecclesiastic who had an interest in a land-grant was on occasion bidden to use his own scriptorium or scribe to draw up his own grant; this was over and above the many known examples of houses making their own copies of grants—and of embroidering them (perhaps even forging them, as Westminster was to do).[84] Bishops also acted at the king's request and on his behalf: a writ of the 1050s declares that King Edward had granted land in Oxfordshire to Saint-Denis in Paris, and the bishop of Dorchester had his full permission to draw up a charter for it.[85] The king also indubitably travelled accompanied by his own chaplains and relics.[86]

Whatever the case earlier, in the eleventh century characteristics of the later writing office were becoming discernible; a glossary, produced at Abingdon, associates the office of custodian of the relics with that of chancellor, and links both to the 'treasure-chest' and chamberlain.[87] The keeper of the king's seal was the chancellor's deputy or the chancellor himself: the royal priest, Regenbald, attested King Edward's charters, on one occasion as 'keeper of the king's seal', perhaps on another as 'chancellor', just as he occurs in Domesday Book.[88] Later, in the 1080s, the keeper of the king's seal, Rannulf Flambard, served under the chancellor,[89] and the same functionaries are linked together in an early twelfth-century text, the

[80] P. Chaplais, 'The royal Anglo-Saxon "Chancery" of the tenth century revisited', in H. Mayr-Harting and R. I. Moore (eds), *Studies in History presented to R. H. C. Davis* (London, 1985), 41–51.
[81] S. Kelly, *The Charters of Abingdon Abbey*, Anglo-Saxon Charters VII, Part I (Oxford, 2000), provides a nuanced discussion of the question, lxxii–lxxxiv, cxxii–cxxxi, quotation at cxxxi.
[82] Keynes, *Diplomas*, 39–83, 134–53.
[83] Dover, GDB:1a (KEN:D3); Torksey, 337a (LIN:T,1).
[84] *Writs*, 286–339.   [85] *Writs*, no. 55; S.1105; also *Writs*, no. 7; S.1067.
[86] *Waltham Chronicle*, 46.   [87] Keynes, *Diplomas*, 145–50.
[88] S.1033; S.1036, possibly spurious, but demonstrates the credibility. GDB:180d (HEF:1,46).
[89] *Hugh Chantor*, 6.

Constitutio Domus Regis: in outlining Henry I's household, it opens with the chancellor, followed by the master of the writing office who is closely associated with the seal, followed by the chaplain in charge of the chapel and the relics—who has two men and four servants beneath him.[90]

The king's seal effectively represented his authority at a distance and authenticated royal instructions; the Domesday Inquiry not infrequently sought the evidence of the imprint of the king's seal, whether of Edward or of William, sight of which was affirmed, or lacking.[91] It is known from 990 that the king might send an envoy with a seal to a key case in a shire court.[92] In Domesday itself, old charters are surprisingly rarely cited or their contents quoted as authority; on occasion they were cited to substantiate a tax rating rather than for verifying tenure.[93] The authority of the seal of King Edward does gain mentions;[94] but it seems that the shire and hundred also required or preferred evidence from King William.[95] It was the shire's or hundred's witness of a seal or writ of King William (and they seem to be treated as synonymous by 1066[96]) or the arrival of his seal-bearing envoy, that appears to have been demanded as the touchstone of validity for the post-1066 transfer of land: thus Domesday not infrequently notes when men of the locality have, or have not, seen a seal, writ, envoy, or 'deliverer'.[97] Such references might well have been to writ-charters delivered to the shire-court or hundred, not necessarily to a document retained by the landholder: albeit one priest was expected to produce either a document or local witness to an envoy if his tenure was to be upheld.[98] The emphasis on the witness by the shire of a royal order seems to correspond with the function of writ-charters delivered to the shire court whenever a new king or a new incumbent took over.[99] After the Norman Conquest, Harry Cronne observed, 'the important thing for a litigant, or a potential one, was not so much to possess an ancient charter as evidence, especially if it were a pre-Conquest one, as to have its contents embodied in a charter of confirmation'.[100] Whilst literacy was not confined to churchmen in eleventh-century England,[101] the seal with the image of the English king was itself memorably impressive. Earlier English kings had aspired to the title *basileus* in charters; but Edward's unusual double-sided seal bore the image of the king 'in majesty', and was inscribed: 'the seal of Edward, king of the English', *Anglorum Basilei*.[102] Doubtless influenced via the German imperial tradition, the

---

[90] EHD2, no. 30; see also J. H. Round, 'Bernard, the king's scribe', *EHR*, 55 (1899), 417–30
[91] e.g. GDB:60d (BRK:21,22).   [92] Charters, no. 66; S.1454.
[93] GDB:175cd (WOR:10,10).   [94] e.g. GDB:208a (HUN:D1).
[95] GDB:59b (BRK:7,38); 374a (YRK:CW39).
[96] *Writs*, 543–5.   [97] GDB:376c (LIN:CK10); 36a (SUR:21,3).
[98] e.g. GDB:211a (BDF:14,1). References listed Fleming, *Law*, 547.
[99] Exemplified by Bury St Edmunds and illuminated importantly by R. Sharpe, 'The use of writs in the eleventh century', *ASE*, 32 (2004), 247–91.
[100] H. A. Cronne, 'Charter scholarship in England', *University of Birmingham Historical Journal*, 8 (1961), 26–61, at 33.
[101] Williams, *The English*, 84.
[102] Barlow, *Confessor*, Plate 6, 135; T. A. Heslop, 'English Seals from the mid-ninth century to 1100', *Journal of the British Archaeological Association*, 133 (1980), 1–16, at 9–10.

term *basileus* betrayed its ultimate derivation from the Byzantine imperial style in which the depiction of the Christian Roman Emperor was intended to reflect on earth the authority of the reigning Christ in Majesty in heaven.

Turning to the Conqueror's reign, the various sources of scribal expertise and record, royal and ecclesiastical, were similarly not divorced; there was flexibility. In 1069, a clerk who was also active at Saint-Denis drew up a royal charter with Old English features in Winchester for Saint-Denis.[103] David Bates' unique knowledge of the documents of William of Normandy gives us a fully measured assessment of 'chancery' activities in William's reign—one that also seems applicable earlier. The term chancery 'should be used to describe an organization responsible for the validation of *acta*, rather than, necessarily, for their production'.[104] 'Everything points' to the chancellor 'having a vital role in the production of documents in the king's name', which did not prevent a charter being drawn up in the locality and sent to William for confirmation and signature.[105]

The assets of the Winchester minsters were obviously dedicated to royal service, and vice-versa. In addition to the royal charters recorded by the monks of Old Minster, its own business was witnessed by the highest in the land: one lease of land to a layman was witnessed by King Edward and his mother, as well as by named archbishops, bishops, earls, and other 'many good men, both clerics and laymen'.[106] Abbot Aelfwig of New Minster was sufficiently identified with King Harold to have been killed in battle at Hastings along with twelve of his monks and twenty knights, with the consequence that William took punitive action against the abbey.[107] (The house was permitted to elect another abbot only in 1068 or 1069; and he, Wulfric, was deposed by Lanfranc.) In Domesday, the lands of the erstwhile minsters, like their churches, buildings, and cemeteries, were indiscriminately at the mercy of royal needs. By 1086, Hugh de Port, royal official and probably Hampshire's sheriff, held not a few of New Minster's manors (and was entered, along with his wife, in its *Liber Vitae*), and deployed several to fund royal officials: one being held by Oda, a *Dapifer* of native birth, another by a chamberlain, and another by a royal huntsman.[108]

Under King Edward a body of royal clerks existed who were 'his' men, some recruited from abroad, whose early years were spent on his business. A considerable measure of continuity between his reign and William's early rule obtained in both the writing office and in the Winchester treasury. Regenbald, King Edward's chancellor, continued to be given lands and so presumably to function at the highest levels during William's first years,[109] when writs and charters continued

---

[103] *Acta*, no. 254.
[104] The essential discussion for William's reign is David Bates, introduction in *Acta*, 96–109, quotation at 96.
[105] Bates, *Acta*, 102, 105–6.   [106] Charters, no. 98; S.1391, dated 1043–4.
[107] *Liber Vitae*, 41.   [108] GDB:42c–d (HAM:6,1).
[109] He received 38 hides worth about £46. He held about 50 hides, worth around £40, before 1066, Keynes, 'Regenbald', *ANS*, 10 (1987), 194–6, 210–21; *Acta*, nos 223, 224; EHD2, nos 33, 36.

to be issued in Anglo-Saxon. Many royal clerks remained in harness through 1066 and afterwards; and in 1086 at least thirty priests and clerks are mentioned in Domesday as currently being 'the king's'.[110] Even lacking a Domesday account of Winchester itself, the Survey shows at least eleven royal officials, probably clerks, holding lands in the surrounding county, and the long list of all sorts of land-holding functionaries are witness to the city's still paramount position. These officials bear the hall-marks of continuity in office: in Domesday they were even categorized as 'king's thegns', a high echelon of royal service in the Anglo-Saxon period, with no less than seven chamberlains, one marshal, a treasurer, and two priests so listed in Hampshire.[111] One treasurer, Henry, had received his two properties in Winchester before 1066 and had several manors in Hampshire in 1086.[112] The important-sounding 'Oda of Winchester' had been a treasurer under Edward and had held land in Wimborne, Dorset; as a member of an Anglo-Saxon family who continued in the Conqueror's service, he did not retain his earlier estate under William but was given different landed assets, presumably in order to focus his new loyalties: no less than 38 hides in four shires.[113] He was, in all likelihood, the same Oda who held New Minster lands and the Oda enlisted in New Minster's Book of Life. The body of royal officials visible in and around Winchester in 1086 was unlikely to have been newly instituted there.

EXPERTISE IN THE REGIONS

Other centres of literacy offered halfway houses between royal offices and religious foundations. Successive Anglo-Saxon rulers drew on colleges of canons as resources for recruiting and rewarding clerks; several had a special relationship with crown service and their members proved of value to the maintenance of the government of Edward the Confessor and of Harold. Regenbald, King Edward's chancellor, held estates in seven counties and many churches, including up to nine minsters on royal estates, stretching across Berkshire, Wiltshire, Gloucestershire, and Somerset, and possibly Northamptonshire.[114] Spirtes, a richly endowed royal clerk, already employed under Cnut and Harthacnut, had held canonries at St Martin's, Dover, and St Mary's, Bromfield, and was near enough to the centre of power to fall from favour into exile in 1065, his lands being given to other leading functionaries such as Robert fitzWimarc, the Staller.[115] The status of such men was high and

---

[110] Listed, Barlow, *English Church*, 131, 156–8.

[111] GDB:48a–50d; Biddle and Keene, in *Winchester*, 390–1, 475–6; Williams, *The English*, 109–16.

[112] GDB:49a (HAM:56,1–4); *Winchester*, Survey I, ed. F. Barlow, no. 184.

[113] e.g. GDB:75c (DOR:1,21), 'treasurer' in *Exon*; B. J. Golding, introduction in *The Hampshire Domesday*, Alecto 1989, 24–5; Williams, *The English*, 115–16.

[114] J. Blair, 'Secular minster churches in Domesday Book', in *Reassessment*, 124; Keynes, 'Regenbald', 194–7.

[115] GDB:1d (KEN:M21), 252d (SHR:3d,7); M. F. Smith, 'The preferment of royal clerks in the reign of Edward the Confessor', *Haskins Soc. Journal*, 9 (1997), 159–74, at 169–70.

acknowledged to be so. Regenbald was formally given the legal worth of a bishop in an individual writ, 'that his *wite* [the legal compensation for injury by another] be equivalent to that of a bishop of a diocese in all things'.[116] Royal chapels might well have supplied possible bases for drawing up Domesday's regional returns.[117] However, during the Confessor's reign the indications are that such houses were drawn upon as sinecures for largely non-resident royal clerks, leading directly or indirectly to their economic decline;[118] but they afforded bases for itinerant royal servants when needed. And, with their *ius scholarum*, as at St Oswald's, Gloucester, they might still have raised personnel suitable for royal tasks.[119]

Harold Godwineson—William's immediate predecessor whatever William might argue—both as earl and as king had close links with several religious houses that were almost certainly maintained for practical as well as devotional reasons. He established a dean and twelve secular canons at Holy Cross, Waltham, and built them a splendid church, filled with ornaments, dedicated around 1060.[120] Harold was known to have been a friend of Wulfstan, the long-surviving monastic bishop of Worcester;[121] and he appears in the Bayeux Tapestry as having a special relationship with the Church at Bosham, which overlooked the protected harbour. Although its lands were in the hands of Edward's Norman kinsman, Osbern, Harold's father, Earl Godwine, and presumably in turn Harold too, had held land there, as did a royal clerk.[122] Harold also maintained close links of mutual support with the powerful abbey of Abingdon, whose thegns died fighting for him at the battle of Hastings. He also travelled with his chaplains and relics.[123]

Thus Anglo-Saxon kings kept some contact with regions of diverse character and history via the incumbents of colleges of canons, as well as through abbots and bishops, and the alliance between Church and State was probably as close as, or closer than, anywhere in Europe. Eminent amongst those collegiate churches that funded a royal secretariat in the eleventh century was the long-established St Martin's, Dover; such houses of secular canons were originally established to share a dwelling site as well as a church. St Martin's evidently provided for, and was in contact with, a formidable range of expertise: the five, possibly six, priests and clerks of King Edward known to have held its canonries were all men of stature, allocated lands and churches elsewhere.[124] The Normans, in turn, took full advantage of this inherited expertise, especially useful as the wing of power towards Normandy could only enhance the strategic position of Dover; and several of these clerks, whilst quite possibly non-resident, were still landholders in 1086.

---

[116] *Writs*, no. 44; S.1097; EHD2, no. 34.

[117] Their tenure continued to be associated with officeholders such as Roger of Salisbury and Henry of Blois, J. H. Denton, *English Royal Chapels 1100–1300* (Manchester, 1970), 4, 23–4.

[118] Lennard, 396–404.   [119] Denton, 51–3.

[120] *Waltham Chronicle*, xix–xxv, *cap.* 14 and *cap.* 15.

[121] *The Vita Wulfstani of William of Malmesbury*, ed. R. R. Darlington, Camden Soc. 3rd ser. (London, 1928), 13.

[122] GDB:17b–c.   [123] *Waltham Chronicle*, 46.

[124] Barlow, *English Church*, listed, 156–8.

Perhaps the making of Domesday, despite its many uncertainties, can throw some shadowy light back onto the debate about the Anglo-Saxon writing office. Scribes belonging to Bishop Osmund's circle at Salisbury who collaborated to produce books for the community at Salisbury also participated in the copying of the regional Domesday return in Exon Domesday (hereafter *Exon*).[125] Yet *Exon*, with three or more of its scribes now identified as belonging to the newly consti-tuted cathedral at Old Salisbury, has survived only via the archive of Exeter Cathedral, although no one doubts that it represents a stage in the making of the government-organized Domesday Inquiry. The entries for the lands of St Martin's, Dover have distinctive characteristics in Domesday. Royal and other ecclesiastical writing offices existed, and were employed: it was the art of the possible. That Giso, bishop of Wells, a former royal clerk, was given responsibility at the end of Edward's reign to draw up a charter for his house does not indicate that there was no royal writing office.[126] It signifies rather that Giso, because of his bishopric in Wells—not despite it—was still part of the team under Edward, Harold, and William. Royal clerks became bishops, members of the witan and council, com-missioned for multitudinous tasks until their infirmity and death. Certainly, for the reigns of the Confessor and the Conqueror it seems unwarranted to push distinc-tions between royal, collegiate, and episcopal scriptoria too far, and use was made of all three.[127]

RECORDS

Clerks and relics were certainly portable; but for reserves in silver and gold, stable storehouses and records were essential. While Winchester was the home of the principal treasury of the kingdom, and royal access to it an essential route to royal power in the eleventh century, the question affecting the making of Domesday is one of records. Was it a treasury with documentation, as opposed to a mere deposit?

All grants of land, and tolls, potentially held consequences for the collection of national taxation. Grants stated the number of hides—the unit of assessment for public works and taxation—granted and listed the beneficial assets, and the necessity for writs of confirmation suggest that royal officials took over judicial rights during vacancies.[128] In the Winchester archive, charters were often briefly endorsed with the names of the estate, the donor, the recipient, and often the hidage of the estate conveyed.[129] It would have been easy for royal clerks to amend fiscal lists in similar fashion, thereby keeping central records up to date and, if some

---

[125] Webber, 1–18.   [126] *Writs*, no. 68; S.1115.
[127] The Carolingians expected bishops and abbots to produce further copies of their enactments, McKitterick, *The Carolingians and the Written Word*, 32.
[128] N. Brooks, 'The Archbishopric of Canterbury and the so-called introduction of knight-service into England', *ANS*, 34 (2011), 41–62, esp. 49–51.
[129] Hart, 'The Codex Wintoniensis and the King's Haligdom', 20–4.

central fiscal register were then altered, there was no need to make or keep a copy of the charter itself. A recurring formula in grants was 'as fully and to the same extent as' a predecessor; thus, all that was required was the updating of a list.

Apart from the two great volumes of Domesday Book, it remains true that during the reigns of the Confessor and the Conqueror, as earlier, evidence of land transactions and taxation survives largely in the archives of the great churches. It continues predominantly true indeed of records for almost a century afterwards, but we know that in the first half of the twelfth century this did not preclude the evolution of a central base, first at Winchester, then at Salisbury, and later Westminster. It is now becoming more generally accepted that there were practical government documents of this period that survived only via monastic not central archives: amongst other 'public' documents, a preliminary draft of the Worcestershire Domesday and a late eleventh-century county list of hides for Gloucestershire—from around 1086, updated to around 1100—have survived only via two later cartularies of Evesham Abbey.[130] One list of hides *c.*1104, surviving via Evesham, refers to the roll of Winchester, *rotulum de Winton*, thereby echoing similar references to the rolls of Winchester elsewhere—in other words, to rolls held in the Winchester archive.[131] Moreover, landholders were also careful to keep some record of their fiscal responsibilities, a chore surely concomitant with an equally informed and demanding royal fisc. Long known and little discussed, but highlighted recently, is a record of the archbishopric of York, *c.*1020, concerning its multiple estates of Otley, Ripon, and Sherburn, and their numerous tributary vills. Not a record of the food-farms or rents, it is a memorandum of hidages and ploughlands, distinguishing inland, workland, 'priests' land', sokeland, and waste, and so was fiscal and tenurial in basis.[132] As the survey was written into a Gospel book, the volume was undoubtedly conserved on ecclesiastical premises.

Further references of various dates in the later eleventh century exist to lists of hides in the 'writings of the treasury', or 'rolls of Winchester', which are not to Domesday, although some may well have been to the detailed, and perhaps more useful Domesday returns.[133] A session of barons and officials in Winchester in 1111 was called upon to determine to which hundred the Abingdon Abbey manor

---

[130] Evesham A and K in a cartulary written up between *c.*1130 and *c.*1200. Further analysis is to be found in *Evesham A*. Also relevant here are Evesham P and Q from a second cartulary written up *c.*1206. Evesham A, P, and Q are translated in *DB Worcestershire*, App. IV. Evesham K is translated in *DB Gloucestershire*, Appendix EvK. Their contents are outlined in these two publications. I am indebted to Howard Clarke for numerous informal discussions about these texts.

[131] Evesham P.

[132] W. H. Stevenson, 'Yorkshire surveys and other eleventh-century documents in the York Gospels', *EHR*, 27 (1912), 1–25; Charters, no. 84; tabulated and mapped in S. Baxter, 'Archbishop Wulfstan and the administration of God's property', in M. Townend (ed.), *Wulfstan, Archbishop of York* (Turnhout, 2004), 161–205, 179–86.

[133] For instance, two mid twelfth-century references *temp*. Henry I–Henry II, to the 'rolls of Winchester', one of which is clearly not to Domesday, J. H. Round, 'The Northamptonshire Survey', in *Feudal England*, 2nd edn (London, 1964), 175–80, 175; Harvey 1971, 765–7; Harvey 1975, 176–9; D. Roffe, 'The Historia Croylandensis: a plea for reassessment', *EHR*, 110 (1995), 93–108.

of Lewknor belonged and they consulted 'the book of the treasury'.[134] There is, however, no information on which was Lewknor's hundred in Great Domesday itself, so the court was seemingly referred either to the fuller regional version or to a hundredal hidage schedule.[135] The latter, some containing earlier data, some later, might be commonly referred to in the context of tax assessment, and contrasted with the *descriptio*: from Worcester, we hear of the *exemplar* of the royal record, which is conserved in the royal treasury, together with the *descriptio* of the whole of England.[136] (A Worcester cartulary also contains a list of hides, possibly earlier than Domesday, more probably later, which concludes with a reference to the 'old hidage which is in the Roll of Winchester'.[137]) The preamble to a late copy of an Abingdon list of hides says it is copied from writing in 'the royal treasury' 'arranged by hundreds'; the following extract containing hides and tenants is attributed to a different source: 'from another book of the royal treasury, of the time of King William which he ordered to be made . . . it contains an *abbrevatio* of hides and a *descriptio*'.[138]

Before the Domesday project was launched, schematic Domesday-type data and documentation were in use for reference on matters of tenure and tax.[139] Before the Domesday project was in any position to make returns, tax collectors were sending money to Winchester and accounting 'before the king's barons'.[140] Whilst even in the Conqueror's reign relatively few records attributable to royal scribes survive, Exon Domesday, some 532 folios, a regional Domesday text and its Geld Accounts, written up partly by scribes based at an important but incipient ecclesiastical scriptorium, stands as a substantial reminder that the resources that the royal treasury and a few officials might activate were almost limitless in scope.

WINCHESTER, THE BISHOPS, AND THE TREASURY

According to the minimalist view, the Winchester treasury was merely one of several depositories in the Anglo-Saxon and early Norman periods. But an archive relating to the main treasure-store should be beyond question. Tenth-century Byzantium was 'one of the most bureaucratic states of the medieval world', yet most of its imperial and administrative documents in the original have disappeared,

---

[134] *per Librum de Thesauro*, HistAbbend 2, 169–70, no. 169; *Regesta* 2, no. 1000.

[135] GDB:156d (OXF:9,1).

[136] *Ad huius rei confirmationem exemplar eius in autentica regis cartula . . . scriptum est, quae in thesauro regali cum totius angliae descriptionibus conseruatur*, Hemming, 287–8; *DB:Worcestershire*, App. V, Worcester F.

[137] *Red Book of Worcester*, vol. 4, ed. M. Hollings, Worcester Historical Society (1950), 442–3; but see *The Cartulary of Worcester Cathedral Priory*, ed. R. R. Darlington (*PRS*, ns 38, 1968 for 1962–3) for evidence for later dating, xlvi–vii.

[138] D. C. Douglas, 'Some early surveys from the Abbey of Abingdon', *EHR*, 44 (1929), 623–5; *HistAbbend* 2, App. III, Texts 1 and 2, at 379–86.

[139] Harvey 1971; further, see below pp. 27–31, 67–71.

[140] 20s was allowed for William the Usher and Ralf de Pommeraye in order that 'they should carry the geld to the treasury at Winchester', DB4, f.71; *vadiaurunt foris ante barones regis*, f.76b; 'not able to render account', *nescierunt reddere rationem*, f.81b. The accounting comments are interlined.

surviving only as copies in the monastic houses they concern.[141] In England before 1066, and thereafter, there was unquestionably specific knowledge of the lands, jurisdictional revenues and fiscal concessions granted to individual landholders, and of the receipts due from royal estates, royal gelds and dues, and coinage. There was a taxation system that was capable of setting national targets in time of threat and that was imposed on counties at a varying rate according to the level of returns necessary.[142] The complex demands of the hidage system that raised man-power for borough defences and military service, taxation, and revenues from royal lands required records of shire liability for reference.[143]

Whilst the importance of the king's word and actions required ever-moving facilities for issuing charters and other documents, the audit and receipt of revenues had a least one fixed site well before Domesday. Early in William's reign, William of Poitiers wrote as if the king had inherited a recognized treasury that was more than the sum of various deposits: 'William set a limit that was not oppressive to the collection of tribute and all dues owed to the royal treasury', *regius fiscus*.[144] The same formal term was adopted at Abingdon when linking the Treasury to the oversight of tenure: the chronicler looked back to the aftermath of 1066, to the time when many English exiles 'fled to foreign kingdoms taking a restricted amount of money with them and when their lands became forfeit to the royal treasury', *in regium proscripte sunt fiscum*.[145] Long before that there are hints of a Winchester overview. In the mid tenth century, when King Eadred's will, *c*.951–5, left £400 each, to relieve the people of their regions from famine and from the distress caused by the heathen army, to the archbishop of Canterbury, to the bishop of Dorchester 'for the Mercians', and to the bishop of Winchester for the people of Hampshire, Wiltshire, and Dorset; £200 was assigned to the abbot of Glastonbury for Somerset and Devon. The king also requested that another £200 be kept at Winchester 'for whichever shire may need it'.[146]

Under the Confessor, many indications, albeit no categorical statement, point to Stigand, bishop of Winchester, having been the royal treasurer, just as the Norman Walkelin, his successor at Winchester, was to be. Stigand prolonged vacancies in no less than five monasteries, was reported to have received payments openly for appointments to bishoprics,[147] and was known to have accumulated churches, leases, and treasure: all of which was consistent with his having been in charge of the Treasury.[148] Significantly, the Treasury or *fiscus*—the same term again—was

[141] R. Morris, 'Dispute settlement in the Byzantine provinces in the tenth century', *Dispute Settlement*, 125, also 209.

[142] *ASC*, 1051, D; M. K. Lawson, 'The collection of danegeld and heregeld in the reigns of Æthelred II and Cnut', *EHR*, 99 (1984), 721–38.

[143] See Ch. 8.   [144] *WP*, 161.

[145] *HistAbbend* 1, 372–3; cf. *HistAbbend* 2, no. 52.

[146] S.1515, EHD1, no. 107.   [147] *LE*, 2, no. 98; *HistAbbend* 2, 196–7.

[148] Perhaps even running 'the whole late Saxon administrative machine by 1066', P. Stafford, *Queen Emma and Queen Edith* (Oxford, 1997), 113; Barlow, *English Church*, 77–81; J. Campbell, 'Some agents and agencies of the Anglo-Saxon state', in Holt, *Studies*, 218.

accused of not providing for Stigand after his deposition.[149] Stigand's expertise in this position, however questioned and questionable, might explain why Queen Emma sought his counsel and was able to withhold her Winchester treasure from her son, why Stigand retained Winchester with Edward's approval when appointed to Canterbury, continuing to base himself there rather than at Canterbury, and why the widowed Queen Edith visited Stigand in prison after his deposition. It would also explain why five kings found him indispensable: the Confessor tolerating the hard-headed pluralist in Winchester and the Conqueror allowing the pluralist to continue there. Importantly, William did not replace Stigand as bishop of Winchester until 1070; and, when he did depose him, his successor Walkelin—a canon of Rouen, and a known and trusted confidant of the king—was nominated and consecrated the following month, suggesting that an incumbent in post was vital. And why, despite Stigand's notoriety amongst censorious chroniclers, his name was inscribed in New Minster's *Liber Vitae* and he was honourably buried at Winchester.[150]

Stigand's indispensability and role is suggested even by his falls: he fell, temporarily, with Queen Emma in 1043, when she refused to give up the treasure she held in Winchester. Despite that, he was back in favour by 1046 and was regarded as a useful ally by all parties, with status enough to act as a mediator and conciliator between the king and the Godwine family after the latter's armed confrontation with their royal lord.[151] Stigand had evident influence in secular circles: more than a thousand thegns and freemen in East Anglia owned Stigand as lord in one way or another and another hundred elsewhere.[152] He was expert in negotiating advantageous leases on lands outside his own bishoprics and, judging by Domesday values for 1066 at Tidenham, did not feel obliged to fulfil all the terms of the lease.[153] Public affairs rather than ecclesiastical duties determined his conduct; his own hoard of precious metals was reputed to have included records of the weights and qualities of the various types of metals collected, thereby indicating his technical Treasury expertise.[154] His extravagant tastes as patron also placed him in the same line as the treasurers Roger of Salisbury and Henry of Blois.[155] Stigand's retention of the bishopric of Winchester alongside that of Canterbury and the extent of the wheeling and dealing that he was permitted outside the two bishoprics—his farming of the royal manor of Tidenham, possibly indeed the very existence of the late Anglo-Saxon survey of Tidenham, and his possession of some formerly

[149] *GP*, 37.
[150] *Liber Vitae*, ff. 16r, 28v; *AnnWinton*, 29.   [151] *VitaÆdw*, 22.
[152] M. F. Smith, 'Archbishop Stigand and the eye of the needle', *ANS*, 16 (1993), 199–219, at 205.
[153] GDB:164a (GLS:1,56); cf. *Charters*, no. 115. Stigand held lands in 10 counties of £755 in value by 1066: in addition, the bishoprics of Canterbury and Winchester were worth over £1,000 each annually, Smith, 'Stigand', 218–19; R. Fleming, *Kings and Lords in Conquest England* (Cambridge, 1991), 81–2.
[154] *qualitatem metallorum et quantitatem ponderum*, *GP*, 37.
[155] Smith, 'Stigand', 217.

royal manors[156]—seem explicable only in terms of a shrewd grasp of the potential of the treasurer's office.

Scholars are continuing to piece together links in the chain of authority from king to shire—links crucial to accessing resources in manpower and money and in effective royal power. It is now more generally appreciated that in the eleventh century ecclesiastical landholders traditionally received written reconfirmation of their land and its fiscal concessions or responsibilities from each new ruler, and preserved these documents, or copies of them. The pattern of Bury writ-charters, surviving from the time of Cnut until the end of the eleventh century, suggests that rulers followed the practice of informing the relevant shire courts of the accession of new abbots and bishops and of the prerogative rights temporarily alienated, so that those courts would know that the newly elected incumbent was entitled to these estates and fiscal privileges and, in the case of the less privileged than Bury, be aware of their concomitant obligations.[157] These texts presume equivalent knowledge at the documents' source, and moreover, the crown's retention of these profitable rights when the office was vacant.[158] The sequence of writ-charters at Bury St Edmunds show that King Edward and his Norman successors were precisely aware of which hundreds they and their predecessors had temporarily alienated to the abbey of Bury St Edmunds, and of the extent of abbey's exemptions from gelds and rights to local jurisdiction, and of its control of a one-moneyer mint.[159] The Northamptonshire Geld Roll of the 1070s used the assessment in hides of each hundred in King Edward's day as the departure point from which exemptions were made. The issue of grants, writs, and instructions also presupposed such data; and the updating of these royal records, together with the collection and accounting for the nationwide geld and regular county farms, would have surely sufficed to keep a nucleus of eleventh-century clerks occupied—quite distinct from current enact-ments of the king and council and the demands of an itinerant royal household. Perhaps significant here is that in the 1090s all enactments witnessed by Rannulf Flambard, save one, are precepts to other royal officers, not charters.[160] Some separate scribal expertise based in Winchester is surely a sound inference, given that even the geld collectors of the 1080s had a cash allowance for scribes.

Domesday's own data shows that three sources of royal revenue demanded accountability before 1066 as well as in 1086: the geld, the royal estates, and the coinage. On geld, any particular manor or landholder could have their assessment changed, as could a hundred, or a county.[161] For obvious reasons, such powers could not rest entirely within the county concerned and its landholders. By the time

---

[156] e.g. Barham: 'Archbishop Stigand held this manor, but it was not the archbishopric's, but was of King Edward's demesne farm', GDB:9d (KEN:5,138); cf. *Charters*, no. 109; *EHD2*, no. 174.

[157] e.g. *Writs*, nos 28–33; Sharpe, 'Use of writs', 247–91.

[158] Brooks, 'The archbishopric of Canterbury', 41–62, esp. 49–51.

[159] Sharpe, 'Use of writs', 280–1, quotes the change made concerning 'heregeld'; *Writs*, no. 15, cf. *Acta*, no 35; *Writs*, nos 8–25.

[160] In the 1180s, the treasurer had his own scribes, *Dialogus*, 29–31, 70.

[161] See Ch. 8, esp. pp. 214–17.

of the launch of the Domesday Inquiry, the Geld Accounts in *Exon* show tax-conveyors, *portatores*, of landholding status, who were responsible for bringing the geld to Winchester, accounting to the king's barons, and giving pledges when the amount was insufficient.[162] The so-called Geld Accounts of 1084 or 1086 are not themselves full accounts, but audited balances recorded after account had been made, interim or final, before the king's barons; it was not feasible that receipts were thus checked and controlled, without the aid of basic documentation.

The historic character of the Winchester minsters and their personnel provided a credible environment for the production of Domesday, and Winchester was certainly the first known site of its conservation and usage, alongside other fiscal data, and perhaps the regional returns.[163] Although *sui generis*, Domesday did not spring out of thin air. Until the completion of a stone Norman castle in Winchester, perhaps Domesday was kept—along with the skeletal records of liabilities of counties and estates which constituted a framework for the collection of Domesday data—in the *Domus Dei*.

---

[162] DB4, ff. 71, 526b; also ff. 76b, 81b.

[163] As in Van Caenegem, *Writs*, no. 70. The acres, the meadow, and the smallholders enumerated are as described in LDB:216b–17a (NFK:17,14;17,29).

2

The Architects of the Inquiry:
The Bishops and the Royal Clerks

The king was completely shaken and summoned a council and threw open discussion on what should be done.

William of Malmesbury[1]

Then at Christmas, the king was at Gloucester with his Council, and held his court there for five days, and then the archbishop and clerics had a synod for three days. There, Maurice was elected Bishop of London, and William for Norfolk, and Robert for Cheshire – they were all clerics of the king. After this, the king had much thought and deep discussion with his Council about this country.

Anglo-Saxon Chronicle, 1085

The occasion was not planned as the grand finale of a successful reign. Only in retrospect did it become this, and only for some historians. It was a period of crisis, when, for the fourth time in William's reign, a hostile fleet from a king of Denmark threatened; on this occasion, it was not a contingent endeavouring perhaps to regain the north of England, but a full invasion force of a thousand ships, several hundred supplied by William's one-time ally, Flanders.[2] The Norman subjugation of England had involved extensive slaughter in battle, reprisal killings, and enforced exiles. In the two decades that had elapsed since the Conquest, the productive agrarian sector of the population had been taxed to the hilt, their rents raised to maximum tolerable levels, and above. With the Norman establishment's hold on their highly profitable kingdom in jeopardy, it seems that the king's council had already considered the invasion threat at an emergency autumn council, which decided on the billeting of knights, and might well have prepared the ground for further decisive action at Christmas.[3] Here, the next four chapters seek to explain how the conquered country with its predominantly English and Anglo-Danish population was mobilized to co-operate in this remarkable Survey and how the enterprise could have been successfully completed in such a context, given the difficulties in communication and the lack of native incentive.

---

[1] WM, *Saints' Lives*, 106–7, my translation.   [2] *ASC*, 1069; 1070; 1075, D, E; 1085.
[3] J. R. Maddicott, 'Responses to the threat of invasion, 1085', *EHR*, 122 (2007), 987–91.

THE ROLE OF THE BISHOPS

The bishops, as key players in William's administration, were at the pinnacle of the circle of authority that produced Domesday, provoking the intriguing search for a single mastermind amongst them. Leaving that question aside for the moment, what is interesting is that we can perhaps discern elements of their individual inputs to the Domesday project from their careers.

William I, in addition to consulting his normal retinue of a varying group of magnates, bishops, and clerks, held formal 'great councils': councils that were attended by major ecclesiastics, landholders, and sheriffs. They were convened at the great feasts of the year; the Conqueror spent eleven Christmases of his reign, including that of 1086, in Normandy, but when in England, Christmas might be celebrated at Gloucester (twice), Whitsun at Westminster or Windsor (twice each), or Winchester, where he spent five Easters.[4] Easter, or Lady Day, was adopted as the terminus for at least one of the gelds, becoming the point for half-yearly accounting in the twelfth century. Other religious festivals, Michaelmas and Trinity Sunday, for instance, also became landmarks for agricultural rentals.

To coincide with these great occasions, William convened formal ecclesiastical synods that took decisions on matters of marriage, clerical simony, parish organ-isation, vagrant monks, recognition of Anglo-Saxon saints, and much else. These meetings, following the great Christian feasts, encouraged a certain group solidar-ity. A number of the men who were to direct the Domesday project were thus largely present together at the 'deep speech' of the Christmas council of 1085 when it met at Gloucester and launched the project. The election of three new bishops drawn from amongst the royal clerks was the sure sign that the king was particularly focused on the bishops' administrative experience in royal service: the chancellor, Maurice, now became bishop of London, with royal chaplains appointed to Lichfield and Thetford. Occasionally, the king had turned to the monastic church to supply candidates, but even they were monks of steel of wide abilities: in 1080 he had appointed William, monk and prior of Saint-Calais, to the tough post of Durham after the murder of its previous incumbent. William of St Calais arrived with considerable experience of the world, one of the Bayeux 'mafia', educated within Odo's chapter there, and the duke-king's negotiator in France, Maine, and Anjou.[5]

The most powerful sheriffs and the greatest lay landholders, particularly those whose lands formed strategic enclaves, were also members of the king's council. The mechanics of the Survey would not only have been in the council's hands, but would have evolved at its suggestion. The project required the landholders' en-dorsement: the essence of feudal kingship being that it relied on great landholders given high positions and wide powers. Their advice had to be sought, given, and heeded before action. These men in turn sought and heeded advice from their own respective councils: Bishop Robert of Hereford and Roger de Lacy, one a great

---

[4] Introduction in *Acta*, 84.   [5] Barlow, *Anglo-Norman Church*, 64.

ecclesiastic, the other a great secular landholder, are known to have done so in 1085.[6] The bishops and abbots stood in a somewhat different relationship to the king from the lay magnates. Usually able and educated men, they were initially more dependent on him than on their families for position and promotion. Once appointed, however, they were difficult to remove, and as they had, officially, no heirs to disinherit, the king had fewer sanctions over them. Hence they were men of power and stature.

The bishops and royal clerks had an instrumental role at each point of the Domesday procedure. William's bishops of 1086 were impressively experienced: charged with the direction of administration, education, and cure of souls in their bishoprics, they had also functioned as the new regime's commissioners, or legates, in the several legal cases already launched by churches in an effort to regain lands lost through confiscation or newly enforced tenancies. Their influence on the Domesday Inquiry was all embracing: one bishop certainly served on the one commission whose members are known and there are indications that two others did similarly; each circuit in 1086 might well have included an experienced bishop as commissioner, a pattern practised in subsequent judicial commissions.[7] By 1085, the appointees to the episcopate numbered several of considerable achievement—and, perhaps just as important, considerable stamina and longevity—which had enabled them to build up the administrative expertise and authority on which William relied in this final crisis of his demanding take-over of England.

William had early recognized the central role of ecclesiastics in his administration in Normandy.[8] As a young duke, he made several pro-active ecclesiastical appointments designed to recover the authority of his rule and at the same time reversing the disintegration of the Norman church prevailing earlier. He took an interest in the spiritual functions of bishops, holding several reforming synods, from Lisieux in 1064 onwards; by 1080, at the ecclesiastical Council of Lillebonne, 'outstanding' churchmen of 'professional quality' were enacting important provisions of high principle.[9] Support for the Church and its strong leaders repaid a ruler a thousand-fold. The consent and aid of ecclesiastics was, after all, an essential: more particularly for one, as William, born illegitimate and who had made a marriage alliance too close in affinity to bear the scrutiny of the newly enforced papal rules on these matters. In 1066, papal approval and a papal banner were perhaps as crucial to maintaining the support of the episcopate as they were to retaining the support of fighting men.

---

[6] T. S. Purser, 'The origins of English feudalism? an episcopal land-grant revisited', *Historical Research*, 73 (2000), 80–93; for text photographed and discussed, see also V. H. Galbraith, 'An episcopal land-grant of 1085', *EHR*, 44 (1929), 352–72.

[7] H. R. Loyn, 'William's bishops: some further thoughts', *ANS*, 10 (1987), 223–35, esp. 224–5.

[8] D. Bates, 'The Conqueror's adolescence', *ANS*, 25 (2002), 11.

[9] D. Bates, *Normandy before 1066* (London, 1982), 208–12.

The ethos of reciprocal support between Church and ruler had an even stronger tradition in England. Bishops or their deputies presided in the shire courts. All men, including slaves, had a strong theoretical link with their bishop, who was deemed responsible for the welfare of the men on his not-inconsiderable estates as part of the cure of souls within his diocese. In England, the principles and practice of a bishop's leadership were set out in a tract called *Episcopus*: peace, law, and practical concord were of first concern, and a high priority was to give his flock godly instruction; the tract called upon bishops to address all sorts of practical as well as spiritual concerns, including the supervision of weights and measures and their manufacture, as well as all spheres of justice.[10] In parts of France at the same period—Narbonne, Cluny, and later Soissons and Beauvais—bishops were trying to launch the 'Peace of God', a movement designed to protect Christians, clerics, churches, and the vulnerable. In the Truce of God, they attempted to limit hostilities, seeking to exclude fighting on feast days, holy days, and the days preceding them. Authorized by ecclesiastical authorities, these ideas had been introduced as a limited way of bringing respite to a fractious society—although they were largely a dead letter. Yet individual bishops continued to make efforts; and in 1082 the bishop of Liège in Lotharingia proclaimed the Truce of God, and was even backed by the barons of the diocese.[11]

Certainly, England was much in need of peace and concord. The country had endured two conquests—Danish and Norman—in less than fifty years, and had been drained of its wealth by tribute and heavy taxes. In addition, rebellions against William had achieved no bargaining position for the native population—rather the reverse, for the reprisals they encountered had brought further deprivation and misery. Indeed, the rebellions of 1069 seem to have provoked a swing away from the use of Anglo-Saxon in official documents and towards a policy of cultural as well as political and economic domination. It is not surprising that bishops without either Norman or Anglo-Saxon affiliations, educated in imperial Germany or with experience elsewhere on the continent, conceived it as part of their duties—as well as an excellent career move—to bring stability to the exploited country, especially in the context of this major Danish challenge of 1084, since Denmark was still viewed as a partly non-Christian country.[12] Their perspective in administering the Domesday Inquiry was to include native men from the localities in order to foster an element of stability. And those who had been monks in Normandy would have been inculcated with the Benedictine principle of *stabilitas*.

---

[10] Liebermann, 477–9; H. R. Loyn, *Anglo-Saxon England and the Norman Conquest* (London, 1962), 237–8.

[11] M. Bloch, *Feudal Society*, tr. L. A. Manyon (London, 1962), 412–19.

[12] William of Malmesbury saw Cnut and the Danes as barbarians, *GP*, 190; also WM, *Saints' Lives*, 106–7: the latter may reflect the feelings of his subject, Wulfstan of Worcester, obtained from Coleman, Wulfstan's chaplain and biographer.

CONTINUITY, EXPERTISE, AND THE LOTHARINGIAN CONNECTION

Continuity in the royal clerical service provided strong links between the reigns of Edward and William and, importantly, between royal and provincial centres of literacy and administration. Under Edward, the late 1040s and 1050s had witnessed a significant rise in the number of secular clerks appointed to bishoprics: at one point the episcopate numbered ten former royal clerks to three monks. Several of Edward's clerks went on to become bishops under William, amongst them, the Norman Peter, who became bishop of Lichfield, 1072–85. Osbern, a Norman relative of King Edward, became bishop of Exeter, 1072–1103, holding valuable churches in Sussex, Hampshire, and Wiltshire, while the Norman William of Jumièges remained bishop of London from 1051 until 1075. The bishops included some natives: amongst Englishmen with similarly unbroken career paths were Wulfstan II of Worcester, bishop 1062–95, and Stigand of Selsey, 1070–87. In 1085–6, there were appointees surviving from Edward's reign who would have known how to involve the native population in the Domesday proceedings.

The bishop who stood out pre-eminently in the continuity that William ensured for a time was Wulfstan of Worcester. Born in 1008, bishop of Worcester 1062–1095, Wulfstan endeavoured in a life both active and ascetic to maintain peace on the western borders for William, while at the same time celebrating English cultural tradition in liturgy and chant at Worcester and mitigating the persecution of English practices within and without monastic life.[13] His very longevity testifying to his cunning resilience in the face of events, Wulfstan was a dominant administrator of his triple hundred and diocese, and the veteran manipulator of several lawsuits.[14] He exerted leadership in both the learned and the military world. Despite his ascetic regime, he maintained a contingent of household knights, dining with them and the monks alternately—so that the knights' behaviour might be kept within the limits permissible in an ecclesiastical environment—and he shared responsibility for guarding the Severn crossing at Worcester with sheriff Urse d'Abitot.[15] With the help of the Lotharingian bishop at Hereford and the efforts of the border earls, Wulfstan strove, mainly with success, to sustain the English borders against Welsh incursions, and the growing jurisdiction of his bishopric against challenges.

Even more influential for an enterprise such as the Domesday Inquiry were the Lotharingian personnel, with their upbringing in a much more metropolitan environment than that of Normandy or England. The western sector of the Ottonian empire, largely run by bishops, was at the height of its powers when

---

[13] E. Mason, *St Wulfstan of Worcester c.1008–1095* (Oxford, 1990), 204–32.
[14] A. Williams, 'The cunning of the dove: Wulfstan and the politics of accommodation', in J. S. Barrow and N. P. Brooks (eds), *St Wulfstan and his World* (Aldershot, 2005), 23–38.
[15] *GP*, 281; Mason, *St Wulfstan of Worcester*, 151–2, 2.

Edward the Confessor recruited the services of their scholar-clerks. Under the Ottonians there was a beaten path that cathedral canons and chaplains in noble households could follow into imperial administration and bishoprics. There, monks and chapters of canons became the intellectual leaders of monastic reform. Utrecht, Liège, Toul, Metz, Trier, and Gorze all offered centres of study in the tenth and eleventh centuries.[16] Edward the Confessor had appointed several Lotharingian royal clerks who, rising to bishoprics, continued their career path unbroken in William's reign. They included Walter, bishop of Hereford, 1060–79 and his successor, Robert, 1079–95; Herman, bishop of Ramsbury/Sherborne/Salisbury, 1045–78; Giso, bishop of Wells 1060–88; and Leofric, the learned bishop of Exeter, 1046–72 who, although a Cornishman, was educated at Liège.[17] They did not all survive until 1086, but they brought certain traditions and perspectives. Under Otto I, the prominent schools in Liège, in particular the cathedral chapter of Saint-Lambert and the abbey of Lobbes, had introduced a type of education that gave not simply a religious and theological education, but one in classical and new learning: the *trivium*, covering rhetoric, dialectic, and grammar, and the *quadrivium*, consisting of arithmetic and geometry, as well as music, and astronomy; the teaching there was particularly open to science and mathematics.[18] Most relevant here was the room made for intellectual reflection on the exercise of power and on respect for archives, and Liège became almost 'a training centre for the imperial episcopate'.[19]

Lotharingia included many small territories with advanced economies situated in that corridor across Europe to the Rhine that formed the western tranche of the Ottonian empire from Utrecht to Toul and Metz; it embraced the episcopal rulers of Trier, Metz, and Cologne with their inherited Roman administration and Tournai and Cambrai with their influential cathedral schools. It was a commercial and intellectual corridor for merchants, pilgrims, and armies moving between the regions of the North Sea, Burgundy and northern Italy—with the metal workers of the upper Meuse renowned for industrial products, and for their work in gold, silver, and enamel.[20] Bishops in Germany were lords of territorial principalities that equalled duchies in size and power; they undertook administrative duties at court, and led their contingent of vassals to the host of the imperial army.

By contrast, leading English cathedrals and the episcopate heading them had been monastic since Bishop Æthelwold, until King Edward adopted a different source of recruitment. One of the several irregularities in Archbishop Stigand's position was that he headed monastic sees at Winchester and Canterbury without

---

[16] M. Parisse, 'Lotharingia', in *NCMH* 3, 322–7.

[17] V. Ortenberg, *The English Church and the Continent in the Tenth and Eleventh centuries* (Oxford, 1992), 58.

[18] C. Renardy, 'Les écoles liégeoises du IXe au XIIe siècle: grandes lignes de leur évolution', *Revue belge de philologie et d'histoire*, 57 (1979), 309–28.

[19] Parisse, 'Lotharingia', 325–6, quoting J.-L. Kupper, *Liège et l'église imperiale, XIe–XIIe siècles* (Paris, 1981), 119.

[20] Parisse, 'Lotharingia', 325–6.

having taken monastic vows himself. The continental and imperial tradition was somewhat different: bishops were active, powerful men, with archdeacons to assist them; they were accustomed to episcopal seats in cities perhaps of Roman origin and certainly of some status. Indeed, three of King Edward's Lotharingian appointees, Leofric, Giso, and Herman, as well as King William's appointee, Remigius, appear to have been disappointed by the modesty of their cathedral seats—and all took radical measures to remedy the position. Leofric moved his seat from Crediton to Exeter in 1050 and gave his house the rule of St Chrodegang, favoured of secular Augustinian canons in Lotharingia, so changing Exeter from a Benedictine house to a cathedral of secular canons. He collected and imported manuscripts assiduously, maintained the canons at his own expense, at least at first, and re-stocked the manors.[21] The policy of seeking out important centres for episcopal seats was raised again at the council of London in 1075, and more re-sitings eventually followed, including Dorchester to Lincoln, and Lichfield to Chester.[22] An influential stratum of both Edward's and William's episcopate came from a continental-imperial context; such men were unlikely to draw any line between their responsibility to keep the records of their house and their participation in the rule of a Christian kingdom and its record-keeping.

The Lotharingian connection, clerical or commercial, was an important facet of England's strength. There was already an established permanent trading base in London protected by laws of Æthelred II.[23] Contacts with the German empire had been for some time characterized by respectful diplomacy, with a marriage alliance made by Cnut, whose own baptismal name was Lambert from St Lambert of Liège.[24] Duduc, a senior royal priest under Cnut, was said to be Saxon or Lotharingian. He was appointed bishop of Wells in 1033, and was respected enough to head the delegation sent by King Edward to the important reforming Council of Rheims of 1049.[25] Edward's own life of exile on the continent had added to these contacts, offering him the opportunity to recruit broadly educated clerks and, ultimately, bishops, independent of the factional aristocracy of England or Normandy. Certainly, in the first ten years of his reign, he took full advantage of this opportunity.[26] These men, drawn from the court chapel, often of good constitution and long-lived, cannot but have provided wide-ranging perspectives, as well as contacts with the intellectual mainstream of interest in mathematics and philosophy. The longevity was important not simply because of the respect it carried, but for the wealth of administrative and political expertise that educated men of stamina might contribute to a hard-living, hard-fighting political elite, not itself always long-lived. Certainly, the financial and administrative capacity of

---

[21] *GP*, 201; Keynes, 'Giso', 209; Barlow, *English Church*, 83–4, 214–15; Ortenberg, *English Church*, 58.

[22] Barlow, *Anglo-Norman Church*, 47–8.   [23] IV Æthelred, 8–10.

[24] M.K. Lawson, 'Archbishop Wulfstan and the homiletic element in the laws of Æthelred II and Canute', in A.R. Rumble (ed.), *The Reign of Cnut: King of England, Denmark and Norway* (Leicester, 1994), 108–9, 136–8.

[25] *ASC*, 1049, E; Ortenberg, *English Church*, 238.   [26] Graph in Barlow, *English Church*, 63.

William I and William Rufus depended much on the long-serving careers of men such as Wulfstan of Worcester, Walkelin, the treasurer, and bishop of Winchester, and Rannulf Flambard, eventually bishop of Durham.

Giso of Wells, bishop 1060–88, supplied continuity of direct significance to the Domesday project. The Lorrainer bishops-elect, Giso and Walter, far too canny to allow themselves to be consecrated by Stigand, had gone to the reforming Pope Nicholas II for the ceremony, Giso returning armed with a splendid papal privilege forbidding kings, dukes, and marquises 'to disturb or defraud' the bishopric:[27] most useful in the context of the regime changes of 1066. He was also adept in gaining privileges and patronage from members of different royal families, and, in keeping them through good times and bad.[28] His contacts included Queen Edith, King Edward's widow, and William's queen, Matilda; and he successfully preserved the only original writ to survive from King Harold. It declares, via the shire court of Somerset, that Bishop Giso of Wells is to have various jurisdictional and financial rights over his lands and his men 'as fully and completely' as ever he had 'in the time of King Edward'.[29] It is ironic that this phrase 'the time of King Edward', used by Harold to ensure continuity, was later adopted throughout the Domesday Inquiry as the legal point of departure for tenures and rents, precisely in order to erase Harold's own reign.

International contacts were not confined to the personnel of the established church, nor were they simply one way. Edward sent Bishop Ealdred of Worcester (later archbishop of York) in 1054 to the imperial court on a diplomatic mission, where he stayed for nearly a year, as a guest of the archbishop of Cologne and the Emperor Henry III.[30] There were cross-influences of saintly cults promoted by noble contacts, and royal English and imperial marriages. Over and above the exchange of manuscripts and gifts of relics, such gatherings irradiated political and aristocratic life.[31] Yet, unique to kingship was the link created between consecration and promises, between the established church and political reality.[32]

On a practical level, English aspirations were linked to imperial Germany through functionaries close to the royal family. Albert the Lotharingian was Edith's chaplain and also a canon of St Paul's.[33] Others included Otto, the goldsmith and moneyer, and Theodoric, the moneyer associated with cutting Edward's Great Seal and thereby possessing the secret of its crafting. They managed both to retain contacts with the former Queen Edith and to prosper under King William; Otto still held lands in 1086;[34] and Theodoric was present together with many English

---

[27] EHD2, no. 76; Keynes, 'Giso', 228.   [28] Keynes, 'Giso', 241–8, App. I.

[29] *Writs*, no. 71; S.1163.   [30] *ASC*, 1049, C; 1050, D.

[31] Ortenberg, *English Church*, 54–94.

[32] On the evolving character of the link see J. Nelson, 'Ritual and reality in the early medieval *ordines*', in *Politics and Ritual in Early Medieval Europe* (London, 1986), 329–39. Changes in England and their long-term implications are discussed by G. Garnett, 'Coronation and propaganda: some implications of the Norman claim to the throne of England in 1066', *TRHS*, 5th ser., 36 (1986), 91–103, and in Garnett (*Conquered England*), outlined, vii–viii.

[33] Barlow, *English Church*, 157.

[34] GDB:190a (CAM:1,18); LDB:3b, 97b–98a, 106b (ESS:1,11–12; 81,1; B3j), 286b (SUF:1,97).

witnesses, including Queen Edith, when Giso of Wells completed the purchase of twenty hides of land at Combe, Somerset.[35] The evocative record sites the transaction in an upper storey of the new stone church of Wilton Abbey, while the nuns sang *Reminiscere miserationum*—the office for Ember Wednesday in Lent. Bishop Giso's insistence on the presence of English witnesses to a major land transaction in 1072 illustrates the political perspective that churchmen of international education could bring to the Norman tenurial revolution.

Giso's purported 'autobiography' claimed that his achievement was to bring to Wells 'in praiseworthy manner, all those things which I knew to be appropriate for the purpose, according to the custom of my country'. This confident assertion of his superior traditions is in character with what we know of his policies. He was reputed to have made a list of the lands of Wells in order that 'it may be known what belongs peculiarly to the use of canons and what to the demesne and disposal of the bishop; and so, posterity being freed from all uncertainty on this subject, one party may not encroach upon the rights of another'.[36] Here are both the language and the intent of the Domesday Inquiry. As Giso had been in post since 1060 and was known to have contested matters tenurial with Earl Harold, the bishop might well have compiled his own list of manors long before William's Survey was in prospect, but it remains the case that the present form of this text is of the twelfth century.

Other Lotharingians moved easily from centre to centre and provided a force for continuity. Herman, a native of Lotharingia, served first in the household of Harthacnut and then in that of Edward the Confessor, prior to his appointment as bishop of Ramsbury. He, too, was not content with the seat of his bishopric and tried to move it to Malmesbury. Failing to achieve this, he left the country to become a monk in Flanders for three years; but by 1058 he was back, managing to move his seat to Sherborne. Still not content, he removed the seat of the see to the citadel-like site of Old Sarum in 1075, dying three years later as 'bishop of Berkshire and Wiltshire and Dorset'.[37] Bishops were thus attuned to operate in more than one county court: groups of shires, as adopted for the Domesday circuits, were already familiar administrative units to them.

The Anglo-Norman kings had a strong interest in maintaining the means to enable their royal clerks to live off their prebends, and secular canonries were important to governmental recruits throughout the reigns of the Norman kings.[38] Nigel, William I's physician, succeeded Spirtes to a plurality of minsters. Bishop Maurice of London remodelled and then made use of the prebendal system

---

[35] Keynes, 'Giso', 243–7, 259; App. III, 262–3.

[36] The 'autobiography' may have been concocted to make a case for the division of canons' lands, under contention in the mid twelfth century onwards; yet it may also have incorporated some of Giso's carefully kept records. Several points of its detail accord with the evidence of Domesday Book; others do not, Keynes, 'Giso', 213–26; App. IV, 263–8.

[37] Barlow, *English Church*, 156, 224; Keynes, 'Giso', 209, 253.

[38] J. Blair, 'Secular minster churches in Domesday Book', in *Reassessment*, 132.

at St Paul's and its canons included Robert, Bishop of Hereford, and Rannulf Flambard.[39] Colleges of canons provided both incomes for royal clerks and educated clerks for royal service. Ingelric, himself one of King Edward's clerks, and one of King William's early land commissioners, had endowed St Martin's-le-Grand, London, which in turn became a foundation for recruiting and then providing income for the many royal clerks who were the 'civil servants' of the twelfth century. A royal chaplain, Samson, later bishop of Worcester, headed the house of secular canons at Wolverhampton at the time of Domesday—possibly a useful base in Staffordshire, that low-value Mercian region.[40]

The co-operation of the 'public' and the 'private' sectors was seamless, and personnel at the level of the episcopate often identical. Salisbury's bookish bishop, Osmund, had formerly been the royal chancellor and retained his links with the up-and-coming raft of worldly royal clerks, giving the young Rannulf Flambard a tax-free manor to hold of the bishopric.[41] And we have seen that scribes of the newly constituted cathedral at Salisbury co-operated with both the Domesday record for the south-west and in the record of tax-collection in the region.[42]

THE KING'S NEW MEN

Despite all continuity, 1070 marked a watershed in William's reign. The rebellions of 1069–70 provided the cause, and the death of Archbishop Ealdred of York in 1069 the opportunity; Thomas, the new appointee to York, a former canon and treasurer of Bayeux, found his cathedral church destroyed and his diocese ravaged by war, but rose to the challenge to become a great patron of scholars and of effective clerks.[43] The year 1070 also saw the dethronement of Archbishop Stigand and the elevation of the renowned Lanfranc of Bec. Investiture by rulers had not yet become the controversial issue that it was by the end of the eleventh century: the mid-century debate on reform in England was still centred on pluralism and simony. But in order to get the support of a range of able men, William was compelled eventually—one might say belatedly—to divest himself of the continuity offered by the uncanonical Stigand. Stigand was probably of little positive support as archbishop—although many indirect clues point to his Treasury expertise—but certainly a born schemer, with contacts, whom William was perhaps wise to accept and neutralize at the beginning of the reign. The harsh reprisals and change of language following the several and general uprisings in 1069–70 marked a general change of direction in William's policies.[44] The monasteries were plundered of their treasures and other bishops removed.[45] Canterbury was left

---

[39] *John le Neve, Fasti Ecclesiae Anglicanae, 1066–1300*, vol. 1, compiled by D. Greenway, Institute of Historical Research (London, 1968), 42.
[40] GDB:247d; *Acta*, no. 265.   [41] GDB:58b (BRK:3,3).   [42] Webber.
[43] Barlow, *Anglo-Norman Church*, 61–2.   [44] Williams, *The English*, 24–69.
[45] Williams, *The English*, 45–6.

temporarily vacant; East Anglia went to Herfast, William's chancellor, and Selsey to another Stigand. Winchester immediately went to Walkelin. All three appointees were royal chaplains.[46]

Lanfranc, monk and scholar, had reason to be appalled by the harsh reprisals consequent on the rebellions of 1069–70. He was known later as William I's principal adviser, and his involvement in the English Church may well have been concomitant with, perhaps even conditional on, a more balanced rule from William as well as on the employment of reforming councils and synods in the English Church: he was later unwilling to crown William Rufus without promises that Rufus would 'maintain justice, mercy and equity', defend the Church, and observe Lanfranc's counsel.[47] Although the events of 1069–70 showed William's complete disregard for his early promises of good kingship sworn to Archbishop Ealdred 'on Christ's book' before his coronation, the Conqueror appears to have become more susceptible to the civilizing influence of his own respected churchmen in his later years, when he sought Anselm's friendship: customarily 'fierce and formidable', it was remarked that 'when Anselm was present he became, to the astonishment of all, an altogether different person from what he usually was'.[48] Even ecclesiastics from Normandy may well have found themselves unable to acquiesce in the persistent confiscation of land, and certainly in the loss to the Church of its leasehold land held by laymen, and have induced, eventually, some kingly consideration, for instance, for the plight of Ely Abbey. Anselm, as abbot of Bec, and concerned for its English endowments, had travelled to England for the Domesday Survey. Even a native chronicler, whilst providing a devastating critique of William's rule, nevertheless acknowledged that William was 'gentle to the good men who loved God'.[49]

Lanfranc's background and education, according to the somewhat slight evidence, was in the intellectual and legally conscious environment of Pavia—a cosmopolitan city occupying a strategic position on major land routes. In Lombard and Carolingian times a capital city, modelling itself on Constantinople, it had then contained the leading school of Lombard law, but became less favoured than Ravenna or Rome under the Ottonians.[50] Lanfranc's father appears to have been attached to the law-court, where the church and the royal writing office of the imperial palace in Pavia fostered a close-knit group of judges, possessed of practical knowledge of the laws of Justinian and of the Lombards, whose function it was to preserve the rights and laws of the city.[51] Lanfranc, probably born about 1010 and based in Italy until about 1030, as a youth was likely to have witnessed the revolt that swept northern Italy in 1024, when the city of Pavia rose against imperial rule.[52] Yet despite a period of chaos, Pavia remained the renowned centre for the study of Roman law and its lawyers maintained their position as the leading

---

[46] Barlow, *Anglo-Norman Church*, 62.   [47] *Eadmer*, 12, 25.

[48] *ASC*, 1066, D; *Eadmer*, 23–4, *Eadmer's History of Recent Events in England*, tr. G. Bosanquet (London, 1964), 24–5.

[49] *ASC*, 1087.   [50] J. K. Hyde, *Society and Politics in Medieval Italy* (London, 1973), 46–7.

[51] Hyde, *Society and Politics in Medieval Italy*, 34.

[52] M. Gibson, *Lanfranc of Bec* (Oxford, 1978), 4–6, 15–16.

interpreters of Lombard law.[53] As a chaplain at the Ottonian court claimed that all Italians sweated out their youth in legal studies,[54] debates about civil law and imperial rule and its deficiencies are unlikely to have passed the young Lanfranc by and may well have contributed to his devotion to established order.[55] The separate legal status of urban political centres that Domesday acknowledges, if only by default—by skirting around the greatest cities—is surely one with the principles with which Lanfranc grew up. His experience of Pavia's developing civic identity may have contributed to sparing the boroughs from an inquiry into anything but crown and archiepiscopal interests.[56]

More tangible evidence suggests Lanfranc's contribution of the Domesday project. One of the great legal projects of the period was the rearrangement of the Lombard Code into subjects, the *Expositiones*. One dispute cites Lanfranc, identified as the subsequent archbishop, who loses the argument.[57] The issue—proof of inheritance—is of central interest to the Domesday legal processes. It raised a legal conundrum of several centuries standing[58] and of lasting import: what weight can be given to written records when those who witnessed them are no longer alive to substantiate whether coercion or forgery had a part in their making? An extract from the moot reads:

ARCHBISHOP LANFRANC to BONFILIO the *iudex*   If a man presents a charter in court, and it is challenged; and if both the notary who wrote it and the witnesses are dead, how can he defend the validity of his charter?

BONFILIO   By custom, he may call twelve oath-helpers, and show two other charters written by the same notary.

LANFRANC   Does custom allow no other way?

BONFILIO   No.

LANFRANC   Then custom is in conflict with the law; for Otto I declared this custom to be 'detestable, dishonest and inadmissible'.

ANOTHER answered LANFRANC   It was not the custom itself that Otto I thought detestable, but its abuse; for men were drawing up false charters deliberately and then perjuring themselves in their defence. So Otto gave to the challenger the option of trial by battle.

The subject under debate—what evidence constituted a good basis for a rightful claim—was being tested out in the courts in many parts of western Europe.[59]

---

[53] Gibson, *Lanfranc*, 46–7, 63.

[54] A chaplain of Emperor Henry III (1024–56): Hyde, *Society and Politics in Medieval Italy*, 34, 63–4.

[55] Gibson, *Lanfranc*, 191.   [56] See Ch. 9 in this volume.

[57] 'The editor of the *Expositiones* (or, at the worst, the scribe of the only manuscript) must have believed that his defeated disputant was the archbishop of Canterbury at an earlier stage in his career', Gibson, *Lanfranc*, 7–8.

[58] The force of charters, witness, and oaths on relics is discussed by R. McKitterick, *The Carolingians and the Written Word* (Cambridge, 1989), 67–73.

[59] The respective proofs, and the pressures behind them, are discussed by P. Wormald, 'Charters, law and the settlement of disputes in Anglo-Saxon England', *Dispute Settlement*, 149–68, and in 'Conclusion', *Dispute Settlement*, 213.

In Anjou, in 1074, a land plea before five ecclesiastics held that the Church's claim could be defended either 'by witnesses, or by proof of investiture, or by charter'.[60] But the moot point raised and its resolution may well have influenced Lanfranc's thinking on the Norman land settlement and the conduct of Domesday Inquiry in several ways. First, in the adoption of the customary twelve oath-helpers to provide witness: central to getting the English to acknowledge the new regime and the legitimacy of the tenurial revolution it had imposed (albeit with half the witnesses made up of men brought in by the new regime). Second, in the Normans' introduction of trial by battle to England.[61] And third, in the Inquiry's apparent lack of consistent interest in the proffering of old charters as evidence.

The Domesday Inquiry needed to circumvent the difficulty of sanctioning the transfer of land legally to an illegal regime. In particular, ecclesiastical institutions, which did possess charters, had lost leasehold land in the widespread confiscation of lay estates, leading to injustices that the Inquiry needed to address—which it did not entirely succeed in doing. But, as the quoted debate recognized, charters might be falsified or witnesses function under duress.[62] In fact, as we have noted, old charters are invoked a mere handful of times in the two Domesday volumes, whereas there are over eight hundred references to oral witness, many regarding tenure.[63] Even a charter belonging to the bishop of Bayeux was not acceptable without substantiation by witnesses, and was gainsaid anyway by subsequent action.[64] It has also been pointed out that the Domesday record left the efficacy of verbal witness in doubt in many cases.[65] But the Domesday Inquiry was not an equal and open process; at the local level, it simply ventilated the steam from an explosive situation; in modern terms it conducted a process of 'disclosure', revealing and airing the relative strengths of conflicting claims between incomers themselves, or between incomers and the Church. The main impulse at work appears to have been to uphold the king's will in replacing the Edwardian landholders—unless their expertise had been found to be in demand. Domesday itself refers to a previous inquiry made about land of the church of St Petroc (lost to first Harold and then to Robert of Mortain), wherein either the king's actions have been conflated—quite likely, as that occurs elsewhere—or the outcome dictated beforehand: King William had 'ordered a judicial enquiry to be held, and the Saint to be repossessed by judgement'.[66] Even William's splendid bilingual diploma for St Martin-le-Grand, David Bates observes, evidently had 'no standing as a confirmation of title'.[67]

Traditionally, Lanfranc's influence has been seen as that of a lawyer versed in ecclesiastical rather than strictly secular administration, albeit his clearly written

[60] *testibus, an investitura, an carta, Cartulaire de Saint-Aubin d'Angers* I, ed. Comte B. de Broussillon and E. Lelon (Paris, 1903), 120.
[61] See Ch. 10 in this volume, pp. 282–303, 315.
[62] N. Brooks, *The Early History of the Church of Canterbury* (Leicester, 1984) 191–7.
[63] Discussed further and similarly, Fleming, *Law*, 61–5; Garnett, 15–18.
[64] GDB:375a (LIN:CS13).
[65] Wormald, 70. Discussed further, Chs 3, 9, and 10 in the present volume.
[66] GDB:121b (CON:4,21).   [67] *Acta*, nos 181, 597.

arguments were, throughout his varied career, a continuing source of expertise.[68] Whilst the *Expositiones* point to his influence in the field of tenurial recognition, George Garnett has strongly argued a much more fundamental role for Lanfranc: as the pragmatically legal brains behind a ready-prepared 'template for regime change', wittingly drawn up before the invasion while working closely with the Duke when abbot of William's monastic foundation of St Stephen's, Caen, which resulted in a pre-prepared brief, constructed to gain papal approval for an invasion, and commonly available to William's apologists, William of Jumièges and William of Poitiers. Key to this argument is Lanfranc's surviving canon law collection, which he demonstrably marked at over 200 points, drawing upon it for his letters and to marshal the canonical authority for particular points currently at issue in ecclesiastical councils. On his own record of the seventh-century Fourth Council of Toledo, Lanfranc marked the margin, arguably to note the strength it gave William's claim to the English crown and to William's moral stance, at the decree that 'anyone who with tyrannical assumption has usurped the pediment of the kingdom should be anathema in the sight of God the Father and the angels, and should be excommunicated from the catholic church'.[69] In particular, Lanfranc's input included the Domesday adoption of the canon law term 'antecessor' that usually denoted the previous holder of an ecclesiastical position; he certainly employed the term in about 1080 for his rebuttal of Pope Gregory VII's 'claim for fealty from the English king'.[70] In the Domesday Inquiry, and surviving in detailed Little Domesday, the term 'antecessor' was employed to denote an accepted Edwardian landholder from whom the king or his deputies had transferred the land. Most importantly, it was Domesday Book's acknowledgement of the Edwardian holder, if only to confirm his replacement, that gave a superficial appearance of lawful sequence to the land transfer, and to the whole Domesday edifice. At some point, Lanfranc saw to it that similar copies of his canon law collection were circulated amongst other bishops; two copies survived in Hereford Cathedral library, one 'has been there always', another was at Salisbury, and Durham's copy is written in a Christ Church hand.[71] Lanfranc regarded his copy as essential; it contains, in a Canterbury hand, an anathema on anyone who removed it from Christ Church.[72] Thus, through calculating premeditation, the lawyer and theologian Lanfranc was prepared to transform the Conqueror's takeover and re-dispersal of land into a legal succession allegedly derived from a moral authority, in which Domesday was to play its effectively crucial part.[73]

---

[68] Gibson, *Lanfranc*, 192–3.
[69] Garnett, 24–44, 36–40.   [70] Lanfranc's Letters, no. 39; EHD2, no. 101.
[71] Z. N. Brooke, *The English Church and the Papacy* (Cambridge, 1931), 57–70, 78–82. Contrast H. E. J. Cowdrey, *Lanfranc: Scholar, Monk, and Archbishop* (Oxford, 2003), 140–1.
[72] Garnett, 39.
[73] But it did not convince Flemish and other contemporaries, E. M. C. van Houts, 'The Norman Conquest through European eyes', *EHR*, 110 (1995), 832–53.

Lanfranc was originally an academic, applying his skills to the study of canon law, theology, and biblical commentary; but tackling practical problems also captured his interest. His presence while prior as a teacher at the school of Bec brought in clerks, sons of dukes, pupils from Germany, as well as pupils sent by Pope Nicholas II. Margaret Gibson has indicated how Bec 'caught the market in the 1050s, when the area under Norman control expanded at an unprecedented rate', generating 'a new demand for the trained administrator'.[74] Lanfranc himself was a proven administrator: his letters, one important to Domesday, are in his own style, not deputed to a clerk with a formula book. He re-built the cathedral at Canterbury and founded one hospital for lepers, another for the sick and aged poor. He took an interest in Canterbury's commercial development, and during this period its mints were amongst the most productive in the country, two of its seven moneyers belonging to the archbishop.[75] He also took a carefully manipulative interest in the tenurial problems of Canterbury estates.[76] At the time of the making of the Domesday Survey Lanfranc was, of course, *in situ* as archbishop, as he was at the time of making the original of the *Domesday Monachorum* of Canterbury. A Canterbury list of tax assessment changes on whose order the *Domesday Monachorum* is formulated has been dated to a short time earlier than the Domesday Inquiry. It is not impossible that Canterbury's Domesday-like survey might indeed have constituted some sort of trial-run exemplar that was updated.[77] The Domesday Inquiry was central to Lanfranc's concerns.

Many of William's bishops became similarly engaged on enormous enterprises, re-building their cathedrals with a fusion of ruthlessness and vision, amongst them Walkelin of Winchester, bishop 1070–1098, Remigius of Lincoln, bishop 1067–1092 (who had served under Abbot John of Ravenna), and William of St Calais.[78] They also became a closely knit administrative team. Gundulf was appointed under Lanfranc's aegis to the bishopric of Rochester, 1077–1108, to transform the impoverished diocese. He had been educated as a cleric at Rouen, became a monk of Bec, where he formed a life-long friendship with Anselm, and accompanied Lanfranc first to Caen, and then to Canterbury; his achievements included not only building a substantial monastic community at Rochester from a handful of clergy into more than sixty monks, developing its archival tradition while continuing to function as Lanfranc's deputy, but also overseeing the transforming of Rochester's architectural context, planning the cathedral, the castle, and the town. His wide-ranging practical expertise was subsequently enlisted for works on the White Tower in London and to conduct a variety of reconciliatory negotiations: between Archbishop Anselm and two successive kings, and between

---

[74] Gibson, *Lanfranc*, 34–8.   [75] Gibson, *Lanfranc*, 183–6.
[76] P. Taylor, 'Domesday Mortlake', *ANS*, 32 (2009), 225–9.
[77] *DMon* survives as a polished manuscript of *c*.1090; but its evidence on the farm of Sandwich suggests that this version was updated during the year following Michaelmas, 1086, *DMon*, 89.
[78] e.g. *Acta*, no. 177.

Henry I and his brother Duke Robert, after the latter's invasion in 1101. He was known for providing food during famine and accommodation for the poor, and for withstanding the demands of royal officials during the vacancy of the archbishopric of Canterbury.[79] Two other bishops, Maurice of London and Osmund of Salisbury, had both held office as chancellor. Walkelin, bishop of Winchester, as well as re-creating Winchester's cathedral and living to see it consecrated, was also William I's treasurer, and his Winchester base was patently central to his office. Certainly Walkelin became one of the chief work-horses of the new regime, a specialist in finance under both William I and Rufus. The substantial backlog that he was owed from the moneyers of Colchester and Maldon suggests that his role as the treasurer gave him control of moneyers' dues and of the issue of dies.[80] He was often found with other magnates acting as a commissioner, as in a 1096 commission with William Capra and Harding, son of Eadnoth the Staller, to hear the pleas of the crown in Devon, Cornwall, and Exeter.[81] Under Rufus, Walkelin acted as the king's main administrative deputy, aided by a group of justiciars.[82] Like his colleague, William of St Calais, he died in harness: in Walkelin's case, from a collapse provoked by receiving an urgent demand from the king for £200 as he celebrated mass on Christmas Day.[83]

Lanfranc was certainly not unmindful of the secular responsibilities of his fellow bishops. The archbishop-elect allowed Remigius, William's early appointee to Lincoln—who as almoner of the prestigious Fécamp Abbey under the great ultramontane, John of Ravenna, had acquired extensive financial experience—to accompany him to Rome in autumn 1071 to seek re-consecration, since Remigius had been suspended then deprived of office by papal authority in 1070, because of his consecration by Stigand. Once in Rome, Remigius found himself accused of simony for supplying Duke William extensively in preparation for the invasion.[84] Lanfranc, however, defended the appointments of Thomas of York and Remigius to Pope Alexander II on practical grounds: 'first, that they had a sound basis of knowledge of a wide range; secondly, that they were very necessary to the new king in making the new dispositions of his kingdom'.[85] These were the criteria essential in the appointment of bishops: their value in governance enhanced by the logistical demands that confronted the ruler of two separate states, England and Normandy. Even an English monk, merely a generation after the Norman Conquest, could portray king and archbishop as a ruling working team. Eadmer relates how Anselm, a former confidant of William I, addressed the bishops and magnates in 1093:

[79] R. A. L. Smith, 'The place of Gundulf in the Anglo-Norman church', *EHR*, 58 (1943), 257–72; M. Brett, 'Gundulf (1023/4–1108), bishop of Rochester', *Oxford Dictionary of National Biography* (Oxford, 2004–13).

[80] LDB:107b (ESS:B6).   [81] *Regesta* 1, no. 378.   [82] Barlow, *Rufus*, 205.

[83] *AnnWinton*, 39; Barlow, *Rufus*, 257.

[84] D. Bates, *Bishop Remigius of Lincoln 1067–92* (Lincoln, 1992), 5–6, 13–14.

[85] *Eadmer*, 11.

This plough in England is drawn by two oxen outstanding above the rest, the king and the archbishop of Canterbury. These two drawing the plough rule the land, one by secular justice and authority, the other by divine learning and instruction.[86]

King and archbishop ploughed the same furrow—in theory, but soon to be abandoned in practice! Despite the confrontations that developed between Anselm and William II, the close coherence between royal service and episcopal office continued: by the end of the reign, almost three-quarters of the bishoprics were held by former royal clerks.[87]

Bishops close to William who had already worked with him in establishing authority in Normandy were in a category all their own. In England they acted with almost secular authority but with the added aura of consecration. Both Odo, bishop of Bayeux, and Geoffrey, bishop of Coutances, were assertive, even military, characters. Odo was William's younger half-brother and a partner in the family consortium—a *mafioso* no less: of a worldly nature, pompous, headstrong, and without scruples. He had already fallen from favour sometime before the date of Domesday, being imprisoned in late 1082–3 for having attempted to raise some sort of military force independently—just why is unknown, but a bid for the Papacy was rumoured to be a possibility.[88] He therefore played no part in the Domesday proceedings; yet, since he took part in the 1088 rebellion that followed close on the Domesday Inquest, he may well have reacted to the policies it embodied and the comments on his activities enshrined in the Book. Odo, like William, had had substantial responsibility from his earliest years. He was appointed bishop far below the canonical age—certainly before his twenty-first year—and he built up an educated establishment in Bayeux, even if the emphasis was on administrative skills.[89] After his half-brother's successful invasion he was quickly given judicial and even regency functions in England; and, despite his late imprisonment, Odo's influence still pervaded via his followers, several of whom had been educated in Odo's cathedral school or amongst his knights and were well placed to attend the 1085 Christmas council: the sheriffs Hugh de Port, Roger Bigod, Haimo of Kent, and William de Courseulles of Somerset had all held land from Odo in Bayeux, and two of his contacts in England, Robert d'Oilly and Urse d'Abitot, also became sheriffs.[90] Several of his Bayeux-educated clerks were installed as royal officials and no less than nine eventually became bishops:[91] they included William of St Calais, Rannulf Flambard and Samson of Worcester—all candidates for the Domesday mastermind—and also Archbishop Thomas of York.

---

[86] *Eadmer*, 36.   [87] Barlow, *Anglo-Norman Church*, 318.

[88] Odo was accused of 'misleading my knights whose duty it was to guard against Danes and Irishmen and other enemies', Van Caenegem, *Lawsuits*, no. 11; OV 4.40–4; discussed, D. Bates, 'The character and career of Odo, bishop of Bayeux (1049/50–1097)', *Speculum*, 50 (1975), 14–18.

[89] Bates, 'Odo, bishop of Bayeux', 2, 12–15.

[90] J. Green, 'The sheriffs of William the Conqueror', *ANS*, 5 (1982), 136–7.

[91] Barlow, *Anglo-Norman Church*, 58.

William's appointees to the English sees have been recognized by historians as strong in every sense. Several had scholastic claims, and many had been educated outside Normandy. Beyond that, these men were schooled in a tradition of bringing law and order, as well as Christian living to western Europe.

LAND PLEAS AND DOMESDAY COMMISSIONERS

By 1085, William had available a body of veteran advisers and, in Geoffrey, bishop of Coutances, in particular, a man of considerable experience. To illustrate the range of experience Geoffrey could bring to the 1085 council, some of his achievements are worth rehearsing. In 1049, as a young, probably simoniacal appointee to the bishopric of Coutances from the Norman baronage, he revived the fortunes of an almost derelict see, using his contacts amongst the Norman conquerors of southern Italy and their plundered wealth to re-build the cathedral and reconstruct its defunct diocesan organization. Written and cultural achievements were of obvious importance to him since he was said to have maintained grammarians, dialecticians, and organists at Coutances at his own expense.[92] He was party to some of William's most ambitious plans, being present at the battle of Hastings and playing an important part in the coronation at Westminster. Over and above his activities within William's close circle, Geoffrey took on tasks of active military leadership: in 1069 he led forces that defeated the rebels in the south-west,[93] and in 1075 helped to suppress the revolt of the earls of Hereford and Norfolk, being amongst those who occupied Norwich Castle after its surrender.[94] His career indicated his capacity for innovation, his wide-flung contacts, and his far from claustral forcefulness.

Long before the Domesday initiative, Geoffrey had gained relevant administrative and judicial experience. William employed groups of royal commissioners or justices in both Normandy and England; several included Geoffrey: on one occasion, around 1081, he heard a case before 'the king's court' at Cherbourg along with the bishops of Avranches and Lisieux and Vicomte Eudo.[95] Geoffrey was given authority with Robert of Mortain to hear one or more of the series of land pleas concerning the lands of the once-powerful abbey of Ely.[96] Similarly prolonged over a number of years was Ramsey Abbey's series of law-suits conducted against the bishop of Thetford.[97] Experience of these prolonged disputes over tenurial possession encouraged the evolution of a procedure and the shaping of a framework employable in the great Domesday Inquiry and the expertise jointly

---

[92] J. Le Patourel, 'Geoffrey of Montbray, bishop of Coutances, 1049–1093', *EHR*, 69 (1944), 129–61.
[93] OV 2.228.   [94] *JW* 3.24–5.
[95] *Acta*, no. 201; Le Patourel, 'Geoffrey of Montbray', 149.
[96] *Acta* nos 119, 120; *IE*, 192–5.   [97] *Acta*, nos 221, 222.

built up by those in charge enabled later proceedings to be set up speedily. Five features seem especially noteworthy.

First, a recognisable chain of command seems to have evolved in the appointment of justices. Those very close to the king—Lanfranc, Odo of Bayeux, Geoffrey of Coutances, Robert of Mortain—might initiate proceedings, appoint justices, and convene shires. At times, too, they appeared in a judicial role themselves as one of a small panel, or as deciding presidents. Their precise role varied. A hierarchy of authority is known from a court in Normandy constituted sometime between 1070 and 1079: set up by Archbishop John of Rouen, heard by William and Matilda, and judged by Archbishop John and Roger de Beaumont, and other barons.[98] In England, on one occasion, Odo of Bayeux was commanded to arrange commissioners who were to hear and do right in a land dispute;[99] on another, Odo himself had allocated the land, somewhat questionably, 'by the seal of the bishop of Bayeux'.[100] At the time of the Domesday project itself, however, Odo's unavailability, still in prison, was a striking sign of how few were the magnates in whom the king retained confidence.

As previous pleas had involved a hierarchy of presidents and commissioners, in groups of varying size, they offered experience of a tier of courts—some for a specific purpose, some for general witness—to collect, collate, and authorize Domesday data.[101] One pre-Domesday group of commissioners contained three laymen, although the leading local ecclesiastics would undoubtedly have witnessed proceedings, since 'all the shire' were present and 'a great gathering of men from the neighbouring counties and barons assembled at Worcester' and the judgement was 'witnessed by the knights of the Church of Worcester'.[102] Another mission, to Ely in the 1080s, comprised three justices of the highest prestige—Archbishop Lanfranc, Geoffrey of Coutances, and Robert of Mortain, the king's half-brother. Their mission, interestingly, included the charge to restrict the landed ambitions of Remigius of Lincoln—himself commissioner at another Ely hearing, and a Domesday commissioner in Worcestershire.[103] An earlier Ely hearing, between 1071 and 1075, saw no fewer than five commissioners detailed to sort out Ely's problems: Bishops Geoffrey and Remigius, Earl Waltheof, and Sheriffs Ilbert and Picot.[104] The disputes from Ely, Worcester/Evesham, Ramsey and the Canterbury/Odo litigation all necessitated several hearings with different commissioners and not even the Domesday Inquiry and the resulting Great and Little Domesdays were able to enforce closure to the problems of these churches' endowments, Canterbury's losses stemming from actions by Earl Godwine and his men well before 1066, as well as from actions by Haimo the sheriff and Odo of Bayeux in William's

---

[98] *Acta*, no. 29; D. Bates, 'The origins of the justiciarship', *ANS*, 4 (1981), 1–12, 167–71, at 7.
[99] *Acta*, no. 118, probably a conflated account.
[100] GDB:342a, (LIN:4,1).
[101] e.g. *Acta*, no. 350; this writ about a previous plea was addressed to the Domesday commissioners.
[102] *Acta*, no. 349.   [103] *Acta*, no. 123.   [104] *Acta*, no. 117.

reign; many were never retrieved.[105] Some infringements, indeed, may well have resulted from a deliberate royal tactic to replace the lay Edwardian lessees of great religious houses with royal followers.[106] Certainly, by 1085 William's tenurial take-over had provided a body of leading men with sufficient experience to provide the core expertise for numerous panels acting simultaneously in different parts of the country.

Second, a decision required the proper witnesses to past situations and to present agreements—as many as possible. Moreover, whilst the men of the shire were essential, land pleas were not necessarily confined to a single shire. One text (a conflation, maybe supplemented later), attempting to resolve the Ely land pleas, emphasizes the range of people present: assembled at Kentford in the presence of the king's commissioners, *legati*, were four abbots with their Frenchmen and Englishmen, the sheriffs Picot and Eustace with their men, Ralph and Winer on behalf of two other sheriffs, and 'many other proven French and English knights from the four counties of Essex, Hertford, Huntingdon and Bedford'.[107] Assemblies of groups of shires supplied weight and witness to proceedings; the Domesday Inquiry similarly banded together groups of counties to make up a judicial circuit that patently drew on a common mode of proceeding. The number of shires assembled varied. One instalment of the case between the bishop of Worcester and the abbot of Evesham was held 'before seven shires' by Bishop Odo at the Four Shire Stone—the meeting place of Warwickshire, Worcestershire, Gloucestershire, and Oxfordshire.[108] Assemblies of more than one shire had been features of tenth- and eleventh-century England, and were a familiar part of the judicial landscape.[109] One purported writ of Edward the Confessor confirms the tenure of two West-minster estates by the judgement of nine shires.[110] The historic ability to summon representatives from varying groups of shires was an important facility amongst the range of procedures brought into play at speed for the Domesday Inquiry, and the publicity of the process was of the greatest import for the success of the enterprise. Routine procedures were established, but flexibility was available if needed.

Yet a third feature of these land pleas affected Domesday procedures—the possibility of partial judgement or partial pleading. Whilst the king now had a body of personnel with proven expertise at his disposal, several prominent magnates had proved themselves capable of manipulating procedures. Lanfranc had sought to claim or restore Canterbury lands both by means of hundred and shire courts; and no lesser

---

[105] D. R. Bates, 'The land pleas of William I's Reign: Penenden Heath revisited', *Historical Research*, 51 (1978), 1–19, esp. 9–19; E. Miller, 'The Ely land pleas in the reign of William I', *EHR*, 72 (1947), 438–56, esp. 452.

[106] e.g. GDB:191b (CAM:5,24); 200b (CAM:32,5). To restore Ely's lands which were in demesne at King Edward's death 'excepting those which men claim that I have given them': *Acta*, no. 120.

[107] *Acta*, no. 118, 1075/6 × 1081/2.

[108] *Acta*, no. 135, probably *c*.1078–9.

[109] A. L. Kennedy, 'Law and litigation in the *Libellus Æthelwoldi*', *ASE*, 24 (1995), 131–83; Fleming, *Law*, 13–17.

[110] *Writs*, no. 79; S.1123.

pillars of the Anglo-Norman establishment than Odo of Bayeux, along with Hugh de Montfort, Richard fitzGilbert, and others had been brought to court by Lanfranc, for taking over Canterbury lands and installing their followers therein.[111] Yet when William was in Normandy in 1075, Richard fitzGilbert had himself been, with William de Warenne, appointed as a 'justiciar' in charge of 'the affairs of the kingdom'.[112] Despite his post as a commissioner in one of the Ely land pleas, as a neighbouring landholder fitzGilbert could well have proved unsuitable: he was certainly named by the abbot as suspect of taking over Ely land illegally when it was vulnerable.[113] When Archbishop Lanfranc, Geoffrey of Coutances, Robert of Eu, Richard fitzGilbert, and Hugh de Montfort were ordered to ensure that sheriffs restored to the Church its lands that they had wrongfully taken over, the same writ required these great men to make similar restitution if guilty.[114] Legal disputes with former commissioners such as Richard and Odo doubtless provoked the requirement that the Domesday commissioners be 'sent into counties which they did not know and where they themselves were unknown': information supplied by a curial bishop.[115] Odo, was, after all, a figure on whom William had placed almost total reliance, entrusting him with a regency that included many of the functions of a later justiciar, whereas Domesday records him as guilty of giving out royal and other lands to his contacts.[116] Yet Odo himself was well able to recognize an instance of partiality and to manipulate it thereafter to suit a bishop within his earldom; he ordered a second hearing of the court case between Gundulf, bishop of Rochester, and Picot, sheriff of Cambridgeshire, following allegations that the sheriff had intimidated the jurors. To the new hearing in London, before 'many of the most important barons in England', Odo summoned the representatives of the county and, finding them to be guilty of perjury, the court imposed severe penalties and gave the disputed estates to the bishop.[117] Magnates had evident influence over the choice of hundred jurors, since both they and sheriffs were strongly represented by their own tenants on hundred juries.[118] Whether a witness currently held land from a litigant was known to matter to contemporaries, but often to a limited degree. One man permitted to give evidence for Bishop Wulfstan of Worcester in his case against the abbot of Evesham was—of all people—the bishop's former steersman, supposedly an impartial witness since 'on the day the oath was taken, he held nothing of Bishop Wulfstan'.[119] Such practices suggest that impartiality was neither possible nor, indeed, intended.[120]

[111] *Acta*, 69; F. R. H. Du Boulay, *The Lordship of Canterbury* (London, 1966), 25–51.

[112] OV 2.316.   [113] *Acta*, 119.

[114] *Acta*, no. 129, quoted in Ch. 9 in this volume, p. 256.

[115] W. H. Stevenson, 'A contemporary description of the Domesday Survey', *EHR*, 22 (1907), 72–84; EHD2, no. 198.

[116] e.g. GDB:139b (HRT:31,8); Bates, 'The origins of the justiciarship', 3–4.

[117] Fleming, *Law*, 17–21; *Acta*, no. 25.   [118] Fleming, *Law*, 20–8.

[119] *Acta*, no. 349.

[120] cf. the machinations of Bishop Wulfstan, and others, inside and outside courts, and the packing of this one, portrayed by Williams in 'The cunning of the dove', 23–38, esp. 35–7.

Such were the limitations and deficiencies of the shire court—and they were already patent to the ruling group, who evidently took steps, perhaps insufficient ones, to surmount them. The only known group of Domesday commissioners held no land in the circuit where they operated, save for a single manor, Lechlade: and for that, Henry de Ferrers, the commissioner, had recently obtained a royal confirmation of quittance of geld for six hides![121]

A fourth feature of the land pleas employed in the Domesday Inquiry was the adoption of the last day of King Edward's reign rather than that of Harold II as the departure point for tenurial rights, by establishing who held the lands in the time of King Edward and to whom the king had subsequently gifted them. One writ of 1080 had directed that Ely Abbey was 'to have all its liberties over all its men as it had them on the day on which King Edward was alive and dead'—that is, to ignore Harold's short reign.[122] That was the formula used by Exon Domesday; Great Domesday used the briefer 'TRE'—often adopted by historians—standing for *tempore regis Edwardi*, 'in the time of King Edward'. It largely bypassed the difficulty of supplying a legally acceptable date for William's slaughter of the crowned king, sometimes surmounted by such euphemisms as 'when the king crossed the sea', adopted at Penenden Heath.[123] The new establishment had evidently come to the view that the legal standing of Domesday was better served by a general reference to King Edward's reign as its baseline than by reference to his victory at Hastings. Probably in 1082, Geoffrey of Coutances and Robert of Mortain were directed 'to put an end to the pleas' brought by William d'Eu, Ralph, son of Waleran, and Robert Gernon, 'if they are not willing to plead as they would have done in the time of King Edward'. The same writ ordered Bishop Remigius to cease his claim to rights over Ely since the king 'does not wish him to have anything there which his predecessor did not have on the day that King Edward died'.[124] To establish this baseline—rather indeed a springboard—the Inquiry enlisted the men from the villages, the hundreds, and the shires to pronounce on conditions in the time of King Edward. Reference was not confined to jurors or the men of the locality. At the king's command, the deposed bishop of the South Saxons, the aged Æthelric, was brought to a Penenden Heath plea in a cart in order 'to expound and declare the ancient customs of the laws, and with him several other English skilled in ancient laws and customs'.[125]

Fifthly and finally, the land pleas instruct us that, whatever the exigencies of the Conquest's aftermath, in the later part of his reign William, or his punctilious deputies, insisted upon written confirmation of decisions. Odo of Bayeux had held the Worcester/Evesham plea before seven shires, yet he still notified the result in writing to the three sheriffs concerned by name—although undoubtedly these

---

[121] GDB:169a (GLS:59,1); Hemming, 288; *DB: Worcestershire*, App. V, Worcester F.

[122] *Acta*, no. 120, 1081 × 1083; also Acta 121, possibly 1070 × 1086, probably 1081 × 1086.

[123] Du Boulay, *Lordship of Canterbury*, 38–40, but cf. GDB:154d (OXF:1,6).

[124] *Acta*, no. 123.   [125] *Acta*, no. 69.

officials would have been there present or represented.[126] Similarly, after Bishop Geoffrey of Coutances had conducted a plea in this dispute in open court at Worcester, probably between 1083 and 1085, it was later deemed necessary for him to issue a written certificate stating the results of the case. Geoffrey confirmed the authorized record of the outcome in 1086 to the four known Worcestershire Domesday commissioners in the command form of a routine text; after the greeting, it begins simply 'know', *sciatis*, although Urse, sheriff of Worcester and Osbern fitzScrob, a Worcestershire and Herefordshire landholder, had been there present with 'the whole shire'.[127] Whilst the usefulness of Domesday Book, and its earlier versions, comes into question from time to time, all were intended as a record of acceptance. The Domesday Inquiry should be distinguished, but cannot be divorced, from the written record.[128] The fact that ecclesiastical houses made their own copies or extracts of Domesday was, as Janet Nelson has put reception of the written word, 'the litmus test of political loyalty'.[129]

Ely had allegedly been the shelter of rebels, and the lands of all those who fought against William were forfeit. Experience of the Ely land disputes alone seems almost sufficient to inform the Domesday Inquest, given the prolonged and inconclusive nature of previous proceedings. In general, the intention seems largely to have been to accommodate the new holders as tenants, not to make complete restitution: at Ely, the abbot was to be 'seised of those thegnlands which belonged to the abbey on the day of King Edward's death, if those who hold them cannot come to an agreement with him':[130] the last phrase seems crucial. William's successful effort to legitimize his new land settlement via Domesday demonstrates his realisation that it was patently not in his long-term interest that harm should come to the title of the Church's proper holdings: support from the church hierarchy and of churchmen was too invaluable. When these well-educated, worldly-wise, but well-intentioned men had given William their counsel (*communicato concilium* as the *Dialogus* put it), they formed the essential personnel in panels of commissioners sent on circuit through the kingdom; they were truly royal legates *a latere*.[131]

Anglo-Saxon England was never part of the Carolingian empire but, admiringly, and curiously belatedly, came to imitate not a few of its practices.[132] Charlemagne had experienced a similar need to oversee and rectify the local authority of counts and other officials, by instituting literally 'messengers of the lord king', representing direct lines of royal authority. The same term, *missi*, was in use for Carolingian ambassadors; *missi dominici* could act as judges in court, and such hearings were one stage in the appeal process; they could punish criminals and receive oaths; and

---

[126] *Acta*, no. 135.   [127] *Acta*, no. 350.
[128] Contrast Roffe, *Inquest*, 224–51 and Roffe, *Decoding*, 104–8.
[129] J. L. Nelson, 'Literacy in Carolingian government' in R. McKitterick (ed.), *The Uses of Literacy in Early Medieval Europe* (Cambridge, 1990), 294–6.
[130] *Acta*, no. 119; Fleming, *Law*, 70.
[131] *discretissimos a latere suo destinavit viros per regnum in circuitu, Dialogus*, 63.
[132] J. Campbell, *The Anglo-Saxon State* (London, 2000), xv–xvi, 7, 16; C. Wickham, *The Inheritance of Rome* (Penguin, 2010), 460–4.

they could inspect and check the behaviour of clergy and laity. Men of the highest status, with archbishops, abbots, dukes and counts regularly amongst their number, they usually acted in pairs, one lay and one cleric, in a specific territory; they covered any matter concerning the administration of justice, insisting on written law and administering oaths of loyalty.[133] These established procedures were not forgotten: collections of Carolingian capitularies were copied and circulated amongst the ecclesiastics of Lotharingia and France in the tenth and early eleventh centuries. In the Domesday context, the equivalent of the *missi* were designated *legati*—again the contemporary term for ambassadors. Such commissions were thereafter to become established in England and to prove powerful agencies of royal authority.

William's control lines were immediate and direct, and, whereas between 1072 and 1080 almost all of his time was spent outside the kingdom, he clearly spent most of 1086 travelling around southern England while the Domesday Survey was in progress.[134] Bishops and royal clerks, who provided widely trained expertise and European perspectives, were the key to the Domesday enterprise. Their role as commissioners earlier in the reign was substantially innovatory and thereby they constructed a tested framework that obviated some of the Inquiry's potential pitfalls. Working towards reconciliation and stability—within the limits of the military regime and the damage already done—these men contributed their expertise to facing the tenurial complications resulting from the Conquest and from William's last great endeavour to legitimize his actions.

---

[133] R. McKitterick, *Charlemagne* (Cambridge, 2008), 258–63.
[134] Introduction in *Acta*, 76–7, 82.

3

Who Wrote Domesday? Resources and Expertise in the Localities

The commissioners appointed, the assembly of data remained to be co-ordinated with shire, hundred, and landholders. The Domesday Inquiry was always intended to result in a written record, not merely a series of hearings. William was ever suspicious, and intent on allocating responsibility, and by the 1080s he required a written report to conclude a hearing. About the time of Domesday, or earlier, Lanfranc instructed Bishops Geoffrey of Coutances and Walkelin of Winchester that it was to be noted 'who had the lands of St Ætheldreda [of Ely] written down and sworn, how they were sworn and by whom, who heard the swearing, and what the lands are, how many there are, what they are called and who held them'; Lanfranc would then let the king know the truth (*veritatem*) in a letter.[1] Verbal assurances and witness alone were now adjudged insufficient.

The main sources of the Domesday material are largely agreed: great landholders, representatives of shire and hundred, pre-Domesday and perhaps pre-Conquest documents all played a part. What is not agreed is the order in which these eleventh-century actors come on stage and their precise role—they all have their respective supporters. Nor is there agreement as to *when* the final act was played out, with the two volumes of Domesday Book as the last scenario. Only relatively late in Domesday studies have historians begun to consider in depth the question of *who* produced the regional Domesdays and Domesday itself. Yet knowledge derived from the handwriting and input of individual scribes has made great strides in recent years, aided by the rebinding of Domesday and the republication of a facsimile edition. Aiming to be realistic in a somewhat arcane field, this study seeks to ferret out the personnel charged with mustering Domesday's written data.

Language and communication were major obstacles, but were evidently not insuperable. Domesday is an encyclopaedic agricultural compilation whose information was gathered from English- and Anglo-Scandinavian-speaking peoples and written down in Latin, under the supervision of a ruling elite who spoke French; it was also an abridged tax assessment with the legal force of a title deed. Moreover, many members of the new Norman lay elite were illiterate even if, in theory, all churchmen read Latin—the prevailing medium for the literate. Certainly, relatively

---

[1] *Acta*, no. 127 (1081 × 1087, probably 1085 × 87).

few spoke three languages, although their calling demanded continual translation between the language spoken locally and the Latin record. A century later, it was still worthy of mention that Gilbert Foliot, bishop first of Hereford, then of London (died 1187), was 'a man thoroughly at home in three tongues, Latin, French, and English,' and clear and eloquent in each of them,[2] and that Abbot Samson of Bury St Edmunds had mastered the local dialect.[3] Most needed help: five French-speaking royal justices, including Peter de Valognes—sheriff of Hertfordshire at the time of Domesday—when requiring information in court from the twelve lawmen of York in 1106, needed the reeve of the North Riding, Ansketel of Bulmer, later sheriff of Yorkshire, to act as interpreter.[4]

The indispensable interpreters and latimers—those skilled in Latin—only rarely appear in Domesday, although such men were probably an integral part of most great households and, perhaps surprisingly, held lands from ecclesiastical houses as well as from lay barons.[5] One *Godricus* appeared as *Latunarius* (*sic*) in the *Inquisition of St Augustine's*, but without his title in Domesday, suggesting that more went unrecorded there.[6] Several held small lands from the king: Ansgot the Interpreter was listed first amongst the trained functionaries called *servientes* and later 'thegns' in Surrey.[7] Hirokazu Tsurushima has suggested that they earned their titles from their official functions in county courts, where their interpreting and literacy skills were essential, as well as on honorial business.[8] Two latimers were present at a legal agreement, a *conventio*, in the early twelfth century, whereby the abbot of Ramsey gained land from an Englishman in return for a payment in cash and kind: one of the two was of the abbot's own household.[9] Domesday shows one Englishman, Robert, widely known as *Latinarius* or Latimer, taking on lands, largely at farm, for the king, the archbishop of Canterbury, Odo of Bayeux as earl of Kent, and Richard fitzGilbert, and holding a small amount of land from St Augustine's Abbey;[10] and a writ shows him working with Haimo the sheriff.[11] As Robert's activities were certainly not confined solely to the household of any one of

---

[2] Walter Map, *De nugis curialium*, ed. M. R. James, rev. C. N. L. Brooke and R. A. B. Mynors (Oxford, 1983), 36–7.

[3] *The Chronicle of Jocelin of Brakelond*, ed. H. E. Butler (London, 1962), 40.

[4] Van Caenegem, *Lawsuits* 1, no. 172; Green, *Sheriffs*, 90.

[5] Interpreters, GDB:36d, (SUR:36,8), 73c (WIL:66,8), 83b (DOR:54,7), 99b (SOM:45,9–11). Latimers, GDB:50d (HAM:NF10,3), 180c (HEF:1,36); LDB:101a (ESS:90,42); GDB:6c (KEN:5,19). H. Tsurushima illuminates these 'hinge-men', outlining their holdings, associations, and possible functions, 'Domesday interpreters', *ANS*, 18 (1995), 201–22.

[6] GDB:1d (KEN:M24); *An Eleventh Century Inquisition of St Augustine's, Canterbury*, ed. A. Ballard, British Academy Records, Records of Social and Economic History, vol. 4 (London, 1920), 30; also (CAM:5,37).

[7] GDB:30a; 36d (SUR:36,6).

[8] Tsurushima, 'Interpreters', 208–22.

[9] *Cartularium monasterii de Ramseia*, ed. W. H. Hart and P. A. Lyons, vol.1, RS 79 (London, 1884), 137; Tsurushima, 'Interpreters', 214.

[10] *DMon: Rodbertus interpres*, 87: *Rodbertus Latimer*, 101.

[11] *Textus Roffensis*, ed. P. H. Sawyer, Early English Manuscripts in Facsimile, vol. 11 (Copenhagen, 1962), ff. 211v–12; Williams, *The English*, 83–5.

these magnates, he seems to have profited from his language skills by conducting, in effect, an estate-management service for magnates in Kent. Certainly Domesday shows several of the lands he managed were paying more than their worth, including Boxley, which was worth £30 and paying £55, and Chatham, where Robert's brother, Ælfwine, was reeve, worth £15, and paying £35.[12]

THE LANDHOLDERS' WRITTEN RETURNS

> The survey is made by counties, hundreds, and hides. The king's name is written down at the head of the list and then other top people placed by name (followed by those of nobles who hold of the king in chief), placed according to their order of dignity. Moreover, they were placed in numbered order, using which they can the more easily find what belongs to them further on in the sequence of the Book.
>
> Richard fitzNigel, *The Dialogue of the Exchequer,* describing Domesday[13]

Listed first after the king were the ecclesiastics. The bishops, whether those seated in monastic cathedrals reformed under King Edgar or in the newer secular cathedral foundations of William's reign such as Lincoln, were heads of literate communities. Monastic communities preserved, rewrote, augmented, or even forged the solemn charters and wills that confirmed the lands of their house. Their narratives and annals were the repository of the history and culture of the eleventh century, including that of warfare and of politics, and within such institutions far more continuity was permitted following the Conquest than in the world of lay land-holders. Several Anglo-Saxon bishops and abbots were deposed in 1070 and thereafter, but none immediately, an important tactic in William's success: Bishop Wulfstan survived at Worcester until his death in 1095. Many of the rank and file of the remaining religious and clergy were of native extraction; Eadmer, a native Englishman in the Christ Church monastic community, served Archbishop Anselm as a chaplain and secretary and took notes of Anselm's activities which he wrote up after his master's death. Whilst many leading honorial officials tended, of course, to be also incomers, lower down the economic scale we have few names; but some large lay and ecclesiastical estates in Domesday record clerks and knights as minor subtenants with reeves and beadles alongside, who seem likely to have functioned as agricultural support teams.[14] Ecclesiastical institutions, which continued to hold, but not necessarily control, between a fifth and a quarter of the land by value, faced no intractable obstacles in responding to a set of questions

---

[12] GDB:8d (KEN:5,102), 8c (KEN:5,89).

[13] This translation I owe to F. Thorn. *Fit autem descriptio per comitatus, per centuriatas et hidas, prenotato in ipso capite regis nomine, ac deinde seriatim aliorum procerum nominibus appositis secundum status sui dignitatem, qui videlicet de rege tenent in capite. Apponuntur autem singulis numeri secundum ordinem sic dispositis, per quos inferius in ipsa libri serie que as eos pertinent facilius occurrunt, Dialogus,* 63.

[14] e.g. GDB:180a (HEF:1,10a); Harvey 1988, 88–9.

about their lands, seeking information from the locality in English, and writing it up in Latin.

Lay landholders appear, at first glance, to have been less well equipped to provide written information. By 1085, only four named Englishmen held more than 100 hides or carucates of land and many of the new landholders spoke a language alien to those who worked their acquisitions. But Norman landholders, like their predecessors,[15] often maintained practical links with religious institutions for their mutual interest, as well as retaining chaplains as members of their households. Moreover, the Anglo-Saxon minsters with their non-monastic clergy did not fade from the scene immediately following the Conquest: similarly, small colleges of secular canons, who had close social links and supplied practical clerical support for their patrons and founders, had not been uncommon in Normandy between 990 and 1066—albeit their popularity in both England and Normandy was short-lived.[16]

Such colleges of clerical communities were often set up anew in England on chief residential estates, and particularly fortified sites. Some alien priories, St-Florent from the Loire in particular, seemed to relish the opportunity to plant communities in strategic border regions under the protection of a castle and patron, as in Sussex and in the Welsh borderland.[17] One of William's most trusted followers, Earl Roger of Montgomery, who was allocated two of the more autonomous blocks of land in strategically vulnerable regions, was acclaimed for setting up new clerical communities, and extending their influence through assigning churches to them. At Arundel, the fortified focus of his Sussex land, Roger established the clerks of St Nicholas; in Shropshire he founded, in addition to Shrewsbury Abbey, a college at Quatford alongside a castle and a new, probably collegiate, chapel in Shrewsbury Castle. The earl's chaplains held portions of his demesne manor of Morville. One of these 'wise clerks' or chaplains, Godebold, was a man of status, holding in 1086 several manors of St Alkmund's Church, Shrewsbury, as well as other land and preferment. A second clerk, Herbert, who like Godebold witnessed the founding document of Quatford Church, has been identified with Herbert *Grammaticus*, archdeacon of Shropshire within the Lichfield/Chester diocese.[18] A third 'wise clerk', Odelarius of Orléans, was the father of the well-known chronicler, Orderic Vitalis, who describes him as an eloquent and learned man and Earl Roger's confidant; he had encouraged the earl to found Shrewsbury Abbey. Odelarius must have become bilingual since his son, Orderic, recalls being unaccustomed to hearing spoken French until he left home for the monastery at Saint-Evroult.[19] Richard de

[15] S. Baxter, 'The Earls and the monasteries of Mercia', in *The Earls of Mercia: Lordship and Power in Late Anglo-Saxon England* (Oxford, 2007), 152–203.

[16] J. Blair, 'Minsters in a changing world, c.850–1100', in *The Church in Anglo-Saxon Society* (Oxford, 2005); J. Blair, 'Secular minster churches in Domesday Book', in *Reassessment*, 131–7.

[17] J. Martindale, 'Monasteries and castles: the priories of St-Florent de Saumur in England after 1066', in C. Hicks (ed.), *England in the Eleventh Century*, Harlaxton Medieval Studies, vol. 2 (Stamford, 1992), 135–56.

[18] J. F. A. Mason, 'The officers and clerks of the Norman earls of Shropshire', *Trans. Shropshire Archaeological Society*, 56 (1957–60), 244–57, at 252–6.

[19] OV 2.262; OV 6.552–5.

Belmeis, another of Earl Roger's clerks and a landholder, was later to serve his son, Robert of Bellême. Although his exact office is uncertain, his status was high, for he later became bishop of London for nineteen years.[20] There was no insuperable career divide between secular and ecclesiastical service, nor between that of great feudatory and crown.

Earl Roger could certainly provide men to supervise and record the details of his manors, and organize responses from his subtenants, or on their behalf—and he held most of Shropshire. One of the few lay landholders with discernible policies of estate management and demesne agriculture,[21] he and his two sons had the ability to keep control of their finances over wide distances, ordering revenues from lands in one dominion to be paid regularly to monasteries in another.[22] With other magnates, too, the coincidence of patronage of houses of secular clergy with discernible estate policies suggests the interdependence of the two, reflecting the worth of literate Englishmen to the greatest of the lay newcomers. Richard fitzGilbert, holder of the honours of Clare and Tonbridge, inherited at Clare both a college of secular canons and an estate organization from a powerful Anglo-Saxon family. Richard continued to maintain the demesne agriculture he found there and also the patronage of the religious foundation, albeit transforming the prebends into a Benedictine priory in 1090.[23] William of Briouze, with a large portion of Sussex in his charge, founded a college alongside his fortified administrative headquarters at Bramber—though, like many another, this clerical college was not long-lasting. The role of these short-lived institutions in the first decades of the Norman period was largely unappreciated by the rule-observing monastic writers; yet at the time of Domesday, they represented a widespread source of clerical personnel 'linked to the patron's household, the service of his chapel, and perhaps the staffing of his secretariat'.[24]

Some magnates—Roger of Montgomery, Robert of Mortain, and William of Briouze—and several others, even boasted their own 'sheriff' on their widespread lands and greater jurisdictions, an official who held regional responsibility for the geographically dispersed estates of the greatest tenants-in-chief,[25] just as did the stewards of the great Anglo-Saxon ealdormen.[26] Although great men entrusted with key strategic areas were hardly typical of lay landholders generally, lesser tenants-in-chief, too, had permanent officials; thirty-four estates betray evidence of a steward—an impressive number given that their small chance of survival in

---

[20] Mason, 'Officers and clerks', 253–4; *AnnWinton*, 43.

[21] Harvey 1983, 56–7; Harvey 1988, 115–21.

[22] OV 3.138–43; *Calendar of Documents preserved in France, 918–1206*, ed. J. H. Round, Public Record Office (PRO) (London, 1899) nos 665, 668.

[23] R. Mortimer, 'The beginnings of the Honour of Clare', *ANS*, 3 (1980), 119–41; Harvey 1988, 116.

[24] Blair, 'Secular minster churches in Domesday Book', in *Reassessment*, 135.

[25] J. F. A. Mason, 'Barons and their officials in the later eleventh century', *ANS*, 13 (1990), 243–62, esp. 248; but see Green on Turstin: *Sheriffs*, 33.

[26] D. Whitelock, *The Beginnings of English Society* (Harmondsworth, 1965), 90.

record depended on the regional *Exon*, since Great Domesday largely omits functionaries.[27] Even mesne tenants had a steward, responsible both for the administration of estates and for provisioning the household. While the honorial officers known from 1086 appear largely of Norman origin, they themselves probably employed native subordinates, just as Norman sheriffs employed English as well as French reeves. Several decades after the Conquest, the Worcestershire sheriff, Urse, had a chaplain with an English name who seems to have assisted with the administration of his estates.[28]

Variants in 'Domesday diplomatic'—the terms, order, and phrases used—as well as in content, all leave indications confirming that the greatest landholders produced individual Domesday returns;[29] they were able to amass their own data and influence its content and format. To name a few clear examples, the recorded entries for the lands of St Martin's of Dover, of the former bishop of Elmham, and of the bishopric of Worcester, all exhibit distinctive characteristics of content, order, and forms of expression.[30] The ploughland formula—a main item of information that varies in character according to county—might also vary by fief; and its variants in Shropshire, Leicestershire, and Yorkshire have been tabulated.[31] Domesday entries for Roger de Lacy's own fee in Shropshire share features with his tenancies from Earl Roger, from the bishop of Hereford, and from Rainald the sheriff.[32] The individual character of the bishopric of Worcester's lands, the domain of the influential stalwart Wulfstan, is shown in its data on tenurial rights and dues, which are distinctive in position and content from the rest of the shire: it is the only fief in Worcestershire and in Circuit V that consistently refers to the payments and services owed by its pre-Conquest tenants.[33] The data on the privatized borough of Bury St Edmund's are uniquely valuable.[34] In thirteenth-century governmental inquiries too, the descriptions of ecclesiastical estates showed every appearance of separate origin: those of Thorney and Peterborough Abbeys diverge in terminology from other lands in the same hundred, despite the crucial role of hundredal jurors: and one entry depended upon material supplied by Ramsey Abbey.[35] One of the few direct allusions to the collection of information in the shire court is a Gloucestershire entry which ascribes its lack of manorial data to the fact that 'no one rendered account (*reddidit rationem*) to the king's

---

[27] Mason, 'Barons and their officials', 244–8.

[28] *The Cartulary of Worcester Cathedral Priory*, ed. R. R. Darlington, PRS, ns 38 (1968 for 1962–3), no. 338.

[29] For analysis, with interpretations, of some Domesday variants see Roffe, *Inquest*, 187–216. For variations on tenure, see tables in S. Baxter, 'The representation of lordship and land tenure in Domesday Book', in Hallam and Bates, 95–102.

[30] Harvey 1975, 191–2; Baxter, 'Lordship and land tenure in Domesday Book', in Hallam and Bates, 83–92.

[31] H. C. Darby, *Domesday England* (Cambridge, 1977), 347–51.

[32] C. P. Lewis, introduction in *The Shropshire Domesday*, Alecto 1990, 7–9. There are references to Roger Bigod's *breve* or return LDB:277b (NFK:66,81); and to the king's return, GDB:178a (WOR: X3); and to Ely Abbey's return LDB:205b (NFK:13,1), 238a (NFK:23,9).

[33] Baxter, 'Lordship and land tenure in Domesday Book', in Hallam and Bates, 83–92.

[34] LDB:372a.   [35] Raban, 78.

commissioners nor came to this *descriptio*'.[36] Either a written return or a personal appearance was expected from each landholder as perhaps, indeed, each vill.[37]

Oblique allusions survive to backroom work undertaken by the landholder's men on his behalf. The 'men of William de Warenne' state that the values of the churches on his manors are subsumed into the total value.[38] The remissness of a landholder's officials in supplying details is castigated in the Herefordshire snippet: 'concerning 33 hides [of the bishopric's 300], the bishop's men gave no account'.[39] We need to accommodate this evidence alongside a recently revived emphasis on the men of the shire, the earlier equivalent of the knights of the shire, and on jurors, as 'responsible for the collection of much of the data'.[40] Indeed, in the manorialized western districts, the reliance upon written returns by landholders may well have been stronger.[41] The Domesday working blend of the two elements were recognized in the *Leges Henrici* of thirty years later as the approved mode of inquiry: in the county courts, the lord, or his steward, could represent all the land he held in that county; 'if both are unavoidably absent, the reeve and the priest and the four most substantial men of the vill shall attend on behalf of all who have not been summoned by name to court'.[42] In 1086, great landholders, punctiliously careful of their assets, most probably sent their men *and* a written return—if truly influential, they might have by-passed a preliminary session altogether.

Two major surviving texts suggest returns from individual landholders: the *Inquisitio Eliensis*, a detailed Domesday description of the church of Ely's lands in six counties, and Exon Domesday, arranged by landholders across several counties. Then there is the *Domesday Monachorum* of Christ Church, Canterbury, which includes a Domesday-like text with impeccable landlord provenance and shows its autonomy by its different order. And the text known as Evesham A appears to represent a compilation of data submitted by tenants-in-chief, arranged in hundreds ready for the hundredal meetings: a text made for a single shire.[43]

One noteworthy aspect of the Canterbury and Evesham texts, one from the south-east and one from the west midlands, is that both houses divided their tenanted from their demesne lands in a different way from that in the Domesday record.[44] They had one notion of the project, but their material became rearranged on different lines. Those heads of major religious houses debating the launch of the Domesday process at Christmas 1085 understood some, but

---

[36] GDB:164b (GLS:1,63).

[37] *Inde nullum responsum*, GDB:22b (SUS:10,82), where hides and ploughlands but no people, ploughs, or value are enumerated.

[38] LDB:172a (NFK:8,136); also GDB:238a (WAR:B2).

[39] GDB:182d (HEF:2,7).   [40] Roffe, *Inquest*, 117–18, 121–3.

[41] Minster survival, mapped in Blair, *The Church in Anglo-Saxon Society*, 296, might well suggest the sources of different styles of Domesday returns.

[42] *LegesHP*, 101.   [43] *Evesham A*, esp. 8.

[44] For Westminster Abbey, *Evesham A*, 6–7. The lands of Canterbury's tenants by knight-service were described separately in GDB, but not in the main Canterbury Cathedral survey known as *DMon*, 81–95: the knights are listed separately later, 105.

not necessarily all, of the uses to which the data might be put; possibly the future fiscal significance of demesne versus tenanted manors only emerged once the Survey was in progress. The extent of the king's power over subtenancies was to be a battleground for action and legislation by the strongest rulers for the next two centuries. Certainly, one official sought clarification directly from Lanfranc on this very point, when he asked if any Canterbury estates in certain counties were held in demesne.[45]

Great landholders, lay as well as ecclesiastical, employed sufficient clerical assistance to submit their own returns to the shire, or circuit, there to receive the shire format impressed upon them. Some returns, however, received individual treatment: St Martin's, Dover, and the bishopric of Worcester, with more continuity of leadership than was general, may have acted quickly after the Christmas council at Gloucester to assert or conserve their rights. The eccentricities in their accounts may also reflect an indulgence already given officially to those at the centre of affairs, institutionalized into the fiscal concessions given to barons of the Exchequer—as well as a recognition of the art of the possible.

THE LOCAL COMMUNITIES

> Here follows the inquiry concerning lands which the king's barons made according to the oath of the sheriff of the shire and of all the barons and their Frenchmen, and of the whole hundred court, the priest, the reeve and six men from each village.
>
> Preface, *Inquest of Ely*[46]

The shire

The shire and the sheriff

The most powerful sheriffs were surely present at the Christmas council and knew directly of the decision to launch the Inquiry, whose terms of reference were likely to be communicated to all shires via writs published in the shire court. Pre-1066 shire courts met at least twice a year and those of the boroughs three times a year.[47] We have no direct knowledge of the timing of the shire meetings in the eleventh century, but later shire meetings took place after Easter and after Michaelmas. The Domesday writs may have demanded the data to be gathered in time for presentation at the spring meeting. In 1274–5, instructions went out to sheriffs and to commissioners simultaneously, and commissioners were commanded:

> to hold these inquests according to the contents of the said articles, at fixed days and places, which you shall appoint for the purpose ... We have also commanded our sheriffs of the said counties to bring before you at the fixed days and places, which you

---

[45] F. Barlow, 'Domesday Book: a letter of Lanfranc', *EHR*, 78 (1963), 284–9.
[46] *IE*, 97; EHD2, no. 215.   [47] III Edgar, 5,1; II Cnut, 18.

shall signify to them, so many good and lawful men of their bailiwick that by them the truth of the above-mentioned may be well ascertained.[48]

In the somewhat more literate and inquiry-rehearsed society of the late thirteenth century, the earliest dated return came back, amazingly, within one month of the issue of the commission; others were dated nine months later.[49] In 1086, given the external pressures on the ruling group, speed was of the essence and England, as a conquered country, could be directed at will, within the limits of weather and rebellion. The questions asked in 1086 are directly represented only in the Inquest of Ely—a later copy of a detailed Domesday-like text for the lands of the abbey of Ely in six counties—opening with the questions quoted in my Introduction.[50]

The constitution of the shire court is known. Traditionally, the earldorman or earl had presided over the shire court together with the bishop; the 'shire-reeve' or 'sheriff' had been his paid official, perhaps of his own kin, or perhaps of the bishop's.[51] But the Anglo-Saxon earls who survived 1066 lasted no later than 1071. William I created earldoms only in the vulnerable border counties of Cheshire, Shropshire and, briefly, Herefordshire with Worcestershire, and in strategically important Kent and Sussex. With the extinction of the other earldoms, the sheriff—in the absence of a count or earl and in Norman Latin, *vicecomes*,—became the king's chief officer at county level employed in executive, policing, and military tasks as well as in levying taxation and the organization of revenues from royal lands, large tracts of which he 'farmed' in both the modern and the historical sense of the word. Yet, Judith Green sums up, it was their presence in the shire and hundred courts that gave sheriffs their 'crucial role, for it was there that many of the disputes arising from the vast transfer of land to the Normans took place'.[52]

Sheriffs were primarily men of action, frequently castellans of royal castles, but they were nevertheless accompanied by household clerks and chaplains, and were even patrons of colleges. Whether shire-reeves or their subordinates, the men termed 'reeve' in Domesday were often of substantial means; some combined the role of bailiff with the ability to take on large-scale farming contracts and therefore had the wherewithal to present an account.[53] For them, recording the outcome from deliberations of shire assemblies was not difficult to arrange.

After 1070 most sheriffs were Normans, but not all. Strands of continuity in personnel remain from the Anglo-Saxon kingdom. Robert fitzWymarc, son of a Breton mother, whose castle at Clavering dated from before the 1050s and who had possessed substantial estates in Edwardian England, served as sheriff of Essex after the Conquest and was succeeded by his son, Swein.[54] William Malet, an early

---

[48] Cam, App. I; EHD3, no. 45.   [49] Raban, 82–4.
[50] *IE*, 97, quoted in this volume, p. 1.
[51] A. Williams, 'A vice-comital family in pre-Conquest Warwickshire', *ANS*, 11 (1989), 279–95.
[52] J. Green, 'The sheriffs of William the Conqueror', *ANS*, 5 (1982), 127–45, at 127.
[53] Reeves and their functions are discussed by J. Campbell, 'Some agents and agencies of the Anglo-Saxon state', in Holt, *Studies*, 210–18, at 205–9, 215–16.
[54] Williams, *The English*, 10; Green, *Sheriffs*, 39.

Norman sheriff of Yorkshire, was thought to have had an English mother.[55] Edward of Salisbury's name is not the only indicator of the English origin of the sheriff of Wiltshire, who by 1086 held no less than 300 hides of land in nine shires—his lands held in chief were worth over £400 (more than half in Wiltshire, by value); Ramsey evidence shows him functioning in a shire-court before the Conquest, and three of his Wiltshire manors record no pre-Conquest tenant.[56] He held lands of the temporarily vacant Glastonbury Abbey.[57] Although an enigmatic figure, Edward's more than substantial estate of over 300 hides and his solo issue of writs around 1087–8 suggests that he held a key position at that time in the fast-developing administrative expertise established in the Conqueror's new citadel at Salisbury, and so quite probably in the Domesday Survey itself.[58] In addition, sheriffs retained Anglo-Saxons as auxiliary officials, able to keep some land conditionally, by earning it through service, as the Exchequer expert, Richard fitzNigel, later insisted was the sole justification.[59] One Godric Dapifer seems to have been the most successful of these, holding 32 carucates and farming other royal land. The shrieval group was close-knit, even endogamous. Robert d'Oilly, sheriff of possibly three counties—Berkshire, Oxfordshire, and Warwickshire—is thought to have married the daughter and heiress of the powerful Wigot of Wallingford, its custodian, and related to the Confessor.[60] William Malet's son, Robert, was sheriff of Suffolk before 1086. Ivo Taillebois' father was Ralph, probably sheriff of two, or even three counties, whose niece married Ranulf, brother of Ilger, a future sheriff of Huntingdonshire.[61]

Despite their eclectic origins, the coherence amongst the members of the shrievalty might well have helped their prompt action in the Domesday Inquiry. It was not unusual for one sheriff to hold more than one county, or to hold several in quick succession. Roger Bigod held Norfolk and Suffolk; Ansculf of Picquigny, Surrey and Buckinghamshire; and Hugh fitzBaldric, Yorkshire and Nottinghamshire. Hugh de Port was sheriff of Hampshire, and earlier of Kent;[62] in both counties he held lands from Odo of Bayeux; he also held royal manors in Northamptonshire at farm.[63] Personnel seemed to have been moved around more frequently than was subsequently the case under the Conqueror's sons,[64] thereby familiarizing officials with several counties and keeping them distanced from local vested interests. A limited number of men proved both pro-active and trustworthy.[65] Giving sheriffs

---

[55] Green, 'Sheriffs of the Conqueror', 132.
[56] Williams, *The English*, 105–6; Green, 'Sheriffs of the Conqueror', 141–2.
[57] e.g. GDB:66c (WIL:7,7; 7,12).
[58] *Regesta*, nos 292–4; probably dated autumn 1087 or spring 1088, Sharpe, 'The use of writs in the eleventh century', *ASE*, 32 (2004), 266–7, 275–7, 285.
[59] *Dialogus*, 54.
[60] Green, 'Sheriffs of the Conqueror', 132; Green, *Sherrifs*, 26, 69, 83; Williams, *The English*, 100–1.
[61] Green, 'Sheriffs of the Conqueror', 132–3.   [62] Green, *Sheriffs*, 44, 50.
[63] GDB:219b (NTH:1,1–1,2).   [64] Green, 'Sheriffs of the Conqueror', 133–4.
[65] e.g. *Acta* 129.

lands to farm in counties other than their own was perhaps a ploy to prevent any one sheriff having sole custody of the royal lands in his own county. Yet, their wide-flung responsibilities imply that sheriffs were capable of accounting for the revenues of their office in more than one county.

Many of the sheriffs were 'new men', not infrequently linked to those other new men par excellence, Odo, bishop of Bayeux and Robert, count of Mortain, the king's half-brothers (both born like William to Herlève, daughter of a prosperous tanner, but unlike the king, the legitimate sons of her subsequent marriage to Herluin, *vicomte* of Conteville).[66] Both half-brothers were fostered as leading administrators by William, and were able to influence the promotion of those with prior experience in their service: we noted that sheriff Roger Bigod, founder of a powerful dynasty in England, and Hugh de Port had held land in Normandy by knight-service from Bishop Odo.[67] These two, in turn, drew on local expertise: one Northmann by name, a pre-Conquest and early Norman sheriff of Suffolk, was still a tenant of Roger Bigod in 1086.[68] Completing the links in the chain of command, two of the king's more important clerks, Rannulf Flambard and Samson, who both arguably had a hand in the Domesday project, were Odo's protégés, reared in his cathedral school.

In the shire court, the sheriff was all-important. He was expected to summon the court, often to co-preside over it, and, on occasion, adjudicate there.[69] He also gave sworn testimony.[70] Moreover, the sheriff might also influence the selection of jurors: a total of seven Cambridgeshire jurors, across four different hundreds, had Sheriff Picot as their lord.[71] Many sheriffs had ample opportunity to dispense extensive patronage. Seventeen Norman sheriffs held lands worth at least £100 yearly: five held lands worth between £450 and £650, and Geoffrey de Mandeville held lands worth almost £800.[72] But some sheriffs held little land in chief in their county of office, or were only in possession of sub-tenures or borough properties.[73] A sheriff's varied instructions gave him plenty of scope—or headache. For much of William's reign the sheriffs, or their powerful associates, the 'deliverors', *liberatores* as Domesday calls them, were the agents of large-scale land redistribution. The latter were drawn from the same group as the sheriffs: twice mentioned was Hubert de Port, probably the sheriff's brother, or cousin, who, like Hugh, held extensive lands in Hampshire; others were themselves sheriffs or land commissioners.[74] The sheriff was ordered to execute judgements, restore fugitives to their lords, or 'to do right' in a particular matter. On the authority of a royal writ, probably accompanied by a prestigious messenger, he took lands 'into the king's hand' as Domesday

---

[66] Douglas, *Conqueror*, 15.   [67] Green, 'Sheriffs of the Conqueror', 136–8.
[68] LDB:331b; 338b; 339b (SUF:7,10; 7,70; 7,77); Green, *Sheriffs*, 76.
[69] *Acta*, no. 350.   [70] *IE*, 97.   [71] Table, Fleming, *Law*, 24–5.
[72] Green, *Sheriffs*, 15; table, Green, 'Sheriffs of the Conqueror', 140–1.
[73] GDB:30a (SUR:1,1c).
[74] LDB:377a, 450a (SUF:16,34; 77,4). Garnett considers the functions and persons of these *liberatores* in *Conquered England*, 66–74.

phrases it, as magnates fell and were replaced,[75] and he proclaimed new landholders in the presence of the men of the shire and the hundreds.

Documents in the shires: Fiscal lists

The shire retained the supervision of fiscal responsibilities, and it is maintained here that shire lists were a *sine qua non* for its collection of geld and its production of man-power, if only because the level at which a shire, its hundreds, and its manors were rated was often revised and adjusted: Northamptonshire had its level of taxation changed three times in the mid eleventh century and, probably because of the changes, there survives a brief list, in Anglo-Saxon, probably datable between 1070 and 1078, of each hundred's liability in hides.[76] In it, the few names cited of those that have not paid geld—in one case 'not a penny'—are not those of the land's occupants, but of the well-known landholders, Richard Engaine, the king of Scotland, and the king's wife.

It was maintained in Chapter 1 that lists of hides that were part of the normal texts of central administration have in part survived, but have largely gone unrecognized or unaccepted. A list of hides with Edwardian data only is extant for Christ Church, Canterbury,[77] and for Abingdon Abbey, a comparable list is headed: 'Of the hundreds and hides of the church of Abingdon in Berkshire according to the writings of the king's treasury arranged by hundreds'.[78] Whilst it is true that later abbreviations of Domesday customarily retained Circuit I's Edwardian hide assessments in preference to those of 1086, criticism of my pre-1070 or 'TRE' dating of Bath's hidage list, Bath B, does not satisfactorily explain why, if the list was derived from Domesday (as all its figures could be), it included the manor of Tidenham, which in Domesday is firmly in royal possession and unmentioned in Bath's Domesday lands;[79] it was lost temporarily to Bath Abbey before 1066, and permanently after Stigand's fall in 1070.[80] If indeed Bath produced the list only to argue the case at the Domesday Inquiry, as David Roffe suggests—for he agrees that Bath B and the Kentish Assessment List 'almost certainly pre-date the compilation of Great Domesday'—

---

[75] e.g. LDB:223b (NFK:19,20), 290b (SUF:1,222f).

[76] F. H. Baring, 'The pre-Domesday hidation of Northamptonshire', *EHR*, 17 (1902), 470–9; C. Hart, *The Hidation of Northamptonshire* (Leicester, 1970), esp. 45. Charters, App. I, 1, no. 3, 230–7. The dating would extend to 1083 if the reference to 'the Lady, the king's wife' were to Matilda, not Edith.

[77] *DMon*, f.2r; Harvey 1971, 756–9.

[78] *HistAbbend* 2, App. III, Texts 1 and 2, 379–80. Harvey 1971, 759–60; similarly, F. F. Kreisler independently came to the same conclusions, 'Domesday Book and the Anglo-Norman synthesis', in W. C. Jordan, B. McNab and T. F. Ruiz (eds), *Order and Innovation in the Middle Ages* (Princeton, 1976), 3–16, at 13–14.

[79] *Domesday Book: Somerset*, ed. C. and F. Thorn (Chichester, 1980), Appendix, 'Two Texts from a Bath Cartulary', designated Bath B, albeit it occurs earlier in the MS than that designated Bath A, a recognized Domesday satellite.

[80] GDB:164a (GLS:1,56); Charters, no. 117; Harvey 1971, 760–1.

then it was still composed *before* Domesday, yet evinces a similar order.[81] Further, other tenurial and fiscal lists survive incorporated into Domesday itself.[82]

Yet in practical terms, there now seems more consensus than is openly acknowledged. For whilst holding a different view of the process of collecting data, Roffe accepts that these fiscal lists included in Domesday Book are 'demonstrably earlier than the Yorkshire folios' and 'the formal archetype of the GDB text'; but, he argues, they are not to be dated earlier than the process of the Domesday Inquiry itself.[83] Thus, these Yorkshire lists are agreed to be Domesday 'satellites', contributing to the make-up and arrangement of Domesday material, by four current scholars.[84] However, the contents of such fiscal lists originate, not in the Domesday Inquiry, but older public records. On two folios, probably inserted into the original gathering, are lists of lands of former thegns now mostly waste and uninhabited, all now in the king's hands.[85] There is also the evidence of the lists of the former lands of the Earls Tostig, Edwin, and Morcar incorporated into the account of the royal lands.[86] Tostig had been exiled in 1065, and killed in battle in 1066, and the other earldoms had disappeared by 1071. To take the last full column of the inserted folios: it starts with the lands in Craven that were Earl Edwin's and their fiscal data—taxable carucates and possible ploughlands; however, as the lands were waste in 1086, unpopulated, and without value, no theory of landholder or wapentake furnishing data will account for them. Similarly, the lands in Lancashire that were Earl Tostig's: Domesday lists the carucates for fifty-nine named places belonging to Preston, but no other data; Domesday tells us 'how many people living there is not known', just 'a few'; the rest is waste (see Figure 2).[87] Such data could only derive from old fiscal lists incorporated into Domesday. The alternative hypothesis is that these lists were prepared *ab initio* for the Inquiry; but such a complex antiquarian exercise on a depopulated group of wasted lands is implausible. From Yorkshire too, a much earlier tenurial and fiscal list also survives. Ascribed to a date between 1023 and 1069, with a preference for the 1030s, it lists the estates of the archbishopric, with hides, ploughlands, and sokelands noted.[88]

It was relatively straightforward to use such skeletal administrative documents to construct the Domesday framework, as they were amenable to arrangement either by hundred or landholder. Even when the Yorkshire fiscal lists were arranged by wapentakes—the northern equivalent of the hundred—it was possible to draw on them to get a feudal arrangement. In some, each tenant-in-chief's name sits above

---

[81] Roffe, *Decoding*, 55–6. Roffe, *Inquest*, 108–11.

[82] e.g. GDB:379a–382b, added after the Claims section of Lincolnshire.

[83] Roffe, *Decoding*, 269. Roffe gives a useful analysis of Domesday texts, *Inquest*, 101–12.

[84] H. B. Clarke, 'The Domesday satellites', in *Reassessment*, 50–70, at 67, 69–70; F Kreisler, note 78 above.

[85] *Domesday Rebound*, HMSO (London, 1954), App. I; GDB:300–1.

[86] GDB:300–302a; Harvey 1971, 761–3; Harvey 1975, 176–80.

[87] GDB:301d (YKS:1,290–6).

[88] W. H. Stevenson, 'Yorkshire surveys and other eleventh-century documents in the York Gospels', *EHR*, 27 (1912), 1–25; Charters, no. 84; S. Baxter, 'Archbishop Wulfstan and the administration of God's property', in M. Townend (ed.), *Wulfstan, Archbishop of York* (Turnhout, 2004), 179; see also Ch. 1 in this volume, p. 26.

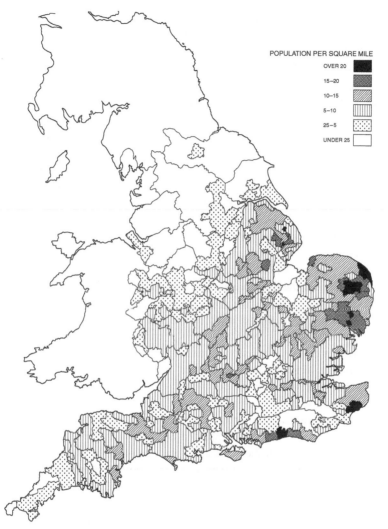

POPULATION PER SQUARE MILE

OVER 20

15–20

10–15

5–10

25–5

UNDER 25

Figure 2. Population estimated from Domesday Book (after H. C. Darby, *Domesday England* (Cambridge, 1977)).

the line and stands out, so a user could achieve the Domesday order of landholders in hundreds simply by travelling through these names in sequence.[89] Such lists could be readily deployed as 'conversion tables'—as Howard Clarke succinctly explained it—to rearrange material from wapentake to landholder order, or vice-versa.[90] Similar hidage lists might well have been copied and issued to a tenant-in-chief to use as a pro forma in assembling his data. Evesham K, arranged according to landholder which largely prefigures the order for Domesday Gloucestershire,

[89] GDB:379a–382a for list; cf. 305b–308c, 309a–313b, 315a–318.
[90] Clarke, 'The Domesday satellites', in *Reassessment*, 67; also Harvey 1971, 771–3.

might be just such a list created for and utilized in the Domesday Survey.[91] Even the Exon text, despite its arrangement by landholder and its lack of hundred headings, reflects some ordering into hundreds.[92]

Because lists with both hundredal and tenurial data were in existence already, tenurial material could receive aural verification by shire and hundred without necessarily rewriting the data for every occasion. The creator of the Canterbury text, the *Domesday Monachorum* of Christ Church, evidently used a fiscal list on which to base its order, whereas the creator of the Canterbury fief in Domesday itself drew on another list, with more recent hidage figures and a different order of 'lathes' (the Kentish grouping of hundreds), on which to model the Domesday information.[93] From such lists, more comprehensive sets of data could be produced for a particular purpose—either for shire or hundredal verification or for landholder usage—with labour and expertise, but without excessive difficulty. The Inquest of the County of Cambridge, the *ICC*, offers an example (of a copy) of a detailed Domesday survey, with demesne livestock, arranged by hundreds; moreover, it survives in the same manuscript alongside one of three copies of the landholder-arranged Inquest of Ely, the *IE*.[94] In the *ICC* the royal lands are absent, entirely explicable if utilizing a shire taxation list.

With tax lists as guides, information could be arranged and reviewed in a manner both speedy and flexible. In William's reign, as earlier, the relevant shire or hundred expected written orders to be sent both to landholder and shire, and such gatherings expected to monitor the taxes due from the landholder. Skeletal documents indicating the responsibility of both landholder and hundred were necessary throughout, and the evidence of earlier lists of liability peep through the Domesday data in, for instance, the arrangement of the fief of the bishopric of East Anglia. In 1047, Bishop Æthelmaer had succeeded his brother Stigand to the bishopric of Elmham, and, like Archbishop Stigand, was deposed in 1070. But, although sixteen years had elapsed since Æthelmaer's deposition, the bishopric in Domesday retains a strong semblance of the layout of the estate created during his tenure of the see. The first section is headed 'Land of the Bishop of Thetford belonging to the bishopric in the time of King Eadward'.[95] Next, is a heading 'Land of his (the bishop's) fief', containing Æthelmaer's family lands and his personal acquisitions.[96] A third section, called 'Of the Encroachments of the same Fief', consists of lands once belonging to men commended to Æthelmaer, a number of which, but by no means all, no longer form part of the bishop's lands.[97] It is hard to see how this last could have been constructed *de novo* in 1086, as the current holders of these lands

---

[91] Clarke, 'The Domesday satellites', 63–5, 70; partially translated in *DB Gloucestershire*, Appendix EvK.

[92] Finn, *LExon*, 37–8; but Finn also contrasts *Exon* with the vill structure of *ICC*, 74.

[93] *DMon*, 80–1, cf. 81–98; Harvey 1971, 755–60.

[94] All are late twelfth-century copies, R. W. Finn, *The Eastern Counties* (London, 1967), 81–95; Roffe, *Inquest*, 100–1; Galbraith, 123–45.

[95] LDB:191a (NFK:10,1–19).   [96] LDB:193b (NFK:10,20–47).

[97] LDB:197b–201b (NFK:10,48–93).

are multitudinous. The order of the hundreds in all three sections reflects that characteristic of Norfolk, apart from one deviation in the lands of the bishopric and which is repeated in the 'Encroachments'. Rather, the 'Encroachments' seem to reflect a culling from pre-1070 lists, arranged both by tenure and by hundred, those lands needing to be queried in the presence of the Domesday commissioners.[98] Without such older lists, the Domesday Survey could not have been conducted so speedily or so thoroughly.

Bishops in the shire court

Routinely, the bishops too presided in the shire court—'Christ's sheriffs', Archbishop Wulfstan of York called them earlier in the century.[99] Episcopal authority came ultimately from Christ through apostolic succession and commanded the highest respect. In a high-profile shire meeting from Cnut's reign, a Herefordshire court heard and determined a land-plea in the presence of the bishop, the earl, the local nobility, the sheriff, and 'all the thegns of Herefordshire', the president was clearly the bishop, and the court's judgement was recorded in a Gospel book.[100] Archbishop Lanfranc presided with the earl of Kent, Odo, at a judicial session in Kent held 'before the king's barons' to consider customary dues.[101] Leading bishops might adjudicate as well as preside: Lanfranc appeared as a judge in the shire court that met at Bury St Edmunds in the late 1070s, to deal with a prolonged dispute between the abbey and the bishop of Thetford.[102] Whereas spiritual cases were taken out of the shire into separate ecclesiastical courts in 1070, there is no indication that bishops or their representatives ceased to officiate in the shire.[103]

The wide range of demands made upon episcopal energies, by Church, State, and diocese, created logistical difficulties, especially so in England, where dioceses were larger than in Normandy, and where several bishoprics extended over a range of shires. Nevertheless, it was expected that every shire had its bishop: Giso was known as 'Bishop Giso of Somersetshire'.[104] Some ecclesiastics held their own multiple hundred or borough courts; in 1086 the bishop of Winchester's pleas were held routinely three times a year at the borough of Taunton.[105] Yet with bishops in demand in the king's council, in the English Church synod, in continental Church councils, and for administrative and spiritual duties in their own dioceses, their absence from the shire court was as likely to be felt as their presence. In practice, their place was not uncommonly taken by a representative. The diocese of Lincoln,

---

[98] See also B. Dodwell, 'The making of the Domesday Survey in Norfolk: the hundred and a half of Clacklose', *EHR*, 84 (1969), 79–84,

[99] *Die Institutes of Polity, Civil and Ecclesiastical, ein Werk Erbischof Wulfstans von York*, ed. K. Jost (Bern, 1959), 144–5.

[100] Charters, no. 78.   [101] GDB:2a (KEN:C8).

[102] D. Bates, 'The origins of the justiciarship', *ANS*, 4 (1981), 6.

[103] But there is a reduction in the appearance of bishops in the address clause of writs, Bates, *Acta*, 107.

[104] *Writs*, no. 72.   [105] GDB:87c (SOM:2,2).

which covered nine counties from Lincolnshire to Oxfordshire, more than five days' ride across, soon acquired seven archdeacons.[106] If Herbert *Grammaticus*, archdeacon of Shropshire, acting within the diocese of Chester was indeed, as suggested, one of the 'three wise clerks' of Earl Roger of Montgomery in Shropshire, he was, serviceably, both an official of Earl Roger and the representative of the bishop in that borderland county.[107]

Bishops not only presided in the shire courts but also provided a secretariat and a place of safe-keeping for documents of judgement and record. It was a traditional charge: the later Carolingians had expected certain bishops and counts to take note of their capitularies, and had expected bishops and abbots to produce further copies within regional writing offices under their auspices.[108] The commissioner, Remigius of Lincoln, was accompanied on his Domesday mission into Worcestershire by his clerk Nigel, a priest, and two monks, the priest and one monk being English.[109] Christopher Cheney concluded that twelfth-century bishops' secretariats made no distinction between business belonging to the bishop himself and that of the chapter, and members of the cathedral chapter would copy documents for what was often purely bishop's business. It was standard practice for the bishops' clerks to make use of cathedral buildings for the preservation of muniments; at Chichester, there was one muniment room only—the cathedral treasury—for all.[110] At least three pre-Conquest documents attest the bishop's role as guardian of agreements of land disputes. An agreement between Bury St Edmunds and Wulfgeat (1043–47) was recorded in 'three documents: Wulfgeat himself has one; the second is at Bury St Edmunds; Bishop Stigand [then of Elmham] has the third'.[111] After the resolution of a dispute between the bishop of Hereford and two laymen, a triple record was kept—by St Mary's, Worcester; by the Church of Hereford; and by the possessor of the estate.[112]

Others of the shire

Leading abbots, members of the king's council particularly in the Anglo-Saxon period, normally attended the shire court. Monks from their institutions often accompanied them—many being accustomed to administrative duties. In Kent, in one pre-Conquest case, the monastic community of Christ Church, amongst others, witnessed with the men of East Kent and West Kent; in another, the monastic community of St Augustine's witnessed together with the citizens of Canterbury and the community of Christ Church and others.[113] Domesday notes the presence of

---

[106] Barlow, *Anglo-Norman Church*, 49; HH, 590–1.
[107] Mason, 'Officers and clerks', 253.
[108] R. McKitterick, *The Carolingians and the Written Word* (Cambridge, 1989), 32.
[109] Hemming, 75–6, *DB: Worcestershire*, App. V, Worcester H, no. 5.
[110] C. R. Cheney, *English Bishops' Chanceries 1100–1250* (Manchester, 1950), 139–40.
[111] Charters, no. 100; S.1470.   [112] Charters, no. 83; S.1460; also Charters, no. 98; S.1391.
[113] Charters, nos 41, 69; S.1458, 1456.

monks from Abingdon and Chertsey at relevant hearings; and, on the question of the tenure of Badlesmere, monks of St Augustine were again publicly supportive of their abbot and the men of the hundred.[114] Monks as well as knights of the monastic cathedral at Worcester assembled for Worcestershire pleas.[115]

Integral to the shire court were the leading men of the shire—in Anglo-Saxon terms 'the leading thegns', in Norman terms *barones* or *fideles*, who were still sometimes referred to in William's writs as 'his thegns'. Those who attended went by many titles: 'proven knights, French and English', *optimates*, the 'best' or 'richest men' (a term much used in Italy for the higher echelons who elected city councils), and 'officials and faithful men'.[116] The shire court routinely met twice a year, but writs of William I show that shire meetings were frequently ordered to consider specific problems of tenure, and convened for the purpose. Shire courts were respected; whilst they could on occasion be directed by the powerful, they could also challenge them. Domesday records that the sheriff and great landholder, Edward of Salisbury, holds the farm of Gloucestershire 'wrongfully'.[117] After Domesday, it was still the shire courts that, in the twelfth century, decided most disputes between different lordships about land.

In the 1086 Inquiry, the occasion and the personnel of the shire meetings seem distinct from those of the county town and the major boroughs.[118] This, despite some early eleventh-century land transactions which involved a range of witnesses: as one prestigious Canterbury transaction put it, 'many men, both ecclesiastics and laymen, from within the city and without'.[119] In the great thirteenth-century inquests, borough and county sometimes met as one, and sometimes not.[120] Although in Domesday there are numerous instances of burgesses giving witness, none occurs outside the borough description; nor, vice-versa, does the shire give witness on any borough matter: although information on the county farm is sometimes added to the borough account.[121] There is only one instance of a joint Domesday meeting: it concerned one of the Kentish lathes—administrative units—when the burgesses of Dover, the hundred, the men of Eastry Lathe, and the men of the abbot of St Augustine's, all gave witness on disputed land at Atterton, just outside Dover.[122] Otherwise, the Domesday evidence suggests that the sheriffs' assemblies for borough and for shire were distinct occasions.

The new rulers had reason to avoid a borough or great church venue for a general shire meeting with its drastic implications for the tenure of land. The king's peace traditionally obtained in churches, and on main roads,[123] yet under the Normans, towns had the reputation of being awkward centres of resistance and rebellion:

---

[114] GDB:10b (KEN:5,149); also 59b (BRK:7,38).
[115] *Acta*, no. 349.   [116] *Acta*, nos 118, 88, 331–3, *ministris et fidelibus*.
[117] GDB:164b (GLS:1,63).   [118] Contrast, Fleming, *Law*, 13.
[119] Charters, 101; S.1471; R. Fleming, 'Rural elites and urban communities in late-Saxon England', *P&P*, 141 (1993), 22–3.
[120] 1274–5 differed from 1279, Raban, 48–9, 69–70.
[121] GDB:280b (DBY:B15).   [122] GDB:13a (KEN:9,9).
[123] I Cnut, 3,2; Leis Willelmi, 26.

York rebelled on several occasions and, shortly after Domesday, even the regime stalwart, Geoffrey of Coutances, defended Bristol against William II. Traditionally, moreover, great gatherings of the shire, or indeed several shires, or perhaps several hundreds, often convened at advantageously placed sites—conjunctions of Roman roads or great earth-works.[124] The two hundreds of Ely met at Witchford in 1086.[125] They were perhaps still a safer option than towns or castle baileys for all concerned under the new, still-vulnerable regime. Kentford, selected for one of the Ely land pleas, was located on the boundary of the two relevant counties, on a major east–west route and adjacent to north–south routes. In 1086, open sites offered an opportunity to publicize the new order as widely as possible and gain oaths to acknowledge it: a later tenth-century record of a land grant made in the presence of men of East and West Kent had asserted that a 'good thousand men gave the oath', and that further shires took cognisance of the decision—although the numbers themselves should not be taken too literally.[126] Yet such assemblies offered a security challenge as well as a logistical one; the more so, as groups of seven shires, like that at the Four-Shire Stone on a Roman road at the confluence of Warwickshire, Worcestershire, Gloucestershire, and Oxfordshire, might amount to a great muster.[127] The Abingdon portrayal of the adjudication over a water-sluice shows the royal clerk, Peter, attending to the judicial defence of royal rights accompanied by the probably indispensable band of well-armed mounted men.[128] Moreover, the *murdrum* fine expressly protected 'all the men' whom William had brought with him or who had come afterwards.[129]

The hundred, the wapentake, and the Domesday jurors

The *IE* terms of reference specify the *prepositus*, the usual Latin term for reeve, as one of those required at the Domesday Inquiry. Since the early tenth century, royal reeves had been particularly responsible for regular meetings associated with peacekeeping, and those who managed royal estates were at the hub of a primary unit of royal rule and administration.[130] How much reliance was still, by the eleventh century, concentrated on what had been the royal manor, or to what extent the meetings of hundreds had achieved roles and momentum of their own, is uncertain.[131] Domesday indicates that the reeve of the hundred held land from and

[124] A. Pantos, 'On the edge of things: the boundary location of Anglo-Saxon assembly sites', *Anglo-Saxon Studies in Archaeology and History*, 12 (2003), 38–49.

[125] *IE*, 100.   [126] Charters, no. 41; S.1458; *LE*, II, *cap.* 25.

[127] GDB: 238c (WAR:3,4); Acta, no. 135.

[128] *HistAbbend 1*, 372–5, quoted in this volume on p. 279.

[129] *Willelmi Articuli Retractati*, c.1110–35; Liebermann, 486–8; *Laws*, 238–43, *cap.* 3, 4, 6.

[130] e.g. H. M. Cam, 'Manerium cum hundredo', *EHR*, 47 (1932), 353–76; P. Sawyer, 'The Royal Tun in pre-Conquest England', in P. Wormald, D. A. Bullough, and R. Collins (eds), *Ideal and Reality in Frankish and Anglo-Saxon Society: Studies presented to J. M. Wallace-Hadrill* (Oxford, 1983), 273–99.

[131] e.g. Pantos, 'Anglo-Saxon assembly sites', 38–49; investigated in A. Reynolds, *Late Anglo-Saxon England, Life and Landscape* (Stroud, 1999). The topic is currently being tackled by a multi-discipline research project.

worked to the king's sheriffs.[132] In all probability the collection of customary dues fell to such officials and they presided over local courts and the imposition of works of service. The office of reeve might be onerous, and lucrative: some who held office before 1066 were king's thegns and of high status, such as those who held the royal manors of Chedworth and Arlington: Arlington by Cynewig Chelle, who was certainly a king's thegn, and Chedworth by Wulfweard, who was of similar status if he is identified as Wulfweard White.[133] They seem to have held these manors as royal officers paying, as Domesday notes, 'what they wished' in 1066. However, in 1086 reeves were often nameless, even when French and even when in charge of considerable assets—one had charge of Dartford, a royal manor worth near-ly £100.[134] But some reeves of all gradations were evidently native. The *Laws of Henry I* mention various local officials who attended the shire court, from men in charge of the hundred down to village reeves, some of whose titles were perhaps synonyms: *centenarii, aldermanni, prefecti, prepositi, vavassores, tungrevi.*[135] The reeve of the vill might, or might not, be the same as the reeve of the hundred and the same man might, or might not, be the deputy of the sheriff himself; however, he bore the same title. It is context alone that betrays the role and status of such officials—as with 'secretary' in modern usage.

The functions of local assemblies and the penalties they might exact continued to be defined and refined in written edicts, particularly during Edgar's reign. One such held that each large borough and shire was to have thirty-six chosen witnesses and each small borough and hundred twelve witnesses, who were to swear the truth of what they saw and heard.[136] From 997 the wapentakes (the Danelaw equivalent of the hundreds) also presented and indicted criminals: a jury of twelve leading men from the locality was required to swear, together with the reeve, that they would accuse no innocent man nor conceal any guilty man.[137] By 1066, the tasks of the hundred, including manpower for defence, were established and wide-ranging. A particular concern of Edgar's reign was straying and stolen cattle. The danger of theft obliged men of the hundred to witness the buying, selling, and keeping of cattle, and a body of standing witnesses were appointed; it meant that villagers, reeves, and landholders knew not only the numbers of their own cattle, but also the numbers involved in transactions made by their neighbours; herdsmen were required to monitor any strange animals.[138] This traditional concern helps to explain why the most regular item of all in Domesday, one never in dispute, is the number of ox-teams on the manorial demesne and the number belonging to the peasantry. Cattle were a main avenue to any increase of assets and returns for small

---

[132] 60 acres were given to the reeve of the hundred, LDB:120a (NFK:1,75).

[133] GDB:164a (GLS:1,57–8); A. Williams, introduction in *The Gloucestershire Domesday*, Alecto 1989, 6.

[134] GDB:2c (KEN:1,1).

[135] *LegesHP*, 98. Reeves are discussed in P. D. A. Harvey, 'The manorial reeve in twelfth-century England', in R. Evans, ed., *Lordship and Learning: Studies in Memory of Trevor Aston* (Woodbridge, 2004), 125–38; and in Campbell, 'Some agents and agencies of the Anglo-Saxon state', in Holt, *Studies*, 201–18, at 205–8, 215–16.

[136] IV Edgar, 4–5.   [137] III Ethelred, 3.1.   [138] I Edgar, 4; IV Edgar, 8–11.

and large landholders alike, particularly for the former. They were more mobile than grain and it is no accident that a contemporary Latin word for 'livestock' was *pecunia,* whose other meaning was 'money'.

Men of the locality also needed to know who was responsible for local contributions to national imposts. This tax was not solely the money payments due from an estate, but involved the triple duties of maintaining bridges and roads, manning borough walls, and contributing men to the army in time of need. Since it was the duty of the hundred to raise taxation and men for this *trimoda necessitas,* men of the shire and hundred knew who held the land and the level of their responsibilities in hides or carucates—the Danelaw equivalent of a hide—again a regular feature of Domesday data. A landholder had material reason for being recognized by the hundred and shire as fulfilling his responsibilities. A law of Cnut stated: 'He who, with the cognisance of the shire, performed the duties demanded of a landowner . . . shall hold his land unmolested by litigation during his life and after his death shall have the right of disposing of it.'[139] Evasion of these burdens was not a wise tactic: if a tax or fine went unpaid, forfeiture of the land might well follow.[140] The men of the hundred and shire thereby became in effect the witnesses to the validity of tenure. Tenure and public responsibilities linked landholder to hundred and shire—links that created the complex construction that is the Domesday Survey.

The Domesday jurors

Whether the jury of the locality functioning as a fact-finding or verifying body—a jury of recognition as the lawyers term it—owes its origins to Norman or to an Anglo-Saxon practice has aroused much debate. The strands are difficult to separate. England was governed by Norman rulers during the later eleventh and earlier twelfth centuries, just when rulers in western Europe generally were making strides in their regular exercise of authority; and both England and Normandy were ruled by a common Angevin house in the later twelfth century, when that authority was being worked out in detail, with England in the van of such developments. Yet even Edward the Confessor's reign, particularly before 1051, was in some ways that of the first Norman ruler, since he ruled with the help of Normans and Lorrainers— contacts from his days in exile. Employment of a jury from the hundred in judicial and fiscal inquisitions dated back to Carolingian times, however, the Viking invaders had caused considerable social and governmental disruption in Normandy. When, in the twelfth century, the jury was drawn upon as freely in Normandy as in England, it was fully fledged in both by that time.

Despite the time-gap, some historians understand that 'as an administrative tool the Carolingian inquest survived without too many difficulties, especially in Normandy',[141] and indeed the Fontenay pancarte, dated 1070 × 1079, describes

---

[139] II Cnut, 79.   [140] LDB:98a (ESS:83,2); see Ch. 8 in this volume.
[141] E. van Houts, 'Gender and authority of oral witnesses', *TRHS*, 6th ser., 9 (1999), 207.

William as duke of Normandy launching a settlement of disputed land in a way that offers precedents for the role the Domesday jurors were called to perform. As the abbey of Fontenay's honorial tenants had begun to repossess the lands donated to the abbey by their fathers, Duke William ordered the *vicomte* of Avranches to summon the barons of the honour 'to record accurately on oath' what had been given to the abbey. Once assembled at Caen, four lawful men, *legitimi viri*, one being the reeve, *prepositus*, were named in the document; they were to swear upon the Holy Gospel that it was truthfully recorded. The other three jurors were nominated at the assembly. The inquiry prefigured the Domesday procedure in several ways: it was summoned by the *vicomte*; the lands and payments under discussion were identified by their previous holders or tenants; and the outcome of the assembly was widely known, since William and Matilda, William's two half-brothers, Roger of Montgomery, Roger de Beaumont, and the *vicomte* were among the many signatories.[142]

Nonetheless, the employment of the sworn oath on matters of tenure is documented earlier in England; similar to the Domesday juries' role in the matter of landholding rights was the jury summoned in the litigation between Ramsey Abbey and Thorney Abbey, *c.*1054, on the extent and boundaries of their fen pastures. Four abbots were present, accompanied by their named monks and retainers. It was, however, agreed that 'old men' of the neighbourhood known to both parties should give the verdict.[143] Each side included a fisherman, undoubtedly expert on the extent of fen, in their list of names. Thus the use of a jury to provide decisive evidence in a case of land tenure is documented in the England of Edward the Confessor before its increased appearance in the reign of the Conqueror. But contacts between Lotharingia, England, and Normandy were frequent; the importance for Domesday is that men on both sides of the Channel were not unfamiliar with the process.

Function in the Inquiry

The men of the hundreds and vills, the so-called 'juries', were long understood to be the first and main source of information; but V. H. Galbraith's emphasis on landholders' returns as the primary source of data has placed the landholders to the fore in many historians' thinking.[144] The jurors' role had been inferred from the surviving Domesday text, *ICC*, which preserves not only the names of some Cambridgeshire jurors, but the livestock details; there the cows, sheep, and pigs, omitted from Great Domesday, point to an earlier origin for this Cambridgeshire text. In Domesday however, traces of the jurors' contributions are uneven and the

---

[142] *Acta*, no. 149.
[143] Discussed, *Writs*, 252–6; Van Caenegem, *Writs*, 69–72: 'Their sworn verdict was at once a fact and an adjudication', 71.
[144] Galbraith, 166–7.

precise weight of their contribution to the furnishing of information remains a source of debate.[145]

Domesday notes evidence from the men of the hundred or wapentake most often on the issue of land tenure, particularly, of course, that before the Conquest—a vast field to review and of the essence of Domesday, and such witnesses occasionally provide vivid details on the fate of earlier holders.[146] Few secular lands—at least at the higher echelons that Domesday records—remained in the same hands after the processes of death, conquest, and rebellion that followed William's victory at Hastings, and the terms of reference of the Inquiry assume that a change has been made. Although William, as Conqueror, sooner or later had the disposal of most estates in England, the question of the extent of displacement is a vexed one, hampered by the lack of detail in Great Domesday; a few Anglo-Danes, for example, survived in Yorkshire and Lincolnshire and were recognized as landholders.[147] Yet since the preservation of some agricultural continuity was essential to ensure the Conquest's economic profitability, it seems likely that the sons and brothers of those who had died in the battles of 1066 and afterwards were permitted to continue their agrarian routine—as rent-payers.

The Domesday jurors, in particular, were asked to affirm who had held the land in King Edward's day and, evidently, if a dispute arose about the present-day holder, whether they had seen any writ, or messengers, authorizing that holder. Men of the hundred—in over three-quarter of cases—or of the shire testified as to whether the present holder was indeed the person named by the writ or royal messenger.[148] Mention of the witness of the hundred survives in over half the counties Domesday covered, featuring most frequently in the eastern half of England. Sussex, Middlesex, Buckinghamshire, Cambridgeshire, Norfolk, and Suffolk all feature witness of the hundred, but not witness of the shire; however, evidence given by the shire occurs in Essex, but not as often as that by the hundred.[149] In all, in Great Domesday, the hundred's testimony is recorded three times more often than the shire's; even individuals give testimony twice as often as does the shire. (Only on geld liability does the verdict of the shire appear more frequently than that of the hundred.) Testimony from the hundred certainly predominates in matters of the Anglo-Saxon *antecessor* and their outlawing or fleeing, in remembering writs or messengers, in the mortgaging of land, and in knowledge of woods and pastures.[150] When the men of the hundred cannot validate the transfer of land, action is occasionally immediate and the land taken into the king's hand, indicating that a shire or hundredal reeve was present and active;[151] but this is usually the case for small acreages only. Influential landholders

---

[145] Discussed, Roffe, *Inquest*, esp. 118–22.   [146] e.g. GDB:377cd (LIN:CK3–17).

[147] H. M. Thomas, 'A Yorkshire thegn and his descendants after the conquest', *Medieval Prosopography*, 8 (1987), 1–22; D. Roffe, 'Hidden lives: English lords in post-Conquest Lincolnshire and beyond', in D. Roffe (ed.), *The English and their Legacy, 900–1200: Essays in Honour of Ann Williams* (Woodbridge, 2012) 205–28.

[148] Fleming, *Law*, 40–6.   [149] Galbraith, 71.

[150] Frequency charts in Fleming, *Law*, 41–3.   [151] LDB:25b (ESS:18,44); 54b (ESS: 27,17).

often held onto the lands they had acquired, at least in the short term. It remains, however, important for the interpretation of the Domesday enterprise that the opinions of the hundred are sought and recorded, even when they state that they have *not* seen a writ or messenger from the king; and even when nothing appears to come of this information.

Yet those occasions when the hundred say that they do not know or have not seen a writ or messenger may have signalled how hazardous it was to be put into the position of being asked to verify one claim or another: when 'caught between a rock and a hard place, struggling to navigate their way between two enormously powerful Normans', as Alan Cooper put it.[152] The Domesday scribe, a master of concision, successfully confronted a similar problem when relaying what sounded like mere assertion by an interested party: he deftly managed to put the evidence into question simply by adding 'so he says' after an item.[153]

It is surprising how much reliance had been placed on the co-operation of the hundreds even before Domesday, as in the case of various miscellaneous landed claims that Lanfranc asserted against Odo, as earl of Kent, and Hugh de Montfort. After debating the tenurial history of entire manors, reference is made to other claims—perhaps to smaller lands and pastures, which not infrequently appear in contention in Domesday also—which should be 'determined (*difiniri*) in the hundreds'.[154] Their decision would be a *veredictum*, that is 'a verdict not a judgement'.[155]

Pressures on the men of the shire, hundred, and vill

Not that, for men of shire or hundred, it was simply a matter of volunteering comment: attendance at both shire and hundred courts was a duty concomitant with landholding. Domesday records that before 1066, in the land between the Ribble and Mersey, an area of low returns in Domesday, anyone who stayed away from the shire moot without reasonable excuse was fined 10s—the annual revenue from 120 acres (49 hectares) of land thereabouts. If he stayed away from the hundred, or did not go to the hearing of pleas when the reeve ordered, he was fined 5s.[156] And once in attendance, testimony was on oath and the penalties associated with false witness or perjury were harsh.

---

[152] A. Cooper, 'Protestations of ignorance in Domesday Book' in R. F. Berkhofer, A. Cooper, and A. J. Kosto (eds) *The Experience of Power in Medieval Europe, 950–1350* (Aldershot, 2005), 169–81, at 179.

[153] e.g. GDB:246a (STS:B12).

[154] Printed in D. C. Douglas, 'Odo, Lanfranc, and the Domesday Survey' in J. G. Edwards, V. H. Galbraith, and E. F. Jacob (eds), *Historical Essays in honour of James Tait* (Manchester, 1933), 51–2, there dated to *c.*1078 or 1079 as also F. R. H. Du Boulay, *The Lordship of Canterbury* (London, 1966), 38–9. An 'original' printed by C. Flight, *The Survey of Kent*, BAR, British Series, 506 (Oxford, 2010), 214–16, dated to 'soon after 1070'.

[155] F. Pollock and F. W. Maitland, *The History of English Law*, vol. 1, 2nd edn (Cambridge, 1968), 143–4.

[156] GDB:269d (CHS:R1,40d).

There was of course the perennial influence of great men in court, to which the conquerors added the pressures of the ordeal to ascertain whether witness was partial or not. Sometime, probably between 1077 and 1080, in a plea between the bishop of Rochester and the Cambridgeshire sheriff, Picot, representing the king, the court of the men of the shire found for Picot, but the Rochester source reports that that was only 'through fear of the sheriff'. Odo of Bayeux, interested because the diocese of Rochester lay within his earldom, was subsequently informed by a reliable source that the jurors were perjured. At a second hearing in London called by Odo and held before the leading barons, the representatives of the county— probably from the hundred concerned since five of the named jurors were—were found guilty of perjury, as were the second jury empanelled who failed to convince the court of their integrity. Threats of the ordeal were raised, and the unfortunate jurors, and their county, then received the swingeing fine of £300 pounds; the original decision was reversed and Rochester given the case.[157] The size of fine alone suggests the stature of some of these men: perhaps, it was intended simply to enforce the loss of their land, but one Ordmær of Badlingham survived the process to feature as a juror in the Domesday Inquiry itself.[158] The case illustrates just how constrained were the jurors by the powerful men present during court proceedings. Yet outside times of crisis, invasion, or huge imposts, meetings of the hundred and groups of hundreds quite probably offered a welcome break from routine, and allowed opportunities for buying and selling—with the appropriate reeves and witnesses ready to hand—as well as for games and horse-racing.[159]

A later graphic description of court proceedings between St Augustine's and Christ Church, Canterbury, over the dues of the port of Sandwich supports the evidence from the Rochester case of the jurors being selected from the people assembled, after the issue was stated, and with that in mind. In the less contentious tenurial context of Henry I's reign, the truth on the ownership of the tolls was sought from twelve lawful men of Dover and twelve lawful men of the neighbour-hood of Sandwich 'who are neither the men of the archbishop nor the men of the abbot'; they were elected 'from among the men of the king and the barons, twenty-four wise old men, full of years and having good testimony'. The twenty-four then gave their testimony and 'the great multitude agreed'. Each juror swore individually on the Holy Gospels. Many magnates, including the contesting parties, were present; plus 'very many others, both clerk and lay, of whom the multitude cannot be numbered'.[160] Important for any decision was to gain general acceptance,

---

[157] *Acta*, no. 225; Fleming, *Law*, 18–20. One jury was threatened with the ordeal; it seems uncertain as to whether it was carried out.

[158] *ICC*, 1.

[159] A. Pantos, 'The location and form of Anglo-Saxon assembly-places: some "moot points"', in A. Pantos and S. Semple (eds), *Assembly-Places and Practices in Medieval Europe* (Dublin, 2004), 166; R. H. Britnell, 'English markets and royal administration before 1200', *ECHR*, 2nd ser., 31 (1978), 183–96.

[160] Text in D. M. Stenton, *English Justice between the Norman Conquest and the Great Charter, 1066–1215* (London, 1963), 116–23.

even approval. In 1086, the Conqueror's concern was to gain passive acknowledge-ment for the tenurial changes by as many inhabitants as possible. The *IE* and the *ICC* both affirm, after naming the jurors, that 'all the other Frenchmen and Englishmen swore'.[161] Vill, hundred, and shire often functioned alongside each other, although the selection of jurors in a crowded court would doubtless have favoured the more well-connected of those assembled.

The names of the Domesday jurors for the fifteen hundreds of Cambridgeshire and for three Hertfordshire hundreds fortunately survive in the *IE* and the *ICC*. Each hundred jury was composed half of English and half of newcomers. The names represent 158 individuals—eighty Englishmen and seventy-eight foreigners (two foreigners serving twice). At first glance, this balance seems surprisingly even-handed, yet—given the much smaller number of French inhabitants—the deal was skewed. Even so, it seems clear that the new regime intended that Englishmen should participate in established practices alongside the newcomers; and that natives as well as incomers should explicitly acknowledge and sanction the whole-sale predation of land.

Robin Fleming's analysis of the tenancies of these jurors makes it less surprising that they proved co-operative. Landholders who held an entire hundred inevitably had their own tenants as jurors: all the jurors in the two hundreds of Ely lived on abbey land. In contrast, the known jurors of three Hertfordshire hundreds held land from between five and eight different lords. In Cambridgeshire eighty per cent of the jurors held tenancies from the top seven barons, and their provenance is telling: the lands of the abbey of Ely provided 20 jurors; those of Picot, sheriff of Cambridgeshire, 8; those of Earl Alan of Richmond, 12; and those of Geoffrey de Mandeville, sometime sheriff of London, Essex, and Hertfordshire, 4. It is unsurprising that Sheriff Picot's notorious land-grabbing propensities attracted no recorded complaint in Domesday in the four hundreds that met in his presence.[162]

Whilst the majority of these jurors are untraceable in Domesday—almost certainly because their holdings were not of sufficient substance—Christopher Lewis has identified 35 out of 78 alien jurors and 11 out of 80 English jurors. These were all of some economic standing, including Englishmen who are 'known survivors' from amongst the thegns and greater freemen of pre-Conquest Cam-bridgeshire and Hertfordshire. On average, alien jurors held just over 5½ hides, the English held just over 4 hides; the aliens had 20 demesne plough-oxen (say 2½ teams), the English 15 plough-oxen (almost 2 teams). The aliens' lands were worth on average about 130 shillings a year, the Englishmen's about 90 shillings. Yet the identified jurors spread over a wide economic spectrum: ranging from Humphrey d'Anneville, with over 25 hides worth more than £40 a year, to Lovet, a man with only ¾ hide worth 8s 8d; typical of the more substantial men were those with about 10 hides worth £10–£15. The men with more land were evidently well connected: Humphrey d'Anneville was a tenant of two great lords and Sigar was the English

---

[161] *ICC*, 1; *IE*, 97.   [162] Fleming, *Law*, 27.

steward of Geoffrey de Mandeville, a man powerful in the new establishment. Not a few jurors also held land outside the hundred for which they swore, almost half of these in an adjacent county.[163]

Yet, the tenurial identity of the majority of known jurors is missing from Domesday and remains an enigma. The higher proportion of traced aliens to traced English is in itself revealing of the loss of English lands. It should be remembered that it was the smaller landholders, susceptible to pressure from their lords, who were included in the juries, not the magnates whose cause they upheld, who had to bear the physical ordeal and the ensuing fines if their decision or witness were called into question.[164]

Women were not jurors, although they occasionally gave evidence on their former tenures.[165] In the desperate attempt to hold onto land after the Conquest, perhaps as tenant, the ordeal became a vital resort in maintaining a case, even over small parcels of land. One woman was prepared to undergo the ordeal in support of her claim that eight acres (three hectares), mostly woodland, that she had held TRE, were free of a gage (a vif-gage, mort-gage, or debt).[166] Men with English names, followers of Guy de Craon and Count Alan of Brittany respectively, each pledged to uphold their own lord's claim to fourteen bovates of land by ordeal or by combat.[167] To uphold the freehold of just one carucate of land, one man of Hermer de Ferrers was prepared to go to combat or to the judicial ordeal, whereas another was prepared to defend 'in the same way' that the land belonged to the abbey of Ely.[168] Trial by battle for land pleas was, in fact, a Norman innovation and was supposed to be accessible only to disputes over lands worth more than 10s (according to *The Laws of Henry I*, an amalgam of eleventh- and early twelfth-century legal practices).[169] The loser faced a substantial fine at least and was, either way, physically at hazard. The signs are that, at the time of Domesday, the pressure of a potential ordeal was general.[170]

The temptation for those present to succumb to worldly pressure and take the line of least resistance was counterbalanced by the presence of the priest, as stipulated in the Ely terms of reference. An ecclesiastical presence was essential for the administration of oaths, and 'oath-helpers' might be called upon to conclude a case.[171] General fear of the penalties attached to perjury put oath-helping, witnessing, and the inquest all into the same spectrum.[172] Before 1066, perjury carried severe penalties whereby lands and livelihoods were clearly at stake.[173] If a man swore a false oath on the relics (*on haligdome swerie*) and was convicted, he might forfeit a hand or half his wergeld or be exiled.[174] The priest was essential in

---

[163] C. P. Lewis, 'The Domesday jurors', *Haskins Society Journal*, 5 (1993), 17–44.
[164] II Cnut, 37; Fleming, *Law*, 16–20.   [165] GDB:173d (WOR:2.67).
[166] LDB:137a (NFK:1,213).   [167] GDB:377d (LIN:CK66).
[168] LDB:213a (NFK:15,2); other examples in Ch. 10 of this volume.
[169] *LegesHP*, 187–8.   [170] See Ch. 10 of this volume, pp. 280–6.
[171] P. Wormald, 'Charters, law and the settlement of disputes in Anglo-Saxon England', *Dispute Settlement*, 160.
[172] 'Conclusion', *Dispute Settlement*, 221.
[173] VI Æthelred, 7, 36; VIII Æthelred, 27; II Cnut, 6, 36.
[174] II Cnut, 36.

the conduct of ordeals: he exorcized and blessed the instruments of ordeal with elaborate ritual, and with many prayers that the righteousness of justice should prevail.[175] Perhaps in the courts of the Domesday Inquiry, if it came to the ordeal, the priest's discretion would have weighed in favour of the Church's claim, if that were an option—particularly if there were a presiding ecclesiastic—as finally proved the case for Rochester.

HUNDRED VERSUS LANDHOLDER AS SUPPLIERS OF INFORMATION

On who furnished the manorial details, historians' opinions are divided. Plough-teams apart, it was the demesne livestock that was recorded in Exon and Little Domesday, so these data were presumably supplied by landholders or their agents—stewards, reeves, and the like. As far as agricultural assets went, the function of the men of the locality seems primarily to have been to listen to the details and to agree them—apart from a few brave challenges on points of tenurial history and the level of payments demanded.

There are signs, however, that input from men of the hundred was more positive than mere commentary. Woodland in Domesday Shropshire, for instance, is measured in two different ways varying according to hundred, suggesting that the source was the men of the hundred: in four hundreds the data are given in linear measurements, whereas in nine other hundreds Domesday gives the number of swine the woodland could support. However, the fact that the demesnes of Earl Roger used the linear measurement throughout indicates that his returns were made separately.[176] Since the small freeholders relied upon the pannage and grazing resources of woodland, their knowledge was sometimes turned to account. The incidence of the parallel terms for smallholder, 'cottar' and 'bordar'—the first of English derivation and the second of Norman—is instructive as to the nice balance between landholder and hundred as Domesday sources. In Surrey, usage varies by hundred: cottars in Emleybridge in the west, Wallington in the east, and Godalming in the south. But the separate submissions of large landholders also leave their dominant traces: the bishop of Bayeux's large manor of Bramley has cottars, whereas the rest of the hundred has bordars, with the converse the case on the king's estates in Godalming hundred.[177] Thus the men of the hundreds and the scribes of large landholders each made their contribution.

Regional variants in Domesday might well reflect the structure of sources, or real difference in practices or, confusingly, both. The more frequent quotation of the

---

[175] See Ch. 10.   [176] Lewis, introduction in *The Shropshire Domesday*, 10.
[177] F. H. Baring, *Domesday Tables* (London, 1909), 9; other examples, Roffe, *Decoding*, 50–2.

men of hundred and wapentake in the heavily populated eastern counties may well represent a significant difference in social structure (see Figure 2).

In contrast, the counties of the south-western circuit (Wiltshire, Dorset, Somerset, Devon, Cornwall), the west midland circuit (Gloucester, Worcester, Hereford, Shropshire, Cheshire), and the central circuit (Oxford, Northampton, Stafford, Leicester, Warwick), seldom cite the evidence of the hundred.[178] And in Great Domesday for the south-west, there is no labelling of the hundreds by rubrics, as in the rest of the volume. It might well be inferred that in these less populous and hilly western and midland counties the men of the hundreds played a less conspicuous role in the Inquiry than they did in eastern England— where the high density of freer population gave the hundred a stronger presence.[179] But it is arguable that this undoubted regional difference is over-emphasized by our sources: for Great Domesday cites 'reeves' and 'men of the king', when claiming customary dues from the lands of the Count of Mortain in Devon, whereas Exon refers to the same body as 'the hundred and the king's reeve'.[180] Whilst lacking hundred labels, Domesday in the south-west shows traces of a recurring order of hundreds—particularly in the earlier Exon text; and the hundreds are self-evidently important in the Geld Accounts of the south-west.[181]

Did hundreds or groups of hundreds hold initial sessions or was their witness called for in the shire court after backroom sessions? Procedures may well have varied with local custom and the terrain. Regular meetings of local courts had long been recognized as desirable; it was ordained under Edgar that the shire court should meet twice, the borough court thrice, and the hundred court twelve times a year.[182] In the Domesday Inquiry, the employment of all three assemblies seems to have been both frequent and flexible. In the Lincolnshire 'Claims', the testimony of the wapentakes, shire, and riding often recurs randomly: 'the wapentake and the county say', 'the wapentake and the riding say', 'the men of Hoyland say', 'the North Riding and the whole county testify'. Such varying combinations conjure a picture of plenary sessions that included both men of the wapentake and the shire, certainly during the review of tenurial disputes.

One ambiguity has lain over the number of men of the locality required at the hearings.[183] Were 'the men of the vill' included in or additional to the jurors chosen to represent the hundred? The *IE* stipulates six men from each *vill*, plus priest and reeve;

---

[178] However, once in Devon and once in Gloucestershire, the men of the hundred assign a holding to its parent hundred or manor, without being able to furnish other data, GDB:107a (DEV:16,74); 165d (GLS:11,14); Galbraith, 71–3.

[179] Galbraith, 75–6.   [180] GDB:105c (DEV:15,67).

[181] F. R. Thorn, 'Hundreds and Wapentakes', in *The Devonshire Domesday*, Alecto 1991, 26–42 (charting evidence for the complicated evolution of hundreds), at 31–4; also C. Thorn and F. Thorn, *DB Somerset* (Chichester, 1980), and *DB Dorset* (Chichester, 1983), Appendices. Cornwall and Wiltshire are 'probably' in a consistent order; some have undergone arrangement by subtenant, P. H. Sawyer, 'The "original returns" and Domesday Book', *EHR*, 70 (1955), 177–97, esp.181; also Lewis, introduction in *The Shropshire Domesday*, 8–10.

[182] III Edgar, 5; II Cnut, 17, 18, envisage all three might be needed more frequently.

[183] Numbers of representatives discussed by Roffe, *Inquest*, 122–3.

yet the *IE* and the *ICC* list the eight men from each *hundred*, and some commentators have assumed that the references represented one and the same group. It is now evident that they did not.[184] Locals, who are not classified as 'men of the hundred', are quoted in Domesday several times as having a divergent opinion on manorial or hundredal profits,[185] and indeed, in one Suffolk case on the matter of soke, 'the men of the vill' testify against 'the hundred'.[186] In another Domesday dispute, one between two sheriffs, as to whether land was held as a tenancy or not, 'men of the hundred' and 'men of the vill' maintain different opinions on tenure and were on different sides. On the Hampshire sheriff's side, were men of the whole county and of the hundred; whereas the Cambridgeshire sheriff's claim had the support of the men of the vill and the common people (*villani et vili plebe*) and the reeves.[187] Such incidents strengthen the likelihood of two distinct groups of witnesses, the vill and the hundred, at least in the more populous counties. Thus the *IE*'s requirement of 'six villeins from each vill' was not a gloss for the men of the hundred; the presence and assent of both groups at some or all stages was generally required.

The Domesday Inquiry in 1086 certainly established the hundredal jury firmly as an institution on which the new rulers could continue to rely. The Domesday Inquiry could be regarded as a forerunner of the possessory assizes established in Henry II's reign after years of civil war, when juries were used extensively in conditions of conflicting tenures and when, in order to achieve a stable tenurial settlement from which claims could be pursued by legal channels rather than by force, four possessory assizes were set up. For these, juries of twelve free and law-abiding men of the neighbourhood, assembled by the sheriff in the presence of royal justices, were asked questions of recent fact about tenures; but a consideration of best right rather than recent dispossession was separated for later determination in the court of grand assize. Henry II was imaginatively reported to have devised these procedures only with the help of 'many wakeful nights', although three of the four assizes were in some respects successors in function to the hundred juries of the Domesday Inquiry;[188] and indeed actions arguably similar to the twelfth-century *novel disseisin* appear early in William II's reign.[189] In that assize, as in Domesday, ultimate 'right' was often left for later decision in the king's court.

In Domesday, local jurors were asked apparently straightforward questions as to the Edwardian holder, with the immediate purpose it seems, of ascertaining whether the previous holders had had affiliations of any sort which might be profitably converted into paying rent or service, as in Morden where eight sokemen

---

[184] Also, S. Baxter, 'The making of Domesday Book and the languages of lordship', in E. M. Tyler (ed.), *Conceptualizing Multilingualism in England c.800–c.1250* (Turnhout, 2011), 271–308, at 285–8, including table of those recorded as giving evidence.

[185] See Ch. 7 of this volume, esp. pp. 200–2.

[186] LDB:285b (SUF:1,77).   [187] GDB:44d (HAM:23,3).

[188] Stubbs, *Charters*, 165–6, 179–80, 194; Pollock and Maitland, *History of English Law*, vol. 1, 143–9, quotation at 146; Van Caenegem, *Writs*, 51–103.

[189] Van Caenegem, *Writs*, nos 52–5, 62–70; cf. Garnett, 338–52.

of various affiliations appear to have been converted into eight villeins.[190] But the varied types of Anglo-Saxon tenures were in practice disregarded, despite the jurors' efforts to represent them. When land had been 'held' or leased from a church, the church had a claim; but by 1086 the church's lay lessee had often already lost possession as a result of William's arbitrary reallocation. When the Domesday hundreds were asked who had held the land in King Edward's day and whether the current holder was the appropriate successor, the permitted answer was evidently never 'his son'. Rather, recorded replies from men of the hundred largely concerned whether they had, or had not, seen the king's writ, seal, or messenger that 'delivered' the land to its current holder. Before 1085, precedents can be found for turning to local juries to provide evidence in both England and Normandy, but it was the countrywide Domesday Inquiry that entrenched the use of juries; and, in Henry II's reign, juries were to be given a range of functions: in fact-finding surveys, in the Grand Assize, and in criminal cases.

Whatever purpose was uppermost in the Domesday Inquiry, its logic demanded a full record of the Norman land settlement. Only with the allocation of tenure established could assets be attributed and taxation pursued or reassessed. It is unsurprising that the Domesday Inquiry itself failed to resolve every claim and counter-claim; and it is over-punctilious to deny Domesday its status as a 'Register of Title' simply because it records several hundred apparently still-disputed cases.[191] Much there was laid out for easy reference later;[192] furthermore, cases may have been made public, then withdrawn, as compromise or realism set in.[193] After all, something approaching 13,000 Domesday entries, and many smaller holdings, were confirmed by what were in effect possessory assizes; although many might have awaited action in the king's court, disclosure had been effected. The ruler died while the document was being completed and he or his successor took prompt executive action on some claims before then facing rebellion.[194] Given that the Conqueror had established his position by sheer military force, many claims could not be resolved 'rightfully'—whatever procedures were followed through to their propaganda-driven conclusion.[195]

---

[190] e.g. GDB:200b–c (CAM:32,8).

[191] As by Maitland, 5, and Wormald, esp. 75–6, who differ from P. Hyams, '"No register of title": the Domesday Inquest and land adjudication', *ANS*, 9 (1986), 127–41.

[192] As in Van Caenegem, *Writs*, no. 70; also V.H. Galbraith, 'Royal charters to Winchester', *EHR*, 35 (1920), 383–400, 388–9, no. 12, cf. GDB:43c (HAM:10,1); and no. 10 cf. GDB: 87c (SOM:2,9).

[193] 'Conclusion', *Dispute Settlement*, esp. 234–7.   [194] *Acta*, no. 352, 1086 × 1088.

[195] Garnett (*Conquered England*), investigates the short- and long-term implications of the illegal position.

4

Who Wrote Domesday?
The Returns and the Book

The mighty king, thereafter sent his justices through every 'shire', that is province, of England, and made them enquire on oath how many 'hides' (that is yokes (*iugera*) sufficient for one plough per annum) there were in every village and how many animals.[1]

Henry of Huntingdon

Some of the more trustworthy personnel who took part in the decision-making process were sent on circuit to preside at official sessions of approval and verification. The chief function of these commissioners, launched into the counties, was to act as arbiters in the tenurial decisions that were essential in the layout of Domesday and its enumeration of resources and indeed for the stability and legalization of the Conquest itself.

The circuits on which the Domesday commissioners or justices travelled to oversee the Domesday project are broadly known; however, there is internal evidence of smaller working units within these circuits and, in some counties, of a degree of autonomy. In this field more work may prove fruitful; and computer technology may be able to clarify differences in terminology, presentation, and information as between putative circuits, counties, hundreds, and tenants-in-chief, and so enable us to determine the input of various bodies or localities, whether originating from regional terms of reference, or features important to the local economy, or merely the concerns of a particular scribe.

DEFINING THE CIRCUITS

Over and above the shire, groups of shires—often neighbours in the two Domesday volumes and geographically—share similarities in terms of information, phraseology, and content. Using these common features, several attempts have been made to allocate counties to a 'circuit' that shared the same justices or commissioners,

---

[1] *Misit autem dehinc rex potentissimus iusticiarios suos per unamquamque scyram, id is est provinciam, Anglie, et inquirere fecit per iusiurandum quot hide, id est jugera uni aratro sufficientia per annum, essent in unaquaque villa, et quot animalia,* HH, 400–1.

such judicial circuits becoming normal practice in succeeding centuries. One such allocation breaks the Survey down into nine such groups, another into seven.[2] The following list numbers the counties according to their present order in Domesday (not necessarily the original order), with Roman numerals denoting the circuits of counties thought to have shared commissioners.

     I 1.Kent, 2.Sussex, 3.Surrey, 4.Hampshire, 5.Berkshire

     II 6.Wiltshire, 7.Dorset, 8.Somerset, 9.Devon, 10.Cornwall

     III 11.Middlesex, 12.Hertfordshire, 13.Buckinghamshire, 18.Cambridgeshire, 20.Bedfordshire

     IV 14.Oxfordshire, 21.Northamptonshire, 22.Leicestershire, 23.Warwickshire, 24.Staffordshire

     V 15.Gloucestershire, 16.Worcestershire, 17.Herefordshire, *VIII 25.Shropshire, 26.Cheshire

     VI 19.Huntingdonshire, 27.Derbyshire, 28.Nottinghamshire, 29.Rutland, *IX 30.Yorkshire, 31.Lincolnshire

     VII 32.Essex, 33.Norfolk, 34.Suffolk

    * My suggested additional 'circuits': conventionally included in the preceding group

Three circuits—I, II and VII—are not currently in dispute (although, in Circuit I, Kent and Sussex certainly exhibit characteristics peculiar to themselves): an incomplete earlier recension for Circuit II survives in Exon Domesday and those counties called Circuit VII—Essex, Norfolk, and Suffolk—exist together in a separate volume called Little Domesday. For the rest, reconstruction of the circuits is based on inference—grouping together counties, mostly juxtaposed in Great Domesday, which have common features, such as values recorded for three dates rather than two. Counties in Circuit III have several items of information common to them alone, including the way the ploughland is calculated. Elsewhere, some counties have a regular order of data in common—for instance, each entry starts with the name of the Edwardian holder, as in Derbyshire and Nottinghamshire. A separate circuit for the enormous territory of Yorkshire and Lincolnshire was suggested by Galbraith,[3] and the similar layout of the two counties in Great Domesday gives some justification for this, as also does the ruling and pricking of the folios.[4] Moreover, in Great Domesday, the county of Yorkshire begins the first of several quires and overlaps quires with Lincolnshire; whilst three blank folios divide Yorkshire from the preceding group of Derbyshire, Nottinghamshire and Rutland.[5]

---

   [2] e.g. C. Stephenson, 'Notes on the composition and interpretation of Domesday Book', *Speculum*, 22 (1947), 1–15, repr. in B. Lyon (ed.), *Medieval Institutions* (Cornell, 1954), 184–205; tabulated in V. H. Galbraith, *Domesday Book: its place in administrative history* (Oxford, 1974), 38, where Nottinghamshire is erroneously assigned.
   [3] Galbraith, 59.
   [4] M. Gullick, 'The Great and Little Domesday manuscripts', in Erskine and Williams, 148.
   [5] *Domesday Rebound*, HMSO (London, 1954), App. IA.

The grouping of the five western counties in Circuit V is illustrative of the debate. It has been observed on the one hand that the measurement of woodland in Cheshire differs from that in Shropshire, Herefordshire, Worcestershire, and Gloucestershire; the counter-argument is that all five counties have a defining common interest in parks and hawks' nests, and might simply reflect a feature important to the regional economy, rather than the particular interest of one group of commissioners.[6] Of course, the scribe who compiled Great Domesday from the county returns was aiming to straighten out as many variations as possible in the interest of uniformity. Yet, even within circuits, not every trace of longstanding differences of custom, terminology, and social structure could be ironed out by the panels of commissioners. To quote Galbraith, 'in our efforts to distinguish the circuits we are at all times balancing two factors: one, the tendency of the *legati* to impose a certain uniformity of procedure, nomenclature, and formulas; the other, the age-long difference in custom between even neighbouring counties'.[7]

There could be a third dimension to defining the circuits: the terminology that distinguished the component counties could have perhaps stemmed simply from a shared regional centre of record. It is usually assumed that provincial Domesdays were co-extensive with the circuit of a particular group of commissioners, yet this is only an assumption. Given the variation in groups of counties and commissions evident in previous court hearings under the Conqueror, it would seem unwise to take for granted that the two were invariably co-terminous. Excepting those counties in the highly organized Circuits II and III, single counties in Great Domesday have their own characteristics more often than not. The final descriptions of the counties of Leicester, Cheshire, and Kent, to take three of the more individualistic, do not marry with those of other counties in their putative 'circuits'. On the other hand, Nottinghamshire and Derbyshire, often jointly administered in subsequent centuries, shared similarities of layout: that they were dealt with jointly by the Domesday commissioners is borne out by the recorded testimony of *two* shires after Derby's account which is entered under Nottinghamshire.[8]

There may well have been 'mini-circuits' within our accepted circuits, either at the launching stage of the Inquiry or in the regional gathering together of information. Study of the hands employed in the Salisbury scriptorium—a likely site for the production of Exon Domesday—does not contradict the other evidence in the *Exon* text that the five counties of Circuit II had already been divided into two subgroups beforehand. The booklets concerning Devon and maybe Cornwall could even have been copied elsewhere, with the scribes travelling afterwards to Salisbury with the booklets to complete their task there, in collaboration with the Salisbury scribes.[9] William's commissioners had drawn upon a varying range of shires in

---

[6] A. T. Thacker and P. H. Sawyer, 'Domesday Survey', VCH *Chester*, vol. 1, ed. B. E. Harris (Oxford, 1987), 293–7; contrast, Roffe, *Inquest*, 125.
[7] Galbraith, *Domesday Book: its place in administrative history*, 38.
[8] GDB:280b (DBY:B15).   [9] Webber, 10.

earlier land pleas and we have seen that more than one set of commissioners had earlier been sent to sort out complex legal disputes.

The hypothetical nature of circuits—'intelligent guess-work' as Galbraith put it—needs emphasis. In the meantime, my suggestion is that the number of circuits should be increased at least to nine. They would differ from the currently accepted grouping by separating Gloucestershire, Herefordshire, and Worcestershire from Shropshire and Cheshire, and in putting Yorkshire and Lincolnshire into their own circuit. Cheshire and Shropshire, Kent and Sussex, all had good reason not to share identical processes with their neighbours: all were border seats of strategically important earldoms, and the individuality of their Domesday accounts reflects the powers of the chief landholders within those counties. The astonishingly brief time-scale of the Inquiry, with the short notice of its likely *terminus ad quem* at the Salisbury gathering of all significant landholders on 1 August, argues for the most effective and least complicated procedure.

THE ROLE OF THE DOMESDAY COMMISSIONERS

Several questions about the commissioners remain. Did they preside over the initial collection and review of data held in the shire? Or was that process simply left to the sheriffs, with the commissioners coming in at a later stage, in particular to preside over legal pleas arising from conflicting evidence on tenure? If so, did they then meet several shires together at one venue?

Two further complications exist: they arise from the Domesday evidence of a recent reassessment of tax liability, particularly evident in Circuit I, and of a checking of officials' actions, both of which called for comparable structures of adjudication. Robert, bishop of Hereford, implied that at least one such process was linked to the Survey:

> Other inquisitors followed the first; and men were sent into shires (*provincia*), which they did not know and where they themselves were not known, in order that different men should check the others' survey and arraign the accused parties before the king. And the land was vexed with many disputes arising from the collection of the royal revenues.[10]

Some check-up was probably envisaged from the beginning of the enterprise, as argued in Chapter 2. Shortage of reliable officials was an endemic weakness. Only a couple of decades or so after Domesday, a small group of men had charge of 'a particularly large number of counties'. By 1110, five sheriffs were in charge of two or more; Hugh of Buckland was said to have been in charge of eight—which suggests that the king was indeed pressed to find effective and loyal officials.[11]

---

[10] I have adapted Frank Thorn's translation, kindly given by correspondence. W. H. Stevenson, 'A contemporary description of the Domesday survey', *EHR*, 22 (1907), 74; EHD2, no. 198; discussed further in this volume, pp. 226, 249.

[11] J. A. Green, *The Government of England under Henry I* (Cambridge, 1989), 199–200.

Many incidents in King William's rule show his suspicions at work and it is unsurprising to see that the Domesday Inquiry erected a system of checks and balances, so pitting vested interests against each other. Little Domesday shows that men of the shire had been totally unable to withstand not only the wholesale confiscations of land, but also the wheeling and dealing in small freeholders. The appointment of churchmen provided an immediate counter-weight, but ultimately contained its own inherent disadvantage for the crown. It soon offered opportunities for the Church's developing claims of autonomous authority, as William II was shortly to discover in his dealings first with the contumacious bishop of Durham, and later, with Anselm, archbishop of Canterbury.

Certainly, the personnel of the only group of commissioners known upholds Robert of Hereford's statement that those without interests in the region presided over the *descriptio*. The four commissioners officiating in Worcestershire and neighbouring counties are named in Hemming's cartulary: Remigius, bishop of Lincoln and former royal clerk, Walter Giffard, Henry de Ferrers, and Adam fitzHubert, brother of the king's steward, Eudo. They 'were dispatched by the king himself to inquire into and write down the possessions and the customary dues not only of the king, but also of his magnates in this shire (*provincia*) and in many others, at the time the same king had the whole of England surveyed in writing'.[12] (Here, *provincia* cannot be taken to be 'province' or 'circuit' as it is sometimes translated,[13] since it would imply that Hemming's four commissioners officiated in more than one region—most unlikely on the grounds of time and on the distribution of their lands; it would also negate any differentiation of circuits by their characteristics.) None mentioned at Worcester held land in Circuit V, save only Henry de Ferrers—with a single large manor in Gloucestershire—thus fulfilling Robert of Hereford's criterion of impartiality for the checking commissioners.[14]

Each group of commissioners might well have included one senior bishop in each circuit.[15] As well as our knowledge of Remigius of Lincoln in the Worcestershire circuit, it seems likely that William, bishop of Durham, participated in that for the south-west: Bishop William is mentioned 'with colleagues' in the Wiltshire Geld Accounts, and *Exon* and Domesday both record that after the Salisbury meeting, the bishop of Durham was to inscribe a grant to Winchester in the returns, *in brevibus*.[16] Possibly Bishop Osmund of Salisbury was functioning as a commissioner for Circuit III or for the eastern circuit, as a writ of 1085 × 1087 requested him, along with Robert d'Oilly, sheriff of Berkshire and Oxfordshire, and Peter of Valognes, to put into effect the grant of the castle of Bishop's Stortford (in Hertfordshire, and close to the Essex border) to the recently appointed bishop,

---

[12] Van Caenegem, *Lawsuits*, no. 15, 39–41; Hemming, 75–6; *DB Worcestershire*, App. V, Worcester H, no. 5.

[13] *provincia* was specifically used for 'shire' in a nearly contemporary copy or forgery, *Acta* no. 14, II.

[14] Lechlade, GDB:169a (GLS:59,1).

[15] H. R. Loyn, 'William's bishops: some further thoughts', *ANS*, 10 (1987), 228–30.

[16] DB4, ff. 1b; 175b, GDB:87c (SOM:2, 9).

Maurice of London.[17] Osmund's bishopric held no land in the vicinity, yet Peter, as sheriff of Essex and Hertfordshire, would have been a partial commissioner in either circuit. However, it was certainly the case that in the great 1279 Inquiry eleven former or current sheriffs were enlisted as commissioners.[18]

To summarize: the likelihood is that a small number of senior persons of the rank of Geoffrey of Coutances set in motion the Domesday Inquiry, by initiating writs sent to the shire court laying out the terms of reference; however, distinctive regional features in Domesday might reflect the concerns of an initiator, or of a bishop or an earl, or of one of their scribes, or of features important to the local economy, not only of a common group of itinerant commissioners.[19] It appears as though the first round involved the sheriff, with material collected for review in the shire court. Since the nature of these shire proceedings, with the sheriff as convener, was likely to be partisan, others whose interests lay outside the county were commissioned to investigate evasions and attempt to resolve disputes.

A formal regional review seems to be reflected in a letter from Lanfranc to a mysterious 'S', perhaps a commissioner, or senior official, to whom Lanfranc appears to have accorded high respect and who was obviously entrusted with the overview of several counties. In reply to 'S', Lanfranc's negative answer about Canterbury lands held in demesne 'in those counties' indicates that the enquiry concerned only a part of the Canterbury lands, maybe those of Circuit III or Circuit VII.[20] The query obviously arose after most data had been collected and indicates some review of content.

REGIONAL DOMESDAYS

The survival of *Exon* and Little Domesday suggests an interim stage in the writing up of Great Domesday, in which groups of counties were written up into drafts at various unknown provincial centres. Each region offered ecclesiastical institutions with strong ties to the decision-makers: Exeter and Salisbury in the south-west, Winchester in the home counties, Worcester and Hereford in the west, Abingdon and Dorchester in the Oxford circuit, and Wolverhampton for Staffordshire, and the new episcopal seat at Lincoln and the archiepiscopal seat at York in the north. Eastern England offered several possibilities: the new cathedral at Norwich, the centrally placed Bury St Edmunds, and the old abbey of Ely where William was trying to repair his fractured reputation—certainly the abbey was to show its expertise in the Inquest of Ely. Yet the two major regional sources surviving are different in character and a precisely parallel interim stage for the whole country is hypothetical. *Exon* is yet more landholder in arrangement than Great Domesday,

---

[17] *Acta*, no. 189.
[18] Raban, 60–7.   [19] Contrast, Roffe, *Inquest*, 125.
[20] F. Barlow, 'Domesday Book: a letter of Lanfranc', *EHR*, 78 (1963), 284–9.

the lands of the tenants-in-chief being grouped together across county boundaries; while Little Domesday—apparently an extant 'regional Domesday' itself—is derived from returns yet more hundredal in arrangement.[21] So, even if regional Domesdays were uniformly a stage in proceedings, they were not necessarily uniform in character.

Alternatively, it is still possible that the returns, *Exon* apart, were abbreviated county by county, since many counties in Great Domesday begin a separate folio and most counties in Great Domesday were written up on independent gatherings of sheets, not shared with another county. In Little Domesday, each county begins a new gathering of sheets as well as a new folio. The counties with overlapping gatherings are Yorkshire with Lincolnshire, Shropshire with Cheshire with 'Land between the Ribble and the Mersey', Devon with Cornwall, and Gloucestershire with Worcestershire.[22]

The handwriting of Little Domesday—covering Norfolk, Suffolk, and Essex— has been analysed and the scribes identified as seven in number: six concerned with the meat of the material; the seventh simply added the famous final colophon.[23] Two or three seem to have been the workhorses who took on the brunt of the task. That four of the seven hands in Little Domesday recur in two or more shires suggest that its composition took place at a single regional centre, even though Norfolk and Suffolk share textual characteristics not displayed by Essex. Alexander Rumble concludes that its inscription was, in general, well organized, within a writing office that had the capacity of handling material from all three counties simultaneously.

Pointers to the native language of the Little Domesday scribes are ambiguous. On personal names, Little Domesday 'preserves a greater number of traditional Old English spellings than is found in Domesday Book'.[24] The place-name evidence, however, is conflicting. On the one hand, there are numerous instances where the Old English suffix *-ford* is preserved as a final element, mostly with a Latin case ending to form *-forda*; on the other, nearly as many instances change the final *-d* to *-t*, as French-speakers were likely to do.[25] Yet, now that the seven separate scribal hands have been distinguished, work on their individual treatment of names may well produce further clarification. There seems to be no inherent institutional reason why the several scribes at work should have been of similar origin, training, and tradition; rather the reverse, as the Domesday enterprise would have meant enlisting all hands to the writing-desk. Content, although rarely of a personal slant, can also be used as evidence. It seems to me that Scribe 2, using Rumble's numeration, however trained, has the perspective of a native, since the dating he

---

[21] Finn, *The Eastern Counties*, 54, 59; Roffe, *Inquest*, 177–80.

[22] *Domesday Rebound*, App. IA and IB.

[23] A. R. Rumble, 'The Domesday manuscripts: scribes and scriptoria', in Holt, *Studies*, 79–99, hands tabulated, 98–9.

[24] O. von Feilitzen, *The Pre-Conquest Personal Names of Domesday Book* (*Nomina Germanica* 3, Uppsala, 1937), 6.

[25] P. H. Sawyer, 'The place-names of the Domesday manuscripts', *BJRL*, 38 (1955–6), 483–506, at 495–7.

gives in one place—'after King William conquered England'—betrays his perspective: for this scribe at least, William's succession was not one of good title.[26] In contrast, Scribe 1 was almost certainly not English, but probably Norman—or else more wary than his colleague—since he records a landholder, Alric, who 'went away to a naval battle against King William' and later writes of 'when the king came to this land'.[27] According to handwriting criteria, however, it is Rumble's Scribe 3 who has 'an undistinguished hand of English type', whereas the other scribes possessed 'equally undistinguished hands of Norman type'.[28] Yet, some twenty years after the conquest, those of native birth and upbringing may well have received their scribal training from incomers.

Could Holy Cross, Waltham, and its canons have provided the site of the production of Little Domesday, or at least of Essex?[29] Harold's head of house here, Adalbert, was a native of Liège who had studied at Utrecht, which meant that Waltham contained men of diverse backgrounds. Was there a trace of resistance in Little Domesday's insistence on recording the many small freeholders who, incidentally, made the regional return virtually uncondensable? (See Figure 2.) At any rate, its library carefully preserved two Gospel books in Anglo-Saxon.[30]

Exon, with no known scribal connection with the city that gave it its name, does have some regional connections. It was a working document produced in the course of the Inquiry, arranged across counties according to landholders, and written in a variety of hands. Since *Exon* has survived in the Exeter Cathedral archives and Exeter was an obvious centre for the making of a description of Somerset, Devon, and Cornwall, it was for long natural to assume that the regional *Exon* was composed at Exeter, the home of the diocese of Devon and Cornwall since 1051. Its incumbent from 1072 to 1103 was Osbern—a Norman cleric who had formerly been in Edward the Confessor's service—and so was likely to have appointed non-English members to his household. Expert work on *Exon*'s handwriting has however changed the perspective completely. At least fifteen scribes worked on *Exon*; three, possibly four, hands are identified as those of the lively and assiduous group of clerks and scholars at work on the cathedral archive at Old Sarum, where seventeen different scribes were active before 1099. Whilst no 'house style' prevailed either at Salisbury or in *Exon*, the hands in *Exon* share similarities in patterns of collaboration with those of the Salisbury scribes, whereas the Exeter scriptorium under Osbern imported manuscripts—or writing styles—from Durham, Fécamp, and Jumièges, and none of its known hands is represented

---

[26] LDB:124b (NFK:1,120).

[27] LDB:14b–15a (ESS:6,9). For scribes, Rumble, 'The Domesday manuscripts', in Holt, *Studies*, 98–9.

[28] Illustrated in *Domesday Book Rebound*, PRO (London, 1964) Plates V, VI. Gullick, in Erskine and Williams, 168–9.

[29] Henry I issued 14 charters at Waltham: S. Mooers Christelow, 'A moveable feast? itineration and the centralization of government under Henry I', *Albion*, 28 (1996), 187–228, at 199. See Ch. 5 in this volume on Domesday's unique Waltham entry, pp. 113–14.

[30] The source is a sixteenth-century Waltham inventory, N. R. Ker, *Catalogue of Manuscripts containing Anglo-Saxon* (Oxford, 1957), xlviii.

in *Exon*. The Salisbury connection resurfaces in the Geld Accounts for the hundreds of the south-west bound up with *Exon*. One of the hands of the Geld Accounts for Wiltshire, whilst taking no part in writing up the Exon Domesday Survey, wrote 15 manuscripts for the library of Salisbury cathedral, founded in or after 1075. Moreover, apart from the handwriting, there are links with the quality of parchment and the physical construction; the frequent changes of hand suggesting that the scribes were accustomed to copying tasks.[31] Although professional itinerant scribes were employed for special commissions at this period at St Albans and Exeter, there is no evidence of them at Salisbury.[32] Thus scribes associated with Salisbury produced some at least of this regional Domesday. Indications are that the hands of many of the *Exon* scribes were not English, although one scribe, who possibly also worked at Salisbury, wrote in a variant of the English Caroline miniscule.[33]

The scribes of Salisbury seem to have had a director, who might have been Bishop Osmund himself, who was appointed to Old Sarum in 1078 and continued until late in 1099. A sometime royal clerk and former chancellor of England, Osmund appears to have placed the services of the learned chapter he had created at the disposal of the king's business. He headed a house famed for its canons' production of copies of patristic works and, according to William of Malmesbury, 'did not disdain to copy and to bind books' himself.[34] The study that Teresa Webber has made of scribes and scholars at Salisbury shows the new community to have been interested from the first in patristic studies, particularly Augustine, and also in secular and pagan authors. Augustine himself had been a proponent of the view that secular studies formed an essential preliminary to sacred studies; clerics interested in his works often felt motivated to contribute practically to establishing a stable Christian state. Some authors represented in the Salisbury library seem to have been sourced directly from the continent, betraying an interest in the studies current at the schools of Liège, Tournai, and the Low Countries.[35]

Careful comparison of *Exon* with Great Domesday has unearthed clues that the scribe of Great Domesday used this very source, not a fair copy. Sometimes whole lines of the source are missed out; sometimes an entry that turns the page in *Exon* is not completed in Great Domesday.[36] Eccentric material, or material corrected in *Exon*, is so reproduced in Great Domesday. Most revealing, two omissions were added to *Exon* in the Great Domesday scribe's own hand onto previously blank folios: the single entry for the bishop of Bayeux's fief in Somerset with Samson as his subtenant, and the two manors comprising the fief of Robert fitzGerald in

---

[31] Webber, 1–18.
[32] e.g. *Gesta Abbatum Monasterii Sancti Albani*, ed. H. T. Riley, RS (1867), 57–8; Rumble, 'The Domesday manuscripts', in Holt, *Studies*, 94, cf. T. Webber, *Scribes and Scholars at Salisbury Cathedral c.1075–1125* (Oxford, 1992), 29.
[33] Webber, 7–8; Sawyer, 'The place-names of the Domesday manuscripts', 491.
[34] *GP*, 184.   [35] Webber, *Scribes and Scholars*, 42–68.
[36] F. and C. Thorn, 'The writing of Great Domesday', in Hallam and Bates, 37–72, at 67–9; 200–1, n. 8.

Somerset.[37] The close working relations between the two manuscripts and the amount of orderly rearrangement achieved by the single step from *Exon* to Great Domesday suggest that similar provincial Domesdays were indeed generally assembled and compiled prior to abbreviation.

In sum, the hands present in *Exon* and Little Domesday suggest that these manuscripts were constructed in the provinces: each the work of a group of scribes whose stints changed and recurred. It seems likely that similar provincial centres for other circuits redrafted the county returns. But there was nothing, after all, to stop the records of individual counties being sent directly to Winchester, or being produced in twos and threes by many more centres of literacy: as indeed *Exon* is divided into two sub-groups—Dorset and Wiltshire forming one, Somerset, Devon, and Cornwall the other.[38] Nor can Little Domesday be regarded as typical, as it was patently not dealt with in the same way as the bulk of the returns that became condensed into Great Domesday, albeit the evidence of the hands indicate that it was produced in a single regional scriptorium.

THE DATE OF GREAT DOMESDAY

Exactly when the two volumes of Domesday Book were written up is not agreed. Although their contents were undoubtedly the Conqueror's enterprise, some scholars have argued that Great Domesday was not actually written up during William I's reign. Various *termini ad quem* for its production have been adduced, from a completion date as late as the reign of Henry I, to the recent contention that it was written up as a book only in the mid-part of William II's reign.[39] More moderate is the proposition that work on the returns from the Inquiry continued into the reign of William II, only halted, on the eve of completion, by the rebellion early in 1088 of some of the central figures of the establishment—Geoffrey of Coutances, Odo of Bayeux, Eustace of Boulogne, Roger of Montgomery and his twin sons, and the bishop of Durham.

Yet both Domesday volumes, monumentally impressive as they remain, evidence the urgency in their production and even Great Domesday contains clues as to the haste with which it was accomplished. First, there are the gaps left, often for accounts of boroughs: sometimes too large a gap has been left, as for Buckingham, sometimes too small a gap, as for Exeter, or one unfilled, as at the start of Sussex.[40] Occasionally, notably in the cases of Winchester and of London, no comparable borough account was drawn up, or perhaps never transcribed, to our great loss: one folio stands vacant at the head of Middlesex for London, another at the head of Hampshire for Winchester, with only the index of tenants in the last part of

---

[37] DB4, ff. 153v; 436v. Entries similar to those of GDB:87d (SOM:4,1) and 97a, (SOM:33,1–2).
[38] F. and C. Thorn, 'The writing of Great Domesday', in Hallam and Bates, 58.
[39] Roffe, *Inquest*, 242–8.   [40] GDB:143a, 100a, 16a.

each. Dorset indeed does not conclude with the end of an entry, but breaks off in mid-sentence.[41]

The magnitude of the task might well suggest long years of ordering and abbreviation, yet the Anglo-Saxon chronicler tells us that King William I saw the returns in some form: 'all these writings were brought to him afterwards',[42] most probably, though not necessarily, before he left England for the last time in the autumn of 1086—which suggests completion of the gathering exercise by then.[43] By 9 September 1087, William was dead. Neither of these pieces of evidence dates the condensed Great Domesday, however, but only the full returns from the Inquiry. Whilst Anglo-Norman kings and officials became used to frequent Channel crossings, and documents were readily transportable, it was a hazardous crossing and unique documents were unlikely to be despatched in this manner, at any rate not before copies or summaries had been made. There remained a year after William's departure for Normandy in which to convert the returns into Great Domesday before his death. One twentieth-century penman, Alfred Fairbank, concluded after experiments that Great Domesday could have been written in 240 days by a devoted and assiduous scribe, whilst a recent study of its handwriting estimates a minimum of 330 days (at a rate of 200 lines a day) for the process of writing alone.[44] It would seem that, allowing for high days and holy days, more than a year would have been necessary for abbreviating and editing the variously ordered returns. Work on abbreviating the returns, however, may have already started in summer 1086.[45]

Little Domesday, containing the description of Essex, Norfolk, and Suffolk, was never tidily arranged and abbreviated, as was its companion volume. A scribe who did not contribute to the copying of Little Domesday added its grand finale—the famous colophon—in vermilion red: 'In the one thousandth and eighty-sixth year from the Incarnation of our Lord, the twentieth of the reign of William, this *descriptio* was made not only throughout these three counties, but also throughout others', thereby fixing at least the assembly of material for that volume firmly in 1086.[46] The colophon of Little Domesday is not the only pointer to early completion. One small but vital clue, long unnoticed, shows that the abbreviated, well-ordered Great Domesday, for Hampshire at least, was written up in William I's lifetime. Interlined above a royal chamberlain's name and title in the Hampshire account is 'to the king's daughter'(see Figure 3);[47] this addition would have made sense only in the time of the first William, who had several daughters, not that of the second, who had none and who remained notoriously unmarried.[48]

---

[41] GDB:85a (DOR:57,22).   [42] *ASC*, 1085.   [43] *Acta*, 78, 82.

[44] *Domesday Rebound*, 34–5; F. and C. Thorn suggest a total of between 17 and 24 months, 'The writing of Great Domesday', in Hallam and Bates, 72.

[45] cf. Raban, 82–4.   [46] LDB:450b.

[47] GDB:49b (HAM;67,1); S. Harvey, 'Recent Domesday studies', *EHR*, 95 (1980), 127.

[48] Douglas, *Conqueror*, 391–5; Barlow, *Rufus*, 328–9.

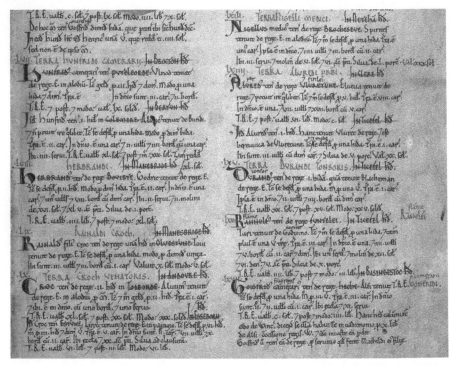

Figure 3. Geoffrey the Chamberlain's entry, which dates Great Domesday, follows Rannulf Flambard's highlighted entry in Hampshire, GDB:49b. Great Domesday Book, folio 49r. TNA.

Two further pieces of Hampshire evidence indicate immediate construction. A leaf had to be inserted into the standard quires' arrangement for the whole volume in order to accommodate an omission of church, chapels, and land: there would have been little need to add a leaf years later to accommodate a case conducted in the Conqueror's reign or early in the next.[49] The second relates to a recent dispute between two sheriffs, relayed in some detail, even giving the status of the witnesses from both sides; but in Domesday it has been added at the end of a folio, is unsettled, and awaited judgement.[50] Thirdly, a writ of William I, halving the hidage of Pyrford, Surrey, is dated as 'after the *descriptio* of all England'; and the relevant Great Domesday entry was amended in the margin as a consequence, indicating that its Surrey folios were already written-up.[51] The writ was issued under William I, and when it was already too late to incorporate the data into the main text of the final volume. After all that labour expended in seeking and assembling information, something brought the work of abbreviation to an abrupt

---

[49] GBD:42; *Domesday Rebound*, App. I and II; the writ restoring the hide 'can only be dated to between the making of Domesday Book and bishop William's rebellion in 1088', *Acta*, no. 352.
[50] GDB:44d (HAM:23,3).   [51] *Acta*, no. 326; GDB:32b (SUR:6,5).

and final halt within an ace of its completion. That event is most likely to have been the death of William the Conqueror in September 1087, following an internal injury at the siege of Mantes.

It remains possible, however, that what provoked cessation of work on the great project was the revolt of the magnates in 1088, portending that Domesday's data might soon be obsolete, its tenurial record out-dated by confiscations.[52] Two Domesday snippets have suggested that work on the project might have continued into the reign of William II: the two references to an 'Earl William' as a landholder, identified as William de Warenne, who was only created earl by William II.[53] But there are uncertainties over this identification: in the nine counties where William de Warenne holds in chief he is nowhere called 'Earl' in the fief headings;[54] and the Warenne title in England was more personal than territorial.[55] Moreover, William de Warenne was not created Earl of Surrey until shortly after 16 April 1088, and was mortally wounded before the end of May, fighting on the king's side at the siege of Pevensey, dying on 24 June;[56] this leaves little credible time for writing up his two mentions as earl in two Domesday circuits. And, a later writing-up would be curious, as Great Domesday pillories Warenne for dispossessing a landholder without the king's writ and for taking away two horses from the landholder's men, which he has 'not yet given back':[57] an unlikely comment about a recently killed or injured hero. The political context, moreover, argues for putting the weight of Domesday's abbreviation firmly into the first William's reign. There was only a matter of months between the death of the first William and the rebellion against the second. The bishop of Durham seems already to have had some outlying estates seized in March, although the rebellion continued through the spring and early summer.[58] And although the rebels' ravages included the great royal manor of Berkeley in Gloucestershire, the burning of Gloucester, and the taking of Hereford, there are no signs of these actions in Domesday.

Whilst the writing-up of the Domesday volumes belongs completely or almost completely to William I's reign, William II and the determined administrative team who were in charge were not slow to follow up the intended use of the data. Two Ramsey writs show prompt action in the first weeks of William II's reign; first to convene a shire court to settle a dispute over land at Isham, and then to give effect to its decision made in favour of the abbey and against the sheriff.[59] Again, the text of Great Domesday was not affected, where the item lies in the fief of the erring sheriff Eustace, suggesting that it was already too late to change it.[60] Like the

---

[52] The rebellion and its significance is discussed in Ch. 9 in this volume, pp. 268–70.

[53] GDB:205d (HUN:14,1); 26b (SUS:12,9); C. P. Lewis, 'The earldom of Surrey and the date of Domesday Book', *Historical Research*, 63 (1990), 329–36.

[54] F. and C. Thorn, 'The writing of Great Domesday', in Hallam and Bates, 71.

[55] D. Crouch, *The Image of Aristocracy in Britain, 1000–1300* (London, 1992), 58.

[56] Keats-Rohan, 480.   [57] GDB:211d (BDF:17,1).   [58] Barlow, *Rufus*, 75–85.

[59] D. Bates, 'Two Ramsey Abbey writs and the Domesday Survey', *Historical Research*, 63 (1990), 337–9; Van Caenegem, *Writs*, no. 185.

[60] GDB:228a (NTH:55,1).

Pyrford writ, the two Ramsey writs indicate that the bulk of Great Domesday was already written up.

Whether work on Great Domesday came to a halt at William I's death or very early in his successor's reign, no later date is compatible with the mass of evidence that the project was that of William I. Although formal Domesday headings were likely to be copied from one text to another, it remains true that throughout Domesday 'the king' or 'King William' is always William I; 'the queen' can only be Queen Matilda. More tellingly, incidental references bear this out: 'King William' has given land in Hertfordshire for 'the soul of his son, Richard', who was deceased; whereas William II appears only once, as 'W. the king's son', accused of illegally giving away a small parcel of Sherborne Abbey land—not the sole mention a ruler would appreciate.[61]

THE ORDER OF GREAT DOMESDAY'S INSCRIPTION

Whilst the topic is of import to those wishing to understand the evolution of the abbreviated text, for the general historian its import is perhaps as an indication of the priorities of the Domesday enterprise. It is currently argued that the northern circuit, Circuit VI, containing five of the six counties now placed last in Great Domesday, was the first to be abbreviated. The reasoning rests on the variety of formulas adopted, the changing principles of abbreviation, the varying number of lines on the Yorkshire pages, and on the incorporation of documents of varying origins.[62]

Whilst acknowledging the interest of this work on Yorkshire Domesday, it may be questioned whether the variations in that county necessarily meant that Yorkshire was the first county to be tackled and condensed, and became the standard. Formulae continued to vary in the Great Domesday text—between counties and between fiefs. No set litany was ever finalized, although Circuit II, for the southwest, comes closest; and it was this circuit's style that was adopted in late entries in Great Domesday.[63] Indeed given its size, the unrest there, and the extent of depopulation and devastation it had endured, it would be surprising if surveying Yorkshire were an easy task. Some variations may well have reflected the skeletal tax lists adopted as *pro forma*s for seeking and ordering information, or the lack of them.[64] York and its minsters had been burnt to the ground in 1069/70, which might well have meant that some fiscal data no longer existed. Other patterns of work might provide alternative practical explanations for the Yorkshire observations. Perhaps the Yorkshire returns were late, and the Domesday scribe was forced to reflect the phraseology without revision as the drafts came to him; then, nearing

[61] GDB:141c (HRT: 36,19); 77a (DOR:3,6).
[62] Roffe, *Inquest*, with tables, 191–204; on rulings, Gullick, in Erskine and Williams, 147–50.
[63] Personal communication from Caroline Thorn.
[64] Harvey 1971, 755–69; H. B. Clarke, 'The Domesday satellites', in *Reassessment*, 50–70 at 67.

completion, he allowed himself more time to standardize. Or, the returns from the north were behindhand, and more experienced scribes were sent to help in completing the returns, with knowledge of the end product. The Great Domesday scribe could not regiment his final version further than the material from the counties warranted. There was little time for the county to become a model, and as a model it was not representative: a number of questions were irrelevant because few people and no assets survived to enumerate.[65] Indeed, the whole argument for circuits rests on the evident lack of a single common character in the Great Domesday text. And if the abbreviation into Great Domesday had been tackled years later, as Roffe envisages, when all data were to hand, there would be no reason for the variations in layout, nor for the discrepancies that exist between the county indexes and the county descriptions.

The best argument for the Yorkshire Domesday being made early and condensed first is a political one: York had been a provincial capital linked to the Danish kingdom and the Danish threat of 1084–6 enhanced its alien aura. The north generally, and Yorkshire in particular, had proved difficult to rule and William's devastating reprisals severely limited its ability to raise taxes—which could well have made the county a focus of interest in an inquiry about revenues.

THE GREAT DOMESDAY SCRIBE AND HIS SCRIPTORIUM

Informed study of the handwriting in Great Domesday by successive scholars has reinforced the astonishing conclusion that the volume was the work of one scribe, or rather one scribe with a second scribe working with him, making some 530 corrections and additions. (A further four scribes made a few additions and a fifth added a series of quire signatures.[66]) There is no discernible 'curial' hand or likeness that might be attributable to a common training. That the abbreviation of the returns and the production of Great Domesday took place at Winchester is an inference derived from its first title, 'the Book of Winchester'.[67] Even so, that title might derive simply from the Domesday volumes' place of keeping and the Treasury's location.

Great Domesday's scribe might well have moved to places other than Winchester to condense the circuit returns. The only pointer to this tactic is the pattern of parchment rulings, which are observed to vary according to circuit; however, it seems all to be the work of the same hand.[68] Centres not far distant from normal royal household itineraries could well have hosted six out of the seven or more putative regional returns: Salisbury, Winchester, Gloucester or Worcester,

---

[65] Even William of Jumièges stresses the extent of the vengeance William wreaked in York where the Normans 'massacred almost the entire population' from the young to the aged, *GND* 2.180–1.

[66] F. and C. Thorn, 'The writing of Great Domesday', in Hallam and Bates, 38–40; for the assistant or supervisor, 48–55.

[67] GDB:332c.

[68] R. W. Finn, *An Introduction to Domesday Book* (London, 1963), 89–92; Gullick, in Erskine and Williams, 148–50.

Dorchester or Abingdon, and in the London area, Westminster, St Paul's, or St Martin's, with Waltham for Essex and East Anglia. Edward the Confessor as king had never travelled further north than Gloucester.[69] When in England, which was probably for little more than a third of his reign, William's great councils tended to meet at Winchester, Gloucester, and Westminster or Windsor: most of his activities further afield were military and crisis-driven.[70] Complete Norman rule arguably progressed from the south and south-east northwards and westwards, becoming more 'colonial' as it moved further from Normandy.[71] William had allocated the college of canons at Waltham, refounded by King Harold, to the bishopric of Durham, and Domesday shows that Waltham was retained as a major base by the forceful William of St Calais. Salisbury offered a prime site as it was of good access from much of the land-based regions of the kingdom and—perhaps most important in the invasion crisis of 1084–6—inland and eminently defensible. Salisbury was only some twenty miles from Winchester with roads from Winchester, London, Cirencester, and Exeter converging at its gate, and a western route nearby.[72] The site chosen for the Norman castle was Old Sarum which, set atop the vast hill-fort, made it one of the most secure in the kingdom. As the chosen venue for the demand for oaths of loyalty from all landholders in 1086, Sarum was arguably the immediate destination of the Domesday returns which may well have played a vital role in the reciprocal element, in fact bargain-making, that the oaths of loyalty and acts of homage imposed there assumed.[73] If the regional returns were already assembled at Salisbury for the Oath, there was no need for the scribe to go further; but to assemble returns from the shires by 1 August was an unsparing demand. The additions to the text in Hampshire and Surrey already mentioned indicate that work began on Great Domesday before all inquiries were completed. (Indeed the evidence for these counties being in Great Domesday form early is more direct than that for Yorkshire.)

The scribe's work-place poses one question; his training and expertise—both self-evidently impressive—pose another. Painstaking detective work, quite recently, has identified his hand in four manuscripts—apart from the addition to *Exon.*[74] Yet their contents have aroused little interest as clues to the identity of the scribe or of his master or background institution. One manuscript is a copy of the *Apologeticum* of Tertullian, a pagan lawyer who later became a Christian and the first theologian to write in Latin.[75] According to one authority, Tertullian 'created the language of

---

[69] D. Hill, *An Atlas of Anglo-Saxon England* (Oxford, 1981), 94–5.

[70] Itinerary, *Acta*, 76–8; York in 1069, Durham in 1072; around 145 months were spent in northern France out of a total of 239, D. Bates, *William the Conqueror* (London, 2004), 164–5.

[71] A theme in J. Le Patourel, *The Norman Empire* (Oxford, 1976).

[72] J. McNeill, *Old Sarum*, English Heritage Guidebooks (London, 2006), 1–40, Map 26.

[73] J. C. Holt, '1086', in Holt, *Studies*, 56–64; Harvey 1975, 190.

[74] Identified by Michael Gullick and Caroline Thorn; F. and C. Thorn, 'The writing of Great Domesday', in Hallam and Bates, 38, 200 n. 8.

[75] Bodleian, Lat th.d.34, ff. 1v–28r; Tertullian's works were transmitted through the ninth century *Codex Agobardinus*, the work of a ninth-century scholar-archbishop of Lyon.

western theology, which owes its characteristic precision to his legally trained mind'.[76] A second example of the Great Domesday scribe's hand has been found in a transcription of the Life of St Katherine,[77] a Greek-speaking princess, regarded as the patron saint of theological learning and debate, who was martyred in Alexandria and whose most prominent western shrine in the eleventh century was Holy Trinity, Rouen.[78] Perhaps our scribe attended a master with affiliations to Rouen, which suggests the treasurer, Walkelin of Winchester, who came from Rouen and was known to have had an interest in relics. Winchester, moreover, had already displayed a pre-Conquest interest in St Katherine and she featured in a Winchester Calendar by the 1060s.[79] Thirdly, the Domesday scribe's hand is evident in a manuscript from the library of Winchester Cathedral.[80] It copies a sermon of the sixth-century monk and archbishop, Caesarius of Arles, an effective administrator, instrumental in gaining primacy for his diocese in Gaul which, in discussing the commandments, concludes with the precept not to covet your neighbours' goods:[81] a precept that had a certain poignancy in Winchester, as towards the end of his life Walkelin confessed to having commandeered the revenues of many of the monastic lands.[82]

The Domesday scribe's hand has also been detected in the list of contents of a Hereford Cathedral manuscript;[83] the manuscript contains a group of texts with predominantly continental interests, viz. a text of Didymus, a fourth-century Alexandrian theologian, three of Augustine, and three of 'Pseudo-Augustine' (one Vigilius), of which one is also to be found in Salisbury Cathedral Library, the texts themselves being written in 'five expert English protogothic bookhands'.[84] These intellectual interests of the Domesday scribe's master again seem to be more in the mould of a man of Lotharingian education, rather than someone in the English or

---

[76] *The Oxford Dictionary of the Christian Church*, ed. F. L. Cross (London 1958), 1334.

[77] BL Harley 12, ff. 141r–143v; F. and C. Thorn, 'The writing of Great Domesday', in Hallam and Bates, 38.

[78] Both Canterbury and St Albans—where a nephew of Lanfranc was abbot—were also known to revere her by the end of the century: C. Walsh, *The Cult of St Katherine of Alexandria in Early Medieval Europe* (Aldershot, 2007), 109–15, 120.

[79] Walsh, *St Katherine*, 70–8, 101–4.

[80] Trinity College, Oxford, MS 28, ff. 89v–91r; M. Gullick and C. Thorn, 'Scribes of Great Domesday', *Journal of the Society of Archivists*, 8 (1986), 78–80. The MS contains a range of authors: Bede; Rabanus Maurus, archbishop of Mainz, died 856, who, as abbot of Fulda created an influential school in Europe; and Eucherius of Lyon, a fifth-century monk and bishop of Lyon, died *c*.449. This MS was in Winchester Cathedral Priory library in the later middle ages: Rumble, 'The Domesday manuscripts', in Holt, *Studies*, 96.

[81] 'Sancti Caesarii Arelatensis Sermones', ed. D. Germani Morin, Sermon 100, in *Corpus Christianorum*, series Latina, 103 (Turnhout, 1953), 406–13, at 411–12; I thank Richard Gameson for this reference. On Caesarius, see Cross, *Oxford Dictionary of the Christian Church*, 215.

[82] *Ann Winton*, 39–40. In Domesday, both houses had evidently suffered. Under the heading 'for the support of the [Cathedral] Monks' most manors are held by 'the bishop himself'; the monks are recorded as holding only five items, four worth £5 or less. Many of New Minster's lands have been allocated to royal officers.

[83] Hereford Cathedral MS P.i. 10.

[84] The MS seems to have come to the Hereford Cathedral library, with others from monasteries of the region, as a result of the activities of a commissioner for the dissolution of the monasteries: R. A. B. Mynors and R. M. Thomson, *The Catalogue of Manuscripts in Hereford Cathedral Library* (Woodbridge, 1993), 69–70.

Norman monastic tradition. In the hands of a local monastic house for one reason or another, this manuscript provokes a speculation that the Domesday scribe was at some point employed by Robert, bishop of Hereford, who is thought to have worked in harmony with the surviving Old English scholarship at Hereford,[85] and thus would have appreciated a man of English training close at hand. As Robert constructed a two-storey chapel one of whose levels had a chapel dedicated to St Katherine shortly after his appointment to Hereford, the appearance of the Domesday hand elsewhere, transcribing a Life of St Katherine, strengthens the idea of a link with Robert;[86] possibly the Domesday scribe worked for him at some point.

Differently, on the strength of the three manuscripts then known to him, Chaplais identified the hard-working Domesday scribe as almost certainly holding 'a position of some importance in the Durham scriptorium'.[87] Whilst the Domesday scribe wrote only the 'table of contents' for the Hereford manuscript, two hands in the texts themselves share 'the same unusual suspension-sign for -*us*' with the Domesday scribe. The layout and decoration of the manuscript, too, have characteristics redolent of Durham.[88] Further, the royal writ halving the hidage of the manor of Pyrford was, we remember, witnessed by William of St Calais, bishop of Durham (also by Ivo Taillebois), and the corresponding correction is in the hand of the principal Domesday scribe.[89] That writ's physical characteristics prop up a Durham connection, argues Chaplais: in particular in the form of its wrapping tie, which was virtually without parallel at the time, except for two other cases, both associated with Durham: a grant of Henry I to Durham, and a vernacular writ for the monks of Durham issued by Rannulf Flambard, bishop of Durham from 1099 to 1128, and the bishopric's custodian beforehand.[90] On the other hand, the content and dates of these two texts associate the technique with Bishop Rannulf's service, not with St Calais. Moreover, Durham, remote from London and Winchester and not covered by Domesday Book, could hardly have provided a geographical base for the Domesday scribe. In 1075, even after the rising of Earl Ralf and the Bretons was quashed, Lanfranc wrote to warn the bishop of Durham of the Danes' incursion.[91] The dangers inherent in taking unique returns to that remote site in 1086, and perhaps encountering marauders or invading Danes en route, are so obvious as to render it out of the question.

As to the background of the single-minded official, responsible for writing up Great Domesday, Galbraith's thought that his hand had 'an old-fashioned air, more characteristic of a native scribe': an impression that has been not been contradicted by specialist studies since, although they remain tentative as to the official's cultural

[85] Barlow, *Anglo-Norman Church*, 63–4 attributes this to Robert, but without source. He certainly remained a close friend of Bishop Wulfstan and he attended the formal translation of St Oswald's bones at Worcester: E. Mason, *St Wulfstan of Worcester c.1008–1095* (Oxford, 1990), 119.

[86] *GP*, 300; Walsh, *St Katherine*, 116–17.

[87] P. Chaplais, 'William of Saint-Calais and the Domesday Survey', in Holt, *Studies*, 65–77.

[88] Chaplais, 74.   [89] *Acta*, no. 326; GDB:32b (SUR:6,5).

[90] Chaplais, 'William of Saint-Calais', in Holt, *Studies*, 76.

[91] Lanfranc's Letters, no. 36, 126–7.

origins and training.[92] Chaplais noted the hand's several distinctive characteristics, two of which, he concluded, 'entitle us to regard his hand as English': the scribe's almost invariable use of the Tironian *nota* for *et*—resembling an Arabic 7 as opposed to an ampersand—and his use of the horned '*e*'. Yet, his hand 'was strongly influenced in other ways by continental practice'.[93] The expert consensus now is that the Great Domesday scribe was of native origin or trained in an English scriptorium. It seems that any candidate must meet several requirements: a man experienced in writing and ordering material, and familiar enough with Old English to feel confident about altering place-names, but strangely inconsistent over English personal names, which often fare less well in Great Domesday. Additionally, there is a second, amending scribe, whose handwriting indicates that his cultural origin was 'distinctly Norman'.[94]

Could other monastic institutions with experience of long-standing ties with comital houses or with meetings of the witan have offered a venue? Could collegiate centres of excellence or the newly established cathedrals staffed with secular canons equipped with the latest learning have provided such a scriptorium? The formulae employed in the document resulting from the Fontenay land inquiry in Normandy, suggests that it was written by a scribe of the abbey of St Stephen's of Caen, a monastic scriptorium which belonged to neither interested party but was closely affiliated to the duke/king.[95] It is sensible to look for the Domesday scribe within the extraordinary expertise developed earlier in the century at Winchester, yet he might have been a young native clerk of talent reared elsewhere. There were, for instance, four or five pre-Conquest scribes known to be working at the influential St Augustine's, Canterbury, for a considerable period after the conquest.[96]

In the absence of a Domesday account of London, any clues as to whether scribal expertise or facilities were afforded by St Martin-le-Grand, St Paul's, or indeed the abbey of Westminster remain 'known unknowns', although the first two institutions both boasted canons who were at the centre of affairs or to become so. St Martin's itself was an institution patently at the mercy of the ruler's political needs.[97] Both college and cathedral provided canonries for royal clerks and curial bishops of the twelfth century and for their education, whilst St Paul's list of canons from around 1090 onwards shows that a few *curiales* held positions in both.[98] The links of St Martin-le-Grand with royal service were contemporary and close. Its founder, Ingelric, had been a prominent royal clerk and a prospering landholder under the Confessor; he acted for the Conqueror, witnessing royal charters early in

---

[92] Galbraith, 203; Chaplais, in Holt, *Studies*, 70; Gullick, in Erskine and Williams, 152–4; Rumble, 'The Domesday manuscripts', in Holt, *Studies*, 84.

[93] Chaplais, 72.   [94] Gullick, in Erskine and Williams, 158–60.   [95] *Acta*, no. 149.

[96] A. Lawrence, 'Manuscripts of early Anglo-Norman Canterbury', in N. Colstream and P. Draper (eds), *Medieval Art and Architecture at Canterbury before 1220: The British Archaeological Association Conference Transactions for the Year 1979* (Leeds, 1982), 101–11.

[97] P. Taylor, 'Ingelric, Count Eustace and the foundation of St Martin-le-Grand', *ANS*, 24 (2001), 215–37; *Acta*, no. 181.

[98] John le Neve, *Fasti Ecclesiae Anglicanae, 1066–1300*, vol. 1, compiled by D. Greenway, Institute of Historical Research (London, 1968), 42.

the reign,[99] and was one of a trio of royal commissioners enforcing the buying back, or 'redemption'—as Domesday terms it—of Englishmen's lands in East Anglia, early in the reign.[100] In the early twelfth century, St Martin's curial character was reinforced by the fact that the deanship was held successively by Roger of Salisbury and Henry de Blois and, in Stephen's reign, a scribe of St Martin-le-Grand produced a succession of royal writs.[101] Alternatively, Westminster Abbey was to become adept at charter forgeries in the late eleventh and twelfth centuries; even in Domesday it had tried to hold one hide of land *per falsam brevem*, which was, consequentially, then claimed for the king;[102] perhaps the Conqueror's Domesday provided the house with a precedent for its activities.

The scribe's master—perhaps one of a succession of masters—should have had the intellectual interests displayed in the non-Domesday texts surviving in his hand. A right-hand man of such as Osmund of Salisbury or Robert of Hereford, too young to have yet gained high preferment in Edward's reign, may be the man we seek. Is the contents list surviving at Hereford Cathedral a vital clue? The bishop of Hereford, Robert, was a former royal clerk from imperial Lotharingia, whose closest friend was the English bishop Wulfstan; his cultural aide could well have been English, or familiar with English scripts. On the other hand, the link between this manuscript and the Hereford bishopric may well be late and fortuitous.

The detective work will no doubt continue. Although the intellectual interest of his master, or former master, may well afford important clues to the scribe's background, the connection between the two at this period was not necessarily life-long or confined to a single institution: besides the masters of religious scriptoria in the great abbeys, there were well-trained clerks who moved from episcopal to royal service, and vice-versa. Yet the search for the Domesday mastermind tells us much about the range of expertise and even renaissance abilities of the ecclesiastics on whom William relied to support his regime: so we turn to consider one or two candidates further.

[99] e.g. *Acta*, nos 138, 159, 181; S. Keynes, 'Regenbald, the Chancellor (sic)', *ANS*, 10 (1987), 218–20.

[100] LDB:360b (SUF:14,39), 367b (SUF:101), 423b–424a (SUF:39,3); Williams, *The English*, 8–10.

[101] R. H. C. Davis, 'The College of St Martin-le-Grand and the Anarchy, 1135–54', in *From Alfred the Great to Stephen* (London, 1991), 237–54.

[102] LDB:14a (ESS:6,4). *Writs*, 286–339, discusses the Westminster tradition of evolving royal writs and charters.

5

The Mastermind

PERSONALITY AND ANONYMITY IN DOMESDAY

Domesday is an agrarian gazetteer that openly betrays little of the human element. Great and Little Domesday alike afford no identity for the mastermind who thought up the idea of a survey as the response to the king's queries, the editor who determined and supervised its shape, or the scribe who penned almost all of Great Domesday. The dramatic depositions of schismatic bishops—among them the archbishop of Canterbury, Stigand, and his brother, Æthelmær of East Anglia—are reduced to dry allusions to 'former' holders of large estates.[1] Even the timings of the falls or deaths of earls, English and Norman, are difficult to gauge from Domesday Book. We must turn to other sources to learn that Bishop Odo of Bayeux, earl of Kent, the king's half-brother and regent of England in the king's absence, was in disgrace at the time Domesday Book was made, his estates confiscate, and he himself in confinement after some political and military activity independent of the king.[2] In Domesday Book his lands still lie under his name, with little to bear out his dramatic fall from grace. Likewise, we hear regularly of the holders of land in King Edward's day, but rarely of the fate that befell them, such as the freeman who 'was killed at the Battle of Hastings', or of the thegn who 'went to a naval battle against King William'.[3]

Nor does Domesday Book contain more than a few personal glimpses of the dynamic characters who defeated and killed many of England's inhabitants at Hastings and afterwards. There, King William is not William the Conqueror—except when, with a slip of the pen, a Little Domesday scribe wrote 'after King William conquered England'. (The same scribe, however, a few lines later remembered to use the more politic 'after King William came to this land'.)[4] Generally, William is 'the king' or even, at the opening of Little Domesday where it would be noticed, 'King of the English'—thereby proclaiming his lawful succession to his kinsman, King Edward.[5] Similar contradictions lie in Great Domesday; King Harold II, a crowned king after all, is reported on the same folio in successive entries, but from different hundreds, as having 'invaded this kingdom', and as

---

[1] LDB:191–201.
[2] D. Bates, 'The origins of the justiciarship', *ANS*, 4 (1981), 2–4; 'The character and career of Odo, bishop of Bayeux (1049/50–1097)', *Speculum*, 50 (1975), 7–10, 15–17.
[3] LDB:275b (NFK:66–41); LDB:14b (ESS:6–9).
[4] *conquisivit*, LDB:124b (NFK:1,21–2).   [5] LDB:1a; also Suffolk, 281a.

'reigning'.[6] But in general, the principle was that he was referred to only as 'Harold' or 'Earl Harold'; his reign was simply 'in the time of Harold', or 'after King Edward's death'.[7] The Normans were good at propaganda, and at rewriting history. Great Domesday is uncompromising: harsher even than the Bayeux Tapestry, where Harold is given the title 'duke' before his coronation, and 'king' afterwards, if only to emphasize his perfidy and fall. The Domesday record was intended to ensure that there could be no return to the Danish line or to the Godwinesons; the Conqueror had become the crowned ruler, and his apportionment of the country was to be upheld in the courts, sworn to, and written down.

This severe document occasionally retains signs that the men in Domesday were not, as yet, the established names of some of England's oldest great families, but for the most part an upstart group of landed pirates apt to denote their followers by expressive, even crude names. We see the newness of the group in the useful, indeed indispensable, presence of the few interpreters and those skilled in Latin.[8] The physical vulnerability of even the tough military elite is implied in the several lands given to the king's physician, Nigel, by other great landholders.[9] Uncomplimentary characteristics were perpetuated in such epithets as Hugh Lasne, 'Hugh the Ass', nonetheless a tenant-in-chief in several counties.[10] Norman the Fat held burgages in Lincoln and Richard the Frail in Nottingham.[11] Sobriquets were not uncommon, such as William the Goat and Ralph Crooked Hands: perhaps the latter suffered from arthritis, or from Dupuytren's contracture—common amongst peoples of Scandinavian ancestry.[12] Less respectable activities were commemorated for posterity by the record of land held by 'a certain concubine of Nigel',[13] while Essex landholders included Robert the Pervert—probably to be identified with Robert the Lascivious, Humphrey *Aurei Testiculi*, and Roger May-God-save-the-ladies, *Deus dominas salveat*—or was Roger just a convivial toast-master?[14]

Tiny clues to the lives of successful career women are permitted us. Ælfgyth *Puella* worked successively for King Edward and King William in orphrey—embroidery in gold thread: her work for the former had won the spinster two hides of land in Buckinghamshire from the royal demesne, which she was entitled to sell or dispose of as she wished; and she had held a further half-hide of royal demesne for as long as the Anglo-Saxon Godric was sheriff, in order that she should teach Godric's daughter her skill.[15] One Leofgyth too, was able, despite her marriage and widowhood, to hold her position as embroiderer in gold thread to the king and queen: in 1086 she still held

   [6] GDB:38b (HAM:1,12–13).   [7] e.g. GDB:80d (DOR:34,8); 162d (GLS:1,1).
   [8] Interpreters: GDB:36d (SUR:36,8), 73c (WIL:66,8), 83b (DOR:54,7), 99b (SOM:45,9–11). Latimers: GDB:50d (HAM:NF10,3), 180c (HEF:1,36); LDB:101a (ESS:90,42); GDB:6c (KEN:5,19). Discussed Ch. 3 in this volume, pp. 56–8.
   [9] GDB:73a–b.   [10] GDB:337b, 73a.
   [11] GDB:336a (LIN:C3), 280a (NTT:B16).
   [12] GDB:100b (DEV:1,11); GDB:89c (SOM:6,9).
   [13] GDB:214b (BDF:24–16).
   [14] LDB:15a (ESS:6,12), 66b (ESS:32,28), 100b (ESS:90,30),1a, 96b.
   [15] GDB:149b (BUK:19,3).

three hides of land that her husband had held before the Conquest.[16] Thus, for a few Englishmen and Englishwomen continuity of landholding was possible as the Conqueror and his queen proved keen to retain skilled personnel associated with the Anglo-Saxon monarchy. A king's *joculator* or jester held land in Wales near to the castle of Strigueil; his record occurs in an annex to the city of Gloucester: did his duties include the amusement of the Christmas court held there in 1085?[17] One Adelina, a female jester, *joculatrix*, retained a mere virgate of land—the basic peasant holding—that had been given her by Earl Roger of Hereford, who had forfeited his land in 1075, on the now-royal manor in Hampshire.[18]

Yet, for enlightenment on the characters most vital to Domesday Book—the mastermind who planned the enterprise and the ways its data might be employed, the scribe who laboured to condense it and his assistant, or supervisor, who checked it, we look in vain. In the philosophy of the age, King William had commanded and authorized the Survey. In the words of one writ of William II, the Domesday returns, when consulted, were termed 'my writings in my treasury of Winchester' and, in another writ, 'the royal book'.[19] It recorded the land that William I had gained and bestowed, but not inherited. A few, very few, known landholders with skills useful to the new regime had retained their lands;[20] most survivors were now agriculturalists in social classes below those whose names were recorded in Domesday.

To identify the mastermind who outlined the project to be refined at the Christmas council, 1085, and the writing office, royal or otherwise, that produced Great Domesday, or the scribe and his background and training, would all further our knowledge of the administration of William I. They may well have been closely associated. Thus it is worth looking for any evidence of the administrator whose right-hand scribe may have abbreviated the unwieldy returns into the manageable Great Domesday, and for the possible affiliations of the Domesday scribe—a search that has already led, in the previous chapter, to some mention of Walkelin of Winchester, Osmund of Salisbury, and Robert of Hereford.

ROBERT, BISHOP OF HEREFORD 1079–95

Although he had been given office on a dangerous borderland with Wales, there is every sign that Robert was a man of national affairs also. Prior to his appointment to

---

[16] GDB:74b (WIL:67,86). It remains possible, given the multilingual project and the potential for mis-hearing or mis-copying, that Domesday's *Aluuid*, above, was identical with this *Leuiede*. For the complications possible see J. McN. Dodgson, 'Domesday Book: place-names and personal names', in Holt, *Studies*, 121–37.

[17] GDB:162a (GLS:W4).   [18] GDB:38d (HAM:1,25).

[19] *In meis brevibus...qui sunt in thesauro meo Wyntonie*, Van Caenegem, *Writs*, no. 70 cf. LDB:216b, 217a (NFK:17,9; 17,14); *sicut liber regius hoc testatur*, Galbraith, 'Royal charters to Winchester', *EHR*, 35 (1920), 383–400, no. 12, cf. GDB:43c (HAM:10,1) Hayling.

[20] Listed, Williams, *The English*, 99, cf. H. M. Thomas, 'The significance and fate of the native English landholders of 1086', *EHR*, 118 (2003), 303–33.

Hereford, he had been a royal clerk with a Lotharingian background: an obit links him to the cathedral at Liège, a city remarkable for its study and teaching of mathematics.[21] At Hereford, next to the episcopal palace, his creation of a two-storied chapel was further evidence of his Lotharingian heritage and he introduced continental scholarship to the dioceses of Hereford and Worcester, and his cathedral was said to be after the pattern of Aix-la-Chapelle.[22] Robert's well-known account of the Domesday Survey, directing attention to its contentious results and to the role of the commissioners, is contained in a short treatise that he wrote on the computational methods of one Marianus Scotus, an Irish ascetic who died in 1082, and who had spent much of his life in study at Fulda. Both Robert's description of the Inquiry and his organization of the bishopric's lands convey his interest in practical affairs; and no less than eight clerics and ten laymen were available to advise him on negotiations about leases and knight-service.[23] Although the Domesday account of the bishopric's lands is not the most consistently laid-out portion of Great Domesday, this may well reflect the fact that, under Robert, the Hereford estates were reorganized to provide each of the canons of the secular chapter with a separate holding.[24] The city of Hereford's account, however, shows more exact knowledge of its moneyers' payments to London than anywhere else in Domesday, perhaps indicative of Robert's knowledge of central financial affairs.[25]

Robert's engagement on all sorts of practical levels at Hereford did not detain him from full participation in the affairs of the kingdom, witnessing several royal charters in the late 1080s and 1090s.[26] (The border bishopric was evidently thought of as an important strategic enclave, as the royal chancellor, Gerard, succeeded him.) Robert was an early canon of St Paul's, London,[27] and only he could be the 'Bishop Robert' that Domesday shows as the tenant of Bampton—a convenient halfway house between London and Hereford—where traces survive of a late eleventh-century double chapel.[28] With his wide-flung and long-standing experience, Robert continued to function amongst the *curiales*, and is found travelling with the king and making decisions in one of the financial pleas amongst the curial *barones* only months before his death.[29] He had truly become almost indispensable, requiring the king's permission for leave to go to the funeral of his great friend, Bishop Wulfstan, in January 1095.[30] Indeed, it might have

---

[21] J. Barrow, 'A Lotharingian in Hereford: Bishop Robert's reorganization of the church of Hereford, 1079–1095', in *Medieval Art, Architecture and Archaeology at Hereford, British Archaeological Association Conference Transactions*, 15 (1995), 29–47, 34.

[22] *GP*, 300–1.

[23] T. S. Purser, 'The origins of English feudalism? an episcopal land-grant revisited', *Historical Research*, 73 (2000), 80–93; V. H. Galbraith, 'An episcopal land-grant of 1085', *EHR*, 44 (1929), 371–2.

[24] Barrow, 'A Lotharingian in Hereford', 34–41.   [25] GDB:179a (HEF:C9).

[26] *Regesta* 1, no. 301, 1088; no. 320, *c*.1091; no. 328, 1092.

[27] *John le Neve, Fasti Ecclesiae Anglicanae, 1066–1300*, vol. 1, compiled by D. Greenway, Institute of Historical Research (London, 1968), 42.

[28] GDB:155a (OXF:5,1); J. Blair, 'Bampton deanery, Oxfordshire: another double chapel built by Robert the Lotharingian?', *British Arch. Assoc. Conference Transactions*, 15, 47–9.

[29] *GP*, 302; *Regesta* 1, no. 338, Gloucester, 1093.

[30] *GP*, 302–3; WM, *Saints' Lives*, 144–6.

well have been Robert's influence that encouraged the adoption of the abacus as an easily visible mode of audit. (The abacus was known in England before the Conquest: what is not clear is when it was employed in the court of audit, 'the Exchequer' being first mentioned in 1111.[31]) Geoffrey de Cambrai, the Winchester cathedral prior, 1082–1107, comments in a verse epitaph for Robert somewhat wryly on his fellow Lotharingian's expertise with the abacus now that his calculating of years has come to an end:[32] a hint perhaps that Robert and his abacus had made their presence felt in Winchester. A mathematician could make himself useful in the Treasury—possibly by obviating the tedious use of roman numerals in postulating the product of different levels of geld. As Robert was not unknown in Winchester, a possible connection with Domesday resurfaces, not only in the evidence of the Domesday scribe's hand from Hereford, but also in the history of St Katherine—we remember that his two-storey chapel contained a level dedicated to her; and in the further example of the Domesday hand held in the library of Winchester Cathedral Priory in the later middle ages.[33] Perhaps the Domesday scribe had been in Robert's employ earlier, assisting with his bishop's interest in surviving Old English scholarship;[34] or perhaps an association was struck later in Winchester after Domesday. Robert's lasting reputation was certainly that of a renaissance figure, with expertise in all liberal arts as well as with lunar and astral computations.[35]

SAMSON, BISHOP OF WORCESTER 1096–1112

V. H. Galbraith's candidate for master-mind was Samson, a king's clerk later appointed bishop of Worcester, who as one of a family of administrators rather than spiritual leaders was a man in the right mould; his brother Thomas had already become the educated but worldly archbishop of York.[36] Samson was a protégé of Odo of Bayeux, married—clerical celibacy not yet being established as a *sine qua non* in the western church—with one son eventually becoming an archbishop, and another, bishop of Bayeux. He himself had been treasurer of the church of Bayeux. At some point, perhaps in 1082 on the disgrace of Odo from whom he still held lands in Somerset in 1086, Samson became a royal clerk. As one of the king's chaplains in minor orders, Samson was ordained priest only the day before he was made bishop, in order to qualify for consecration: to remain in the

---

[31] G. R. Evans, 'Schools and scholars: the study of the abacus in English schools, *c*.980–*c*.1150', *EHR*, 94 (1979), 71–89, esp. 77–8; *Regesta* 2, no. 963.

[32] *Non tua te mathesis, presul Rodberte, tuetur,/Non alios annos aliter dinumerans abacus*, The Anglo-Latin Satirical Poets and Epigrammists of the Twelfth Century, ed. T. Wright, RS (1872), 2.154; *GP*, 172; C. H. Haskins, 'The abacus and the king's curia', *EHR*, 27 (1912), 101–6.

[33] Trinity College, Oxford, MS 28 ff. 89v–91r; A. R. Rumble, 'The Domesday manuscripts: scribes and scriptoria', in Holt, *Studies*, 96.

[34] See in this volume: Ch. 4, pp. 103–4.   [35] *GP*, 300–1.

[36] For Samson, V. H. Galbraith, 'Notes on the career of Samson, bishop of Worcester (1096–1112)', *EHR*, 82 (1967), 86–101.

diaconate until they were offered a high appointment was a recognized course for ambitious young men, particularly royal chaplains, who had too many duties of royal service to be obliged to celebrate mass daily.[37] Any Domesday connection apart, Samson's reward of a bishopric in 1096 was not in itself extraordinary— William II's appointees were commonly royal chaplains and administrators— Archbishop Anselm was the outstanding exception, appointed when Rufus was dangerously ill and somewhat more mindful than usual of the next world.

Galbraith put forward three pointers as evidence for Samson's leading role in Domesday. First, his substantial reward of the bishopric of Worcester: yet that was not until 1096. Second, there is Lanfranc's letter about the Canterbury's lands to an enigmatic 'dear and faithful S'—the sole direct evidence for Samson. But the import of the letter was that 'S' had control of certain counties and their record, implying that he did not have control of all, and the letter's content holds valid best for the eastern circuit covered by Little Domesday.[38] A more obvious candidate to resolve the enigma of 'S' was Swein, sometime sheriff of Essex, one of the two counties in question, who had followed his father in the shrievalty there; and whilst Swein was not in post in 1086, he had not fallen from favour: he still held significant estates there. However, given that it was intended that Domesday commissioners were appointed to circuits in which they had no personal interest, Swein's candidature as a commissioner in the eastern circuit is not without obstacles. Third, Galbraith pointed out that, in two counties in Great Domesday, the record of Samson's lands was visibly altered. Yet these demotions in the course of the preparation of Domesday Book, with the consequent weakening of his direct relationship to the king as feudal lord, seems to testify rather to Samson's lack of influence at this period; perhaps there were concealed issues at stake.[39]

In short, Samson's claim to be the *éminence grise* we are seeking for the Domesday Survey in 1085–6, whilst not implausible, has yet to be substantiated. Perhaps Samson was the ecclesiastical commissioner on the eastern Domesday circuit. He had certainly collaborated harmoniously with William of St Calais in the past: in 1082 the king had made a grant to the church of Saint-Calais at their joint request.[40]

WILLIAM OF ST CALAIS, BISHOP OF DURHAM 1080–1096

The presence of William of St Calais, bishop of Durham, at Salisbury points to an appropriately disinterested cleric for the supervision of the *magnum opus*, Chaplais argued;[41] and other specialists now incline to agree.[42] Whilst St Calais had the

---

[37] J. Barrow, 'Grades of ordination and clerical careers, c.900–c.1200', *ANS*, 30 (2007), 41–61, at 51.
[38] F. Barlow, 'Domesday Book: a letter of Lanfranc', *EHR*, 78 (1963), 284–9.
[39] See Appendix to this chapter.   [40] *Acta*, no. 253.
[41] P. Chaplais, 'William of Saint-Calais and the Domesday Survey', in Holt, *Studies*, 65–77.
[42] F. and C. Thorn, 'The writing of Great Domesday', in Hallam and Bates, 71; the evidence is, however, 'circumstantial'.

initiative to serve successfully in a dangerously remote location, it was just at this time that Durham was becoming drawn more directly under royal authority—participating for the first time in the issue of coinage with the *Paxs* type of *c.* 1086.[43] Yet Durham was beyond the territory covered by the Inquiry—although St Calais did hold valuable lands elsewhere—and the fact remains that Durham itself was not a practicable base for the production of Great Domesday.

Two directives from King William, previously quoted, offer clues to his background presence. One is the writ for Pyrford, Surrey, witnessed by St Calais and Ivo Taillebois, whose entry was amended accordingly in Great Domesday in the hand of the main scribe.[44] Another is the direction to St Calais at Salisbury to record the concessions given to the bishop of Winchester's manor of Taunton *in brevibus*, and these duly occur at the end of the Winchester section in *Exon* in a distinctive hand and were repeated verbatim in Great Domesday.[45] Chaplais considered that this second hand, not found elsewhere in *Exon*, shares characteristics with that of the Domesday scribe attributable to a common training in Durham; and, of course, St Calais, as bishop of Durham, was likely to have been accompanied by a Durham scribe.[46] Even so, this royal order might indicate simply that St Calais was a commissioner in the south-west circuit, and present at Salisbury.

The political context gives some circumstantial evidence to the claim that William of St Calais and his scribe were responsible for Domesday. That first he sided with, then deserted, William II, as the new king faced a regime-threatening rebellion early in 1088, suggests that St Calais was under the impression that he had some leverage with the king. Prominent also among the rebels involved were, surprisingly, the influential work-horse, Geoffrey of Coutances, and a later chapter here will suggest the direct effect that the Domesday Inquiry had in provoking the rebellion. William of St Calais' resulting trial took place in the Salisbury citadel of Old Sarum in November 1088, leading to his three-year exile: a further drama at the same scene that had witnessed his presence in 1086 at what was probably the destination of the Domesday returns. Moreover, the stand that St Calais took at his trial in 1088 might explain the copy that the Domesday scribe made of an account of the stand that St Katherine of Alexandria upheld to the death against the secular power.[47] But that was hardly the stance of the Domesday Inquiry.

Yet Domesday itself does hint of suitable headquarters for St Calais and the project: the valuable base of the canons of Waltham. The Conqueror, irregularly, had originally given control of Waltham Holy Cross to Walcher, bishop of Durham, as a nearby base so that he could receive Walcher's counsel, resulting in a mere half hide of this substantial manor remaining for the canons.[48] Here

[43] P. Grierson, 'The monetary system under William I', in Erskine and Williams, 112–18.

[44] GDB:32b (SUR:6,5); M. Gullick, 'The Great and Little Domesday manuscripts', in Erskine and Williams, 157–8.

[45] Rumble, 'The Domesday manuscripts', in Holt, *Studies*, 93; GDB:87c (SOM 2,9); DB4, f.175v.

[46] Chaplais, 'William of Saint-Calais', in Holt, *Studies*, 73–5; also Ch. 4 in this volume.

[47] BL Harley 12, ff. 141r–143v; C. Walsh, The Cult of *St Katherine of Alexandria in Early Medieval Europe* (Aldershot, 2007), 115.

[48] *Waltham Chronicle*, 58–61.

Domesday blatantly falsifies the record in stating that Harold was the holder TRE: rather, the estate had been Earl Harold's widely witnessed donation to the canons, confirmed *c*.1062.[49] In Domesday, it is evident that the current bishop of Durham made great use of it as a base; a number of the bishop's retainers, *homines*, were resident at Waltham, presumably consuming much of the head manor's income. The revenues from the substantial manor were 'appraised' by the bishop's men at just over £63, whereas the 'other men of the hundred' testified it was worth £100.[50] This is the only Domesday entry where the locals protest that a larger sum is being produced, and it looks as though the bishop's followers were taking much more from the manor than they were prepared to own. Furthermore, two regime stalwarts, William de Warenne, the magnate who made the most careful returns in Domesday on values, and Ranulf, brother of Ilger, possibly sometime sheriff, certainly a later commissioner of pleas, were both given a toe-hold within the manor.[51] If St Calais did have a supervisory hand in Domesday, Waltham, with its artificially created Durham connection, would offer a prime location for the task: at the very least for Little Domesday.

OSMUND, CHANCELLOR 1070–8, BISHOP OF SALISBURY 1078–1099

Osmund, the former chancellor, had credentials of royal service second to none; and the bishop and his chapter brought with them the intellectual interests of the Continent. The removal of the seat of the see of Sherborne to Old Sarum, a large manor of the bishopric as well as the site of a Norman royal castle, had created a citadel in which the king sojourned to conduct affairs: in 1081 a grant was made there *in camera regis*.[52] As we have seen, the secular canons of its newly constituted house had experience of working as a team, copying a range of texts, and in assisting in assembling *Exon* (Old Sarum and its bishop continued in importance to governance and to the Exchequer in the early twelfth century, when Roger, bishop of Salisbury, became chancellor and regent in the king's absence, rebuilding both cathedral and bishop's palace in grand fashion.[53]) In all, an almost impregnable site seems to have been chosen with deliberation and developed with facilities appropriate to secure either defensive or aggressive governmental policies, a fitting site amongst the dangers of 1084–6 and the pro-active response to them—which included the Domesday Inquiry. On the other hand, in 1086–7, Salisbury was, like many another castle and cathedral town, a building site: the cathedral not ready for consecration until 1092.[54] Cathedrals throughout

---

[49] *Waltham Chronicle*, xxiii–xlviii; *cap*.12, 20–3: S.1036; cf. Ch. 10 in this volume.
[50] LDB:15b (ESS:7,1).   [51] On Ranulf, Green, *Sheriffs*, 48.
[52] *Acta*, no. 268.
[53] J. McNeill, *Old Sarum*, English Heritage Guidebooks (London, 2006), 1–40, at 32–3, 6–10.
[54] *GRA* 1.568–9; McNeill, *Old Sarum*, 15–18.

the middle ages managed to function under similar conditions, yet the late addition of two small entries in the hand of the Domesday scribe to *Exon*, to which Salisbury scribes also contributed, might suggest that its writing office was one the Domesday scribe visited, rather than his continuous workplace, particularly as Great Domesday itself was not an example of the 'co-operative style of manuscript production that was practised at Salisbury'.[55]

RANNULF FLAMBARD, BISHOP OF DURHAM 1099–1128

Rannulf (also known as 'the Chaplain') was called 'Flambard', Orderic Vitalis relates, because he and his policies were 'like a devouring flame': a name given by one of the governmental financial team, and earned and established by the time it appeared in Domesday.[56] As Galbraith said, 'the man who compiled' Great Domesday 'must have been the greatest living authority in 1087 on both tenure and tenants, and as such as invaluable to William II as William I'.[57] On this reasoning, Rannulf, famous as justiciar and 'exactor' in the reign of William II, deserves to start favourite for the title of Domesday mastermind.

Rannulf's strident role in William II's reign has long been acknowledged—by Freeman, as the hated fiscal innovator; by Stubbs, as the architect of feudalism and its feudal incidents; and more recently by Southern, for his contribution to the 'vigorous administration' of William II's reign.[58] Whilst historians have not bothered much with Rannulf's career under William I,[59] contemporaries were in no doubt of his influence under the Conqueror. His already-earned nickname apart, his impact was already documented: it was the Ely view that 'the iniquitous plunderer' was able to ride rough-shod in Ely because he was in the same favour with 'the young successor king' as he was with his father: a view which must carry weight, as royal justices intervened to hand Rannulf the supervision of Ely's treasury and the monks' allowances for some years during the senility of its ancient incumbent, Abbot Simeon (abbot, 1082–November 1093), and Rannulf continued to administer Ely in the vacancy that followed Simeon's death. Exactly when Abbot Simeon became bedridden and called in the king's justices to prevent the further take-over of Ely lands by laymen is unclear, but the indications are that Flambard's consequent take-over occurred between 1086 and 1088; Rannulf's and Simeon's joint issue of a decree on the monks' provisioning being most likely datable to 1086–7.[60]

---

[55] On Salisbury, *Fasti Ecclesiae Anglicanae* ed. D. Greenway, vol. 4 (London, 1991), xxiv.
[56] OV 4.173.   [57] Galbraith, 'Samson', 93.
[58] Southern 1933, and a later version in Southern, *Humanism* (1970).
[59] But see Harvey 1975, 190–3, and Barlow, who devotes considerable attention to Flambard's part in the developing financial administration, *Rufus*, 191–210; cf. also Roffe's afterthought, *Inquest*, 249–50.
[60] Dating of no. 136 by its latest editor, J. Fairweather, *Liber Eliensis*, (Woodbridge, 2005), 263. A date of 1086–7 accords with 'the oldest Ely tradition'; later dates up to 1093 possible, *LE*, 220 n.1. Cf. *JW* 3.317.

Like several of William's lay and clerical appointments, Rannulf came from the right stable: the diocese of Bayeux. As his father was a priest of Bayeux, who later became a monk at St Augustine's, Canterbury, the young man's earliest patron was almost certainly Bishop Odo; and his path to prominence in the king's service may then have been eased by his sometime entry into the service of Maurice, who became chancellor in 1078.[61] That Rannulf attained high office no later than 1083 is suggested by the dedication for a church and hospital that he built in Durham: done, he wrote, for the salvation of his own soul, for the salvation of William II who elevated him 'to the honour of this bishopric', but also 'for the redemption of the souls of King William the Conqueror and Queen Matilda who gave me promotion'.[62] As the queen, who had not infrequently presided at legal assemblies, died in 1083, Rannulf's rise to prominence in royal service was before that. Incidentally, we observe here at first hand the 'verbal subtleties' with which Flambard was often credited: at the same time as he acknowledges his debt to William I who raised him from obscurity, Rannulf deftly manages to put himself on a parallel plane by dubbing the king 'Conqueror'; both King William and Bishop Rannulf became known by their sobriquet as much as by their title: both the Conqueror and the 'Flaming Torch' were *arrivistes*.

Certainly, Domesday shows that by 1086 Flambard had already achieved enough prominence to establish holdings in seven counties. Whilst not of great value, they were strategically sited for administrative purposes: his houses and churches in Guildford, Godalming, and Oxford served him with halfway houses: Guildford and Godalming conveniently midway between London and Winchester and the south-coast ports, Oxford conveniently between London and Gloucester.[63] Like many another official connected with the collection, receipt, or disbursement of monies, and whose activities centred on Winchester, Rannulf also held lands in Hampshire.[64] At one point he engulfed a street in Winchester by enlarging his holding there.[65] He administered the estates of New Minster for a period (and his name was inscribed in its Book of Life—at the top of a crowded page).[66] There were bases in other cities. Rannulf held part of the bishopric of London's great manor of Stepney—as did William the Chamberlain—and prebends at St Paul's, London, at Lincoln, and, 'for as long as he shall live', at Salisbury.[67] Rannulf's tenure at some point of the mastership of St Martin's, Dover, a house of secular canons with royal affiliations, enabled him to conduct the king's business there and would have given him contacts with news from across the Channel.[68] The range of

---

[61] Barlow, *Rufus*, 194–5.

[62] *Durham Episcopal Charters 1071–1152*, ed. H. S. Offler, *Surtees Society* 179 (1968), no. 9.

[63] GDB:30a (SUR:1,1b), 30d (SUR:1,14–15), 154a (OXF:B9).

[64] GDB:51b (HAM:NF8,1–2), 49b (HAM:66,1), not far from Portchester.

[65] *Winchester*, Survey I, c.1110, no. 163.   [66] *Liber Vitae*, f.28v, plate VIII.

[67] GDB:127b–c (MDX:3,4); *Fasti Ecclesiae Anglicanae*, vol. 4, 73–4.

[68] H. E. Craster, 'A contemporary record of the pontificate of Rannulf Flambard', *Archaeologia Aeliana*, 4th ser., 7 (1930), no. XVI, 47–8; e.g. *Regesta* 1, no. 315, 1091.

Domesday properties that Rannulf was holding already points to a man with logistical foresight who could effectively pursue his ends.

Flambard was shortly in charge of much greater estates. These charges, a testimony to Rannulf's ability to administer several great estates widely dispersed across the country, followed closely on the Domesday Survey. He may have received charge of New Minster, after Abbot Riwallon's death, as early as January 1088.[69] Before the end of the year, he was also supervising the lands of Ramsey Abbey, to which was added Canterbury the following year.[70] The speed with which these responsibilities accrued suggests that the intention to record the revenue for that very purpose had already been formulated, and Rannulf's early prominence at Ely as a controller of its affairs temporal a part for him in its formulation.[71] Indeed, the policy—standard practice by the early twelfth century—whereby 'at the news of the death of any bishop or abbot, a royal clerk was at once sent down to make a written inventory of all he found and bring all subsequent income into the royal treasury' was attributed to Flambard's own invention.[72] Immediate advantage was taken of the opportunities for stepping in and managing these newly regularized regalian rights, whose yearly returns were now accessibly assembled in the Domesday data on assets and values.[73] Even single manors fell to his and the treasurer's surveillance, seemingly as a matter of course: Rannulf and Walkelin the Treasurer were responsible for redirecting the late Dereman's manor, with orders as to its stock and men, to the charge of Eudo Dapifer.[74] Despite his controversial reputation, there is no evidence that Rannulf's management, whilst stringent, undermined the long-term viability of the assets; the £300 a year that he took from Durham when it was added to his portfolio of custodies in 1096 was about half the amount taken in the vacancy after his death.[75]

Rannulf's established nickname shows his already-resented influence under William I; yet his activities in the next two reigns are better documented. His professional undertakings were brilliantly drawn together by Richard Southern who concluded that, 'wherever land, or justice, or finance . . . were involved there is the possibility of finding Ranulf'.[76] He was the key official in all three spheres, originating more writs solo than any other official: of the thirty-five writs he is

---

[69] *AnnWinton*, 36.

[70] New Minster, Winchester, 1088; Canterbury, 1089; Lincoln and Chertsey Abbey in 1092, *AnnWinton*, 36–7; Salisbury, *JW* 3.94–5. Ramsey, D. Knowles, *The Monastic Order in England*, 2nd edn (Cambridge, 1963), 612–13.

[71] *LE*, II, no. 140; above, p. 115.

[72] *fisco regio*, *GRA* 1.558–9; E. King, 'Economic development in the early twelfth century', in R. Britnell and J. Hatcher (eds), *Progress and Problems in Medieval England* (Cambridge, 1996), 1–22, at 2–4.

[73] Harvey 1975, 184–6; Barlow, *Rufus*, 233. See also the use of a royal chaplain to oversee the bishopric of Dorchester, *HistAbbend* 1,372–5, quoted Ch. 10, p. 279.

[74] Van Caenegem, no. 66.

[75] *Symeon*, 266–7, cf. PRS, 57 (2012), 102–3; M. Howell, *Regalian Right in Medieval England* (London, 1962), 20–9, discussed C. W. Hollister, *Henry I* (Yale, 2001), 383–6.

[76] Southern 1933, 105.

known to have witnessed, fifteen were witnessed by him alone. Most important here, they include the writ containing the first reference to Domesday as a 'book'; and he witnessed the other two earliest referrals to Domesday data.[77] He was also a frequent addressee.[78] Rannulf was several times a member of a group of commissioners or justices assigned to hear land pleas, serving on two bodies of itinerant justices: one in Bury St Edmunds in 1095, and the other for Devon and Cornwall and Exeter in 1096.[79] He acted on a commission with the bishop of Lincoln, Haimo, and Urse to assess Thorney Abbey for gelds, knight-service, and all customs 'as leniently as any honour is assessed in England'.[80] He was quite ruthless in his discharge of legal duties, and appeared at Canterbury to institute a plea on the very day of Anselm's enthronement.[81] Until the last two years of his long life, he showed an unflagging interest in the minutiae of judicial administration: Southern compares his work in Durham with that of his predecessor in incisive terms: 'Of William of St Calais there remain only formless charters; Ranulf has not only left writs but also evidence of a constant body of officials who issued them.'[82] As bishop of Durham, he served three of the earliest known writs of naifty in England for peasants who had fled from taxation; but before that, between 1093 and 1097, he was organizing similar action on a manor that had fallen into the king's hands.[83] His assiduity in the hearing of land disputes earned him a number of titles: *placitator totius Anglie* and *regni Anglie iustitiarius*.[84] Later, these titles were applied to Roger of Salisbury, chief justiciar in the twelfth century, in overall charge of the Exchequer, whose upper chamber was a court of land title.

Rannulf was concerned with all aspects of the royal fisc. In the field of general taxation, he was held to be behind a drive to reassess agricultural and arable land, thereby producing a doubling of the fiscal liability of the former hidage.[85] William of Malmesbury's verdict on Rannulf was that 'when a royal edict went forth taxing England at a certain sum, it was his custom to double it'.[86] Nor can these words be dismissed as merely the hyperbole of a literary source. Domesday Book records

---

[77] *Liber regius testatur*, Galbraith, 'Royal charters to Winchester', 388–9, no. 12; and no. 10 (1091×1096), *per breves meos*, referring to GDB:87c (SOM:2,9); Van Caenegem, *Writs*, no. 70. See n. 19 in this chapter for contents. Sole witness, *Regesta* 1, no. 322, 1087×1091, and no. 390. As one of the financial management team at Winchester in 1093, *Regesta* 1, no. 337.

[78] Barlow, *Rufus*, 192–3.

[79] Hermannus, 'De Miraculis Sancti Eadmundi', in *Memorials of St Edmund's Abbey*, ed. T. Arnold, vol. 1, RS (London, 1890), 86–7; one of four *optimates* sent to Devon *ad investiganda regalia placita*, *Regesta* 1, no. 378; M. M. Bigelow, *Placita Anglo-Normannica* (London, 1879), 69–71; Barlow, *Rufus*, 207–8.

[80] *admensuratis Abbatiam de Thorneia de geldis, scotis et servitio militum et de omnibus consuetudinibus*, *Regesta*, 1, no. 422; Southern 1933, 107–8. The monastic settlement at Thorney, like that of Crowland, is unrecorded in Domesday. Rannulf was one of the four 'justiciars of England', *Regesta* 1, no. 424.

[81] *Eadmer*, 41.

[82] Southern, *Humanism*, 126; see Rannulf's series of episcopal charters, *Durham Episcopal Charters 1071–1152*.

[83] Van Caenegem, *Writs*, nos 106, 107, 111; 70; P. Hyams, *Lords, Kings, and Peasants in Medieval England* (Oxford, 1980), 226–7.

[84] HH, 446–7, also *JW* 3.94–5; *HistAbbend* 2, 54–7.

[85] OV 4.172.   [86] *GP*, 274.

manors in the East Midlands and tracts of the Welsh borderland where the record of ploughlands doubled the number of the former hidage.[87]

Over royal revenues from direct sources, such as those of crown lands and lands in the king's hands, Rannulf reigned supreme. By 1097, he was alleged to be in charge of sixteen abbeys and bishoprics, all held vacant so that the king could receive the revenues; during Rufus' reign thirteen royal abbeys and nine bishoprics endured vacancies.[88] Labelled *exactor* by several chroniclers, the expression was not so much defamatory as designating his position in charge of incoming revenues for the fisc:[89] a style recalling earlier continental parallels and looking forward to the *rotulus exactorius*—the Exchequer record of royal farms—of a hundred years later.[90] Items from just such a document were evidently incorporated into Domesday in the statements of farms of boroughs and counties. The term *procurator* was also applied to Flambard; it implied responsibility for expenditure on necessities and on military action.[91] Nevertheless, Salisbury and Winchester continued to be a focus of Rannulf's activities under William II; ten out of the twelve writs and notifications that bear his name and a location were witnessed in the south-east of England between Kent and Hampshire, several originating in Hampshire or Salisbury.[92]

In matters that concerned the purview of the twelfth-century Treasury, Rannulf possessed an acknowledged expertise, and that included war finance. In 1094, William II, aiming to stir up rebellion against his brother in Normandy, caused Flambard to raise the traditional English military force of one man for every five hides, which was summoned to Hastings for service overseas. This traditional force was obliged to defend the kingdom but had never been engaged in aggrandizement overseas. However, Rannulf Flambard met the host at Hastings and took from each man the ten shillings furnished by his neighbours to provide for his maintenance (20 shillings for two months was required by the Edwardian Berkshire customs in Domesday) and sent the men home, resorting to continental mercenaries after all.[93] It was a speedy means of raising a substantial sum. He was unceasingly ingenious at extending existing principles to unprecedented profit, straining them until they became another tax entirely. From manipulating Anglo-Saxon countrywide obligations, Rannulf turned to feudal customs. Witnessed by Rannulf and two other officials, a writ of 1095 required that following the death of the bishop of Worcester a relief should be exacted from the Worcester subtenants and paid to the king, on pain of loss of land and goods.[94] This relief was distinct from the demesne revenues

---

[87] Harvey 1985, 96–8; Ch. 8, pp. 223–5 in this volume.
[88] OV 4.174–6; revenues discussed, Barlow, *Rufus*, 237–40.
[89] e.g. *negotiorum regni*, *JW* 3.90; HH, 446–7.
[90] Dom. du Cange, *Glossarium Mediae et infimae Latinatis*, vol. 3 (Paris, 1884), 335–6; *Dialogus*, 125.
[91] *totius regni procurator*, Symeon, 266; *summus regiarum procurator opum et iusticiarius*, OV 3.310; *GP*, 274. Cf. *Constitutio Domus Regis* subtitled *De Procurationibus*, in *Dialogus*, 129.
[92] *Regesta* 1, nos 337, 429, 385, 427.   [93] *ASC*, 1094; *JW* 3.72–3; GDB:56c (BRK:B10).
[94] Hemming, 79–80; J. H. Round, *Feudal England*, 2nd edn (London, 1964), 241–3; E. Mason, 'Brothers at court: Urse de Abetot and Robert Dispenser', *ANS*, 31(2008), 64–89, at 76; *Regesta* 1, no. 387.

of the bishop that went to the king during a vacancy, and was an imposition on a level of tenure on which a feudal ruler, arguably, had no direct rights. But, the whole Domesday Inquiry was based on that premise—that the king had a right to information on, and even command of, the subtenancies of the great feudatories.[95]

Finally, for two years, 1097–99, Rannulf was effectively regent on the king's absences abroad, his co-regent at first being the treasurer, Walkelin of Winchester, with whom Flambard had frequently co-operated.[96] In 1099, Rannulf succeeded William of St Calais to the powerful and independent bishopric of Durham—northern England being the main region to which the Domesday record did not extend. The expansion of effective Norman rule into the area around Newcastle was a major objective of William II who forcibly removed peasants from further south to colonize the region and authorized the construction of New Castle itself, marking the foundation of a town. The first Norman bishop of Durham had come to a violent end. It required a man of courage and enterprise to officiate effectively there.

On the death of William II, his younger brother Henry had won support and was crowned, notwithstanding any claim of the eldest, Robert, duke of Normandy; but it was at the cost of a series of promises about the character of his future reign, promises perpetuated in a charter that formed a precedent for Magna Carta a century later. In this Coronation Charter, Henry agreed to get rid of numerous of his father's and brother's grasping financial practices, many named and specified, especially those concerning vacancies, wardships, reliefs, leasing or selling church lands, and other payments.[97] As regards the perpetrators of such policies, it appears to have sufficed to target Flambard alone, since his colleagues all passed into Henry I's service.[98] Ten days after the coronation, Flambard was incarcerated in the Tower of London, from which few have escaped. In early February, however, at Candlemas, he cajoled someone to smuggle in a rope in a wine-barrel, and, having managed to get his gaolers drunk, at the age of about forty plus climbed down the outside of the White Tower, probably from the second floor (it then comprised one basement and two upper floors) to join friends waiting with horses to ride to a waiting boat, and sail to Normandy.[99]

This was by no means the end to Rannulf's career, although he was deprived of his bishopric at Henry's Whitsun court, 1101, and accused of simony by Anselm in a letter to the Pope.[100] Within months, he had turned his thwarted talents to advising Duke Robert of Normandy, Henry I's elder brother, on the organization of an invasion of England.[101] The depriving of the eldest son of the English

---

[95] For William I's reign see 'An early charter of enfeoffment for Bury St Edmunds', EHD2, no. 220; for William II's reign, *Eadmer*, 39–4; for Henry I's reign, *PRS Henry I, 2012*, xxvii, 90, 71, 101; for earlier kings, N. Brooks, 'The archbishopric of Canterbury and the so-called introduction of knight-service into England', ANS, 34 (2011), 41–62.

[96] Southern, *Humanism*, 189; with Walkelin, *AnnWinton*, 39.

[97] Stubbs, *Charters*, 117–19; EHD2, no. 19.   [98] Southern 1933, 117.

[99] OV 5.310–15; HH, 450–1; *Symeon*, 272–3.   [100] *Anselmi Opera*, vol. 4, no. 214.

[101] Southern, *Humanism*, 196–8; C. W. Hollister, 'The Anglo-Norman civil war: 1101', *EHR*, 88 (1973), 322–33.

inheritance was not, in fact, a total abrogation of current Norman practice. From their fathers, who were a generation of military colonizers, the eldest sons often inherited the patrimony in Normandy, while younger sons were handed the *acquêt,* or acquired land.[102] Anyway, on William I's death, Robert had held onto Normandy and Maine, while the much more valuable England was allocated to the second surviving son, William Rufus. Nor was inheritance of the throne by a younger son in conflict with English custom, where the king's successor might be chosen from amongst the male descendants of former kings. Direct descent by primogeniture was not indeed established until the succession of King John's son, Henry III, whose minority succession provided a council of Regency with a welcome opportunity for power. But once Henry I had been accepted in England, and crowned, Robert had no over-riding claim to the English throne.

This fact did not deter the opportunist Flambard. The Anglo-Saxon chronicler wrote: 'it was chiefly through his contrivance and instigation that Count Robert had come to this country with warlike intent'.[103] In July 1101, the force from Normandy set sail, not for Pevensey in Sussex where Henry awaited the invasion, but for Portsmouth, convenient for securing Winchester and its treasury. In the end, after shielding London, Henry intercepted the now hesitant invading army in Hampshire and bought Robert off with a pension. Astonishingly, the king also made his peace with Rannulf, who recovered his bishopric and eventually received absolution from Archbishop Anselm, yet nevertheless remained in Normandy for a further five years. In the values of a feudal society, Rannulf's turning to Robert was not necessarily unjustifiable: he had served two successive kings of England well, whereas Henry, in turning against Rannulf simply for political expediency, had failed to fulfil his duty as a good lord: Rannulf was therefore entitled to seek another. What Henry's reconciliation meant is not so clear. Did Rannulf's apparently extraordinary restoration mean that he returned to Normandy as Henry's agent, or as no less than a double agent?[104] Or was it the price Henry paid to put an end to fraternal strife and to secure the support of key men whose interests were divided between the two states.[105] Whatever the understanding between Flambard and the king, the former was free to return to Normandy, where he became a leading adviser to the duke and took charge of the bishopric of Lisieux, putting first his brother, and next his own young son into the bishopric.[106] This situation ended only when Henry invaded Normandy in 1106 and gained the duchy in battle at Tinchebrai from his elder brother, Duke Robert, who was then captured and imprisoned for life. Rannulf, however, was now permitted to shift his main attention to England and to his restored bishopric in Durham. Henry had achieved

---

[102] It seems it was a convenient practice, rather than a principle; certainly the Conqueror's sons themselves did not accept the practice. J. Le Patourel discussed the question in *The Norman Empire* (Oxford, 1976) 180–95; also J. C. Holt, *Colonial England 1066–1215* (London, 1997) 120–2.
[103] *ASC,* 1101.   [104] Southern 1933, 119–24; Southern, *Humanism,* 197–8.
[105] Hollister, 'The Anglo-Norman civil war', 314–34, esp. 326–9; Hollister, *Henry I,* 40–5.
[106] OV 5.318–23; Southern 1933, 118–24.

his Normandy objective; but experience had taught him to be wary of the more than capable Rannulf and while Henry continued to develop his administration under Roger of Salisbury, he saw to it that Rannulf expended his energies and ingenuity advantageously in Durham.

The heritage Rannulf left in the field of architecture and its financial planning remains as imposing reminders of his capability to think anew. Given Rannulf's activities in raising levies from the counties in cash and manpower, both the building of Westminster Hall and the rebuilding of London Bridge came within his competence.[107] Rannulf accompanied Bishop Walkelin of Winchester, and Roger Bigod, in planning the new cathedral and its site at Norwich and in sorting out the legal and tenurial problems of its lands.[108] It seems likely that, as its master, he was concerned with the rebuilding of the church of St Martin-le-Grand, Dover. As the dean, he launched the rebuilding of the collegiate church of Twynham, Hampshire, situated on an estuary important to seafaring, and later known as Christchurch.[109] There, he reorganized the revenues of the canons, allowing their numbers to decline and demolishing existing churches and chapels, in order to rebuild the church with the revenues.[110] He was the right man to persevere with the construction of the remarkable Durham cathedral—much of the nave was built under his supervision— and with the complete destruction and redesign of its urban environment; he also built new buildings for the monks, translated St Cuthbert's body grandly to a new shrine, launched the financing and building of another church and hospital in Durham, built a major arched stone bridge to cross the Wear, and a castle at Norham to discourage Scottish incursions.[111] Yet William of Malmesbury alleged that after Rannulf's initial respect for the legacy of St Cuthbert, he exhibited a sceptical approach and went so far as to remove, 'without hesitation', criminals who took refuge in the saint's church.[112] Such actions seem to fit with his pursuit of fleeing peasants with writs of naifty, which we have noted both during his bishopric and before.

Besides great ecclesiastical buildings, Rannulf left other posterity. He was assiduous in securing appointments for his sons: several became clerics in the household of Archbishop Theobald of Canterbury; one received a canonry; another held a couple of knight's fees. His energies were diverse and almost insatiable: in the north of England Flambard became established as a surname in the middle ages.[113] It may be recalled that the Domesday scribe's hand has been found in a copy of Tertullian's work *Apologeticum*; whether any link with Rannulf existed or not, he evidently took literally the well-known dictum therein: *semen est sanguis*

---

[107] *ASC*, 1097 and see Ch. 8 in this volume; F. Barlow, *Feudal Kingdom of England 1042–1216*, 5th edn (London,1999), 135.

[108] *Regesta* 1, no. 385.

[109] J. H. Clapham, *English Romanesque Architecture*, II (Oxford, 1964), 35–8; *Regesta* 1, no. 361, 1093 × 1094.

[110] Williams, *The English*, 128.

[111] *GP*, 275; *Symeon*, 274–9; *Durham Episcopal Charters*, no. 9.

[112] *WM Bishops*, 416–17. See cover.   [113] Southern, *Humanism*, 201–2.

Christianorum.[114] During the reign of William Rufus, Rannulf Flambard had an English wife or mistress, called Alveva who seems to have borne him several sons. After he was appointed bishop of Durham in 1099, he married her off to a burgess of Huntingdon, but relations remained good: he gave help to her relatives and at the same time found a convenient staging post when riding between his northern diocese and London.[115]

Vivid stories survive of his adventures. In the course of celebrating mass at Huntingdon, he was driven to distraction by, and planned to seduce, his former partner's niece, apparently with Alveva's complicity. For once, however, his plans were unsuccessful—the young lady in question being the future eremite, renowned as Christina of Markyate, with a notable religious vocation.[116] His behaviour was still scandalizing contemporaries as late as 1125, when he had been holding high office for well over forty years and a papal legate was sent to England to unfrock the bishop for his mode of life. Legend relates that Rannulf schemed to deny him his mission: the legate being lured into bed with a young woman, only to be publicly discovered with her by a carousing party of companions led by Flambard. True or not, the legate departed hurriedly, with no further consequences.[117]

Whilst many people were antagonized by Rannulf's vigorous policies, three relevant traits recur in unconnected incidents during his long and active career. Foremost was Flambard's ingenuity and capacity to innovate. Orderic Vitalis, the scholarly Anglo-Norman chronicler, complained of 'the innovative practices he imposed on the people, by which he cruelly oppressed the country and turned the daily chants of the Church into lamentations'. As we have seen, he was particularly associated, under William II, with the practice of keeping important ecclesiastical appointments vacant, so that the king in his capacity of feudal lord could keep the lands of the office in his own hands and receive the returns from them, which now became a regular and permanent policy, and constituted an extension of the royal fisc.[118] Prior to Domesday, administrators might have faced a difficult accounting exercise, but once the values of ecclesiastical lands were there enshrined, it was not hard to make demands realistic. Second, there was Rannulf's driving energy: the source of a nickname that was established in the Conqueror's reign and remained as a sort of surname. His reputation at Durham, which he held until his death in 1128, was that Rannulf was 'impatient of leisure, that he moved on from task to task, thinking nothing of what he had achieved, only that new tasks should take the place of those already accomplished'.[119] Third, was the remarkable force of his personality. His invaluable services apart, it was the strength of his presence, noted by contemporaries, that enabled him to escape the normal consequences of outrageous actions

---

[114] *The Oxford Dictionary of the Christian Church*, ed. Cross, 1334.
[115] Southern, *Humanism*, 201–2; Barlow, *Rufus*, 197.
[116] *The Life of Christina of Markyate*, ed. C. H. Talbot (Oxford, 1987), 40.
[117] *AnnWinton*, 47–8; *GP*, 274, describes similar carousing.
[118] OV 4.170–5.   [119] *Symeon*, 276–9.

and dangerous situations, to carry novel and daring projects to completion, and to persuade others to assist him.

THE DOMESDAY CONNECTION

In all, Rannulf Flambard had the originality, the energy, and the initiative to conceive of just such an unprecedented inquiry as Domesday, and the unquestionable administrative ability to see it through to completion, however unpopular.[120] Domesday's threefold concerns—to establish the platform of Norman tenure, to record the values of all land for use in fiscal feudalism, and to re-evaluate the current assessments for taxation—were precisely those of Rannulf's professional expertise.[121] Underlining the affinity between Rannulf's interests and those of Domesday Book is the detailed Domesday-like text, the Inquest of Ely, for the abbey's lands in six counties, its preface supplying the only known version of the questions asked by the Domesday inquiry—its 'terms of reference'.[122] Although only late twelfth-century copies survive, the original text was certainly drawn up by someone with access to the early returns of the Domesday Inquiry, as it contains information on demesne livestock and the names of the jurors in fifteen Cambridgeshire hundreds and four hundreds in Hertfordshire who bore witness in the court session of the Inquiry: neither of which are preserved in Domesday. The *IE* was, it appears, constructed from the returns of three different Domesday circuits.[123] An Ely source records how, on Rannulf's 'personal initiative, the estates belonging to the jurisdiction of St Æthelthryth were recorded fully in writing and defined by the sworn testimony of reliable men'.[124]

Moreover, the Ely Inquest supplies three other categories of information not routinely included in Great Domesday.[125] Importantly, it contains a précis of the total extent and annual value of the Ely lands in each of six counties and by how much the annual value had been augmented in the hands of Abbot Simeon, who was appointed in 1082. There were summaries of the sizes of holdings of the knights; of the men of the estate and their ploughs; and their values—in different counties and also in total.[126] The text also includes the abbey's claims to estates that had been alienated.[127] In fact, the *IE*'s concern with values and claims reflect those items in its 'terms of reference' whose answers are not routinely covered in Domesday itself: 'How much has been added to and how much taken away from

---

[120] Roffe suggested that Rannulf conceived the late creation of the abbreviated Great Domesday between 1087 and 1100, *Inquest*, 242–8.

[121] Harvey 1975, 183–93; Barlow, *Rufus*, 199–202, 233–5; Barlow's graph of estimated revenues from ecclesiastical custodies, 261.

[122] *IE*, 97; EHD2, no. 215.

[123] Galbraith, 141–2.   [124] Fairweather, *Liber Eliensis*, 267; *LE*, II, no. 139.

[125] Described Galbraith, 136–40; R. W. Finn, *The Eastern Counties* (London, 1967), 81–95; Roffe, *Inquest*, 100–1.

[126] *IE*, 121–4, also for the Ely lands of Picot the sheriff and Hardwin de Scales.

[127] *IE*, 184–9.

the estate?' 'And if more could be had from the estate than is now being had'. There is no direct statement that it was the Ely text as we have it that Rannulf command-ed, or exactly when in his custodianship he had the survey made, but as we have seen, the ancient abbot appears to have been incapable by 1088 and Flambard was certainly in command of the temporalities of the abbey well before Simeon's death in his hundredth year, and remained in charge until 1100. Rannulf remains the most likely person responsible.

These are the more obvious points about Rannulf and Domesday; but the folios of Great Domesday hold covert evidence in the individual and unexplained character of the survey that currently opens Great Domesday. Most shires in Great Domesday conform approximately to a model layout: first, a numbered list of the tenants-in-chief of the shire, starting with the king, followed by the eccle-siastical landholders and continuing with the lay landholders; these lists constitute an index to the shire. There follows a description of their lands, largely in the same order, with minor variations. The primary position of the king's lands is the rule, with the single exception of Kent. There, primacy of place goes neither to the king, nor to the archbishop of Canterbury, nor even to Odo of Bayeux, the king's half-brother and earl of Kent. In first place, together with the descriptions of Dover and Canterbury, appear the lands of the canons of St Martin's, Dover. Layout and spacing give reason to think that the write-up of the Index of tenants-in-chief in each county preceded the transcription of the boroughs, but in the case of Kent it appears as though the St Martin's survey preceded the Index: it might well have functioned as a pilot survey. This primary position of St Martin's was indeed felt to be an anomalous breach of precedence by the copyists of two thirteenth-century shortened versions of Domesday Book: carefully penned, one brilliantly illumin-ated, in both the account of St Martin's has been removed from its leading place and placed later, amongst the lesser ecclesiastical houses of Kent.[128] The mastership of the canons of St Martin's, Dover, which was in the king's gift, and where other royal clerks of eminence had held canonries, was possibly one of the earlier positions assigned to Flambard.[129]

Close examination of the St Martin's description shows it to differ in two respects from that characteristic of the county of Kent and the rest of the Domesday in ways that indicate a date in advance of the rest of the Domesday Survey. The south-eastern circuit of counties in Domesday feature the fiscal assessments for two different dates: for King Edward's day and for a more recent date. On the St Martin's lands, however, no second assessment is given, but only a statement of the number of sulungs (the unit of land measurement and tax in Kent) that the canons *used to* have, suggesting that the account was drawn up at a time when some new assessment was anticipated. There is also the absence of the ploughland category,

---

[128] In National Archives Miscellaneous Books E.164/1, called the *Breviate* of Domesday; National Archives E36/284 (formerly Museum Case 6) called the *Abbreviatio*. Harvey 1975, 191–2.

[129] Craster, see n. 68 in this chapter.

arguably the new rating made in the course of the Inquiry.[130] The rest of Kent either enters a ploughland figure, or a blank is left for its insertion: on the lands of St Martin's there is no mention of the item.

Moreover, in common with the Inquest of Ely, the St Martin's account follows two questions in the terms of reference on possible revenue more closely than Domesday does itself. The second section of St Martin's lands concludes with an estimate of the value of its lost assets: 'if the canons should have their right, all these things would be worth £60 each year to the canons, but now they have only £47 6s 4d'. St Martin's Domesday text includes claims—even of parcels of land worth 20d—and rehearses which elements in the St Martin's portfolio are quit of tax and which do not yield the full amount to the canons but to some other party.[131] It is not difficult to understand that probing such matters before a large court hearing, when most units in the country had changed hands by compulsion in the previous twenty years, could generate almost endless evidence, totally unsuited to the making of a country-wide survey, let alone to making it quickly. Yet in the St Martin's lands, as at Ely, we see these questions answered.

By 1086, Rannulf was influential enough for contemporary churchmen to aspire to count on his goodwill or services. He was a subtenant of the Church in several counties: he held land in Stepney from the bishop of London, and land from Bath and Malmesbury Abbeys. He also held land in Wiltshire from the abbey of Glastonbury: as the abbey had been leaderless since Abbot Thurstan's disastrous rule had led to his exile in 1083, this tenure hints that Rannulf might have already been gaining experience in administering custodies.[132] Rannulf's own landholdings exemplify how partial the workings of the current fiscal system could be: his tenancy of Winterbourne from the bishop of Salisbury in Berkshire was no longer liable for tax at the time of Domesday, although formerly it had been;[133] and his two churches and his Surrey holding were not liable for geld either.[134] On his property in the borough of Guildford, the Domesday text permits itself an unparalleled comment: Rannulf retains sake and soke, that is, he does not owe the minor fiscal and jurisdictional obligations from it to another, but retains them himself with, Domesday says, 'the exception of the community geld, which no one can evade':[135] this last phrase might well reveal the only way a hard-pressed clerkly colleague or underling of Rannulf's could quietly give vent to his feelings. Whereas Rannulf's total Domesday estate was not of great value, whoever finalized the production of Great Domesday was concerned that his lands should stand out. In four of the counties where Rannulf held land, 'Flamme' or 'Flambard' has been inserted later between the lines in red. In Hampshire itself the marking is indeed 'flamboyant'. Rannulf wielded enough influence for a scribe to insert a late flourish

---

[130] Harvey 1985, 86–103.   [131] GDB:1c,d; 2b (KEN:P18).
[132] GDB:127b–c (MDX:3,4), 89d (SOM:7,12), 67a (WIL:8,6).
[133] GDB:58b (BRK:3,3).   [134] GDB:30b (SUR:1,14–15).
[135] GDB:30a (SUR:1,1b).

by putting in large letters 'Rannulf Flamme' in red in the right-hand margin besides his holding in Domesday Hampshire: he is the only person so treated in Great Domesday, apart from his colleague, Geoffrey the Chamberlain, who gets similar treatment, in smaller letters, just below (see Figure 3 in Chapter 4).[136]

Rannulf's can probably be ruled out as the 'assistant's' or 'supervisor's' Norman-style hand, since in the autumn of 1086 he was present, according to York tradition, as one of three key witnesses of an agreement on archiepiscopal metro-politan status made on the Isle of Wight, by the court en route for Normandy.[137] Whilst the Anglo-Saxon Chronicler affirms that the king saw some version of the Inquiry—most probably before he left England in October—the time constraint can only have meant that these were unabbreviated returns, not Great Domesday itself. There was, however, sufficient time for Rannulf and others to have engaged in deliberations on the mode of the abbreviated record before the king left for Normandy, and Rannulf obviously had influence on the embellishment of the final product.

Rannulf's official position at this time was keeper of the king's seal. As such, he had functioned in all probability as the deputy of the chancellor, Maurice, and also as the master of the writing office.[138] The two offices certainly went together in Henry I's reign.[139] It seems that while holding this post as keeper of the seal, which involved him in the transaction of the king's administrative acts and grants, a remarkable incident occurred. Some landholders who deemed Rannulf's notions—not specified in the account—intolerable, kidnapped him and took him on a ship down the Thames intending to throw him overboard at sea. Rannulf, however, kept his presence of mind; he argued successfully with his captors, and throwing his signet ring over-board (the successor ring survives at Durham Cathedral), got his accompanying notary to do the same 'with his master's seal'—which might refer to the king's seal or the chancellor's—so that they could not be used by the conspir-ators, and contrived, somewhat incredibly, to get them to return him to land again unhurt. The man whom Rannulf persuaded to save him was told he could name his own reward. He brought Flambard to safety and received him in his own house, but then 'placing no credence at all' in Flambard's promises, took himself into permanent exile. To the amazement of all, Rannulf then returned to his post and 'while the king was alive no one could ensnare him'.[140] The incident is recorded only in the Durham chronicle, and its high drama doubtless lost nothing in the telling, its source being most probably Flambard's own reminiscences in Durham, yet it illustrates contemporaries' reactions to Flambard's initiatives. If Rannulf were

---

[136] GDB:49b (HAM:66,1).   [137] *ASC*, 1086. With Maurice of London and Gilbert Crispin, future abbot of Westminster, *Hugh Chantor*, 5–6.

[138] *Hugh Chantor*, 5–6. The writing office is discussed in Barlow, *Rufus*, 146–7, 195; also by N. Karn, 'Robert de Sigillo: An unruly head of the royal scriptorium in the 1120s and 1130s', *EHR*, 123 (2008), 502–53: the keeper of the king's seal had 'no superior but the king', at 553.

[139] *Constitutio Domus Regis*, in *Dialogus*, 129.

[140] *Symeon*, 268–73.

the architect of the Domesday Inquiry, it would indeed have provided a motive for an assassination attempt that has been dated from 1085 onwards.[141]

He held the appropriate office to be in charge of a vast written project. As keeper of the king's seal, he held a role in the writing office second only to the chancellor. The writing office was very much more than a group of clerks: it was an influential body of men. No less than seven clerks of the chapel of William II's reign subsequently became bishops.[142] Witness of the king's seal was much quoted in Domesday as the authentic touchstone for the transfer of land, and a century later the *Dialogus* insisted that Domesday Book was 'the inseparable companion in the Treasury of the royal seal'.[143] At the same Christmas council that set in motion the Domesday Inquiry, Maurice, the chancellor, received the usual reward of a bishopric—in this case, London. But as it is not certain just when Gerard, Walkelin of Winchester's well-educated nephew from Rouen, succeeded Maurice, both Rannulf and Maurice may well have continued to function together for some of 1086.

The only chronicler to associate Rannulf with the Domesday Survey is Orderic Vitalis, who connects him with a 'revision' of the country-wide survey, not of a survey from the beginning. But, since I have argued that some skeletal documentation of fiscal liability already existed, Orderic's use of the so-called 'revision' does not preclude a reference to the Domesday volumes. Orderic states explicitly that 'with the king's consent, he [Rannulf] had all the ploughlands which are called hides in English measured by the rope and recorded, setting aside the larger measurement which the generous English had apportioned by order of King Edward; to increase the royal taxes, he reduced the size of the fields belonging to the peasants'.[144] Historians have dismissed Orderic's account of such a remeasuring as a 'fabulous tale'—albeit William of Jumièges alleged that Richard fitzGilbert's district of Tonbridge was measured 'by the rope' in order to counterbalance lands that Richard had lost in Normandy.[145] But Orderic, although circuitous in expression, stands vindicated on two points. The Domesday Inquiry did record a revision of existing fiscal lists, and, in beginning a new estimate of the fiscal ploughlands, it did set out to double, approximately, the general fiscal liability based on land so as to halve the size and scope of the former measurement. The hides, or carucates, in those Domesday counties that contain ploughland data, number approximately 32,000. The ploughlands in the same counties amount to about 60,000. Significantly, the increased assessment in ploughlands lies mainly in the counties where the value of land averaged higher than £1 per hide—the fiscal unit.[146]

A remaining objection to the acceptance of Orderic's attribution of Domesday to Rannulf was his association of the survey with William II, rather than William

[141] Southern, *Humanism*, 187; Barlow, *Rufus*, 197–8; cf. *Symeon*, 268, where the editor's note places the incident in William II's reign.
[142] Barlow, *Rufus*, 147–8.   [143] *Dialogus*, 61–3.   [144] OV 4.172–3.
[145] *GND* 2.228–9; the leuga of Battle Abbey and its subdivisions was also measured with a rope, *funiculo, Chronicon Monasterii de Bello*, ed. J. S. Brewer (London, 1846), 58.
[146] Harvey 1985, esp. 99–100.

I. Yet a close look at Orderic's account may challenge the interpretation usually placed on it. Orderic reads: 'This man unsettled the young king with his fraudulent suggestions, inciting him to revise the survey of all England', or, in Latin: *Hic iuvenem fraudulentis stimulationibus inquietavit regem incitans ut totius Angliae reviseret descriptionem.*[147] Here the force of 'young' agreeing with 'king' places the reference into the reign of William Rufus, not William I. Now, Orderic was a boy of about eleven at the time of Domesday, he was setting this down in the 1130s, so his editor tells us 'his recollection of exact dates may be uncertain . . . In fact his method was to move from one theme to another in some way associated with it, treating each one in depth, and often covering a considerable number of years before he left it'.[148] It does seem strange that William Rufus, probably about thirty years of age when he came to the throne, should be called 'young' in juxtaposition to Rannulf, of similar age, particularly as it directly follows Orderic's comments on the precocious initiatives of Rannulf's early years under William I. Moreover, in the ecclesiastical sphere, *iuvenis* might imply someone in minor orders, perhaps under the age of twenty-eight or before consecration as priest.[149] Further, the original of Orderic's text has not survived. What we have comes largely from a Caen copyist, not totally accurate, and incomplete.[150] It could be that Orderic had originally put the occasion into King William I's reign, and the copyist had abbreviated the case-endings mistakenly writing *hic iuvenem* rather than *hic iuvenis*. It is only the matter of a single stroke of the pen that puts the 'revision' into the reign of Rufus and, with their appetite for exploiting ecclesiastical assets and their eccentric life-styles, Rufus and Flambard appeared to monkish chroniclers somewhat as diabolical twins.

The Domesday project fits with everything known of Rannulf's career. As an administrator, the weight of the evidence is that he did more than St Calais in Durham to organize its estates and household, whose liberty he placed under two sheriffs and two archdeacons, and more of Rannulf's actions are evident from his peremptorily practical writs than for St Calais.[151] As for Domesday, the influential college of St Martin's, with its array of canons in the royal service, might well have provided a pioneer survey from which the concept of the Domesday Survey could be developed. With the fall of Odo from power, the Earl's depredations in and around Dover could be safely chronicled: the Domesday description of Dover, which lies adjacent to St Martin's fief, takes the opportunity to describe how Odo's mill-race had detracted from the value of the harbour.[152] The 1085 emergency meant that the depleted reassessment in hides, or sulungs, in the south-eastern counties became a problem. The general obligations of military defence, crucial in time of danger, were also determined by hidage. In 1085, the great tenants-in-chief had been obliged to maintain additional forces 'each in proportion to his land' as

---

[147] OV 4.172–3.   [148] Chibnall, OV 4.xix, xxiii.

[149] Albeit Rannulf seems to have become a priest some time before he became bishop, perhaps accounting for his appellation 'chaplain', *JW* 3.94–5.

[150] Chibnall, OV 4.xiii–xiv.

[151] Southern, *Humanism*, 200–3.   [152] GDB:1a (KEN:D10).

the Anglo-Saxon chronicle put it, a controversial allocation whichever existing figures were drawn upon. Maybe Rannulf then suggested the idea that both English husbandmen and their lords could be made to pay more taxes, if they were more securely rooted in economic reality, based perhaps on arable land.

In all, the weight of the evidence for fiscal ideas lies with Rannulf. But the important conclusion here, more important than any identification, is that the candidacy for 'ideas man', architect, or backroom supervisor, could well be made for half a dozen of the ecclesiastics and royal clerks who surrounded the king at the time. And, once the idea of confronting a number of issues was mooted, a not inconsiderable number of literate men of energy and experience, ability and clout, of all-round, even renaissance capabilities, could see the point of the project, augment or modify its scope, and contribute to its fulfilment.

Samson and Rannulf

No direct evidence points to Samson's connection with the making of Domesday Book except the letter addressed to 'S'. Yet, it still might be that he played a direct part in the Domesday enterprise.

As noted, during the evolution of the Domesday project, Samson suffered demotion in his status as landholder. He merits a mention in the Domesday tenant-in-chief index of Staffordshire, as head of a college of secular canons at Wolverhampton—and the indexes are thought to be entered early in Great D-omesday—but in the county's main text, the heading is of the canons alone. (Although the canons hold several manors 'from Samson', Samson himself appears holding three manors only towards the end of the entries for the lands.[153]) The net effect is that Samson is not easy to find as a tenant-in-chief.

The other instance of the 'demotion' in the record of Samson's lands has more intrinsic interest: his single and substantial manor in Somerset, Templecombe, worth more than £10 yearly.[154] In *Exon* it was placed amongst the small but independent category of 'French thegns' holding directly from the king; but in both the Exon and Great Domesday manuscripts a correction has been made to show that Samson held this manor as a subtenant of Odo of Bayeux, and Samson himself no longer heads the entry. Moreover, the adjustment in *Exon* was made in the hand of the scribe of Great Domesday himself (only found once elsewhere in *Exon*), thus connecting Samson directly with the Domesday scribe.[155]

Whereas the character of the script of the main Domesday scribe is not Norman, the hand of the secondary, revising, scribe in Domesday is.[156] Thus, Samson might have participated in the revision of material, making him a possible addressee of Lanfranc's letter. But, as supervisor, he seems unlikely to have authorized the demotion of his own land, not unless, that is, there were fiscal advantages to being a subtenant of an absentee tenant-in-chief, rather than a landholder holding directly from the king, as perhaps indeed there were. With one of King William's five daughters, Constance, to be married in or about 1086, the acute former treasurer of the cathedral of Bayeux might well have reckoned that it was better to appear as a subtenant than to be liable for the 'aid' usually demanded on such occasions. In short, Samson's possible association with the project is not excluded.

Some rivalry may well have existed between Flambard and Samson. Flambard's later taking of reliefs from the tenants of the bishopric of Worcester would have

---

[153] GDB:246a, 247d.   [154] GDB:87d (SOM:4,1).

[155] Galbraith, 'Samson', 89–91; GDB:87d (SOM:4,1).

[156] M. Gullick, 'The Great and Little Domesday manuscripts', in Erskine and Williams, 158–60.

rendered similar aids from them to the next bishop less profitable. Rivalry is also hinted in the twelfth-century survey of Winchester, where Samson had taken over Flambard's former much-enlarged tenement. Outside the North Gate 'there was a street there in King Edward's day along which the burgesses used to lead their horses to water. And the bishop of Durham incorporated that street into his tenement. Now the bishop of Worcester holds the tenement'.[157] It is tempting to imagine the two ambitious royal servants, both Odo's protégés from Bayeux, both concerned with the Domesday project behind the scenes: Rannulf, younger, more innovative; Samson, overseeing the painstaking redrafting of the regional returns; each trying to annoy the other without overstepping the mark: Samson contriving the 'demotion' of his own lands so that he was not liable for the feudal aids, based on realistic land values, that Rannulf was planning; Samson persuading the scribe to slip into the record on Flambard's property 'the tax which no one can evade' and to leave out the distinguishing 'Flambard' from Rannulf's fiefs (which might well have led to his being confused with the unimportant Surrey sheriff); Rannulf, noticing this omission, then causing a very large red heading to be added afterwards in the margin to his Hampshire lands.[158] Fanciful, yet compatible with the evidence.

[157] *Winchester*, Survey I, *c.*1110, no. 163.
[158] See Figure 3; GDB:49b (HAM:66,1), cf. GDB:37d.

6

Coinage, the Treasury, and the 'Exchequer'

The Domesday record's intense interest in revenues from land and in the effectiveness of taxation must be set in the context of the progressive shortage of silver in Europe and the Middle East. Supplies were diminishing from the 1040s onwards, as the chief source of German silver production at Goslar, Saxony, became depleted and remained so until the opening up of alternative sources at Freiberg in Meissen and in northern Italy in the mid twelfth century.[1] A decline in the quality of Byzantine gold currency began in 1034, later becoming so pronounced that around 1090 gold had virtually disappeared from the content of its coins, signalling that gold too had become scarce.[2] Meanwhile, conquest and demands for tribute and tax from first Danes and then Normans were draining both silver and gold from England. Even so, eleventh-century England relied much on its silver currency; the number of active moneyers and dies represented in the surviving English coinage was extraordinary, and the very period of the Domesday Survey was marked by a surprisingly large issue of coin.

The economy was geared to foreign trade, and monetization clearly reached into the life of every village before the Norman Conquest. Not only landlords but reeves and men of the hundred could estimate the returns from large herds in terms of pounds, shillings, and pence, and occasionally in marks. Although a round halfpenny was to be issued briefly in Henry I's reign, and the occasional gold coin minted for ceremonial occasions, the only standard currency was the penny, a small high-quality silver coin, with halfpennies simply that—pennies cut in half.[3] Pounds, shillings, and marks were units of account, with twelve pence to the shilling and twenty shillings to the pound; the mark was 13s 4d. And although the relationship between a 'pound' of 240 minted pennies and a pound weight of pure silver might fluctuate, the link was never lost sight of in eleventh-century England. Indeed, it was precisely at this time that the term 'sterling' was first applied to English currency (the term may derive from Old English *steor*, firm, because of its weight which now became stable for over two centuries, or from 'Easterlings', merchants from Germanic regions whose trade brought in silver), and

---

[1] P. Spufford, *Money and its Use in Medieval Europe* (Cambridge, 1989), 94–101, 109–12, hereafter, *Money*.

[2] M. F. Hendy, *Coinage and Money in the Byzantine Empire* (Washington, DC, 1969), 5–7.

[3] M. Blackburn, 'Coinage and currency under Henry I: a review', *ANS*, 13 (1990), 63–4; Metcalf, *Atlas*, 84.

it continued to be known as such in Europe throughout the middle ages—since what constituted a 'pound' weight varied with states and cities across Europe.[4]

The abundance of silver coin mobilized from the monetized economy by a high-yielding taxation system was not without drawbacks; it made England attractive to foreign invaders, magnifying its vulnerability to plunder. As it seems that England itself had few native sources of silver and lead apart from those in Derbyshire,[5] English exports, tin and cloth, but mainly agricultural goods and in particular raw wool to the manufactories of Flanders, were clearly sufficient to ensure an inflow of silver for much of the eleventh century.[6] Evidence on the wool trade is direct, yet limited: Domesday provides only figures for some demesne sheep flocks in up to eight counties. It seems probable that corn, wool, and salt—important known exports in both the Roman period and the high middle ages—were being shipped from eastern England to the more developed urban populations of Flanders and the German empire who could offer European silver in return. Certainly, the inexplicably large number of Domesday plough-teams at work in eastern England could well represent the working capital of a corn trade; and the oxen enumerated in Domesday—over half a million in all—seem more than sufficient to provide arable crops for the resident population.

Control of currency is a benchmark of effective rule and so it was traditionally acknowledged in both Æthelred's and Cnut's legislation where the integrity of the coinage was directly linked to public peace and security, *frith*, and placed alongside the repair of fortifications and military service.[7] The surviving coins provide refreshingly independent verification of the efficacy of the controls which ensured that imported silver was transformed into current English coin. In late Anglo-Saxon England, the coinage had been more closely controlled than anywhere else in Europe and the Normans, whose currency was of poor quality, avidly took over the system in its entirety. Even when William made a clean sweep of the moneyers at Wilton, where Harold II's minting activities were already substantial, he replaced them with native personnel.[8] Thanks to the English system of imposing both the name of the moneyer and his place of work on the coins, and to the plentiful survival of *Paxs* coins, about 165 moneyers working in the 1080s are known by name. Two decades after the conquest, there had apparently been no increase in the proportion of Norman or continental Germanic moneyers—eighty-four per cent have Old English names and twelve per cent Old Norse.[9] From the time of

[4] P. Grierson, 'Sterling', in R. H. M. Dolley and D. M. Metcalf (eds), *Anglo-Saxon Coins* (London, 1961), 266–83.

[5] GDB:272b–c (DBY:1,11–15); I. Stewart, 'The English and Norman mints', in C. E. Challis (ed.), *A New History of the Royal Mint* (Cambridge, 1992), 61; other possible sources lie in the Mendips, Wales, Devon, and Cornwall, primarily known for mining other minerals.

[6] P. Sawyer, 'The wealth of England in the eleventh century', *TRHS*, 5th ser., 15 (1965), 145–64. HH, 10–11.

[7] V Æthelred, 26; VI Æthelred, 32; II Cnut, 8,10.

[8] H. E. Pagan, 'The coinage of Harold II', in K. Jonsson (ed.), *Studies in Late Anglo-Saxon Coinage*, Numismatiska Meddelanden, 35 (Stockholm, 1990), 179–205, esp. 179, 187.

[9] D. M. Metcalf, 'Taxation of moneyers under Edward the Confessor and in 1086', in Holt, *Studies*, 284.

Æthelred II, a network of mints for the issue and change of coinage had extended to all county towns and included many southern and south-eastern ports from Ipswich to Exeter. There was also a scattering of mints across the west country— probably for the convenience of the royal household—between Bridport and Gloucester. The number of mints known to have been operating—at least seventy- two under Edward the Confessor and at least sixty-five in William I's reign—were close to the peak reached under Cnut.[10] Under William, the reliance on pre- Conquest expertise was almost total;[11] it was the taxation of mints that changed.

Once well established in England, William did not shrink from making changes in monetary practice, fixing a high weight standard, which was fully enforced in his last issue. As the stabilization of weight of the penny arguably reduced crown profits from the charges levied when coin was reminted, a new tax called *monetagium* was introduced to compensate for this. As both these developments took place in the later part of William's reign, they may have been part and parcel of a coherent policy; but the timing of their introduction cannot be determined exactly as the coins bear no date, being dated only by their juxtaposition to succeeding types. But the coin-type bearing the inscription *Paxs*—the issue most probably contempor- aneous with Domesday—with its uniformity of weight standard at all mints throughout the life of the issue certainly constituted a 'radical reform'.[12]

Coinage was a major source of crown revenue: a prerogative that in England was regularly exercised, and, whilst the possession of a mint was granted occasionally to the highly privileged, it was always the king's coin that was minted. Moreover, the Domesday texts supply the bulk of the documentary evidence on moneyers and on the crown's income from coinage in the eleventh century, and on the crown's control of the dues for the recoinage, *renovatio*, that took place every two or three years. The system continued unbroken under William's rule, marked chiefly by a tighter control over the standard weights of coins and an increase in the profits taken from the crown monopoly of dies. The element of propaganda, moreover, was not entirely missing: in what seems to be the last issue of his reign—coinciding with the Danish threat and Domesday—William issued coins bearing the inscrip- tion *Paxs*, in addition to the customary images of a cross and of the king.

In passing, Domesday provides sufficient data, albeit in fragmentary fashion, to indicate that control over the receipt of monies was, when William came to the throne, already anticipating some methods described in the late twelfth-century *Dialogue of the Exchequer*. In fact, the eleventh-century government's powers over coinage seem comparable to those of the twelfth-century Exchequer, lacking only the eponymous chequer board. Perhaps because the payments recorded in Domes- day included new arrangements alongside those of earlier systems, they reflect a

---

[10] J. J. North, *English Hammered Coinage: Early Anglo-Saxon to Henry III* (London, 1980), mints and moneyers listed 122–8, 131–5; 142–4.

[11] Four moneyers of Harold II disappeared from Cambridge: M. Allen, 'The Cambridge mint after the Norman Conquest', *The Numismatic Chronicle*, 166 (2006), 239–40.

[12] Metcalf, *Atlas*, 188.

complexity that one numismatist has called 'Byzantine': indeed some practices might even have had links to Byzantium.[13]

THE COMPLEXITY OF CROWN RECEIPTS IN THE ELEVENTH CENTURY

In 1086, as in 1066, the Treasury was in command of several means of taking payment and checking coin: by tale, by weight, assayed, newly minted 'white' pennies—all of which could be further required to be at 20d *in ora*. The origin of the different methods is probably historic, each mode fulfilling a requirement current at the time of introduction (see Table 1).[14]

Methods of payment in coin and silver in Domesday

Domesday is generally acknowledged to incorporate three forms of money payments, or 'specifications':

1. by counting at face value (*ad numerum, ad compotum*)—also known as 'by tale'
2. by weight (*ad pensum, ad pondus*)
3. assayed or blanch or white (*ad arsuram et pensum, arsas et pensatas, blancas, candidas, albas,* and other variants of these)

The third set of specifications—'melted/smelted and weighed', 'blanch' and 'white'—are often taken to refer to the assay: melting down the coin, removing impurities, and weighing the resulting silver.[15] Yet this category may have been over-simplified: these Domesday references are not identical, but seem to refer to different stages of the process of ascertaining standards of weight and purity. Here it is suggested that it should be sub-divided into (a) assayed (b) bullion (c) new coin at the new fixed standard, and perhaps also (d) a fixed surcharge replacing the assay.

A fourth, more enigmatic, specification describes payments at '20 pence in the ora' (*de denariis xx in ora, xx in ora*). It is confined to Domesday texts alone, and may well be associated either with the change to the new standard introduced with

---

[13] M. Dolley, in *Anglo-Saxon Coins*, 155; developed by P. Nightingale, 'The evolution of weight standards and the creation of new monetary and commercial links in northern Europe from the tenth to the twelfth century', *ECHR*, 2nd ser., 38 (1985), esp. 195–209.

[14] P. Stafford, 'The "farm of one night" and the organization of King Edward's estates in Domesday', *ECHR*, 2nd ser., 33 (1980), 491–502.

[15] S. Lyon also argues that 'weighed and smelted' was not the same as 'white' silver, but with different conclusions, 'Silver weight and minted weight in England *c.*1000–1320 with a discussion of Domesday terminology, Edwardian farthings and the origin of English troy', *BNJ*, 76 (2006), 233–7.

Table 1. Distribution by county of Domesday mentions of coinage specifications

County	By counting	By weight	*xx in ora*	Smelted and weighed	*albus*	*candidus*	*blancus*	Royal estates only?	Gold
Kent	6	1*	4*	2*				1 Bp of Bayeux	2
Sussex	2	3*	1*	1*				1 Battle Abbey	2
Surrey	2	3*	1*	1*				2 Eustace	2
Hampshire	5	3*	6*	1	2*		1 = *xx in ora*	1 Eustace	1
Berkshire	3*	1*							1
Wiltshire	7	8*							
Dorset					1*	1* *Exon*			
Somerset	5*	30	10*		15* + 11qr			1 Rouen Abbey	
Devon	10	8*	1*	11* + 5qr					
Cornwall	1*			4*					
Middlesex									
Herts.	7	1 *albus*		3	1			1 Eustace	1
Bucks.	8			3*	4				
Oxon	6*	2*	3*						
Gloucs.	5	1*	5*	1*	2 = *xx in ora*	1 = *xx in ora*			
Worcs.	2*	6*	5						
Hereford					3*				1
Cambs.	9		2*	9*	7*	5			2
Huntingdon	1*								
Bedford		5*			3*				3
Northants	5	1 = *xx in ora*	4*		1 = *xx in ora*				
Leicester	1*	1*	2						
Warwick		3*						2 Countess Godgifu	2
Stafford									1
Shropshire									
Cheshire									
Derbyshire					1 *puri argenti*				
Notts.	1								
Rutland		1*			1*				
Yorkshire	1*	3*							
Lincoln	1*	3*		2*		1*			
Essex		2*			1*		2*	3 Eustace	4
Norfolk	26	6*					36	1 Ralf de Todeni	2
Suffolk	10	10					4*		1

Note: mention at two dates is counted twice.

* numbers all apply to 1086.

qr numbers 'when received'.

Paxs, or with a mercantile weight for bullion, adopted by the crown.[16] There is a Domesday example of this phrase being applied at one point to each of the main categories listed above.

1. Payment by counting

Payment by counting needs no further explanation, except for the single reference to counting 'at 20d to the *ora*'. It is here suggested that this last specification was intended to check that coin measured up to the new standard.[17]

2. Payment by weight

King Edgar's coinage reform in the late tenth century had sought to enforce the observance of one coinage and one weight standard—those in use in London and Winchester.[18] From his reign onwards the design of the coinage was changed every two or three years or so, weight changes were directed, and the old coinage required reminting. Each coin showed the moneyer's name and was thereby traceable. The authorized moneyers in county towns and ports were required to collect the necessary dies of new design and pay for them centrally—traditional sources of royal revenue that feature in Domesday Book.[19] Domesday shows that the dies for Worcester were sourced from London at the end of the Confessor's reign;[20] perhaps London was the venue for former Mercia and places further east; perhaps control over dies was separated from the general mint taxes.[21] For, under William, it was evidently the Winchester mints that took the lead in standards: during the 1070s they consistently adhered to what seems to have been the official weight for coin, and in the 1080s it was Winchester that furnished the stable weight standard that was eventually enforced countrywide with William's last issue.

Moneyers were responsible for purity and weight; and the port-reeves and sheriffs in charge of boroughs were to see that all weights were marked according to 'the weight by which my money is received'. The ounce normally contained 16 pence, showing strong Danish influence.[22] Nevertheless, the weight of coins did vary: it might fluctuate according to type, or mint, or even within a type or mint. It seems that 240 silver pennies of any one type of the second half of William I's reign

[16] Rarely tackled, see Harvey 1967, 221–8; but debated recently, Lyon, 'Silver weight', 227–41, esp. 232–8; P. Nightingale, 'English medieval weight-standards revisited', *BNJ*, 78 (2008), 177–93; S. Lyon, 'Comments on Pamela Nightingale, "English medieval weight-standards revisited"', *BNJ*, 78 (2008), 194–9.

[17] Harvey 1967, makes a different suggestion, whilst not incompatible with the current one, I am less convinced by my earlier argument than I was. The article does, however, lay out the problem and evidence fully.

[18] III Edgar, 8.   [19] GDB:179a (HEF:C9).   [20] GDB:172a (WOR:C1).

[21] Excavations from London found dies from Northampton indicating that old dies needed to be returned, M. M. Archibald, J. R. S. Lang, and G. Milne, 'Four medieval coin dies from the London waterfront', *Numismatic Chronicle*, 155 (1995), 165–200; M. Allen, 'Mints and money in Norman England', *ANS*, 34 (2011), 12.

[22] IV Æthelred, 9.

would have required the addition of anything between 15 to 28 pence to make up a pound of 240 pennyweights of the median weight.[23] When a number of mints, as in some earlier issues, operated at a lower weight—or even two standards[24]—a central weighing of coin might well have demanded more. Payment taken by weight was obviously designed to compensate for light or worn coins, the discrepancy between that and payment by counting, of course, depending on the weight of any particular group of coins handed over. We remember that Stigand had kept by him at Winchester a record of the quality and weights of precious metals.[25]

The quality of coin in England was high, but even so there were problems, and given the ubiquity of county mints with their facilities for testing and weighing, Æthelred II's code declaring that coin should be 'pure' and 'of the proper weight' might well have carried practical force.[26] Mints cut numerous halfpennies, despite the danger of loss through leaching, fractions of London coin being found far and wide.[27] Yet, everyone, apart from the crown, was obliged to accept coin at face value and, indeed, minted coin had a small premium in value over and above that of pure silver. Certainly, for everyday transactions within England its official, theoretical value remained constant, since it derived not from intrinsic worth, but from its validation by the king.[28] Whilst for the crown, for moneyers, and for merchants abroad a penny's value might be in line with the amount of metal it contained, for most normal purposes a penny was a penny.[29] But moneyers were evidently involved in sufficient transactions to be able to manipulate the system enough to become wealthy men of status.[30]

A feature of the English system, distinguishing it from contemporary coinages in western Europe, was that from the death of Cnut in 1035 onwards a different type and design of coin was issued at least every three years, and coin-hoards prove that much coin was indeed reminted fairly soon after a new type was introduced. This remarkable renewal of money, *renovatio*, gains brief mention in Domesday.[31] The crown is assumed to have profited from the practice of reminting and changing weight standards; yet, just how, apart from a fee from the moneyers, plus a charge for the dies, is not known. However, one of two recently published contemporary agreements from Empúries, in north-east Spain, which had a long tradition of minting and commercial exchange, permitted the supervising party to take a

[23] Calculated from data in G. C. Brooke, *Catalogue of Coins in the British Museum*, vol. 1 (London, 1916); n. 35 in this chapter.

[24] Examples in Metcalf, *Atlas*, 178, 186, 171.

[25] *qualitatem metallorum et quantitatem ponderum*, GP, 37.

[26] IV Æthelred, 6, 9; Metcalf, *Atlas*, 65–6.   [27] Metcalf, *Atlas*, 76–84.

[28] Spufford, *Money*, 94.   [29] Metcalf, *Atlas*, 57.

[30] P. Nightingale, 'Some London moneyers and reflections on the organization of mints in the eleventh and twelfth centuries', *Numismatic Chronicle*, 142 (1982), 34–50; see also M. Biddle and D. J. Keane, 'Winchester in the eleventh and twelfth centuries', in *Winchester*, 400–15, 421.

[31] GDB:26a (SUS:12,1), 75a (DOR:B1), 172a (WOR:C1), 179a (HEF:C9), 252a (SHR:C11), 262d (CHS:C19).

seigniorage at recoinage of fifteen pence in the pound:[32] a rate which tallies remarkably with recent calculations about English coinage (see below).

Payment by weight had a further practical advantage for the crown. Sums laboriously counted out at 240 pence to the pound were at risk from human error, and even fraud: the simplest way to verify a large payment was to weigh it. Bearing this out, in Domesday many of the largest payments made to the crown are paid by weight, and are usually in round sums of pounds, rarely with shillings, and never with pence.[33] Not only were payments by weight easy to administer; they retained the flexibility demanded by a coinage of varying weight standards that prevailed until near the end of William I's reign. But the difference for the small payers might make for hardship: it certainly incurred demur from Englishmen, recorded in Domesday at Aldham, Corsham, and Melksham, Wiltshire.[34]

With the *Paxs* issue of the 1080s, real uniformity was imposed; it reached a modal weight of over 21 grains (1.36 g—a mean of 21.15 and a median of 21.2 grains) for the first time in William's reign; yet even these needed the addition of 15 pence to make up the pound weight. Was 15 pence a pound taken as seigniorage by minting 255 pence to the pound, as other calculations by Stuart Lyon might also suggest?[35]

The *Paxs* issue and the reform it represents has not, however, been dated precisely: the dates suggested range from 1083 to 1087. From the historical context, there is much to be said for placing its introduction in 1084–6 and the stresses and achievements of those years—the threatened invasion of England by the Danes in 1084–6, the heavy geld, and the great administrative process of the Domesday Inquiry.[36] Yet, as both Edward the Confessor and Harold II opened their reign with 'peace' inscriptions, it has been argued that the motif *Paxs* was selected especially to mark William II's accession in 1087;[37] but since Henry I's *Pax* issue was certainly not the first type of his reign, that argument is not water-tight.[38]

3. The assay and Treasury practices

Assaying was a complicated procedure, the refining process demanding skill to minimize loss of silver. The entire sum owed might be subjected to an assay, or a

[32] S. P. Bensch, 'Lordship and coinage in Empúries, *c.*1080–*c.*1140', in R. Berkhofer, A. Cooper, and A. J. Kosto (eds), *The Experience of Power in Medieval Europe, 950–1350* (Aldershot, 2005), 73–89.

[33] Of the 77 weighed payments recorded, many large, three only have sums running into shillings: GDB:65a (WIL:1,12), 172a (WOR:C,2), 230a (LEC:C3).

[34] GDB:65a (WIL:1,10–12).

[35] S. Lyon, 'Silver weight', 232–4, 237. Earlier, I calculated 14, Harvey 1967, 221.
The large Beauworth hoard of predominantly *Paxs* coins contains a number of Types V–VII, but not a great percentage, Metcalf, *Atlas*, 189.

[36] P. Nightingale offers historical arguments for William I's reign, 'English medieval weight-standards revisited', *BNJ*, 78 (2008), 180.

[37] R. J. Eaglen, *The Abbey and Mint of Bury St. Edmunds to 1279*, British Numismatic Society Special Publication, no. 5 (London, 2006), 53–8.

[38] Blackburn, 'Coinage and currency', 57–8.

sample taken as a guide to the quality of the rest. The accuracy of testing depended on the temperature of the furnace, the amount of lead used, and the concentration of base metals in the melt, and was hard to achieve.[39] The twelfth-century *Dialogue of the Exchequer* warned the assayer to be 'diligent, watchful and attentive': he 'must be careful not to stop before it is done, nor to heat it too much, so that it is consumed; the former would be a loss to the king, the latter to the sheriff'.[40] The minimum unavoidable loss was later variously calculated at between one and seven pennyweights in the pound;[41] and, as these were official figures, it seems likely they proved optimistic! In the 1180s the smelter himself was due twopence for the task and, in all, as much as forty-four shillings had to be at hand for the process of assaying a pound, in case it was to be repeated.[42]

Arcane as these processes seem, they were not so alien to medieval people. In Old English a 'mint' was a literally 'mint-smithy';[43] the work of a blacksmith's forge was familiar to all, and the art of moneyers and silversmiths, or 'whitesmiths', largely a refined version of it. Monks and canons regularly sang from Psalm 12: 'the words of the Lord are pure words, as silver tried in a furnace of earth, purified seven times', whilst, in the scriptorium one manuscript illustrator portrayed a mint furnace within a scene of the Day of Judgement, with balances nearby.[44]

English coin had high standards of fineness. In fact, in the eleventh century the proportion of alloy in English coins was small: of 30 pennies analysed, the great majority fall into the range 90 per cent to 97 per cent silver, with most being 93 per cent to 94 per cent; and an analysis of the coins of 1087–1125 proved similar.[45] Given the eleventh-century system of borough mints, a central or regional system for the issue of authorized dies, and regular reminting, it would seem needful for the crown to assay only imported coin or bullion; simple weighing would compensate for wear or clipping and also compensate for official weight changes, unless, that is, the assay was envisaged as a check on the moneyers—which, given the enforcement of a single weight standard at this very time, seems not unlikely.

---

[39] *Dialogus*, 36–40; C. Challis, 'Assays and assaying in the reigns of Henry III and Edward I', in N. J. Mayhew and P. Spufford (eds), *Later Medieval Mints*, BAR International Series 389 (Oxford, 1986), 76.

[40] *Dialogus de Scaccario: The Dialogue of the Exchequer/Richard fitzNigel*, ed. E. Amt (Oxford, 2007), 57; *Dialogus*, 37.

[41] Challis, 'Assays and assaying in the reigns of Henry III and Edward I', in *Later Medieval Mints*, 76; Nightingale, 'English medieval weight-standards revisited', 181: 'wasted 6d in the pound in the late twelfth century'. Normally 7d in the pound was lost in combustion alone in 1230–1, J. D. Brand, *The English Coinage, 1180–1247*, BNS Special Publication 1 (London, 1994), 65–6.

[42] *Dialogus*, 36–8.

[43] See *mynetsmidde* f. mint: *A Concise Anglo-Saxon Dictionary*, J. R. Clark Hall, 4th edn (Cambridge, 1960), 243.

[44] *The Canterbury Psalter*, ed. M. R. James (London, 1935), f.25b; other Judgement scenes contain scales and furnace, for instance, in illustrating Psalm 101.

[45] J. S. Forbes and D. B. Dalloway, 'Composition of English silver coins (870–1300)', *British Numismatic Journal*, 30 (1960–1), 82–7; D. M. Metcalf and F. Schweizer, 'The metal contents of the silver pennies of William II and Henry I (1087–1135)', *Archaeometry*, 13 (1971), 177–90, esp. 179, 181.

In the context of the new concern to enforce a weight standard strictly, the curious and still mysterious Domesday specification that coins should be at 20d to the ounce might perhaps be explained by a later known practice. Used coin, in subsequent centuries, was officially permitted a more lenient discrepancy between counted and weighed coin than was permitted to new coin—leeways that clearly changed with time and circumstance.[46] Underweight in used coin ran the risk of confiscation by the Treasury as not legal tender. But, when new coin was underweight, the moneyers stood culpable for their work, and penalties were severe. Before taking a sample for the assay, the knight silversmith in the *Dialogus* first counted 'the number of pence to see from their number whether they are of lawful weight'.[47] Certainly, during the 1248 coinage reform, newly issued money was examined and assayed in order to check its standard.[48] Just such a practice might well lie behind the unique Domesday requirements for payments of pennies '20 *in ora*'.

Yet, in reality, the various modes of payment may have been more similar than all these distinctions might suggest, since weighing was key to every practice, from assaying to a check on counting: in the *Dialogus* counted coin was weighed in bowls 'lest there should have been an error in the counting'.[49] When William I died and his youngest son Henry was bequeathed £5,000 from the Treasury, Henry insisted on 'having it carefully weighed to make sure that nothing was withheld'.[50] Demands for new pence involved weighing when the money was changed and the assaying process itself, of course, involved weighing at several points. All large Domesday sums received by the crown were probably weighed as part of the successful drive to stabilize the weight of coin in the contemporary *Paxs* issue. Some form of weighing, therefore, was almost always on the cards. Few Domesday revenues exceeded £150, and so presented no insuperable difficulties in handling or transport.

By the end of his reign, William had tightened up royal control. Precise dating aside, the administrative success of the second part of the Conqueror's reign can be measured by the general enforcement of a single weight standard. As far as we can gather from Domesday, the aim seems to have been to maintain a high standard and to use various methods to check on the sheriff's supervision of moneyers in his locality and the number of pence in the pound weight. The introduction of a stable weight in the *Paxs* issue that, once up and running, reduced the loss involved in exchanges, might also have formed part of a belated attempt to placate the English people.[51]

---

[46] Money underweight by more than 6d in the pound ought not to be legal tender; new and used rates discussed, *Dialogus*, 39. In *c.*1248, new money of less than 6d in the pound underweight was acceptable; old money was allowed to be deficient by up to 10d in the pound before it went to the assay; different rates were set in 1280 and 1284: *The De moneta of Nicholas Oresme, and English Mint Documents*, tr. and ed. C. Johnson (London, 1956), 52, 54; 'Money must be cut so that there are not more than six heavy and six light in the pound': *Mint Documents*, 87, cf. 92.

[47] *Dialogus*, 36.   [48] *Mint Documents*, 53.   [49] *Dialogus*, 9.
[50] OV 4.95–7.   [51] See Ch. 10 in this volume, pp. 311–12, 319, 325.

RENOVATIO, THE TREASURY, AND THE HUNDRED

Almost all Domesday payments with special stipulations regarding coinage come from royal estates or boroughs—and from some estates in the king's hands, such as those of Odo.[52] It was not just a matter of 'the king's book' concerning itself more with the king's receipts than those of other lords. Only crown officials could make the stipulations discussed above; everyone else was obliged to accept the king's coinage: no one was to 'refuse pure money of proper weight in whatsoever town in my kingdom it be coined'.[53] Regulations were enforced and reinforced. The Christmas council of 1100 exhorted the shire authorities of Worcestershire—bishop, sheriff, and barons, French, and English—to enforce the laws against false coining, a directive doubtless circulated to all shires.[54] Later, the sheriff's accounting commitments obliged him to supervise the mints and to keep check on the moneyers to ensure that their weights were good.[55] But supervision was not simple; many counties had several minting sites, and even in the county town moneyers functioned from independent premises. At Winchester no less than six different workshops with eighteen forges operated; however, until the Norman castle was built, five of them worked in the busiest street, near the Anglo-Saxon governmental nucleus.[56] Mints were also moveable, sometimes necessarily so.[57] Portable mints followed armies, enabling regular payment—an effective means of containing indiscipline, desertion, and looting: the Hereford moneyers were obliged to follow the king's army into Wales, not a greatly popular place for English soldiers.[58]

In practice, it might well have been the payment of borough and hundredal dues and revenues from royal manors via the sheriff and his deputies that ensured recoinage was enforced in the eleventh century and through which it spread through the economy.[59] Local and borough reeves, required to witness sales over 4d, could have insisted that the dues of 1d or 4d paid to them by both buyer and seller for witnessing the sale of a horse or a slave were in coin of the latest type, bearing the current image.[60] They were evidently expected to be in a position to detect forgers.[61] Their supervisory role could also have extended to the coins handed over to the seller, enforcing their up-dating, too; indeed, in near-contemporary Empúries, in 1102, the right to a seigniorage on minting accompanied the power to require that only newly exchanged money was used in the local market.[62] Five of the

---

[52] e.g. GDB:6a (KEN:5,1).   [53] III Edgar, 8; IV Aethelred, 6.
[54] *Regesta* 2, no. 501.   [55] *Dialogus*, 9.
[56] *Winchester*, Survey I, nos 59–65, Biddle and Keene, in *Winchester*, 398–9.
[57] Spufford, 'Conclusioni', in *I Luoghi della Moneta* (Milan, 2001), 157–8.
[58] GDB:179a (HEF:C10).
[59] Raised in I. Stewart, 'Coinage and recoinage after Edgar's Reform', in K. Jonsson (ed.), *Studies in Anglo-Saxon Coinage*, Numismatiska Meddelanden, 35 (Stockholm, 1990), 455–85, esp. 466–8. But he concludes that legislation on witnessed sales was unlikely to have been observed and so played little part in the process.
[60] e.g. Lewes, GDB:26a (SUS:12,1).   [61] II Cnut, 8.2.
[62] Bensch, 'Lordship and coinage in Empúries', 78, 88.

Winchester mints that had been destroyed, apparently in order to extend the Norman royal palace, were 'in the market'.[63] Through the reeves' known powers, effecting the remarkable renewal of the coinage may well have been less daunting than it otherwise appears.

Domesday shows the combination of royal reeves and coinage requirements at work. Royal manors that paid by weight, or in assayed or new coin, were often also boroughs, or sometimes, heads of the hundred;[64] many of these contained markets. In this way, the reeves' currency responsibilities could be quite readily discharged. Several of the largest payments for the pleas of the county were demanded by weight: Warwick paid £145 by weight yearly from royal manors and pleas of the county.[65] Those old royal manors, once charged with supplying the royal household with provisions for a day or a night, feature prominently amongst those with surcharged payments, and, in 1086, not infrequently paid in the same mode as the very groups that once combined to supply the royal household. Ten small minting sites in Somerset were based either in royal manors or boroughs.[66] The moneyers of Hereford themselves held rights of jurisdiction (sake and soke) which might have meant that they were required to exercise a supervisory role over coinage when receiving soke dues.[67]

The hundred afforded the means through which royal revenues might be easily changed or augmented. Some royal revenues were changed in the course of William's reign from royal sustenance—'the farm of a night'—into reminted coin or coin at 20d in the ora, probably a reflection of the little time that William spent in England.[68] Dues, amassed at hundred manors, had all the characteristics of 'a public tax, a tax upon the hundred, the farm of a hundred, the hundred identified with that of capital manor'.[69] It has indeed been argued that 'hundred silver', 'hundred pennies', the 'farm of a night' of Wessex, and the royal customary dues of East Anglia, and the farms of manors with hundreds situated between the Ribble and the Mersey, were regional forms of synonymous levies.[70] However that may be, it is the case that the counties of Devon, Somerset, Norfolk, and Suffolk contain the highest number of coinage specifications in Domesday.

The sheriffs, Domesday clues suggest, were certainly keen to hand down to their subordinate farmers the financial burden concomitant with the change of coinage; in Domesday, lesser reeves and farmers of borough and hundredal dues, who are

---

[63] Survey I, *Winchester*, no. 58.   [64] Cf. Cam, App. IV.

[65] GDB:238a (WAR:B4), also 230a (LEC:C3).

[66] North, *English Hammered Coinage*, 14.   [67] GDB:179a (HEF:C9).

[68] e.g. GDB:86b–c (SOM:1,1–6;1,8–9). In 1086, seven of these pay *albus*.

[69] E. B. Demarest, 'The hundred-pennies', *EHR*, 33 (1918), 65.

[70] Demarest, 'The hundred-pennies', 62–72; 'The *Firma Unius Noctis*', *EHR*, 35 (1920), 78–89; '*Consuetudo Regis* in Essex, Norfolk and Suffolk', *EHR*, 42 (1927), 161–79 and '*Inter Ripam et Mersam*', *EHR*, 38 (1923), 161–70. A qualification to be made is that the *firma* or *consuetudo regis* included several sources of revenue, not only hundred pennies. Belonging to the bishop of Winchester from Taunton in King Edward's time were 'church-scots and borough-rights, hearth pence and hundred pence, and a tithe of eight pence from every hide; house-breaking, stealing, peace-breaking, thieves, oaths, ordeal, fyrd-wite', Charters, App. I, no. 4.

seldom mentioned by name, were required to pay in specified coin. Haimo, the sheriff, was officially in charge of the extensive royal manor of Milton, Kent; yet the anonymous 'he who holds it' was making several payments, including £140, to be assayed, a responsibility that was surely Haimo's.[71] It did not stop at the large-scale farmers. The high surcharges of William I's reign were widely passed on to freeholders, sokemen, and burgesses, via levies on boroughs and hundreds. Henry of Huntingdon's comment on William's rule was: 'Sheriffs and reeves, whose office was justice and judgement, were more frightful than thieves or robbers and more savage than the most savage.'[72] Even some small agriculturists were held responsible for possible discrepancies of weight: in Domesday Witchingham, three free men with 1½ carucates of land paid 30s blanch, and sokemen on royal land in two Norfolk hundreds paid £8 blanch.[73] Once imposed, these surcharges, like many archaic dues, became immoveable; they became 'added to the farm or estates of king or other lord', and 'from then onwards the royal custom would be paid into the render of that estate and thus might be lost sight of as a distinct contribution'.[74] A charter of 1228 shows a sheriff customarily compensating himself by taking an extra 1s in the pound from taxpayers 'for the blanching'.[75] As late as 1549, blanch surcharges were unwarrantedly passed down the tenurial ladder: one of the demands of the Norfolk rebels led by Ket was to rescind

> the payments of castleward rent and blanch fferme and office land, which hath been accustomed to be gathered of the tenements, whereas we suppose the lords ought to pay the same to their bailiffs for their rents gathering and not the tenants.[76]

In Domesday, the county of Norfolk records far and away the highest number of 'blanch' payments, and specified payments of all sorts.[77] The link of blanch farm with surcharges was preserved in local memory or lord's excuse for an unconscionably long time.

The link made in the twelfth century between the profits of the hundred and the requirement to pay blanch was explained in Richard fitzNigel's study of the Exchequer:

> when the king confers an estate on anyone with the hundred or the pleas which arise in the hundred court, that estate is said to be granted blanch. But when the king retains the hundred court... and merely grants the estate without specifying 'with the hundred' or 'blanch', it is said to be granted by tale.[78]

Already in Domesday the profits from hundredal jurisdiction or soke rights appendant to royal manors affected the character of payments. At Finedon,

---

[71] *ad ignem et ad pensum*, GDB:2d (KEN:1,3).
[72] HH, 403.   [73] LDB:131b; 129b (NFK:1,187; 1,163).
[74] Demarest, '*Consuetudo Regis*', 164–6.
[75] *Calendar of Charter Rolls preserved in the Public Record Office*, HMSO (London, 1903) vol. 1, 68, quoted P. Nightingale, 'The King's profit', in *Later Medieval Mints*, 65.
[76] F. W. Russell, *Ket's Rebellion in Norfolk* (London, 1859), 50.
[77] See Table 1.   [78] *Dialogus*, 85–6.

Northants, the payment in King Edward's time was £20 by tale; in 1086, fifty sokemen in various hundreds owe sake and soke of over £8 to the manor, which was now required to pay £40 by weight at 20d *in ora*.[79] At Hitchin, £40 of revenues from sokemen contributed to the total payment that was 'smelted and weighed'.[80] By 1086, maybe before, a causal relationship existed between payment specifications and royal hundredal jurisdiction. Winchcombe borough, which had paid a set charge (*firma*) of £6 in Edward's time, later, 'together with the whole hundred', was paying £20; in 1086, with three adjacent hundreds, it paid £28 at 20d *in ora*.[81] Thus the holders of jurisdictional powers were already being held to some financial account.

It seems likely that sheriffs in the eleventh century were obligated to bring in coins from their own local mints to render their account, so completing the circle of control. In the Confessor's reign, it was the moneyers who completed the circle: they had to travel in person to London, or some other centre, to collect their dies, for which they paid;[82] and Domesday tells us that before 1066 moneyers were required to pay a further 20s a short interval after they had received the new dies, over and above the 18s paid for the dies themselves: Shrewsbury says 'like the other moneyers in the country'.[83] Surely the second instalment was intended to check the quality of their new product? In 1086, the mints of both Oxford and Leicester paid their dues at 20d *in ora*—thereby ensuring a check on the weight of their coins.[84] The ruling under Henry I forbidding moneyers to coin outside their own county appears to be directed to the same ends (as does the later concession that only Northumberland and Cumberland might present coin from any county, since they did not have a mint of their own).[85]

If the king's interest were fully protected by assaying, the *Dialogus* was anxious to convey the message that it protected the interests of the people too, in that the sheriff, fearing loss from the assay when he paid his farm, took 'good care that the moneyers working under him did not exceed the established proportion of alloy'. If caught, 'they are so punished as to discourage the others':[86] for moneyers, the traditional penalty for false coining was loss of a hand, but under Æthelred they might incur the death penalty, or, under Henry I, loss of both hands and castration.[87] For the sheriff, his standing with the crown, indeed his continuance in office, might depend on his success in maintaining standards. Given that even a skilled assay lost a percentage of the silver concerned, sheriffs, farmers, and rent-payers were all anxious to avoid the process.

---

[79] GDB:220a (NTH:1,32).   [80] GDB:133b (HRT:1,19).

[81] GDB:162c (GLS:B1).

[82] GDB:172a (WOR:C1). Some regional production and dispersal of dies took place in the first part of the eleventh century at Lincoln and York, P. Stafford, 'Regional production of dies under Æthelred II', *BNJ*, 48 (1978), 35–51, at 51.

[83] At Hereford, one month, GDB:179a (HEF:C9); at Shrewsbury, 15 days later, 252a (SHR:C11).

[84] GDB:154d (OXF:1,12), 230a (LEC:C5).

[85] *Dialogus*, 9; Stewart, 'Coinage and recoinage', in *Anglo-Saxon Coinage*, ed. K. Jonsson, 468.

[86] *Dialogus*, 43.   [87] III Æthelred, cap. 8; *ASC*, 1125.

MINT TAXATION: *DE MONETA* AND *MONETAGIUM*

Domesday supplies much of the mid and late eleventh-century manuscript evidence on minting; yet, erratic in its borough accounts, it mentions a mere twenty-eight of the sixty-five or so mints known for William I's reign, recording some for 1066 or 1086 only.[88] Discrepancies too, occur in its citation of mint fees, perhaps representing different arrangements, perhaps simply incomplete. The annual fee paid by each moneyer in Edward's reign was a mark of silver, plus a fee at the change of type. Domesday provides this information clearly for the four, quite small, Dorset borough mints.[89] Other Domesday entries—for Chester, Lewes, Shrewsbury, and Worcester—mention the £1 per moneyer due 'when the money changed'.[90] It is evident that Edwardian payments were small, regular, and paid directly by the moneyers when, and after, they collected their new dies. William dramatically increased these levies and it is suggested that William was attempting to raise income of the order of £750–£1,000 a year from minting activity. Domesday shows that the 1086 levy *de moneta*—often of the order of £5 a year per moneyer—was substantial in comparison with the Edwardian arrangements, not to say punitive.[91] In King Edward's day, the Ipswich moneyers had paid £4 yearly; in 1086, the borough owed £20 yearly, but had managed to proffer only £27 in all over the last four years.[92]

Another crown levy or indeed 'second tax-reform' imposed upon the boroughs has been discerned: *monetagium*.[93] It seemed to be one of the few indisputable Norman innovations, as later codification of Norman law sees *monetagium* as a hearth-tax levied every third year: a ducal charge for not changing the weight of the coinage.[94] Nonetheless, it is by no means proven that there were two distinct levies in William's reign in England, *moneta* and *monetagium*. Whilst Haskins dated some Norman material from not long after William I's death, Thomas Bisson discovered that 'it is hard to find it in a reference to a tax before 1205'.[95] Mention of *monetagium* occurs only twice in all, and in fact Domesday gives us just enough evidence to indicate that its characteristics were also those of William's raised *moneta* and that both were identical to the *monetagium commune* rescinded, at least at the unsustainably high level set by William, in the Coronation Charter of Henry I.

---

[88] Domesday entries for both dates are tabulated in P. Grierson, 'The monetary system under William I', in Erskine and Williams, 112–18, at 115.

[89] GDB:75a (DOR:B,1–4).

[90] GDB:262c (CHS:C19), 26a (SUS:12,1), 252a (SHR:C11), 172a (WOR:C1).

[91] Metcalf, 'Taxation of moneyers', in Holt, *Studies*, 291–3.

[92] LDB:290b (SUF:1,22g); Grierson, 'The monetary system', in Erskine and Williams, 117.

[93] The phrase of P. Grierson, 'Domesday Book, the geld *de moneta* and *monetagium*: a forgotten minting reform', *BNJ*, 55 (1985), 84–94, at 90–1.

[94] A thorough treatment is T. N. Bisson, *Conservation of Coinage: Monetary Exploitation and its Restraint in France, Catalonia, and Aragon c. AD 1000–c.1225* (Oxford, 1979), esp. 14–28.

[95] C. H. Haskins, *Norman Institutions* (New York, 1960), 277–8; Bisson, *Coinage*, 91.

The sole occurrence of *monetagium* in Domesday in that form shows that it was known 'as the king's tax', that it was levied upon urban property, and that it was the one tax the king did not grant away: William excluded *monedagium* from property and taxes that he had gifted in Lincoln.[96] Similarly, the heavy mint tax *moneta* also was now levied via property, and was not always the moneyers' obligation, but imposed on communities: during William's reign, the borough—or even the county, in the case of Oxford—became primarily responsible for paying it, pre-sumably for the facility of a mint.[97] Moreover, the identity of this with *monetagium* is reinforced by Henry I's Coronation Charter, which expressly rescinded the *monetagium commune*, 'levied by counties and boroughs', 'which was not in the time of King Edward'.[98] Domesday Guildford also refers to a *commune geldum* as the tax 'which no one can evade', even when other taxes are exempted[99]—as with *monetagium* at Lincoln. By 1100, *monetagium* evidently proved unpopular enough in England for the powerful to seek its repeal, amongst other taxes, before accepting William I's youngest son, Henry, as king. Its novelty lay in both the punitive level of the tax's imposition and the mode of levying it—in the continental fashion—with the onus being placed on boroughs rather than absorbed by the moneyers.

The evidence of Domesday thus suggests that the 'two' taxes, *moneta* and *monetagium*, were indeed one and the same, and that by 1086 it was a levy mainly paid by the urban community—and at a much increased level. But in England *monetagium/moneta* could not and did not continue at the level imposed by William I and, apparently, William II. It was already unrealistic in the 1080s in Ipswich, even given its prosperous hinterland and trading connections; it became impossible amid the growing European-wide silver shortages, after the run of poor English harvests that limited exports. Like other fiscal experiments of the two Williams, the mint tax had to be retracted as unworkable in the long term—at least at the new Norman level. The features of this tax in Normandy should not condition our view of its characteristics in England. The first documentation of *monetagium* in Normandy is later than its mention in Domesday and it seems unlikely that Normandy's degraded currency provided the model for changes to the English system. Moreover, not all the characteristics of the Norman *monetagium* were relevant to England for, in Normandy, barons, clergy, knights and their followers, border counties, and the indigent, were exempt from *monetagium*.[100]

However, magnates and clergy, poised for the coronation of Henry I, were unlikely to have put a tax for which they were not liable high on their agenda. Furthermore, the prohibition of *monetagium* in Henry I's Coronation Charter, a forerunner of Magna Carta, does not necessarily mean that its abrogation was permanent: the numerous reissues and recastings of Magna Carta are sufficient to

---

[96] GDB:336c (LIN:C23).
[97] GDB:154d (OXF:1,12), also Huntingdon, 203b (HUN:B15).
[98] Stubbs, *Charters*, 118, *cap.* 5; EHD2, no. 19.
[99] GDB:30a (SUR:1,1b).   [100] Bisson, *Coinage*, 20–7.

show that a royal promise was not necessarily the end of a matter. And although the presence of *moneta* in the Pipe Rolls suggests a similar tax—sometimes paid by the burgesses directly for their town's minting privileges and sometimes via the sheriff and county—the 'allowances' accounted recall the more moderate levels of Anglo-Saxon times: when the number of licensed moneyers fell short of target, the allowance *de moneta* was commonly £1 per moneyer or die.[101]

The effect of William I's extension of the minting tax was probably to lessen minting charges for the travelling merchant community by transferring the onus of payment onto the resident community. In Æthelred II's time, Norman merchants from Rouen appear to have paid higher tolls in London than any other significant trading group: those who came up-river with wine or blubber-fish paid duty of 6s for a large ship and five per cent of the fish, whereas merchants from elsewhere who came as far as the bridge with a boatload of fish paid one penny for a large ship and a mere half-penny as toll, and subjects of the German Emperor with ships had the same privileges as Englishmen.[102] In imposing the mint tax, the vengeful Norman duke was more than evening up the score.

COINAGE AND TRADING POLICIES

The more lasting changes in coin weight standards of the first half of the eleventh century have been given various *raisons d'être*, and one is trade.

With the restoration of Harold Godwineson's family to power following the crisis of 1051–2, the trade pendulum had certainly swung—or, more probably, been directed—to the east and north-east.[103] In the mid eleventh century, production from the Lincoln mint soared to nearly twenty-four per cent of the total coin production and that of both Norwich and York rose substantially, whilst Winchester's diminished and Dover's fell to a low point.[104] However, some multi-type hoards, particularly of the period 1052–65, point to variable levels of control or, perhaps, a conscious policy of permitting several types to circulate together.[105] During 1066, political events again changed patterns of trade and of minting activity; Southwark, the great trading manor of the Godwine family, was burnt to the ground, so it is unsurprising that the activity of the port's mint became thin and sporadic until late in William's reign. Production also fell at the mints of Lincoln and York, the latter's hinterland devastated by reprisals and political

---

[101] W. C. Wells, 'The Pipe Rolls and "Defaulta Monetariorum"', *Numismatic Chronicle*, 5th ser., 11 (1931), 261–90.
[102] IV Æethelred, 2.8.
[103] The crisis itself might have involved trading politics and coinage weight standards, S. Harvey, 'Eustace II of Boulogne, the crises of 1051–2 and the English coinage', in D. Roffe (ed.), *The English and their Legacy, 900–1200: Essays in Honour of Ann Williams* (Woodbridge, 2012), 149–57, esp.151–3.
[104] Tables in Metcalf, *Atlas*, 294–301.
[105] Spufford, *Money*, 92–3; discussed Metcalf, *Atlas*, 94–9.

instability and by the severing of contacts between the Danelaw and its natural trading partners across the North Sea.[106]

For reasons not yet understood, different mints, and some regions, appear to have operated at somewhat different weight standards, yet whatever policies lay behind the Anglo-Saxon system of determining coin types and weight standards, they were likely to have been compromised by the variations that prevailed at individual mints until *Paxs*.[107] Coins of the second half of Edward's reign reveal that the western mints maintained higher and less variable standards than those in the east—the ports of the south-east coast excepted.[108] In Domesday, there was some tendency for 'weighed and smelted' payments and new white pence to be requested from the western boroughs, and for 'blanch' payments to be sought from eastern England.[109] That said, the scatter of Domesday evidence on the changes made in payment specifications between 1066 and 1086 suggest that, whatever the impetus was, it was not predominantly regional, but reflected policy changes from the centre.

High coin production was characteristic of mints at the points of entry to a kingdom, particularly where there was a favourable balance of trade.[110] Coins from ports with mints, small and large, exemplify the control that kings of England, before and after the Norman Conquest, maintained over mints, and over trading activity in general. An analysis of the balance of minerals in coins of William II and Henry I points to an inflow of foreign silver to the ports and mints of London and the south-east.[111] William, like his predecessors, was directly tapping into trading activity and its stock of silver; and, whatever else was achieved, the constant revision and adjustment of coin design and weight standard probably helped to keep much of the controlling impetus with the crown, rather than with the unscrupulous. Certainly, coin finds from the period certify that legislation compelling the reminting of foreign coin was effectively enforced.

Coinage in Normandy, on the other hand, had been of poor quality early in the eleventh century and remained so under William: weak in weight at *c*.0.80 g (12.3 grains) and about fifty-five per cent to sixty-five per cent fine: a contrast to the previous century under Richard I of Normandy (942–96), when it had been of remarkable quality, being 1.2 g (18.5 grains) in weight and three-quarters fine.[112] Indeed, under Duke William, the coinage was barely under control: there are no moneyers' names on the coins and only the occasional mint location; it is not

---

[106] Metcalf, *Atlas*, 188.   [107] e.g. Metcalf, *Atlas*, 178, 184, 186.

[108] See the wide ranging discussion of weight variation, its incidence, and possible significance, Metcalf, *Atlas*, 56–9.

[109] See Table 1.

[110] D. M. Metcalf, 'Coinage and the rise of Flemish towns', in N. J. Mayhew (ed.), *Coinage in the Low Countries 880–1500*, BAR International series, 54 (Oxford, 1979), 12, 15.

[111] Based on the proportion of gold traces in the silver, Metcalf and Schweitzer, 'The metal contents of the silver pennies of William II and Henry I', *Archaeometry*, 13 (1971), 177–87.

[112] F. Dumas, 'Les monnaies normandes (Xe–XIIe siècles) avec un répertoire des trouvailles', *Revue Numismatique*, 6 ser., 21 (1979), 84–140, 89–91.

possible to distinguish the succession of types; and coins could be made at Rouen, Bayeux, or places unknown. Coins of the third quarter of the eleventh century are described as degenerate, evidencing negligence in the making of flans, and engraving. At less than half fine and only about 0.68–0.75 g in weight, those roughly contemporaneous with the English *Paxs* type bear 'un aspect exécrable'.[113] Norman coinage continued to be poor until William's death and beyond, and in general a Norman penny was worth only a third of its English counterpart.[114] Ducal control was certainly not evident in the quality of coin production and coins continued to weaken in weight in the early twelfth century, before being supplanted by the money of neighbouring statelets.[115]

The forcefulness with which William promulgated raised standards in England points to a different attitude to coinage regulation in the conquered country from that prevailing in the home duchy. Well might the English chronicler, in William's obituary, feature the king's stark actions whereby he 'deprived his underlings of many a mark of gold and more hundreds of pounds of silver that he took by weight and with great injustice from his people with little need for such a deed'.[116]

THE 'EXCHEQUER' AND WINCHESTER

Various signals suggest a revival in the financial ascendancy of Winchester under the Conqueror.[117] Winchester offered easy access to Normandy by sea. (Harold had originally expected William to head for the coast in the region of the Isle of Wight, and this might indeed have been William's initial plan.[118]) It was the Winchester mint that, with William's Type IV, ushered in tight weight standards— 19.6 grains (*c.*1.27 g) rising to 22.1 (*c.*1.37 g)—which it upheld for most of the reign.[119] It was to Walkelin, the treasurer as well as bishop of Winchester, that the burgesses of Colchester and Maldon owed arrears of £40 for the mint,[120] pointing to the likelihood that mint accounts were held at Winchester or London but only sporadically brought into the Domesday record: just as Winchester in the early twelfth century could produce data on rents of King Edward's day although Winchester itself was omitted from Domesday.[121] An increasing proportion of the reformed *Paxs* issue was struck in places associated with governmental authority: Winchester's fifteen per cent share of surviving coins overtook London's eleven per cent, while that of Old Salisbury, a mere thirty or so miles away, more than doubled.[122] And, after Winchester's earlier weight standard became enforced

---

[113] Dumas, 'Les monnaies normandes', Group B/C, 92–3; Group C, 93–4.
[114] Grierson, 'Monetary system', in Erskine and Williams, 112.
[115] Dumas, 'Les monnaies normandes', esp. 92–9, 103.   [116] *ASC*, 1087.
[117] Metcalf, *Atlas*, 184–90.   [118] *ASC*, 1066, C.
[119] Metcalf, *Atlas*, 177–90, esp.177, 184.
[120] LDB:107b (ESS:B6).   [121] *Winchester*, 9–10, 1.406–8.
[122] Metcalf, *Atlas*, 188. But the large Beauworth hoard of predominantly *Paxs* coins contains its own bias, having been found in Hampshire.

country-wide, reaching London with *Paxs*, Type VIII, that standard was followed throughout William II's reign.[123] In short, it was the Winchester mints that led the way in reforming and stabilizing the coinage.

Several studies have pushed the presence of an Exchequer-like department from the twelfth century firmly back into the reign of William II,[124] yet Domesday shows that its currency and accounting functions were well developed even earlier. Our sporadic Domesday fragments present a range of competences recognizable to those familiar with the twelfth-century Exchequer. Whilst past debts on dies issued were referred to only in passing in Domesday, they were evidently known and accounted for elsewhere.[125] The link between jurisdictional revenues and blanch surcharges, formally enunciated in the late twelfth century, already existed in the late eleventh century and the Treasury at Winchester levied mint taxes, revised coinage standards, and brought tax collectors to account. In carrying out its activities, the Treasury shared with royal sheriffs the supervision of moneyers and of incoming royal revenues in bullion, and assayed silver, and coin, new and old. Between 1074 and 1082, probably nearer the latter date, William I imposed a single new mint tax generally upon boroughs and counties, simplifying the payment of mint dues, and inflating them.

CONCLUSION

Royal receipts were collected and accounted for in a variety of ways: in kind, in coin by weight, in assayed coin, in coin at face value, or in new coin. Similar methods are recorded in different parts of the country, so these were not the regional devices of a particular county or sheriff, but more likely the preferred mode at the time when the revenues came into the king's hands, or when they were handed over to a reeve. To regulate the new coin standard of the 1080s, it was perhaps particularly necessary to have more frequent recourse to weighing and assaying than when the higher standard became firmly established: hence the complications visible in Domesday and the close control exerted over the weights of coins the crown received. Weighing was common; assaying an ever-present possibility; and 'blanching' became a process at the Treasury, perhaps demanding an assay, perhaps demanding a compensatory rate.[126]

Before the Norman Conquest, England had a coinage of the highest standards and royal control was unparalleled: there was centralized supervision of the issue

---

[123] Metcalf, *Atlas*, 61, 177, 182–8.

[124] Barlow, *Rufus*, 134–213; recently, E. Mason, 'Brothers at court: Urse de Abetot and Robert Dispenser', *ANS*, 31 (2008), 64–89. Cf. similar conclusions on law, in 'Conclusion', *Dispute Settlement*, 228. See further discussion Ch. 9 in this volume, pp. 265–6.

[125] Probably in what fitzNigel calls the *rotulus exactorius* or *breve de firmis*, *Dialogus*, 62; Harvey 1975, 179–80.

[126] See Appendix 2.

and design of coin dies, together with some influence over coin weights. But William did not rest content with its takeover. In the last years of his reign, he increased mint taxation and spread it out to the community. Furthermore, the Domesday texts support the numismatic evidence that the last years of his reign saw William extending his control of coinage to a degree without parallel in his home duchy.

Domesday's details on coinage demands give some indication of how far it was possible for England's rulers to govern the minutiae of dues paid yearly or quarterly by many people. Moreover, Domesday's evidence on sheriffs' revenues from hundred and borough suggests that it was by these means that the inherited system of recoining was enforced. The variety of methods quoted in Domesday for calculating revenues in coin seems to reveal a group of practices in the process of becoming more streamlined, probably concomitant with the enforcement of fixed weight standard. All mints now produced coin at the same weight, making English currency abroad an accepted commodity; but the borough communities, it seems, had been made to pay for this. Moreover, whereas the king and other major landowners, who spent much of their money overseas, stood to gain from maintaining a 'strong' coinage, the rising scarcity of silver made it harder in real terms for rent-payers and tax-payers to meet their obligations.[127]

The period of escalating returns in silver from land was soon to be over. The Domesday Survey may well have recorded its peak, its very launch perhaps reflecting the strains emerging in the economy and the rulers' revenues. Domesday's record of revenues from land, however, furnished countrywide data which the Exchequer could turn to account for decades ahead. It is to the ways in which the land produced these revenues that we now turn.

---

[127] Blackburn, 'Coinage and currency', *ANS*, 13 (1990), 49–81, at 74.

APPENDIX 1

Gold payments in Domesday

There was no regular native gold coinage in western Europe at this time, though first the 'mancus' and later the 'bezant' make the journey to appear in western documents.[128] Nevertheless, English sources in general and Domesday in particular supply a considerable portion of the documentary evidence on gold in western Europe in the tenth and eleventh centuries; 'marks' of gold, as well as silver, occur in both Domesday and the Pipe Rolls.[129]

Gold had a role to play in the media of exchange. In western Europe as a whole, including England, payments were recorded in 'gold and silver', or expressed in terms of—often unavailable—gold, sometimes with alternatives in kind; so in practice their calculation rested on a known ratio between gold and silver. An enactment of Æthelred, for instance, implied a workable ratio when it stated that '22,000 pounds in gold and silver have been paid out of England to the Viking fleet as the price of the truce'; and a 1023 confirmation of a sale of land referred to payment of a weight of gold weighing one pound of silver.[130] It seems that the weights for silver were used also to measure gold and then the current recognized multiplier between the two metals was applied.[131] Ideally, the ratio was regarded as fixed unless a radical change in supply took place.

Gold was likely to have been in particularly short supply in England in the latter part of William's rule.[132] As there was no known source of gold in England for the medieval period, and as, looting apart, gold would be exchanged amongst only a small sector of the population in western Europe, relatively small changes in supply could have a noticeable impact. Whilst the Normans acquired treasuries in England, Italy, and Sicily, the chief users of gold in Europe—the Byzantines—were in difficulty with their gold coinage, reflecting the scarcity of the metal and, for Anglo-Saxon England, 'the record of English finds of Byzantine coins is indeed a sparse one'.[133] When considering the values of precious metals, scholars tend to assume that the unusually moderate ratio of 1:9 of gold/silver at the end of Henry I's reign

---

[128] R. S. Lopez, 'The dollar of the middle ages', *Journal of Economic History*, 11 (1951). 209–35, esp. 228.

[129] M. Bloch, 'Le problème de l'or au moyen age', *Annales d'histoire économique*, 5 (1933), 1–32, esp. 12.

[130] II Æthelred, 7–2; S.960. Also Charters, App. II, no. 9.

[131] *In thesauro vi libras pro I marca auri*, PRS Henry I, 2012, 25.

[132] 'Bezants' are assumed to be Byzantine gold coins; they first appear in English documentation in 1130, and in Norman texts by 1100, P. Grierson, 'Carolingian Europe and the Arabs: the myth of the mancus', *Revue Belge de philologie et d'histoire*, 32 (1954), 1059–74.

[133] P. D. Whitting, 'The Byzantine Empire and the coinage of the Anglo-Saxons', in R. H. M. Dolley (ed.), *Anglo-Saxon Coins: Studies Presented to F.M. Stenton* (London, 1961), 33.

obtained during that of William I.[134] Yet, there is a clue in Domesday that a historically more usual differential obtained, and that the ratio of gold to silver in William's reign was rather of the order of 1:15. A thegn is obliged to give the payment of two hawks or two marks of gold (the mark being the weight of 13s 4d) to avoid trial by battle;[135] as £10 is given as the alternative for a hawk in six other places in Domesday, this entry might suggest a ratio 1:15 of gold to silver.[136]

In Domesday, gold appears particularly in association with sales and with unusual, sometimes dubious, transactions in land: all—nearly fifty—of its gold payments being expressed in ounces or marks. The visible presence of gold made a transaction particularly memorable to witnesses, just as the king issued an occasional gold coin for ceremonial and religious occasions. A substantial proportion of gold payments in Domesday were made to the queen or to people of high status.

Many of Domesday's other mentions of gold arose over questioned title to land, citing a sale, or a gage.[137] The payment of gold further features in rental demands made over and above a manor's normal value.[138] In numerous cases it seems to have been given, often as a bribe, to acquire assets or land from earl or sheriff or reeve.[139] Gold was handed over as a pledge or gage on several occasions:[140] sometimes under evident duress, as when one Eadric had come to an arrangement with the abbey of St Benet's at Hulme over his land whereby he paid £7 and a gold mark 'to redeem himself from arrest by Waleran' (probably the royal official making confiscations after Earl Ralf's rebellion); but by 1086 it was Waleran's nephew who was holding that land from St Benet's.[141] Englishmen and English institutions had evidently been compelled to de-thesaurize their gold and silver in order to try to retain or acquire assets. A *gersuma* of an ounce of gold was required for one three-year agreement for men to farm Blakenham at £12 a year: unsurprisingly the farmers' agreement led to their ruin as the land they obtained was worth only £3, plus freemen worth 45s.[142] Gold frequently featured as a quick fix in desperate circumstances. The bishop and monastery of Worcester had paid considerable sums of money to be allowed by King William to keep their crosses and sacred vessels: 'for the incense bowl, £10', 'for the candlestick, £10', 'for the crosier, 33 marks, and in addition to all this, 45½ marks of gold'.[143] When Æthelwig was abbot of Evesham, he paid the king gold to come to an agreement over a manor which Odo had

[134] P. W. P. Carlyon-Britton, 'A numismatic history of the reigns of William I and II', *British Numismatic Journal*, 1st ser., 51 (1905), 89; Lyon, 'Silver weight', 239.
[135] GDB:36d (SUR:36,1).
[136] GDB:64c (WIL:B2), 154d (OXF:1,12), 172a (WOR:C2), 219a (NTH:B36), 230a (LEC:C4), 238a (WAR:B4).
[137] e.g. GDB:75d (DOR:1,24), 376b (LIN:CW4).
[138] e.g. GDB:5c (KEN:4,1), 23a (SUS:11,3), 44d (HAM:21,6).
[139] e.g. GDB:2b (KEN:P19), 50a (HAM:69,12), 197b (CAM:22,6); LDB:217b (NFK:17,22).
[140] e.g. GDB:31c, 32b (SUR:5,6; 6,4).
[141] LDB:217a (NFK:17,18), cf. 170b (NFK:8,120); also, GDB:75d (DOR:1,24), 137d (HRT:19,1).
[142] LDB:353b (SUF:9,1).
[143] Charters, App. I, no. 6.

purloined notwithstanding.[144] Other monastic houses as well as small English landholders were undoubtedly forced to yield their precious metals to military conquerors who proceeded to expend these finely worked treasures on military ambitions or to endow monastic houses of their own founding.

[144] GDB:176a (WOR:11,2); also, *HistAbbend*, 2, 13, 347 and Williams, *The English*, 9.

APPENDIX 2

Assaying, blanching, and ingots

The four Domesday terms often classed together as 'blanch' seem, on closer consideration, to be referring to three different stages in the process of determining quality.

1. *ALBUS* AND *CANDIDUS*

Albus and *candidus* are both classical Latin: meaning white or bright. Sums *albus* or *candidus*, Domesday indicates, were synonymous;[145] and, as they were often specified *ad numerum*, demanded rather newly minted pennies, to be paid 'by counting'; they were not payments assayed at the Treasury.[146] Several Cambridgeshire royal manors paid significant round sums 'smelted and weighed', differentiated from other sums paid 'by counting in white pennies' (*ad numerum de albis denariis*)—not in rounded sums;[147] the latter could not be clearer in their distinction from the 'smelted and weighed' preceding them and were evidently different in form.[148]

2. *BLANCUS*

Blancus is not classical: often, as in the French, *blanchir*, it is associated with the activity of whitening, as in to lime-wash, to wash dirty laundry, and to refine metal—silver and pig iron. It seems that *blancus* becomes synonymous with the process of purifying a payment: *either* by an assay, *or* by adding on a number of pence in the pound to make a sum in worn money nominally equivalent to a sum in new money. In the early twelfth century, the farm of Exeter is given in one charter as £25 blanch, in another as £25 'according to the scale' (*ad scalam*), whilst the Pipe Roll of 1130 shows the actual payment made was £25 12s 6d by tale, that is, 'blanch' at the rate of 6d in the pound.[149] Yet half a century later, a blanch farm (*firma blanca*) was made white by

---

[145] GDB:75b (DOR:1,1), cf. DB4, f.26a.

[146] e.g. five payments of pounds and shillings of 'white pence', *de candidis denariis*, GDB:179c–180a (HEF:1,1–4;1,6). In Gloucestershire three payments are in 'white' pennies as well as at 20 to the *ora*, GDB:164a–b (GLS:1,56,58,61). A payment from Hereford is in 'white' pence 'by counting', GDB:179a (HEF:C15).

[147] GDB:189b–c (CAM:1,1–1,5).

[148] Nor do they occur together in the same group of payments with other sums *ad numerum*. Contrast, P. Nightingale, 'The ora, the mark, and the mancus: weight-standards and the coinage in eleventh-century England, part 1', *Numismatic Chronicle*, 143 (1983), 254–5.

[149] *Regesta* 2, nos 1514, 1493. The *Medieval Latin Dictionary* (Oxford, 1975 onwards) gives 1172 as the first use of 'scala' in the sense of weighing.

weighing or 'testing' *(facto examine, dealbatur)*.[150] Thus, the term seems likely to have originated in the assaying process, but altered in practical import according to current practices.

In Domesday, payments 'blanch' share features with 'smelted and weighed': first, most payments are in round sums.[151] Of the thirty-six instances of 'blanch' payments in Norfolk—the county's most characteristic mode—several seem deliberately to avoid including awkward or additional amounts in the blanch sum, the odd sums being counted normally. In 1086, Acle was 'worth £14 13s 4d: 53s are paid by counting *(ad compotum)* and it pays the rest blanch'.[152] Perhaps significantly, 'blanch' does not occur in the same *group* of payments as 'smelted and weighed'. Moreover, *blancus* never occurs in the same sum with 'by counting', nor with the reiteration of pence, in contrast to payments *albus* or *candidus*.

Thus, payments 'blanch' appear to indicate sums needing to undergo an assay, in order to be 'whitened', perhaps into bullion of known fineness. In the use of this term, Domesday and twelfth-century practices were not identical; but what they apparently had in common was that 'blanching' was a process of 'making white' acknowledged by the Treasury.[153]

3. PAYMENTS 'SMELTED AND WEIGHED'

'Smelted and weighed' was a cumbersome phrase in the highly abbreviated Domesday text that could only apply to the product of an assay. It was not a new requirement in William's reign: four estates in Devon had rendered 'weighed and smelted' at the time when they had changed hands as well as in 1086: information for the earlier date preserved only in *Exon*.[154] But use of the process seems to have been extended in the course of William's reign; three Hertfordshire payments were demanded 'smelted and weighed' in 1086, yet only one had paid this way in King Edward's day.[155] The significant extra burden in demanding payment 'weighed and smelted' is indicated by Godalming in 1086—valued at £30 by tale, it 'nevertheless' paid £30 'weighed and smelted' *(ad pensum et arsursam)*—the difference between the two being enough to gain record.[156]

Use of ingots was already normal for large payments by the time silver supply was increasing from the 1160s onwards; and, later in the middle ages, the term 'smelted silver' implied ingots. Unminted silver, provided its fineness was known, was obviously more convenient for substantial sums than minted pennies that required weighing, or counting out in thousands and tens of thousands. Ingots were often

---

[150] *Dialogus*, 85, for text, not translation.
[151] Of 43 instances of *blancus*, 35 are in pounds alone, with 4 more including half-pounds.
[152] LDB:128b (NFK:1,151), 127a (NFK:1,139).
[153] *per hanc taleam combustionis dealbatur firma vicecomitis*, *Dialogus*, 38. For a similar but not identical argument, Grierson, 'Monetary system', in Erskine and Williams, 114.
[154] GDB:100b (DEV:1,11), 100d (DEV:1,34), 101b (DEV:1,54), 101a (DEV:1,45).
[155] e.g. GDB:132a–133b.   [156] GDB:30d (SUR:1,14).

marked with the mint of origin—in effect an assay mark, since the standards prevailing in different localities were known. Most ingots were of a fineness usable, if desired, for crafting silver objects and probably because of this handy character-istic few medieval examples have survived.[157] In the 1180s, ingots of tested silver were conserved in specially marked sacks that were set aside to make silver vessels for the king or to send money overseas.[158]

That Domesday's 'smelted and weighed' refers to bullion, not coin, is by far the 'best fit' explanation, one that has the merit of making sense of the phrasing and of the rounded sums.[159] Dover and Bosham supply the two items of difficult Domesday evidence about this process: both major ports where receipts in un-coined silver and foreign coin were common and required transformation into coin or, for the crown, into bullion of known standard.[160]

---

[157] Spufford, *Money*, 209–24, esp. 220–2.   [158] *Dialogus*, 11.

[159] Nightingale, 'English medieval weight-standards revisited', 178; cf. P. Nightingale, *A Medieval Mercantile Community: The Grocers' Company and the Politics and Trade of London, 1000–1485* (London, 1995), 302.

[160] Cf. R. Duncan-Jones, *Money and Government in the Roman Empire* (Cambridge, 1994), 243–4.

An interpreted translation of silver payment phrases

Smelted and weighed	silver bullion of a high standard
Smelted and weighed at 20d *in ora*	bullion refined to the latest standard
By counting	current coin at face value
By counting at 20d *in ora*	coin at face value, individually up to weight: close to new standard, otherwise not legal tender.
By weight	weighed
By weight at 20 *in ora*	coins by weight in coins of the full weight, in contrast to old pence that were 'legal' at a lower weight.
20d in ora	coins of new universal standard weight
White pennies	newly minted coin
White pennies at 20d *in ora*	new coin at new standard
Blanch	sum of money 'blanched' at the Treasury. Perhaps adopted in order to discipline eastern mints, which had operated to lower standards. Or perhaps due to different terminology used in the two Domesday volumes: there is no mention of 'smelted and weighed' in Little Domesday, but many mentions of 'blanch' there.

7

The Valor: The Definition and Import of Values in Domesday

> He ruled over England, and by his cunning it was so investigated that there was not one hide of land in England that he did not know who owned it and what it was worth and then set it down in his record.[1]
>
> *The Anglo-Saxon Chronicle*, 1087: obituary of William I

The international respect, indeed cupidity, for quality English coin remains the essential setting for the sums featuring in almost every Domesday entry. The major objective of the Domesday Inquiry was to find out precisely, in cash terms, what returns were obtainable from land; and defining what these Domesday values represented is central to any account of the agricultural economy of the later eleventh century. This 'value', in Domesday as in other medieval documents, was not a sale value: it referred to the annual income that accrued from land—although such figures, multiplied by the appropriate number of years, were often adopted as the basis for determining the price of a sale or lease.

The 'value' of each landed unit is the most consistently recorded item in Domesday Book. The 'terms of reference' of the Inquiry required all data to be 'given thrice': 'as it was in the time of King Edward, as it was when King William gave the estate, and as it is now'.[2] Given the geographical scope and the disruptions in tenure, the aspiration to collect a complete set of data for three points in time was impractical, yet it was the values that came closest to compliance: thirteen Domesday counties regularly provide manorial values for three dates— those comprising circuits I, III and VII;[3] the remaining counties normally record values for two dates. The only other category of information supplied at all regularly for more than one date is the tax assessment of manors in the counties of Circuit I, albeit Little Domesday records some changes in demesne livestock over twenty years.

---

[1] *ASC*, 1087.   [2] EHD2, no. 215; *IE*, 97.
[3] Tabulated in the regional *Domesday Geographies*, but Cheshire is better placed amongst those giving two dates, as it rarely gives an interim value, contrast H. C. Darby and I. S. Maxwell, *The Domesday Geography of Northern England* (Cambridge, 1962), 497.

THE CENTRAL QUESTIONS AND SOME INTERPRETATIONS

In common with other Domesday terms, the general import is fairly obvious—
valet, 'it is worth': the value was *either* the best approximation of the net profit
from a manor with its associated peasant agriculture *or* the payment of a set return,
or 'farm', whether in cash or kind or both.[4] It was the appropriate level of payment,
valid for the long term, not simply in good years alone. Yet, in common with other
terms, its precise basis is elusive, and conflicting concepts abound.

Wide understandings depend on the interpretation of these Domesday data.
Did the many increased Domesday values mean that the new landlords brought
markedly increased agrarian productivity, or were the Normans, to put it bluntly,
rack-renters?[5] The value data has also been put to use alongside the fiscal data
to judge for whom taxation was regressive, and how regressive. However, when
different scholars make different assumptions about the level of peasant contributions to the money economy and taxation in general, and to the value of Domesday
manors in particular, their calculations produce stimulating debate but conflicting
results.[6]

Several fundamental questions of interpretation still remain open. One concerns
the tenurial status of the valuation. If the value represents the annual worth to
the 'holder', in cash or kind, to whom in Domesday's hierarchy does this refer? Was
it the tenant-in-chief, whose name heads the list of manors and who appears in
the index of each county? Or was it one of his vassals, sons-in-law, nephews, or
officials, who was the manor's subtenant and was often, but not invariably, named
in Domesday. Or was it the man who took the manor on a long-term lease or
a short-term 'farm' (from *firma* meaning 'fixed' or from *feorm* meaning 'provisions'), thereby hoping to make a living or profit? In other words, did the annual
'value' benefit whoever worked the manor—who was able to pocket it, in return for
paying a rent or service to the lord? Or was it the rent he paid?

A more obvious question arises from the, relatively few—albeit some of
the largest holdings—that give not only a 'value', *valet*, but also a 'render', *reddit*
(at its simplest, 'it pays'); they both appear together on over 200 manors in eastern
and south-eastern England, often on the largest manors. In Circuit I, there are 172

---

[4] R. Lennard, *Rural England* (Oxford, 1959) is the important study of most land management
questions, but it does not yield quick answers. Good short treatments of the subject include J. Palmer,
'The wealth of the secular aristocracy in 1086', *ANS*, 22 (2000) 279–91; H. C. Darby, *Domesday
England* (Cambridge, 1977), 208–31.

[5] Contrast Harvey 1983, 65–72, with 'larger estates tending to be more efficient', J. McDonald,
Production Efficiency (London, 1998), 157.

[6] In R. H. Britnell and B. M. S. Campbell (eds), *A Commercialising Economy: England 1086 to 1300*
(Manchester, 1995): G. Snooks, 'The dynamic role of the market in the Anglo-Norman economy and
beyond, 1086–1300', and 'Appendix 1: a note on the calculation of GDP and GDP per capita in 1086
and *c.*1300', 27–54 and 194–5; N. Mayhew, 'Modelling medieval monetisation' and 'Appendix 1: the
calculation of GDP from Domesday Book', 55–77 and 195–6; and C. Dyer, 'A note on calculation of
GDP for 1086 and *c.*1300', 196–8.

instances, representing about 12 per cent of locations; in the three eastern counties, there are some 46 (2.5 per cent)[7]: in terms of acreage both percentages are most probably higher. The value was quite evidently what the estate was or should be worth; but what then was the higher render?[8] The very presence of the contrasting sums calls the straightforward definition of values into question, asking how an agricultural enterprise could 'render', pay, or hand over considerably more than it was 'worth'.[9] Satellite Domesday texts have but added to the confusion. Exon Domesday often employs 'render' where Great Domesday uses 'value', seemingly without particular import or rationale;[10] in *Exon* too, clerks frequently wrote *valet*, struck the word through, and substituted *reddit*.[11] A number of entries quoting two different sums employ a third term, *appreciare*, literally to put a price on or to appraise or 'estimate'—the last is employed here. (*Pretium*, or price, is linked linguistically, but is more down-to earth.)[12] The Domesday usage of the three terms ('put a price on', *appreciare*, 'to be worth', *valere*, 'to pay/return', *reddere*) was not absolute or uniform: just as in modern English, any one of the three terms might be used alone to express a single appraisal of worth or, in contrast with another term, to express a second opinion. Comparison with contemporary texts has not greatly assisted. In Kent, both Domesday and the Domesday of the Monks state a 'value' of £100; whereas a Canterbury cathedral farm schedule shows Wingham returning a *firma*, or set payment, of £100, plus rent (*gablum*) of £29 10s and customary dues of £3.[13]

The character and constituents of these contrasted sums have provoked varied interpretations. In the 1980s, in the *Agrarian History* and elsewhere, I argued that the major part of the revenue from large estates came from the rents and dues of peasant agriculture, but that the demesne core was an important element in the structure of agricultural activity and its returns, particularly on small manors.[14] There were also a few great demesne enterprises of real importance to the magnate class. Yet, studies in the last thirty years have assumed different bases, without mutual critical review, and thus nice but core differences of interpretation remain almost hidden to their readers.

The traditional view on values accords primary importance to the demesne, assuming little contribution directly from the peasants; and this continues to be the basis of two pioneering statistical volumes on the Domesday economy, one by John

[7] Darby, *Domesday England*, 211.
[8] 'although they are worth less', *quamvis minus valeant*; GDB:52c (HAM:IoW1,11) cf. 'would be worth' *valeret*, if the canons should have their right, *ius*, 2b, (KEN:P18).
[9] The difficulty was outlined clearly in R. W. Finn, *An Introduction to Domesday Book* (London, 1963), 230–2, and discussed by J. L. Grassi, 'The lands and revenues of Edward the Confessor', *EHR*, 117 (2002), 254–8.
[10] e. g. Cerne Abbey, DB4, ff. 36–38b.   [11] Finn, *LExon*, 136.
[12] In 1086, a freeman's berewick with demesne and villein land is accounted for *in pretio de Sporle*, to which he now doubtless pays rent, LDB:126b (NFK:1,137).
[13] DMon, 98, 83, GDB:3d (KEN:2,21); also Appledore, *DMon*, 91, GDB:5b (KEN:3,20). Lennard discusses Domesday farms and values, 142–75.
[14] Harvey 1983, 53–65; Harvey 1988, 79–80.

McDonald and Graham Snooks, one by the former alone.[15] In contrast, the theories of A. R. Bridbury and David Roffe emphasize peasant contributions in cash to the exclusion of all else.[16] A. R. Bridbury, known for his refreshing views on the economy of the later middle ages, developed Hale's observation that for the manors of St Paul's the Domesday values 'bore an astonishingly close relationship to the cash totals [of rents] of 1181 and 1222'. Thus, Bridbury considers that Domesday values were 'not the aggregate income that the manorial lord derived from produce and sale of produce, from court dues and rents in kind and in service and from seigneurial perquisites and levies, but merely the cash yielded by those rents that were paid in money'.[17]

For David Roffe, the 'value' of a manor was 'a sum that went out of the estate to an overlord in recognition of a soke relationship', and were 'in origin probably shares of a royal farm'; moreover, 'they represent that part of the issues of the estate that are in coin'.[18] But there are difficulties with a general application of the soke theory definition—a perspective on Domesday values that seems coloured by Roffe's deep knowledge of Yorkshire, Lincolnshire, and the Danelaw. The revenues of royal manors did indeed derive from soke-type payments; yet as these often present their information in terms of 'renders', not 'values', this interpretation does not necessarily help with the Domesday 'values' on small, non-royal manors, which did not possess soke or hundredal revenues. Second, in 1086 some royal manors with extensive soke paid a 'farm of one night'—twenty-four hours' maintenance for the royal household—and nothing else, which certainly was in kind and not in coin.[19] Third, the text of Domesday was always influenced by the regional character of English society: whilst the small free-holders' and villeins' agricultural enterprises might well account for almost all of the 'value' of land in Norfolk and Lincolnshire—counties known for their many small free- and soke-holders—the soke theory does not fully take into account the functioning of great demesne enterprises in the south and west of England. Notwithstanding, Roffe concurs with Bridbury's view that the agriculture of the demesne and its products played no part in Domesday values.[20] Thus current views of Domesday specialists on the source of landed returns are now further apart than ever before. Certainly, recent controversies serve to highlight the point that any definition must give due attention to evidence on the contributions of the richer and freer peasants to Domesday returns.

All definitions of Domesday values provide a departure point for current theories on the rise of population and the growth of the economy, thereby affecting our

---

[15] See n. 90 in this chapter.

[16] A. R. Bridbury, 'The Domesday Valuation of Manorial Income', in *The English Economy from Bede to the Reformation* (Woodbridge, 1992), 111–32.

[17] Bridbury, *The English Economy*, 112–24, at 113, referring to the rentals in *The Domesday of St Paul's*, ed. W. H. Hale, *Camden Soc.*, 69 (London, 1858), 73–4, 140–52.

[18] D. Roffe, introduction in *The Norfolk Domesday*, Alecto 2001, 30.

[19] GDB:64d (WIL:1,1–4).

[20] Roffe, *Inquest*, 139. Yet, presumably he does not concur with Bridbury's exclusion of court dues—precisely those arising from soke jurisdiction, however see, Roffe, *Decoding*, 243.

views of the long-term functioning of the English economy.[21] If indeed, as Bridbury argues, Domesday's values generally equated with thirteenth-century rents and were at a similar level, current tenets on growth between the eleventh and thirteenth centuries could be called into question. Furthermore, one definition of Domesday values may provide a projected model of GDP perhaps double that derived from another definition.[22]

Because of the centrality of current differences over the meanings of Domesday values, the intention here is to argue their basis from first beginnings. My conclusion remains in a partway position between contemporary extremes. Whilst the demesne was a vital constituent of the 'value', yet the bulk of manorial cash revenues came from peasant agriculture: both from that subservient to the demesne, and from freeholders and sokemen—those within an attached jurisdiction. In fact, by recognizing the respective sources of these cash incomes, we can also answer the 'value' versus 'render' question: in that the higher 'renders' usually cover those newly augumented dues from rents and jurisdiction that were being levied over and above the more customary rents and services due to the demesne.

THE BENEFICIARIES

The identity of the value's recipient is perhaps the issue least capable of general resolution, as Domesday seldom says whether a tenanted manor was leased for cash or held in return for service;[23] and there is reason to think that manors held for military service alone were much fewer than historians used to envisage. Indeed, the evidence, admittedly sparse, points to no sharp tenurial divide between cash payments and specialized services, but rather to some combination. Wisely satisfying a range of their needs, tenants-in-chief seem to have relied on 'mixed' rentals, often featuring two of three forms of return—provisions, cash, and service of all kinds.[24] Service, moreover, covered an extremely wide range of benefits, some commercial, others unmeasurable.[25] One motive in bestowing tenancies, often unmentioned because it does not fit into the neat pyramid shape of tenures, was to obtain favours from those in power—or simply to avoid disfavour. 'Out of love for the king', the abbot of Ramsey gave a hide of land to a royal falconer.[26] It was 'for the sake of his advice in the matter of business' that, during the abbey of Abingdon's four-year vacancy in the 1090s, the monk in charge granted an under-

---

[21] Mayhew, 'Modelling Medieval Monetisation' 61–2, 73, 74.

[22] Mayhew, 62; Bridbury's interpretation would lead to 'guesstimating' a 1086 GDP far in excess of Mayhew's uppermost estimate.

[23] The Geld Accounts, and *Exon*, occasionally, record persons, unmentioned in Great Domesday, who hold land at farm, VCH *Dorset*, 3.121–3.

[24] Cf. after 1106 and before 1113, sokemen of Felsted, Essex, rendered cash and carried the farm four times yearly to Winchester, *Caen*, Chibnall, 34.

[25] Also, Harvey 1970, 8–14.

[26] *ob amorem regis*, GDB:208a (HUN:D8).

tenancy to the royal chamberlain, Herbert; he was probably the same Herbert the Chamberlain who appears in Domesday Hampshire holding land from the king, from Hampshire's sheriff, and from New Minster.[27]

Yet, whoever was the immediate beneficiary, the 'value' of all lands can be safely credited to its tenant-in-chief: even if the tenant-in-chief did not receive cash, he received services and support instead by forgoing that sum. During the two decades that Domesday covers, the tenure of all followers was still flexible, indeed precarious. Yet, when giving a verdict on production, efficiency, or taxation levels, or deciding whether exploitation had reached the point of diminishing returns, it does matter whether the value is the rent, or whether it is the net income to the tenant after rent has been paid. On this matter, again contrasting views prevail. One view holds that Domesday valuations reveal the *entire* annual value of the lords' holdings;[28] the other, that the 'values' are the amount paid over as rent.[29] Yet the two were currently confused anyway at this time since the conquerors were able temporarily to enforce unrealistic terms. Here it will be argued that demesne estates—those managed directly by the tenant-in-chief—handed over to him the full value as recorded in Domesday; whilst for service tenancies, usually the net rental value is given. However, whether this was the actual return received by the tenant-in-chief or the amount received by his subtenant remained a matter for negotiation. Anyway, as demesne manors were managed directly, and as other, perhaps lesser, more dispersed manors, were given out for more nominal sums or for longer-term agreements, their economic returns or 'values' are directly comparable only within limits.

In contrast to the confusion over interpretation, access to the values themselves in digestible form is good: Domesday usually places the value data accessibly at the end of each entry. General patterns in the distribution and rise or fall of values have long been tabulated and published.[30] There now exists a valiant general indexing of the rise and fall of values.[31] All entries are available online.[32] It is a field ripe for computer studies, but the ability to manipulate the data on values is not yet publicly available, and in any case there is still the need to establish the parameters within which the data can be employed. Whilst values were not mapped in detail for the regional *Domesday Geographies*, H. C. Darby's discussion of them in his final

---

[27] *HistAbbend* 2, no. 53; GDB:48d (HAM:55,1), 45c (HAM:23,35), 42c–d (HAM:6,16).

[28] Snooks, 'The dynamic role of the market' and 'A note on the calculation of GDP', in Britnell and Campbell, *A Commercialising Economy*, 27–54, 194–5.

[29] Mayhew, 'Modelling medieval monetisation', in Britnell and Campbell, *A Commercialising Economy*, 55–77, esp. 60–6, 72, and notes by Snooks and Mayhew, 194–6.

[30] F. H. Baring, *Domesday Tables* (London, 1909); Maitland, 400–3; maps and discussion throughout R. W. Finn, *The Norman Conquest and its Effects on the Economy: 1066–1086* (London, 1971).

[31] J. D. Foy, *Index of Subjects: Domesday Book*, 38 (Chichester, 1992), 240–55.

[32] *Digital Domesday* (Alecto, various edns) supplies translations of the text, the 1783 transcription, and photographs of the original. A translation of the text is available online as Hull Textbase (Phillimore, Chichester); some figures are obtainable via *Domesday Explorer*, University of Essex, online data store (1986–2008), <http://www.domesdaybook.net/> (accessed 20 Jan. 2014). The manoeuvrability of earlier versions was reviewed by R. Fleming and A. Lowerre, 'MacDomesday Book', *P&P*, 184 (2004), 209–32.

volume, *Domesday England*, remains the most carefully concise treatment of the subject, despite his somewhat weary conclusion: 'we cannot be surprised that commentator after commentator has been puzzled over the implications of the Domesday *valet* and *reddit*'.[33]

There is no case, however, for a counsel of despair. One point that commentators seem agreed upon is the worth of the data on values. Several historians of legal procedures have emphasized the stringent character of court proceedings, and in making Domesday values central to their statistical analysis of the Domesday economy McDonald and Snooks reassuringly rate the quality of data collected above that normally available to modern economists.[34] Roffe describes values as 'the *raison d'être* of DB', although he also disparages them as 'very clearly conventional'.[35] There are indeed some instances of stereotyping amongst the assets directly held by the crown but given that these represented centrally organized long-term arrangements they are few enough not to cause unease: the farms of the ancient royal estates of Wessex are well known;[36] the Kentish ports of Rochester, Sandwich and Folkestone, and Bosham and Eastbourne in Sussex, all have farms or values of £40, as do two districts on the Welsh borders.[37] 'Values' meant so much to the Conqueror and his advisers that to obtain them they were prepared to set up one of the largest investigations known to western Europe; and the Conqueror's two successors put them to profitable use. For the most part, Domesday values are precise; if they were thought to yield information to contemporaries, they should be capable of sufficient definition to be of service to historians, particularly when set in the context of the tradition of evaluation of landed income in the medieval period.

PROBLEMS OF TERMINOLOGY AND TIME

Historians have found it convenient to assign values from 'the time of King Edward' and 'now' to the dates 1066 and 1086 respectively and the full wording in *Exon* refers back vividly to 'the day on which King Edward was alive and dead'; but strictly speaking, for values, neither 1066 nor 1086 was likely to have been the year in question. King Edward died on 5 January 1066, so the last 'year' of his reign is more properly regarded as 1065 than 1066: the last agricultural year and harvest was certainly 1065. The same argument applies to 'now', the year of the Inquiry. The returns from the 1086 harvest would be known only at Michaelmas 1086 at the earliest, whereas the bulk of the Domesday information was collected earlier that year. Only if the manor were leased, and payment due at Lady Day, 25 March, would the 1086 value be available; even then, the sum quoted would relate to an agreement made in 1085 and

[33] Darby, *Domesday England*, 208–31, 225.
[34] McDonald and Snooks, 35–6, 120–1; Fleming, *Law*, 17–19.
[35] D. Roffe, 'From thanage to barony', *ANS*, 12 (1989), 163, 173.
[36] In Hampshire, £76 16s 8d recurs.
[37] Archenfield, GDB:197b (HEF:A10); Rhuddlan, 269b (CHS:G1).

its profits, or pressures, which may help to explain the high returns recorded in Domesday, despite the notoriously poor harvest, cattle disease, and famine of 1086.[38]

Moreover, on estates with broken tenurial history, Domesday's data on past values were likely to vary in time.[39] Across half the counties, Great Domesday records one figure only for the past valuation; and *Exon* reveals the ambiguities surrounding the dating, often referring, not to King Edward's day, but to the time when the newcomer was granted it, *quando recepit*, which depended upon circumstance:[40] one entry cites the sum charged when 'the queen was living', another 'when Hugh acquired it'.[41] In Great Domesday the wording is often simply *valuit* or *olim*, with no date quoted; so this information did not necessarily apply to the last year of Edward's reign. The change of tenure was a serviceable baseline in regions of widespread revolt, with extensive loss of life and so disruption of tenure, memory, and documents. Such discrepancies and ambiguities over dates advise caution in the statistical use of 'values': there is always the possibility that, unless Edward's day is mentioned explicitly, *valuit* may refer to 'when received', a date varying with the progress of the Conquest, the pathways of revolt, and the survival of people or documentation.

WHO WERE THE VALUERS? WHO RECEIVED THE VALUE?

Who provided these manorial values? Here, we encounter Domesday's complex structure: dependent both on the traditional shire and hundred and on returns from newly enfranchised landholders. Moreover, those key figures, the sheriffs and reeves, not only had their official role to play in returns, they had their own vested interests to defend.

The role of shire and hundred

Sales of land and long-term leases were not simply matters to be left to the contracting parties: thus landholders had long operated within the context of shire and hundred. Agreements on the terms of a lease were traditionally witnessed by the men of the vill, hundred, or shire, as well as a reeve, who could thereby supply a collective memory of its value: the shire, for instance, had witnessed a son's agreement to provide lifelong maintenance for his father by paying him a 'farm'.[42] With the bishop or other ecclesiastics present, agreements came with high sanctions—fines in this world and the possibility of damnation in the next; and

---

[38] *ASC*, 1086.

[39] See also P. Taylor, 'Ingelric, Count Eustace and the foundation of St Martin-le-Grand', *ANS*, 24 (2001), 215–37, esp. 226, for instances of the inaccuracy of TRE data on tenure.

[40] Other variations include GDB's use of *olim* for Devon and Cornwall: Finn, *The Norman Conquest and its Effects on the Economy*, 283.

[41] DB4, 29b; 31b; GDB:75c,d (DOR:1,17; 1,27).   [42] GDB:59b (BRK:7,38).

such witnessed agreements, *conventiones*, were referred to in and outside Domesday.[43] From the late tenth-century under Anglo-Saxon law, sales of land or cattle
required authoritative witness, which might be charged for. These witnesses might
include a reeve or priest; later, each hundred was to provide at least twelve
sworn witnesses to sales.[44] Other law codes specified that nothing worth more
than 4d was to be sold except in the presence of four trustworthy witnesses, thereby
including quality sheep and pigs—for instance, rams and boars—as well as all oxen
and horses.[45] Buyer and seller each paid a toll—in Lewes, 1d on a horse—for this
witness.[46]

Before 1066, local and shire courts, meeting regularly, were used to publicize
agreements when lands in the king's farm were leased, when the sheriff acquired
rights on royal lands, and when land was granted out in the king's service. Reeves
farming the royal estates and managing their hundreds might be important people,
perhaps even king's thegns, and were well used to working with witnesses from the
hundred.[47] Certainly, one of the most remarkable achievements of Domesday was
its record of the values of most manorial units either 'in King Edward's day'—at
least twenty years and a military conquest prior to the Inquiry—or, failing that, when
the manor had last changed hands. Yet however finely tuned were the meetings
and memories that put Anglo-Saxon law into effect, they were always liable to be
vitiated by powerful men resolved to determine matters in their own favour.[48]

It is indeed the hundred that Domesday quotes more often than the shire in
concerns over manorial appurtenances, misdeeds of reeves, and the selling, leasing,
and granting of land before 1066.[49] As we have seen, some sheriffs influenced the
selection of the jurors, yet given the weight of the witness of the whole hundred,
coram totius hundredti testimonio, a phrase recurring constantly in the *Inquest of Ely*,
the sheriff needed to work with, sway, or intimidate, the gatherings of shire and
hundred, too.[50] In practice, the relative importance of hundred and landholder
seems to have varied from region to region.[51]

The men of the hundred were certainly knowledgeable—and expected to be—
about the contributory rights, dues, and assets that made up the Domesday value
and the render. In the Shropshire Domesday, the mode of measuring woodland—
whether by linear dimensions or by numbers of pigs fattened—varies according
to hundred.[52] Moreover, once the process of public assembly was under way, the
sheer weight of opinion in the populous eastern counties (see Figure 2) might have
given more say to the dissenters present and somewhat restricted a sheriff's or

---

[43] When Roger Bigod wished to prove how much a royal manor paid that he had farmed, he aimed
to do so 'through those men who were present at his agreement', LDB:287b (SUF:1,103); GDB:47a
(HAM:29,9); also, Van Caenegem, *Lawsuits*, no. 15.
[44] III Edmund, 5; IV Edgar, 3–11.   [45] II Cnut, 24.   [46] GDB:26a (SUS:12,1).
[47] e.g. IV Edgar, 13,1; VII Æthelred, 2, 5; Lennard, 271–7. J. Campbell, 'Some agents and agencies
of the Anglo-Saxon state', in Holt, *Studies*, 205–8, 215–17, is important on reeves.
[48] Fleming, *Law*, 13–14, 20–8.   [49] Fleming, *Law*, 40–3.
[50] Discussed Fleming, *Law*, 18–19, 27–8.   [51] Discussed in Ch. 3 in this volume.
[52] C. P. Lewis, introduction in *The Shropshire Domesday*, Alecto 1990, 10.

landholder's opportunities for manipulation: for whatever reason, it is certainly the case that what the manor actually paid out—the 'render'—was more frequently recorded in the southern and eastern circuits.

The landholders

As for the source of the 'values'—particularly those of 1085–6 and those when the estate had changed hands—it was the landholder's duty to respond to the Inquiry for the lands he claimed, but sometimes his responses were permitted to vary. A telling example comes from Staffordshire—a county whose descriptive detail often falls short of Great Domesday's high standards. Most Staffordshire manors record values for two dates, yet those of the lands of three royal officers, Henry de Ferrers, Robert de Stafford (whose land occupies over four columns in Domesday), and Rainald de Bailleul, Shropshire's sheriff, record only the current one.[53] Great lay landholders, as well as ecclesiastics, did keep accounts at the time: sometime between 1087 and 1095 Roger de Beaumont granted the Abbey of Preaux twenty pounds of English money annually 'from the tithes of his revenues overseas'; Eustace of Boulogne possessed his own weights for the receipt of coin.[54] Earl Hugh of Chester was remarked upon just because he 'kept no accounts of his receipts and expenditure', yet the reeve of Chester—Hugh's semi-autonomous possession—evidently kept good tally for him of the most important fines and tolls.[55] Although, Domesday apart, evidence for landholders' accounts is merely indirect or fragmentary, nonetheless the same is true of crown accounts for these decades.

Though few pre-Domesday estate accounts survive, there are two working texts of a kind possibly usual amongst landholders and their representatives: ecclesiastics were perhaps more likely to keep such records, and theirs were certainly more likely to survive. One such, of the first quarter of the eleventh century in Anglo-Saxon, contains an inventory with valuations of livestock, seed, and farm implements supplied by Ely Abbey to the neighbouring Thorney Abbey:[56] transferred from Milton were eighty swine 'valued at one and half pounds and the swineherd at half a pound'; later, money for improvements was disbursed. Written in four different hands, they seem to be working jottings of an ephemeral kind, not entirely dissimilar to estate memoranda from the see of Dorchester-on-Thames. The latter consist of the briefest notes of monies received and disbursed, probably in the early 1070s, recording, for example, that 'the laymen of Banbury, who have five ploughlands of land, should give £4. And a certain youth who is reeve [£]3'.[57]

---

[53] GDB:248c, 248d–249d, 250c; Green, *Sheriffs*, 71.

[54] *Calendar of Documents Preserved in France*, ed. J. H. Round (London, 1899), no. 321; GDB:137b (HRT:17,1).

[55] *nullam rationem tenebat*, OV 2.260–2, cf. GDB:262c–d; J. F. A. Mason, 'Barons and their officials in the later eleventh century', *ANS*, 13 (1990), 259–62.

[56] Charters, App. II, no. 9.

[57] J. Blair, 'Estate memoranda of c.1070 from the see of Dorchester-on-Thames', *EHR*, 116 (2001), 114–23.

Reeves and stewards of the largest estates would probably have kept similar cursory notes, as would the sheriff, who was responsible for shire revenues; alternatively, in 1086, perhaps native bailiffs memorized figures, supplying them along with other agricultural details to the landholder employing them, who in turn supplied the Inquiry.[58] The lord's reeve was certainly required to be one of the representatives of the vill.

The general tenor on the great landholders' demesne manors in Domesday is that 'values' were the revenues as seen from their perspective, and accruing to them, and not the revenues of the sitting tenant, lessee, or farmer. On royal lands, they were the payments expected by the king. York's entry is explicit: 'TRE the city was worth to the king £53; now £100 by weight'.[59] In *Exon*, one Reginald is named as 'rendering £24 to the king's farm', whereas Great Domesday records a 'value' of £24 by weight without mention of Reginald.[60] The clearest evidence of the landholder's perspective comes from the Devon lands of the Abbey of Sainte-Marie, Rouen, which paid an annual sum expressed in Domesday in Rouen pence: a sum obviously recorded from the view-point of the tenant-in-chief, not that of the sitting tenant or farmer.[61]

Whilst it is usually assumed, often rightly, that in Domesday named followers of the tenant-in-chief concerned were in receipt of the manors' values, yet there are indications that they too, like a *firmarius*, might pay the 'value' of the land to the tenant-in-chief in cash as an alternative to service. A unique charter of 1085, relating to Roger de Lacy's land-grants from the bishop of Hereford, states that Roger pays £1 a year to the bishop for the tenure of Onibury: precisely its current value in Domesday.[62] The case of his second tenancy, Holme Lacy, was less straightforward: the land-grant demanded the service of Roger and two knights, whereas the Domesday value was £8—a realistic costing of such services.[63] The document also shows that conditions of limited duration were laid on the tenure—and subsequently ignored! In fact, wherever we are blessed, or cursed, with evidence other than Domesday, we are confronted with complex details that have been simplified for the Survey. Behind Domesday's relative baldness and uniformity of costing lay all manner of agreements, unknown to us and, for the most part, unknowable. The value was often the bottom line from the tenant-in-chief's point of view and, in that first generation after the Conquest, he was able to allocate his resources to supply whatever personnel, goods, services, or cash he required.

---

[58] Harvey 1971, 771–2; H. B. Clarke, 'The Domesday satellites', in *Reassessment*, 55; S. Baxter, 'The representation of lordship and land tenure in Domesday Book', in Hallam and Bates, esp. 81–92.
[59] GDB:298b (YKS:C20).
[60] DB4, f.97b; GDB:101b (DEV:1,56).   [61] GDB:104b (DEV:10,2).
[62] V. H. Galbraith, 'An episcopal land-grant of 1085', *EHR*, 44 (1929), 353–72; EHD2, no. 221. For the latest helpful discussion, T. S. Purser, 'The origins of English feudalism? an episcopal land-grant revisited', *Historical Research*, 73 (2000), 80–93; GDB:252b (SHR:2,2).
[63] GDB:181d (HEF:2,12); approximately £5 for a man of status, and 30s for each professional subordinate knight: Harvey 1970, 23–8.

The layout of the Domesday Summaries, however, reinforces the traditional dimension of service due, and revenue to the tenant. The Summaries are under-discussed texts that give us some insight into the usage intended for Domesday's data. Their partial survival, most notably via *Exon*, shows how outline Domesday information was condensed for some major fiefs, by adding up the hides, plough-lands, and values of the lands of each tenant-in-chief. In so doing, they separate the lands of the tenant-in-chief's followers from those of his demesne. In the case of the Count of Mortain, the distinction is unambiguous: the value of his supporters' lands in four south-western counties is stated to be the value 'to them'.[64] A similar Summary of core data makes a similar division for the knights on 'Lands between Ribble and Mersey' formerly held by Roger of Poitou, and for Alan of Richmond's followers in Yorkshire.[65] Evidently the values on many tenanted estates did go to the recognized subtenant, in return for fulfilling his functions as steward, knight, or whatever he happened to be.

It seems that the Domesday values showed to the king and his tenants-in-chief the product of their lands, and indicated the cost to them of the services they currently enjoyed. In the first three decades after the Conquest, whilst the regime was still establishing itself, there is every indication that such tenures were expected to be conditional and renegotiable.[66] Then, as the de Lacy agreement shows, the rent might well be renegotiated—and the annual value provided a basis.[67] Four sokemen had land 'valued' at 13s, and this was the rent, *census*, that Richard fitzGilbert took from them while they remained in his hands.[68] Moreover, there are hints that if professional services were not performed, rent was paid, just as the king himself expected during the minorities of lay tenants-in-chief or in ecclesias-tical vacancies. Whilst the alternatives of a cash payment or service were standard requirements from Domesday sokemen;[69] and commutation was already common-ly employed before 1066 for the armed men due from every five hides and from boroughs, such costings extend contemporaries' habits of estimating landed values and their equivalent in service into another sector of landholding. Azur, a pre-Conquest tenant of Pershore Abbey, gave service to the church plus an annual 'recognition' of either a 'farm', or 20s.[70] It was surely one way of trying to ensure that the land, as in the Lacy agreement, was not assumed to be hereditary once services could no longer be rendered. That service and rent might be alternatives is

---

[64] *eis*, DB4, ff. 527b–531; VCH *Wiltshire*, 2.218–21; VCH *Dorset*, 3.148–9.

[65] GDB:270b (CHS:R7,1), 381b (YKS:S402); also, *IE*, 121–4.

[66] J. C. Holt, 'Feudal society and the family in early medieval England II: notions of patrimony', *TRHS*, 5th ser., 33 (1983), 214–15.

[67] Perhaps the meaning behind the curious Cerne entry, *ista terra valet* [deleted] *reddit c. solidos per annum. Et iste tegnus reddit per annum xxx solidos ecclesiae quo minus excepto servitio*; DB4, f.36a, cf. GDB:77d (DOR:11,1, and note). Three Dorset 'thegns' who hold 3 hides of land 'pay £3, apart from service', GDB:75c (DOR:1,16); cf. also TRE under Cropthorne with Netherton, GDB:174a (WOR:2,73).

[68] LDB:6a–b (ESS:1,27).   [69] e.g. GDB:189b (CAM:1,2).

[70] GDB:175b (WOR:9,1b).

suggested in an Essex dispute over who was the proper overlord: Ralph Pinel had 'rendered service' to Geoffrey de Mandeville, because 'Geoffrey had told him how the king had given him the service (*servitium*) of that land; but he [Ralph] has twice given his rent (*censum*) to the king's officials'.[71] In supplying a large household, food-farms from the whole manor were of course another alternative in the mix of returns, but these are well known from the good documentation of monastic histories and the ancient royal estates and I shall only acknowledge them in passing here.

Landholders were fully aware of the cost to themselves of military protection, and occasionally we see it wittingly deducted from the lord's own revenues. In the Welsh borders, Domesday explains why Westhide's value had decreased by fifteen shillings: Ralph de Tosny 'gave ½ hide of this land to one of his knights, therefore the manor pays less'.[72] The *Exon* Summaries add the values of knights' sub-holdings on demesne manors to those of their undertenancies proper; but Domesday does not always value such holdings separately, simply supplying the size. Several small functionaries who hold from the king pay no farm because of services rendered, but apart from their professional titles—huntsmen, goldsmiths, and so on—we know little specific about the extent of these services. Before 1066, many who 'could go where they wished' with their land were making no payments for their land; the best Domesday could aim at was some sort of standardization. In Welsh lands recorded under Gloucestershire, 'Berdic the king's jester has 3 vills, and there are 5 ploughs. He pays nothing'.[73] We may instead imagine him performing at crown-wearings in Gloucester, including the Christmas Council that set in motion the Domesday Survey.

Leaving aside exploitative deals with the conquered, one possibility may be that, for service, each layer in the tenurial hierarchy expected to make similar levels of remuneration out of rents and farms. The Hundred Rolls suggest that bailiffs often sought for themselves an amount about equal to their contracted payment—although the locality thought it should be less. The Domesday case of William the Chamberlain's land suggests similar 50/50 levels obtained when first he received a manor from the queen: he paid the queen £3 a year for a holding then worth £6, and although *Ebury*'s 'value' had risen to £8 by 1086, the £3 yearly farm remained the same.[74] (We only know all this because for the last four years the farm was unpaid.) It is at least clear that the Chamberlain was supposed to pay an annual farm set at half the value of the land when he received it, allowing him the rest of the value. The case shows too that royal officers did not necessarily hold rent-free in return for service and that, although the profits from this manor were divided between two tiers of the tenurial hierarchy, they still represented the net amount paid out from the manor to the ruling elite.

[71] LDB:97b (ESS:77,1).
[72] GDB:183b (HEF:8,8); cf. a knight has a ½ hide which pays 12s 'to him', 264b (CHS:2,2).
[73] GDB:162a (GLS:W4).   [74] GDB:129c (MDX:9,1).

Domesday procedures

Domesday procedure is perhaps illustrated by a case in which the opinions of the men of the hundred and those of the lord—or putative lord—were both invoked. A disputed Norfolk holding was listed, wrongly, in Domesday under William de Warenne's name and it seems that he was expected to supply a valuation, but 'William's men say he had nothing from it'. The men of the hundred then attested that, after Earl Ralph had forfeited it, the sheriff had held it on the king's behalf, and his deputy Godric had accounted for it to the royal treasury;[75] besides, they had seen no authentication of William's possession. The normal mode of pronouncing on a manor's worth was through the landholder, or his men; however, the men of the hundred had knowledge that was sought, and carried authority.

Yet, when the tenant-in-chief did not supply a value, the men of the locality were not always able to provide the missing figure: it was not known what one Herefordshire manor was worth in King Edward's day, because it had not then been put out to rent.[76] Before 1066, in several Gloucestershire cases, the royal reeves had been simply entrusted to provide the best returns: and, as 'the sheriff used to render what he wished, therefore they do not know how to evaluate it', and no Edwardian value is given.[77] Similarly positioned were the reeves of Chedworth and Arlington: one estate probably, the other certainly, being held by king's thegns of high status in 1066.[78] The very act of an agreement on a sum or payment in kind meant witnesses; without that, local memories could not always supply figures twenty years later. On occasion, the men of the locality were able to comment so knowledgably that their divergent opinion was not merely heard but formally recorded as that of 'the English' or 'the men'.[79] Generally, however, the sources of the values remain anonymous.

The majority of Domesday values tend to be given in sums of pounds alone, or rounded to five or ten shillings. They indicate rounding at some stage, either because they were the regular farm paid, or were the tenant-in-chief's best estimate of the worth of services or farm provided. On the other hand, not a few of the largest manors returned values or renders precisely in pounds, shillings and pence. There are no hard and fast rules. Outside Domesday, the Ely Abbey valuation of assets handed over to Thorney included mostly rounded items: £1 for mill-oxen at Yaxley, and 5 mancuses of gold for a smith and a slave dairymaid. Even commissioned tasks involved rounded sums: 'The bishop in the first instance gave three pounds for improvements at Yaxley, and then 3 pounds of gold was given.' But the final figure for assets was expressed as '£16 pounds in gold and silver,

---

[75] *in thesauro regis in brevi suo*, LDB:276b (NFK:66,64).   [76] GDB:179c (HEF:1,2).

[77] *De hoc manerio reddebat quod volebat vicecomes TRE. Ideo nesciunt appreciari.* GDB:163a, (GLS:1,10), 164a (GLS:1,53).

[78] Wulfweard White and Cynewig Chelle, A. Williams, introduction in *The Gloucestershire Domesday*, Alecto 1989, 6; GDB:164a (GLS:1,57–8).

[79] GDB:2c (KEN:1,1), 66c (WIL:7,1).

less 40 pence', so there was precision also.[80] Some figures were deliberately rounded up for the Domesday record: a Gloucestershire column of rounded values includes one manor, Upleadon, 'scarcely (*vix*) worth 30s.' and another, Ampney, 'scarcely worth' £1.[81] Similarly, twelfth-century grants and agreements show that land was frequently designated in 'librates' or 'solidates' of income per annum from the reign of Henry I onwards. Six separate rents constituted the 'marcate' of land at Nyton, Isle of Wight, given to the Canons of Christchurch, adding up in all to a safe 13s 10d, rather than the strict 13s 4d that made up the mark.[82] Many levels of the community were practised in the art of appraising. Sherrington, in Domesday Sussex, had lost a half hide to another rape; in King Edward's day it had been worth £3, and now £2, 'for the half hide that is not there they deduct, *decidunt*, £1'.[83] 'They' might be the local representatives of the rape or one of its hundreds, or the followers of its lord, the Count of Mortain: both groups needed to approve the record and both, here in Sussex, were likely to hold land ultimately from the Count.

To provide the Domesday 'value', the holder or his official was expected either to submit written returns, or attend in person; however, in the absence of such returns, the 'render' was still known to local men—because this was what they were required to pay. In the case of a disputed holding, listed under Gloucestershire, and lacking 'value' or details, the entry explained: 'Concerning this manor, no one rendered an account to the royal commissioners, nor did any one of them come to this *descriptio*.' Even so, those present could affirm that it currently paid £7 'unjustly' to the farm of Wiltshire.[84] Such fragments are consistent with the process laid down in the *Leges Henrici Primi*, whereby the lord or his steward represented all the land he held in that county; and 'if both are unavoidably absent, the reeve and the priest and the four most substantial men of the vill shall attend on the behalf of all who have not been summoned by name to court'.[85]

Whilst landholders normally supplied the present-day and 'when received' value, the local community were the default suppliers of the values of Edward's day—and of the renders; through the latter, local men might question the validity of the 1086 landholder's valuation, by supplying details of their own rental contributions or their own estimate.

THE CONSTITUENTS OF THE VALUE

The majority of the 14,000 or so agricultural units valued in Domesday were not simply groups of rents, but made up of two constituent parts:[86] the demesne,

---

[80] Charters, App. II, no. 9.   [81] GDB:165c (GLS:10,10; 10,12).
[82] F. M. Stenton, *The First Century of English Feudalism*, 2nd edn (Oxford, 1961), 166; other examples 35, 108, 165–91.
[83] GDB:20d (SUS:10,18).   [84] *reddit*, GDB:164b (GLS:1,63).   [85] *LegesHP*, 101.
[86] Values in 1086 recorded in 14,198 instances according to the Coel data base. According to *The Domesday Book Online*, September 2009, <http://www.domesdaybook.co.uk/index.html>, devised

with arable land, livestock, and manpower kept in hand by a petty lord, or a great lord and his deputies;[87] and the non-demesne sector, consisting of villeins, small-holders, and small tenants with their own plough-teams, contributing various rents and services to the demesne as well as cultivating their own holdings. Forms of freer tenure were as diverse as were their rents, and some of their services, such as escort duties, might be of a prestigious nature. Beyond the traditional bounds of the estate, further levies in cash or kind might be raised for access to a wide range of assets within a soke or hundredal jurisdiction, and imposts levied for failure to comply with these levies. Within such a jurisdiction, the suitors themselves, those obliged to attend court, witness, and declare local custom, could be a source of profit—they could be amerced for absence, unpunctuality, or other technical offences.

To discover what revenues were appraised for the Domesday record, I shall look first at the demesne and its livestock; second, at rents (though of course the two sectors were not run independently); and third, at the option to lease the whole manor. This may seem otiose, but one eminent historian of agricultural organiza-tion has recently disclosed:

> What is not clear at all is how lords drew profits from their manors before the mid-twelfth century. For long it was an all but undiscussed question: historians wrote about manorial demesnes, their grant or sale, their expansion or contraction, as though everyone knew how they were run, how manorial demesnes were translated into seigneurial profits, when in fact no one really knew at all.[88]

Moreover, given the disagreement still current over the interpretation of Domesday values, it is worth questioning the evidence yet again to discover how revenues were obtained from land, whilst largely leaving aside the much-studied great monastic houses that had particular year-round needs of provisions in kind.

The demesne

According to Lennard, 'except in the rare cases where there was no manorial demesne, it was not merely a matter of collecting customary rents and dues from the *villani* and other manorial tenants. The demesne was involved. When a manor was put to farm, the farm represented primarily what the lord received from the

by The National Archives at Kew, 13,418 settlements are recorded. Over 21,106 units of landholding have been identified in all by the Hull University's Open Domesday project, but many of these are small, contributory units. See <http://www.domesdaymap.co.uk/about/> accessed 20 December 2013. The Hull database allocates separate entries as in Phillimore edition; this total presumably includes urban sites.

[87] G. Duby, *Rural Economy and Country Life in the Medieval West* (London, 1968), 200; how many freemen or free tenants were omitted by Domesday Book is, by definition, largely beyond the scope of our evidence, but see J. F. R. Walmsley, 'The "censarii" of Burton Abbey and the Domesday population', *North Staffordshire Journal of Field Studies*, 8 (1968), 73–80; Harvey 1988, 46–9.

[88] P. D. A. Harvey, 'The manorial reeve in twelfth-century England', in R. Evans (ed.), *Lordship and Learning: Studies in memory of Trevor Aston* (Woodbridge, 2004), 134.

demesne.'[89] McDonald's work too is based on the premise that the annual values were 'usually the net revenue gained from directly working the demesne'.[90] In complete contrast, as we have seen, are the recent claims that Domesday values derive only from cash revenues in rent, or soke payments. With views so diametrically opposed, this study aims to determine the bases of revenues in the Domesday period without assumptions. Yet specific evidence is sparse because, whatever those bases were, they were taken for granted by contemporaries. But, the evidence indicates, first, that demesne agriculture did indeed play a role in these values—though a smaller one than traditionally assumed; second, the corollary, that the preponderance of the wealth in Domesday values came from the transferred surpluses of the small agriculturalists, in cash, kind, services, and jurisdictional dues.[91]

Whilst demesne revenues formed part of the monetary value, there is a major qualification: what the resident household consumed of the manor's basic produce was not represented in the valuation. For Tockington, Gloucestershire, the residence of a king's thegn in King Edward's day Domesday records, 'this manor paid no farm TRE, but he to whom it belonged lived off it'. The thegn had evidently been sufficiently independent for the level of returns to be unknown; certainly, in 1086, Tockington was a substantial manor, paying £24, with a substantial demesne sector of five ploughs and ten slaves; a further twenty ploughs belonged to the men attached.[92] Some leading centres of fiefs tended to have huge agricultural resources or a relatively low value, sometimes both. In Staffordshire, adjacent to the site of Henry de Ferrers' castle, Henry had four ploughs in demesne, worth a mere 24s a year and, most unusually, no manpower or peasant ploughs.[93] Its low value was probably attributable to the bulk of the demesne output being consumed by the honorial centre, and the demesne oxen-teams recorded were as likely to have been employed in the transport of household provisions and building materials as on the arable. On the Evesham manor of Offenham were 'oxen for one plough, but they are drawing stone to the church', for the rebuilding of Evesham Abbey.[94] We must assume that the drastic rebuilding of abbeys and cathedrals, and the erection of mottes and castles, occupied many of the recorded plough-teams. But unfortunately the regular workforce of lordly households, along with their ancillary horses, hunting dogs and so on, went almost entirely unrecorded in Domesday: that is apart from the unique entry of the seventy-five bakers, ale-brewers, tailors,

---

[89] Lennard, 142; contrast P. Vinogradoff, *English Society in the Eleventh Century* (Oxford, 1908), 353–8.

[90] McDonald and Snooks, 98; McDonald, 62.

[91] Harvey 1983, 45–72; Harvey 1987, 253–6, discusses further the balance between demesne and tenants, and the relatively few great demesne manors for which Domesday supplies evidence.

[92] GDB:164b (GLS:1,61).

[93] 'Burton', GDB:248c (STS:10,2 and Notes); the identity of the castle site, possibly that at Tutbury, is uncertain.

[94] GDB:175d (WOR:10,5).

washerwomen, robe-makers, and others who 'daily served the Saint, the abbot, and brethren' of Bury St Edmunds.[95]

Along with household personnel, the number of riding horses appropriate to a household—whether that of reeve, knight, or baron—usually went unrecorded in Domesday. Those horses logged amongst the livestock of the two regional Domesdays—Exon and Little—were certainly too few to transport the personnel of lordly households: they can only have related to the year-round stock. Swein, for instance, sometime sheriff of Essex, a possible Domesday commissioner, listed only five horses and two colts at his head manor and castle of Rayleigh: the five can scarcely have been the only rideable animals at his household's call.[96] The riding, fighting, and sumpter horses were, by their nature, only transient manorial residents.

Some assets were devoted to supplying the resident demesne household, unvalued; fisheries and mills were indeed almost invaluable. Whereas they might well have furnished a substantial income, the household needs of lordly landholders came first. At Taunton, half the peasants' fish catch went to the bishop;[97] at Swanscombe, where five fisheries paid 30d, the fishery 'serving the hall' went unvalued.[98] Two mills attached 'to the hall' at Winkton produced not cash, but 450 eels.[99] At Badlingham one mill paid 6s, the other 'grinds for the demesne'.[100] Indeed, sustenance took priority at all tenurial levels: one mill 'paid nothing, except the food of the man in charge'.[101] Thereafter, mills might provide a good rental income: sums of between 15s and £1 are not uncommon, and are occasionally much higher. In its unique position, the Abbey of Westminster derived no less than £42 9s 8d, 'or corn of the same price', from its seven mills at Battersea, thus enabling the monks either to ensure their own food supply or to reap rewards from the proximity of the London market.[102] Both fisheries and mills—they were watermills—needed frequent maintenance and, with the political turmoil, many mills fell out of use TRE to TRW, particularly in the north and Yorkshire.[103] However, provided corn was still grown in the locality, mills had a certain economic resilience: one small landholder, Alsige, survived as a subtenant on land in the West Riding that had been worth 60s in 1066, but by 1086 its only paying asset was one mill 'rendering' 6s.[104]

But Domesday could not document the standard of living in kind enjoyed by the holders or lessees of lands, or only exceptionally: for the Æthelric who still

[95] LDB:372a (SUF:14,167).
[96] LDB:43b (ESS:24,17). Compare the 70 brood mares and foals maintained by Burton Abbey in the early twelfth century, EHD2, no. 176. Exceptionally, two of Ranulf Peverel's Suffolk manors tallied 16 horses 'for the hall', LDB:416a–b (SUF:34,3).
[97] Charters, no. 21.   [98] GDB:6a (KEN:5,2).
[99] GDB:48b (HAM:45,1).   [100] GDB:195c (CAM:14,67).
[101] GDB:179d (HEF:1,7).   [102] GDB:32b (SUR:6,1).
[103] e.g. GDB:292d (NTT:30,19); *wastum*, 284b (NTT:8,2); 299c (YKS:1,9); M. L. Faull, 'Late Anglo-Saxon settlement patterns in Yorkshire', in M. L. Faull (ed.), *Studies in Late Anglo-Saxon Settlement* (Oxford, 1984), 133–4.
[104] GDB:283b (NTT:5,8), 315d (YKS:9,41).

held a four-hide, five-plough Buckinghamshire manor, now 'oppressedly and miserably', *graviter et miserabiliter*, at farm; his ability to lead a thegnly lifestyle had clearly vanished.[105] Appropriate subsistence was expected.[106] After the decease of the landholder, Dereman, in the 1090s, his brother had temporarily managed his land until a royal official took possession: then it was officially ruled that the manor must be 'stocked as on the day when Lefstan first received it after the death of his brother, except for what Lefstan himself consumed from his demesne'.[107]

We should not disparage our eleventh-century source for not costing production consumed at source. One Devon farming family I once knew completely eluded the ability of late twentieth-century bureaucracy to measure income. They 'lived of their own' on seventy poor acres (twenty-eight hectares) and a kitchen garden, producing only what the family of seven or their animals ate, and they paid many of their bills in kind. Reprimanded for not producing tax returns, the family was able to show that not only were there no net profits, there were no gross receipts. Although, by working long hours, they undoubtedly attained a higher standard of living than many waged labourers compelled to pay tax—they ate well and maintained a borrowed horse for their teenage daughter to ride—they remained untaxed. Domesday could not impose a tighter grip on agricultural returns than could the late twentieth-century Inland Revenue.

Supportive of the reasoning given here for the Domesday era is the *Rotuli de Dominabus et Pueris et Puellis*—the 1185 record of the lands of widows, heirs and heiresses temporarily in the king's custody (here called the Roll of Heirs). That collection of data—sworn in the hundreds, county by county, in the presence of four royal justices in eyre—had much in common with Domesday,[108] and provides a better idea of how a 'value' was arrived at. In it the manor's gardens were often excluded from the 'value'—there the amount to be paid to the crown—presumably because they were earmarked to sustain the resident household, whether reeve or knight: Whitchurch, for instance, was worth £20 a year 'without aids, demesne, or orchard'.[109] The Roll of Heirs did not dispute the basic produce consumed, but did censure excess, with the jurors from the hundreds able to bring the farmers' misdemeanours to light, such as those of one Richard Rufus, taking oxen, cows, and work-horses from the demesne and 222 oaks from the wood to make 'a hall and chamber' for himself elsewhere. Yet, despite Richard's depredations, a rise in the annual 'value' paid to the crown at Kimbolton from £32 to £40 is documented.[110] The principle harks back to Charlemagne's Capitulary de Villis, *cap.* 63, where

---

[105] GDB:148d (BUK:17,16).   [106] See also *LE*, vol. 2, no. 136.

[107] Van Caenegem, *Writs*, no. 66.

[108] An enquiry probably of 1185, the second of Henry II's reign; cf. The Assize of Northampton, clause 9, charged 'justices to make enquiry concerning escheats, churches, and women who are in the gift of the lord king'. Only the returns for twelve counties survive. J. Walmsley, Introduction, *Heirs*, x–xiii.

[109] *Heirs*, nos 84, 71.

[110] At Kimbolton, head of its hundred, the 'assised rents' made up just one element in the farmer's revenue, and were distinct from the annual 'value' he paid to the crown, *Heirs*, no. 106.

before the production and sales were accounted in detail, 'all the things that a man might have in his house or on his estates, our stewards shall have on our estates'.

The sustenance of the resident household being the first call on the demesne, and one largely unvalued, to what extent did demesne revenues contribute to the cash value? The Domesday evidence is scanty. Domesday records that the canons of Chichester held 'communally' sixteen hides with four demesne ploughs on land valued at £8.[111] Since there was no dependent tenantry at all, the labour presumably being done by full-time servants or brethren, there were no contributive rents; its value must have derived from demesne profits. Most demesnes would hope that, over and above household needs, a good year would see surpluses marketed. It was long-established practice. Carolingian administrators had demanded that royal estates not only delivered a set quantity of products, but also stored or sold the surplus and recorded the gains.[112] The 'best' assets were often therefore retained for the demesne; at Sporle, Norfolk, the monks of St Riquier reserved 'the best woodland, arable, and uncultivated land, and the meadow land, which was exceptionally suitable for the cultivation of all crops' and, in East Winch, they held on to a mill, a wood, and 'a good fishery'.[113] On one Domesday manor, the most regarded product was precluded from marketing, and went unaccounted for. Rayleigh, in Essex, had earlier been worth £10 and the same in 1086, 'besides the wine from its vineyard'—although, we are told, the vines rendered as much as 20 *modii* of wine 'in a good year';[114] the tacit assumption being that saleable demesne produce over and above household needs normally contributed to the value but that when it came to wine the household consumed whatever was produced—understandable in that Rayleigh was the site of Swein of Essex's castle.

Whilst lay resident households took their subsistence in kind before determining the sums entered in Domesday (as all peasant households hoped to do before paying rent), yet something of a 'mixed system' was practiced, since they all needed cash to supply other needs. The needs of the much-studied stable religious institutions were of course particular; their primary requirement was for twelve months' or more food supplies so that they were not subject to the vagaries of the market. As the farm was not normally consumed on the manor, the month's farm was usually costed and accounted for, so that individual manors could be run efficiently: thus the costed amount could appear in Domesday. The monks' lands of Christ Church, Canterbury, were all valued in monetary terms in Great Domesday and *Domesday Monachorum*. However, one in-house Canterbury list of 'farms' owed divides the manors between 'those which rendered corn and

[111] GDB:17a (SUS:3,10).

[112] *Capitulare de villis vel Curtis Imperialibus*, in H. R. Loyn and J. Percival, *The Reign of Charlemagne* (London, 1975), no. 15, *cap.* 44, 62, 65; *MGH Capitularia Regum Francorum*, ed. A. Boretius (Hanover, 1881) no. 32, *cap.* 44, 62, 65.

[113] *Acta*, no. 259.

[114] LDB:43b (ESS:24,17); cf. *LE*, II, no. 136, 'if there should be wine in sufficient quantity'.

money, and those which rendered money alone'. Here 'corn' was evidently a generic term for supplies in kind, as the 'farm of a month' denoted not merely wheat, but also oats, barley, cheeses, honey, peas and beans, salt, fuel and lights, bacon and cows. Cash too was an integral part of the month's farm, in that £8 'in pennies' were required 'for the kitchen'.[115] The twenty-five bacon pigs and four cows submitted had evidently to be of high quality—the former 'ought to be worth 2s' and the latter 'worth 3s'; moreover, 'it is the reeve's choice whether he takes the livestock or the money'—so both cash and beasts had to be ready to hand. This last requirement in a system introduced at Canterbury under Lanfranc, archbishop 1070–1089, reminds us that it is anachronistic to differentiate too sharply between cash revenues and saleable foodstuffs in kind. The legal dispute over Queen Edith's broken farm agreement stated that she had not been paid her rent 'in honey and money'.[116] Honey, the major source of sweetness, invaluable for its healing properties, and in the brewing of mead, was more precious to the ruling elite than coin (as were horses, hawks, and gold); the individual landlord's needs were paramount.

As literate institutions were demanding consumers, they often costed their households' foodstuffs in their own records, but it was rare that they were costed in Domesday. Yet, from the great manor of Leominster, with its highly organized demesne agriculture and network of supervisory riding-men, we learn that the manor, which contained a nunnery, was 'at farm' for £60, 'besides the food of the nuns'.[117] Domesday also says that Leominster should have been worth £120, 'if the manor is delivered' from that burden, evidently thought excessive for a religious house of doubtful worthiness, the abbess having been famously abducted in 1046 by Earl Swein![118] Unusually, foodstuffs are valued on land held by the priory of St Neot's from the wife of Richard fitzGilbert; it was worth £21, 'besides the food of the monks, which is estimated (*appreciatur*) at £4'.[119] (The expenditure on food was important to the fitzGilberts, since Richard became a monk there before April 1088.[120]) The Bath Abbey estate of Tidenham was given no Edwardian Domesday value 'except the food of the monks'; but a lease shows that it was then in the hands of Archbishop Stigand, who had agreed to pay the monastery 6 porpoises, 30,000 herrings, and a mark of gold (c. £10) yearly.[121] Whether the abbey received only seafood and no gold from Stigand—quite possible given his known love of the metal—or whether more provisions were substituted for gold, the lease reinforces the sense that tenurial agreements were in reality more varied than appears from the simplified Domesday record.

---

[115] *Canterbury Cathedral MS: Register K*, ff. 69v–70.   [116] *Writs*, no. 72.
[117] GDB:180a (HEF:2,30; 2,33; 2,49).
[118] It was evidently not suppressed in 1046 as supposed in D. Knowles, C. N. L. Brooke, and V. C. M. London, *The Heads of Religious Houses*, vol. 1, 2nd edn (Cambridge, 2001), 214.
[119] GDB:207b (HUN:28,1).   [120] Keats-Rohan, 363.
[121] GDB:164a (GLS:1,56); Charters, no. 117.

The demesne livestock

So very narrowly did he [William] have it investigated, that there was not one single hide or virgate of the land, nor indeed—it is a shame to relate, but it seemed no shame for him to do—not one ox nor one cow nor one pig which was left out, and not put down in his record.

Anglo-Saxon Chronicle, 1085

Amongst a bishop's first and last concerns was to conserve the stock that maintained the viability of the bishopric's demesnes. The will of Thored, bishop of London, 942–951, took as axiomatic that stock came with the episcopal demesne of Hoxne, and required that 'as much as I found on the estate' should be 'left' on it. He felt, however, entitled to dispose of the *increase* in stock made during his episcopate: half was to remain with the minster—and the other half distributed to charity for his soul.[122]

The demesne and its stock being an essential constituent of the value, an obvious way of raising manorial returns was to increase demesne livestock. Livestock, absent from Great Domesday, is recorded in both Little Domesday and Exon Domesday. It has been traditionally accepted that the livestock recorded were those only of the demesne sector of the manor.[123] However, opinion now differs: and some interpret the figures as referring to the entire tenurial unit, including the peasant sector, pointing out that the record of livestock in *Exon* occurs at the end of the account of each manor, and so follows the non-demesne population.[124] But the direct evidence lies with the traditional view. In *Exon* itself, Black Torrington has ten swineherds grouped with the villeins and smallholders, but only thirty pigs are listed in *Exon*.[125] In Little Domesday, livestock figures only where there is a demesne; no livestock other than plough-teams is normally quoted on the lands of freeholders. Moreover, the entry for Weeley does state that the livestock quoted is 'in demesne', and its stocking levels are by no means lower than usual.[126] Indeed, livestock numbers on some large and remunerative manors, with large numbers of villeins and high revenues, were often ridiculously small.[127] In the four eastern counties of Essex, Norfolk, Suffolk, and Cambridgeshire, Domesday recorded under 36,000 pigs in all,[128] yet pannage payments, for access to autumn mast for fattening pigs, for the five counties of Circuit I indicate between 135,500 to 194,000 pigs kept, representing significant numbers belonging to the peasantry.[129]

---

[122] *Wills*,1; EHD1, no. 106.

[123] e.g. H. C. Darby and R. W. Finn, *The Domesday Geography of South-West England* (Cambridge, 1967), 285.

[124] F. and C. Thorn made the point about *Exon* by correspondence. Similarly, McDonald and Snooks, tacitly, 85–9.

[125] GDB:101a (DEV:1,37) from DB4, f.93b.

[126] LDB:51a (ESS:25,2); also Snailwell, in *ICC*, f.76b.

[127] e.g. LDB:92a (ESS:55,1), and herein, nn. 136 and 159. On livestock and values, see P. Sawyer's review of Darby, *ECHR*, 2nd ser., 16 (1963–4), 155–7.

[128] Darby, *Domesday England*, 164.   [129] Harvey 1988, 127–30.

It is demesne livestock, along with rents and services, which are recorded in the surveys of the English lands of the abbey of Holy Trinity, Caen not long after 1106.[130] Plough-teams apart, it seems that the detailed Domesday texts recorded only demesne livestock.

Little Domesday sometimes records livestock at two dates and, on occasion, values appear to reflect stocking levels. At Flitcham in Norfolk, where most of the land was in demesne, the loss of the sheep flock appears to be the major factor in the reduction in value: 'Then 1 packhorse and now also. Then 3 cattle [probably cows] and 27 pigs, now 32. Then 180 sheep, now 1. Then and afterwards [worth] 40 shillings, now 1 shilling.'(See Figure 4.)[131] The effect of this flock's loss is echoed by numerous estimates in the 1185 Roll of Heirs that 100 extra sheep should add £1 in value.[132] Then, £1 was also seen as the net return expected from the working of a team of oxen.[133] In the *Leges Henrici* of the early twelfth century, it was accepted that demesne stock and assets were as relevant to a manor's value as the rents of tenants. When a manor was returned to its lord at the end of an agreement, 'inquiry must be made of the herdsmen' whether the animals were 'in full quantity and equal value'; 'they must be questioned about increases in the number of men and cattle, about whether the manor has decreased in value in respect of demesne land or tenants, pastures or woods'. Importantly, particulars of rents increased or unjustly exacted and of stocks of grain were also sought.[134]

Disease in cattle and sheep as well as political turmoil and foraging troops could, of course, have a devastating effect on herds.[135] The Pipe Roll of 1130 shows sheriffs empowered to restock royal manors and those of a vacant bishopric, and to sell surplus animals from others.[136] Similarly, the *Herefordshire Domesday* of Henry II's reign, looking back to Henry I's time, assumed that the level of livestock was integral to the level of returns: 'Stanford used to render (*reddebat*) £5 with this stock, that is to say, 6 oxen and 1 cow and 1 draught horse.'[137]

Indeed, there was enormous expenditure on restocking royal estates in the first four years of Henry II's reign, £1,178 in 1155–6 alone.[138] In the Roll of Heirs, the great majority of valuations, some fifty-two cases, were related specifically to the levels of livestock: a further eight were evaluated both with and without stock, and only six 'without stock'. In that text, one value was based on 'reasonable' stocking levels; another manor could 'not sustain further stock' nor could it 'be worth more' (*nec plus valere*).[139] In 1085, as in 1185, evaluation was a skill common to farmers

---

[130] *Caen*, Chibnall, 33–8.   [131] LDB:173a–b (NFK:9,6).

[132] *Heirs*, nos 61, 69, 70, 90, 99, 109, 111, 143, 144, 165.   [133] *Heirs*, no. 91.

[134] *LegesHP*, 175; cf. J. L. Nelson, 'Dispute settlement in Carolingian West Francia', *Dispute Settlement*, 50–1, discussed Ch. 10, nn. 219, 250.

[135] e.g. 'cattle disease', LDB:1b (ESS:1,3).   [136] *PRS Henry I, 2012*, 96, 102–3.

[137] *Herefordshire Domesday*, ed. V. H. Galbraith and J. Tait, PRS, 63 (1947–8); ns, 25 (1950), 75.

[138] E. Amt, *The Accession of Henry II in England* (Woodbridge, 1993), 141–8; the costs of restocking are tabulated at 144.

[139] *Heirs*, nos 187, 188.

Figure 4. William's army foraging: slaughtering livestock, by special permission of the city of Bayeux and the Bayeux Museum.

of manors and jurors alike, who were evidently familiar with the prevailing costs and anticipated returns from restocking. Given that the only native coin in use in 1086 was the silver penny, it is impressive how many people were able to estimate returns in terms of large sums of pounds and shillings.

In Domesday, numbers are usually specific for large animals—horses and oxen—and rounded for the smaller: a unique and telling entry in Great Domesday mentions 68 cattle, 350 sheep, 150 pigs, 50 goats, and a mare—together with woodland for 50 pigs.[140] On royal land in Devon, numbers of sheep are frequently rounded, with a sequence of 200, 300, 500, 500 on the larger manors,[141] and many other flocks noted in multiples of 10, 50, or 100. Sometimes round numbers hint of a policy: on Richard fitzGilbert's great demesnes in Suffolk, two manors had 480 sheep and one 960 sheep, perhaps suggesting a planned ratio of sheep to shepherd.[142]

The rounded numbers of smaller animals reflect the hard truth that, in terms of revenues, it took progeny and profits from flocks of a great size to improve the cash income of a manor dramatically. Neither pigs nor sheep, both smaller than today, were of much individual value: the Laws of Athelstan had valued a sheep at 5d, a pig at 10d, a cow at 20d, an ox at 30d.[143] Levels changed little until the late

---

[140] GDB:139b (HRT:31,8).

[141] e.g. DEV:1,34–1,40.

[142] LDB:289b (SUF:25,1–2), 390a (SUF:25,3). Harvey 1988, 87–121, discusses demesne agriculture in greater detail.

[143] VI Athelstan, 6.1–2.

twelfth century.[144] The *gebur*, or tied peasant, of the *Rectitudines* paid a young sheep or 2d at Easter, and the dues from Hurstborne Priors equate two young sheep with one fully grown.[145] In Domesday itself, instances occur of oxen reckoned at 24d and 30d and sheep at a mere 2½d.[146] Thus, the many great leaps in values between 1066 and 1086 were unlikely to have had increased sales of demesne progeny as their source.

Where land was suitable, investment in grain production seems to have brought returns comparable to those from investment in sheep, although grain demanded more manpower at two full-timers for each plough. As oxen were priced at some 30d or 2s each, the capital cost of a full team of eight was about £1—about the same as that of 100 sheep.[147] Of course the grain and livestock sectors also interacted—most probably the pasturing of sheep on fallow was important to both—but on this Domesday provides little evidence. Before 1066, an acre of 'grain', delivered, was valued at 4d.[148] Given that land returned values of between 10s to £1 per Domesday plough-team in most reasonably fertile counties, these prices suggest that in a good year gross returns might be as high as fifty per cent of the outlay on stock. Even more essential than cash was, of course, the subsistence of the peasant cultivators of the land and their dependents, and this, except when rents threatened to encroach upon it, did not figure in the records, any more than did the subsistence of the occupants of the demesne.

Domesday's livestock figures provided an agricultural context for changes in value. Once these values were authenticated, the novel details of the pigs and other demesne animals that so offended the educated Englishman who chronicled William's last years could then be excluded. Livestock of small freeholders and peasantry were ignored, except for plough animals, which not only represented working capital, but also served as a guide to the extent of the arable that could be cultivated, and the services requited. The request for annual values was a revolutionary demand in 1086; thereafter however, such information continued to be sought by royal officials. The plough-teams, too, were retained, for good fiscal and economic reasons. All went much according to plan: and the product, Great Domesday, was well summed up by the Anglo-Saxon Chronicler:

> Also he [William] had a record made of how much land his archbishops had, and his bishops and his abbots and his earls – and though I relate it at too great length – what

---

[144] A. L. Poole, 'Live stock prices in the twelfth century', *EHR*, 55 (1940), 284–95; D. L. Farmer, 'Some price fluctuations in Angevin England', *ECHR* 2nd ser., 9 (1956), 40–1.

[145] EHD2, nos 172, 173. The estimated cost of 100 sheep on the Glastonbury estate in 1189 was 4d per head, N. E. Stacey, 'The state of the demesne manors of Glastonbury Abbey in the twelfth century', in Evans (ed.), *Lordship and Learning* (Woodbridge, 2004), 114.

[146] Ox, GDB:116d (DEV:43,1), 117d (DEV:51,2), 120c (CON:1,15), 263a, (CHS:B2); '24 sheep or 5s', DB4, 473. Hence McDonald and Snooks found that livestock were only a marginally positive source of income, 'The determinants of manorial income in Domesday England: evidence from Essex', *Journal of Economic History*, 45 (1985), 541–56. *Domesday Economy*, 85–9.

[147] Table of prices in Harvey 1988, 57.   [148] GDB:143d (BUK:3a1).

or how much everybody had who was occupying land in England, in land or cattle, and how much money it was worth.[149]

Rents and dues

> King William had a record of the whole of England made (*fecit describi*) ... and what renders each estate was able to pay and the country was vexed with the many disasters that proceeded from this survey (*et quantum red[d]itus queque possessio reddere poterat: et vexata est terra multis cladibus inde procentibus*).
>
> John of Worcester[150]

The terms in the texts were a matter of standpoint: one person's piece of rented-out land was another's demesne or land-in-hand. Many free and subordinate holdings on large manors were well over a hide in size (120 fiscal acres or thereabouts) and might well require their own workforce of smallholders, with some land reserved for them. On the difference between renting, leasing, and paying a farm, *ad firmam*, Domesday itself draws no hard and fast line.[151] Here, however, I use the term 'rent' for landed units smaller than manors, and 'lease' or 'farm' to denote the renting of the whole manor, usually with a demesne. The distinction is, of course, necessarily arbitrary, given that Domesday deals with at least 14,000 distinct landholding units—themselves the simplifications of conquerors—in which every conceivable gradation was represented.

Broadly speaking, two sources of rents and dues augmented the demesne's own revenues: on the one hand, the dependent tenures of smallholders and villeins; and on the other, the rents of free tenants and the dues of landed freeholders who might be regarded as within the jurisdiction of the manor or hundred. The dues themselves were, however, multitudinous: witness the numerous payments and gelds owed to the bishop of Winchester's jurisdiction of Taunton.[152] Until relatively recently, the contribution of peasants to the manorial economy in the eleventh century was not fully appreciated: the statistical summaries and maps of the *Domesday Geographies,* for instance, do not distinguish between the plough-teams of the demesne sector and those of the peasants.[153] Yet we should not be misled by Domesday's orientation to the lands and incomes of the great landlords: England at the time was primarily a land of small agriculturalists, who contributed to the demesne directly, by their labour and working capital and, indirectly, through rents and dues. In fact, on the Domesday demesnes there are over 22,000 plough-teams recorded compared with over 59,000 for the manorial villeins and small landholders together;[154] thus the peasantry owned more than two and a half times as many plough-teams as the demesnes.

---

[149] *ASC,* 1085.   [150] *JW* 3.44, cf. vol. 2, n. 184.

[151] e.g. some knights, *milites,* held 'villein land', Harvey 1970, 23–4.

[152] GDB:87c (SOM:2,2–4); Charters, App. I, no. 4.

[153] Nor does Maitland, 400–3. But Baring's *Domesday Tables* tabulates them separately, also Vinogradoff, *English Society in the Eleventh Century,* App. IX.

[154] The AHRC Open Domesday project supplies county totals and calculates 22,155 demesne ploughs, compared with 57,344 ploughs held by 'the men'. All recorded ploughs total 81,262, leaving

The virtual absence of demesne plough-teams from some of the richest royal manors points to the high returns extracted from peasant agriculture, and to the viability and profitability of small-scale agricultural units in the eleventh century. The royal manors of Kent and Suffolk were at the extreme end of the spectrum: Dartford and Milton had only two and three plough-teams respectively in demesne; yet with 220 peasant teams together they were worth nearly £300.[155] Although some manors in the west of England had a high proportion of demesne, the norm for royal manors across the country was approximately 1:5 or 1:6 of demesne to tenants' plough-teams; however, ploughing and carrying services for the demesne were undoubtedly required in many places. The foundation charter for Blyth priory, *c.*1088, shows that the men of the vill—in Domesday four villeins and four smallholders—were rendering Roger de Builli services of ploughing, carrying, mowing, reaping and haymaking, paying merchet, and making ponds.[156] Yet within vast manors embracing several communities, peasant ploughs were not necessarily close enough at hand for regular ploughing services: at Leominster the 224 husbandmen ploughed only 125 acres (51 hectares), or less.[157] Nor, with the exception of sheep-rearing, did the demesnes of royal manors necessarily concentrate on animal husbandry rather than arable: there is little sign of large numbers of demesne cattle in either eastern England or in the south-west (although some royal manors of the south-west did have substantial flocks of sheep); and on those manors that did have a marked number of demesne plough-teams, they were particularly associated with slaves.[158] Some large royal manors had had no significant demesne in King Edward's day, and seem since to have run down what they had. Thorney in Stowmarket had rid itself of its single demesne plough-team by 1086; it had no other stock, moreover, and no longer kept slaves. Its value of £40 blanch must have been produced entirely by rent- and due-payers.[159] The preference of many large landholders for accumulating rents rather than managing land directly is easy to comprehend; for a recently arrived elite who spoke an alien tongue, the preference was often an imperative.

It has been suggested that the peasantry, living at no more than subsistence level, were largely non-contributory to the cash sums in Domesday.[160] Yet, as payers of both geld and dues for decades, peasants needed coin. There had long been various cash poll taxes and compulsory giving of alms: the *chevage* of Peter's Pence, for instance, was supposedly annual, payable by free and unfree.[161] Domesday *villani*, recognized holders of land within the vill, were liable to tax on their portions

---

1,763 ploughs on small independent free-holdings—which are under-recorded in Domesday. I thank John Palmer for help with these figures.

[155] Also Faversham, GDB:2c–d (KEN:1,1;1,3–4).

[156] *Cartulary of Blyth Priory*, ed. R. T. Timson, Thoroton Society Records, 27 (1973), vol.1, no. 325. GDB:285b (NTT:9,49).

[157] GDB:180a (HEF:1,10a).

[158] Harvey 1988, 88–91.   [159] LDB:281b (SUF:1,1); Harvey 1983, 63–9.

[160] McDonald and Snooks, 98; see debate on p. 162 and at note. 6 of this chapter.

[161] e.g. VII Æthelred, 2, 5; I Cnut, 9; *Acta*, no. 288.

of a hide.[162] Further, analysis of the Domesday plough-team data shows that over 300 villeins were part of a group averaging one plough-team each or more, and so more than a hundred acres (forty hectares); and that well over 2,500 villeins were members of a group averaging at least half a plough-team or more.[163] Indeed throughout the eleventh century peasants were also contributing to the market in order to acquire iron tools, pottery, and other necessities.[164] The shoemaker in Aelfric's *Colloquy* asserts that the shoes, reins, bottles, and flasks he sold were essentials: 'Not one of you could pass a winter except for my trade'.[165]

In theory, the Conquest made it easy for incoming landholders to increase rents and dues from native freeholders; but their continued success depended on these smaller units remaining both profitable and viable. True, small producers were always handicapped by their inability to access the more profitable long-distance markets directly, but studies of later centuries now understand that, contrary to previous tenets, the smaller agricultural units were actively effective in extending production, and in providing the wherewithal for numerous local markets.[166] The statistical computer study based upon the lay landholders of Essex suggested that agricultural methods were much the same whatever the landholder and the size of the estate.[167] Yet arguably the similarities derive from the fact that many great lay landlords of eastern England were not running large enterprises, but amassing rents, and their estates were simply agglomerations of freeholders.

In fact, even the greatest Anglo-Saxon estates had acknowledged boundaries of features such as streams and pagan burial sites, so that even distant assets could be converted into revenue, with the aid of an enterprising population. At Benson in Oxfordshire, 'the meadows and pastures and fisheries and woodland' returned £18 15s 5d each year; at Shipton-under-Wychwood, £12 17s came 'from meadows, pannage, rents, and other customary dues'.[168] The jurisdiction of several hundreds was attached to each of these manors, bringing their returns up to £85 in the case of Benson and £72 in the case of Shipton; the size of these sums alone helps explain why the commitment of great estates to demesne arable farming was not axiomatic. Access to rough pasturage and woodland came into the category of rights whose lines were easily blurred, so raising grazing dues to the level of rents became an easy matter in the wake of conquest. The *Dialogus* long ago distinguished between 'farms' (often the equivalent of the 'value'), which ought to stay steady—and rents

---

[162] e.g. GDB:203b (HUN:B21); Maitland, 120–8; E. Searle, 'Hides, virgates and tenant settlement at Battle Abbey', *ECHR*, 2nd ser., 16 (1963–4), 290–300.

[163] R. Lennard, 'The economic position of Domesday *villani*', *The Economic Journal*, 56 (1946), 244–64, important tables at 262–4.

[164] Dyer, in *A Commercialising Economy*, 197.

[165] *Ælfric and the Homilists*, ed. N. G. Garmonsway (London, 1939), 183.

[166] B. M. S. Campbell, *English Seigneurial Agriculture 1250–1450* (Cambridge, 2000), 3, 11, 55–7; C. C. Dyer, 'The hidden trade of the Middle Ages: evidence from the West Midlands', in *Everyday life in Medieval England* (London, 1994), 283–303.

[167] J. McDonald and G. D. Snooks, 'Determinants of manorial income in Domesday England', *Journal of Economic History*, 45 (1985) 541–56.

[168] GDB:154c (OXF:1,1;1,5).

(*census*), particularly from woodland, which 'rise and fall' as they 'are cut down daily and shrink each year'; but its clarity has been somewhat muddied by translating *census* into the obscure 'cesses' in both editions.[169] In short, the bulk of revenues from large manors with small demesnes came not from any direct agricultural effort, but from the efforts of smaller enterprises within their bounds. And when, nearly a hundred years after Domesday, Abbot Samson ordered a *descriptio generalis* in writing of the hidages, dues, and revenues in each hundred of Bury St Edmunds, it was because these 'in great part had always been concealed by the farmers'.[170]

Although many hundreds were still attached to royal manors, some jurisdictions were temporarily reallocated.[171] The Abbey of Bury St. Edmund's had a liberty of eight and a half hundreds attached to its lands; the bishopric of Worcester had a triple hundred; Richard fitzGilbert of Tonbridge, a 'banlieu' in Kent; and the county of Sussex was carved into five jurisdictions. With two sets of rights held by the same landholder, it soon became difficult to discern where hundredal dues ceased and manorial rents began. Other hundreds were held by royal deputies. A manor with hundredal jurisdiction collected dues not only for pasture, but also the profits from hundredal jurisdiction and infringements of the peace owed to the king, for which the hundred provided the most convenient collecting vehicle.[172] The former freeholders' contribution to manorial incomes in 1086 was substantial, and the easiest way for the landlord—especially for an office-holder in the new regime—to raise his profits was from converting freeholders into sokemen (those who owed jurisdictional dues), and both into full-scale rent-payers. Between 1066 and 1086 the value of Buckenham in Norfolk, one of the demesne manors forfeited by Ralph Guader, Earl of East Anglia, after his rebellious plotting in 1075, had risen fivefold, the main change being the manor's acquisition of forty-three sokemen.[173] At Mutford, held formerly by Earl Gyrth, a number of freemen paying a mere 13s 6d in King Edward's time, were made to pay a total of £30 by 1085, imposed on them by Ælfric the reeve under Bigod the sheriff, although their assets in plough-teams had declined.[174] Little Domesday provides striking testimony to the way in which the people of the former lands of 'Earl Harold', or of his brother, Gyrth, were hit by the crippling impositions on free- and soke-holders. A succession of sheriffs, working with Anglo-Saxon reeves, appear to have deliberately impoverished those who might hold old loyalties. Certainly, the sheriffs' politicized action against the

---

[169] *Dialogus*, 30–1; *Dialogus de Scaccario: The Dialogue of the Exchequer/Richard fitzNigel*, Amt, 47.

[170] *The Chronicle of Jocelin of Brakelond*, ed. H. E. Butler (London, 1962), 29, resulting in *Kalendar, Abbot Samson*. With full jurisdiction, Wye 'would be worth £20 more', GDB:11d (KEN:6,1).

[171] It has been estimated that some 130 were in private hands by 1086, H. M. Cam, *Liberties and Communities in Medieval England* (Cambridge, 1944), 59; but see *Writs*, 124–31: many alienations took place under Henry I.

[172] e.g. LDB:120a–b (NFK:1,73;1,75). [173] LDB:126b–127 (NFK:1,139).

[174] LDB:283a (SUF:1,23–30); also 110a (NFK:1,3), from 12 ploughs to 3.

followings of former magnates makes an across-the-board statistical manipulation of Domesday's monetary sums more hazardous.

The tactic, commonly visible in East Anglia, of putting freemen and their holdings within a manor 'in order to complete the sum' expected, appears to have amounted to a deliberate policy of post-Conquest control.[175] At Benfleet, Essex, a free man with half a hide was 'made into one of the villeins' and was then included 'in the above calculation' of Benfleet's value;[176] such controversial additions as his were likely to be at the source of the 'render' versus 'value' data we see there. The lands of twenty freemen were put at rent, *adcensavit*, first by Ralph Guader, earl of East Anglia, then by Ivo Taillebois.[177] Their value had been £4, now it was £8. Between 1066 and 1086 the directive on rents from many officials seems to have been 'double, or quit'! The steepness of these demands on freemen should be measured by the number of additional animals required to be raised and marketed in order to produce such returns. This extortion increased cash returns temporarily, but in the long run militated against increased output.

Nevertheless, in 1086, Domesday speaks of a change of policy, with the actions of some officials now felt to be excessive.[178] A range of lands, several of whose free holders were formerly commended to Earl Gyrth, had rendered 20s at farm before 1066. Now in the king's hands, Roger Bigod's reeve increased them first to 100s; then, under Hugh de Houdain, to £50, 'as the men say', a phrase suggesting that someone was sceptical of the leap in returns alleged.[179] Yet, unsurprisingly perhaps, we later find Hugh de Houdain reported as being 'in royal custody'.[180] Similarly, it went on record that at Combs, Suffolk, held by the king's half-brother, Robert of Mortain, fifty freemen whose obligations had once been 'commendation only, in the king's soke', were worth formerly £16, now £31, 'but they cannot bear it without ruin'.[181] Retaining only half their former ploughing animals, their returns, even if temporary, were astounding: the increase in levels of rent being equivalent to, say, raising and marketing an extra thirty-six young sheep per freeman. Other freemen at Fodderstone in Suffolk were newly obliged to pay customary dues 'because they could not do without their pasture'.[182] Domesday contains more examples.

Thus higher monetary demands did not necessarily enforce higher efficiency on the peasants and small landholders: they often resulted in the depletion of livestock—the working capital—and diminished ploughing power. It was not in the interest of long-term productivity to demote the economic status of peasants to the point of limiting their grazing and forcing them to sell their livestock—especially as they provided the bulk of the ploughing-power. Nor was it beneficial to long-term receipts to raise rents and dues to the point of diminishing returns

[175] LDB:173b (NFK:9,8).   [176] LDB:1b (ESS:1,1).
[177] LDB:125b (NFK:1,31).   [178] See Chs. 9 and 10 in this volume.
[179] LDB:283b–284b (SUF:1,44–60).   [180] LDB:448b (SUF:76,14).
[181] LDB:291a (SUF:2,6).   [182] LDB:274a (NFK:66,15).

since payments in the form of hens, sheep, and pigs formed consistent elements in the supply of food to manorial lords; one pig in seven, or in ten, was commonly paid by small producers to the manor in return for pannage, or for pasturage—nearly 20,000 pigs were so paid in Circuit I.[183] Only the most spendthrift of heirs, or the most recent of military conquerors, would overlook the force of these points. Unsurprisingly our sporadic evidence suggests a flattening out in landholders' returns for the eighty years following 1086.

Forfeitures and fines offered easier and quicker returns from landholding than demesne agriculture: in comparison, putative demesne profits from maintaining a hundred sheep or from two men working an eight-oxen plough paled into insignificance—witness the known scale of fines for shire jurisdiction. The soke jurisdiction of just one man produced 4s of revenue for the king's reeve.[184] At Dover, £8 was chargeable for a breach of the peace and 100 shillings for felling a tree or branch on the king's highway and carrying off the wood or foliage. Similarly, 100s was payable for the non-appearance of landholders at the shire moot.[185] In the 'land between the Ribble and Mersey', where returns from land were much lower than in Kent, anyone absenting himself from the shire moot without reasonable excuse was fined 10s, and anyone absent from the hundred, or the hearing of pleas on the reeve's order, was fined 5s.[186] Many hundredal manors drew fifty per cent or more of their cash income from sake and soke and other dues. One of the sheriff's deputies farmed Stow Bedon, Norfolk, for £13 13s 4d and a 20s premium, *gersuma*, for 'as long as he had the soke; now, since he lost the soke, it pays £7'.[187]

Whilst information about changing levels of rent, and expected levels of profit, is crucial to any assessment of the land market, generalizations about 'normal' rental levels can be precarious; the Roll of Heirs contains examples of how profit margins might differ. In 1185, one young heir had 'a mill for which he pays 30s and 3½ burgage acres for which he pays 6s 6d and the surplus is worth 1s 6d to him'. In contrast, his mother held land for which she paid a mere 28d, 'and it is worth 15s a year more than this'.[188] Simple circumstance, as well as regional social structures and politics, often played its part.

The demesne was important in determining the value of a property to the sitting tenant as a means of livelihood—and to his overlord in rent; but it was less easily productive of soaring revenues than were rents and widespread jurisdiction over woodland and pasture. It was these last that determined whether high levels of profit were to be obtained from a manor; the devastating verdict of the Anglo-Norman chronicler, Henry of Huntingdon, was no hyperbole, but a pretty accurate view of what was happening in the agricultural sector:

---

[183] e.g. at Hurstbourne Priors, EHD2, no. 173; Harvey 1988, 127–30.
[184] LDB:360b (SUF:14,37).   [185] GDB:1b (KEN:D12, D14–15).
[186] GDB:269d (CHS:R1,40d).   [187] LDB:126a (NFK:1,135).
[188] *Heirs*, no. 77.

Their [the Normans'] character is such that when they had brought their enemies so low that they can cast them down no further, they bring themselves down, and reduce their own lands to poverty and waste . . . And so in England they increased, in those times, unjust tolls and very evil customary dues *(pessime consuetudines)*. All the leaders had been so blinded by desire for gold and silver . . .[189]

The scenario was long to remain familiar: an unusual record of a dispute in 1341 concerned 'certain customs' which the steward and bailiffs were demanding from the tenants, who claimed that the exactions were new and unjust. It was finally determined that the lord, or his steward, did have powers to exact entry fines at will on customary land—but with the proviso that 'the law of God and of the land wills that the fine be made reasonably',[190] a proviso that the English tenantry and former freeholders of 1086 would have endorsed wholeheartedly. But eleventh-century conquerors and their agents had too much room for manoeuvre.

Ancillary assets

Unfortunately, Domesday is not clear whether separately valued assets—woodland, meadow, mills—were always computed within the total Domesday value. It was obviously possible to sub-let various components of the manorial economy: three mills were leased separately from the manor two decades later on the manor of Horstead belonging to the abbey of Holy Trinity, Caen.[191] We are on safe ground with the royal manor of 'Coton' near Warwick, farmed out to the sheriff, Robert d'Oilli: in 1086 its value was £30, 'with everything that belongs to it'—'everything' here obviously included 100s from two mills, £4 from meadows and pastures, and 50s paid by 100 bordars, probably market-gardeners, for their garden-plots *(hortulis suis)* outside the borough of Warwick. Thanks to the same punctilious sheriff, Domesday was equally careful about the barons' burgages in Warwick, as we are told explicitly that they have been priced in with their manors.[192] The question is: were this punctilious sheriff's methods of accounting unusual? Or confined to royal officials? Or can we infer that they were general practice?

Sub-let assets were indeed more likely to be recorded separately, which may explain geographical aberrancies in the recorded distribution of mills and churches, visible capital assets that undoubtedly often went unrecorded in Domesday.[193] Income from mills was often recorded separately, and sometimes they were recorded as either kept in hand or rented out.[194] In 1185 too, mills with land were often separately rented out.[195] Major assets, like churches and mills, were no doubt given

[189] HH, 402–3.

[190] J. Birrell and D. Hutchinson, 'An Alrewas Rental of 1341', in *A Medieval Miscellany: Collections for a History of Staffordshire*, Staffs Record Society 4th ser., 20 (2004), 76.

[191] *Caen*, Chibnall, 36.   [192] *appreciatae sunt*, GDB:238a (WAR:B2).

[193] A Canterbury list of churches records many more eleventh-century churches than either Great Domesday or *Domesday Monachorum*, DMon, 78–9. On mills, Darby, *Domesday England*, 272–5, 261.

[194] e.g. *Acta*, no. 266 for demesne mills.   [195] *Heirs*, nos 36, 41.

a separate valuation for good reason: both were specialist structures requiring investment and trained personnel; both normally levied their own dues. The calculations of McDonald and Snooks clearly indicate that the mill renders given were not subsumed in the annual values.[196] A profitable mill might be subject to a hierarchy of payments: Odo, as earl of Kent, took a mark of gold from Herbert fitzIvo for allowing him to appropriate a mill belonging to St Martin's, Dover, without its consent:[197] Herbert sought to profit from it, as did the miller he needed to operate it.

Not many churches were valued separately but on Winchester land even a church worth 40s 'nevertheless' had 50s paid from it.[198] Unusually, William de Warenne's fief in Norfolk explains the rationale on his lands: 'all the churches are appraised with the manors';[199] and indeed, no sums of money are mentioned there connected with his churches, although their presence, and their glebe—up to sixty acres (twenty-four hectares)—is regularly recorded, as is one church that is 'without land'.[200] Similar practice applied on the royal lands in Norfolk: 'all the churches are priced (*in pretio*) in with the manors',[201] also to the Norfolk lands of Hermer de Ferrers.[202] Warenne and Hermer helpfully inform posterity of their policy but, as both men moved within the circle of high office-holders, our difficulty is to know whether their accounting practices are the exception or the rule in Domesday.

At the very least, these rare details demonstrate that contemporaries were aware it was current practice to calculate such assets either way. The Lichfield entry for the bishopric—until his recent death held by Bishop Peter, a former royal clerk—states that the value of the additional berewicks, sub-tenures, and mill of this large manor, 'is calculated in with the manor', *valentia in manerio est computata*.[203] The largest manors not uncommonly declare that the sum is the 'total value', *in totis valentiis, inter totum*, an indication that behind the value was an agglomeration of payments for assets; as Great Domesday is an abbreviated text, it seems justifiable to take such signals literally.[204]

Leases and other agreements

The hazardous yet highly profitable venture the Normans had embarked upon was still not secure in 1085, so social, military, and political solidarity within their own group was vital. As ever, personal contacts expected to receive land on better terms than those short-term leases or farms negotiated with the conquered or with asset-stripping reeves. As ever, too, supposedly 'safe' agreements with acquaintances did not always turn out as intended: a post-Conquest writ shows no lesser

---

[196] *Domesday Economy*, 86–90. [197] GDB:2b (KEN:P19).
[198] GDB:41d (HAM:3,18). [199] *appreciatae sunt*, LDB:172a (NFK:8,136).
[200] LDB:169b (NFK:8,108). [201] LDB:116a (NFK:1,60).
[202] LDB:208 (NFK:13,23).
[203] GDB:247b (STS:2,22); *in eodem computo et pretio*, LDB:328b (SUF:6,308).
[204] Also the working hypothesis in Grassi, 'The lands and revenues of Edward the Confessor', *EHR*, 117 (2002), 258–9.

personage than Queen Edith seeking 'just judgement, *richte dom*, concerning Wudumann, to whom I entrusted my horses, and who for six years has withheld my rent, both honey and money'.[205] Wheeling and dealing in leases for favour and for the favoured was common both before and after 1066: brothers and nephews of an abbot or bishop commonly held lands on lease or for services from religious houses. However, when the conquerors negotiated a lease or subtenancy, *force majeure* was often given an apparent legitimacy: Hugh de Montfort, a leading landholder employed as a justice, simply took over six manors of Ely Abbey that had been loaned to a previous abbot's brother and held on to them, despite the abbey's protests.[206]

There were multifarious ways of going about renting and leasing, and one obstacle to a clear definition of land management at this period is that 'one type of management shades into another'.[207] Domesday detail has encouraged historians to try to establish the norms of land exploitation; however, practices and landlordly requirements varied widely. One brave historian of agrarian rental values between 1500–1914 has stressed the invalidity of simply averaging all available rents: only those agreements made 'in a competitive market' in any single year represent current market conditions; for the rest, 'land was held on a bewildering variety of terms: . . . customary leases well below market values, leases for lives where the current rent has little relation to market conditions, and, renewable leases with low annual rents, but large entry fines and so on'.[208] This range of tenures, and consequent cautions, all apply to Domesday: our text reveals a competitive market, but also hints of the play of undocumented personal and political factors.

A lease, the alternative to direct supervision, obviated the problems and costs of management. As the majority of Domesday landholding units had a demesne, then demesne revenues inevitably formed part of its market value, especially when there was every sign of a competition for land between newcomers, residents, and dispossessed. The essential ingredients for an agricultural enterprise, after land, were labour and stock. Three mid eleventh-century charters transfer land 'with produce and men', *mid mete* and *mid mannum*, one adding 'with everything as the estate stood at the time', and another, 'exactly as it stands'.[209] Bishop Giso's purchase of land in 1072 has the same phrases.[210] One transaction in Great Domesday, recorded only because the land was wrongly appropriated, actually lists the livestock thereby lost.[211] Domesday records elsewhere that, after the third heir, a leased manor should return to St Peter's, Winchester, and with all its livestock.[212] Not only the demesne livestock, but also the men and all their stock

---

[205] *Writs*, no. 72.   [206] *LE*, II. no. 97; *Acta* no. 129.   [207] Lennard, 111.
[208] G. Clark, 'Land rental values and the agrarian economy: England and Wales, 1500–1914', *European Review of Economic History*, 6 (2002), 281–308, at 281.
[209] Charters, nos 105, 114, 101.   [210] Keynes, 'Giso', App. III.
[211] GDB:139b (HRT:31,8); Lennard, 189–96, gives early twelfth-century examples of stock and land leases.
[212] GDB:46d (HAM:29,3).

were required to be restored to Dereman's manor when it was taken into royal hands in the 1090s.[213]

At times, the better option was to lease land without stock; the farmer, in the course of building up his flocks and herds, would then supply his own. Certainly, a few uninhabited and waste manors in Yorkshire still produced rental income from grazing, presumably utilized by the flocks and herds of neighbouring vills.[214] Alternatives were certainly seriously costed in the Roll of Heirs: Great Chesterford in Essex was worth £12 a year 'without stock'; 'if there were 2 ploughs, 100 sheep, 6 cows, 1 bull and 7 pigs it would be worth £20'.[215] Obviously, additional livestock should give higher returns but, equally, more livestock necessitated additional investment, labour, supervision, and marketing, and precluded the possibility of renting out surplus land for cash.

The extent of commercial leasing before the Conquest is uncertain, although life-leases, or longer, of ecclesiastical lands were usual: but whether the relationship between the Edwardian holder and his lord was tenurial or personal went unrecorded in many Domesday counties. In 1086, the evidence is that landholders had a mix of motives and sought a variety of returns. After consulting his council over his agreement with de Lacy, the bishop of Hereford preferred to continue with the service of knights as a return for one manor and to take money for the other. An agreement of Archbishop Eadsige of Canterbury, *c*.1045, recorded the option to renew a lease after two lives 'agreeably to the archbishop, at a fair rent, *to rihtan gafol*, or in accordance with such arrangements as may be devised at the time'.[216] His compromising tone contrasts with that in Archbishop Stigand's surviving leases for two lives that insist on renewal 'for as much money as he [the lessee] could furnish at the time'.[217] Stigand, archbishop 1052–70, in addition to his revenues from the bishoprics of Winchester and Canterbury, had built up a landed fortune, with landed interests in ten counties producing over £750, using his influence to take on leases from many religious houses—Ely, Bury St Edmund's, Peterborough, St Albans, Bath, and Abingdon—and drawing income from the churches of St Oswald and St Martin's, Dover. All this made him, perhaps in the office of treasurer, one of the wealthiest of landholders; and some leased lands were not returned to these institutions on his fall—or only with the greatest difficulty.[218]

In 1086, the evidence suggests that many of the greater landholders' demesne manors were indeed 'farmed out' or leased for shorter periods than before, perhaps for terms of three or four years. The clout of the conquerors meant increments, and between 1066 and 1086 terms changed frequently: in the favoured south-east, revenues from land often dipped then rose dramatically. Moreover, it appears that the revenue policies of the *curiales*—of leading ecclesiastics, of Odo of Bayeux,

[213] Van Caenegem, *Writs*, no. 66.
[214] e.g. GDB:329c (YKS:25,21–2), 330a (YKS:28,19).
[215] *Heirs*, nos 189, 190; also, nos 132, 133.
[216] Charters, no. 101.   [217] Charters, nos 106, 107.
[218] M. F. Smith, 'Archbishop Stigand and the eye of the needle', *ANS*, 16 (1993), 204–14, 219.

of Walkelin, and of the crown officers, Roger Bigod, Edward of Salisbury, Oda of Winchester, and Eudo Dapifer, and even those of Lanfranc, archbishop of Canterbury, particularly in the south and east of England, were more aggressive than those of other landlords: perhaps because they, their deputies, and their manorial reeves or lessees, all needed to be satisfied. The archbishop's Pagham of Pagham hundred, formerly worth £40, now had a value of £60, and was paying £80, 'but it is too heavy'.[219] Large rises in Wiltshire values took place on the estates of the sheriff, Edward of Salisbury, and on the estates of Glastonbury Abbey. The abbey was in a state of vacancy, so its Wiltshire estates may well have come under the supervision of a royal official, perhaps of Edward himself. But ruthlessness had also been the rule at Glastonbury under its abbot, Thurstan. (The vacancy had come about from the abbot's removal after the murderous riot he caused in his monastery in 1083 when, to ensure his monks' obedience to his changes to their chant, he had sunk to calling in his household knights, who killed several monks in the church itself, wounding yet more.[220])

It is those Domesday tenants-in-chief who were working *curiales* who are responsible for most of the non-royal 'renders' that are higher than values, and for the most dramatically raised values. Eudo Dapifer, for instance, had contrived that the farm of two of his Essex manors virtually doubled: Munden had been worth £10 TRE; when Eudo himself was the farmer it produced £19, and was 'now' worth £17;[221] Weeley had been worth £8, and was now worth £17 and an ounce of gold.[222] Not only officials but royal clerks took on the farming of vacant ecclesiastical estates and it seems to have become the apprenticeship for a bishopric, sometimes leading to the new custodian calling for a *descriptio* of the estate. Peter, a royal chaplain, bishop of Lichfield/Chester 1072–85, was put temporarily in charge of the bishopric of Dorchester/Lincoln,[223] possibly in 1070–1 when its bishop was suspended. William of Malmesbury observed that no 'priest became rich unless he was—to use a somewhat foreign word—a rentier (*firmarius*)'.[224] Importantly for understanding Domesday, the pre-Domesday practice for leading *curiales* to supervise the revenues of vacant lands and ecclesiastical offices provided an obvious motive for Domesday's collection of data on assets and values.

Among the entrepreneurial lessees of 1086, some have native names,[225] and like Swein, sometime sheriff of Essex,[226] seem to have been content to exploit their countrymen for the benefit of themselves and the invaders—countrymen obliged, as twelfth-century Exchequer tradition had it, 'to purchase the favour of their lords by devoted services'.[227] Godric, a deputy shire reeve, was in charge of many royal lands in Norfolk which have dramatically raised values. He also features in Domesday in an apparently more beneficent role, contributing to the survival of one of

---

[219] *sed nimis grave est,* GDB:16c (SUS:2,5).   [220] *ASC,* 1083.
[221] LDB:49b (ESS:25,5).   [222] LDB:51a (ESS:25,22).
[223] *HistAbbend* 1, 372–5; cf. Van Caenegem, *Lawsuits,* no. 222. The perquisites of vacancies generally are considered by Barlow, *Rufus,* 232–5.
[224] *GRA* 1.558–9; cf. church lands *vendita et ad firmam erat posita, JW* 3.94–5.
[225] Lennard, 154–5.   [226] Green, *Sheriffs,* 39.   [227] *Dialogus,* 54.

his countrywomen who had fallen upon hard times, a certain widow who existed on 20s worth of land, which used to have two ploughs but now there were none: 'now [she] pays nothing because [she] has nothing: then, Godric pays the rent for it'.[228] We do not know whether she was the vulnerable subject of his charity or perhaps a member of his once-influential family.[229]

Post-Conquest lessees, like the enterprises they managed, were under economic as well as political pressure by 1086, several desperately holding on to land and status that they had formerly enjoyed as of right. Baldwin and Æthelric, two tenants of William fitzAnsculf in Buckinghamshire, exemplify what was probably the unrecorded undercurrent. Both had held their land before the Conquest, and Baldwin had been once entitled to sell it if he wished. By 1086, they both paid a farm for their former manors, and Æthelric was, as we have seen, in a sorry state.[230] Like the freer tenants and rent-paying villeins of various grades, lessees too could be losers. Whilst the down-grading of smaller free-holders into *villani* is a recognized feature of post-Conquest England, the spiralling cost of leases was also hitting lessees like William fitzStur, who paid £60 for four royal manors on the Isle of Wight, 'although they are worth less'.[231] Similarly, we glimpse the predicament of an anonymous Englishman, albeit one with entrepreneurial substance enough to take on a large contract. Richard fitzGilbert's substantial manor in Essex was worth £50, 'so the French and English say'—in tune on values for once in Domesday; 'but Richard gave it to a certain Englishman at rent (*ad censum*) for £60, but each year [the rent] is deficient by at least £10'.[232]

Smaller units were often more viable and profitable (apart from anything else, they had fewer layers of farmers' profits and peculations to take account of), and on occasion, even groups of peasants were tempted to take on a manor: men of the vill of East Clandon in Surrey, 'rendered' £6, although the land was worth only £4.[233] In the few clear cases of a group of men taking on the 'farm' of a manor, Domesday either enters no demesne ploughs—itself unusual—or states that there is no demesne or no hall.[234] The phenomenon may well have been more common in the eleventh century than the occasional case mentioned in Great Domesday would indicate;[235] however, the sporadic evidence suggests that by 1086 the high rents demanded by the new elite made such ventures vulnerable.

Later eleventh-century evidence made no sharp distinctions between rents, farms, and leases, and Domesday shows that the level of payments—unless to a follower with social or political connections—tended to fluctuate. In contrast to the first half of the twelfth century, the later eleventh was a time of rapid change:

---

[228] LDB:121a (NFK:1,80).
[229] Godric possibly belonged to a thegnly dynasty, Williams, *The English*, 108–9.
[230] Marsh Gibbon, GDB:148d (BUK:17,16).
[231] GDB:52b–c (HAM:IoW1,11).   [232] LDB:38b (ESS:23,2).
[233] GDB:34a (SUR:8,29).   [234] e. g. GDB:41d (HAM:3,17), 127d (MDX:3,17).
[235] R. S. Hoyt, 'Farm of the manor and the community of the vill in Domesday Book', *Speculum*, 30 (1955), 147–69.

the archbishop of Canterbury's demesne manor of Charing, Kent, was valued before 1066 at £24; £60 was paid for it in 1086, although its true value was £34; it fell back to just over £46 in the 1090s, and the family who remained its tenants for much of the twelfth century paid a fixed £32.[236] If many Domesday values were indeed actual payments for farms and leases, as most commentators seem to agree, then the fluctuations in value in the two decades between 1066 and 1086 show that they were not permitted to remain fixed for long.

The *gersuma* that appears in Domesday and contemporary documents was a separate levy: in Old English, *gærsuma*, 'treasure', 'profit of office'; in Middle English, *gersum*, 'a premium', 'a fine'.[237] It appears emblematic of the pressure on a whole hierarchy of farmers and reeves, and peasants.[238] The premium was, in fact, sought occasionally in the Confessor's reign as an acknowledgement of an agreed lease for one or two lives; and seemed rare enough then to need explanation: a *respectum quod gersume dicunt* was given by a lessee of Ramsey Abbey.[239] Another was paid to Stigand and Old Minster in order that Wulfweard White might have five hides for life at Hayling Island.[240] In the course of William's reign, however, this premium seems to have become transformed into an annual, biennial, or triennial payment—over half the thirty or so Domesday cases were sums of either 20s or 100s—functioning as an additional consideration cementing a short-term commercial agreement, rather than a one-off recognition of a life-long lease or tenancy.[241] It features particularly on the royal estates in Little Domesday, where its record might simply reflect the government's current interest in the honesty of officials. It also occurs occasionally as a payment in gold. A *gersuma* of an ounce of gold was required for one three-year agreement for men to farm a manor at £12 a year: the farmers' agreement led to their downfall (*confusi*), as the land they obtained was only worth £3 yearly, together with freemen worth 45s.[242] It seems to imply digging deep into reserves.

As a measure of secular trends in demand for land, the length of leases offers a good yardstick; and over the Domesday decades, the Conquest evidently allowed leading landholders to renegotiate quite frequently from a position of strength. Leases in the tenth century had often been granted for at least two, or perhaps three, lives, and they survive until 1066.[243] (In the twelfth century, too, leases were

---

[236] GDB:3d (KEN:2,19); Lambeth MS.1212, 212; F. R. H. Du Boulay, *The Lordship of Canterbury* (London, 1966), 198–202.

[237] *Dictionary of Medieval Latin from British Sources*, ed. D. R. Howlett, British Academy (Oxford, 1975–), 1071.

[238] Lennard, 180–5.

[239] *Chronicon abbatiae Rameseiensis*, ed. W. D. Macray (RS, 1886), 175.

[240] 'gersumen', Charters, no. 114.

[241] Canterbury Reg. K records 13 manors with an additional *gersuma*, ff. 69–70. The schedule of farms in *DMon*, 98–9 shows additional gablum and customary dues.

[242] LDB:353a–b; see 'Appendix 1: Gold Payments in Domesday', Ch. 6, pp. 154–6 in this volume.

[243] e.g. TRE, 'for the lives of three men', GDB:72b (WIL:41,4), 66c (WIL:7,2); Charters, nos 16, 106, 107; Lennard, 159–66.

frequently granted for one or two lifetimes, although their future heritability then became an issue.[244]) However, we have seen that in 1085 a lease might be granted for one lifetime, and with conditions. Although most manors, unsurprisingly, experienced a drop in value in the period after the Conquest, Domesday indicates that by 1086 the pressure on the land market in eastern and southern England was such that even short-term arrangements at a high price were an accepted, if far from acceptable, proposition, and, rents and leases were being set at the highest sustainable levels—sometimes higher. There were signs that the land market had been under pressure, even before the Norman Conquest imposed additional strains. Leases or farms were even renegotiated annually and for a period were tilted in favour of the landlord. Before 1066, Hereward had leased land from the abbot of St Guthlac's at a payment that was 'to be agreed between them each year', and the land had reverted because Hereward had not kept the agreement.[245]

The conquerors had enjoyed a land bonanza, yet there were elements of realism in their demands.[246] The lower values often observed on subtenanted manors reflected strategic as well as market forces determining rents. Although some small manors, remote from possible markets and route-ways, tended to be of lower value per hide or per plough team, others similarly remote had strategic value, including as travelling posts. A multiplicity of considerations on both sides affected the formation of a tenancy: witness the Lacy request to retain the bishop of Hereford's small manor at Onibury, a day's journey from both Hereford and Shrewsbury, worth only £1. Yet, for Roger de Lacy, a Marcher lord, Onibury was strategically placed, on the direct route between the two county boroughs, at a river-crossing close to Stanton Lacy—a main de Lacy manor and the largest in Domesday Shropshire—and close to the site of the planned Lacy castle at Ludlow. Equally, the bishop of Hereford's willingness to continue to lease Holme Lacy and Onibury to Roger depended more on immediate services than cash. Bishop Robert was an experienced administrator, concerned to defend his diocese on the Welsh Marches where his predecessor had come to a violent end. The bishop, after weighing up the relative merits with his council, decided to require Roger's military support with two fully armed men, not cash, as the return for Holme Lacy;[247] Roger was young and the chief tenant of Roger of Montgomery, Shropshire's earl. It would be futile to discuss Domesday assets and their values without acknowledging the importance of strategic factors.

---

[244] Lennard, 172–5.   [245] GDB:377b–c (LIN:CK48).

[246] 'The process of leasing was adapted to circumstances and parties': G. Brunel, 'Leasehold in Northern France in the twelfth and thirteenth centuries: economic functions and social impact', in B. J. P. van Bavel and P. R. Schofield (eds), *The Development of Leasehold in Northwestern Europe, c.1200–1600* (Turnhout, 2008), 81–98, at 87.

[247] Galbraith, 'An episcopal land-grant of 1085', 371–2.

RENDERS AND REEVES

The high rents demanded from Domesday lessees and former freeholders depended on good harvests and adequate access to rough pasture and woodland for livestock: woodland and fenland offered opportunities for many small agriculturalists confronted with high levels of national taxation, but over-exploitation could spell dangerously diminishing returns. At Glastonbury Abbey's largest Wiltshire manor, the burden was too great: Damerham, a hundredal manor once worth £36, was now rendering £61, but 'the men' did not value it at more than £45, 'because of the deterioration of the land and the farm which is too high'.[248] Glastonbury's disgraced abbot, Thurstan, was able to buy back his position in the next reign for £500;[249] yet the exorbitant farms paid meant that such an outlay was worthwhile for great landlords.

Nor was it difficult for shire officials to build themselves an income, what with premiums and suchlike. In practice, the crown depended upon assertive agents in the localities to harvest the profits from jurisdiction: under Henry I, jurisdiction provided more than a third of the crown's revenue from the counties, yet, in the Exchequer year 1129/30, more than half of the revenue from pleas was still outstanding.[250] From the crown's perspective, there was also the reverse danger—that sheriffs, farmers, and bailiffs might be complicit in undervaluing its assets when it suited their purposes. In the great Inquiry of 1274, the crown sought to discover whether these men have 'made inadequate valuations of any person's land in favour of himself or of some other person . . . thus deceiving the lord king'; or 'for prayer, for bribe, or for favour have agreed or advised that the lord king's wardships should be sold at a lesser price than they should be by their true value (*secundum verum valorem*)'.[251] In effect, Domesday's data exposed exactly this situation by seeking information from men of the locality about the renders paid by royal manors and comparing them with what the sheriff accounted for to the crown and with the value in King Edward's day. Report of land insufficiently exploited almost never occurs in Domesday;[252] however, officials were occasionally reported for siphoning off assets to contacts: for the royal demesne in Ewell, Surrey, 'the men of the hundred testify that 2 hides have been subtracted from this manor, which were there TRE, but the reeves let them to their friends, and a woodland dene, and a croft'. Ewell's 'value' was consequently lower in 1086 than in 1065, 'nevertheless' it was rendering a higher sum, despite the reduction in size.[253]

---

[248] GDB:66c (WIL:7,1).   [249] *GP*, 197.

[250] County farms totalled £9,166, of which £1,931 was owing. Pleas (excluding forest pleas and murder fines) totalled £3,583, of which £2,164 was owing, tabulated, J. A. Green, *The Government of England under Henry I* (Cambridge, 1989), 223.

[251] Cam, App. I, 254–5.

[252] Aldwincle, worth 20s; but 'if it were worked well, it would be worth £5', GDB:222a (NTH:6a,27).

[253] *tamen reddit*, GDB:30c (SUR:1,9); similarly, 42a (HAM:4,1), 30a (SUR:1,1e).

In 1086, as in 1274, there was an underlying expectation by the locality, sporadically recorded, that the render from the hundreds and vills should be closely related to their value; although it was on such profits or management charges for administrative services that the farming system depended (as does modern retailing). In 1274, a jury reported that one William de St Omer paid a 'farm' of £12 to the king and yet farmed out the bailiwick for £18.[254] In 1086 similarly, an extra 50 per cent to 100 per cent was not infrequently exacted in the central and eastern counties: Newton Toney, in Wiltshire, for example, 'was worth £10; now £18. By the English it is estimated (*appreciatur*) at £12'.[255] When a man of position, like sheriff Hugh de Port, took on the farm of several manors in 1086, he expected a portion appropriate to his station, as did his local agent; so of course the total sum produced by a community was expected to be higher than the farmer's contracted sum. Occasionally, Domesday reflects a dispute between officials, exposing possible profiteering and collusion with the sheriff, or his under-reeve. One argument was immensely complex—quoting the dealings of three sheriffs, a reeve, and the crown with East Bergholt and its attached hundred and a half. Amid contradictory assertions about premiums of gold, and sums due to sheriffs past and present, the reeve Aelfric insisted that his agreement was to account directly to the king, and that no premiums figured in his contract.[256] When Henry I's Queen Matilda (d.1118) wished to increase her income, her officials advised her to lay a range of demands (*calumnias*) upon her peasants (*coloni*), which then redounded to the officials' great profit also.[257] In 1086, the recording of the 'renders', the actual payment, as well as the value, served to expose officials' extortionate practices, not all of which contributed to the royal coffers.

In the administration of the largest manors and towns *in absentia* there existed a whole hierarchy of payments of which we see rarely see more than the peak, particularly in the abbreviated Great Domesday. In Kent, reeves on three royal manors paid £5, £3, and £12 respectively to the sheriff over and above what was owed to the crown.[258] Tewkesbury in 1086 is estimated at (*appreciatur*) £40, but Ralph, the farmer, rendered £50.[259] Dover illustrates something of the system. 'At [William's] first coming to England this city was burnt down and therefore it is not possible to reckon (*computari*) how much it was worth (*valebat*) when the Bishop of Bayeux received it; now it is estimated at (*appreciatur*) £40.' Nevertheless it was the reeve who 'renders' from thence £54', to the king and the earl.[260] He obviously hoped to make up the difference between the estimated value and the render, and to provide for himself also. The hundred manor of Witham, Essex, was formerly worth £10, now £20, 'but the sheriff receives from his customary dues and the pleas of the half hundred, £34, and £4 premium'.[261] Unmentioned was the highest sum

---

[254] Cam, 143; *Rotuli Hundredorum*, vol. 1 (London, 1812), 512b.
[255] GDB:70b (WIL:26,5).   [256] LDB:287b (SUF:1,103).
[257] *GRA* 1.756.   [258] GDB:2c–d (KEN:1,1–3).
[259] GDB:163d (GLS:1,38).   [260] GDB:1a (KEN:D7).   [261] LDB:1b–2a (ESS:1,2).

of all, the total of all sorts of dues, licit or novel, that the men of Witham paid the local reeve. After 1066, the socio-political support of freemen and sokemen, once invaluable in the waxing of comital and kingly power, became of less importance than cash to often-absentee magnates, except in so far as the services of native-speakers were needed to manage the land that the newcomers had acquired.

We are not able to quantify the extent of either leasing or 'farming' in Domesday, but we have enough evidence to discern the trends which, as often, were regional in their impact and nature. Except in the devastated north, the terms on which William and his followers 'granted' and 'received' land were what would be aptly described in today's terms as leasing by competitive tender.[262] Cash, services, and provisions, all had their place in the bargaining process.

VALUES, RENDERS, AND ESTIMATES

This consideration of the Domesday evidence on landed revenues makes the 'value' versus 'render' conundrum explicable. Most Domesday 'values' represent the payment—on various terms—made to the listed tenant-in-chief or tenant for the use of the land, unless he had assigned it elsewhere in return for service. They were the viable payments expected for the traditional exploitation of traditional resources. The higher 'renders' were the payments currently demanded by the king, a tenant-in-chief, or his intermediary, often after a veritable auction, and rested particularly on additional rents and jurisdictional dues from freeholders.

The terms on which different people took on crown lands could vary significantly as to which assets and dues were included.[263] At Southease, near Lewes, land belonging St Peter's, Winchester, had been worth £20 and was now appraised at (*appreciatur*) the same, 'but nevertheless' was rendering £28; here we are told directly that £9 comes 'from the fines of the villeins'.[264] Dues, old and new, customary or otherwise, were variable extras in a farm agreement.[265] Unfortunately, similar variations may affect the strict comparability of Domesday values. In *c*.1126, a record probably made when the manor of Beckford reverted into the king's hands shows that the 'farm' continued to be steady at £30—its Domesday 'value'; but in 1126 Beckford was also paying customary dues of 27s 8d, plus £2 to the sheriff.[266]

Whilst the demesne sector was normally central to a manor's value, it was not the largest contributor on the largest manors; indeed, royal manors—some heads of

---

[262] e.g. *ASC*, 1087; GDB:134a, (HRT:4,22).

[263] Cf. in 1185, the value given for Wolverton was 'with the demesne and without pleas and tallages', no. 10.

[264] *pro forisfactura villanorum*, GDB:17c (SUS:7,1).

[265] This resolves the problems set by the variations in the Canterbury evidence discussed by Lennard, 119–20.

[266] GDB:164b (GLS:1,59–60). Evesham L, printed and dated in H. B. Clarke, 'Evesham J and Evesham L: two early twelfth-century manorial surveys', *ANS*, 30 (2007), 62–84, at 73–84.

their hundred—are prominent amongst the Domesday entries either with a render alone or with a render higher than their value. Of the 120 or so entries in Surrey, Sussex, Hampshire, and Berkshire that have a render higher than value, many are on manors with evidence suggesting headship of hundreds.[267] Furthermore, in 1086 these were often manors belonging to, or in the charge of, a small group of *curiales*. 'Render' tends to be the term employed when registering soke rents, customary dues, and service levied over and above the value of the manorial unit.[268] One royal manor and extensive royal soke in the freer Danelaw uses the two terms precisely: Rothley in Leicestershire, is worth per year (*valet per annum*) 62 shillings; whilst the 204 sokemen, 157 villeins and 94 bordars all render (*reddunt inter omnes*) £31 8s. 1d.[269] On large or hundredal manors, jurisdictional payments, aids, and forfeitures from tenantry constituted a major item and these profits were reflected in the render.

'Renders' also represented payments from the freer tenants, particularly for the use of pasture and woodland rights. In Worcestershire, the sheriff, Urse d'Abitot, was able to 'render' £24 by weight from Bromsgrove 'so long as he had the woodland'.[270] He was also to 'render' £65 by weight and two loads of salt from Droitwich 'while he had the woodland', whereas 'if he does not have the woodland, he says he cannot pay that amount'.[271] Eling, in Hampshire, with a 'value' of £20, nevertheless pays (*reddit*) £52 6s 1d 'with those assets which lie in the Forest'.[272] So effectively had freemen—and their assets—been attached to manors over the period of the Norman Conquest that the few in the freer society of eastern England who were not so attached posed a puzzle: they were listed in a separate category in Domesday as 'the freemen of the king who do not belong to any farm': a category now fast becoming an anachronism, for these freemen were now being absorbed into royal or shrieval land.[273]

The 'renders' of 1086 related particularly to exploitable assets over and above the demesne that were able, for a time, to supply the exorbitant sums recorded; they were integral to the dramatically raised values. The efforts of the inherited resident slaves and many villeins were already largely committed within existing manorial structures, so the sums obtainable from converting free and soke men into rent-payers offered more scope to amass returns than did the demesne. The Conquest provided a host of opportunities for unprecedented, and therefore unlawful, charges and rents; and these high returns came about largely through targeting the freeholders and sokemen, as part of a political and economic strategy. Of course, agreements on leases and terms should, traditionally, have been

---

[267] Headship is listed, mainly from later evidence, in Cam, *The Hundred*, App. IV, 260–85.

[268] Cf. Davis, 'sokemen *rendered* soke', *Kalendar, Abbot Samson*, xl.

[269] GDB:230b–c (LEC:1,3). Contrast, 'freemen and sokemen made only a minor contribution to demesne output': J. Macdonald, 'Using William the Conqueror's accounting record to assess manorial efficiency', *Accounting History*, 10, no. 2 (2005), 129–44, at 137. True, but 'demesne output' is being measured by Domesday values and renders—to which their contribution was often not minor.

[270] GDB:172b (WOR:1,1b).   [271] GDB:172c (WOR:1,3b).

[272] GDB:38d (HAM:1,27).   [273] e.g. LDB:109a, 272a; 446a–447a.

witnessed by the men of the hundred, by its reeve, and perhaps by 'men of the shire' as well; but in the reallocation following conquest, such niceties were not necessarily observed. Yet the Domesday Inquiry importantly provided a rare opportunity for some men of the locality to voice an opinion.

Although contemporaries' usage of the respective terms was to some extent variable, nonetheless, there is a thought-provoking effort in Great Domesday to use 'value' for the norm, *reddere* to express contentious excess, and *appreciare* in connection with the opinion of men of the locality. When 'the men of the shire' of Gloucestershire supply the worth of a holding for which no one responded, it is 'estimated' at £8.[274] In quoting the evidence of local witnesses, Domesday employs 'estimate' in eight counties, spanning four circuits, so seeking the opinion of the local men was a widely accepted process, and several times it was used of the evidence of 'Englishmen'.[275] Nor were such estimates mere 'guesstimates'. They could be specific and show the men of a locality actually withstanding pressure from landholder or sheriff effectively enough to go on record. On the royal lands in Wiltshire, the English get the bit between their teeth, three times insisting that their estimate was for coins at face value, in contrast to the alleged value by the more exacting measure in weight.[276] The French reeve who farmed the royal manor of Dartford in Kent, 'valued' it at £90, whereas the English 'estimated' the manor at £60—the same sum as it used to be in King Edward's day.[277] The term 'estimate' was not entirely an English monopoly: it was used by 'Frenchmen' in valuing the home manor of the nunnery of Barking, Essex—possibly in the king's hands due to a vacancy—who supplied a high 'estimate' and were opposed by Englishmen asserting the value to be the same as TRE.[278] It was also used on occasion when estimating the returns if assets had not been removed from a holding, or if assets were added.[279]

Even when unattributed, the lower sums in the 'estimates' suggest that they originated from the Englishmen of the locality. It was 'the men of the hundred' who twice in Little Domesday asserted an estimated value in opposition to the landholder's figure; in one entry they estimate the appropriate income from the lands of a number of freemen at 48s, whereas they were paying £6.[280] Usually the thrust is that the payment is too much: Pettaugh, in Suffolk, 'was at farm for £3 15s, but the men from there were ruined (*confusi*)' 'now it is estimated at 45s'.[281] As values were of the essence of the Domesday enterprise, and the level of rents and fines paid made all the difference to peasants' subsistence, it is unsurprising that

[274] GDB:166c (GLS:28,7); also *Heirs*, no. 4.
[275] Five entries. Four in Wiltshire, GDB:65a;70d (WIL:1,10–12; 26,5); and by Frenchmen at Barking.
[276] GDB:65a (WIL:1,10–12).   [277] GDB:2c (KEN:1,1).
[278] LDB:17b–18a (ESS:9,7). The Abbess Aelfgyva's dates are given as 1066–87 in Knowles, Brooke, and London, *The Heads of Religious Houses*, 208; contrast comment on *Acta*, no. 10.
[279] *appreciantur* GDB:2b (KEN:P13); *plus appreciaretur*, 11d (KEN:6,1).
[280] LDB:343a (SUF:7,121).   [281] LDB:440b–441a (SUF:67,3).

there were differences of opinion over the level viable. Much more surprising is that dissent was recorded.[282]

SUMMARY AND CONCLUSION

'Values' were the viable returns expected from a working agricultural unit with demesne and tenantry. 'Renders' were associated particularly with rents and judicial dues. It was also the usual term for urban rents. But complications and qualifications lie behind the simplified data, particularly on the matter of sub-tenures and lessees, so that these definitions, sadly, are still not invariably precise, simply because Domesday does not always supply enough tenurial data for us to be sure who receives the value of the land; nor are we given full data on substituted, or additional, benefits in kind and services—after all, benefits in kind defeat record and taxation even in modern bureaucracies. Nevertheless the space, effort, and ease of visibility given to the values shows them, after tenure itself, to be the single most highly sought-after item of the Domesday Inquiry; and their central record was undoubtedly innovatory.

The qualifications have implications for the study of revenues from manors, large and small, because the proportion of the product consumed in kind, and the extent of the jurisdiction attached to each unit, might vary. In making comparisons of agricultural activity, the large hundredal demesne manor held by a *curialis* should be differentiated from the small subtenanted unit: the former was not only more likely to have ancient dues attached, it was also in a good position to enforce new ones on its extensive assets. Thus, economic comparisons and judgements on the progressive or regressive nature of taxation should take these differences into account. The new conquerors had seemed to assume that the resources of pasture and woodland were infinite and could be increasingly exploited for the benefit of lords; however, there was a limit to the cash that these resources could generate when excessive demands might necessitate the contributing peasants selling their livestock capital. But it is important that in 1086 even the abbreviated Great Domesday permitted the recording of the lower estimates coming from the men of the locality, contrasting them with the inflated revenues exacted by royal farmers and by alien ecclesiastics intent on their rebuilding programmes.

How these valuations were made up is of central importance to our understanding of one of Domesday's major functions. A contemporary charter—an original document written by a royal chancery scribe—supports the conclusions reached here.[283] When in 1085, King William set out to reimburse the abbey of La Trinité,

[282] Discussed further, Chs 9 and 10 in this volume, pp. 245–53, and 320–2.
[283] P. Chaplais, 'Une charte originale de Guillaume le Conquérant pour l'abbaye de Fécamp', *Essays in Medieval Diplomacy and Administration* (London, 1981), 93–104. The scribe continued to function under William II.

Fécamp, for its lost revenues from Hastings—presumably ruined by military action—he granted the monastery the manor of Bury, Sussex, on the basis that

> if the manor should be worth (*valet*) more than the rents (*redditus*) which they had lost in Hastings, then they would still receive it with all laws and customs and with sake and soke. Should the manor be worth less (*non valet*), then he would discharge his obligation to them through an exchange of equivalent value (*escangium eque valens*).[284]

Thus, just before Domesday, William was obliged to face the contingency that the land and rights he had given might not enable Fécamp to make up the short-fall in value. He patently needed to know not merely the location and hidage of what he was giving out—available via hidage lists—but its *value*: gaps in the royal data were circumscribing his actions. The charter points to an important motive for the collection of Domesday values. It also suggests that thoughts of reparation to the Church were evidently in the Conqueror's mind at this time of crisis (perhaps even an awareness that disparity in the 'guesstimated' value of the grant might shortly show up in the Domesday Survey).

It *was* within the capacity of the great Domesday Inquiry to find out and record the expected annual returns from land at two or three crucial dates. It was *not* within its capacity to estimate the full potential of land in cash terms, especially where land had been laid waste. But there were other ways of approaching this problem: waste land could be appraised in terms of past or future arable capacity, and other tangible assets—the demesne livestock, the demesne plough-teams, the plough-teams of the peasantry—used to assess the strength of resources.

As it turned out, any hopes placed in production potential were largely disappointed: at existing levels of cultivation, there was not, as the Ely terms of reference put it, a great deal 'more could be had, than is now being had'—except in repossessing excess profits taken by the sheriffs and their deputies, or by removing existing concessions in taxation.[285] The conquerors, their reeves, and their bailiffs were already doing all they could to obtain cash. Only if and when deliberately wasted lands were restocked was there much chance of increased productivity. In 1086, regions which had suffered reprisals for rebellion in the course of the Conquest were still recording much lower values than in 1066; moreover, some eastern parts of the country had been wasted on royal orders as recently as 1085 in a scorched-earth policy, anticipating the threatened invasion from Denmark.[286] Even so, there were general rises in value between 1065 and 1086: 20.5 per cent in Suffolk, 20 per cent in Essex, 29 per cent in Kent, 25.5 per cent in Warwickshire, and 22 per cent in Oxfordshire; while land values in Norfolk rose by as much as 38 per cent.[287] Not a few royal manors had doubled their returns in the course of

---

[284] *Acta*, no. 144; worth £24 in 1085–6, GDB:17b (SUS:5,3). A grant of William I of land, tithes, *cum aliis redditibus*, was inserted into New Minster's *Liber Vitae*, *Acta*, no. 344, 1072 × 1086.

[285] *si potest plus haberi quam habetur*: but see also Chs 8 and 9 in this volume.

[286] *ASC*, 1085.

[287] Finn, *The Norman Conquest and its Effects on the Economy*, 35; cf. F. Barlow, introduction in *The Devonshire Domesday*, Alecto 1991, 11, who estimates a slightly higher rise in some counties.

twenty years, although these relied on punitive exactions from former freemen on comital demesnes—not a tactic that could be employed indefinitely.

By the time of Domesday, England was already an old country, and rents in the south and the east of the country, easily accessible to continental and home markets, now overstepped a viable level. A *nouveau riche* ruling class, spending what they had neither inherited nor cultivated, largely on buildings and war— felling woodland and confiscating draught livestock to cart building materials— seems to have caused painful reductions in the all-important ploughing capacity in some regions, such as Yorkshire, and price inflation on still-productive arable in other counties, such as Norfolk. The Norman building boom in keeps, castles, and cathedrals demanded much mature timber.

The Domesday agrarian economy was characterized by the contrast between pressure on good land in the right place, particularly in the southern and eastern areas of the country, and low values in the more northerly regions. We saw that almost all the manors delivering 'renders' higher than their 'value' are located in two circuits: Circuits I and VII, the eight counties of the south-east and east. Apart from the administrative influence of circuits, three possibilities might account for the disparity: first, because of the link with Normandy, there was pressure for lands and rents in the south-east of England; second, as the Inquiry elicited only disputes when it put the question on potential in the more prosperous circuits, commissioners further afield might have felt it politic to drop it; third, the influence of the royal presence: whereas, between 1072 and 1087, William spent less than a quarter of his time in England, he clearly spent much of 1086 travelling around the southern counties while the Domesday Survey was in progress.[288]

The Norman kings were desirous of taking considerable quantities of silver out of the country for Norman military ambitions elsewhere. A senior numismatist has estimated the effects during the reign of Henry I in terms that apply equally to the closing years of his father's reign, when silver bullion was already scarce in Europe. 'When the value of silver bullion and hence of the English penny was rising, prices of commodities other than silver would have been falling. Rents and other obligations denominated in money such as taxes and fines would thus have become more valuable in real terms, while incomes derived from the sale of goods would have fallen.' Thus lessees and rent-payers suffered.[289] Unfortunately, few financial records survive from the reign of William II but, to judge by chroniclers' complaints of over-heavy taxation and poor harvests, an insufficient surplus remained after paying rents, leases, and taxes to prevent a period of diminishing returns in agriculture. In 1086 itself, 'God sent plagues of sickness and famine to England, and those who escaped the fevers died of hunger. Nor did he (William) care how

---

[288] *Acta*, 82; D. Bates, *William the Conqueror* (London, 2004), 164–5.
[289] M. Blackburn, 'Coinage and currency under Henry I: a review', *ANS*, 13 (1990), 49–81, at 74.

great an injury was done to the poor by the reeves.'[290] There is little to substantiate theories of a Norman-led increase of efficiency in agriculture.

In the late eleventh century, sitting tenants and lessees seemed to have had small scope to retain comfortable margins, as some longer-term lessees had done earlier, and were to do again later. Yet always there was scope for greed, resulting in peculation by officials, even if returns were short-term. The Anglo-Saxon Chronicler was quite clear about this:

> The king and his chief men loved gain much and over-much – gold and silver – and did not care how sinfully it was obtained providing it came to them. The king sold his land on very hard terms – as hard as he could. Then came somebody else, and offered more than the other had given . . . Then came the third, and offered still more, and the king gave it into the hands of the man who had offered him most of all, and did not care how sinfully the reeves had got it from poor men, nor how many unlawful things they did.[291]

Some lands and offices had been sold outright. William, bishop of London 1051–75, added in this way to the land which went with his office: Stortford is described as 'of the *feodum* which Bishop William bought' and Throcking as 'of Bishop William's purchase'.[292] Yet, without some indication of former returns, the king and those with whom he made bargains were in the dark.

The king's position as feudal lord entitled him, or his designated appointee, to the income from the lands temporarily in the royal hands after the death of tenants-in-chief who left widows, or an heir who was a minor, or an heiress not yet married. In addition, 'a relief', often based on a year's income from the estate, was payable to the king on the heir's resuming his inheritance. Domesday valuations in particular enabled the maximization of feudal dues: and even when not exacted in full, the data supplied bases for negotiation with heirs and for Treasury expectations during the minorities of heirs and ecclesiastical vacancies.[293] William II immediately capitalized on the ability Domesday gave to levy charges on churches in vacancy and on heirs, and he continued to do so, as the promises forced upon his successor indicate.[294] Henry I too availed himself of the opportunity to exploit the marriage market by giving well-endowed heiresses and widows to his own men.[295] These vacancies and imposts, although a source of grievance to tenants-in-chief, became a major source of crown income. The royal sons were, however, merely regularizing a

---

[290] HH, 404–5, a rearranged version of *ASC*, 1086, 1087. Aelfric twice translates Biblical tax collectors as 'reeves', M. R. Godden, 'Money, power and mortality in late Anglo-Saxon England', *ASE*, 19 (1990), 4–65, at 62–4.

[291] *ASC*, 1087.

[292] GDB:134a (HRT:4,22), 133c (HRT:4,1); P. Taylor, 'The endowment and military obligation of the See of London', *ANS*, 14 (1991), 304–9.

[293] e.g. 'an exchange of equal value', *PRS Henry I, 2012*, 16. To permit marriage to the widow of Edward of Salisbury, £200 was paid, *PRS Henry I, 2012*, 64.

[294] Stubbs, *Charters*, 118, *cap*.1–4.

[295] J. A. Green, *The Aristocracy of Norman England* (Cambridge, 1996), 364.

practice of their father, and perhaps an earlier one; and with Domesday's data to hand the practice became temptingly accessible.[296]

In short, these novel and intrusive data enabled the crown to regularize incidents in the already established history of taxation in England. For tenants-in-chief, the gathering and recording of information about their assets, and their income, was indeed their Day of Account. The 'feudal middlemen', the social and political buttresses of the barons, were similarly revealed to be substantial landholders whose supportive oath was also demanded at Salisbury in 1086, 'no matter whose men they might be'. Domesday values turn out to be the most 'feudal' item in purpose and character. Clearly laid out at the end of entries, and even more usefully and explicitly in the 'Summaries' of total values, they empowered the king to access the wealth that his tenants-in-chief, and their tenants, derived from land.

It is again to the question of cash that we shall turn next in considering Domesday's role in taxation. Appearing to be national and general in character, taxation too turns out to have a discriminatory, 'feudal' dimension.

---

[296] M. Howell, *Regalian Right in Medieval England* (London, 1962), 5–29. For earlier practice, see P. Stafford, 'The laws of Cnut and the history of Anglo-Saxon royal promises', *ASE*, 10 (1982), 173–90, and N. Brooks, 'The archbishopric of Canterbury and the so-called introduction of knight-service into England', *ANS*, 34 (2011), 50–3.

8

Domesday and Taxation

THE GELD

Historians have long maintained that taxation provided the main motive for carrying out the Domesday Survey.[1] The *descriptio*, Domesday's own term, regularly kept fresh its Carolingian fiscal implications with the help of the Vulgate: the decree from Caesar Augustus 'that all the world should be taxed/assessed'—*describeretur*.[2] Yet, the fiscal function of the Domesday information collected is by no means self-evident; and Galbraith and others since have disputed its role in national taxation.[3] Now, a full bibliography concerned with Domesday's evidence on taxation might itself occupy a small chapter.[4]

After arguing that the Domesday was a feudal *valor*, it is nevertheless proposed here, first that the Survey was also intended to reveal the widespread extent of fiscal concessions given to landholders and to prepare a more realistic assessment, and, second, that alongside hundreds, landholders too were agents of tax organization on whom government relied, and with whom it still needed to negotiate. Some reappraisal had become the more necessary against the background of the increasing levels of rents that landlords had sought in the course of William's reign: levels that inevitably affected the viability of general taxation.

Much of what we know about the national tax in specie termed 'geld', literally 'money', draws on material from the 1080s, Domesday and the Geld Accounts. Yet, for nearly a century prior to 1086, the 'hide' was probably the unit on which cash levies were raised; and it had a longer history as a levy on manpower and works: the Burghal Hidage of the tenth, and the County Hidage of the early eleventh century, both public records, survive.[5] Their very existence makes the point that no Domesday Survey was needed before manpower was requisitioned to provide defensive works; before large, even vast, sums were raised in national tax; before

---

[1] Still essential are Round, 'Danegeld', 77–142, esp. 77, 117, and Maitland, esp. 5–8.

[2] Luke 2:1; R. H. C. Davis, 'Domesday Book: continental parallels', in Holt, *Studies*, 15. The import of the Carolingian context is developed in J. Campbell, 'Observations on English government from the tenth to the twelfth century', *TRHS*, 5th ser., 25 (1975), 39–55.

[3] Galbraith, 12–27, 42–3, 87–101.

[4] But H. R. Loyn, *Anglo-Saxon England and the Norman Conquest* (London, 1962), 303–14 and J. A. Green, 'The last century of danegeld', *EHR*, 96 (1981), 241–58, cover much ground. Barlow, *Rufus* provides the best commentary on Domesday's immediate aftermath.

[5] Maitland, 455–60; Loyn, *Anglo-Saxon England*, 306–9.

reeves, communities, and landholders were held responsible for onerous duties; and before county assessments were readjusted. Moreover, in the eleventh century, first with Viking forces threatening, and then with two conquests, many of the levies were of straightforward tribute (*gafol*), rather than taxation (geld and heregeld).[6] Yet even levies of almost-regular taxes—when dictated and collected by an alien elite—felt like tribute.

In the late tenth and early eleventh century England was forced to raise great sums, with monasteries drawing on stores of gold and silver as well as coin for chronicled demands of between £10,000 and £48,000 between 991 and 1014, and even, in 1018, of £83,500—this last constituting the supreme national effort to produce tribute to pay off those Danish forces that by then had become resident.[7] Their magnitude is such that the Anglo-Saxon Chronicler's apparently precise evidence on the progressively exigent demands of the Danes is seriously in question—given medieval chroniclers' consistent exaggeration once numbers reached into the thousands.[8] However, Domesday's specific figures for the annual returns from estates in 1086 do indicate that the surplus from England's eleventh-century agriculture, plus mercantile capital and stored treasure, could indeed have supported a one-off payment of £83,500 in tribute. Moreover, William quite evidently levied tribute when in 1070 he forced 'all the monasteries' to yield, or sometimes to buy back, their sacred treasures, and laymen to 'redeem'—literally to 'buy back'—their lands in order to be permitted to retain possession.[9] But there was an art of the fiscally possible: the texts of William I's reign suggest that however 'stark' he appeared to the native chroniclers of his day and beyond, his national gelds never claimed cash on this scale. A 2s geld might produce some £3,000:[10] the 6s geld thus suggests something in the region of £9,000; but diminishing returns would operate. Even so, the £71,000 plus that the new and largely alien elite took annually from their Domesday estates by the 1080s[11]—much of it spent abroad, or on military fabric, or in the rebuilding of cathedrals unnecessarily—suggests that William's take-over had an ongoing economic impact almost comparable to the largest sums envisaged to pay the Danes' demands.

[6] A distinction I owe to Ann Williams: *ASC*, 1040, C, gafol; cf. *ASC*, 1041, 1051, E geld/heregeld and *fere importabile tributum*, Hemming, 248–9.

[7] M. K. Lawson, 'The collection of danegeld and heregeld in the reigns of Aethelred II and Cnut', *EHR*, 99 (1984), 721–38, esp. 736–7, and '"Those stories look true": levels of taxation in the reigns of Aethelred II and Cnut', *EHR*, 104 (1989), 385–406.

[8] J. Gillingham, '"The most precious jewel in the English Crown": levels of danegeld and heregeld in the early eleventh century', *EHR*, 104 (1989), 373–84, and 'Chronicles and coins as evidence for levels of tribute and taxation in late tenth- and early eleventh-century England', *EHR*, 105 (1990), 939–50.

[9] *ASC*, 1070; Charters, App. I, no. 6; LDB:360b (SUF:14,39). Williams, *The English*, 8–19.

[10] In the financial year 1129–30, a 2s danegeld meant that £4,355 12s 7d was demanded; £2,374 12s 11d was paid; £1,810 17s 1d was pardoned and £170 odd was owing, J. A. Green, *The Government of England under Henry I* (Cambridge, 1989), 223.

[11] Rural estates in 1086 have been totalled at £71,573: H. C. Darby, *Domesday England* (Cambridge, 1977), 359, which is certainly a net valuation, not GNP.

National threats, followed by successive stern and alien regimes, meant that rulers were uncompromising over tax compliance. Resistance to payment faced grim measures: when two tax-collectors were murdered in Worcester, King Harthacnut sent a force to ravage the county.[12] The late eleventh-century Worcester historian reported how relentlessly the link between tax-paying and tenure operated in practice: in Cnut's reign those who had not paid their tax within four days lost their land to whoever gave the geld due to the shire reeve—sometimes to an acquisitive reeve himself.[13] Lawson argues that the practice led even major landholders to lose their land, temporarily or permanently, through seeking loans and mortgages.[14] The sanction of loss of land leaves its signs in Domesday: land was 'in the king's hands, because no one rendered account'; other land confiscated by a sheriff because of non-payment of tax had in fact, according to men of shire, been exempt.[15] Picot and other sheriffs had been busy grouping freemen into 'manors' for ease of collecting rents and taxes:[16] some might have lost their autonomy when unable to pay taxes or to 'redeem' their lands. (The thesis connecting taxation to decline in status is perhaps supported by the converse situation in prosperous Domesday Kent: its exceptionally low tax rating did little to disrupt the survival of its small freeholders.) In all, following the Norman conquest, it seems likely that taxation contributed to the down-grading of freeholders into the subordinate peasantry, as it had in the hard times experienced under pressure from the Danes.[17]

THE ASSESSMENT AND COLLECTION OF GELD UNDER WILLIAM I BEFORE 1086

The national geld, though an ancient levy, was by no means a dead letter under William I, but rather a recurrent source of distress: heavy gelds were taken in 1066 and 1067, another in 1084 and, also, seemingly, in 1086.[18] Smaller gelds might well have been levied more frequently as a matter of course, without incurring special comment—and, confusingly, many types of levy might be labelled 'geld'.[19] Annual 'gelds' were certainly levied in some boroughs in William I's reign; however, some cities paid less often than others;[20] but we are unsure as to whether there was an annual country-wide geld.[21] Nonetheless, an assessment for a land-tax

---

[12] *ASC*, 1041, C.

[13] Hemming accused the shire-reeve of taking 3 estates from Worcester after Æthelred's death, Hemming, 276–7; *DB:Worcestershire*, Worcester G, no. 29.

[14] *EHR*, 99, 724–32.   [15] LDB:279a–b (NFK:66,99); GDB:141a (HRT:36,9).

[16] e.g. GDB:190b (CAM:3,4), 193c (CAM:13,8), 200b (CAM:32,4).

[17] Hemming, 391–2.

[18] *ASC*, 1066 D; 1067 D; 1083, 'after Christmas'; 1086, 'a very great amount of money'.

[19] GDB:30a (SUR:1,1b); also *Regesta*, vol. 2, no. 851, 1103 × 1107, quoted in n. 46 of this chapter.

[20] They were probably levied as constituent elements of the boroughs' customary dues, GDB:246a (STS:B11),100a (DEV:C4).

[21] Galbraith, 97, 87–101.

in hides (in 'carucates' in the northern Danelaw, and 'sulungs' in Kent, both terms deriving from the amount of land that could be cultivated by a plough in one season, but fiscal in meaning before 1066) is one of Domesday's more consistent items.[22] As both shire and landholders' lists of hides survive from the second half of the eleventh century and from the twelfth century—several of obviously 'official' origin[23]—Domesday's country-wide record marks just one point on the long path of noting, and readjusting, the liability of estates; but was it a major milestone?

Despite the regularity with which Domesday records hidage, or carucage—even for lands that lay 'waste'—its message on taxation is not transparent. Only in four counties—Surrey, Sussex, Hampshire, and Berkshire—does it record two different tax assessments with regularity, notwithstanding the injunction in the 'terms of reference' to provide data for TRE, for 1086, and for the interim time when the king regranted the manor. Most counties merely record a single assessment: for 1086, or 1066, or give a figure, date unspecified. The character of data on hides varies so much according to circuit, county, and its status as crown land, that historians have suspected some new fiscal policy was afoot—aided by the mention of an enigmatic *inquisitio gheldi* in the *Exon* volume;[24] but whether the 'inquiry' alluded to was the Domesday Inquiry itself, its forerunner, or its aftermath, remains unresolved.

The answer depends partly on the vexed dating of the Geld Accounts for the south-west:[25] arguments can be made for 1084 and for 1086, but neither is watertight.[26] There certainly was a heavy geld of 6s in 1084; but whether these accounts concern a second geld at that rate taken in 1085–6 or even 1086–7 is uncertain.[27] However, the important point here is that the surviving Geld Accounts appear largely independent of Domesday; and that, with three stages of collection and audit in Wiltshire, they suggest some difficulty in so doing.[28]

Whilst its data on hides and carucates vary, Domesday's very landholding units, manors, were themselves arguably fiscal entities: long ago, Maitland's magisterial investigation concluded that the Domesday manor was the unit against which geld was charged, through which peasants rendered their geld.[29] Domesday consistently

---

[22] The geographical extent of the Domesday use of hides and hundreds, carucates and wapentakes, as also data of the Burghal Hidage and the County Hidage, is mapped by D. Hill, *An Atlas of Anglo-Saxon England* (Oxford, 1981), 98, 86, 96. Some districts 'carucated' in Domesday had used hides earlier.

[23] e.g. The Northamptonshire Geld Roll, Charters, App. I, no. III; Evesham M, *c.*1095 and Evesham K, *c.*1100, the latter discussed in Chs 1 and 3 in this volume.

[24] Not within the Geld Accounts themselves but in an incomplete list of 26 landholders: DB4, ff. 532–532b; Finn, *LExon*, 2–3; discussed Roffe, *Inquest*, 134–9.

[25] J. F. A. Mason, 'The date of the Geld Rolls', *EHR*, 69 (1954), 283–9; Galbraith, 87–101; contrast R. R. Darlington, 'Introduction to the Wiltshire Domesday', VCH *Wiltshire*, vol. 2, ed. R. B. Pugh and E. Crittall (Oxford, 1955), 174–7.

[26] Finn, *LExon*, 97–122.

[27] Discussed A. Williams, 'Introduction to the Dorset Geld Rolls', VCH *Dorset*, vol. 3, ed. R. B. Pugh (Oxford, 1968), 115–23, at 119–120.

[28] Discussed, VCH *Wiltshire*, 2.171–2.

[29] See Maitland's excellent discussion of collection and exemptions, 120–8.

distinguished manors which were centres for geld collection: simply putting 'M' in the margins in Yorkshire and Lincolnshire, and elsewhere relying on its layout to distinguish between manors and their ancillary berewicks.[30] However, even if the Domesday Inquiry utilized fiscal lists as a skeleton for collecting data, as argued in earlier chapters, it was not necessarily for fiscal purposes. The role of fiscal lists of places, wapentakes, and carucates in the construction of Yorkshire Domesday is now severally acknowledged.[31] Moreover, the lists seem patently to originate from various dates and, in the case of the listings of lands of Earls Tostig, Morcar, and Edwin, much earlier.[32] (Indeed, several Domesday features are better explained as an inquiry utilizing existing skeletal fiscal lists, rather than an inquiry starting from a blank parchment: the manors or townships of the abbeys of Crowland and Thorney, for instance, were supposedly exempt from geld[33] and neither appear in Domesday.) In East Anglia, taxation was recorded in a different way from the rest of the country in that contributions were noted according to each pound levied on the hundred. But, even in Norfolk, it is argued that the Domesday clerks initially worked from a geographical list of hundreds, villages, and tax-payers, in order to produce the Norfolk county return.[34]

Neither the mechanism for levying geld, nor its assessment, had ossified by 1066. Administrative units, with defence as the primary objective, had been carved anew in William's reign: in Sussex, in Kent, on the Welsh borders, and in Holderness.[35] The hundreds, major units in the organization of tax and manpower, continued to adjust their boundaries.[36] On rates, 'heavy' gelds at 6s or 4s on the hide are chronicled in 1084 and 1096, leaving open the likelihood that unremarkable near-annual gelds of one or two shillings were levied under both Williams—as it seems they were under Henry I, since sheriffs account for consecutive years of geld in Henry I's first surviving Pipe Roll.[37] As for assessment, striking instances of continuity can be found—Sedgeberrow, Worcestershire, occurs in Domesday as four hides, the same rate as that contained in a charter of Offa more than three centuries before;[38] in other cases, also exceptional, Domesday notes no fewer than four different rates in the recent past.[39] More general changes had taken place in the total county assessment of Northamptonshire, once between the County Hidage and the Northamptonshire Geld Roll (the latter in English and datable to between

[30] J. Palmer, 'The Domesday manor', in Holt, *Studies*, 139–53.

[31] GDB:379a–382b, 300–302a, 332a–b; Harvey 1971, 761–3; H. B. Clarke, 'The Domesday satellites', in *Reassessment*, 67, 70; Roffe, *Inquest*, 84–7; Roffe, *Decoding*, 85, 269.

[32] e.g. GDB:301d.

[33] *The Chronicle of Crowland Abbey by Ingulph*, ed. Walter de Gray Birch (Wisbech, 1883), 141.

[34] B. Dodwell, 'The making of the Domesday Survey in Norfolk: the hundred and a half of Clacklose', *EHR*, 84 (1969), 79–84.

[35] J. F. A. Mason, *William I and the Sussex Rapes*, with maps, Historical Association (London, 1972).

[36] e.g. H. B. Clarke, 'Evesham J and Evesham L: two early twelfth-century manorial surveys', *ANS*, 30 (2007), 66–8; F. R. Thorn, 'Hundreds and Wapentakes', in *The Wiltshire Domesday*, Alecto 1989, 31–4; *Kalendar, Abbot Samson*, xxix–xxx.

[37] Discussed Green, 'Danegeld': 'certainly', 242; *PRS Henry I, 2012*, 28.

[38] GDB:173d (WOR:2,63); S.113.   [39] e.g. GDB:58d (BRK:7,15).

*c.*1070 and 1075, possibly a reduction reflecting the devastation of the county area at the hands of the followers of Earl Morcar in 1065);[40] and again radically between the 1070s and 1086, the result of a reappraisal of several hundreds;[41] similarly a reduction of about forty per cent took place in six hundreds of Cambridgeshire.[42] Just as William's officials did not require a Domesday survey before they levied a geld, nor did they before they readjusted its assessment.

As ever, both royal and official influence persisted: witness Pyrford's twenty-seven hides, lowered TRE to sixteen hides 'by Harold's will'.[43] The hidage of three manors, including Portchester, of William Mauduit, later to be Chamberlain, was halved.[44] In Westminster Abbey's hands by 1086, Pyrford's hidage was lowered again after the Domesday Survey to eight hides—at King William's command:[45] perhaps to show that his piety was greater than Harold's, or motivated by a self-interested wish to draw on its hospitality, as three of its hides were in the adjacent royal forest.[46] Queen Matilda remitted geld on one hide of a widow's rented land for the sake of her dead son's soul.[47] The Domesday commissioner, Henry de Ferrers, contrived a tax remission of six hides in Lechlade—the only manor he held in his circuit of office: he not only produced the king's seal for the county to see, but in Great Domesday *rex* has been inserted above 'himself' in the line recording the adjustment, so that the transaction was beyond reproach.[48]

Concessions recorded in Domesday do point to the principles by which geld was collected—or waived. Tax collection followed a similar path, posing similar questions, to those already encountered with the assembly of the Domesday material itself: that is, it depended on both shire and hundred—traditional local administrations— and on landholders, now mostly new. The Geld Accounts show the prime unit of collection was the hundred, acting together with the king's tax-collectors. But, in practice, the sheriff and the men of the shire were prime movers and, well before the Conquest, landholders were wont to answer for their own lands within the shire, and to accept the consequences. An edict of Cnut, already quoted, emphasized the link between tenure and the obligation to provide military man-power.[49] The inter-dependence of tenure and tax is shown in William's writ ordering that the dispute over jurisdiction, and land, between Evesham and Worcester was to be determined as on the day before 1066 when tax was last received for ship-building.[50] Certainly, the

---

[40] *ASC*, 1065, D, E.

[41] C. Hart, 'The Hidation of Northamptonshire', *English Local History Occasional Papers*, 2nd ser., 3 (Leicester, 1970), 38.

[42] C. Hart, 'The Hidation of Cambridgeshire', *English Local History Occasional Papers*, 2nd ser., 6 (Leicester, 1974), 26–30.

[43] *ad libitum Heraldi*, GDB:32b (SUR:6,5); one freed virgate had King Edward's seal, 50b (HAM:69,30).

[44] GDB:47c (HAM:35,1–2; 35,4).   [45] *Acta*, no. 326.

[46] Under Henry I, 8 hides of Pyrford were confirmed freed as they were 'within the park and forest of Windsor', including from the 'new geld on account of the hidage', *Regesta*, vol. 2, no. 851.

[47] DB4, f.18, VCH *Dorset*, 3.128.

[48] GDB:169a (GLS:59,1).   [49] II Cnut, 79; quoted in Ch. 3 of this volume, p. 76.

[50] Hemming, 77–8.

occasional mention of a landholder who does not pay tax in the Northamptonshire Geld Roll is a great name—'the king's wife' or 'the Scottish king'—not their local tenant or reeve.[51] The 1080s Geld Accounts from the south-west, too, show that hundred by hundred, the 'king's barons' might have their geld waived.

The national geld and other burdens were imposed, or excused, in a variety of ways.[52] Some concessions reflected ancient precedents and privileges: Chilcomb, a great multiple estate of Old Minster, had had its long-standing reduction to one hide confirmed by Æthelred II and, although worth altogether around £100 by 1086, so it remained.[53] Other concessions were given by Edward and confirmed by William.[54] Under the first two Normans:

a *manor* might be
—waived geld on its assessment[55]
—waived geld on part of its assessment[56]
—excluded from geld altogether but still assessed for works[57]
—held liable for the 'king's geld', but freed from other gelds[58]
—assessed at one figure, but required to respond to a king's summons or geld
at a different rate;[59]
a *hundred* might have its assessment modified;[60]
a *county* might have its assessment modified;[61]
an *estate*, an *individual*, or an *institution* might
—remain assessed for geld, but permitted to collect and retain the proceeds[62]
—arrogate exemption to itself[63]
—retain some gelds, but not possess an immunity from all gelds[64]
—redistribute geld between manors[65]
—redistribute the geld within the manor onto the peasants' land. *Terra villanorum*, was a term denoting tax liability in Domesday and the Geld Accounts;[66]

---

[51] Charters, App. I, no. 3, 233, 237.
[52] P. Vinogradoff, *English Society in the Eleventh Century* (Oxford, 1908), 177–96.
[53] e.g. *Writs*, no. 107; GDB:41a (HAM:3,1).
[54] Two five-hide manors of Bath Abbey were each reduced to three hides, GDB:165b (GLS:7,1–2).
[55] Odiham, where the king held court on tenures, defended itself for 38 hides, now for nothing, GDB:38a (HAM:1,1).
[56] Under King Edward also, GDB:60d (BRK:21,16).
[57] GDB:368a (LIN:57,43). Many royal manors were in this category, e.g. 30a–b (SUR:1,2–3).
[58] GDB:203a (HUN:B9).
[59] Ditchford, Gloucs., 1051 × 1055, was assessed at 1½ hides for the lord's service and at one hide for the king's, Charters, no. 111; EHD2, no. 185; S.1409. In the twelfth century, *danegeld* or *geldum regale*, was paid at a different rate from hidage, *Kalendar, Abbot Samson*, xxxvii–xlv.
[60] F. H. Baring, 'The pre-Domesday hidation of Northamptonshire', *EHR*, 17 (1902), 470–9; Hart, *Hidation of Northamptonshire*, 38.
[61] Hart, *Hidation of Northamptonshire*, 38.   [62] GDB:252a (SHR:C14).
[63] e.g. GDB:215c (BDF:32–1); 'William Peverel does not wish to give tax', 40d (HAM:2,20). Gerard the Chamberlain at Kemerton and Boddington withheld geld and service: 166b (GLS:19,2).
[64] GDB:30a (SUR:1,1b).
[65] e.g. Clarke, 'Evesham J and Evesham L', *ANS*, 30 (2007), 67–9.
[66] Finn, *LExon*, 105–14; Harvey 1970, 23–7; Harvey 1987, 260–1. For the complex evolution of fiscal inland see R. Faith, *The English Peasantry and the Growth of Lordship* (Leicester, 1997), esp. 48–55.

and *reeves*, or *tax-collectors*, might appropriate their due portion, or more, in the course of collecting geld.[67]

Only additional contemporary explication can indicate the conditions on the ground: the Domesday record in general remains enigmatic. Strategically placed manors appear to have a privileged status: the king's great manor of Dartford, Kent, worth over £120, 'defends itself' for only one and a half sulungs; similarly, with the port of Fareham, on the Hampshire coast: ten of its hides were made exempt 'because of the Vikings, since it is on the sea'.[68] Yet, whilst cash taxes were waived, it seems likely that such estates of necessity furnished almost unlimited manpower and boats for land and sea defence.[69] Otherwise, Domesday does not explain all the circumstances of liability, but seems rather to have offered an occasion to probe concessions.[70]

Meanwhile, the Conqueror's rule had further distorted whatever balance between tax and the economy had prevailed. Most obviously, extensive lands had been laid waste; just how far Yorkshire had been pushed backwards economically by William's reprisals for its 1069 uprising in support of a Danish fleet is indicated by the number of wasted settlements with little or no value in Domesday, and by its record of the fiscal carucates prior to 1069. Mapping the latter suggests that, before William's military action, the fertile districts of Yorkshire had been amongst the most densely peopled in England.[71] William's 1069–70 campaign had by no means been confined to Yorkshire: his army had crossed the Pennines in winter to deal with uprisings in Lancashire, Cheshire, Shropshire, and Staffordshire; the unusual midwinter campaign had probably wrought more than the usual damage on agriculture, through his forces' easier access to stored corn, seed, and livestock. Certainly the effects can still be seen in Domesday Book some twenty years later, as can the impact of his army's encircling approach to London in 1066, before reaching agreement with the remaining Anglo-Saxon elite and venturing to take command of the great trading port and its nearby abbey at Westminster. Although laying waste was an oft-adopted tactic of aggressive warfare, and even of alien rule, it was likely—apart from supplying his troops' victuals—to prove detrimental to a ruler in the long-term. But perhaps William's actions in the North had been as much strategic as ireful: as a recognized tactician having just repulsed one Danish challenge, he might well have been ensuring that future challenges from that direction could access few resources and that the ravaged northern province provided little incentive to establish a Danish kingdom there. In anticipation of the Danes in 1085, he certainly deliberately devastated land 'near the sea', 'so that if his enemies landed they should have nothing to seize on quickly'.[72]

---

[67] VCH *Wiltshire*, 2.170; Finn, *LExon*, 97, 101–3, 108.
[68] GDB:2c (KEN:1,1), 40c (HAM:2,15).   [69] Cf. *Dialogus*, 55.
[70] e.g. GDB:58d (BRK:7,15).
[71] J. Sheppard, 'Pre-Conquest Yorkshire: fiscal carucates as an index of land exploitation', *Transactions of the Institute of British Geographers*, 65 (1975), 67–78.
[72] ASC, 1085; R. W. Finn, *The Norman Conquest and its Effects on the Economy: 1066–1086* (London, 1971), 250, charts the fall in value of Essex coastal hundreds 1066–86.

Whatever the reasoning, 'waste' was already an official term in the Northamptonshire Geld Roll (and in the York archbishopric in the 1020s) and Domesday further consolidated the term's status in Treasury accounting. Although the precise meaning of 'waste' has been debated,[73] it quite evidently refers to uncultivated or depopulated land—not necessarily both and not necessarily entirely without value, perhaps as rough pasture[74]—that was unable to sustain and account for regular taxation. If, for fiscal reasons, Yorkshire were indeed the first county to be investigated in 1086, little could be done towards making its depopulated and stockless acres fiscally productive as, sixteen years after the rebellion, much land was still 'waste'.[75]

William's other doings were more susceptible to remedial action: besides the changes made in Northamptonshire and also Cambridgeshire, Domesday shows that in Sussex, Surrey, Hampshire, and Berkshire, all Domesday Circuit I, tax rates had quite evidently been pruned between 1066 and 1086. Whilst particular settlements and regions had suffered repercussions from military action during the Conquest, hidage had been adjusted during William I's reign mostly for other reasons. Geld was indeed regressive in its incidence, not arithmetically nor logarithmically, but in a political and *ad personam* manner, for the benefit of lordly landholders in general, but most particularly for prominent individuals whose great estates maintained crucial strategic positions.[76]

But Domesday set out to effect a turning point in the policy by laying bare the extent of the concessions granted to men influential in the regime or to institutions of great symbolic importance. Battle Abbey's fifteen-hide manor in Berkshire was exempt.[77] In Surrey, the Boulogne dynasty, Battle Abbey itself, Chertsey Abbey, St Peter's, Winchester, and Richard fitzGilbert were all treated particularly indulgently at some point under William; indeed, Odo of Bayeux had paid no geld at all on his great demesne manor of Bramley, worth almost £80, since taking possession.[78] Robert, William's other half-brother, was obviously ranked similarly: some of his Sussex demesne manors—West Firle, Willingdon, and Westburton—became completely exempt, whether they had forty-eight hides, fifty and a half, or two.[79] These exemptions for William's inner circle were almost certainly the outcome of personal concessions from the ruler himself; but their estates, many on the coast, might also have borne a heavy responsibility for defence—Surrey is less explicable, although its role may have been to protect the southern approach to London. Moreover, each shire in Circuit I reduced its assessment on slightly different lines,

---

[73] See, for instance, J. A. Green, *The Aristocracy of Norman England* (Cambridge, 1996), 236, and references therein.

[74] e.g. GDB:187b (HEF:29,2).

[75] H. C. Darby, 'Devastated land', ch. 8 in *Domesday England* is useful.

[76] Cf. McDonald and Snooks, 74, 119–20. On other aspects see Harvey 1987, 258–61; J. D. Hamshere, 'Regressing Domesday Book: tax assessments of Domesday England', and 'Domesday Book, cliometric analysis and taxation assessments', *ECHR*, 2nd ser., 40 (1987), 247–51, 262–6; H. B. Clarke, review in *Agricultural History Review*, 36 (1988), 206–7; R. A. Leaver, 'Five hides in ten counties: a contribution to the Domesday regression debate', *ECHR*, 2nd ser., 41 (1988), 525–42.

[77] GDB:59d (BRK:15,1).   [78] GDB:31b (SUR:5,1a).   [79] GDB:21a.

reflecting its autonomy: in Sussex, which William knew from his own experience to be vulnerable, the powerful men in charge of the consolidated units each distributed their reductions on individual lines.[80] Aside from concessions to those made great and saddled with great responsibilities, others were granted to lesser men, professional huntsmen and the like, including Anglo-Saxons who still held land as royal functionaries.[81] By 1086, certainly in four of the southern counties that were at the heartland of Norman rule, hidage concessions had become applicable to demesne manors generally.

The Northamptonshire Geld Roll, in Anglo-Saxon and assumed to provide some continuity with pre-1066 practices, shows the hides of each hundred divided into four types: 'warland', 'inland', land producing the king's farm, and 'waste', the last three being exempt from tax.[82] 'Inland' denoted land directly managed by a lord, and was a term employed occasionally in the Domesday record. In the Northamptonshire Geld Roll, 'inland' is used to denote acknowledged exemptions from the king's geld; it was 'demesne' with a publicly recognized status. 'Warland' was land liable to the burdens of public works and geld. The net effect was that, in twenty-three out of the twenty-eight accounted hundreds in Northamptonshire, the 'inland' or 'demesne' exceeded the paying hides; and in all hundreds the total of the three classes of non-paying hides—royal, inland, and waste—exceeded the paying. This general picture from the 1070s is largely repeated in the Geld Accounts for the south-west of the mid 1080s. Here waste was not a factor, but royal manors that rendered a night's farm were not accounted and, as in Domesday, the liability of subtenanted manors is largely maintained. In these Accounts, around forty per cent of hides were non-paying. In Devon, only 613 of its 1,028 hides paid geld;[83] while in the south-west generally about thirty per cent of royal and baronial land was exempted as 'demesne', with a further nine and a half per cent not paying for other reasons.[84] Not a situation to be tolerated in the 1084–6 crisis! Amongst favoured names to receive near-total concessions on some demesne manors, it is no surprise to see St Stephen's, Caen, the countess of Boulogne, and the count of Mortain.[85] Yet even the abbot of Caen was expected to balance his account on time: the tax on his manors in Frampton hundred was noted as late, settled after the date set.[86]

During William's reign, as before, perhaps more so, landholders as well as hundreds were fiscal entities with whom officials might deal directly. The later Geld Accounts show that landholders with lands in more than one hundred occasionally paid some geld in another, leaving the unfortunate collectors to

---

[80] Harvey 1987, 256–60; Round, 'Danegeld', 110–13.
[81] GDB:63c–d.
[82] Charters, App. I, no. 3; J. H. Round, *Feudal England*, 2nd edn (London, 1964), 125–30.
[83] Barlow, *Rufus*, 242.   [84] Finn, *LExon*, 110.
[85] 'Text and translation of the Dorset Geld Rolls', ed. A. Williams, VCH *Dorset*, 3.124–49, at 146–7, DB4:f.24.
[86] VCH *Dorset*, 3.116.

account as best they might for surpluses in one hundred and deficits in another.[87] In addition, great landholders made use of hides for all sorts of local levies of their own: in the case of Taunton, for exacting payments of tithe.[88] They might moreover, like Battle Abbey, create sufficient new tenant virgate holdings to cover the liability for any geld due (from freshly cleared land, calculating eight virgates to the hide) and thereby keep the demesne sector free of geld; and, despite Domesday's efforts, some continued to do so.[89]

Thus, complete concessions aside, powerful landlords were continuing to restructure geld within manors, transferring much of their fiscal burden from the demesne to the peasant and tenanted sector: a principle of taxation which stemmed naturally from the concept of inland, but which the Normans may have extended.[90] That the phrase *terra villanorum*, as employed occasionally in both Domesday and the Geld Accounts, carried fiscal import is made clear in two Domesday entries:[91] the manor of St Constantine, Cornwall, had 'half a hide of land which was quit of all service TRE, but after the count received the land, it rendered geld unjustly, as villeins' land', and in Hurstingstone hundred, Huntingdonshire, where 'the demesne carucates are exempt, but the villeins and sokemen pay geld according to the written list of hides'.[92] Knightly and other tenants received similar treatment, at least until 1100 and the *Coronation Charter*—and probably afterwards too. In its *Notitia Terrarum,* St Augustine's declares of its lands 'the demesne and the monks' part never paid geld or customary dues, but the knights and other men of this honour answered for everything'.[93]

Two principles of taxation, dependent on two definitions of demesne, seem in evidence in Domesday and the Geld Rolls. Whether, post-Conquest, it was the demesne sector of demesne manors of tenants-in-chief generally that were exempt from geld, or whether exemptions applied to entire demesne manors of favoured institutions or individuals, divides commentators; indeed, fitzNigel still felt the need to argue the point.[94] In fact, both practices are widely evident in Domesday and the geld documents. Royal manors paying the king's farm usually had complete exemption, but partial concessions were common amongst tenants-in-chief. What was actually happening on the ground was that, for much of the Conqueror's reign,

---

[87] e.g. the abbot of Abbotsbury in Whitchurch and Uggescombe hundreds, VCH *Dorset*, 3.125–6, DB4, f.17b.

[88] Charters, 236–9.

[89] E. Searle, 'Hides, virgates, and tenant settlement at Battle Abbey', *ECHR*, 2nd ser., 16 (1963–4), 290–300. See also Darlington's discussion, VCH *Wiltshire*, 2.50–1. Barons of the exchequer were quit of geld for assarts made before the death of Henry I, *Dialogus*, 56–7.

[90] Faith discusses the evolution of inland, in ch. 2 of *English Peasantry*.

[91] Harvey 1970, 25–6; Darlington, VCH *Wiltshire*, 2.176–7.

[92] GDB;121b (CON:4,29), 203b (HUN:B21); also Alton, 43a (HAM:6,1).

[93] *dominium et pars monachorum numquam geldavit vel consuetudines fecit sed milites et ceteri homines eiusdem honoris per omnia defendebant*, National Library, Exchequer (K.R.) Miscellaneous Books (E.164), vol. 27, f.16r.

[94] R. S. Hoyt, *The Royal Demesne in English Constitutional History, 1066–1272* (Ithaca, NY, 1950), 52–8; discussed Faith, *English Peasantry*, 53–5. *Dialogus*, 56.

key members of the regime, those in royal service, and tenants-in-chief, were receiving tax concessions. Domesday, however, succeeds in laying the groundwork for the time when such privileges needed to be earned by further service— or paid for in advance.

FISCAL EXEMPTIONS AND DOMESDAY'S NOVEL DIMENSION

Domesday data helped to expose an unwarranted proportion of demesne exemption. As already noted, fiscal demesnes had often been conveniently expanded; and they became exposed when Domesday recorded the number of demesne hides as well as the number of ploughs in demesne. One of St Stephen of Caen's manors, Frampton, was formerly liable for twenty-five and a half hides; it was 'allowed' thirteen hides of fiscal demesne in the Geld Rolls, although Domesday reveals that it was only nine and a half hides.[95] Whereas all counties record the number of demesne plough-teams, particular attention was paid in Circuit III and in Exon Domesday to the size of the demesne sector of demesne manors, thus reinforcing the interpretation that exemption of manorial demesne was indeed being targeted. In both circuits, unhidated ploughlands in demesne were recorded, and exposed. In Middlesex, the demesne hides are recorded; in Buckinghamshire, spare demesne ploughlands might also be recorded. Yet, neither in Buckinghamshire nor Cambridgeshire were any demesne hides recorded for royal manors (often exempt), or for tenanted manors which to date had paid tax anyway. The data collected for Domesday could well have enabled a reversal of the concessionary policy, both towards the demesne sectors of manors, and towards demesne manors.[96] Although Great Domesday was less obviously helpful on this than was *Exon*, Domesday succeeds in showing how common were the overlarge concessions on putative demesnes.

In detail, however, the Domesday figures differ from the figures of the Geld Accounts on exempt demesne. In Dorset, for example, in ninety-five cases where direct comparison is possible, fifty-one instances do not agree.[97] Domesday was more concerned with the exact size of the manor's demesne and its corroborative plough-teams, its ploughlands, and its value. Of importance here is that, when juxtaposed to the Geld Accounts, the details of Exon Domesday reveal the size of the discrepancy between fiscal and actual demesne that the tenants-in-chief were enjoying. As they were preserved in the same volume, perhaps it was exactly this juxtaposition that was intended for all Domesday regional drafts.

On the extent of fiscal exemptions still permissible, Glastonbury Abbey's ancient non-gelding carucates are mentioned in both Domesday and the Geld Accounts

---

[95] GDB:78c (DOR:17.1) cf. 'Geld Rolls', VCH *Dorset*, 3.147–8.
[96] Harvey 1987, 257–61; Round thought that this change in policy was self-evident in the Survey, 'Danegeld', 93–4.
[97] VCH *Dorset*, 3.118.

and were, seemingly, accepted by both.[98] Moreover, there are indications that the phrase 'never paid geld' drew attention to newly exempt as well as ancient privilege, and that Domesday might employ such phrases merely to signify that geld had never been paid by the present holder.[99] (Some fiscal reductions, however, may have been obtained at the time when the incomer was granted the estate and its value was low: the low rates on Earl Roger's demesne manors in Sussex appear to correlate with the Domesday value at the interim date when the estate was received by the newcomer.[100])

Domesday was not a text to be used for collecting tax. Nor for that matter were the Geld Accounts self-evidently the instrument of geld-collection: they were rather the product of particular audits. The Accounts do, however, refer to the collectors' own 'lists' or 'evidence' (*indicis eorum*).[101] Yet the detailed Domesday returns, as contained in Exon Domesday and the *ICC*, when put side by side with the Geld Accounts, there and everywhere else, except East Anglia, would have proved revelatory on the concessions on demesne manors, and on the extent to which demesnes within manors had parcelled out liability onto the peasant sector. And certainly, in the south-western circuit, this data was indeed preserved in the same archive as the Geld Accounts. Both sets of documents assume that the shire or the Treasury held details sufficient to hold collectors to account 'before the king's barons'—the Geld Accounts explicitly and Domesday implicitly.[102] When in England, the king kept Easter at Winchester more often than at any other known venue,[103] so those of his advisers knowledgeable on money matters were available to participate in an audit.

Exemption or cash in hand?

Whether geld exemptions always entitled the landholders to collect and retain the geld for themselves remains unclear, but some Domesday landholders, usually churches, evidently enjoyed this benefit, and it was surely more widespread than its traces suggest. Great Domesday states that lands of St Petroc's church held TRE 'never' paid geld except to the church itself, unusual information given because count of Mortain had taken away the holdings from the church.[104] In 1086 the monks of Bury St Edmunds received a portion of the sum raised in geld from Bury: 'when £1 went from the town, sixty pence went to the provision of the monks'; writs of King Edward and King William, however, indicate that they had been freed

---

[98] 'Summaries of fiefs in the Exon Domesday', VCH *Wiltshire*, 2.218–21, at 218; DB4, ff. 527b–528; 'ancient inlands' were expressed as ungelded or unhidated, Faith, 54–5.

[99] e.g. the Hastings Rape of Count Robert of Eu in Sussex, discussed below.

[100] GDB:23a–b (SUS:11,3–4; 11,6).

[101] DB4, f.18, VCH *Dorset*, 3.127.

[102] DB4, f.76b; see Chs 1 and 9 in this volume.

[103] *Acta*, 84, on five known occasions.

[104] GDB:120d; 121b (CON:4,1–5; 4,22); also Shrewsbury Abbey, 252a (SHR:C14).

of all gelds on their 'inland' or 'demesne'.[105] There are hints that lay landholders, too, availed themselves of this concession. A man, on what is now William de Briouze's land, had formerly 'paid the geld to his lord and his lord gave nothing'. In 1086, as Briouze still gave nothing from this manor of formerly fifty-nine hides, it seems quite likely that he might also have retained the right to receive geld from some of his subtenants.[106] In the early twelfth century, tenanted land of Burton Abbey certainly paid geld to the abbot.[107]

This sort of concomitant benefit begins to make sense of the high payments noted in the Pipe Rolls to obtain freedom from the king's geld. And given that the small freeholder, sokeholder, or peasant bore the brunt of national taxation—as almost all historians now agree[108]—the concessions procured by named landholders seem likely to have implied the right to receive geld themselves, rather than simply to give their own peasantry, or knightly subtenants, a geld holiday (albeit the Winchester survey *c.*1110 shows Herbert the Chamberlain doing just that[109]).

In short, Domesday shows that widespread fiscal exemptions were granted to demesne land for most of William I's reign. More blatant, men of William's inner circle seem to have taken a near-total holiday from geld, although we are in the dark about other obligations. It was not that the hidage was totally out-dated, rather that concessions under William had become so extensive as to make nonsense of the old assessments. The data on the demesne plough-teams served to emphasize the fact that tenants-in-chief did not qualify to benefit on this scale.

Ploughlands

The enigmatic term, the ploughland—*terra est x carrucis*—was the Domesday Survey's novel contribution to the business of fiscal rating in general and the exemption of demesne in particular.[110] It was no new concept: the carucate, and its subdivision the 'yoke', had been adopted as a standard land measure and tax unit from Ptolemaic Egypt and the Roman Empire to Scandinavia and early modern Scotland. Even in regions where the wealth-yielding forms of agriculture were the inappropriate vineyard or livestock, land was measured in carucates and yokes for uniformity's sake. Similarly in Ombersley, a woodland manor of Evesham Abbey, in King Edward's day fifteen hides were reckoned, 'between woodland and open land', *inter silvam et planum*.[111] In Normandy the term 'carucate' was used—not infrequently by Orderic Vitalis—for a notional sixty arable 'acres' with pasture and woodland attached.[112] Closer to home, the 'sulung' of Domesday Kent

---

[105] LDB:372a (SUF:14,167); *Writs*, no. 15; S.1075; *Acta*, no. 35.

[106] GDB:28a (SUS:13,9).   [107] EHD2, 887, 889.

[108] Galbraith, 15; Gillingham, 'Most precious jewel', n. 8, on this 'at one' with Lawson, 'Danegeld', 725–6; excepting McDonald, *Production Efficiency*, 2–3, 147–56, with some reservations, 159–60.

[109] *Winchester*, Survey I, nos 13, 24, 33.   [110] Harvey 1985.

[111] *fuit numerata*, GDB:175d (WOR:10,10).

[112] R. Lennard, 'The origin of the fiscal carucate', *ECHR*, 1st ser., 14 (1944–5), 51–63, at 62; however the Norman 'acre' is accepted to be twice the size of the English acre, and thus akin to the

represented a fiscal ploughland of 200 acres (81 hectares), divided into four 'yokes'; while the Domesday data-gatherers for northern and eastern England retained the Danish 'carucate', grouped in duodecimal units, for the purposes of fiscal assessment.

Understood as a new assessment, the Domesday ploughland was more realistically based than the existing hides and carucates, whether Edwardian or of 1086. In Circuit I it appears to remedy the discriminatory changes of William's reign: in Surrey, for instance, the Edwardian rating, at some 1,800 hides, was high in relation to its average value of under £1 per hide, whereas its 1086 assessment was absurdly low, at about 700 hides; its ploughlands, however, amount to about 1,200. This median position was also true of Berkshire ploughlands. In devastated Yorkshire the assessment in ploughlands was understandably lower than previously, almost halving the former assessment; and Wiltshire, saddled with an enormous Edwardian hidage of over 4,000 hides, produced a ploughland figure of some 3,400. The ploughland adopted different criteria according to region. In the disciplined Circuit III it was usually based on the easiest target, the arable—the total of working plough-teams—plus scope for any more—together with their sustaining meadowland. Some entries relate the existing hides clearly to the new ploughland, for instance '8 ploughlands besides these 5 hides' and three ploughlands in demesne.[113]

But where agricultural wealth lay in sheep and cattle raising—in the Welsh borders, Herefordshire and Shropshire, disrupted by border warfare and rebellion after the Conquest, and anyway known for open rough pasture, reassessment simply doubled the previous hidage. Domesday lists eleven individual holdings amounting to 18 hides, concluding that 'in these manors there is land for 36 ploughs but it was and is waste. It has never paid geld; it belongs in the Marches of Wales'.[114] Examples of fiscal ploughlands doubling hides in this region include three tax-paying hides, which had six 'ploughlands', consisting of a deer enclosure, but no ploughs.[115] What was being 'guesstimated' was primarily fiscal and agricultural land, not arable alone: one valley was described simply as 56 hides and 112 ploughlands that pay geld.[116]

The ploughland item clearly attempted to pry into demesne, and to draw totally exempt lands, and far-flung hillsides, into the fiscal net. And even though there were still exceptions made and exemptions permitted to stand, the link between ploughlands and fiscality is directly discernible. For instance, on many of the small lands without named tenants that 'never paid geld' on land carved out somewhat arbitrarily for William, count of Eu, Domesday records no ploughlands.[117] As these

---

hectare: *Charters and Customals of the Abbey of Holy Trinity, Caen: Part II*, ed. J. Walmsley (Oxford, 1994), 33. Dorchester-on-Thames used *carrucata* for demesne ploughlands; whereas Domesday Oxfordshire does not include 'ploughlands', J. Blair, 'Estate memoranda of *c.*1070 from the see of Dorchester-on-Thames', *EHR*, 116 (2001), 114–23; also *Acta*, no. 101.

[113] GDB:151b (BUK:31,1).   [114] GDB:186d (HEF:24,3).
[115] GDB:186d (HEF:24,6); also 269a (CHS:G3).   [116] GDB:187a (HEF:25,4).
[117] Particularly on three Domesday columns, GDB:19a–c. He was a grandson of Duke Richard I of Normandy, Douglas, *Conqueror*, Table 5.

lands had all sorts of TRE predecessors, the 'never' seems likely to refer only to the tenure of the count, rather than to include his various predecessors, some comital, but some not. Similarly, the link with hides is pointed at Andover, where 'they' express ignorance as to the hides, and a gap is left for the number of 'ploughlands' also—although the number of working ploughs is recorded![118] The Survey's attempts to uncover exempt demesne appears to become tentative at times: presenting the relevant data, but unable to take a fiscal decision: perhaps understandably when it concerned the bishop of Salisbury, a former chancellor, the probable provider of the host site for the inscription of *Exon*, and, possibly, a Domesday commissioner. One of several similar entries on his Dorset manors runs 'land for 6 ploughs, besides this it has in demesne land for two ploughs which never paid geld'.[119]

A few commentators have found difficulty in accepting the ploughland's intended fiscal function, preferring to stay with its literal meaning of a measurement of arable alone, even though it is over a century since Maitland, and Vinogradoff, felt obliged to dismiss 'this simple inference'.[120] The 'ploughland', whilst agricultural, clearly adopted values and population, as well as hides, in its assessment where appropriate.[121] Those who question the ploughlands as an attempted fiscal revision or as an experimental measure of fiscal liability have not, moreover, produced a more convincing hypothesis;[122] indeed, amongst contributors to the individual Alecto county volumes, more have found the fiscal argument helpful or applicable than those who have not.[123] Roffe's objections to the ploughland's fiscal nature are difficult to pin down: first, it was not fiscal in character, mainly because it was never implemented;[124] yet, later, he states, 'the ploughland figures provide a measure of the fiscal capacity of the fee'.[125] If I understand correctly, he now accepts the ploughland as information that might influence future assessment, but disputes that it constituted that assessment. Little evidence is, indeed, available as to which was intended: neither happened in the long term.[126] In favour of a new assessment, there is Orderic's claim that Rannulf Flambard was attempting to double the taxation in hides by adopting the smaller ploughland.

Yet, controversies over taxation are sometimes more apparent than real. What individual texts mean at any one time is now largely agreed, although questions

---

[118] GDB:39d (HAM:1,41).   [119] GDB:75d (DOR:2,2).
[120] Maitland, 418–31; Vinogradoff, *English Society in the Eleventh Century*, 157.
[121] Harvey 1985, 93–7.
[122] N. Higham, 'Settlement, land use and Domesday ploughlands', *Landscape History*, 12 (1990), 33–44.
[123] e.g. J. Bradbury, introduction in *The Buckinghamshire Domesday*, Alecto 1988, 19; F. Barlow, introduction in *The Devonshire Domesday*, Alecto 1991, 7.
[124] e.g. Roffe, *Inquest*, 18–19.
[125] Roffe, *Inquest*, 241; cf. Roffe, *Decoding*, 206–9. Roffe's discussion of the geld itself remains of much interest, 133–7.
[126] See further Ch. 9 in this volume, pp. 268–70.

about their relationship with each other and the precise policies behind them remain to stimulate future research. The scenario that follows is merely my attempt to put together a temporary perspective.

In 1084 a geld was levied at the high rate of 6s on the hide, and maybe another in 1086 at the same rate. The geld documented refers to payments in two instalments, the second of which was quoted alternately as Easter or Lady Day.[127] The dates of the two feasts were quite close in both years: six days separated them in 1084, and eleven in 1086; the heavy gelds earlier in William's reign were also taken after harvest and over winter.[128] (Geld was often levied in two stages: when tax was given before 1066 in Berkshire, the hide gave 3½d before Christmas and the same at Whitsun.[129]) The Accounts' mention of the death of Peter, bishop of Lichfield/Chester, whose successor was nominated at the Christmas council of 1085, might well assign them to the winter of 1085–6. Either way, the geld documented ran into difficulties; and if datable to 1085–6, the fiscal *impasse* naturally became a matter for discussion at that same Christmas council that launched Domesday, and, as long as the regime was in peril, the council could expect co-operation from all great landholders. Domesday's concern in one circuit with the precise extent of the demesne sector on demesne manors of tenants-in chief and its concern with the new assessment in ploughlands that was recorded in several circuits both envisaged a rethink of the existing concessions.

However, putting a drastic revision into practice was a political act, one that might well have proved impossible once the crisis was over. Even of that we cannot be sure—perhaps there was indeed a pioneer attempt to implement it, since Robert of Hereford, one of the inner circle of 'Treasury' bishops, associated the Domesday Survey 'with much violence arising from the collection of the king's taxes'.[130] We can be sure, however, that whilst in the end the Edwardian hidage was revived, great tenants-in-chief could no longer assume the large exemptions that they had enjoyed under William I. A writ of Henry I, seeking the shire's recognition as to whether St Paul's holds a questionable four hides, states that if the canons hold the land, they must pay the geld.[131] We know also that Lanfranc, who knew what he was doing, corresponded directly with one of the officials in charge of a sector of Domesday returns, with the sole purpose of stating that he, that is the estates of the bishopric, as opposed to those of the monks of Canterbury, had 'nothing in demesne' in that region:[132] a good effort to restrict the fiscal implications of current policies on the levy of feudal dues or taxation.

[127] VCH *Dorset*, 3.116–17.
[128] *ASC*, 1066, 1067, D.   [129] GDB:56c (BRK:B10).   [130] EHD2, no. 198.
[131] M. Gibbs, *Early Charters of the Cathedral Church of St. Paul, London*, Camden Soc., 3rd ser., 58 (1939) no. 33, addressed to the sheriff.
[132] F. Barlow, 'Domesday Book: a letter of Lanfranc', *EHR*, 78 (1963), 289.

THE PUBLIC BURDENS

The contribution of the Danish crisis to the increased demand for money and the assembling of data with a view to a revision of tax is obvious. But hidage was not only a tool for levying geld, but also for summoning the three-fold burden of military service, defensive works, and bridge-work.[133] As ever, war entailed extraordinary demands on manpower and cash. In the autumn of 1085, William brought a supplementary military force from France and Brittany to counter the threat: it was a 'larger force of mounted men and infantry', one contemporary thought, than he had ever brought before; and the king 'had all the army dispersed all over the country among his vassals (bishops, abbots, earls, barons, sheriffs and king's reeves)'.[134] As the Chronicler also tells us that the landholders 'provisioned each in proportion to his land', the following Domesday Survey has been made into a key point in the history of quotas of enfeoffed knights. Some preparations, however, were simply a matter of temporary accommodation for mercenaries, for when William realized the invasion had been delayed, some troops were 'sent back into their own country' before the winter. One proposal is that the Survey was intended to reassess landholders for the billeting of mercenaries, William thereby 'conceding an equality of misery for the baronage' and shouldering 'an equivalent share of that misery himself'.[135] Yet, whilst it is undeniable that an imposition of troops on great ecclesiastical houses, landholders, and boroughs did stem directly from the Danish threat,[136] a military emergency has never needed a survey of assets before requisitioning billets, nor required their egalitarian distribution.

Whatever the long-term consequences of the king's actions, they betrayed his immediate desperation for cash and manpower, and, inter alia, the Domesday Survey certainly identified where there were resources in men and traction power that might be mobilized via the traditional functions of the shire, or requisitioned. Whilst the geld and the cash economy has rightly received due attention in recent years, from the sums levied under Æthelred and Cnut to the twelfth-century Pipe Rolls—all satisfyingly specific—the importance of fiscal rights more ancient and more long-lasting than the geld have received somewhat less attention. Yet the shires' contributions, based on hidage, in supplying men for the army and in the construction and maintenance of defences and bridges, and now castles, were likely to prove more crucial than cash in a military crisis.

Such burdens had anciently been regarded as an integral component of taxation.[137] Before 1066, Stamford had paid the geld of twelve and a half hundreds 'in

---

[133] See also Faith, 90–106.   [134] *ASC*, 1085.

[135] N. Higham, 'The Domesday Survey: context and purpose', *History*, 78 (1993), 7–21, at 18–19.

[136] *JW* 3.42–3; *HistAbbend* 2, 16–17; WM, *Saints' Lives*, 130–1.

[137] e.g. *terra libera ab omni regali tributo preter expeditionem et pontis arcisue constructionem*, AD 963, *HistAbbend* 1, 215; S.713.

the army and in ship service and in danegeld': thus Domesday's sole reference to 'danegeld' rather than 'geld', placed military service at the head of the list of burdens.[138] After the 930s, not even kings should have or could have excused landholders from the threefold obligations of supplying manpower for fortifications, bridge-work, and military service. And when kings did set them aside, it seems to have been under Norman influence: witness Emma of Normandy's Winchester marriage portion, whose 'liberty' from demands of taxation, and works, and 'every yoke of worldly servitude', was expressed in grandiloquent and suspiciously uncharacteristic language.[139]

Military manpower

Traditional levies supplied military service based on one man from every five hides, whose expenses were funded by the group of hides, thereby accounting for the predominance of multiples of five hides evident in many fiscal assessments (and of six and twelve carucates in the north of England). Hides had been grouped particularly to supply the military burden, and were therefore partly artificial, but in practical terms they required a firm basis of both men and land. Despite concessions and the many vills divided between multiple holders, vills in multiples of five hides (and six carucates in the north) were still much in evidence in 1086.[140] Some boroughs possessed the privilege of being able to substitute a substantial payment in lieu: Oxford's responsibility to send twenty burgesses or £20 when the king went on expedition shows how costly it was to furnish, or substitute, military manpower in Edward's day.[141] In Berkshire anyone failing to respond for service when obliged forfeited his land; moreover if a substitute failed to appear, his lord might be subject to a heavy fine.[142]

With the Danish king's assassination in July 1086, it turned out that the Conqueror had no need to raise local forces after all. However, the new Norman regime had indeed drawn successfully upon these traditional native levies in an emergency: in 1069 Geoffrey of Coutances led forces that included the men of Winchester, London, and Salisbury to defeat a rebellion in the south-west.[143] And in 1088, the English were to come to the aid of William II against a rebellion within his inner circle; whereupon the king rewarded them with a ban on any unjust tax—which he later retracted. The royal search for cash and for manpower continued to interact. The mobilization of the fyrd for action in Normandy in 1094 showed that the traditional manpower levied on hides was still available, but this time the

---

[138] GDB:336d (LIN:S1).

[139] A. Cooper, *Bridges, Law and Power in Medieval England, 700–1400* (Woodbridge, 2006), esp. 60–5; S.925; S.1153.

[140] R. A. Leaver, 'Five hides in ten counties', esp. 524, 531–2; also G. Loud, introduction in *The Somerset Domesday*, Alecto 1987, 1–31.

[141] GDB:154a (OXF:B2).   [142] TRE 50s, GDB:56c (BRK:B10).

[143] OV 2.228.

objective was ready cash for mercenaries, not military action: on this side of the Channel, Rannulf Flambard simply took from each man 10s of the money given him by the supporting hides to sustain him for service, before sending the men home.[144] In 1101 Henry I, too, in readiness for his brother's invasion, also summoned 'an army of his whole realm'.[145]

Fortress-work

The ancient obligation to construct defensive works came into play both for traditional burghal walls and for the new strongholds of earth, timber, and stone that maintained Norman power. Obligations to build and repair the two castles which defended London, Baynard's and the Tower, and other fortifications, were imposed widely; in 1097, the 'many shires whose labour was due at London were hard pressed because of the wall that they built about the Tower, and because of the bridge that was nearly all carried away by a flood, and because of the work on the king's hall, that was being built at Westminster, and many a man was oppressed thereby'.[146] Freedom from such toils became a prized advantage for a landholder and his men: a writ to all shires where the canons of St Paul's hold lands instructed them to 'leave the cathedral's demesne lands free of all gelds and all kinds of work—for the castle of London and for the wall and the bridge and the bailey and cart-work as the writ of William I commands'.[147] Whilst the writ gave due weight to burdens of works as well as in cash, it certainly assumed no general concession on demesne land extant in the reign of William II, either for geld or for works. Moreover, although it was for the sheriff to implement concessions, the landowner received fiscal adjustments involving several different hundreds and localities.

Bridge-work

Employing this general obligation, innovative government had built up a network of bridges from Alfred onwards. It was, as we have seen for London, an onerous obligation, and widely imposed. It was, moreover, dangerous: a viable structure demanded secure and lasting foundations, hazardous to put in place: the coffer-dams and shuttering required while securing the base might be swept away at any time.[148] The greatest eleventh-century bridges, albeit some of Roman foundation, entailed widely distributed burdens of maintenance—just how wide was shown when Henry I declared Battle Abbey's land at Alfriston in Sussex free of bridge-work in London as well as work on Pevensey Castle.[149] Nicholas Brooks's study of an early eleventh-century text has revealed how the great Watling Street bridge over

---

[144] *ASC*, 1094.   [145] *ChronAbing*, 2.128.   [146] *ASC*, 1097.

[147] *Early Charters of St Paul's*, ed. M. Gibbs, Camden Soc., 58 (1939), no. 13; *Regesta*, vol. 2, *Addenda* to vol. 1, no. 399a, 1093 × 1097; cf. Van Caenegem, *Writs*, no. 27, spurious but contemporary.

[148] Cooper, *Bridges, Law and Power*, 5.   [149] *Regesta* 2, nos 1717, 1718, App. nos 258–9.

the Medway at Rochester, crucial for the London to Dover traffic, was maintained via assessments across the lathe of Aylesford.[150]

Whilst in the eleventh-century the communications linking boroughs, county, and market towns were high priorities for reasons of governance and commerce, bridge-work, along with the other common burdens, came into its own in a crisis. Bridges had functions in a defensive network: they might be fortified; they enabled shire levies to come to each other's assistance; and they could enable those armed only with rocks or wooden staves to make a waterway impassable to a water-borne enemy. Had the Danish invasion fleet actually appeared in 1086, bridge-work, like the other burdens, would doubtless have been in demand.

Bridge-work was a communal burden that in practice fell largely upon the peasantry. But landholder responsibility again overlapped with that of the local government unit; the responsibility for each pier of Rochester's bridge, for example, was on the landholder with the leading estate in each district.[151] Chester Domesday's message from Edwardian times on landholder responsibility was similarly clear: for the repair of the bridge over the Dee, the reeve summoned one man from every hide in the shire; but it was his lord, not the hundred, who incurred the heavy 40s fine if a man failed to respond.[152] William I's first substantial grant of freedom from bridge-work formed part of his thanksgiving foundation of Battle Abbey.[153] And, under Henry I, it became a ready source of patronage or immediate profit, along with other fiscal freedoms, with ecclesiastical institutions often making spurious claims of freedom from it during the twelfth century.[154] Whilst its long-term relevance to the maintenance of the road network is doubtful, since the stone bridges of the high middle ages required more initial skill and landholder investment and probably less renewal, the ancient obligation did good service for the great bridges with timber superstructures on Roman stone piers.

Cartage and transport

These obligations were imposed on boroughs and shires and mobilized via sheriffs; they were defined, in Hertfordshire Domesday at least, in terms of hides.[155] Cambridgeshire and Hertfordshire recorded the obligation on sokemen, and often its commutation rate, with some regularity. The sums involved—set at 8d per service in Cambridgeshire before 1066—were not negligible.[156] For a sea campaign, Leicester was obliged to provide not armed men, but military pack-horses, valued at £1 each, for bringing weapons or supplies to London.[157] Labour

---

[150] N. Brooks, 'Church, crown and community: public work and seigneurial responsibilities at Rochester Bridge', in T. Reuter (ed.), *Warriors and Churchmen in the High Middle Ages*, (London, 1992), 1–20.

[151] Brooks, 'Rochester Bridge', n. 77.   [152] GDB:262d (CHS:C21).

[153] *Acta*, no. 14.   [154] Cooper, *Bridges, Law and Power*, 66–76.

[155] e.g. GDB:141d (HRT:37,14).   [156] GDB:189c (CAM:1,3).

[157] GDB:230a (LEC: C2, 4).

with traction-power was invaluable for purveyance, for royal and shrieval defensive works, and for mobilizing prises generally in times of emergency. Indeed such demands rendered Domesday data on the agrarian workforce and its ox-teams immediately relevant to countering the current problem of the Danish threat. Cartage and escort services were obligatory on many free tenures; even a former Norman sheriff lost the use of some royal land because of his refusal to do cartage.[158] Though not the Survey's prime function, it is irrefutable that Domesday provided precise knowledge on manpower and traction-power that might be vital in a crisis.[159]

All the above burdens, especially if commandeered suddenly by royal officials, were disruptive of commercial and agricultural routine and so, quite apart from the obvious damage they inflicted on lesser cultivators, they aroused resentment amongst great landholders. Sometime between 1072 and 1083, the reeve of the royal vill of Sutton Courtenay became notorious for 'frequently and barbarously' seizing the abbey of Abingdon's men and animals to supply carrying services for royal journeys and for taking wood from the abbot's woods. The annoyance proved so great that it eventually provoked the abbot himself to react physically. While the royal reeve 'yoked the church's oxen to cart lead (which he had demanded for royal use)', he was 'hit with a staff that the abbot happened to be holding'. A second incident with the abbot over cartage ended with the royal reeve in the river. The abbot was constrained to pay compensation, but his forceful action, and a success-ful plea in a royal court, meant 'he shook off forever the tyranny of reeves'.[160] Not everyone could take such action, or afford the compensatory penalties it entailed. But should royal reeves commandeer manpower or cartage at crucial points in the manorial year, disaster could ensue: the foundation grant to Blyth Priory of 1088 placed reliance upon the services customarily owed by the men of the vill for ploughing, carrying, mowing, reaping, haymaking—all activities which depended crucially on timing.[161]

As a rule, liability for geld and works went together: Domesday records that each of the eighty-four carucates of land attached to York paid as much geld as one house in the city and was liable for the king's 'three works' with the citizens.[162] Since hidage or carucage determined the level of manpower owed, these traditional burdens might well have furnished magnates with further incentives to pay the high prices for geld exemptions documented in the twelfth century. One instance amounted to a twenty-year purchase, a ridiculously bad bargain, indeed an 'im-possible rate', if only an exemption from geld is assumed.[163] Eton was twelve hides in Great Domesday, yet eighty marks and two destriers were paid under Henry I to

---

[158] GDB:132d (HRT:1,9).
[159] Cf. Charles the Bald used men and materials recorded in the *breves* of vassals and churches to enable defensive works against Viking attacks, J. L. Nelson, 'Literacy in Carolingian government', in R. McKitterick (ed.), *The Uses of Literacy in Early Medieval Europe* (Cambridge, 1990), 277.
[160] *HistAbbend* 2, 15, Van Caenegem, *Lawsuits*, vol. 1, no. 12.
[161] *Cartulary of Blyth Priory*, vol. 1, ed. Timson, Thoroton Society Records 27 (1973), no. 325.
[162] GDB:298b (YKS:C23).
[163] Round poses the problem, but without answer, in 'Danegeld', 114–16.

have Eton for six hides:[164] it is likely that the manor was particularly susceptible to royal reeves' demands when the king held court at Windsor or when he hunted in the adjacent royal forest.

'Purveyance' and 'prises' as required for sustenance and transport remained an ever-present threat to inhabitants from the ruler—the only limits being the tacit obligation to provide good rule.[165] Yet, even in the constitutional crises of the thirteenth century, such kingly prerogatives—for emergency use—went unquestioned; and it was true at all periods, and as late as the sixteenth century, that royal officers were tempted to commandeer resources, even when no peril impended.[166] In 1097, while William II was simply awaiting better weather to sail to Normandy, 'his court did the greatest damage in the districts where they stayed that ever court or army was reported to have done in a land at peace'.[167] The irony was that on that king's death out hunting his companions were so anxious to avoid responsibility, or to reach the appropriate heir, that it was left to a few *rustici*, quite possibly requisitioned by the sheriff, to carry his forsaken body from the New Forest to Winchester by horse and cart.[168]

DOMESDAY'S AFTERMATH AND FISCAL EXEMPTION

Given that the Conqueror left England for the last time not long after the collection of data, but well before its inscription in Great Domesday was complete, and died the following year, the reigns of the Conqueror's two sons are the place to seek evidence as to the efficacy of the project. The question of fiscal exemption remained a battle-ground between king and landholders in both reigns: witness Henry I's Coronation Charter's promise of concessions on geld and burdens for the demesne ploughs of knights—not, we note, their hides—that much at least the crown had learnt from Domesday.[169] Henry's fiscal promises, however, like those of Rufus before him, do not seem to have been fulfilled in practice. Moreover, the definition and extent of exempt fiscal 'demesne' seems under debate even in the late 1170s: the *Dialogus* then arguing that villeins were part of the demesne, 'both they and the lands which they cultivate as service to their masters', as though the fiscal limits of demesne were not well established.[170]

Galbraith's shift of emphasis from hundredal to landholders' returns does not negate the argument that geld reform was a motive for Domesday. Great landholders, as well as hundreds, had long been directly responsible for ships, for military

---

[164] GDB:151a (BUK:29,2); *PRS Henry I, 2012*, 98.

[165] e.g. 1548, 'Proposal to abolish the royal right of Purveyance', in R. H. Tawney and E. Power (eds), *Tudor Economic Documents*, vol. 2 (London, 1924), 219–22.

[166] e.g. G. L. Harriss, *King, Parliament, and Public Finance in Medieval England to 1369* (Oxford, 1975) 54–70.

[167] *ASC*, 1097.   [168] *GRA* 1.574–5; Barlow, *Rufus*, 429.

[169] Knights' lands, even on great demesne manors, appear subject to geld, Harvey 1970, 25–6.

[170] *Dialogus*, 56.

contingents, and for geld, and the Normans, like their predecessors, saw no watertight distinction between great lords' responsibilities and national dues. The system, or rather the practices, involved both hundred and landholder, and was not so much in conflict as overlapping and partly double-checking.[171] (In Edgar's reign, the hundred and the lord of the land were both assigned responsibilities to deal with infringements of cattle regulations: in one edict, they shared the fine equally.[172]) For fiscal purposes, local units often operated on the same plane, and frequently as one. The king could with impunity draw upon hidage as a basis for assessing landholders: under Henry I, it seems that even a feudal aid for the marriage of the king's daughter might be levied on hidage.[173] Whilst distinctions between national and feudal taxation are helpful to historians, eleventh-century rulers made lords responsible—or waived their responsibilities—in the mode that suited the occasion: not necessarily in the most consistent way.[174]

Domesday data on the manorial demesne and on the ploughland did indeed represent an effort to make taxation more realistic and more productive; but it led to no long-lasting replacement of the hidage and carucage.[175] However, the knowledge gained of the extent of demesne and of magnates' large incomes meant that the concessions of William's day were abandoned also: the old pre-1066 rate reappeared as the basis of geld collection under Henry I, Henry II, and Richard I.[176] And it was the larger 1066 hidages for the south-eastern counties, not those of 1086, that were copied into the later abbreviations of Domesday.[177]

William II certainly rescinded general demesne concessions at some point, although a collection of laws, c.1130–5, states that it was not until the 4s geld of 1096 that the 'demesnes of the church' lost their exemptions.[178] As far as our other evidence goes, the Church's land became liable after Domesday: exemptions thereafter were confined to individual churches and landholders, and, indeed, to individual gelds, only obtainable by royal privilege, and often to be paid for; whilst freedoms had to be claimed at each levy.[179] In Henry I's nightmare, illustrated in John of Worcester's chronicle, peasants with sickles and pitchforks join knights with swords, and clergy and bishops with staffs and crooks, all complaining menacingly about taxation.[180] Certainly a number of profitable fiscal practices

---

[171] Generally, S. Reynolds, *Kingdoms and Communities in Western Europe, 900–1300* (Oxford, 1984), 3.

[172] IV Edgar, 8.   [173] HH, 456–7; T. H. Aston, *Oxford Magazine*, 10th May, 1962, 289.

[174] For the general point, W. L. Warren, 'The myth of Norman administrative efficiency', *TRHS*, 5th ser., 34 (1984), 113–32, esp. 131; Green, *The Government of England under Henry I*, analyses different sources of revenue, 51–94; they are tabulated, 223–5.

[175] Green, 'Danegeld', 243–5. See Ch. 9 in this volume.

[176] *Three Rolls of the King's Bench*, ed. F. W. Maitland, PRS (1891), 24; with variations under Henry II, Green, 'Danegeld', 244–5; Maitland, 400.

[177] See Ch. 9, n. 73 in this volume.

[178] *Leges Edwardi Confessoris*, in Liebermann *cap.* 11, 634–7; *ChronAbing*, 2.38, *HistAbbend* 2, 54–5; cf. *importabile tributum* for which treasures of the church were despoiled, *GP*, 432; Round, 'Danegeld', 83–4.

[179] Green, 'Danegeld', 246–51.

[180] *JW* 3, Plates 1–4; Hollister, *Henry I*, Plates 13–15.

were temporarily pushed to unknown extremes under William II: Flambard charged reliefs from subtenants during an episcopal vacancy, and he collected cash not service from the fyrd. Yet apart from the feudal incomes from minors and vacancies extensively tapped under William II, we do not know what other fiscal innovations were attempted. Not only did the reign prove a turning point on demesne concessions, his administration might well have put Domesday data on men and ox-teams to use when fortifying the Tower of London, and when transporting materials for the construction of Westminster Hall and the recon-struction of London Bridge.

CONCLUSION: DOMESDAY, TAXATION, AND GOVERNANCE

The degree of royal control evinced in Domesday is explicable only by a fiscal rationale, whether narrowly or widely conceived. As Domesday not infrequently discloses, the king and his officials strove to exert a tight control over landholders, insisting that quite insignificant exchanges of land should receive official sanction: a priest hoped to be allowed, 'if the king consents', to give twenty acres (nine hectares) to a church that he had built; the priest will then sing a mass and the Psalter for the King every week.[181] It was expected, it seems, that two contested acres should have had a 'warrantor' or 'deliveror'.[182] Even a royal chamberlain, Humphrey, had sought the king's consent before he gave half a hide of land to the Church.[183] King William had given a carucate of land just outside Lincoln to one Ulfkil 'for a ship which he bought from him. But the man who sold the ship is dead and no one has this carucate . . . except with the King's consent'.[184] It appears that sheriffs, under orders, or their deputies, might be engaged in 'delivering'—giving possession of—fractions of a virgate as part of an exchange; and just over a quarter of a hide was officially 'delivered' to William Speke.[185] Not that such attention to detail was novel: the imprint of King Edward's seal showed that one virgate of land had been freed of geld.[186] That all these transactions actually received the personal attention of the Norman king who spent almost two-thirds of his reign overseas seems unlikely;[187] more likely, the king's reeves and royal officials were constantly updating a meticulously kept land register in the king's name.[188] Like Domesday, such a register would need to be ad hominem, as well as by hundred and shire.

---

[181] LDB:263b (NFK:45,1).   [182] GDB:191a–b, 199b (CAM:5,22 and 26,57).
[183] VCH *Dorset*, 3.140.   [184] GDB:336b (LIN:C12).
[185] GDB:141d–142a (HRT:37,19); 218b (BDF:56,2).   [186] GDB:50b (HAM:69,30).
[187] After 1072, until his death in 1087, he spent around 130 out of 170 months in Normandy or Maine: D. Bates, *William the Conqueror* (London, 2004), 164–5; Itinerary, *Acta*, 76–84.
[188] Also W. E. Kapelle, 'The purpose of Domesday Book: a quandary', *Essays in Medieval Studies*, 9 (1992), 61–2.

After William's widespread tenurial revolution, first and foremost his land settlement needed to be confirmed and upheld.[189] The Domesday 'terms of reference' expected that all land would have changed holders between 1066 and 1086 and that King William would have made the change; he 'had given it'. Any revision or radical reappraisal of taxable capacity, national or feudal, and any new sources of revenue tapped, depended upon confirming the local landholder's responsibility for the payment of tax and the performance of military, defensive, and carrying services. In times of emergency, tenure and tax—including the three defensive obligations—were especially closely linked.

With tenure as the point of departure, the primary objective of the great Survey—largely fulfilled—was to obtain the annual values of estates. These gave William knowledge not only of the extent to which he had enriched his followers, but also of the former landed revenues now destroyed by military action.[190] He now knew the income from lands that he might reallocate, or confiscate: temporarily, when ecclesiastical vacancies or minorities arose, or permanently, after recalcitrance or rebellion.[191] Soon after 1066 royal clerks were functioning as custodians of the lands of vacant bishoprics;[192] with Domesday to hand, such lands became a regular source of crown income under William II.

The other principal incentive was to raise taxation more effectively, to check the fiscal rating assessment of the existing country-wide taxation, and to collect the data for a revision to increase returns. Whilst Domesday Book was just one point in the continuing tradition of recording adjustments in the liability to pay geld, it was aiming at something altogether more ambitious. The ploughland assessment represented the attempt to rebase tax securely on current agriculture and manpower,[193] and to rethink the assessment and to check its appropriateness. In contrast with William's rule before 1086, Domesday supplied data (in the plough-teams and 'ploughlands') that might be employed to prevent the powerful from offloading their own liability in hides onto the peasantry and subtenants, whose dues had already reached their sustainable peak well before 1086. Hereafter, demesnes of whatever sort were only exempt by written evidence.[194] Domesday at least prevented those whom the Conquest made great from consolidating the immunities that they had begun to carve out in England.

The three essential items for governance feature in what alone should be rightly called Domesday 'Summaries'. The number of manors, hides, ploughlands, and values in each county are totalled for a few great landholders at the end of Exon

[189] Harvey 1976; P. Hyams, '"No register of title": the Domesday Inquest and land adjudication', *ANS*, 9 (1986), 127–41; Fleming, *Law*, esp. 17. Contrast Wormald, who argues against it being a register of title, 64–76.

[190] *per exercitum regis*, GDB:239a (WAR:6,13).

[191] Cf. also II Cnut, 69–83 and P. Stafford, 'The laws of Cnut and the history of Anglo-Saxon royal promises', *ASE*, 10 (1982), 176–84.

[192] Peter, bishop of Lichfield/Chester 1075–85, had charge of Dorchester/Lincoln, *ChronAbing* 1.492; *HistAbbend* 2, 372–5.

[193] Harvey 1985, 86–103.

[194] Green, 'Danegeld', 250–1; Cooper, *Bridges, Law and Power*, 66–79.

Domesday. These fragments include the abbey of Glastonbury's lands in four counties, demesne and tenanted, and those of the count of Mortain in four counties; the Cornish lands of St. Petroc, and the lands of five laymen in several south-western counties. Then, for the count of Mortain, the whole four counties are added up.[195] Similar data is likewise included in the Inquest of Ely, and indeed in Domesday itself at two points: for the knights of Roger of Poitou on 'Lands between Ribble and Mersey' (whose fief was in the king's hands at the time of Domesday, and later restored), and for Alan of Richmond's followers,[196] thus suggesting that they were widely calculated once the circuit versions of the returns were amassed. Importantly, they epitomize Domesday's prime interest in the features discussed here separately, concerning the values and the national fiscal assessments, and indicate how desirable it was that such assets should be arranged by tenant-in-chief, as well as by hundred.

Detailed as the Domesday returns were, all the information amassed was relevant to one or more of the three items on its agenda: these were tenure, feudal taxation based on incomes from land, and national taxation, to separate them somewhat anachronistically. These three strands are at the very core of Domesday. None can take sole precedence: Round's and Maitland's interpretation of taxation, Galbraith's of feudal perquisites, and Holt's of title all remain valid.[197] As James Holt has told us, Domesday Book above all else looks like a practical document, the purpose of which was to bind together Treasury, sheriff, and the localities.[198] But, whereas Holt rightly emphasized the reciprocal need of William for military support and the landholders for written acknowledgement of title, the Conqueror needed his own legitimation even more. The first generation of official references to Domesday were to 'the king's book',[199] 'the charter of my treasury'[200] and to 'the king's charter in the king's treasury'.[201] In the Danish crisis, it was fundamentally the Conqueror who needed his charter, even more than the magnates did theirs. Their title derived from his: as his son Rufus soon had cause to remind dissidents.[202]

All three areas of competence were central to the functions of the Treasury or Exchequer. The commonly used term 'Exchequer Domesday' for Great Domesday is not really so much of an anachronism; the Treasury already conducted a range of practices familiar from the twelfth century, although, Domesday apart, not until the happy accident of the survival of the 1130 Exchequer accounts do we have much detailed administrative data still extant. Yet the long-held supposition that

---

[195] DB4, ff. 173; 527b–31; VCH *Wiltshire*, 2.218–21; VCH *Dorset*, 3.148–9.

[196] *IE*, 130–6; GDB:270b (CHS:R7,1), 381b (YKS:S402).

[197] Galbraith, 29–44; Holt, '1086', in Holt, *Studies*, 41–64; also now the important Fleming, *Law*, esp. 5–6.

[198] Holt, '1086', 55.

[199] *liber regius*, V. H. Galbraith, 'Royal charters to Winchester', *EHR*, 35 (1920), no. 12.

[200] *Per cartam de thesauro*, but *non in numero hidarum mearum est, Herefordshire Domesday*, PRS 63 (1947–8), ns 25, 1950), xxvii; *Regesta* 2, no. 1515.

[201] *Descriptio Terrae . . . secundum Cartam Regis quae est in Thesauro Regali*, which heads a text based on the Domesday text, Hemming, 298; *DB:Worcestershire*, App. V, Worcester B.

[202] *GRA* 1.546–7.

the Pipe Roll of 31 Henry I was patently not an experiment is confirmed by the discovery of an extract fragment from the Pipe Roll of 25 Henry I.[203] And the depth of detail held is confirmed by the series of obviously 'official' documents surviving in two Evesham Abbey cartularies. Extracted from various public documents of the late eleventh century or early twelfth century, they include a Domesday satellite record of fiscal liability; and a record of returns from lands in the king's hands.[204]

What actually went on at the great oath-taking at Salisbury on 1 August 1086 is, of course, pertinent but tantalisingly unknowable. Even the chosen date poses an enigma. Was it a tribute to English customs, or irony, to choose 1 August? Lammas was literally the Old English feast of 'Loaf mass', when the first grains from the new harvest were baked, and blessed by the Church. The feast day was also that of St Peter-ad-Vincula, celebrating the imprisoned apostle's miraculous release from his chains, and Anglo Saxon England had built up an affinity with St Peter, expressed materially in the payment of Peter's Pence.

The only element in the proceedings about which we are told is that subtenants as well as tenants-in-chief were required to take part in the exercise of both homage and fealty, a policy at one with the control which William II followed his father in exerting over that class. With the challenging Danish king disposed of in July, the August assembly's agenda was likely to have undergone change, and something of the cohesion of the previous Christmas Council lost. (After Cnut's assassination one of his many brothers succeeded him; but the costs of the preparations for invasion allied to the disbanding of the fleet unlaunched had divided Denmark politically and the opportunity was lost.) William's position was undoubtedly greatly strengthened by the disappearance of the Danish threat and by the acquisition of the Domesday data in some form; yet it was also an opportunity for bishops of stature to attempt to teach lessons and to assert principles of good rule, as Archbishop Wulfstan had done with Kings Æthelred and Cnut (and, earlier, Hincmar of Rheims had done in 877).[205] The agenda certainly shifted in the matter of boroughs; there are strong indications that the discriminatory fiscal concessions in boroughs given to 'French' burgesses and to *curiales*, and taken by major tenants-chief, were under question.[206] But, come what might, the process of legal 'disclosure' had been completed, in a fashion, and the drastic tenurial changes had passed through the courts without provoking further revolt. In this respect, Domesday marked a triumphant finale to William I's English rule; yet it had been a

---

[203] M. Hagger, 'A pipe roll for 25 Henry I', *EHR*, 122 (2007), 133–40.

[204] Evesham A, K, Q, M, and L, *DB: Worcestershire*, App. IV; *DB: Gloucestershire*, Appendix; Clarke, 'Evesham J and Evesham L', *ANS*, 30 (2007), 62–84.

[205] 'The sermon of the Wolf to the English', EHD1, no. 240; D. Whitelock, 'Archbishop Wulfstan, homilist and statesman', *TRHS*, 4th ser., 24 (1942), 25–45, esp. 35–45; given a wider context in M. K. Lawson, 'Archbishop Wulfstan and the homiletic element in the laws of Æthelred II and Cnut', *EHR*, 107 (1992), 565–86; J. Nelson, 'Kingship, law and liturgy in the political thought of Hincmar of Rheims', *EHR*, 92 (1977), 241–79.

[206] See Ch. 9 in this volume, pp. 242–9.

close finish. Hindsight shows that the period of Danish threat and payment of what was effectively tribute was over; but memories of it lingered on: the national tax was hereafter ordinarily called 'danegeld'.

As for the immediate, in some respects meagre, fiscal consequences of the Domesday Inquiry, its political context must be borne in mind. Lack of outcome does not prove lack of intent. However challenging the data-gathering, the eventual implementation of a refreshed land tax, or the failure to implement it, was a matter of politics.[207] The oaths taken at Salisbury were undoubtedly intended to affect the understood ties between the king and his tenants-in-chief and major subtenants; so, as far as understanding Domesday is concerned, we should perhaps distinguish between William's 1085 intentions and his post-Cnut, post-Salisbury policies. Beforehand, the desperate priority had been to locate resources and to extend the scope of taxation, feudal and national. However, kings were answerable to their councillors—new kings and vulnerable kings most particularly—and some councillors who were churchmen were well aware of their double responsibility at their own Judgement Day.[208] It was as essential to preserve law as to make it. Perhaps the matter of good rule arose at Salisbury, launching the investigation into the conduct of office-holders. It is to this undertaking that we turn next.

[207] Cf. the fate of the 1990 Community Charge, 'Poll Tax', in England, despite vast expenditure on collecting data.
[208] Nelson, 'Kingship, law and liturgy', 247–8.

9

'The Checking': The Inquest of Sheriffs and Other Royal Office-Holders

This chapter argues that a separate yet ancillary adjunct to the Domesday Inquiry was, in effect, an 'Inquest of Officials', designed to enquire into and regulate their activities. Mention in 1086 of a tax inquiry—*inquisitio gheldi*—has long been recognized, and its import debated;[1] but this Inquest of Officials was not confined to cash levies. To avoid confusion with the main Domesday Inquiry and with later inquests of sheriffs, I shall call this inquiry into officialdom 'the Checking'.

THE SHERIFFS' RETURNS: THE BOROUGHS AND THE PROBLEM

By 1086, the chief mover in the shire was the 'sheriff', heir of the Anglo-Saxon 'shire reeve', now the Anglo-Norman *vicecomes*. Not only was he a key administrative figure, accounting for the king's revenues from royal estates and summoning—and getting co-operation from—the shire court, but he was also charged with military action and marshalling the shire's resources of manpower: this gave him clout. Although pre-Conquest sheriffs had received lands with their office, King William's sheriffs generally outranked them in terms of social status and the extent of their landholdings;[2] and not a few turned their endowments into hereditary possessions.[3] Edward of Salisbury and Hugh de Port appear in Domesday as literal *vicecomes*: Edward's name prestigiously listed after the earls in the index of Wiltshire tenants-in-chief; Hugh follows the earls in Domesday Hampshire, with no less than two headings in the Index and three sections in the following text—his own lands, the lands of his office, plus the lands of the Bishop of Bayeux which he administered.[4] Having come to England to enhance their status and economic position, these functionaries had faced the administration of a

---

[1] DB4, f.532; Galbraith, 88–9; Finn, *LExon*, 97–111; Roffe, *Inquest*, 133–9.
[2] An important exception was the Edwardian sheriff of Lincolnshire, Mærle-Sveinn, with lands in six counties, Williams, *The English*, 22–3.
[3] R. Abels, 'Sheriffs, lord-seeking and the Norman settlement of the South-East Midlands', *ANS*, 19 (1996), 19–50, esp. 39–40; E. Mason, 'Brothers at court: Urse de Abetot and Robert Dispenser', *ANS*, 31 (2008), 64–89.
[4] GDB:64c, 69a–d; 37d, 44d–46c.

conquest which remained precarious for at least its first decade, and was again in 1084–6; this called for those of strong personality, with energy and ambition; yet their formidable ruler demanded men who also refrained from taking advantage of their position—an unlikely combination.

Sheriffs were key at several stages of the Domesday Inquiry. We have seen earlier that only they can have organized and presided over the meetings of shire and hundred. In the county arrangement of the Domesday volumes, pride of place was usually given to the county borough, often dominated by its castle, newly built by the sheriff. The sheriff's instrumental role in the returns is hinted at in a passage—unique in Domesday—where Peter de Valognes, sheriff of Essex and Hertfordshire, slips in a reference to himself (*dixi*) in recording a holding which had virtually no assets when he received it, but was now stocked and profitable.[5] Peter was a powerful figure in several shires; he also figured as a crown commissioner outside the Domesday process. Edward of Salisbury, with over 312 hides and more than thirty manors, was still more powerful.[6] He was one of the inner financial circle and sole witness to two successive documents, probably at the very beginning of William II's reign.[7] Domesday retains a hint of Edward's personal pride in his 'new church, excellent house and good vineyard' at Wilmot:[8] as sheriff of Wiltshire, Edward presumably launched the Domesday survey of that county. Moreover, he was the person most likely to have been in charge of the summons to Salisbury in 1086 and its arrangements (and remains a likely but mysterious key figure in the Domesday project).

It was not unknown for the sheriff to influence the choice of jurors in the Domesday Inquiry and to place pressure on those chosen, just as other great landholders did. When Picot of Cambridgeshire attended Domesday meetings of the hundreds, his very presence seems to have stifled any recorded criticism.[9] Sheriffs might influence the selection of jurors even outside the shire of their office: the sheriffs Aubrey de Vere, Eustace of Huntingdon and Geoffrey de Mandeville and the wife of Ivo Taillebois, Lincolnshire's sheriff, all managed to have tenants selected as jurors in Cambridgeshire, although Eustace had land worth only £3 5s within the shire.[10]

Yet, despite the sheriffs' powers and their castle seats in the shire town, the descriptions of the county towns in Domesday are both eccentric and jejune,[11] whereas those of the landed assets have a fairly regular layout, in part characteristic

---

[5] LDB:78b (ESS: 36,5–6).   [6] Green, *Sheriffs*, 25, 39, 47; *Regesta* 2, no. 796.

[7] *Regesta* 1, nos 293–4; Sharpe, 'The use of writs in the eleventh century', *ASE*, 32 (2004), 275–7. Edward was occasionally sheriff between 1070 and 1087: identified in writ addressed to Hugh de Port and Edward and Oda and others and all thegns of Hampshire and Wiltshire, *Acta* no. 339, 1070 × 1086.

[8] GDB:69b (WIL:24,1).   [9] Fleming, *Law*, 18–27.   [10] Fleming, *Law*, 21.

[11] 'uneven, incomplete, and anecdotal', R. Fleming, 'Rural elites and urban communities in late-Saxon England', *P&P*, 141 (1993), 3–37, at 5. S. Reynolds concludes that 'It is very hard to know what was in the minds of the clerks and their informants'; 'they were not interested in telling us all that we want to know': 'Towns in Domesday Book', in Holt, *Studies*, 309. Cf. V. H. Galbraith's verdict on Domesday towns: 'the Norman conquerors were very ill-informed about the country they had conquered', *Domesday Book: its place in administrative history* (Oxford, 1974), 151–3.

of their county and circuit.[12] Certainly, the county towns and boroughs stand out from the neat Domesday plan, and from its fairly neat, final execution. Compared with the rhythm of the county descriptions, where for the most part individual fiefs have their own recessional litany, with the more important demesne manors in each hundred often followed by the smaller and subtenanted, the boroughs have no consistent format. At worst, boroughs are a miscellany; at best, a list of properties that do, or do not, pay taxes. Given that sheriffs were a close-knit social group, it is curious that the county towns were, at the least, not more consistently served. A further peculiarity, however, has gone unquestioned. Why, given the undenied status of sheriffs and their pivotal role within the Domesday proceedings, is the Domesday material on boroughs and royal lands—all within the sheriffs' direct responsibilities—so hostile to them?

In Great Domesday, boroughs mostly occur at the opening of the county description; yet it is clear from the space allotted them, sometimes too little, as in Wiltshire, or sometimes too much, that they came late in the sequence of writing up Great Domesday: they appear to have been entered after the Indexes of tenants-in-chief and fitted around them; their placing on a distinct folio, page, or column in both Little Domesday and Great Domesday also separates them from the related county description.[13] The layout of the Wiltshire boroughs highlights the extraneous nature of burghal data in Great Domesday: Malmesbury is squeezed in at the top of the page, whilst data on the farm of all the Wiltshire boroughs—Malmesbury, Wilton, Cricklade, and Salisbury, as well as Bath—are compressed into the foot.[14] It seems that they were made separately, and entered later into Great Domesday: or, in the case of London, Winchester, and Bristol, never entered at all.

The distinction between borough and county texts rested on a distinct procedure. For Domesday, the burgesses in the county towns do not appear to have met together with the shire, as was frequently the custom after Domesday.[15] The unusually well-organized borough of Warwick records that the houses of the barons in Warwick have been valued with the manors, suggesting that the account of the rural shire was completed before that of the borough.[16] Where the urban properties of magnates are listed under the borough, their order departs, often radically, from the order of these magnates' fiefs in the county, further separating borough from county procedures.[17] Moreover, boroughs are notable by their absence from the Ely 'terms of reference' and, much later, in the great 1279 Inquiry, the questions prepared for London and major towns differed from those for the counties.[18]

---

[12] Tabulated in S. Baxter, 'The representation of lordship and land tenure in Domesday Book', in Hallam and Bates, 95–102.

[13] In *Domesday Rebound* (HMSO (London, 1954)), Appendices I and II show the foliation, gatherings, blanks, and insertions.

[14] GDB:64c.

[15] See Ch. 3 in this volume, pp. 73–4; cf. Fleming, *Law*, 13. Tait argued for separate courts of borough and hundred, J. Tait, *The Medieval English Borough* (Manchester, 1936), 45–57.

[16] GDB:238a (WAR:B2).

[17] G. H. Martin, 'Domesday Book and the boroughs', in *Reassessment*, 143–63, at 160.

[18] Raban, 48–9.

The separate origin of the borough and county descriptions may well indicate different objectives. It has been said that what the king and his advisers wanted from the boroughs 'remains mysterious. Yet the answers are there in the text'.[19] Perhaps they are, in part at least. Normally abbreviated and formulaic, Domesday offers precious little comment on the actions of individuals: all the more reason to exploit those instances where space is given to implied censure.

THE BOROUGHS AND 'THE CHECKING'

Not only is a substantial body of shrieval misdoing put on record in Domesday,[20] but other material, whilst factual and impersonal, is anti-shrieval by implication, particularly in the boroughs and on the royal lands, where sheriffs and royal officers are known to have reigned supreme.

But that supremacy, apparently, was the problem. Urban plots in Domesday are listed largely because the non-payment of geld, rent, or customary dues had excited interest, and because sheriffs had been negligent, or complicit with tax concessions for the powerful. Sheriffs had either thought it politic not to collect customary dues from magnates or, perhaps more likely, had allowed these men to collect such dues from their properties for themselves.[21] On the other hand, the upright payers of dues, or those with clearly substantiated concessions, gain scant space. Many towns record burgage holders simply in order to show what concessions were rightfully held—whether implicit or stated. Few of the Domesday borough accounts are descriptive; they are neither a full and proper list of the king's, earl's, or sheriff's dues, nor simply an incomplete list of the urban assets of tenants-in-chief—as at first sight they seem to be. The proposition here is that the primary purpose of the borough entries in Domesday was to expose actions and situations prejudicial to the king's rights, and that this accounts for the eccentric character of the data presented.

The borough accounts fit with the disjointed results returned by commissioners who had been given the task of an investigation into problems in the boroughs—in particular the way the sheriffs carried out their functions—and consist largely of a vindication, or condemnation, of shrieval management. It is not the exemptions of the tenants-in-chief that the boroughs are concerned to record and accept, but their culpability in not paying. They might have thought that their status gave them a tax exemption,[22] but that was not the stance William was taking in 1086. Notwithstanding the large increases in the borough farms since 1066, no traditional customary royal dues were permitted to go astray: Nottingham even records the royal assent, presumably necessary, given to William Peverel 'to make an orchard'

[19] Martin, 'Domesday Book and the Boroughs', 153.

[20] Fleming's exemplary index cites 122 references under 'Sheriff: acted illegally', with further references to their oppression, *Law*, 519.

[21] See discussion in Ch. 8 in this volume.   [22] Contrast Roffe, *Decoding*, 122–3.

of ten acres (four hectares).[23] Burgesses unable to pay a penny per head, and those who could pay only a penny, were counted, whereas burgesses who paid up often went unrecorded.

Great Domesday does not record abbreviated 'borough surveys' in the same way as it records abbreviated surveys of manors; it largely records problems and their explications. Central was the non-payment of royal customary dues or their diversion to the coffers of the feudatories. Guildford has seventy-five urban plots whose revenues are summarized in one short factual entry; however, on the eight properties that present problems Domesday is verbose: one house was attached to a particular manor 'only because the reeve of that village was a friend of the man who had the house and on his death he transferred it to the manor'.[24] Domesday Ipswich contrasts the 538 burgesses who paid customary dues to the king before 1066 with the 110 burgesses now paying the customary dues and the 100 poor burgesses who can pay no more than one penny to the king's tax. Others there fared worse: 328 urban plots which used to contribute to the king's tax before 1066 now lay wasted.[25] York laments the extent of the wasted districts within the city—and the consequent disappearance of customary dues: one of the six districts had completely disappeared 'for the castles'; of the 400 uninhabited plots, 'the better ones' pay one penny, others less, and '540 are so empty that they pay nothing at all'.[26]

Investigating the reason behind the loss of crown revenues—ground-rents, royal customary dues, and all sorts of gelds—occupies much space and attention. Lincoln and Norwich list those who have not paid geld as they ought. Malmesbury has twenty-five burgage plots where the houses pay 'no more geld than wasteland'.[27] Geld concessions to French burgesses figure as a major grievance in Norwich and in Cambridge, where the immigrants may also have eluded customary dues. In York, where Frenchmen hold 145 urban plots, their record following the non-payers of customary dues suggests that they, like other Frenchmen, had up to now been allowed exemption.[28] Wallingford seeks to explain, or explain away, all non-payment of customary dues: eight plots have disappeared under the castle; the moneyer has a holding free for as long as he operates; one claims a royal concession; another claims the authority of Henry de Ferrers, which is disputed by the burgesses, and so on.[29]

Tax lost owing to the destruction of property for the building of castles seems to function as an explanation: one that is only partly acceptable. The hardships consequent on the remaining taxpayers were real enough: 100 houses have been 'completely destroyed' in Dorchester, Dorset, leaving only 88 to produce the dues; 133 houses had been destroyed at Wareham and 80 houses at Shaftesbury.[30] In Gloucester, 'where the castle stands were 16 houses which are not there now', and

[23] GDB:280a (NTT:B18).   [24] GDB:30a (SUR:1,1e).
[25] LDB:290a (SUF:1,122c).   [26] GDB:298a (YKS:C1b).
[27] GDB:64c (WIL:M1).   [28] GDB:298a (YKS:C1b).
[29] GDB:56b (BRK;B1).   [30] GBD:75a (DOR:B1,3,4).

'in the fortified area of the city 14 houses are waste', explaining why they are no longer paying tax.[31] Whilst Wallingford lost customary dues through castle construction, other dues are said to be non-payable by royal concession; the borough still, however, ended up having to find £20 more than its worth.[32] In contrast, the unusual case of Clifford, an incipient borough and Welsh border castle which formed part of Ralph de Tosny's fief but was held by a sheriff at farm, is instructive. Domesday here is firmly defensive on the matter of the sheriff and possible royal dues: the castle had been built by Earl William, deceased, 'on waste land', was 'not subject to any hundred or customary dues', and 'these men, and whoever else has anything there, hold from Ralph'.[33] No missing royal payments here.

In Domesday, the establishment seems to assume that more tenurial continuity should prevail in the boroughs than in the rural sector; it was only rarely that the sheriff was accused of tenurial change by force. However, two cases of the sheriff, Eustace, taking urban property from women in Huntingdon are recorded in some detail. King William's grant to the widow and sons of an Anglo-Saxon sheriff has been ignored by the present sheriff, although an 'impoverished man' and his mother claim it.[34] Eustace also took 'by force' a house from one Leofgifu and gave it to Oger of London.[35] The new Norman kingdoms in the eastern Mediterranean were shortly to adopt somewhat comparable tactics to the first two decades of the conquerors in England: the non-Franks in the towns were discriminated against simply by taxation, whereas, outside towns, non-Frankish peasants were classed as 'villeins' and the Franks themselves became 'more rentiers than anything else'.[36]

Gloucester illustrates the role of much of Domesday's borough data. Despite being fuller than many accounts, Domesday Gloucester's extensive list of properties is incomplete: its 54 houses and 81 burgesses do not tally with the numbers in a survey of the city *c*.1100, known from the Evesham Abbey archives.[37] In that survey, the king's demesne alone was reported to have as many as 194 burgesses paying ground-rent, and there were at least 310 urban plots. In the Evesham text, the unmistakable Hugh the Ass had two plots, although he does not appear in Domesday's Gloucester; nor do the earl of Chester's burgesses figure in Domesday Gloucester, although the earl's rural account mentions eleven burgesses attached to his manors. Domesday's role was largely to supply a statement on the fifteen men who were not paying all the customary dues that they should, among them, notably, Durand the sheriff, who held four urban plots. Domesday was not undertaking a total account of the city's landholders; the rationale of its Gloucester compilation is made plain at its end: the burgages listed were those which

---

[31] GDB:162a (GLS:G4).   [32] GBD:56b–c.
[33] GDB:183b (HEF:8,1).   [34] GDB:203a (HUN:B10).   [35] GDB:208a (HUN:D2).
[36] J. Prawer, 'Social classes in the Latin Kingdom: the Franks', in K. M. Setton (ed.), *A History of the Crusades*, vol. 5, ed. N. P. Zacour and H. W. Hazard (Wisconsin, 1985), 117–92, at 130.
[37] Printed in H. Ellis, *General Introduction to Domesday Book* (London, 1833) vol. 2, 446; *DB Gloucestershire*, Appendix EvK.

rendered the royal customary dues TRE. Now King William has nothing from these, nor does Robert, his minister. These plots were in King Edward's farm on the day on which he was alive and dead. Now they have been removed from the king's farm and customary dues.[38]

The record of Winchcombe which accompanies it may tell a similar story: whilst Domesday mentions no burgesses for Winchcombe itself, it does record twenty-nine burgesses in scattered references from various manorial entries. Winchcombe's burgesses in the Evesham text again number about five times those in the Domesday Survey, that is, 141 to Domesday's twenty-nine (some burgesses in both texts were mentioned, but not numbered).[39] Importantly for Domesday's role in the history of taxation, its revelations of exemptions were, in Gloucester's case, evidently acted upon: in the *c.*1100 survey—in contrast to 1086—'the king has jurisdiction over all' the properties.

Shrieval activities in the boroughs were minutely questioned, the Checking spending time, and space, on finding out who exactly was responsible for loss of revenues, and when. The destruction in the four Dorset towns was attributed to 'the time of Hugh the sheriff'. Lost royal assets were investigated. In Malmesbury, Ernulf de Hesdin 'insolently', *incaute*, took possession of a burgage plot—one of two that no longer rendered service to the king's farm; Roger de Berkeley had the other.[40] The Cambridge burgesses accuse Sheriff Picot of all sorts of prerogatives wrongly exercised: whereas in 1066, they had 'lent the sheriff their plough-teams three times a year, now they are demanded nine times'; also, they had 'provided neither cartage dues nor carts in King Edward's day, which they now do because a custom has been imposed'. The Cambridge burgesses even sought to 'reclaim from Picot the sheriff, nevertheless, the common pasture taken from them through and by him. Picot himself has built 3 mills there, which have taken up the pasture and destroyed many houses'.[41] Despite the powers of sheriffs in general and this sheriff in particular, the Cambridge burgesses were given the chance and occasion to report their grievances and have them duly recorded.

Whilst Domesday also puts on record the dramatic increases in borough farms over the previous twenty years, these are for the most part given factually and without question of shrieval blame: the royal treasury itself had surely demanded the higher sums.[42] Nevertheless, some boroughs make plain the acquisitive activities of royal officials in their collection of crown demands. The subordinate reeves were entitled to take some cut; the sheriff certainly thought he needed his: that was how officials were paid; but now the amount was out in open court. By 1086, Colchester paid £80, plus honey, plus £20 for the mint, and was producing an additional 100s

---

[38] GDB:162a (GLS:G4).
[39] EvK, above; I have used Table 28 in H. B. Clarke, 'The Early Surveys of Evesham Abbey: An Investigation into the Problem of Continuity in Anglo-Norman England' (Ph.D. thesis, University of Birmingham, 1977), 262.
[40] GDB:64c (WIL:M16).   [41] GDB:189a (CAM:B11).
[42] As in LDB:276b (NFK:66,64), Bradenham.

premium for the sheriff. Even the royal treasurer is not spared a query: on Colchester's £40 debt to Bishop Walkelin of Winchester for inflated mint charges, the burgesses called upon the king himself to substantiate the fact that that he had pardoned them £10.[43] For a reeve or farmer keen to get an agreement to manage a borough or large royal estate, one hundred shillings was about the going rate for shrieval favour: from Dartford the sheriff got 100s and from Canterbury, 110s.[44] Of one sheriff's receipt of £4 and a 'local hawk', Yarmouth records 'the burgesses give these freely and with friendship': gratuitous input that could surely only be a reply to questioning as to whether the sheriff had forced this increment upon them.[45]

In an earlier chapter, we saw that sheriffs were accountable for the products of moneyers and for the quality and weight of silver in the revenues they submitted to the crown. It is possible that the Checking was the logical culmination of a coherent royal policy that included improvements in the consistency of coinage weight, since, in the centuries following, administrative action on monetary standards coincided with scrutiny of royal officials. In 1166 the Inquest of Sheriffs was concurrent with a reform of the coinage, was pursued through a general eyre, and was followed up by a replacement of sheriffs—although by no convictions.[46] In the following century, the detailed Hundred Inquiry of 1279 was contemporaneous with a recoinage of new weight standard, a new round-cut farthing, and severe action against coin clippers.[47]

Many Domesday borough items are explicable as the outcome of the questioning, and the justifying, of exemptions. Lincoln's account shows the Checking considering whether sake and soke, dues of toll, land-gafol, and market rights lie with the king or with the landholders: enough of a bone of contention to provoke a difference of sworn opinion between the burgesses and the priest Wulfgeat, who even offered an ordeal. It mentions by name the fifteen overlords who have 'not paid the king's geld as they ought', and records the great number, 240, of uninhabited urban plots, together with a most instructive explication: 'of these, 166 were destroyed because of the castle; the remaining 74 are unoccupied outside the castle's perimeter, not because of the oppression of the sheriffs and officers (*ministri*), but because of misfortune, poverty and the ravages of fire'.[48]

Other curious explications relate well to a Checking. Domesday Oxford explains that two-thirds of the houses were so wasted and destroyed that they could not pay any geld and that all 'wall houses' are free from obligations apart from military service and repairing the wall.[49] Their holders stand largely vindicated but, with so many holdings unoccupied, or exempt on account of wall-duties, Oxford's remaining property-holders were obviously struggling to cope with a farm which had multiplied threefold since 1066. Urse, sheriff of Worcester, whose revenues were

---

[43] LDB:107a–b (ESS:B6).   [44] GDB:2c–d (KEN:1,1), 2a (KEN:C1).
[45] LDB:118a–b (NFK:1,67).
[46] Stubbs, *Charters*, 174–8; cf., possibly, in the 1120s also, M. Blackburn, 'Coinage and currency under Henry I: a review', *ANS*, 13 (1990), 49–81, at 51; J. A. Green, *The Government of England under Henry I* (Cambridge, 1989), 215–16.
[47] *Mint Documents*, 55–61.   [48] GDB:336b–c (LIN:C20, C26).
[49] GDB:154a (OXF:B4, B9).

squeezed by the bishop of Worcester who had successfully argued for the exclusion of his hundreds from shrieval jurisdiction, seemed to think that a plea for sympathy was his best line of defence. Seven of the twelve hundreds in this shire are so quit, the shire says, that the sheriff has no rights in them 'and therefore as he says he loses much on the farm': and 'if the sheriff does not get so much from the hundreds, he has to pay of his own'.[50] Similarly, a piece of self-justification, even a little whingeing, appears in Edward of Salisbury's statement on the farm. He was responsible for producing £80 a year, and in a poor year had to make up the difference himself, should his own receipts be insufficient.[51]

The interpretation of borough data as the product of an inquiry into missing revenues certainly fits the most comprehensive of Domesday borough accounts: Norwich records the 665 English burgesses in Norwich who do pay customary dues, and 480 bordars who, because of their poverty, pay none.[52] The empty plots are contrasted with the pre-1066 position of 1,320 burgesses, and investigated. Domesday has most to say on the tenurial details of the '50 houses from which the king does not . . . have his customary dues', the offenders being listed by name, with their houses and plots; the bishop's substantial exemption, however, is exonerated, as he held 'by the king's gift'. Functionaries, amongst them a watchman and a loriner, held non-paying plots—their callings seemingly self-explanatory of their exemption, like the moneyer in Oxford.

A follow-up inquisition also accounts for some of the borough descriptions' peculiarities. The Dover entry records its obligations to the king in ships, shipping, and cash payments, and makes clear that in 1086 it was no part of the king's plan that great feudatories and their associates should be exempt from borough dues.[53] It lists only the twenty-nine borough plots 'from which the king has lost the customary dues'; their holders, however, all appeal to the bishop of Bayeux as their warrantor who granted it to them, thereby passing the responsibility for their status to Odo, in his capacity as earl of Kent. No Dover holdings other than improper tenures gain a mention: Rannulf de Colombières holds land which belonged to an exile, an outlaw, so half that land rightly belonged to the king; Humphrey the Bandy-Legged holds one plot, half of which was forfeit to the king; Roger of Westerham has built a certain house on the king's stream, where none stood in King Edward's day, and has, so far, kept back the king's customary dues. At the harbour entrance is a mill which wrecks nearly all the ships through its great disturbance of the sea and causes very great loss to the king and his men: it was not there in King Edward's day and Herbert fitzIvo's nephew testifies that Odo permitted his uncle Herbert to build it.[54] The next Domesday column begins

---

[50] GDB:172a (WOR:C3, C2).   [51] GDB:69a (WIL:24p,1).

[52] LDB:116b–117b (NFK:1,61).

[53] Cf. the dues to which the king and the archbishop were entitled in York, F. Liebermann and M. H. Peacock, 'An English document of about 1080', *Yorkshire Archaeological Journal*, 18 (1905), 412–16; D. M. Palliser, *Domesday York*, Borthwick Paper, 78 (York, 1990), 6–8.

[54] GDB:1a (KEN:D9–10).

with a section on the customs of Kent, seemingly extraneous to the central concerns of Domesday. But these customs were included, not because their presence was required by the Domesday terms of reference but, as Alan Cooper shows, because they recorded the resolution of a dispute so recent that, uniquely in Domesday, all ten rules on fines are stated in the future tense.[55] In contrast to the Kentish antics of Odo, the Sussex reports of Robert of Mortain's borough of Pevensey and William de Warenne's Lewes were exemplary. Although Pevensey no longer seems to be paying anything to the royal treasury, nevertheless tolls, rents, and mint are all well accounted for. After starting with only twenty-seven burgesses, Robert's demesne now boasts sixty burgess rent-payers; and the burgesses whose plots pertained to other landholders were also paying up.[56] Lewes lists all its Edwardian customs and says that they are all now paid, part to the king and part to the holder, and 38s *de superplus*—a good Exchequer term.[57]

In the context of their Domesday functions and powers it remains extraordinary that royal officials are permitted curiously little say in this fiscal 'Checking', although others—and especially the burgesses—are permitted theirs.[58] The 'English burgesses of Shrewsbury' shared a number of grievances with borough dwellers elsewhere and were allowed to give voice to them. It was, they declared,

> very hard on them that they pay as much tax as was paid before 1066, although the Earl's castle has taken over 51 premises and 50 other premises are unoccupied and 43 French burgesses hold premises which paid geld before 1066 and the Earl himself has given to the Abbey, which he is building there, 39 burgesses who once paid tax likewise with the others. In total there are 200 premises, less 7, which do not pay tax.[59]

Despite Earl Roger of Montgomery's all-powerful control of county, borough, and former royal lands, the burgesses are left with the last word on the matter. Picot of Cambridgeshire had arrogated almost royal rights to himself in levying a heriot, a death-duty, on the Cambridge lawmen of £8, a horse and a set of arms, whereas the sheriff had formerly required simply 20s.[60] Again, Picot, powerful as he was, was not permitted a recorded response. At York, William de Percy faced some blame for the disappearance of a tenement, but he laid the responsibility at the feet of Hugh fitzBaldric, sheriff from 1069 to about 1080; the burgesses and William have their say, but Hugh, although still living, was not permitted a recorded reply.[61]

---

[55] A. Cooper, 'Extraordinary privilege: the trial of Penenden Heath and the Domesday Inquest', *EHR*, 116 (2001), 1167–92.

[56] GDB:20c (SUS:10,1).   [57] GDB:26a (SUS:12,1).

[58] Baxter ascribes direct shrieval testimony to 8 occasions only, in comparison with 'burgesses' and 'Englishmen' with 11 quotes respectively. Men of the 'shire' and 'county' are given 117, and the hundred, 311, quotes, S. Baxter, in 'The making of Domesday Book and the languages of lordship', in E. M. Tyler (ed.), *Conceptualizing Multilingualism in England c.800–c.1250* (Turnhout, 2011), 271–308, Table 8, at 285. My gleanings indicate that sheriffs gave testimony in indirect or direct speech on 30 issues (several on undoubtedly the same occasion). Fleming, *Law*, charts the distribution of testimony, 42–3, and gives indexes, 539–43.

[59] GDB:252a (SHR:C14).   [60] GDB:189a (CAM:B13–14).

[61] GDB:298a (YKS:C10); Green, *Sheriffs*, 89.

But the principle of the Checking does not invariably help with the interpretation of every borough; perhaps some circuits had a different remit as the inquisition aspect is less true of Leicester, Warwick, and Northampton—all in Circuit IV, and less relevant for Somerset, Devon, and Cornwall—a possible subdivision of Circuit II. Or perhaps nothing untoward was found. Northampton does go into considerable detail: it does have a few unoccupied burgages, but all seem to be paying their share of the substantial farm.[62] As do Leicester and Warwick; and from 'all' Stafford's holdings 'the king has geld each year'.[63] Similarly, Buckingham accounts for all necessary payments, apart from two burgesses who held from the bishop of Bayeux.[64] In Wallingford, attention is drawn to the 'closes' of the great William de Warenne and Henry de Ferrers (a known Domesday commissioner) that used to contribute to the king's farm, but 'now give nothing'; but there is also much unproblematic data.

For some county towns the record was mixed. Given that a castle—not mentioned in Domesday—had been built at Nottingham, the sheriff had done well to limit the damage to the town. Hugh fitzBaldric, its sheriff, had found there 136 men, now diminished to 120, but he had erected 13 houses on the Earl's land, in a new French borough. The burgesses, however, are on record complaining that they are prevented from fishing in the river Trent as was customary.[65] Nottingham and Derby both seem concerned with the question of the extent of the king's jurisdiction.[66] Derby's account also makes plain the difficulties that Norman policies have created in the borough, where 103 unoccupied urban plots no longer paid dues, but it does not ascribe blame or responsibility for this state of affairs. Hereford, as one might expect of a city with a curial bishop, Robert, a mathematician, presents an exemplary front: all dues are paid and onerous levies listed. Its Lotharingian-educated bishop is our only chronicle source for what seems to be this secondary Checking of officials, when he wrote:

Alii inquisitors post alios, et ignoti ad ignotas mittebantur provincias, ut alii aliorum descriptionem reprehenderent et regi eos reos constituerent. Et vexata est terra multis cladibus ex congregatione regalis pecuniae procentibus.[67]

This may be rendered:

Other inquisitors followed the first; and men were sent into shires which they did not know and where they themselves were not known, in order that different men should check the others' survey and should arraign the accused parties before the king. And the land was vexed with many disputes arising from the collection of the royal revenues.[68]

The borough accounts take the secure possession of basic data elsewhere for granted. When the burgesses of Torksey claimed the same customs as those of

---

[62] GDB:219a (NTH:B1, B37).   [63] GDB:246a (STS:B11).

[64] GDB:143a (BUK:B11).   [65] GDB:280a (NTT:B3, B6).

[66] GDB:280c (NTT:S5), 280b (DBY:B2).

[67] W. H. Stevenson, 'A contemporary description of the Domesday survey', *EHR*, 22 (1907), 74.

[68] See Ch. 4 in this volume, pp. 90–1.

Lincoln and 'much more', only the additional privileges were spelt out, even though Lincoln's customs themselves are absent from Great Domesday, its account concentrating on waste, on shrieval actions, and on the destiny of dues and tolls.[69] Core data, with something of the character of incipient Pipe Roll entries, such as former and present borough farms and customary crown dues, were sometimes incorporated, but often assumed.[70] The absence of basic data from most Domesday boroughs thus becomes explicable—also if no less frustrating, and may well excuse the absence of the major boroughs: London, Winchester, and Tamworth—a royal borough of ancient status—the less-often cited Bristol, farmed by Geoffrey of Coutances (and, of course, Durham, held by William of St Calais). Maybe, too, their reviews were unfinished or, like Durham, their status gave them immunity from review. Working details *were* undoubtedly held elsewhere: when the survey of Winchester was carried out in 1110 by eighty-six of the more important burgesses in the presence of five great officials—chamberlains and justiciars together with the former chancellor—it drew on records from King Edward's day.[71] That the borough presence was not of the essence of Domesday is supported by the fact that the later, 'tidied up', abbreviations of Great Domesday omit most of the urban data altogether.[72]

'THE CHECKING' IN THE LANDED SECTOR

Boroughs had traditionally been closely linked economically with Old English royal and comital estates.[73] The borough properties of the great landholders offered bases for their reeves to market surpluses and acquire supplies, and to make contacts with merchants and the lucrative longer-distance markets.[74] Major royal estates, like many boroughs, paid their revenues in assayed or new coin, presupposing liaison with mints and markets. The Domesday accounts of royal lands, like those of the boroughs, are often distinct in character, but unlike the boroughs, their entries are not dominated by a rehearsal of problems, being often more informative about their agrarian economy than those of the tenants-in-chief. Yet here, too, Domesday took a critical view of the self-seeking of sheriffs and here, too, there is evidence of a secondary investigation or 'Checking'.

In the rural sector, as in the urban, concerns other than those of simple justice motivated the king's interest in administration. In the long term, it was not in the king's interest for his officials to make potential contributors 'too poor to pay any

---

[69] GDB:337a (LIN:T1).   [70] Some tabulated in Roffe, *Decoding*, 128–9.

[71] *Winchester*, Survey I, 33.

[72] In the two British Library volumes, the borough details are not copied, except that York appears in the Arundel MS. Other boroughs are ignored or present only basic royal customs and hidage: BL Arundel MS 153, and BL Cottonian MS Vitell CVIII, ff143–56. In National Archives volumes, E 164/1, 'Breviate', temp. Edw. I, and E 36/284 'Abbreviatio', temp. H. III, the borough hidage and the customary duties of burgesses only are copied; except in the latter the full Domesday entry of York is copied.

[73] Fleming, 'Rural elites and urban communities', 3–37.

[74] e.g. St Edmundsbury, LDB:372a (SUF:14,167).

geld'. Maintenance of the peasants' plough-teams was also essential to revenues, crown and seigneurial.[75] Small agriculturists were contributing more than their fair share to fiscal returns and, after twenty years, perhaps the reliance placed on them was coming to be appreciated by some in high quarters.[76]

Nor did the king wish to hand to his sheriffs completely autonomous command of the 'farms', a traditional source of revenue, and now largely distinct from geld. As in the boroughs, so in the rural sector, royal officials were generally taking much higher returns than in King Edward's day. Despite the shrieval hand on the tiller of the Inquiry, Domesday does not conceal the fact that over and above the raised farms, the sheriffs and their subordinates were levying additional sums that were impoverishing due-paying men to the long-term fiscal detriment of the now twenty-year old regime. The vulnerability of William's regime had already been exposed by the welcoming reception that previous Danish fleets had received in eastern and northern England. By 1084–5, the severe reprisals that had followed earlier uprisings, and higher taxes, were making the prospect of an alternative Danish ruler more attractive to native men. Some change of policy became imperative. Snippets in Domesday, relating more to royal lands than to others, suggest that the Checking investigated situations detrimental to the local community and consequently to the long-term assets of the king. The alliance between ruler and small taxpayer when under external challenge had Carolingian precedents: Charlemagne's Aachen programme for imperial government had stated that all those who had complaints stood under his protection.[77]

The king had an evident interest in finding out about payments received by officials over and above the official demands. We have earlier investigated sheriffs' premiums and the raising of revenues on the use of all sorts of assets for which the hundred provided a convenient collecting vehicle. In the business of negotiating crown leases, the 1274 Inquiry similarly sought to lay bare the practices of which sheriffs and their subordinates might be suspected; it sought information on 'sheriffs who have handed over to extortionate bailiffs, oppressing the people beyond measure, hundreds, wapentakes, or ridings at high farms, so that they may thus raise their own farms'.[78] An anecdote in the Abingdon chronicle illustrates how payments to the sheriff worked. Its abbot, Ingulph, 1130–59, was 'long accustomed to give 100s annually to the sheriff of Berkshire to treat the abbey's men more leniently and help them in pleas and hundreds. Afterwards, the progress of time turned this into a custom, and the sheriff used indeed to receive from the

---

[75] Royal manors, in particular, relied upon them for income, see Ch. 7 of this volume; Harvey 1983, 63–71; Harvey 1988, 85–95.

[76] E. Miller, 'War, taxation and the English economy in the late thirteenth and early fourteenth centuries', in J. M. Winter (ed.), *War and Economic Development: Essays in Memory of David Joslin* (Cambridge, 1975) 11–31, shows that the peasantry were perennially taxed, proportionately, more heavily than their lords, at 17–18.

[77] e.g. M. Becher, *Charlemagne* (London, 1993), 108–9; *MGH Capitularia Regum Francorum*, ed. A. Boretius (Hanover, 1881), no. 33, *Capitulare missorum generale*, *cap.* 1 and 30.

[78] Cam, App. I, *cap.* 18.

abbey the 100s as if they were his rent.'[79] By 1086 there had evolved a hierarchy of pressure and undeclared profits, which were punitive for the peasantry and more-over led to diminishing returns. The noting on royal lands of not only values, but renders also, discussed in Chapter 7, highlighted the over-greedy and corrupt practices of the sheriff and his underlings that were not always channelled to the king's profit. Most of those estates with renders higher than values were on estates, public or private, in the charge of the *curiales*. Henry of Huntingdon's verdict on the Norman establishment, quoted in an earlier chapter, and probably gathered from local tradition and his maternal kinsfolk, concludes: 'Those who were justices were the source of all injustice. Sheriffs and reeves, whose office was justice and judgement, were more frightful than thieves or robbers, and more savage than the most savage.'[80]

Officials and reeves were revealed assisting each other in building up their own estates. One of the hides that Grim the Reeve held in Bowers Gifford had been forfeited to the king, and Grim had added it to his other land, 'through Robert fitzWymarc the sheriff, as Grim says'. Whilst higher farm payments had undoubt-edly been officially sought, sanctioned, and recorded, the Checking was seeking out revenues and policies that had evaded accountability. The enigmatic question in the terms of reference—'if more can be had than is now being had'—might refer to the returns from almost any asset, but it was certainly compatible with asking if more of the sheriffs' receipts should be handed over to the crown.

It was the responsibility of sheriffs and reeves to take the lands of the outlawed into the king's hands, and much land had been confiscated as result of the initial fighting against William or from those who had fled the country or were out-lawed;[81] Grim the reeve held yet other land via Hubert de Port which a 'freeman had forfeited because he could not pay the fine'; however, Grim had paid the 30 shillings fine and taken over the land.[82] Former officials sometimes hung onto such lands. In the Welsh borders, royal thegnland had been changed into 'reeveland' and thus 'this land and the rent from it are being stealthily taken away from the king'.[83] Of the holding of one outlawed freeman, it was said 'Swein's men have taken this land and still hold it', Swein being a former sheriff.[84] Later, Urse, sheriff of Worcestershire, eventually turned farmed royal lands into his own hereditary estate.[85] In 1086, Domesday's Checking exposed this situation by seeking data from the men of the locality on the situation in King Edward's day, and comparing it with what the sheriff accounted for to the crown.

Where livestock on royal land had gone downhill, thereby prejudicing the long-term value of the manor, efforts were made to identify whose was the responsibility; but blame was often spread successfully or allocated to much earlier shrieval action.

---

[79] *HistAbbend* 2, 314–15.   [80] HH, 402–3.
[81] e.g. LDB:176b (NFK:9,49).   [82] LDB:98a (ESS:83,1–2).
[83] GDB:181b (HEF:1,75).   [84] LDB:24a (ESS:18,23).
[85] A. Williams, 'The spoliation of Worcester', *ANS*, 19 (1996), 397; Mason, 'Brothers at court', *ANS*, 31 (2008), 69.

At Hatfield Broad Oak in Essex, the loss of plough-teams, mostly belonging to the peasantry, happened over 'the time of all the sheriffs'.[86] At Witham, the decline in the men's plough-teams, from eighteen to seven, was successfully attributable to previous sheriffs—'this loss was in the time of the sheriffs, Swein and Baynard'— and to 'cattle plague'.[87] Interestingly, sheriffs were being called to account for the non-demesne plough-teams as well as for those of the demesne, their more obvious responsibility. The concern was for revenue and taxation, but the Conqueror was at long last, and for his own reasons, recognizing the essential role of the husbandmen.

The tenurial changes Domesday records in the rural sector were drastic, yet the shrieval misdemeanours to which the Checking objected were small-scale; they concern mainly small lands with which officials furnished their own private contacts. Ilbert, a past sheriff of Hertfordshire, had taken 20s worth of royal land for one of his knights.[88] Even small parcels of land were noted and inscribed: the loss of meadow, an alder grove, a mill, and twenty acres (nine hectares) of land—a mere 20s worth—on the great royal manor of Dartford, where the alienated land was found to have been leased to another reeve before 1066 and to have passed to Helto Dapifer and his nephew. To the same sheriff, Osweard, was also attributed the loss of six acres (over two hectares) of land and a wood by mortgaging it for 40s, with the result that Hugh de Port now held this former royal land.[89] Alwig, a sometime sheriff, was deemed to have alienated land in Oxfordshire 'without the king's permission'.[90] Godric, the Edwardian sheriff of Berkshire, had found all sorts of ingenious ways of taking land out of the king's farm—ploughing some of it with his own ploughs, using it to pasture his horses or simply putting a half-hide 'outside' a manor; he had granted a further half-hide to one Aelfgyth as long as he was sheriff, in order to teach his daughter to embroider in gold thread—a Domesday vignette of a lordly lifestyle.[91] All telling testimony to a meticulous inquiry into the fate of every acre of crown land and into the activities of officials during William's rule.

Sheriffs had been in the front line in implementing the confiscation of the lands of the fallen, the fled, and the antagonistic, and in keeping control of the newly conquered land. We have seen earlier how Little Domesday's data showed shire officials converting freeholders into full-scale rent-payers. Whereas in King Edward's day, for instance, the twenty-six Fulbourn sokemen had paid only 12s 8d or supplied escort duties, their successors were now required to pay Sheriff Picot £8 of assayed silver; moreover, he had 'annexed the excess in despite of the king'.[92] Anglo-Saxon reeves, working to various sheriffs, implemented many such changes. Post-1066, Ælfric, a reeve in charge of large-scale farming of crown lands, had added eighty-three freemen in Wangford hundred to the royal manor: men who

---

[86] LDB:2a–b (ESS:1,3).   [87] LDB:1b (ESS:1,2).   [88] GDB:133a (HRT:1,13).
[89] GDB:2c (KEN:1,1).   [90] GDB:160d (OXF:58,27); Green, *Sheriffs*, 42, 69.
[91] GDB:57c–d (BRK:1,57; 1,26–7), 149b (BUK:19,3); Green, *Sheriffs*, 26.
[92] GDB:190a (CAM:1,14).

formerly did not pay any customary dues there, but who now rendered as much as £15.[93] It was alleged that the payments from a group of freemen had been raised in Hugh de Houdain's time from 100s to £50.[94] It seems likely that Hugh had been a royal officer, or sheriff, as 'in his time' is the manner in which a sheriff's term of office is normally quoted in Little Domesday: moreover, he could not give evidence to the Inquiry as desired because he was 'under royal arrest', *in captione regis*.[95]

In appropriating freemen's revenues, shrieval tactics appeared to have been a calculated policy, one at its most visible in the more detailed Domesday accounts from East Anglia and the East Midlands which 'read like obituaries for the Anglo-Saxon landholding class'.[96] Indications remain that the stratagem was driven directly by the king, and that activities were flagrant on lands that had been held by King Harold, his brothers, and the executed Earl Ralf: Harold's freemen at Saham Toney, who had been worth 53s TRE, were now at farm for £20; others were 'added to this manor by the king's command'.[97] The tactic continued as other survivors of the old regime fell and the king's own supporters fell from grace.[98] Little Domesday offers many examples, amounting to a deliberate intention to impoverish freemen and sokemen with past affiliations to the former king and earls, and push them into economic anonymity.

Even so, in the 1086 Checking, some of those who had suffered at the hands of sheriffs were given a hearing. When Peter de Valogne's men claimed that a certain sokeman had forfeited his land for not paying geld, the men of the shire refused to support the sheriff and, backed up by the hundred, testified that the land had been quit of the geld and other dues as long as the sokeman held it.[99] Ralph de Bernay, former sheriff in Herefordshire, had placed two formerly independent freeholders into the king's farm 'unjustly' and made them pay rent.[100] In the south-west, a great many free-holdings had been 'added to' manors, or merged to form a manor. The Devon sheriff had added the lands of six thegns to the manor of Bridestowe.[101] Moreover, shrieval action was now questioned to the point of nit-picking. Besides attaching freemen who formerly could sell their land to royal manors in Hertford-shire, Ilbert had wrongly enforced cartage from one woman's holding and had refused to supply it himself from one smallholding after he had left office.[102] Even though the last point had already been dealt with to the king's advantage by Ilbert's successor, these points were heard, noted and, surprisingly, not abbreviated out of Great Domesday. Rare it is for an item to reflect the sheriff's view-point: Durand of Gloucestershire had to find 'the whole farm' from what remained of two royal manors, part of whose lands had been alienated or wasted.[103] Yet Durand's cry

[93] LDB:282b (SUF;1,17); also Buckenham, 126b–127a (NFK:1,139).

[94] LDB:283b–284b (SUF:1,44–60).

[95] LDB:405b (SUF:30,3); cf. LDB:448b (SUF:76,14) where he is cited as guarantor for some land held questionably.

[96] Abels depicts the shrieval workings in the south-east midlands, in 'Sheriffs', 19–50, at 19.

[97] LDB:110a (NFK:1,3–4).   [98] e.g. LDB:377a (SUF:16,33–4).

[99] GDB:141a, (HRT:36,9).   [100] GDB:181b (HEF:1,70).   [101] GDB:105d (DEV:16,7).

[102] GDB:132c–133a (HRT:1,6; 1,8–9; 1,11–12).   [103] GDB:163a (GLS:1,13).

rings somewhat hollow, considering that he himself was revealed to have given land from the royal demesne at Westwood in Herefordshire to St Peter's, Gloucester, for the soul of his brother Roger.[104]

Officials seem to have played fast and loose with the tax assessment of the land that they managed or held. Froger the sheriff had made the former sixteen hides of three thegns at Sparsholt into a royal manor, given a nil tax rating.[105] Geoffrey de Mandeville appears to have manipulated the rating of two Surrey manors that he held illegally from thirty-seven hides down to six and a half hides.[106] The practice of conceding beneficial hidation in high places was not, however, novel or confined to William's reign: Archbishop Stigand's onetime manor of Wymondham, worth £70 with 110 villeins and bordars on it in 1086, was assessed at only four carucates, and 'looks like a royal gift'.[107] After 1066, the newcomers exploited such possibilities assiduously in the south-east.

Even when death relinquished the sheriffs' grasp, their widows persisted with their malpractices. Hugh fitzGrip of Dorset took charge of some Abbotsbury Abbey's land 'wrongfully, and kept it'; 'his wife still retains it strenuously'.[108] She, or Hugh, had targeted the resources of other monastic houses, depleting the assets of two manors of Cerne Abbey that were, consequently, worth £5 a year less.[109] Other lands belonging to Hugh were built up from many thegnly landholders who had formerly been independent enough to commend themselves to whichever lord they wished.[110] His widow was apparently not liable for her demesne land in several hundreds, and several of her men followed her example.[111] She might, indeed, have put her husband's eternal life into jeopardy, since a hide of land that her late husband had given to Cranbourne Abbey 'for the sake of his soul' was still inscribed within her fief.[112] More sympathetic is the case of the widow of Godric the sheriff who tried to hold onto a hide of land once gifted to her 'because she kennelled the king's dogs'; she had the support of one Ælfric of Thatcham, who had seen the king's writ, although no one in the hundred would verify that.[113]

The Checking exposed conflicts between sheriffs and their reeves or farmers and led to mutual denouncements about premiums and agreements; and at times royal officials thought it their best defence to cite the king. Roger Bigod, the current controller of most of Norfolk's royal lands, disagreed publicly with the reeve Aelfric as to what had actually been fixed over the revenues from the manor and hundred of East Bergholt, and Domesday uncovers considerable dissension over the sheriff's due of £10 and a mark of gold. While Roger turns to witnesses in support of his agreement with the reeve, the reeve calls no less than the king as guarantor of the

---

[104] GDB:181a (HEF:1,61).   [105] GDB: 57a (BRK:1,10).
[106] GDB:36b (SUR:25,1–2).
[107] LDB:137b (NFK:1,215); M. F. Smith, 'Archbishop Stigand and the eye of the needle', *ANS*, 16 (1993), 210.
[108] *vi detinet*, GDB:78b,c (DOR:13,1 and 4).   [109] GDB:77d (DOR:11,5).
[110] GDB:83c–84a.   [111] DB4; ff. 21b–22; 'Geld Rolls', VCH *Dorset*, 3.138.
[112] GDB:84a (DOR:55,47).   [113] GDB:57d (BRK:1,38); Green, *Sheriffs*, 26.

amount that he is required to pay.[114] Royal lands in Bedfordshire paid one ounce of gold to the sheriff 'by concession of King William'.[115] It was by 'the king's command' that Picot continued to hold lands of the abbey of Ely—although he was now compelled to pay the abbot service for them.[116] The half-share that the sheriff took from the farm in Stafford, rather than the customary third, has been queried, and defended, but not yet corroborated. Domesday notes succinctly: the sheriff, 'Robert [de Stafford] has half the king's own share, by the king's gift, so he says'.[117] Roger d'Ivry, too, held five of his hides from the king, 'so he says'.[118]

Royal officials frequently stand accused of holding onto inalienable Church lands previously held on lease or for service by laymen. In 1086, Picot's tenure of more than six hides of a former lease from Ely abbey was shown to be unlawful, even in a hundred where one of his men served as juror.[119] Eustace, current sheriff of Huntingdon, held some Church land 'without deliveror, writ, or seisor': it had had a chequered history—given to two of the Confessor's priests, who had 'sold' it (possibly a lease) to Hugh, King Edward's chamberlain.[120] Sheriffs had notoriously put pressure on ecclesiastical landholders, even seizing lands by violence. Eustace also stands eternally accused of seizing land 'by force' from Ramsey Abbey and holding it from King William.[121] Even the most powerful of sheriffs did not escape unquestioned. Edward, sheriff of Wiltshire, still held three hides 'which should have returned' to St Albans after the donor, Wulfwynn's, death, 'so the hundred testifies'.[122]

Sheriffs' transgressions had caused concern earlier in the reign.[123] A well-known writ, of no secure dating, but possibly *c.*1077, makes the king's suspicions abundantly clear:

> William requests Archbishop Lanfranc, Bishop Geoffrey of Coutances, Count Robert of Eu, Richard fitzGilbert, Hugh de Montfort and his other noblemen (*proceres*) of the kingdom of England that they summon his sheriffs and on his behalf tell them that they should return to his bishoprics and abbeys all the demesne, and all the demesne land, which the bishops and abbots, either through carelessness, fear or greed, have given them out of the demesne of the bishoprics and abbeys, and which they have agreed to hold, or which they have seized by violence. Unless they return what they have wrongfully held, they are to be compelled to make restitution. And if anyone else, *or any of the addressees who have been given the commission*, is open to the same accusation, he must also make restitution of whatever he holds of the demesne of bishoprics and abbeys, in order that none among them be less able to coerce any sheriff or other person who holds demesne of churches.[124]

Not only were the sheriffs to make reparation, but the very magnates entrusted with the commission, the core of the establishment, were not beyond question. Another

---

[114] LDB:287b (SUF:1,103).   [115] GDB:209c (BDF:1,3).
[116] GDB:191b (CAM:5,24), 200b (CAM:32,5).   [117] GDB:246a (STS:B12).
[118] GDB:242b (WAR:20,1).   [119] Fleming, *Law*, 25–6; GDB:201c (CAM:32,37).
[120] GDB:208a (HUN:D,1).   [121] GBD:228a (NTT:55,1).
[122] GDB:139b (HRT:32,1).
[123] William reprimands a sheriff before Sept. 1069: Van Caenegem, *Lawsuits*, no. 1.
[124] *Acta*, no. 129: my italics.

writ expressly instructs them that the lands of Bury St Edmunds are not to be disturbed; it also instructs Peter de Valognes, sheriff of Essex and Hertfordshire, to free the men of Bury St Edmunds whom Peter holds imprisoned (*in captionem*).[125] Yet in 1086 Peter is still holding various lands of St Edmunds.[126] Magnates who have seized lands forcibly from Ely Abbey also feature in an early 1080s writ and include some usual suspects: William de Warenne, Richard fitzGilbert, Hugh de Montfort, Geoffrey de Mandeville, Hervey of Bourges and Hardwin de Scales are all summoned to court to come to agreement with the abbot.[127] In a writ possibly related to the one quoted, William warns 'all his sheriffs of England' that the abbey of Westminster is to hold freely, with all customs, the lands which King Edward had given them.[128]

Domesday castigates a wide range of sheriffs, past and present, for their misdeeds, yet the great majority of culpabilities concerned only small pieces of land: ancillary portions of manors or lands of small freeholders, some so small that they hardly seem worthy of official pursuit, let alone mention in Domesday, particularly in the context of the cataclysm that had swept over the country's landholders. As many as fifteen sheriffs—Baldwin of Devon, Edward of Salisbury, Peter de Valognes, Godric of Norfolk, Picot of Cambridge, Geoffrey de Mandeville, Hugh fitzGrip and his widow, Hugh de Port, Ilbert of Hertford, Ralph de Bernai, Eustace of Huntingdon, Ralph Taillebois,[129] Robert Blunt, Durand of Gloucestershire and Urse d'Abitot—appear as culpable more than once, most being mentioned in the boroughs as well as in the landed sector; a number of these names reappear in the *IE* with small landed claims against them. Certainly they had appropriated some small holdings to provide rents to fund followers; but for the most part their censurable actions were attributable to the policies that they had been required to carry out as a consequence of the military conquest: policies which are referred to quite openly in Domesday. Careful work has shown how this practice, in some regions, led to the lands of small Edwardian landholders (perhaps remaining themselves as tenants if they were lucky) being parcelled out amongst many new lords.[130] As the sheriffs and magnates who were to become commissioners had been key players in this process, it was not at all surprising if a few freeholders had ended up paying rent to the sheriffs' men, rather than to the crown.

In fact, only three sheriffs, Geoffrey de Mandeville, Picot, and Roger Bigod, stand out as having pursued bigger game. Geoffrey, with lands worth nearly £800, castellan of the Tower of London, and sheriff of London and Middlesex, or on the verge of so becoming, was the only sheriff with the estate of a 'Class A Baron'. He might also have held the shrievalty of Essex at one point.[131] Notwithstanding his position, Domesday notes that Geoffrey 'unjustly' gained two substantial manors,

---

[125] *Acta*, no. 42.   [126] LDB:365b–366b (SUF:14,81–3).
[127] *Acta*, no. 119, 1081 × 1083.   [128] *Acta*, nos 310, 330.
[129] Eleven freemen were put into royal hands by Ralph Taillebois, GDB:218d (BDF:57,13).
[130] R. Fleming, *Kings and Lords in Conquest England* (Cambridge, 1991), esp. fig. 4.4, 119.
[131] Green, *Sheriffs*, 56, 39, and table of values of sheriffs' holdings in 'The sheriffs of William the Conqueror', *ANS*, 5 (1982), 140–1.

amounting to nearly forty hides; men of the hundred and shire having the courage to say and the opportunity to go on record that they have seen neither writ nor 'deliveror' that gave Carshalton, once twenty-seven hides and five manors, to Geoffrey.[132] The nuns of Barking Abbey had lost a small manor to him: the hundred testified that it had been held by a man merely affiliated to Geoffrey's predecessor, who 'could not dispose of the land to any place except the abbey'.[133] Newcomers too, such as Ralph Pinel, were targets of his cupidity.[134]

Tenure was indeed of the essence of the Domesday record, although scepticism has been expressed about its centrality.[135] Even exchanges of land are handled in a manner that implies that they were invalid without royal authorization, and even when the parties were magnates or officials apparently mutually content to make an equal exchange.[136] The action of the Devon sheriff in exchanging a virgate of land, worth 20s, with another, also worth 20s, is duly noted.[137] The Domesday attention to such exchanges, sometimes noted as 'without permission', indicates that all such changes of tenure required acknowledgement by the king or his officials, and possibly, or rather probably, a payment for recognition, as later. Richard *Interpres* had one hide in Roda which he bought 'by permission of the king', *per licentia regis*, from someone who said he held it TRE.[138] The maxim enunciated when the Inquiry learnt about the land of a priest who, on becoming a monk, took with him land held in free alms, tacitly underlies William's whole policy and the Domesday enterprise: 'it is not permissible, *non licet*, for anyone to have the land except by the king's grant':[139] an authoritative statement that sounds like an *ex cathedra* statement from a commissioner. It was intended that the king and his representatives should authorize and endorse the entire landed settlement.

Remedial action, even for small items of land, was evidently expected, if not completed. The Checking resulted in the least-digested section of data in Domesday, because items awaited verification or referral to the king's court. Geoffrey of Bec 'now seeks the king's mercy' for land he is claiming as a successor of Hertfordshire's previous sheriff, Ilbert.[140] This is the present tense; he still has hopes. Sheriff Eustace's appropriation of the houses of twenty-two Huntingdon burgesses belonging to a church leads them to claim the king's mercy; clearly they awaited action.[141]

It is arguable that court sessions for borough checking, and for Claims also in certain counties and circuits, were held later than the hearings for the general county description.[142] In Essex, 'Encroachments' on the king's lands follow the account of the shire, and Colchester's account follows thereafter. The order of the Claims of Huntingdonshire and Lincolnshire differ from their order in the main county text,

---

[132] GDB:36b (SUR:25,2).   [133] LDB:57b (ESS:30,3).   [134] LDB:97a–b (ESS:77,1).
[135] Wormald, 61–102, contrasting with P. Hyams, '"No register of title": the Domesday Inquest and land adjudication', *ANS*, 9 (1986), 127–41.
[136] e.g. LDB:6b (ESS 1,27).   [137] GDB:100b (DEV 1,5).   [138] DB4:466b.
[139] GDB:345a. It also obtained TRE for royal grants in frankalmoign, Barlow, *English Church*, 136.
[140] GDB:132d, 133a (HRT:1,9;1,13).   [141] GDB:203a (HUN:B12).
[142] See also Galbraith, 104; Finn, *LExon*, 146.

suggesting that they were not drawn up on the same occasion; and their contents suggest that further investigating has taken place, or pressure has been exerted, between the two hearings:[143] in Domesday Drayton, in Lincolnshire, the 'witness of the men of the hundred' affirms that 'they do not know through whom the bishop held it'; yet, under Claims, 'the wapentake bears witness' for the bishop of Lincoln, and supplies the antecessor.[144]

There is every sign that the establishment intended to pursue the Inquiry's findings on disputable tenure and official wrong-doing. Even while Great Domesday was being written up, one case was officially recognized and inserted into its account of Hampshire: additional to the quire, a half-page sheet records that the king's reeves have taken away a hide of a manor of the archbishopric of York, allegedly 'without the knowledge of Hugh de Port', the Hampshire sheriff. In this case, a post-Domesday writ, 1086 × 1088, punctiliously confirms the restoration of the hide.[145] Action similarly followed Domesday's report that Eustace, sheriff of Huntingdon, took land at Isham from the abbey of Ramsey 'by force', and early in William II's reign, the shire court settled in Ramsey's favour.[146]

That comparable cases were not followed through methodically was perhaps more to do with the death of one ruler and the succession of another who was challengeable and, shortly, challenged than with any lack of coherent intent. The Checking that followed the collection of data seems intended to address elements in the sheriffs' independence. In the twelfth century, sheriffs were questioned and adjudged in the King's Court in the Exchequer as to whether they had 'acted wrongly'.[147] Yet we should also bear in mind Thomas Bisson's wisdom: 'as late as 1100, accountability is not yet administrative. It is remedial, judicial, moral—and it is occasional'.[148]

'THE CHECKING' OF KEY ROYAL OFFICIALS

Nevertheless, the Domesday Checking challenges the over-bearing activities of a few great individuals who, despite their pivotal positions, were evidently deemed to be exceeding their remit.

Eminent in 1086 was Walkelin, William's treasurer and bishop of Winchester, who proved a zealot for revenues in both capacities. The record of the bishop's borough of Taunton shows that, from paying £50 'when Bishop Walkelin acquired it', it now yields £154 13d with all its customary dues, and Domesday scrupulously minutes the extent of the bishop's jurisdiction.[149] In Hampshire alone, Walkelin's

---

[143] Wormald, 70; cf. also Finn, *LExon*, 58–60.
[144] GDB:348b (LIN:12,59), 377d (LIN:CK65).   [145] GDB:42; *Acta*, no. 352.
[146] GDB:228a; *Regesta* 1, no. 383; D. Bates, 'Two Ramsey Abbey writs and the Domesday Survey', *Historical Research*, 63 (1990), 337–9; similarly *Regesta* 1, no. 291, suggests follow-up: Sharpe, 'Use of writs', *ASE*, 32 (2004), 275–7.
[147] *Dialogus*, 14–15.   [148] T. N. Bisson, 'The "feudal revolution"', *P&P*, 142 (1994), 38.
[149] GDB:87c.

administration was demanding that seven manors of his bishopric and two manors of its priory, which he had taken into his own hands, pay significantly more than the reasonable farm; on five, Domesday says categorically that 'it cannot be borne', including Fareham of Fareham hundred and Meon of Meonstoke hundred.[150] The punitively high rents and dues known on the Winchester estates in the thirteenth and fourteenth centuries had ancient roots.

In the Domesday record, we see farmers of royal estates and sheriffs following this tactic, but not tenants-in-chief as a class. The appointment of hard-headed treasurers, however, to the see of Winchester was already becoming a tradition. Earlier, Stigand, with similar expertise, had exerted pressure during vacancies to enter into profitable agreements.[151] In 1086, Martock, a royal Somerset manor, shows traces of Walkelin's hands-on activity, paying £70, plus a mysterious £5 more 'if Bishop Walkelin bears witness to it'.[152] This entry, too, implies inquiries might not yet be over. As the treasurer, Walkelin appeared to have had the oversight of minting dues; for these, the burgesses of Maldon and Colchester owed him £40, as the mint levy had been set so high that they had been unable to pay more than half.[153] Walkelin—not a monk himself and initially antipathetic towards monks in cathedral churches—was alleged to have appropriated from his monks lands to the value of £300 a year, which he had appropriated to his see, although in his last years he repented of his voracity.[154]

Despite Geoffrey of Coutances' reliable work over many years in endeavouring to resolve land disputes, his own revenues did not go unquestioned. Geoffrey held Bristol, which, like London and Winchester, was not described in Domesday. To Domesday's brief statement (attached to the royal manor of Burton) about the farm that Bristol paid to the king, the burgesses manage to add that Geoffrey took thirty-three marks of silver and a mark of gold—in effect a further third.[155] Earl Roger of Montgomery was another who obviously liked his gold; in 1086, he was noted as the recipient of three payments of an added mark of gold over and above the value of the land.[156] And whilst Roger had achieved the halving of hidage on his own great demesne manors in Sussex in the course of William's reign, his tenanted manors had not.[157]

Over-charging and illicit acquisitions are exposed on the lands of the great Richard fitzGilbert, the founder of the Gilberts of Clare dynasty, who also held the 'banlieu' of Tonbridge in Kent. A leading figure in the eastern region in pre-Domesday pleas, Richard was proving an unsatisfactorily partial commissioner. He had evidently colluded profitably with royal officials: during Swein's shrievalty, annexing four freemen, who had since been taken into the king's hand.[158] He was not above small encroachments onto royal lands: at least seven of Richard's illicit holdings in Suffolk were recorded—he or his tenant being actually called 'bad

---

[150] GDB:40b–41d.   [151] e.g. *IE*, 195; *LE*, II, no. 98.

[152] GDB:87a (SOM:1,27).   [153] LDB:107b (ESS:B6).   [154] *AnnWinton*, 39–40.

[155] GDB:163b (GLS:1,21).   [156] GDB:23a,b (SUS:11,3; 11,7), 44d (HAM:21:6).

[157] GDB:23a–b.   [158] LDB:6b (ESS:1,27).

neighbour', *malus vicinus*.[159] Nor did Richard's interest in agriculture preclude him from over-charging one of his contracted farmers.[160] Yet his tiny, as well as large-scale, infringements did not escape posterity: even his absconding with the virgate of a single *rusticus* was inscribed in Domesday.[161]

Despite Odo of Bayeux's influence amongst the shrieval group, the Domesday record shows no compunction in highlighting his misdemeanours. Odo features in many dubious deals, not just on his own behalf but together with a coterie of magnates and royal officials, many of whom held lands of his earldom in Kent, and, since he was imprisoned at the time of the great Survey, his past machinations could be denounced in safety. On the royal land in Hertfordshire, the Checking, like the record of the county itself, was thorough. Odo had taken charge of land formerly looked after by a royal reeve and given it to Eudo Dapifer, plentifully stocked, 'to the king's loss'.[162] One reeve found himself in an invidious position and did not wish to plead, when the bishop of Lisieux's tenure of land pertaining to a royal manor was called into question and the bishop could cite only the imprisoned Odo as to his possession of it.[163] As well as Odo's misappropriations in Dover, duly noted are the two hides of land that he took 'by force' from a royal chamberlain to fund his own English chamberlain, Æthelwulf.[164] The actions of Odo's brother, the king's half-brother, Robert of Mortain, were likewise subject to scrutiny. The Inquiry does not shrink from questioning Robert's tenure of lands in the south-west, where he was deemed to have taken, in all, four hides from Athelney Abbey.[165] On the other side of the country, at Combs in Suffolk, Robert's doubling of demands, we are told, had led to disaster for fifty freemen.[166]

Domesday questions others of the highest influence. The king's grant of a Waltham manor to the bishopric of Durham does not escape from the hundred's comments unscathed.[167] The great Eustace of Boulogne and his countess had evidently obtained dramatic tax concessions on their Surrey and Hertfordshire demesne lands: between them, they held land that had been assessed at 112½ hides in Edward's day, which were by 1086 reduced to a rating of nineteen hides, one virgate in all.[168] Nonetheless, Domesday records that, in Colchester, the Count has thirteen houses that paid the king's customary dues before 1066, but they 'have not paid since Eustace has had them'.[169]

Various eminent officials were up for questioning. Eudo Dapifer, son-in-law of Richard fitzGilbert, even more than Haimo Dapifer, the sheriff of Kent, appears as

---

[159] LDB:447b–448. It might already have become a name.
[160] Harvey 1988, 119–20; LDB:38b (ESS:23,2).   [161] GDB:30b (SUR:1,6).
[162] GDB:139b (HRT:31,8).   [163] GDB:30b (SUR:1,5).
[164] GDB:216b (BED:40,3).   [165] GDB:91a,b (SOM:10,1;10,6), DB4, f.512a.
[166] LDB:291a (SUF:2,6).
[167] GDB:210c (BDF:5,1). Bishop William also appears in claims in Lincolnshire, GDB:375b (LIN:CS19).
[168] GDB:34b (SUR:15,1–2; 16,1), 137b (HRT:17,1). There were no reductions on his two Kentish manors.
[169] LDB:106b (ESS:B3g).

a recurrent offender. Eudo has twenty-three urban plots in Stamford, which no longer paid the king his customary dues, nor did his two houses in Maldon;[170] he holds land that used to answer for eight hides and now answers for three; he keeps back soke from the king on several of his holdings; quite understandably, he refuses to fulfil the obligations, *wara*, on three acres of woodland that a previous sheriff took from his holding, but it is minuted nevertheless.[171] Both Haimo and Eudo were royal office-holders and *curiales* of note whose actions the Checking exposed elsewhere; Colchester has issues over the lack of royal dues from both their premises there.[172] Certainly, the commissioners took swift action on 80 acres (32 hectares) of arable and 200 acres (80 hectares) of marsh that Haimo Dapifer had purloined: 'we have taken possession of this appropriation into the king's hands'.[173] Nevertheless, Haimo, or his son, continued in office throughout William II's reign.[174] Eudo Dapifer was one of the king's *barones* who held hearings of land pleas together with the bishops of Winchester and Durham, Ivo Taillebois, and Robert Dispenser, early in the second William's reign. He witnessed writs of financial importance together with Rannulf Flambard and Urse of Worcestershire, often witnessed other writs alone, and continued to be given property.[175] Such men were, and continued to be, at the core of the Anglo-Norman establishment.

Edward of Salisbury held over thirty manors, and over 300 hides; but his actions were surveilled and criticised, without his response recorded. He has put land in Gloucestershire wrongfully into the farm of Wiltshire, where he was sheriff.[176] The shire and hundred gave evidence against him in Hampshire; a substantial manor of his in Hertfordshire, that he took over from Wulfwynn (quite possibly his mother), should have returned to the abbey of St Albans; in Wiltshire itself, Edward has ignored the proof that a virgate of land was shown to belong to Croc the Hunter.[177] Ranulf Peverel was another censured in the Inquiry whose dynasty stayed in favour into the next generation. He held several pieces of land claimed by Ely abbey—one of five hides.[178] His Colchester property also does not pay its dues.[179] He, too, was known for demanding extraordinary returns: at Assington, eight carucates that he held with sake and soke had an Edwardian value of £10, yet was given a current valuation of £20: unsurprisingly 'it could not pay 100s of this'.[180]

Hugh de Montfort, royal constable, leader of a contingent of knights at Hastings, a magnate, and plea commissioner in his own right, a sought-after contact by the

---

[170] GDB:336d (LIN:S6); LDB:5b–6a (ESS:1,25).

[171] GDB:47b (HAM:30,1); LDB:239b, thrice; GDB:212b (BDF:21,6).

[172] LDB:106a–b (ESS:B,3b–3d).

[173] *hanc occupationem percepimus in manu regis*, LDB:94b (ESS:66,1).

[174] Green, *Sheriffs*, 50.

[175] J. A. Robinson, *Gilbert Crispin, Abbot of Westminster: A Study of the Abbey under Norman Rule* (Cambridge, 1911), 136, no. 9, 1087 × 1088; Hemming, 79–80; *Regesta* 1, no. 337. Eudo continued to receive property, *Regesta* 1, nos 442, 435.

[176] GDB:164b (GLS:1,63).

[177] GDB: 46c (HAM:27,1), 139b (HRT:32,1), 69b (WIL:24,14).

[178] LDB:19a (ESS:10,3) 73b–74a (ESS:34,19), 75a (ESS:34,30), 384b, (SUF:21,39).

[179] LDB:107a (ESS:B3q).   [180] LDB:416a–b (SUF:34,3).

highest in the land, and in possession of a strategic enclave in East Kent, holding lands from the archbishop of Canterbury, from Odo, and from St Augustine's, was certainly the object of considerable Domesday criticism, overt and implicit. His revenues elsewhere had been augmented by conniving officials: post-1066 the royal reeve Ælfric had added eighty-three freemen from one hundred to Hugh de Montfort's manor, and those who had formerly paid no customary dues now paid £15.[181] Much wheeling, dealing, and exchanging of freemen has taken place—in part authorized, in part now deemed to be 'against the king'.[182] One hide of Hugh's land used to pay dues to the king's manor and now does not.[183] A number of his estates demand renders higher than their values. Moreover, his manor, castle, and developing borough of Saltwood, in Kent, where he was a knightly tenant of the archbishop, was the only Kentish knightly holding to have received a dramatic reduction in its geld rating.[184]

Hardwin de Scales, a commissioner in the Ely pleas, faced widespread censure and questioning; and the Checking looked into the exemption of fourteen of his urban properties from all dues other than 'the king's geld'—which he substantiated by citing the king.[185] He seems to have been a man of influence, maybe an office-holder, who could command men to stand ordeals or face trial by battle on his behalf. Hardwin and his men held various lands formerly belonging to the abbey of Ely;[186] and although the jurors of Armingford hundred included one of his tenants, three different claims were recorded there against him, one of a mere four acres.[187] The inclusion of such small incidental items relating to establishment figures seem only accountable as part of a deliberate process of allowing the locality to complain in public of unwarranted actions by officials. Of Humphrey the Chamberlain, for instance, who had charge of some of Queen Matilda's estates in Gloucestershire, Domesday records that he had taken a relief of 20s from a villein who collected 'the Queen's wool'.[188]

Yet it was not necessarily through acquisitiveness that Norman officials had acquired a few men 'rightfully' pertaining to another; the sheer volume of transactions alone inevitably meant omissions and mistakes. A priest called Snaring and his land, along with other freemen, had had to endure no less than four transfers of lordship since the death of King Edward; one at least on the authority of a king's writ—to put one Ralph de Savenay in possession 'of all the freemen over whom Hubert de Port had seised the bishop' of Bayeux; and Roger Bigod and Earl Hugh of Chester were still contesting the priest and his land in Domesday.[189] The vulnerable freeholders of Anglo-Saxon England had been deliberately enfeebled in a dramatic campaign of downgrading and confiscation, yet this whole process

---

[181] LDB:282b (SUF:1,17).   [182] LDB:407b–409b, e.g. (SUF:31,34; 31:44).
[183] LDB:52b–53a (ESS:27,3).   [184] From 7 to 3 sulungs, GDB:4c (KEN:2,41).
[185] GDB:132a (HRT:B,10).   [186] GDB:198c,199a (CAM:26,30; 26,49; 26,51–7).
[187] GDB:198d (CAM:26,29–30), 191b (CAM:13,2), 196c (CAM:19,4); Fleming, *Law*, 23–5.
[188] GDB:30c (SUR:1,8).
[189] LDB:377a (SUF:16,34); also 114b–115a (NFK:1,52; 1,57).

was largely taken for granted in the Domesday record. The former landholders of Anglo-Saxon England, if mentioned at all, were most often mentioned as 'ante-cessors'—simply vehicles whose names confirmed the validity of the transfer of their land to newcomers. Many sokemen had been 'delivered' to their new lords in the course of making up the number of the newcomers' manors, *in numero suorum maneriorum*, as was the case for one of Hugh de Montfort's misappropriated freemen.[190] Such references suggest that some incomers were awarded a round number of manors verbally by the king, with the implementation left to the sheriff or other delegate. The only pre-1066 landholders that might have been recognized *ipso facto* were the ecclesiastical foundations: many of whom still experienced difficulties in regaining leased or tenanted lands.

Given that they had been charged with the reallocation of tens of thousands of hides and carucates in the aftermath of a military conquest, it is small wonder that royal officers were found to be retaining the odd half-hide and its freeholder wrongfully. Especially in view of their success in assembling the Domesday material, perhaps it is more fitting to appreciate the competence of Norman officials and their aides than rehearse their rapacity. For them, the bar was set unreasonably high: one and a half acres of meadow was claimed against Eudo Dapifer's men and Eudo claimed one acre against Hugh de Beauchamp's man.[191] In the Checking that followed the Inquiry, they were effectively made the scapegoats for Norman unpopularity: it had the potential to set establishment figures against each other and seems to have done so, despite the close relation-ships within the group.

Indeed, lands of the Church apart, most disputes over land were claims and counter-claims between the greatest newcomers and their peers: Geoffrey de Mandeville challenged by Richard fitzGilbert, Ralph Taillebois versus William de Warenne, and so on. Some rivalry seems apparent between the two greatest Dapifers, Haimo claiming forty-five acres (eighteen hectares) from Eudo.[192] Henry de Ferrers, a Domesday commissioner in the west midlands, possibly an earlier royal official or sheriff in Berkshire, was himself faced with several claimants;[193] and he claimed two holdings of a carucate or so of land from Robert Dispen-ser.[194] The men of Count Alan of Brittany and Roger Bigod, as well as the hundred, argue over the rights to the rent of 5s or 10s from a former freeman's land.[195] Perhaps these great *curiales* felt genuinely anxious to prove themselves in the right in the courts; perhaps this tiny elite sought to embarrass each other as a form of diversionary humour amongst the slog of hearings endured and data amassed; perhaps it took an office-holder to catch an office-holder. Yet their public exposure, like their original policies, shows every sign of being driven from on high.

---

[190] LDB:100a (ESS:90,17).
[192] LDB:55a–b (ESS:28,8).
[194] GDB;234d (LEC:19,6; 19,9).
[191] GDB:215a (BED:25,7).
[193] GDB:233a–b; Green, *Sheriffs*, 26.
[195] LDB:176b–177a (NFK:9,49).

BARONS OF THE EXCHEQUER?

These core functionaries constituted a powerful group who had acted, and who continued to act, in a wide range of matters, tenurial and fiscal. They and their associates had already functioned amongst the initial 'deliverors' of land: William's possessory actions had been put into the hands of sheriffs,[196] and their peers, such as Hubert de Port, Sheriff Hugh's brother,[197] or higher, with Bishops Odo and Geoffrey.[198] Thus, not only in the reigns of the Conqueror's sons but in the Conqueror's reign too, we see a group of key barons who acted on the administration of tenure, and who acquired fiscal privileges.[199] Familiar names present in 1086 at the plea between the abbey of Fécamp and William de Briouze, presided over by the king, included St Calais, Walkelin of Winchester, Geoffrey of Coutances, Robert of Hereford, Osmund of Salisbury, Remigius of Lincoln, Maurice of London, the count of Mortain, Roger of Montgomery, Richard fitzGilbert, Roger Bigod, Henry de Ferrers, Eudo Dapifer, and Alfred of Lincoln.[200]

The existence by the 1090s of an experienced and influential group of men working together as a key financial body is brought into focus in a recent study of the Worcestershire sheriff, Urse, and his brother, Robert Dispenser.[201] The writ for the unprecedented 'relief' extracted from the bishopric of Worcester's subtenants in 1095 shows how Urse was in charge of seizing the land and the portable wealth of defaulters, while he and Robert, themselves prominent Worcester tenants, escaped mention amongst those required to pay.[202] The witnesses of Robert's last bequest around 1097 included Walkelin of Winchester, Urse, Herbert the Chamberlain, William the Chamberlain, Peter de Valognes, Ivo Taillebois, and Otto the Goldsmith, who was probably master of the mint—Robert's likely colleagues at the time.[203] Yet before Domesday, as well as afterwards, members of an inner circle were evidently permitting each other to take tax relief whilst others paid. Otto the Goldsmith was amongst those who held houses in Colchester Domesday without paying customary dues.[204]

These men were practised in maximizing their own returns from land: indeed most of the office-holders mentioned in this chapter were those whose manors paid farms set higher than their values. Hubert de Port held one good-sized manor in Hampshire, in the north, close to royal Odiham: its hidage recently halved, it

---

[196] e.g. Peter de Valognes, GDB:141d–142a (HRT:37,19); Ivo Taillebois, LDB:290b (SUF:1,122f).

[197] LDB:377a (SUF: 16,34), 450a (SUF:77,4).

[198] GDB:201d (CAM:37,1), 151d (BUK:40,1).

[199] For William II's reign, those with responsibilities comparable to barons of the Exchequer were already operating, a point developed in Barlow, *Rufus*, 187–92 and by Mason, 'Brothers at court', 64–89.

[200] *Acta*, no. 146, dated 1086, April or after, at Laycock, EHD2, no. 52.

[201] Mason, 'Brothers at court', 77.   [202] Hemming, 79–80.

[203] *Westminster Abbey Charters, 1066–c.1214*, vol. 2, ed. E. Mason, London Record Society, 25 (London, 1988), no. 488.

[204] LDB:106b (ESS:B3j).

rendered more than its value.[205] Oda of Winchester, a senior royal official, held one manor worth 50s, but it rendered 100s.[206] Several of Eudo Dapifer's manors experienced great leaps in rental demands between 1066 and 1086.[207]

In short, we can discern from Domesday that during William I's reign, as well as under his sons', a group of responsible core officers and magnates with vested interests in the new regime were accorded the tasks of barons of the Exchequer as well as the fiscal privileges.[208] The order to leading magnates to supervise the activities of the sheriffs who had purloined church lands might well signify a similar group functioning in that capacity earlier.[209] Other evidence supports the dating of this capacity to William I's reign. The Geld Accounts take note of tax-collectors who have failed 'to render account', *reddere nobis rationem*, or who have given pledges 'before the king's barons', *ante barones regis*, and who remain at the king's mercy.[210] These *barones*, like the Domesday commissioners were also termed *legati regis*.[211] The collectors carried out the collection of tax in a recognized manner. In the case of Devon, a royal sergeant and Ralph de Pommeroy carried the geld to 'the king's treasury at Winchester';[212] Ralph appears to have been in receipt of fiscal concessions: his two Devon manors were together worth £7 10s, yet he paid tax on less than one hide in all.[213] The Somerset collectors enjoyed the services of a scribe, strongboxes, wax for seals, expenses for wagons, and payment.[214] It would seem difficult still to argue that there were no officials to acknowledge and store receipts on arrival. As earlier chapters have argued, the links between counties and Treasury, or treasuries, for crown receipts, were regular, quite technical, and, operative before Domesday.

CONCLUSION

In 1086, when the productive levy of revenues was central to the regime's survival, the conduct of crown agents became a concomitant matter of concern. Yet the public review of their activities was certainly not an inevitable by-product of the collection of Domesday data and, while the Danes threatened, it was against the regime's interests for their activities to receive recorded criticism in this way. But William, who had felt forced to take similar action before, seems to have investigated the very men who had functioned as commissioners on other occasions, and perhaps the likely timing of this investigation was after the July assassination of the Danish king and the August meeting at Salisbury.

---

[205] GDB:46c (HAM:24,1).
[206] GDB:51c (HAM:NF9,2).   [207] e.g. LDB:403a, (SUF:28,1b, 28,2), 51a (ESS:15,22).
[208] In the 1180s barons of the Exchequer and in-post sheriffs had their demesnes officially exempted from geld, *Dialogus*, 56.
[209] *Acta*, no. 129, quoted above, p. 256.
[210] DB4: f.70b. See also the demands of Bishop Osbern, GDB: 101d (DEV: 2,2).
[211] DB4: f.526b.
[212] DB4: f.71; A. Williams, *Kingship and Government in Pre-Conquest England* (London, 1999), 145.
[213] GDB:113d–114a (DEV:34,1–2).   [214] DB4: f.526b; also ff. 76b, 81.

Although the sheriffs and members of the inner circle were the very people who had been in control of the Domesday proceedings, the Checking investigated in public and recorded, mostly in their own counties, the administrative activities of some of the most powerful office-holders and landholders. For them, its Domesday record became both a literal and a metaphorical day of reckoning, where the minutiae of their marginally dubious activities were disclosed for posterity in humiliating fashion. And it may well have helped to tear apart the establishment quite speedily: certainly the sheriffs Hugh de Port of Hampshire and Picot of Cambridge were engaged in litigious contest in Hampshire and it was left for the king's court in the last days of William I, or the first days of William II, to decide.[215] The final entry in Little Domesday refers a dispute between Odo and Robert Malet's mother over the land of four Suffolk freemen to the king's court to be held at the royal manor of Odiham in Hampshire.[216]

Yet, the policy itself of the takeover of the lands of Anglo-Saxon freeholders, great and small, was not in question; that policy can only have been enacted at the Conqueror's instigation: the references by men of the hundred to the king's will, a writ, or a messenger, or occasional lack of them, make that clear.[217] The shrieval policies put into practice during much of William's reign were intended only to impoverish English lay landholders and discourage resistance rather than to enable William to be the good lord that he had promised Archbishop Ealdred. The Conquest had created many opportunities for levying new 'illegal' charges; and not a few royal officials had doubled their returns, on both their public and private estates, in the course of the twenty-year reign, with the smaller freeholders offering easy pickings.

But such a policy could not be pursued indefinitely—especially at a time of challenge. In the Checking, William I, probably mindful of the advice and essential practical support of churchmen in the short term and of the indispensability of their moral and spiritual authority in the long term, demonstrated his intent to supervise those to whom he had given authority. There were precedents for such a line. Those of William's bishops who were conscious of the Carolingian heritage in Lorraine, France, and northern Italy may well have been aware that Carolingian kings, in need of the military and fiscal support of lesser freemen and cultivators, took seriously grievances about raised dues. A royal Carolingian court in 828 in Aquitaine had accepted that the *coloni* were entitled to question new demands, if payments were 'more in rent and renders than they ought to pay and hand over', and had exceeded those traditionally paid over the last thirty years.[218] The lords' dues were rightful only if they were established and the case was judged only after reference to a *descriptio* of twenty-seven years earlier.

---

[215] GDB:44d (HAM:23,3).   [216] LDB:450a (SUF:77,4).
[217] e.g. LDB:377a (SUF:16,34).
[218] J. L. Nelson, 'Dispute settlement in Carolingian West Francia', *Dispute Settlement*, 48–54, at 49.

In the Domesday Inquiry, the 'English' or 'the men of the hundred' were, on not a few occasions, asked to comment on the mode of land transfer or on the values given. The intention, moreover, in 1086 seems to be that their divergent opinion be heard and, not infrequently, recorded. The investigation of the activities of the king's shire reeves and their deputies allowed a limited opportunity to men of the hundred and the English to protest at the level of returns and declare whether the transfer had been properly completed. They were permitted to make public the raised dues and the sheriff's failings. In the record of the boroughs and the Checking, Domesday marks a change in William's policy: the takeover of small freemen and sokemen was temporarily transformed from a policy of carte-blanche encouragement into one in which formal *minutiae* had to be observed.

What is surprising is the sheer triviality of the land deals questioned, given the power he had entrusted to the ruling group. But William did not expect them to take advantage, and did not shrink from *minutiae*. Evidence outside Domesday supports the king's intent: at Salisbury castle, *in camera regis* in 1081, when the king gave formal assent to one Wihenoc of Monmouth's grant to an abbey in Saumur of three ploughlands, he also formally gave his permission for Wihenoc's previous donation of 'a virgate of land for pigs'—about which he previously 'had not spoken to the king'.[219] One of the motives for royal action is perhaps explained in the reasoning given in the Fontenay inquiry held in Normandy: William 'did not wish what had previously been done according to his advice and assent to be diminished'.[220] Thomas Bisson observes: 'nowhere in these lay societies was it possible to delegate power; one could only share it': 'accountability was the last frontier of military lordship'.[221] No doubt the Conqueror's sheriffs would have concurred; yet in the Domesday Inquiry in general, and in the Checking in particular, William I demonstrated his resolve to cross that last frontier and maintain his position there. He had long directed his officials to treat the nuances of English leasehold and freehold in more than cavalier fashion, regardless of the charters and confirmations of religious houses, not to mention their dedications, altars, and relics. Now, for strategic reasons, he confronted his officials with their own Day of Account.

SEQUEL AND REBELLION

The Checking shows real evidence of the crown listening to the fiscal grievances of the boroughs, and perhaps Lanfranc's youthful experience of the Italian towns' revolt against the Emperor had caused him to warn William to go cautiously there. In the rural sector, the Ramsey Abbey writs show that William II began by punctiliously following up his father's controlling policy.[222] Whether any

---

[219] *Acta*, no. 268; similarly, *Acta*, no. 144.
[220] *nolens imminui que consilio eius et nutu ante facta fuerant, Acta*, no. 149.
[221] Bisson, 'The "feudal revolution"', 37, 39.
[222] See n. 146 in this chapter.

discontinuity of sheriffs at the opening of William Rufus' reign was outside a normal pattern of replacement through death and disease, age and accident, the evidence is insufficient—although we know that Henry II and Richard I did conduct purges of sheriffs early in their reigns.[223] Under William II most leading officials reappear, although neither the venal Roger Bigod nor Geoffrey de Mandeville had unbroken tenures in office.[224] Roger may have been removed from the office of sheriff in Suffolk in 1087, but only to be replaced as sheriff by Godric Dapifer or Humphrey the Chamberlain, both mentioned in the Checking;[225] possibly he lost office in Norfolk to Humphrey.[226] He seems, however, to have returned to Suffolk in the 1090s and to Norfolk around 1100.[227] The range of men that William's sons trusted was certainly not wide: Hugh of Buckland had charge of probably five counties under Rufus and eight under Henry I.[228]

Did the likes of Odo of Bayeux and Geoffrey of Coutances, joined by William of St Calais, launch their rebellion of 1088 in disillusionment over the repercussions from the Domesday project? The tenants-in-chief, for their part, were only too aware that if their assets and the annual value of the estate were known precisely, all sorts of feudal dues might well become more onerous. In the heat of the invasion crisis of 1085, many strategies might have been grudgingly accepted as necessary by *curiales* and landholders, but resented deeply in the cold dawn of a new reign when the data could be newly exploited to the full. Odo often acted wilfully, but, curiously, this time his co-rebel was Geoffrey, stalwart of the regime, and veteran of many a legal commission. They were joined, moreover, by the bishop of Durham, whom some regard as the mastermind of Domesday or, at the least, influential in the project; with St Calais' participation, the new king thereby 'lost the resources of the outlying counties'.[229]

Geoffrey, if not himself amongst the Domesday commissioners, most probably had a hand in appointing them; and many shrieval appointees were Odo's men. Did Odo and Geoffrey in 1088 rise up in resentment to oppose the consequences of the Checking that had inquired into their and their protégés' works? Their additional payments in gold,[230] their fiscal concessions, their extortionately high farms, their acquisition of tiny parcels of land unsanctioned, and their premiums for 'goodwill' had all been spelt out in the Domesday returns. Could the very men on whose efforts the success of the Conquest had depended continue to tolerate the public questioning of their reputations, and its public record? The Conqueror's heirs were in danger of losing the support and services of office-holders by pursuing them through the courts. The leaders of the 1088 rebellion against William II—Odo

---

[223] e.g. R. Heiser, 'The sheriffs of Richard I: trends of management as seen in the shrieval appointments from 1189 to 1194', *Haskins Soc. Journal*, 4 (1992), esp. 112–13, 120–2.

[224] Barlow, *Rufus* 170, 187–9.   [225] Green, *Sheriffs*, 76.   [226] Green, *Sheriffs*, 60.

[227] *Regesta* 2, no. 509; Green, *Sheriffs*, 61.

[228] Barlow, *Rufus*, 188; Green, *The Government of England under Henry I*, 199–200.

[229] *GRA* 1.544–5.

[230] Odo of Bayeux was recorded in two such transactions: the bishop, or his men, receiving gold once for an illegal deal, and once allegedly on the king's behalf, GDB:2b, 36d.

of Bayeux; Geoffrey of Coutances; Roger of Montgomery (probably) and his sons; Roger Bigod; Robert of Mortain; Gilbert fitzRichard of Clare; and Eustace III of Boulogne—were almost all receivers of criticism or fiscal scrutiny in Domesday (in the case of the last two, it was their fathers).[231] They were indispensable and they knew it; their great estates, deliberately carved enclaves in Kent and Sussex and on the borderlands, maintained the most strategically important positions. Their lives had been perpetually in danger; and they had, by great effort, supplied the data demanded by William I at a time of crisis when the still insecure and unpopular establishment was in jeopardy. William of Malmesbury states quite explicitly that in 1088, Odo of Bayeux, Roger of Montgomery, and Geoffrey of Coutances were apprehensive that William II was following his father's severe policies too faithfully, and they deduced 'it will not be long before we lose the honour we have earned by long-continued effort; we shall have gained nothing by the father's death, if those whom he made captive are slain by his son'. The rebellion had leverage because of the rival claim of William I's eldest son, Robert; and, in the barons' chronicled debate on the subject, it was indeed pointed out that Robert was known to be of 'milder disposition'—less likely perhaps to pursue administrative minutiae.[232]

Even before the besieging of Odo in Rochester, William Rufus promised the 'desired/desirable laws' at an assembly in London.[233] New rulers adjust policies: especially when confronted with armed opposition from key supporters who could summon up an alternative candidate. Rufus's only riposte was to point out to them, with unanswerable logic, 'he who made you magnates, made me king'.[234] Afterwards, those 'older barons' who had served his father 'long and faithfully' were pardoned, including Geoffrey of Coutances and almost all the magnates mentioned above.[235] Their record in witness lists in the summer of 1088 demonstrates the king's wish to publish their reconciliation: it implied close attendance, and reinstatement in office.[236] However, the loose cannons, Odo and Eustace, were banished, as was St Calais—for the short term. But almost all the officials mentioned in the Domesday Checking resumed office and favour in the reign of the Conqueror's successor. After the dangerous resistance to William II's initial attempts to follow up the Inquiry and its data, it seems that the misdeeds of the king's representatives, questioned in public and perpetuated in Domesday, were not pursued in the king's courts—they were prepared to judge, but they refused to be judged—thereby partly explaining why 'nearly half to more than three-quarters of the evidence as to contested tenure proffered by local opinion on peril of its soul' was ignored.[237]

---

[231] *JW* 3.48–51; Geoffrey de Mandeville and Roger Bigod were possibly 'waverers': Barlow, *Rufus*, 69–93, at 72; the personnel and their vacillations are discussed in R. Sharpe, '1088—William II and the rebels', *ANS*, 26 (2003), 139–57.

[232] *GRA* 1.544–5.

[233] *legesque promisit exoptabiles*, HH, 414; *statuens leges, promittens fautoribus omnia bona*, *JW* 3.50.

[234] *GRA* 1.546.   [235] OV 4.134.   [236] Sharpe, '1088', 145–57.

[237] Quotation from Wormald, 74.

10

The Book of the Day of Judgement

> And I saw the dead, small and great, stand before God, and the books were opened. And another book was opened, which is the book of life. And the dead were judged by what was written in the books, according to their works.
>
> Revelation 20:12[1]

It is in the matter of tenure and the mode of obtaining it that the Book's name resonates. It seems straightforward: 'doom'—the Anglo-Saxon word for a law or judgement, plus the word for 'day'. So the name referred to the written results of the unique Law Day or Days, held in counties across the country, with many of the population swearing as witnesses to the proceedings. The word 'doom' itself carried no necessary sense of disaster: it was the point in time of irrevocable judgement. But there was always a religious dimension to the English name.[2] Whilst the Norman Conquest largely buried vernacular English as an official language for several centuries,[3] two English words arose from the grave when the Englishmen who unwillingly gave authority to our source named the Book 'Judgement Day': hinting that William's now legalized tenure would not be upheld in the eternal balance.

The written word was a contribution to history, especially in the matters of kings and rights to land: ecclesiastics who were historians were aware of their powers and relished wielding them. The names of Bede's 'perfidious kings' remain forever unknown because he deleted them with deliberation from his version of the regnal lists, denying them even notoriety.[4] Apparently, the popular designation 'Domesday' remained unrecorded for up to a century,[5] perhaps with reason: the lawyers and officials of the establishment were all Churchmen, working for stability, and

---

[1] Rev. 20:12–15; also, Matt. 16:27.

[2] Cf. II Edgar, 3 and 5, where *domboc* refers to written legislation on religious observations and ecclesiastical dues.

[3] But see N. R. Ker, *Catalogue of Manuscripts Containing Anglo-Saxon* (Oxford, 1957); D. A. E. Pelteret, *Catalogue of English Post-Conquest Vernacular Documents* (Woodbridge, 1990); also, of course, *The Anglo-Saxon Chronicle (ASC)*.

[4] Bede's *Ecclesiastical History of the English People*, ed. B. Colgrave and R. A. B. Mynors (Oxford, 1972), 214–15.

[5] *et est in regis domesday* appears in *An Eleventh Century Inquisition of St. Augustine's, Canterbury*, ed. A. Ballard, British Academy Records, Records of Social and Economic History, vol. 4 (London, 1920), 1. The *regis domesday* of its heading may be an early reference in that the name of the king is not given; but the extant text is in a thirteenth-/fourteenth-century cartulary and at least two copies removed from an independent document made in or before 1087, and the phrase quoted is in a different hand, National Archives, E 164/1.27. Now edited by C. Flight, *The Survey of Kent* (BAR British Series, 506, 2010), 72–88.

within their consciences. When Richard fitzNigel of the Exchequer, canon of St Paul's and later bishop of London, did finally document the native name, he endeavoured to reduce the Day of Judgement of the Survey to a figure of speech:

> This book is metaphorically called by the native English 'Domesday', that is 'the Day of Judgement'. For as the sentence of that strict and terrible last account cannot be evaded by any skilful subterfuge, so when this book is appealed to on those matters which are noted down, its decisions cannot be quashed or set aside with impunity.[6]

The work was, he wrote, compiled 'in order . . . that every man may be content with his own rights and not encroach unpunished on those of others'. Apportionment of tenure was indeed of the essence yet, although fitzNigel offers a knowledgeable general account of the mechanics and range of the Domesday Inquiry, his reasoning here remains unconvincing: in fact, many 'Claims' lie in Domesday undecided; evidence recorded was apparently ignored; and individual allocations were not infrequently challenged in court in the decades following its composition.[7]

Thus, the 'Book of the Treasury' did not gain its English name because the minutiae of its data and its allocations were unquestionable. Rather the establishment required that the principal tenurial decisions inscribed in the document be regarded as unquestionable and irreversible. The commissioners largely, probably purposefully, had ignored the very real differences between various types of Anglo-Saxon lordship that accompanied commendation, soke, and leasehold;[8] they simply wished to determine each estate's Edwardian 'holder' largely in order to establish which newcomer was to be considered the tenant-in-chief, and which the subordinate tenant—and the royal will in the matter. The returns of the tenants-in-chief had travelled through hundred- and shire-courts, processes familiar to the English, who had been required to witness this change of possession with sacred oaths—a mode of witness that legitimated the Conquest land settlement. Domesday's usefulness to the Exchequer in the long-term was as written evidence of recent possession thereby transformed into proprietary right. Always the king's land was put first, and William's seal, writ, or envoy, seem to have superseded former charters, which were surprisingly rarely quoted in Domesday itself.[9] Bishop Osbern of Exeter had evidently been requested earlier in William's reign to 'show' his bishopric's pre-Edwardian charters, in the presence of the king's barons, *coram*

---

[6] *Dialogus*, 63–4.

[7] e.g. the case of Sandwich, D. M. Stenton, *English Justice between the Norman Conquest and the Great Charter, 1066–1215* (London, 1963), 116–23. Maitland concluded that Domesday did not function as a register of title, Maitland, 3. Wormald reckoned that 'over 80 per cent of seemingly successful plaintiffs are frustrated in so far as their vindicated lands are still ascribed to their opponents', Wormald, 69–71. Granted, several hundred contested cases were either left undecided in Domesday or its recordings disregarded, but given a conquest and the tens of thousands of parcels of land reallocated, the relatively low number is remarkable. Recently, D. Roffe, 'Inquests in medieval England', *Haskins Society Journal Japan*, 4 (2011), 18–24, contrasts with the view here, but comments interestingly on the Claims.

[8] S. Baxter, discusses the possible overlapping of Anglo-Saxon tenure and lordship, *The Earls of Mercia: Lordship and Power in Late Anglo-Saxon England* (Oxford, 2007), with diagram, 204–15, et seq.

[9] A shire writ as well a charter was sought at GDB:375a (LIN:CS13).

baronibus regis (an Exchequer term), but when in 1086 he simply 'spoke' for a manor in Berkshire, his claim was received with some scepticism.[10] Title derived from the king and Domesday supplied the king with his charter. Richard fitzNigel was maintaining Domesday's rationale: the Norman land settlement was not to be set aside or challenged without punishment.

But there was more to the English name. In Anglo-Saxon England, a *land-boc* embodied the legal and tangible transfer of the fullest rights in land: only the royal fisc's right to support with communal defence and its infrastructure was reserved. The holding of land safely was a king-given gift; and the establishment of a king depended on supporters who felt enabled to hold their land safely. Both kings and land-charters were held in veneration after passage through due ritual, and the gravest sanctions were invoked for those breaking the bond. Written documents had an authority all their own and charters were often written up into Gospel books. One royal diploma of Æthelred II for Abingdon acknowledges that 'because of the uncertain changeableness of future years', the words of priests and the decisions of judges 'should be strengthened by the testimony of written documents'. It places an anathema upon anyone who should violate the land-grant: 'he will render account of this in God's presence on the Last Day of Judgement'. The warning was usual; unusually, this grant decreed the same fate for the holder of any former or contradictory document: [he or it] was to be 'deleted from the Everlasting Charter': 'and not be written or heard with the just', adds another Abingdon charter to the same phrase.[11] More sinister, the arbitrary dismissal here of any former charter admits that in the last resort whatever kings decided to confirm, or indeed rewrite, knew no limit.

LAND-GRANTS AND DOMESDAY

The possession of land was the foundation for the earthly life of oneself and one's heirs. It could also be transformed into a sign-post to life eternal: generosity to the church through gifts of land were intended to be gifts in perpetuity, forever to redound to the giver's credit, particularly in the life hereafter. Grants of land to monasteries secured beneficent remembrance and intercessory prayers: the most long-term investment a layman could make. Anglo-Saxon grants of land to minsters traditionally concluded with anathemas, invoking eternal retribution on any who suborned them.

Current notions of the fate of the soul beyond death, powerful in the minds of men and women, were an amalgam of theological teaching and of less learned thinking.[12] The *dies irae* depicted in many churches of human figures falling into

---

[10] GDB:101d (DEV:2,2), 58c (BRK:5,1).

[11] *sed in sempiterno graphio delatur, et cum iustis non scribatur nec audiatur, HistAbbend* 1, no. 101, 156–9; S.896; S. Kelly, *The Charters of Abingdon Abbey*, Anglo-Saxon Charters VII, Part I (Oxford, 2000), no. 128. Also, *HistAbbend* 1, no. 137, 210–13; S.665; Kelly, no. 37.

[12] Bartlett, 612.

flames or devoured by monstrous beasts, were not distant but rather proximate terrors in a hazardous, uncertain, and often short, life. The written context of transactions in land was cosmic in scale. One land-charter opens with a *proem*, or introductory preamble, of over 230 words: beginning with the Creation and the Fall, it covers the Incarnation, with Mary's virtue cancelling Eve's sin, and finishes with a grand anathema, in ninety-six words of Latin. Any transgressor of the grant will, at the Day of Judgement, be relegated to the left hand of Christ, along with Judas; he will never enjoy the heavenly kingdom, but is destined for the eternal fires of hell.[13] Some land-grants recited a succession of unimaginable terrors, and many offered no hope of redemption for the transgressor. Even marginal reductions of the land so granted would incur eternal damnation. At one such ceremony, 'Archbishop Wulfhelm, and all the bishops and abbots who were there assembled, excommunicated from Christ and from all the fellowship of Christ and from the whole of Christendom anyone who should ever undo this grant or reduce this estate in meadow or in boundary. He shall be cut off and hurled into the abyss of Hell forever without end. And all the people who stood by said, "So be it. Amen. Amen".'[14] Anathemas were part of a moral framework accepted by rulers and ruled.

More theologically orthodox land-grants did allow the possibility of repentance and the reparation of any infringement. The tenth-century bishop, Theodred, willed simply: 'whosoever detracts from my testament, may God deprive him of the kingdom of heaven, unless he make amends for it before his death'.[15] Some balanced their anathemas with encouragement to others to emulate their generosity. Earl Leofric of Mercia, and his wife, the Lady Godiva, made a grant of land to the church of Worcester just a few decades before Domesday; 'And if there is anyone who desire to augment or endow it in any way, God Almighty shall grant him a prosperous life and eternal reward. And if on the other hand anyone is puffed up and so greatly covetous of earthly things that he desires to alienate this our gift he shall have the curse of God and St Mary and St Oswald and all the men in Holy Orders here in this life, and he shall be excommunicated on the Judgement Day...and tormented for all time in everlasting punishment along with Judas and his companions, unless he desist and turn to a proper mode of conduct.'[16] Some surviving anathemas were later additions to charters, and some charters that describe their laying on the altar were forgeries,[17] yet these twelfth-century embellishments make the point that men of religion continued to think that such warnings were proper and might inhibit predators who had a high reputation to maintain.

The handing on of gifted land to one's successors was a God-given responsibility. Bishop Godwine, newly appointed to Rochester, *c.*995, immediately set about reclaiming lands lost to his diocese, feeling that he 'durst not do otherwise for the

---

[13] *HistAbbend* 1, no. 37, 60–7, discussed cxcix–cciv; S.658; Kelly, no. 83. Its authenticity is debated; Kelly thinks it 'probably genuine'.

[14] Grant of Land by Earl Æthelstan to Abingdon Abbey, Charters, no. 22; S.1208. It may be spurious, Kelly, no. 28.

[15] *Wills*, no. 1.   [16] Charters, no. 113; S.1232.   [17] *Writs*, 67–70, 168–71.

fear of God'. The resulting agreement chimed with tradition in declaring anathema on anyone who broke the settlement.[18] Such modes of thought did not die out amongst the English after 1066. A post-Conquest record, in Anglo-Saxon, of dues and tithes belonging to the Church at Lambourn warns: 'He who takes this away from the Church at Lambourn and from the Priest shall have the curse of Christ and St Mary and St Michael and St Peter and St Nicholas and all the Saints of Christ'.[19]

Yet, anathemas notwithstanding, churches had seen their lands transferred to churches in Normandy. Robert of Mortain, like many of his fellows and, as the king's half-brother, with more opportunities than most, was particularly prone to this kind of generosity; and also to keep much for himself. No fewer than twenty-four English houses, from the greatest, Glastonbury Abbey and Christ Church, Canterbury, to small houses in Cornwall, suffered from his acquisitiveness; and only a proportion of their lands ended up in the hands of the abbeys of Grestain, Mont-St-Michel and Fécamp.[20] By interfering with the book-land conferred on monastic houses William was risking eternal damnation. But royal predators and their agents were difficult to withstand, and it was perhaps to them that grandiose warnings were especially directed. At a restitution of manors that had been alienated on account of William II's arbitrary actions and fines, the abbot of Abingdon took the opportunity of the presence of Rannulf Flambard—'the king's chaplain and justiciar of the kingdom of England'—to pronounce an anathema safeguarding the lands' future.[21]

For many practical reasons, William could act only with the passive—if not active—consent of churchmen, the most thoughtful and educated of whom generally did their best to direct and mitigate the military acquisitiveness of kings. Their private thoughts may or may not have been kept to themselves while the ruler lived, but only a Gregory VII, an Anselm, or a Bernard of Clairvaux would make public utterance of them. Whether from polity or as a matter of fact, Giso, bishop of Wells, left records that claimed that he had stood up to Harold's acquisitiveness whilst earl: he had 'considered striking Earl Harold, who [had despoiled] the church committed to me, and whom I rebuked sometimes in private and sometimes openly', with a sentence of anathema.[22] However, occasionally, particularly towards the end of his life, there are hints that the Conqueror too was not unmindful of his moral obligations. In private, his archbishop and adviser, Lanfranc, was certainly mindful: his collection of Church Canons was marked in the margin at the decision that a tyrannical usurper of a kingdom should be excommunicated from the church.[23] Yet if Lanfranc had noted it with a view to vindicating William's right to dispossess the usurper Harold, he could not but have been aware that it was a two-edged sword. His successor, Archbishop Anselm, a

---

[18] Charters, no. 69; S.1456.
[19] Charters, App. I, no. 5; two English-style anathemas, 1066–7, *Acta*, nos 159, 216.
[20] B. Golding, 'Robert of Mortain', *ANS*, 13 (1990), 139–44.
[21] *HistAbbend* 2, 54–7.   [22] Keynes, 'Giso', 264–7, *cap.* 2, 6.
[23] Ch. 2 in this volume, pp. 44–5; Garnett, 24–44, 36.

spiritual counsellor regarded with honour by William I, was certainly aware of the moral position: in 1094 he wrote to the archbishop of Lyon of the Normans 'invading' England.[24]

The ceremonies of land transfer

If anyone expels them and alienates the lands from St Mary's, he shall be ejected by God and St Mary and all his Saints on the great Judgement Day (*domes daege*).[25]

Land was transferred according to customary law or on written evidence as to the full legality of the transaction. Anglo-Saxon custom was multifarious, and varied according to locality—radically so, in parts of the Danelaw and in Kent. But the outline framework seems to have been that land was transferred according to custom and with witnesses. Bookland was transferred with custom, witnesses, charter, and due ceremony. The authority of King and Church were of the essence, and witness to this effect was demanded. Grants describe the long-standing Abingdon convention: 'As was then the custom, as a symbol of this gift [the donor] placed the king's charter (through which he had all his right in that land) on the altar of the blessed Mary at Abingdon, in the presence of the king himself and his magnates, with no one contradicting the gift'.[26] The 'shire' gave testimony to the Domesday Inquiry about land that a thegn had handed over to Evesham Abbey by putting a 'text', probably the Gospel, on the altar.[27] In all, the written Domesday, 'the King's Charter', that recorded the transfer of much of the land of England on oath, should not stay distanced from previous transfers of land that Englishmen had witnessed in the shire courts and within the great churches.

The ceremony of land transfer demanded both a public and a religious frame-work, since a text of Holy Gospel was indispensable to the necessary oath-taking and witness. Shire court transactions, indeed, might be recorded and preserved in a Gospel book held at the minster of the county borough.[28] The association of the most down-to-earth land surveys with Gospels was customary in England and the recognition of land tenure was at the heart of ordered governance. The Yorkshire survey of *c*.1020 was, like many another document on land deemed of conse-quence, preserved in a Gospel book: the survey begins on the verso of St John's Gospel, so the association is deliberate. Under the direction of Archbishop Wulf-stan, the Yorkshire survey was followed by homilies on the observance of civil and ecclesiastical laws, and by Cnut's Charter of Liberties.[29] At Christ Church,

[24] *Normanni Angliam invaderent, Anselmi Opera* 4, no. 176.

[25] Charters, no. 115, 1053 × 1055; S.1478.

[26] *HistAbbend* 1, B44, B42, 274–7; S.1021, *c*.1050, is genuine.

[27] GDB:177d (WOR:26,16).   [28] Charters, no. 78; S.1462.

[29] W. H. Stevenson, 'Yorkshire surveys and other eleventh-century documents in the York Gospels', *EHR*, 27 (1912), 3–4; Charters, no. 84; dating in S. Baxter, 'Archbishop Wulfstan and the administration of God's property', in M. Townsend (ed.), *Wulfstan, Archbishop of York* (Turnhout, 2004), 179.

Canterbury, the practice developed of entering royal writs concerning property rights into a copy of the Gospels.[30] The *Domesday Monachorum* of Christ Church, Canterbury, was 'written out on a very grand scale *c.*1100 for inclusion in a huge Gospel-book or Bible'.[31] Ecclesiastics representing fourteen religious houses in at least fourteen counties gave testimony in the Domesday proceedings, indicating perhaps that previous transactions had taken place within a church[32] (when perhaps all the men of the hundred had not witnessed the transaction.[33]) The mode of granting land in Normandy was often somewhat different: the 'customary fashion' consisted of 'placing a piece of wood on the altar of the abbey church' rather than a Gospel book.[34] More forceful was the mode King William adopted at Winchester in 1069; when giving land to La Trinité-du-Mont, Rouen, he handed over his grant to the abbot together with a small knife 'which the king in jest gave to the abbot as if making to drive it into the palm of the abbot's hand, saying "thus ought land to be given"'.[35] The gesture may have been more symbolic than barbaric. Knives had long been in use in land conveyance on the continent, and were to become so in England after the Conquest.[36] The 'little knife', *cultellum*,—not a dagger—wielded by William when granting this charter might well have belonged to the scribe there at work, writing with pen and deleting with knife (see Figure 1). By taking up the scribe's knife in the course of a formal act with witnesses, William's gesture might have signified his preparedness to delete, and rewrite, the charters of English landownership, by force if necessary.

Public transactions and court hearings took place within a strong religious and symbolic framework. Early in Henry II's reign, when the monks of Furness in Cumbria found that their legal suits fared badly in the king's courts, they determined to appeal and to entrust the prosecution of their suit to the blessed St Cuthbert—'to the patronage of a protector whose power no violent plundering predator can withstand'. Consequently, the monks put up an altar to St Cuthbert and, next time they had a hearing before the king's justices, their cause found favour.[37] When Englishmen invoked the judgement of a just deity with reference to the Treasury record of tenurial change, they, too, were likely to be seeking protection from plundering predators.

---

[30] N. Brooks, 'The Archbishopric of Canterbury and the so-called introduction of knight-service into England', *ANS*, 34 (2011), 41–62, at 49–53.

[31] C. R. Cheney, 'Service-books and records: the case of the "Domesday Monachorum"', *Bulletin of the Institute for Historical Research*, 56 (1983), 7–15.

[32] e.g. 'as the monks say', GDB:34a (SUR:8,30), 177d (WOR:26,16); Fleming, *Law*, 47.

[33] e.g. GDB:36a (SUR:23,1).

[34] *Acta*, no. 283. Abingdon records a staff placed on the altar in William II's reign, *HistAbbend* 2, 181.

[35] *Acta*, no. 232.

[36] F. Pollock and F. W. Maitland, *The History of English Law*, vol. 1, 2nd edn (Cambridge, 1968), 84–8; e.g. *Feudal Documents*, no. 172; *Cartularium Monasterii de Rameseia*, ed. W. H. Hart and P. A. Lyons, vol. 1, RS 79 (London, 1884), 256.

[37] *Reginald of Durham, Libellus de admirandis beati Cuthberti virtutibus*, ed. J. Raine, Surtees Society, 1, (London, 1835), 112–14; Bartlett, 465.

RELICS AND COURTS

One of the visible and tangible ways of bringing the reality of heavenly penalties to the consciousness of those who were without conscience was through the relics of saints. Eadmer, Anselm's English-born monk-scribe, spelt out the logic of relics in intercessory prayer—the faithful prayed before the relics of the saints, and the saints prayed before God: 'They prostrate their entire bodies before their relics, go down on the ground on bended knees . . . —and do the saints stand before God unmoving, refusing to hear, caring nothing for them—who would say that?' 'God has provided for us patrons, through whom we may obtain what we would not be able to obtain through ourselves alone'.[38]

For the swearing-in of witnesses, oaths were customarily sworn upon Gospels or upon the relics of saints. Relics were recognized elements in the conduct of courts, having immediate impact and, it was hoped, long-term efficacy. When the monks of Thorney were in dispute with a local landowner, they carried their relics of saints to the disputing landowner for him to swear upon.[39] Saints accompanied their followers to court, even in William I's reign and even Anglo-Saxon saints. The plea of Evesham against Worcester's tenurial and wide jurisdictional claims illustrates the association between oaths and relics. At the first hearing, it was officially requested that 'since the abbot had no witnesses to bring against those of the bishop, the abbot was to bring whatever relics he wished'. The bishop's witnesses were to be named, produced on a designated day, and tested by oath on the relics. 'The abbot brought the body of St Egwin, and the bishop his worthy men (*probabiles personae*), who were prepared to take the oath'.[40] These men of probity were quite prepared to make statements acceptable to the court and take the oath on the body of St Ecgwine, so the abbot, under other pressures also, was obliged to settle with the bishop.[41] But the holdings at Hampton and Bengeworth appear in both Worcester's and Evesham's estates in Domesday Book, with Evesham as the subtenant in Worcester's.[42]

Relics were not simply a moral and spiritual protection. It was believed that relics might safeguard the community against their foes: when the Danish 'great army' came, one edict of Æthelred commanded that 'all should go out with the relics'.[43]

---

[38] Eadmer, *Sententia de memoria sanctorum quos veneraris*, ed. A. Wilmart, *Revue des Sciences religieuses*, 15 (1935), 190–1; tr. Bartlett: 467, 464.

[39] Van Caenegem, *Lawsuits*, no. 193.

[40] *Acta*, no. 349, probably *c*.1078–9, see for dating and other discussion, H. B. Clarke, 'Uses and abuses of foundation legends: the case of Evesham Abbey', in P. Gaffney and J.-M. Picard (eds), *The Medieval Imagination Mirabile Dictu* (Dublin, 2012), 132–45. A second hearing was held before the bishop of Coutances, *DB: Worcestershire*, App. V, Worcester H.

[41] A. Williams, 'The cunning of the dove: Wulfstan and the politics of accommodation', in J. S. Barrow and N. P. Brooks (eds), *St Wulfstan and his World* (Aldershot, 2005), 23–38.

[42] GDB:174a, 175d (WOR:2,74–5; 10,11–12); *DB: Worcestershire*, App. V, Worcester H.

[43] VII Æthelred, 2; also Ailred of Rievaulx, *Relatio de Standardo*, in *Chronicles of the Reigns of Stephen, Henry I, and Richard I*, vol. 3, ed. R. Howlett, RS 82 (London, 1886), 182.

They were known to defend property rights in many practical ways, inflicting punishments even on members of the king's family and his agents. Ordered to send reliquaries to the Christmas court held at Glastonbury, Evesham was suspicious of the royal acquisitiveness and sent only its second-line saint, St Odulf. Even so, when Queen Edith's goldsmith broke into the shrine, the queen was suddenly struck blind; she in turn promised God that she would never do such an injury again if, through the merits of St Odulf, she could recover her sight—whereupon it was restored.[44] Burton Abbey's St Modwenna, was known to have blinded, made mad, or driven to their death royal officials who brought suits against tenants of the abbey, seigneurial foresters who impounded Burton's animals, and local lords who threatened to poach Burton's peasantry.[45]

While the lands of the bishopric of Dorchester were in the charge of Peter, a royal clerk made bishop of Lichfield in 1072, Abingdon relates that the relics of St Vincent effectively protected the waterways of the abbey from his challenge. After a dispute arose over Cuddesdon mill and the river's management, an adjudication was arranged with Peter and his armed and mounted men on one side of the river and the abbot and his following of 'devoted laymen and monks', who 'stood on their own feet', on the other.

> When, indeed, by judgement of those judges (*arbitres*) present, it came about that the abbot was about to make an oath on the relics which he had brought that his side was the more just, he knelt and stretched upwards his right hand. When lo, on the opponents' side the firm ground began to shake, the hard ground to soften, so much so that the feet of the horses became stuck in the softness. Also a very strong wind plucked the spears from the hands of those holding them, and threw them into the air, dashed them against one another and broke them by the force of the wind, in a marvellous sight. Therefore those men, now shocked and despairing of their lives, shouted out and vowed that never again would discussion be started about the case for which they had entered the conflict, nor would any crazed daring impel repetition of these matters. They asked only that they be permitted, by the mercy of the Saint who was present, to return thence safely to their own lands.[46]

Belief in relics was not confined to the uneducated and readily credulous. They were of interest to the most powerful in the land who sought them out to accompany their progresses, to defend their property, and to distribute as patronage—as Queen Emma had delighted in doing.[47] Bishop Walkelin, the hard-headed treasurer of both William I and William II, and the equally tough-minded Rannulf Flambard, travelled together to Suffolk in 1095 to hear land-pleas, enabling Walkelin to officiate at the translation of St Edmund's relics.[48] A later

---

[44] *Chronicon abbatiae de Evesham*, ed. W. D. Macray RS 29 (London, 1863), 317–18.

[45] Geoffrey of Burton, *Life and Miracles of St Modwenna*, ed. R. Bartlett (Oxford, 2002), 190–3, 204–11.

[46] *HistAbbend* 1, 372–5.   [47] P. Stafford, *Queen Emma and Queen Edith* (Oxford, 1997), 144.

[48] *Liber de Miraculis Sancti Eadmundi, Memorials of St Edmund's Abbey*, ed. T. Arnold, RS 96 (London, 1890), 1.86–7.

hard-headed treasurer and bishop of Winchester, Henry of Blois, amassed a personal collection of thirty-seven relics which he kept in his treasury at Winchester along with other objects of interest, several hundred jewels, and his personal seal.[49]

Relics were seen as indispensable for rule and a selection therefore progressed, like the chaplains, with the king. Both William of Poitiers, and the duke whose claim to England he argued, rested part of their case on relics; the canon claimed that William carried around his neck at Hastings the relics on which Harold had supposedly sworn faith to William.[50] Between his victory at Stamford Bridge and his confrontation with the Normans at Hastings, King Harold halted to pray at his foundation of Waltham Abbey. He placed gifts upon the altar, 'together with the relics which travelled with him in his chapel',[51] whose chaplains provided a royal secretariat.

Relics might also figure in the judicial ordeal, which here demands separate attention since it figures in the Domesday proceedings on tenure, and on occasion in the text under the term 'the judgement of God' (*iudicium dei*).

OATHS AND JUDICIAL ORDEALS

Oaths and ordeals were within the Church's jurisdiction, since perjury was a serious ecclesiastical offence as well as a crime, and the livelihoods of those who committed it were clearly at stake.[52] A priest was indispensable in the taking of oaths and the conduct of ordeals. 'Both invoked God. Both brought the supernatural into the courtroom.'[53] The presence of the priest, as well as the reeve and the men of the vill, was laid down in the 'terms of reference' of the Domesday Inquiry, whose every stage demanded the swearing of oaths, even on mere money matters. Domesday recalls an earlier plea before Archbishop Lanfranc, the bishop of Bayeux, and the king's barons, in which a reeve named Brunmann, who had wrongly taken dues from foreign merchants on the land of Christ Church and St Augustine's, swore on oath (*sacramento facto iuravit*) that both houses had received those dues in Edward's day.[54] The understanding at Bury St Edmunds was that involvement in the Domesday Inquiry had been almost universal: 'sworn evidence was then given by almost all the inhabitants . . . whereby each one gave a true verdict when questioned about his own land and substance, and about the land and substance of his neighbours'.[55]

Appraisal of the ordeal's results placed power in the hands of churchmen.[56] The ordeal instrument was placed on the altar prior to celebrating mass and the manifestation of rightful justice (*verissimi iudicii*) invoked, that the iron 'should be a pleasing coolness to those who carry it with justice and fortitude but a burning

[49] F. West, 'Henry of Blois and the arts', *ANS*, 30 (2007), 229.   [50] *WP*, 151–4.
[51] *Waltham Chronicle*, 46.
[52] e.g. VI Æthelred, 36; VIII Æthelred, 27; II Cnut, 6 and 36.
[53] Bartlett, 180.   [54] GDB:2a (KEN:C8).
[55] *Feudal Documents*, 3; EHD2, no. 217.   [56] Bartlett, *Ordeal*, 90–1.

fire to the wicked'. The priest concluded: 'May the blessing of God the Father, the Son and the Holy Spirit descend on this iron, to discern the true judgement of God.' Similarly, the water employed in the ordeal of cold water and the shield and staff used in the ordeal by battle received many prayers and blessings.[57] It was the priest who unwrapped the bandaged hands of those who had undergone the ordeal of carrying hot iron or stone and pronounced the *iudicium dei*; he deemed whether the water in a forced immersion had received an innocent person or rejected a guilty one. Ordeals took place on occasion within the church building, linking the main church of the hundred to the administration of hundredal justice.[58] The ordering of judicial ordeals often prescribed the use of relics, as in five of the sixteen texts surviving of the ordeal in early medieval England.[59] The priest might charge a fee, and penalties supplied revenue for the holders of courts.[60] The bishop of Winchester showed himself anxious to retain his jurisdiction at a suitable central place: on his Somerset estates, Domesday insists, 'those who have to swear an oath or undergo an ordeal', *sacramentum vel iudicium*, were to come to his borough of Taunton.[61] Probably the men of the hundreds gathered in the same way for the Domesday Inquiry.

Cases in western Europe show that the process of threatening the ordeal was sometimes employed merely as a bargaining tool or to bring a case to a conclusion, since some tenurial disputes were quite capable of running for generations.[62] But in the matter of conquerors seeking the assent of the conquered to the changes in tenure, there seems little doubt of the explicit threat. Originally intended to obviate perjury, in 1086 it exerted powerful pressure not to question the changes in land tenure with which the jurors were presented. Its introduction for land pleas possibly an awareness by Lanfranc of Otto I's ruling that there should be recourse to the ordeal when pleas of land depended on witness or the authenticity of documents, since 'those who . . . are not afraid to perjure themselves made acquisitions by oaths with all the appearance of legality'.[63] In 1086, men of the county or the hundred, and maybe also the assembled multitude, swore on the Gospels and on relics; and, if queried, those giving witness might be subjected to the ordeal. This supplied reason enough for the men of the locality to say on occasion that they 'did not know', or had not seen a writ or messenger, and to avoid expressing an opinion.[64] The 'better

---

[57] *The Pontifical of Magdalen College*, ed. H. A. Wilson, Henry Bradshaw Soc., 39 (1910) 179–85, 207–9; tr. Bartlett, 181.

[58] J. Blair, *The Church in Anglo-Saxon Society* (Oxford, 2005), 448; Barlow, *Anglo-Norman Church*, 158–63, describes the practice of the ordeal in the eleventh and twelfth centuries.

[59] D. Rollason, *Saints and Relics in Anglo-Saxon England* (Oxford, 1989), 193. Liebermann, 401–24.

[60] *Pipe Roll, 14 Henry II, PRS*, 12 (1890), 48.   [61] GDB:87c (SOM:2,4).

[62] S. D. White, 'Proposing the ordeal and avoiding it', in T. N. Bisson (ed.), *Cultures and Power: Lordship, Status and Process in Twelfth-Century Europe* (Philadelphia, PA, 1995) 90–125.

[63] M. Gibson, *Lanfranc of Bec* (Oxford, 1978), 7–8, quoted in Ch. 2 in this volume.

[64] 'They', GDB:58c (BRK:5,1), 208c (HUN:D20); 'Men of the hundred', 36a, (SUR:21,3); 'Men of the county and of the hundred', 36b (SUR:25,2). The point is made strongly in A. Cooper, 'Protestations of ignorance in Domesday Book', in R. F. Berkhofer, A. Cooper, and A. J. Kosto (eds), *The Experience of Power in Medieval Europe, 950–1350* (Aldershot, 2005), 169–81.

men of the shire' were obliged to be present at proceedings: in Kent, the fine for non-appearance at the shire moot was £5—a sum perhaps representing the annual profit from a 600-acre estate.[65] Although rarely mentioned in Domesday, the prospect of an ordeal, and possibly a virtually unpayable fine and consequent loss of land, was ever-present in its court proceedings, reason enough to account for the Survey's name amongst the English.

Whilst ordeals were employed in Anglo-Saxon England for criminal cases, they were not employed in 'civil' cases or those concerning property; drawing on the ordeal to substantiate witness in the Domesday Inquiry was thus the more aggressive. Disputes over property were not necessarily black and white affairs and in Anglo-Saxon tradition, resolution was often a matter of compromise and negotiation, involving the community. When the case of the estate of Snodland was settled in Edward the Confessor's reign, negotiations were witnessed by numerous members of recognized communities, monastic and lay—'the citizens of Canterbury and the community at Christ Church and the community at St. Augustine's', as well as by prominent listed individuals.[66] Anglo-Saxon reasoning was often good with relativities. Nor, after the eleventh-century, were ordeals of fire and water in evidence for property cases. Indeed, Robert Bartlett's study of the ordeal found that most of the departures from this tradition in England are recorded in Domesday or in other land pleas of the reign.[67] That a juror, or indeed others, might be liable to undergo the *iudicium*, not as a putative criminal but to authenticate a transfer of land, belonged to the landed inquiries of the Conqueror's reign.

In England in the first half of the eleventh century, it seems that ordeals had been employed extensively for serious crimes such as plotting against the king and false coining. They were also specified in criminal cases, especially theft, for suspects of ill-repute or the servile. For freemen of good and unquestioned repute, oaths and the oaths of compurgators were sufficient.[68] These customary principles may well explain the handling of witnesses, and their responses, in the undecided and enigmatic case, seemingly crammed into the end of a Domesday folio at a late stage. There, Picot the Cambridgeshire sheriff, in challenging a subtenure of the Hampshire sheriff, enlisted the testimony of 'men of the vill and common people, *vili plebe*, and reeves'—all probably Englishmen—who were, apparently, 'willing to maintain' 'by oath or by a judgement day' (the ordeal), that he who had held the land was a free man and could go with his land where he would. On the opposing side, the Hampshire sheriff's putative tenant had the support of the 'better and old men of the whole county and the hundred', but they 'refused to accept any law except the law of King Edward, until it be determined by the king'.[69] Their appeal to the law as practised under King Edward might well have meant that these mature

---

[65] GDB:1b (KEN:D23).   [66] Charters, no. 69; S.1456.   [67] Bartlett, *Ordeal*, 63.
[68] e.g. II Cnut, 22; in contrast to the foreigner, Bartlett, *Ordeal*, 32.
[69] GDB:44d (HAM:23,3). The shorthand at Charford has been interpreted, alternatively, as either 'judgement day' or 'judgement of God': the text indicates the former: either implied an ordeal.

men of standing were not prepared to offer the ordeal as if they were criminals or nobodies. They considered that their oath should suffice.

The process of ordeal did not go unchallenged: leading churchmen had in the past reflected on its logic and had rejected it. Although Charlemagne employed it as a tool, the contemporary Archbishop Agobard of Lyon argued against: 'The faithful should not believe that Almighty God wishes to reveal men's secrets in the present life through hot water or iron.' He was similarly against trial by battle. 'Can it really be that the Highest requires spears and swords to judge cases? We often see a rightful tenant or claimant, fighting in battle, overcome by the superior strength or some underhand trick of the unjust party.' 'We do not deny that God's providence sometimes clears the innocent and condemns the guilty, but it is in no wise ordained by God that this should happen in every case, except at the Last Judgement.' His conclusion was that 'wise judgement, testimony and the oath are sufficient for reaching judicial verdicts'.[70]

Closer in time to Domesday's reference to ordeals was the edict of 1063 of the reforming Pope Alexander II, denouncing 'by apostolic authority that popular proof which has no canonical sanction, namely hot water, cold water, hot iron, or any other popular invention, since these are the fabrications of malice'; they were certainly not to be employed in the judgement of a priest.[71] Nevertheless, following a visit from a Norman delegation, the same pope granted William a banner for the attack on England, together with his blessing.[72] Whether William's convenient interpretation of the banner that trial by battle—*iure belli* as his encomiast William of Poitiers calls it—was well founded is another question, given that both before and after the king's coronation, Norman bishops imposed penances for killings committed during the conquest, penances confirmed by papal authority.[73] Yet portraying battle as a judicial trial of right was an important means of securing support from ecclesiastics and fighting men alike. Even to a supporter of King Stephen, the king's loss of the Battle of Lincoln and capture in 1141 was 'a judgement of God', because of the perfidy of his policies and choice of appointees.[74] Later, formal thinking on warfare laid down: 'if the quarrel is unjust, he that exposes himself in it condemns his soul; and if he dies in such a state, he will go the way of perdition'.[75] The justice of the cause was essential to each partici-pant's hope of personal eternal salvation. Long after trial by battle lost the Church's

[70] Bartlett, *Ordeal*, 111.

[71] *Patrologiae cursus completus, series Latina*, ed. J-P. Migne (Paris, 1844), 146, no. cxxii; Bartlett, *Ordeal*, 82.

[72] *WP*, 104–5; OV 2.142–3.

[73] *WP*, 151–4; EHD2, no. 81; *Councils and Synods with other Documents relating to the English Church*, vol. 1, Part II, ed. D. Whitelock, M. Brett, and C. N. L. Brooke (Oxford, 1981), 582–4; Garnett, 5–6.

[74] *Gesta Stephni*, ed. K. R. Potter (London, 1955) 75, also 77, 88, 153; also *iudicium dei*, HH, 732–3, 738–9.

[75] Christine de Pizan, *The Book of Deeds of Arms and of Chivalry*, ed. C. C. Willard and S. Willard (University Park, PA, 1999), 152–3.

formal sanction, the leaders' claims of a cause's rightfulness retained force amongst fighting men throughout the middle ages.[76]

During the twelfth century, however, thinking churchmen, like laymen, became openly opposed to the practice of ordeals. Burgesses sought the privilege of exemption from this form of trial in their borough charters; and thinking churchmen developed the thesis that to seek His direct intervention in this way was to seek to 'tempt God', discussion finally ending when the Lateran Council of 1215 forbade the clergy to take any part in ordeals.[77] Trial by battle did continue into the thirteenth century and beyond, but with much more limited recourse; it was regarded as a less sacral ordeal than other forms, and the presence of clergy was not indispensable.[78] Domesday adheres to this distinction as, strictly speaking, our source never calls trial by battle a *iudicium dei*, though it does record six occasions on which combat was offered as an alternative to the *iudicium.*[79] Although much-used amongst Germanic peoples in Europe, trial by battle in land disputes was not employed in England before its introduction under the Normans.

As a means of investigating further unresolved problems of tenure, the ordeal was threatened on twenty-one occasions in Great and Little Domesday, though there is no mention of any ordeals having already taken place: the entries merely raise the possibility of using the ordeal in the near future, as a further way of maintaining a case. Signs of the consequent pressure on jurors, Englishmen, tenants, and the local community are there to be read. Once 'an Englishman', and several times men with English names who are 'the men' of Normans, 'offer' to stand the ordeal on a future occasion to support a Norman's claim to tenure.[80] These occasions highlight the dissension and division that the Domesday Inquiry itself created. Thrice, in 1086, Hermer de Ferrers produced a champion, twice certainly English, to offer the ordeal against the evidence of the hundred. On one occasion, 'a certain Englishman' offered the judicial ordeal on the Edwardian tenurial status of Hermer's 'antecessor', which 'the whole hundred disputes, either by battle or judicial ordeal', and the Englishman gave a pledge.[81] On a second occasion, the hundred offers the ordeal against Hermer's man.[82] On a third occasion, the whole hundred defended Ely Abbey's tenure of land, and Hermer's champion, Ulfkil, offered the ordeal or battle against the hundred's champion.[83] In 1086, Hermer was, most probably, already a royal official, since between 1087 and 1091, as sheriff, he was curbed from

---

[76] For the concept's importance in the Agincourt campaign see J. Barker, *Agincourt* (London, 2006), 155, 309–10, 334–6.

[77] EHD3, no. 136, *cap.*18.   [78] Bartlett, *Ordeal*, 63, 121.

[79] Combat has seven mentions in DB; GDB:377d (LIN:CK66); LDB:146b (NFK:4,25), 176a (NFK:9,42), 189b–190a (NFK:9,219 and 227), 213a (NFK:15,2) 277b (NFK:66,81). Its avoidance by Oswald, the abbot of Chertsey's brother, was commuted into a yearly payment to the king of 2 gold marks or 2 hawks, worth *c.* £20, 10 times the annual value of the land charged with it, GDB:36d (SUR:36,1), albeit Oswald held other land from the king.

[80] LDB:190a (NFK:9,227), 310b–311a (SUF:6,79), 332a (SUF:7,13); GDB: 377d (LIN:CK66), also 44d (HAM:23,3).

[81] LDB:189b–190a (NFK:9,219, 9,227).   [82] LDB: 208a (NFK:13,19).

[83] LDB:213a (NFK:15,2).

tampering with the lands and men of Bury St Edmunds.[84] Further, on two occasions a man of the king offered ordeal, or ordeal or battle, against the witness of the hundred in cases involving ten acres and sixteen acres respectively.[85] Only once was the possessor of a Norman name, Ralph, a man of Godric the reeve, put forward for ordeal or battle;[86] the proffered combatants are otherwise anonymous, or have English names. The inclusion of men of the hundred in the Domesday Inquest set locals desperate to be retained in the service of powerful sheriffs or lords into conflict with their less well-placed neighbours.[87]

Whilst these mentions are sparse, we may imagine the social turmoil such incidents generated locally. At base, beneath the apparently ordered process of the great Domesday effort was not so much 'a King working with his barons and the community of the shire to a common end, albeit with an eye to striking as hard a bargain as he could',[88] as a divided and cowed society placed into an effective conqueror's straight-jacket. But it was not the intention of the ruling group to record many such divisions for posterity. Some cases are poignant. One woman offered to verify, by ordeal, the evidence of the hundred on her former sixteen acres of land; another woman, to affirm that her former eight acres, mostly woodland, did not carry a mortgage:[89] gestures obviously made in the hope that some family acres would be returned. In another case too it was the former holder of the land that was prepared to offer the ordeal, perhaps in the hope of returning as a tenant.[90] Yet the possible use of the ordeal to verify witness put all who swore in danger of being treated in the Domesday courts as if they were of criminal repute or servile status. It seems, moreover, that it was permissible for the newcomers to take ordeals, as well as trial by battle, vicariously.[91] A member of the king's household was expected to undergo the judicial ordeal in order to uphold the royal rights over a mere quarter acre and a customary due on pasture![92]

Most references to the ordeal, seventeen of the twenty-one, survive in the less abbreviated Little Domesday, thirteen of these in Norfolk alone.[93] So whether the many tenurial decisions made in Great Domesday had already witnessed the taking of an ordeal or, at the least, its threat, must remain a matter of speculation. Once we are told of the 'judgement' of another hundred, but not specifically that it included an ordeal;[94] otherwise there is no mention of an ordeal having already taken place. Yet we do know of one court case of around 1080, contested between the sheriff and the church of Rochester, in which the men of the shire had made their decision 'in fear of the sheriff', *timore vicecomitis*. When Odo of Bayeux was subsequently

[84] Sharpe, 'The use of writs in the eleventh century', *ASE*, 32 (2004), 275–7; *Regesta* 1, no. 291.
[85] LDB:166a (NFK:8,71), 146b (NFK:4,25).
[86] LDB:176a, (NFK:9,42). [87] e.g. also, LDB:285b (SUF:1,76–77).
[88] Roffe, *Inquest*, Preface, x. [89] LDB:277b (NFK:66,80), 137a (NFK:1,213).
[90] e.g. LDB:332a (SUF:7,13). [91] LDB:176a–b (NFK:9,42); also HH, 408–11.
[92] LDB:110b (NFK:1,10).
[93] In Great Domesday are Taunton, Picot versus Hugh de Port, and two in Lincolnshire, GDB:336a, 377d (LIN:C4; CK66).
[94] GDB:165d (GLS:11,14).

informed of perjury and when, at a second session before the king's barons, the shire's representatives were faced with the ordeal, they received a huge fine for perjury.[95] Domesday, however, makes no mention of the contentious case, the retrial, the ordeal, and the fines, but only of Rochester's possession by Lanfranc's judgement and the king's order.[96] In the dispute between the bishop of Worcester and the abbot of Evesham, knights of the bishop 'were ready to affirm it on oath and by battle if the abbot wished to deny it . . . as well as by holy men, priest and deacons who were ready to confirm it by the ordeal'.[97] For clergy, however, less physically taxing ordeals were normally offered, such as taking communion bread without choking, or repeating prayers without stumbling. In fact, God's judgement had become more than a metaphor in the disposition of land and the settlement of disputes. Under Norman rule and in the Domesday Inquiry, it meant recourse to the ordeal in civil cases, and—for those proven perjured—condign punishment. The fate of English landownership was sealed finally by judgement of the English county courts, duly witnessed by part-English juries under implicit coercion. The oaths sworn and the extraordinary use of the ordeal in 'civil' procedures gave Domesday's court proceedings an apocalyptic atmosphere.

Ordeals were associated with the Last Judgement in popular art. At Stowell Church, Gloucestershire, is a Last Judgement, or Doom, probably late twelfth-century, which includes St Michael weighing souls. Immediately below appear two outline figures, attired for combat: in tunics, bare-headed, carrying square shields, and double-headed picks, as later rules dictated for trial by battle—they perhaps represented an attempt to forge a link between earthly and heavenly justice in a local case.[98] The depiction of Dooms (*Dies Irae*), the weighing up and selection of damned and saved, was a popular subject, even if one likely to have been chosen by the clergy for didactic reasons or by lay patrons for their own disciplinary purposes. Doors, church portals, and west doors of churches in particular, were sites of legal transactions, worldly trials, and places of judgement; they were also sites of artistic depictions of the Last Judgement, sculptured externally or painted on the internal wall.[99] Heavenly penalties bolstered legal codes and moral precepts, and were not necessarily the resort of weak rulers. Robert Bartlett sees the ordeal as a device of strong kingship: 'it could be enforced in an exercise of power, yet it represented

---

[95] *inibi a vicecomite per internuntium conterrit fuissent, Acta*, no. 225, 1077 × 1083. One set of jurors, requested to take the ordeal to substantiate their assertions, were 'not able to do as they promised'; the source seems, understandably, evasive as to whether they took the ordeal and failed, or whether they admitted their bias and confessed their perjury. The claims of Rochester were not clear-cut, Fleming, *Law*, 18–20.

[96] LDB:381a (SUF:20,1).   [97] *iuditio dei, Acta*, no. 349.

[98] E. W. Tristram, *English Medieval Wall Painting* (Oxford, 1944), 35, 45–6.

[99] B. Deimling, 'Medieval church portals and their importance in the history of law', in R. Toman (ed.), *Romanesque, Architecture, Sculpture, Painting* (Köln, 1997), 324–7. The important Christ in Judgement, around 1080, on the west wall of the influential Sant'Angelo in Formis, Capua, comissioned by Abbot Desiderius (Victor III)), is discussed by E. Kluckert, 'Romanesque painting', in Toman, *Romanesque*, 409, 416. Capua hosted a Church Council in 1087.

submission to that power as submission to the deity'.[100] A thirteenth-century chronicler reflected on the Survey's name: 'it is called Domesday, and is called this because no one was spared, just as on the Great Day of Judgement'.[101]

ANATHEMA AND JUDGEMENT

In contrast to the continental tradition of judicial amercements, divine penalties were 'the rule in English anathemas'.[102] In England too, homilies, like charters, were written for audiences wider than the clerical class alone. The influential scholar Ælfric, abbot of Eynsham, who lived c.950–c.1010, had written two volumes of homilies, or sermons, in the vernacular with the encouragement of the earldorman, Æthelweard, and the archbishop of Canterbury, to be delivered to the widest of audiences (and widely disseminated)—enough to cover two years of preaching; he had also translated books of the Bible into English aiming to convert them into 'a simple translation for the sake of avoiding putting off the reader'.[103] He by no means evaded the lessons to be learnt from the prospect of 'the great judgement', when Christ 'will shine for the righteous and burn for the unrighteous': although his own emphasis was upon grace, penance, almsgiving, and masses.[104] Ælfric's work continued to be copied and translated in the twelfth century,[105] and it is in the context of this widely dispersed English tradition that the English name 'Domesday' should be set.

By the eleventh century in western Europe, Christianity framed much authority and most legal precepts: after death, God would judge every man, assigning his soul to Paradise or Hell. Yet, the demands of ruler and faith were often in conflict. On the one hand, canon law deemed that killing in battle was culpable homicide: following the Norman Conquest, a range of penances was imposed in the Penitential of Ermenfrid, distinguishing between operating on ducal and kingly orders and killing for gain or plunder.[106] On the other, the realities of survival in developing kingdoms and small feudatories alike meant that military service was required, particularly from the holders of land. And the Church taught that however many misdeeds a man had committed, he might still obtain salvation—although to obtain forgiveness he might have to perform harsh penances. In practice, many fighting men preferred to defer their confession until their active

---

[100] Bartlett, *Ordeal*, 36.
[101] Matthew Paris, *Historia Anglorum*, ed. F. Madden, RS (1866–9), 1.27, note.
[102] Brooks, The archbishopric of Canterbury, 56.
[103] *Ælfric's Prefaces*, ed. J. Wilcox (Durham, 1996), 9–27, quotation at 130.
[104] L. Grundy, *Books and Grace: Aelfric's Theology*, King's College, London, Medieval Studies VI (1991), 212–75, at 251. See Figure 5.
[105] M. Swan and E. M. Treharne, *Rewriting Old English in the Twelfth Century* (Cambridge, 2000).
[106] See n. 72 in this chapter.

life was over—or even until their last moments—rather than perform protracted and humiliating penances that dominated their mode of life.[107]

The Church called for heavenly blessings on kings; but kings, in turn, were still accountable to God—and, indeed, to their councillors. The support of clergy and magnates was crucial: Æthelred II, sent into exile through loss of magnate support, returned only after having promised 'all the councillors, ecclesiastical and lay', that 'he would govern his kingdom more justly'.[108] Duke William's apologists did their best for him. William of Poitiers, canon and former knight, was concerned to point out that in Normandy William had supported the Truce of God that protected clergy, the poor, and non-combatants, and had forbidden fighting during religious festivals and Lent, and seen to the truce's scrupulous observance; he even maintained that William had gained possession of Maine 'not only by force but also by the laws of justice' (*iustitiae legibus*).[109] The apologist went as far as crediting the arrogant Odo, William's half-brother, with 'a common desire to keep Christian people in peace'.[110] Undeterred by his pre-coronation promises to Archbishop Ealdred of York that he would be an exemplary lord and king, William was, however, acknowledged to be ruthless, even by his panegyrists. William of Jumièges reported the king's slaughter of the population of York 'from the young to the aged'.[111] The Conqueror's sons, regardless of the native support with which they began their reigns, both persecuted key groups of Englishmen. William II seized fifty men of the old nobility and falsely accused them of killing and eating the king's deer,[112] and Henry I seized and mutilated the moneyers—whose profession still relied upon English dynasties—on largely fallacious charges of light-weight coin: probably a populist gesture at a time of a European-wide shortage of silver, poor harvests, and high prices.

Yet rulers, royal judges, knights, and magnates' officials, who could not be gainsaid in this world, still faced the consequences of their acts in the next. Anathemas offered a last protection for the law-abiding from the abuse of power and privilege by 'those seduced by the madness of the love of money'; and the Conqueror's passion for money, *pecuniae cupiditas*, was noted by William of Malmesbury as 'the only point on which he is rightly criticized'.[113] The contemporary sense of retribution is embodied in visions in which the equipment that enabled men to inflict cruelties not infrequently became the instrument of their own torture. The monk-chronicler Orderic tells how a knight, the brother of a priest he knew, appeared after death to the priest in a vision, suffering from a great mass of fire around his heels, lamenting: 'because I used bright, sharp spurs in my eager haste to shed blood, I am justly condemned to carry this enormous load on my heels'. Another sufferer in the next world, in life William fitzOsbern's steward,

---

[107] B. Hamilton, 'Religion and the Laity', in *NCMH* 4, Part I, ed. D. Luscombe and J. Riley-Smith (Cambridge, 2004), 500–2.

[108] *ASC*, 1014, C.   [109] *WP*, 80–1, 58–9.   [110] *WP*, 182–3.

[111] *GND* 2.180.   [112] *Eadmer*, 102.

[113] *HistAbbend* 1, 64–5; Kelly, *The Charters of Abingdon Abbey*, no. 83; S.658; *GRA* 1.508–9.

who had given a poor miller a loan and had confiscated the mill for non-payment, was in death obliged to carry in his mouth a burning mill-shaft 'which seems heavier than the castle of Rouen'. He desired his family to ease his pains speedily by restoring the mill—'from which they have received far more than I ever gave'—to the miller's heir'.[114]

Rulers, too, were expected to be judged and to pay for their sins (see Figure 5). Norman kings were condemned, not only for acts of cruelty and war, but also for extortion—usually after they were safely dead. Rulers themselves were conscious of the link between reasonable exactions and divine approbation. In peril during a storm at sea, Henry I promised a seven-year moratorium on levying geld, and to undertake a pilgrimage to Bury St Edmunds and instantly, on his vow, 'there was a great calm'.[115] The Church's expectations were that a deeply felt generosity was due them from the king: the bishop of London and the canons of St Paul's produced a spurious piece of wishful thinking on taxation that it was Henry I's will 'that the said church be as free as he desires his soul to be on the day of Judgement'.[116] Explicitly, monastic chroniclers besought God to reckon up the arbitrary fiscal exactions insisted upon by William I and his sons, and implicitly, to exact due retribution.[117] The church of Worcester recorded the gold and silver it had paid to redeem its precious plate and crosses from William I's plundering, but refrained from calculating 'the tax on every hide which no one but God alone can reckon'.[118] Such thinking continued to prevail: the Anglo-Norman chronicler Orderic considered that William fitzOsbern, earl of Hereford, one-time regent and noted commander in battle, who was 'the greatest oppressor of the English', causing 'the ruin and wretched death of thousands', received 'just retribution' when he perished in battle and ultimately his 'whole progeny was obliterated in England so thoroughly that . . . they no longer possess a foot of English ground'.[119]

William I's redistribution of land had already earned anathemas. He had adjudged those who had followed Harold into battle as unworthy of recognition as landholders and their lands were confiscate: already, at Hastings, they were 'hostile people who deserved death for rebelling against him, their king'.[120] Those survivors who had not fled into exile had been compelled to swear to the rightfulness of the changes and had received their judgement in this world; that, however, did not prevent them looking for William's judgement in the next. The anathema at the back of Englishmen's minds throughout the Domesday process slipped through onto its record only once: when the 'better men of the whole shire' were bold enough to narrate in faithful detail the true tenurial status of Selly Oak. Like other ecclesiastical property leased for three lives to a layman, it had been

---

[114] OV 4.237–51, esp. 248–9, 244–5.   [115] *JW* 3.202–3.   [116] *Regesta* 2, no. 604.

[117] Tenants took ritual acts of retribution in their fourteenth-century rebellion against the abbey of St Albans, *Gesta Abbatum Monasterii Sancti Albani*, vol. 3, ed. H. T. Riley, RS (London, 1869), 309; R. Faith, 'The great rumour and peasant ideology', in R. H. Hilton and T. H. Aston (eds), *The English Rising of 1381* (Cambridge, 1984), 66.

[118] Charters, App. I, no. 6.   [119] OV 2.318–21.   [120] *WP*, 130–1.

Figure 5. Christ the Just Judge and the King of Kings from Cambridge Trinity College MS B.15.34 third decade of the eleventh century, from *Ælfric's Homilies*, Latin and Anglo-Saxon. By kind permission of the Master and Fellows of Trinity College, Cambridge.

confiscated and regranted by King William—despite the lessee's bequest that it return early to the bishopric of Lichfield/Chester after the death of his widow. Great Domesday rehearses how the men of the shire reported the true tenurial position: Wulfwine, the lessee, had, at 'the end of his life', summoned his wife, family, friends, and bishop, and said: 'Hear ye, my friends. I will that my wife hold this land, which I bought from the church, so long as she lives; and after her death, let the church from which I had it receive it; and let whoever shall take it away from thence be excommunicated (*qui inde abstulerit, excommunicatus sit*).'[121] By 1086, many lands, including Church property, qualified for a similar imprecation.

HAROLD'S TRIAL BY BATTLE

William and his supporters and encomiasts had, in the course of his reign, produced grounds for his military and tenurial takeover, based variously and inconsistently on Harold's perfidy and Williams' own claims.[122] These matters arise here in that they affect Domesday's function, Domesday's name, and the theme of judgement. In common with other military conflicts, William's claims evolved in a pattern still sadly familiar. First, a claim with some legal basis, fragile but arguable; when that was ignored, a moral claim emerged; and, when that failed, came the appeal to straightforward military might, with repercussions and loss of life far beyond anything the claims justified. Yet in order to uphold an apparently legal view of the transition, Domesday regularly offers a verbal obeisance to the tenures of King Edward's day: though the character of its land settlement shows that William adopted rather the *tabula rasa* of an Old Testament king after rebellion.[123] Domesday's allegedly legal foundation would appear to be completely fictitious.

All Norman sources evaded the question of the rightful succession, although in 1066 there were several potential claimants, not only the two protagonists at Hastings. After Harold's death, English nobles had 'elected' one who had a better claim than William or Harold, Edgar Ætheling, Edward's half-nephew, great-grandson in the senior male line of King Æthelred II: in 1066 Edgar was at hand but young, without office, almost without land, and inexperienced.[124] Although West Saxon tradition did not draw upon the female line, others perhaps held a different view. One of Edward's sister's sons by her first marriage, Walter, Count of the Vexin, had been defeated by William of Normandy and imprisoned, dying in 1063 at Duke William's castle at Falaise, where both he and his wife were said to

[121] GDB:177a (WOR:23,1).   [122] For Lanfranc's role, see Ch. 2 in this volume, pp. 42–7.
[123] See Deuteronomy, 20.
[124] GDB:205c (HUN:11,1 and 11,2). Edgar is considered in detail in S. Baxter, 'Edward the Confessor and the succession question', in R. Mortimer (ed.), *Edward the Confessor: The Man and the Legend* (Woodbridge, 2009), 98–103.

have been poisoned.[125] The other, unpropitiously known as Ralf 'the Timid', had died in 1058, although leaving a son. (Another interested party was Eustace of Boulogne—prominent in Domesday in 1086—who had in the 1040s been, like Harold, the brother-in-law of King Edward, having married Edward's sister, and who was for a time a potential father of a possible heir. For one reason or another, he was certainly dangerous enough for William to take a young member of Eustace's family hostage in 1066, and again in 1067.[126]) Yet the only nod early Norman chroniclers gave to the English royal house was to represent the Conqueror's invasion as avenging the murder of Alfred Ætheling, in which Earl Godwine had had a hand.[127] They transformed the succession into a simple issue between William and Harold Godwineson who, having been defeated in battle, might be placed beyond the pale.

The practical reality was that, by 1065, Harold's position as earl of Kent and Wessex had become unassailable: the earldoms of Harold and his brothers covered more than half of England.[128] Unlike Ralf the Timid, Harold had proved himself militarily effective in defending England from Welsh incursions. Moreover, through his mother Gytha, Harold had his own distant claim to the throne of England—as a cousin to King Swein Estrithson, who had succeeded Cnut the Great as king of Denmark in 1047. (Godwine and Gytha had certainly given three of their sons Scandinavian names associated with the royal house.[129]) Other descendants of Cnut the Great had other claims consequent on that king's rule of England, Denmark, and Norway, and kings and men of the two northern nations persistently attempted to assert them: a Norwegian fleet threatened in 1045 and 1058, and there was the realistic threat from King Harold Hardrada in 1066.[130] Even so, it was not the claims of the royal houses of Wessex, Norway, or Denmark that Norman sources were concerned to repudiate. That Harold's coronation swiftly followed Edward's death in January 1066 without apparent question suggests that those at the centre favoured certainty over the destabilizing threat of several claimants, some alien and in arms. The ceremony was not easily gainsaid: as an anointed king, Harold had undoubtedly captured an almost impregnable initiative. Notwithstanding, William's encomiasts, the designer of the Bayeux embroidery and, indeed, the Domesday project itself, aimed to ensure that William's kingship was recognized by churchmen in Europe.[131]

---

[125] OV 2.118, 312. Walter's wife gave him also a claim to Maine.

[126] *WP*, 47; OV 2.206; possibly a grand-child of Eustace's marriage with Goda existed, Barlow, *Confessor*, 307–8; Douglas, *Conqueror*, Table 7. When Edward's sister died is not known.

[127] *GND* 2.168–71; *WP*, 4–7.

[128] Twelve maps of the successive fortunes of the Godwinesons' and other earldoms are provided by Baxter, 'Succession question', between 116–17.

[129] I. Howard, 'Harold the Second: a throne-worthy king', in G. Owen-Crocker (ed.), *King Harold II and the Bayeux Tapestry* (Woodbridge, 2005), 35–52.

[130] *ASC*, D.

[131] European perspectives on the events of 1066 are presented in E. van Houts, 'The Norman Conquest through European eyes', *EHR*, 110 (1995), 832–53. An Anglo-Norman perspective is argued by H. B. Clarke, 'The designer of the Bayeux Tapestry', *ANS*, 35 (2012), 119–39.

We have seen that Harold's own reputation in the Church prior to his coronation was mixed. He was known in the west country as a 'despoiler' of churches, particularly of the see of Wells, incurring at least two anathemas.[132] But the allegations supposedly left by Giso, bishop of Wells, were possibly self-exculpatory: while this Vicar of Bray kept safe King Harold's only original writ-charter to survive, he continued to flourish under King William.[133] Yet despite his faults, Harold as earl had fulfilled the role of patron of religion in the grandest manner. He had refounded Holy Cross, Waltham, as a house of secular canons, endowing it generously with both land and fine objects, bringing in the most up-to-date ideas on the Rule from Lotharingia, and reconsecrating the religious house grandly with King Edward and his court present. Harold's donation of sixty holy relics to Waltham, secured behind substantial masonry, was inscribed by Adelard of Liège in its chapter book, and bears witness to his wide range of contacts.[134] Their origins mostly lay in Flanders, Germany, and northern France, and Ealdred, archbishop of York, had contributed. In the *Life of Edward the Confessor*, Harold was given many qualities—power of body and mind, patience, mercy, and kindness, yet sternness to wrong-doers: the close-up view from a contemporary churchman with a continental education. However, writing soon after Hastings, the author does admit that Harold was 'too ready with his oaths'.[135] Altogether, this was the Harold that had met other rulers, 'and adroitly and with natural cunning... observed most intently what he could get from them if he needed them in the management of business'.[136]

The claim of Harold's perfidy, vividly portrayed in the Bayeux Tapestry, rested on his oaths to William, first as the recipient of arms—implying that he thereby owed William loyalty—and then on oaths made to William upon holy relics. The Tapestry depicts a series of incidents loaded with overtones of lordship and obligation between the two nobles. First, after Harold's boat is untowardly blown to the County of Ponthieu, Duke William negotiates Harold's release from capture by its Count—not a natural ally of either William or the Godwinesons—but perforce William's vassal since his defeat at Mortemer in 1054. Then, William and Harold go on campaign together during which Harold nobly rescues some of William's men from the quicksands around Mont-St-Michel, and William formally gives arms to Harold. As the fighting was over by then, the overt connotation was to confer honour: but it also implied that Harold became William's man, with a tie of fidelity. It might also have represented 'adoption by weapons', especially so, if Harold were agreeing to marry William's daughter, as William of Poitiers asserts—

---

[132] Keynes, 'Giso', App. IV, *cap.* 2, 6; discussed, *Writs*, 275–6; cf. GDB:133a (HRT:1,17).
[133] *Writs*, no. 71; S.1163.
[134] *Waltham Chronicle*, 26–7, 34–8; *VitaÆdw*, 33; N. Rogers, 'The Waltham Abbey Relic-List', in C. Hicks (ed.), *England in the Eleventh Century: Proceedings of the 1990 Harlaxton Symposium* (Stamford, 1992), 162–7.
[135] *VitaÆdw*, 53.　　[136] *VitaÆdw*, 33.

with William swearing to confirm all his lands and possessions.[137] Whilst the Tapestry portrays Harold, initially, as an upright and noble 'duke', this served only to underline the theological and moral significance of his broken oath.

The next development was more sinister, and central to the theme of judgement. The Tapestry shows Harold swearing a second oath to William on two vessels: a shrine-shaped reliquary such as would have held the relics used in the royal chapel and writing office in England for important transactions and a portable altar, carrying the Blessed Sacrament in the form of consecrated bread (see Figures 6a and 6b).[138] This oath-taking depicts William large-size, holding a sword of state on a raised throne, looking down on a thin Harold, who is standing uneasily between the reliquary and the altar, his arms outstretched, trying to touch, or rather trying to avoid touching, both at once. As he swears under duress, Harold is shown with head hanging and in an uneasy stance, an exposed stretched-out posture unusual in Anglo-Saxon art, except to depict crucifixion.[139] On his return, Harold reports to an elderly King Edward, emphasizing that Harold's standing was as Edward's messenger and no more.

Gale Owen-Crocker suggests that if the Tapestry had been designed for decorating a square hall, its over-riding theme becomes the perfidy of Harold contrasted with the upright support for William of Bishop Odo of Bayeux. Hung in this way, four pivotal scenes occur in the centre of each of the walls: with Harold's prayers at Bosham before setting sail on Edward's mission on the first wall opposite Odo's blessing of food and drink before Hastings on the third.[140] The vaunted allusion is not accidental, since Odo's depiction here probably imitates the illustration of a Last Supper in the Gospels that belonged to St Augustine's, Canterbury.[141] Harold's oath on the reliquary and altar would appear central on the second wall, opposite the fourth wall with the galloping Odo, rallying the morale of the younger warriors, brandishing his bishop's staff in the thick of the Hastings battle.[142]

The strictures of Norman propaganda also focused on the English Church. Since 1052 its leadership had been in the hands of Stigand, the pluralist and uncanonical archbishop of Canterbury, with whom King Edward had come to some sort of uneasy compromise, probably because of his undoubted financial acumen.[143] However, Stigand had not only been appointed in the lifetime of the Norman archbishop, formerly abbot of Jumièges, but had also received his archiepiscopal

---

[137] R. Le Jan, 'Frankish giving of arms and rituals of power: continuity and change in the Carolingian period', in F. Theuws and J. L. Nelson (eds), *Rituals of Power from Late Antiquity to the Early Middle Ages* (Boston, 2000), 291–4; *WP*, 70–1, 156–7; *Eadmer*, 7–8.

[138] BT, Scene 29; N. P. Brooks and H. E. Walker, 'The authority and interpretation of the Bayeux Tapestry', *ANS*, 1 (1978), 5.

[139] G. Owen-Crocker, 'Brothers, rivals and the geometry of the Bayeux Tapestry', in *King Harold II and the Bayeux Tapestry*, 109–23, at 114.

[140] Owen-Crocker, 'Brothers, rivals and the geometry of the Bayeux Tapestry', 114–17.

[141] Brooks and Walker, 'Authority and interpretation', 18. BT, Scene 49.

[142] BT, Scene 68, although *pueros* is, probably, and *confortat*, possibly, a reconstruction: Owen-Crocker, 'Brothers, rivals and the geometry of the Bayeux Tapestry', above, 117–19.

[143] See Ch. 1 in this volume, pp. 14–15, 28–30.

Figures 6a and 6b. Harold swearing an oath to William on relics, by special permission of the city of Bayeux and the Bayeux Museum.

pallium from a pontiff who had been condemned and expelled for simony.[144] Yet Stigand's position did not taint the whole English church: he consecrated only two bishops under Edward, Aethelric to Selsey and Siward to Rochester, and was indeed sought out to consecrate William's appointee, Remigius, to the see of Dorchester in 1067.[145] A Norman attack on the schismatic archbishop would have also righted the past insult to the ousted archbishop, formerly abbot of the favoured Norman monastery of Jumièges. After Archbishop Stigand's deposition in 1070, it was in the interests of Norman propaganda to portray him in the Bayeux Tapestry, duly labelled, as officiating at Harold's coronation.

Thus, the Tapestry and the Norman chroniclers—perhaps under Lanfranc's tutelage—unfold the presentation of William as the moral leader of a religious crusade. The papal banner borne at Hastings was a sign of papal blessing,[146] betokening that England was a country that had strayed from St Peter's fold under the influence of Harold's family and Stigand. Yet in imperial Germany— western Europe's super-power and sponsor of papal reform—to bear a leader's banner (*vexillum*) meant to be in fealty to that leader; and in 1072 Pope Gregory VII followed up the logic of the papal gesture, asking William to do fealty to the pope for England. This William refused to do: his predecessors had never done so and he had not promised to do so.[147] Whatever over-vaunted opinions Gregory had about his own stature, he had none about lay rulers: 'Who does not know that kings and princes derive their origin from men, ignorant of God, who raised themselves above their fellows by pride, plunder, treachery, murder?'[148] And in due course he became aware that his earlier support for William's Conquest had arguably given 'sanction for the perpetration of great slaughter'.[149]

The Bayeux Tapestry depicts Harold's perjury adjudged by God:[150] Halley's comet, proof of divine wrath, appears not long after his coronation and, in the margin, ghostly ships on their way to England foreshadow impending disaster.[151] The Tapestry seems designed to convince an audience composed largely of fighting men;[152] its didactic message was bolder than would be accepted by thinking ecclesiastics: forced oaths were invalid and no presiding ecclesiastic is depicted at Harold's oath-taking in Normandy, although, of course, essential. It represents Hastings as a trial by battle, the protagonists having received spiritual sanction from Stigand, the schismatic bishop, in Harold's case; from the papal banner and the exemplary bishop, Odo, in William's. While the Bayeux Tapestry extolled William's co-operation with his half-bother Odo, Norman chroniclers pointed to

[144] *ASC*, 1058, D, E; *JW* 2.584–5, 606–7.
[145] Perhaps because Remigius did not wish the metropolitan of York to exert jurisdiction over the Lincoln diocese, D. Bates, *Bishop Remigius of Lincoln 1067–92* (Lincoln, 1992), 7–8.
[146] *WP*, 105; OV 2.142.   [147] EHD2, no. 101; Lanfranc's Letters, no. 39.
[148] Letter to Bishop Hermann of Metz, 15 March 1081, *MGH Epistolae Selectae: Das Register Gregors VII*, viii, no. 21, ed. E. Caspar (Berlin, 1923) ii, 552.
[149] EHD2, no. 99.   [150] As does *WP*, 100.   [151] BT, Scene 35.
[152] H. E. J. Cowdrey, 'Towards an interpretation of the Bayeux Tapestry', *ANS*, 10 (1987), 64.

Harold's fratricide in slaying his brother Tostig at Stamford Bridge.[153] There seems good reason to credit Orderic when he relates that Tostig, formerly earl of Northumbria, and an exile from his brother's kingdom, visited William and that together they devised a plan to their mutual benefit.[154] Certainly, Tostig's near-simultaneous invasion, in alliance with Harold Hardrada, king of Norway, was crucial to William's victory. For William, to restore Tostig to the northern part of England as earl, or even to split the kingdom with another contender, would have mirrored an earlier precedent, when Edmund Ironside agreed to divide the kingdom with Cnut. Any such plan would be consistent with the impressive range of travel that Tostig undertook—possibly to conjure up support—before he launched his attack.[155] But the Godwinesons had ignored two New Testament warnings: 'if a kingdom be divided against itself, it cannot stand', and 'if a house be divided against itself, it will surely fall'.[156] For William of Poitiers, not only was Harold a perjured vassal and a usurper king, he was a fratricide who rightly lost his trial by battle with William;[157] even if, at the time when William was assembling his invasion forces, no fratricide had yet occurred.

From its very name and foundation, Battle Abbey marked the place as one of martial victory and royal triumphalism. On the new king's insistence, its high altar was sited on the place where Harold had fallen; and William bequeathed to the foundation the relics and the reliquary on which Harold had sworn his oath. (The monastic house later tried to temper the triumphal element, and to promote an understanding that the Conqueror had acted not only in gratitude for his victory, but to pray for the absolution of the sins of those who were killed at Hastings.[158]) Even the native Anglo-Saxon Chronicler allowed that the abbey was built 'in the same place where God permitted [William] to conquer England'.[159]

It seems that Norman propaganda implied that because the landholders of England had acknowledged—and crowned—a perfidious ruler, son of the murderous Earl Godwine, they were justly obliged to forfeit their lands. Recent research on Domesday calculates that by 1086 they held a mere 4.2 per cent of the landed income recorded; most had only small amounts of land. Because of the difficulty of distinguishing persons by Christian name only, Hugh Thomas estimates a range of between 800 and 1,300 surviving landholders, but most had 'miniscule' amounts of land.[160] Only thirteen English survivors are evident as tenants-in-chief: a mere four of these were of magnate status—one held a key office as sheriff in Salisbury,

---

[153] e.g. *WP*, 141.   [154] OV 2.140.

[155] 'Harald Hardrada (the Stern)', *Heimskringla* (Everyman, 1961), *cap.* 78–9.

[156] Mark 3:24–5.   [157] *WP*, 140–1.

[158] 'The *Brevis Relatio de Gillelmo nobilissimo comite Normannorum*', ed. E. M. C. van Houts, *Camden Miscellany* 34, Camden Soc., 5th ser. (1997), 16–18, 32; *The Chronicle of Battle Abbey*, ed. E. Searle (Oxford, 1980), 17.

[159] *ASC*, 1087.

[160] H. M. Thomas, 'The significance and fate of the native English landholders of 1086', *EHR*, 118 (2003), 303–33, at 306–7; Keats-Rohan, 23–4 suggests that around 600 *named* landholders survived (from less than 3,000 known from all records).

and another, Thorkel of Warwick, was probably a retired sheriff; Colswein of Lincoln was evidently a borough official.[161] In all, only about two hundred native men might have been able to sustain a thegnly position.[162] Furthermore, the alien takeover of local soke jurisdiction and of commendation had turned many surviving small freeholders into rent-payers or villeins; the economic and jurisdictional change then became an oppressive combination. The written Domesday enshrined the rights and profits commandeered from the inhabitants; and the name accorded to the book by the English was eloquent of its impact.

WILLIAM'S CLAIM TO BE KING OF THE ENGLISH

William's claim through kinship arose from the fact that Edward's mother, Emma of Normandy, had been William's great-aunt. But Emma had merely married *into* the English royal family as Æthelred's second wife and so William was connected to the English royal family only by marriage, not by blood—hardly an impressive link.

Nor was the moral stance that William and his apologists adopted credible. Harold apart, the 'moral' line of argument was that William, to whose father Edward owed a debt of hospitality while in exile, had been designated heir later by the king himself.[163] According to William of Poitiers, the English magnates recognized William as heir early in Edward's reign and this commitment was conveyed to William by the Norman archbishop of Canterbury, Robert of Jumièges.[164] Whether the matter was indeed settled by delegate, or whether William made a visit in person in 1051 (as the enigmatic 'count William' of the Anglo-Saxon Chronicle[165]), or whether the story was Norman fiction, nevertheless—with no direct heir to England in sight—fury over the powers of influential foreigners in England flared up precisely at that time, with the well-supported Godwine family facing the king in arms on the issue. Whatever claims William advanced in terms of pre-1066 agreements, and whatever arguments his lawyers and chroniclers subsequently confected, the 1051–2 crisis had already demonstrated that a Norman claimant would be generally and strenuously resisted as an outsider: civil war had then been averted in England only by the respective armies refusing to fight their fellow countrymen for fear of exposing the country to its external foes;[166] and the crisis had ended in 1052 with the Norman archbishop of Canterbury being excluded from England. In 1066, Guy of Amiens had recognized perfectly that Englishmen would rather die fighting than acknowledge an alien lord, and even William of Poitiers was aware that it was Englishmen's

---

[161] Williams, *The English*, 98–111; J. Palmer, 'The wealth of the secular aristocracy in 1086', *ANS*, 22 (2000), 279–91.

[162] Thomas, 'Native English landholders', 308–19.   [163] *WP*, 18–21.

[164] *WP*, 20, 68–79; D. Dumville, 'The Ætheling: a study in Anglo-Saxon constitutional history', *ASE*, 8 (1979), 1–33, concludes that there was no regular institution of the 'designated heir'. This affected the claims of both William and Harold.

[165] *ASC*, 1051, D.   [166] *ASC*, 1051, D.

'highest wish to have no lord who was not a compatriot'.[167] The crisis of 1051–2 had publicized unhealthy precedents, exposing the weakness of the English king, while nevertheless demonstrating how extensive was his authority to make and to break earls. An outlaw's land was forfeit to the crown—a sinister feature underlying the Godwinesons' confrontation with Edward and his Norman appointees, and the rise and fall of other earls from established families. William of Normandy, battling to bring order in his duchy, might well have pondered the fact, and felt envy. The events of 1051–2, with the expulsion of high-ranking Normans from the country and the antipathy displayed towards Eustace of Boulogne, were clear and early notice that if William were to assert a claim to the English throne, its success would only come over the dead bodies of the English fighting forces and of the Godwinesons. Little Domesday's unique reference to the time when King William 'conquered' England was all too appropriate.[168]

From the Church's point of view, there were other impediments to William's status within the royal kin. Although the acknowledged son of the duke of Normandy, William was illegitimate, a fact about which he was extremely sensitive; moreover, for some reason his betrothal to Matilda of Flanders was condemned by the council of Rheims in 1049, possibly on grounds of consanguinity. By 1066, he had nevertheless established his power in Normandy. That there was no contemporary recorded clerical opposition to his claim on the grounds of illegitimacy probably reflects simply the circumspection of the chroniclers, rather than lack of concern over his legitimacy; however, after his death, he was quickly given the title 'Bastard', even on parchment,[169] and swiftly termed 'Conqueror', even while respect was paid to his memory.[170] In contrast, in 1135, when no legitimate son of Henry I survived (and when the Church's own jurisdictional strength had gained momentum), Henry's much respected but illegitimate son, Robert of Gloucester, was passed over as a candidate for the throne, despite the alternatives being a daughter—unprecedented—or an alien from Blois. Whilst a king born out of wedlock had a precedent in King Cnut's son, it was not in the English tradition.

'A PLAGUE ON BOTH THEIR HOUSES'

Peace and justice were recognized as the central functions of medieval kings; kings who ruled arbitrarily, with no regard for the law and without consensus, should be and often were resisted.[171] Edward had been lax with both secular and ecclesiastical

---

[167] The *Carmen de Hastingae Proelio of Guy, Bishop of Amiens*, ed. F. Barlow (Oxford, 1999), lines 371–2; *WP*, 146–7.

[168] LDB:124b (NFK:1,120), cf. Great Domesday recorded Harold as 'annexing' land, in the next entry to Harold 'reigning' GDB:38b (HAM:1,12–13); but the lands lay in different hundreds.

[169] OV 2.2–3, 313; Hallam, 50.

[170] *Durham Episcopal Charters 1071–1152*, ed. H. S. Offler, *Surtees Society*, 179 (Gateshead, 1968), no. 9; *Dialogus*, 63.

[171] J. Nelson, 'Bad kingship in the earlier middle ages', *Haskins Soc. Journal*, 8 (Woodbridge, 1999), 9.

magnates: the house of Godwine had been given too much power and freedom; Tostig's rule of Northumbria had been cruel and arbitrary, effected with the aid of a group of Danish housecarls; his brother Swein had abducted an abbess. Ecclesiastical writers considered the Norman coup to be a judgement on English society in general and the Godwinesons in particular, but were soon to apply their high standards of accountability to Harold's Norman successors.

Notwithstanding William's moral and religious claims, neither his propaganda nor his actions stand up to scrutiny. The Norman versions of Harold's coronation by Stigand are highly questionable: when developing the case against Stigand, William of Poitiers added that few noblemen were present at Harold's coronation.[172] The Bayeux Tapestry shows Harold crowned by Stigand, rather than the respected Ealdred, archbishop of York, whom the Worcester chronicler—from a see with strong recent links with Ealdred—records as officiating.[173] Yet it was Ealdred who contributed relics to Earl Harold's refoundation of Waltham, dedicated in the presence of King Edward and Queen Edith, the bishops, leading abbots, earls and leading officials of the royal household and all the court.[174] It was Ealdred who was sent on important missions to Europe. Several bishops in Edward's reign went out of their way to avoid consecration by Archbishop Stigand, going either to Ealdred of York or to Rome. Additionally, Canterbury had not yet established its permanent supremacy over York. For King Edward's biographer, a learned contemporary in holy orders, probably from Lotharingia, eulogious of both Edward and the Godwinesons, and directly in touch with Queen Edith, Stigand was one of those prelates 'who were attracted to the Devil by riches and worldly glory'.[175] He would not have been Harold's archbishop of choice to act at his consecration.

No fewer than five popes had attempted to remove Stigand from his archbishopric;[176] William, nevertheless, left him in office for a further four years after 1066. Whoever had consecrated Harold, Archbishop Ealdred certainly knew the truth of the matter and, significantly, it was only after Ealdred's death in 1069, that William felt able to dethrone Stigand in 1070 and install two archbishops of his choice. Nor did William's appointments to bishoprics in Normandy embody the principles of the eleventh-century movement for church reform. His half-bother Odo, and his second cousin Hugh in Lisieux, had both been appointed to their bishoprics years under the required canonical age. Important here is that at Waltham Holy Cross, Harold's magnificent refoundation in 1062 and, perhaps, his burial place, Little Domesday sanctions one of the most deliberate of illegal acquisitions, resorting to a guilty falsehood. The Conqueror had handed over the estate of Waltham first to Walcher, bishop of Durham—also the beneficiary of Waltham lands in other counties—and then to, his successor, William of St Calais (who had a hand in the Domesday Inquiry, possibly as mastermind, probably as commissioner): severe

---

[172] *WP*, 100; partly followed by OV 2.136.   [173] *JW* 2.600.
[174] *Waltham Chronicle*, xix–xxv; S.1036; see n. 134 in this chapter.   [175] *Vita Ædw*, 77–8.
[176] N. Brooks, *The Early History of the Church of Canterbury* (Leicester, 1984) 307.

treatment presumably designed to stamp out any veneration of Harold.[177] If William of St Calais did indeed play an instrumental role in the great Inquiry, Waltham offered a more suitable base than Durham: the Conqueror had excused the original grant by his need to have the bishop's predecessor close at hand and thereby benefit from his counsel. As Harold had brought to Waltham a *magister scholarum* from Liège, the canons would have possessed appropriate skills. The Domesday courts and Little Domesday certainly felt able to falsify the record deliberately in stating that Harold—not the Canons—held Waltham on King Edward's last day.[178]

For Normans, of course, trial by battle was an acceptable process to decide questions of land tenure. The outcome at Hastings thus demonstrated the right-fulness of William's claim in the final judgement by God. William of Poitiers attempted to assert that before the battle William offered to stand by 'a true and equitable judgement' according to the law of the English, or of the Normans, on the matter of succession. The chronicler adds that Harold, before Hastings, directly sought God's judgement—to his ruin.[179] But that was to adjudge William's claim by the victor's own legal process, one alien to England. William could not evade the verdict of history; and despite the formal registration of the new establishment in Domesday, governmental, monastic, and seigneurial documents later in the middle ages refer as a matter of course to 'the time of St Edward, William the Bastard, and other kings of England'.[180] The epithet designated the illegitimate status of William's tenure in England in a matter-of-fact, irrefutable, almost non-conten-tious way. Soon after his death, and for the present day, any suggestion of a legitimate claim is ignored in the sobriquet of 'Conqueror'.

Ecclesiastical writers maintained that English society deserved censure and punishment, and that ruthless William had been chosen to carry it out. The Anglo-Saxon Chronicler registered that God had granted William victory in 1066 'because of the sins of the people' and another Englishman, Eadmer, later attributed the Norman victory to 'the miraculous intervention of God, who by punishing Harold's wicked perjury, showed that He is not a God that hath any pleasure in wickedness'.[181] In the last year of William's reign, rough justice continued to be accepted as God's will: with plagues, human and bovine, and great storms and famine prevailing in 1086 and 1087, the English annalist asks, 'who is so hard-hearted that he cannot weep for such misfortunes? But such things happen because of people's sins in that they will not love God and righteousness'.[182] Henry of Huntingdon developed this line of thinking in his annal for 1087:

---

[177] *The Early Charters of the Augustinian Canons of Waltham Abbey, Essex, 1062–1230*, ed. R. Ransford (Woodbridge, 1989): no.10 acknowledges some injustice done.

[178] LDB:15b (ESS:7,1).   [179] *WP*, 123, 140.

[180] Raban, 77–8; in 1211, 'William the Bastard', *Annales Monastici*, ed. H. R. Luard, vol. 1, RS (London, 1864), 211; and in a writ of monstraverunt, 1241–2, quoted in J. Birrell and D. Hutchinson (eds), 'An Alrewas Rental of 1341', in *A Medieval Miscellany*, Staffs Record Society 4th ser., 20, (2004), 76.

[181] *Eadmer*, 9.   [182] *ASC*, 1087.

When the Normans had fulfilled the just will of the Lord upon the English people, and there was scarcely a noble of English descent in England, but all had been reduced to servitude and lamentation, and it was even disgraceful to be called English, William, the agent of this vengeance, ended his life. For God had chosen the Normans to wipe out the English nation, because He had seen that the Normans had surpassed all other people in their unparalleled savagery.[183]

Where Domesday detail is sufficient, it bears out this diatribe.

William's encomiast, the educated contemporary chronicler, once knight now canon, writing early in the reign, openly relished the fall of 'those who think that supreme power in this world is the greatest blessing, and who in their wish to be particularly blessed seize power and strive to retain it by force of arms'.[184] But several decades later, the supreme Anglo-Norman chronicler, Orderic, considered the Norman Conquest of England to be morally flawed, in that nearer heirs to the English crown had been set aside. He put such anxieties into the mouth of a learned Norman monk, formerly a pupil of Lanfranc's, who, in refusing King William's invitation to take up office in England, sternly renounced such 'plunder': 'The judgement of God, which is all the more terrible because it is hidden from sight, waits until the day when you must render account, *ad reddendam rationem*, of your stewardship.'[185] Orderic, however, also wrote resignedly of the Conquest as having some positive effect: 'after the Normans vanquished England by their valour, King William brought the country under his laws for its advantage'.[186] William had saved England from falling back into the more barbaric, marginal Christianity of the Scandinavian world: Orderic himself, for example, misguidedly believed that monasteries were not introduced into Norway until the twelfth century.[187]

Military atrocities apart, William's rule in England merited moral condemnation on other grounds. Churchmen and women, native and non-native alike, castigated his execution of Earl Waltheof. As a party to the plans of Earl Ralf of East Anglia and Earl Roger fitzOsbern of Hereford to join forces with the Danes and raise a rebellion, Waltheof had appealed to Archbishop Lanfranc to absolve him from his oath of secrecy to the conspirators and reveal the plot. On the advice of the archbishop, he gave himself up and threw himself on the king's mercy; but that, even in return for first-hand information of the plot's details, was unavailable, and Waltheof was beheaded in 1076. Lanfranc declared Waltheof to be guiltless of any crime; his memory was revered by the nuns of Romsey, which was not far from the site of his execution, and lauded by the chronicler, Orderic. A cult quickly developed around his tomb and, on its translation from the chapter house into the church at Crowland, his body was seen to be uncorrupted.[188] The somewhat sceptical William of Malmesbury later conceded that Waltheof's essential

[183] HH, 402–3.   [184] *WP*, 140–1.   [185] OV 2.270–80.
[186] OV 6.150.   [187] OV 5.220.
[188] *GP*, 321–2; OV 2.346; Williams, *The English*, 58–65; Van Caenegem, *Lawsuits*, no. 7.

blamelessness was supported 'by divine authority, which manifested many miracles at his tomb'.[189] It was not a judgement in favour of William.

William had earned his survival on all fronts not simply as a fighter but as a strategist. His military campaigns were usually swift and often characterized by fearsome reprisals; he was also a schemer, who used diplomatic and covert action to full advantage. He was alleged to have held Harold's brother, Wulfnoth, and another relative, as hostages since 1052, and there is evidence that he made use of Tostig against Harold.[190] He had more than once paid off the Danes, while dealing severely with their English allies. Even William's propagandist could not excuse his devastation of northern and western England in 1069–70. 'He, the chronicler, may not judge him, but God will.'[191] He was known as the severest of military tacticians. Even the vindication of his victory in the Bayeux Tapestry depicts a vignette of the side-effects of war—a woman fleeing from a burning house with a child. Few were secure enough to speak truth to power, but the great Abbot Hugh of Cluny seems to have refused William's request to supply monks for high ecclesiastical office, quoting St Matthew's gospel at him: 'For what has a man profited, if he shall gain the whole world, but lose his soul?'[192]

As to breaking faith with an allegedly religious mission, William's rule stood to be judged harshly. During William's reign, English religious houses were denuded of much of their carefully crafted and precious artistic treasures: gold and silver plate, gold embroidered vestments and hangings, illuminated books and manuscripts, as well as lands, were all seized in order to embellish newly built abbeys in Normandy and northern France.[193] In political terms, William's lifelong practice of terrifying reprisals often proved effective: indeed, a recent study shows how his very ruthlessness in England aided the long-term assimilation of the Normans, because rebellion was quashed and rebels eliminated in the first generation.[194] William persisted with these policies to the end, setting fire to churches, common people, and even hermits, in his final effort to exert his supremacy over Mantes. His death after injury in this Mantes campaign was directly attributed to this unnecessary cruelty: 'God was angered because of all of this, and when the king returned from there He submitted him to sickness, and later, death.'[195]

---

[189] *GRA* 1.268–71.   [190] *Eadmer*, 5–6; OV 2.232.

[191] Duke William's care for cultivators presented in *WP* is contradicted by the chronicler's depiction of William's tactic 'to lay waste the vines and domains' of enemies, *WP*, 61.

[192] D. Bates, *William the Conqueror* (London, 1989), 150, based upon *Patrologia Latina*, vol. 159, cols 923–4.

[193] For lands, see Golding, 'Robert of Mortain', *ANS*, 13 (1990), 119–44, esp. 139–42.

[194] Thomas, 'Native English landholders', 331; H. M. Thomas, *The English and the Normans: Ethnic Hostility, Assimilation, and Identity, 1066–1220* (Oxford, 2003), esp. 62.

[195] HH, 402–5.

TRE AND TENURIAL HIATUS

Implicit in Domesday is the fiction that William was the rightful heir of Edward the Confessor. It does not acknowledge King Harold II, son of Godwine, ruler between January and October 1066, as William's defeated predecessor. In Domesday, he is variously 'Earl Harold', or simply 'Harold'—with an exceptional slip of the pen, which no doubt resulted from the scribe's source.[196] But this official line took time to work out: in a charter of 1066–7 William granted land held by 'King Harold' in Wiltshire to Regenbald, onetime chancellor to King Edward and a key official; and in a gesture to the English establishment, he addressed the charter to Bishop Wulfstan of Worcester, as well as to the local bishop Herman.[197] This enactment, however, did not become a precedent. When William claimed to have been the rightful king from the time of Edward's death, it meant that he could also claim that the lands of all those who had fought against him were forfeit. The Normans drew on the past where it suited them, to construct a text that fortified the future of their regime; and their future policies remained bolstered by the information so gathered.

The legal fiction of William's accession on the day on which King Edward was alive and dead left many issues in contention, and could not be coherently maintained.[198] For instance, a legal hiatus was created between 6 January 1066 and 20 October 1066, although men died, wives and sons inherited, and leases fell in or were granted; moreover, in Harold's and Gyrth's earldoms—legitimately held under Edward—the freeholders were left vulnerable. A rightful transfer of land was a logical impossibility; it remained only to establish under whose authority the changes had been made. Some contorted Domesday phrases reflect the difficulty: one Grimkel, a landholder in the time of King Edward, forfeited his lands 'in the year in which that same king died'.[199] How valid now was Westminster Abbey's tenure of Kelvedon, gifted to Westminster by a man who had fought against William? The perplexed locals report that the donor, Alric, 'went away to a naval battle against King William and when he returned became ill; he then gave this manor to St Peter, but only one man from the shire knows this; and St Peter has held this manor in this way up to now and they [the monks or the shire?] have had neither writ nor servant from the king since the king came to this land'.[200] In the event, probably because of Westminster's symbolic importance to the new king, Kelvedon remained in its possession.[201] The donation to Westminster, by a thegn before 'he went to war in Yorkshire' to fight with King Harold—but not against William—posed another conundrum and needed explaining.[202] Domesday

---

[196] See n. 168 in this chapter.   [197] *Acta* no. 223.
[198] Legal, canonical, and rulership issues and their long-term consequences are pursued by Garnett, in his *Conquered England*. Fleming, *Law*, 53–67, is helpful on TRE conditions.
[199] GDB:376b (LIN:CW12).   [200] LDB:14b–15a (ESS:6,9).
[201] P. Taylor, introduction in *The Essex Domesday*, Alecto 2000, 23.
[202] LDB:15a (ESS:6,15).

mentions only one other man killed in battle against the Norsemen, and his land was taken into the sheriff's possession.[203] If those who fought with Harold against the Norwegian king conveniently forfeited their lands also, perhaps that is another indication that William had colluded with Tostig and the Norwegian invaders.

The way in which William's land settlement transferred tenures wholesale after the Conquest accorded ill with William's claim to be acting as the designated heir of King Edward. Although not openly admitted in Domesday Book, there was no question of restoring the land to the 'antecessor'—or his family; the antecessor merely helped to identify the land and the transfer.[204] Admittedly, the range of tenures and obligations in English custom and in the Danelaw were complex, yet only in Circuit III of Domesday was there any consistent attempt to take note of different types of pre-1066 tenure; some commendations and leases current in 1065 were recorded, but not comprehensively. Leases, soke-rights, and commendation might each be owed to different lords. Once, in a judicial review of land claimed by the crown, the hundred testified that the land in question 'never belonged to that fief, nor did the commendation, nor did the soke';[205] yet rarely was such note taken of Edwardian tenurial considerations.

In the terms of reference, and the Domesday text as recorded, the assumption during the Domesday Inquiry seems to be of tenurial change. If land were disputed, had the men of the locality seen the writ or messenger who had given it to the newcomer? A changeover was taken as read. Further, for the most part—as in modern English courts of law—the men of the locality were permitted to reply only to the questions posed. The apparently straightforward questions on antecessors, and the questions on the witness of transfer that we infer from Domesday, were clever: they concentrated on orderly and king-given succession rather than on preceding and customary rights: Who had held the land in King Edward's day? Who holds it now? The question of who *should* hold the land was, of course, not asked. The men of the locality were not permitted to assert the claims of the sons of the Edwardian holder, and often feared to state the rightful succession of the land. Indeed, there were occasions when those testifying, evidently apprehensive of stating anything definite, refused to commit themselves or take a stand at all on tenure.[206] These can be seen as signs of resistance as well as of fear and 'simple ignorance', as it seems when the men of the hundred of Stowmarket, 'did not know that [the monastery of] St Edmund had been dispossessed' of numerous freemen's soke and commendation after King Edward had granted them, and that King William had given them away.[207] The commissioners themselves seem wary of taking decisive action: although responsibility might be deflected by Domesday recording, 'as he says'.[208] Even when the veracity of a man of the stature of Bishop

[203] GDB:177d (WOR:26,16).   [204] e.g. LDB:246a–b (NFK:29,8), 98a (ESS:82,1).
[205] LDB:447b (SUF:76,2).
[206] e.g. GDB:133c (HRT:4,1), 30b (SUR:1,5), 63b (BRK:58,2).
[207] Cooper, 'Protestations of ignorance', 171–5; LDB:360b (SUF:14,37).
[208] GDB:200c (CAM:32,10), 246a (STS:B12).

Osbern of Exeter was at stake, an unsupported statement was sufficient to refer the matter to the king for judgement.[209] Alternatively, the land was simply taken into the king's hands.[210] As doubt was not infrequently cast effectively, and recorded, when 'they' had 'not seen the writ, seal or envoy', witness of the shire and hundred could not be completely gainsaid. At the least, it was the only way open to local men to avoid sanctioning the changes in tenure that had taken place without endangering themselves.[211] The conquerors, however, might apply pressure through tenancies, and by resort to the ordeal to verify witness.

Despite all difficulties, the tenurial settlement effected during twenty years of Norman rule did not merely have to be verified in order to levy taxes, and dues in vacancies; it also had to be justified in the face of the Danish challenge, as the king had repeatedly wreaked wide vengeance on existing landholders.[212] Some justification was needed to satisfy the literate landholders—the churchmen—who made the country capable of rule and who provided the legal minds of the establishment. Yet William's arbitrary land redistribution of laymen's lands had caused ecclesiastical institutions losses and chaos. In 1066–7, he had granted five hides of Hayling, belonging to Old Minster and leased to Wulfweard White, to the Abbey of Jumièges.[213] William II tried to restore it to Winchester cathedral priory, but Henry I regranted it to Jumièges and the dispute continued.[214] As king, the Conqueror not only confiscated the lands of those who opposed him; their associates also suffered. Lands that William had already confirmed to St Riquier in 1068 were lost, probably because of the rebellion of their donor, Earl Ralph, in 1075.[215] Dispositions made during Edward's reign were not respected: when Stigand was deposed, a number of lands he had held on lease from monasteries in order that 'he should maintain their interests' were redistributed or went to the crown; Folkestone, valued at £110 in Domesday, proved irretrievable, even by Lanfranc.[216] Bury St Edmunds lost Mildenhall because of Stigand's tenure of this important manor and it took the community over a century to recover it, buying it back from Richard I in 1189.[217] Indeed, the Domesday project may well have been strongly promoted by ecclesiastics who were aware of the legal principle of prescription on ecclesiastical claims—thirty-years was the Carolingian limit—and wished to ensure that the problems with church endowments were acknowledged and resolved before the death of the Conqueror.[218] Two decades had already

[209] GDB:58c (BRK:5,1).   [210] LDB:54b (ESS 27,17); GDB:35b (SUR:19,25).

[211] e.g. Kelvedon, above; GDB:209a–b (HUN:D2O, D21), 35d–36a (SUR:21,3); also Cooper, 'Protestations of ignorance', 171–5.

[212] Even as late as 1075, e.g. L. Marten, 'The Impact of Rebellion on Little Domesday', *ANS*, 27 (2005), 132–50.

[213] Charters, no. 114, *c.*1053; *Acta*, no. 159.   [214] *Regesta* 3.417.   [215] *Acta*, no. 259.

[216] e.g. LDB:133b–141b (NFK:1,209–241); GDB:38b (HAM:1,16); M. F. Smith, 'Archbishop Stigand and the eye of the needle', *ANS*, 16 (1993), 206–13.

[217] LDB:288b–289a; Van Caenegem, *Writs*, 436.

[218] 'Thirty year prescription was often offered as proof in Carolingian land disputes; legislation in 829 made it the standard basis for ecclesiastical claims', J. L. Nelson, 'Dispute settlement in Carolingian West Francia', *Dispute Settlement*, 50–1.

elapsed, and while the Conqueror was still active but vulnerable the Church needed action on its lost lands.

Domesday's record of Edwardian data gave, and still gives, a false impression of the legality of William's policies. The chronology and methods of replacing Anglo-Saxon landholders are still debated;[219] probably differing approaches were adopted at different times. It is clear, however, that the lands of those who fought, or rebelled, against William were confiscate.[220] Some lands were taken over wholesale—in areas of rebellion or to create strong enclaves at strategic points.[221] Other lands were reallocated according to 'antecessor'. (County hidage lists and ancient sokes could have assisted in either process.) Many landholders were downgraded and newcomers placed over them because of their former ties: whether leases, commendation, or soke. In some few cases, in Yorkshire and Lincolnshire, a degree of continuity is evident.[222] In contrast to the official and largely impersonal character of the Domesday text, however, vivid incidents from the records of Abingdon, Ely, and even from the more compliant Canterbury, indicate the arbitrary and personal nature of the Norman kings' rule and the way in which the Norman kings' choleric moods, as well as policies, influenced matters. Amongst the landed losses which faced Abingdon Abbey, a stalwart supporter of Harold, were those of an influential priest who had held land from the abbey in Edward's day and fled with Harold's mother into exile in 1068: 'whatever had been his [Blaecmann's] was taken back into the king's hand as a fugitive's' and only 'with great effort the abbot [Ealdred] obtained restitution of the aforesaid lands of the king'.[223] Abingdon Abbey's purchase of land, sanctioned by Odo of Bayeux when regent, was seized by William I when Odo fell into disfavour and given to Richard de Courcy, so the abbot lost both the money and the land: 'everyone who had supposed themselves helped by Odo's power received the king's displeasure'.[224] William II acted in the same way: the widow of Anskill, a leading Abingdon knight who had died in prison following his arrest and maltreatment by William II, was refused a living on a portion of her husband's former land, despite payments made. She was refused, that is, until she became a mistress of William II's younger brother, Henry, and bore him a son, when she was permitted to repossess

---

[219] Contrast P. Sawyer, '1066–1086: a tenurial revolution?', in *Reassessment*, 71–85, with R. Fleming, *Kings and Lords in Conquest England* (Cambridge, 1991), ch. 4, 'Domesday Book and the tenurial revolution'. See also J. A. Green, *The Aristocracy of Norman England* (Cambridge, 1996), 48–99, on the tenurial revolution.

[220] *Acta*, no. 37.

[221] e.g. Alan of Richmond's lands in north Yorkshire and William Malet's lands in east Yorkshire.

[222] D. Roffe, 'Hidden lives: English lords in post-Conquest Lincolnshire and beyond', in D. Roffe (ed.), *The English and their Legacy, 900–1200: Essays in Honour of Ann Williams* (Woodbridge, 2012), 205–28; D. J. H. Michelmore, 'Township and Tenure' in M. L. Faull and S. A. Moorhouse (eds), *West Yorkshire: An Archaeological Survey to ad 1500: Part II: The Administrative and Tenurial Framework* (West Yorkshire Metropolitan County Council, 1981), 231–65, esp. 251–3.

[223] *HistAbbend* 1, 222; cf. 373; F. Barlow, *The Godwins: The Rise and Fall of a Noble Dynasty* (London, 2002), 119.

[224] *HistAbbend* 2, 12–13; Nuneham Courtenay, GDB:159a (OXF:32,1). At Evesham, Odo seized Abbot Æthelwig's accessions after the abbot's death, *Chronicon abbatiae de Evesham*, 96–7.

Bayworth.[225] Yet the Norman rulers' emotive reactions were not invariably ill-intentioned: William I made the abbot give five hides to a former Abingdon knight who had been attacked whilst at sea, and had lost both hands.[226]

The first two Norman kings evidently felt entitled to impose their own candidates onto the lands of their tenants-in-chief. Both William I and William II dealt high-handedly with the estates of St Martin-le-Grand and permitted successive counts of Boulogne to do the same. In the first part of his reign, William had at some point become reconciled with Eustace II of Boulogne and had given Eustace a number of the estates of Ingelric, a royal servant and founder of St Martin-le-Grand, London, that had been allocated as the foundation estate for that house. Eustace, the beneficiary, had been later encouraged to restore the lands of St Martin's by his own followers and officials; but it was a limited restoration that was promised—only five of the twelve manors originally donated to the house. Even more so, in effect: Domesday shows that of those restored, St Martin's appears merely as subtenant in three, and a claim was outstanding on another.[227] The dispossession or down-grading of English landholders resulted from a series of ad hoc decisions as well as from considered policy and, either way, Domesday did a remarkable job of tidying up and presenting the new settlement. Amidst the jockeying for control of the lands of the archbishopric of Canterbury, the danger of the principle was, however, as evident to Archbishop Anselm, Lanfranc's successor, as the practicalities. In 1094, he confided his difficulties frankly to Archbishop Hugh of Lyon over the second William's interference with the Canterbury subtenants: 'the king wishes to assert that he can lawfully constitute as their heirs whom he wishes'.[228] This tactic, of the king asserting rights over subtenants as well as over tenants-in-chief, was one repeated by the strongest English medieval monarchs—as in the late thirteenth-century statutes of *Mortmain* and *Quia emptores*.[229] Awed historians studying Domesday Book have, as Maitland predicted, perforce 'bowed themselves' to William 'and become that man's men';[230] yet we should remain conscious of the deliberate illusion William created when he ordered that his Survey of assets and their new tenures be set down in grandiose formal style.

THE DANISH CRISIS AND DOMESDAY: TIME FOR *PAXS*?

> All men to have the fear of God constantly in their hearts, and day and night to be in terror of sin, dreading the Day of Judgement (*Domesdaeg ondreade*) and shuddering at the thought of Hell and expecting their last day to be close at hand.[231]
>
> I Cnut, 25

---

[225] *HistAbbend* 2, 52–5.   [226] *HistAbbend* 2, 8–9.

[227] P. Taylor, 'Ingelric, Count Eustace and the foundation of St Martin-le-Grand', *ANS*, 24 (2001), 215–37, at 215–17.

[228] *vult asserere se posse iuste quos vult eorum haeredes constituere*, Anselmi Opera, 57.

[229] EHD3, nos 53, 64; *Mortmain 1279* and *Quia Emptores 1290*, Stubbs, *Charters*, 450–2, 473–4.

[230] Final paragraph, Maitland, 520.   [231] I Cnut, 25.

After all, Englishmen were familiar with the sort of sentiments expressed by Archbishop Wulfstan at a time of millenarian fears and invasions, only half a century before Hastings, when his views became incorporated into legislation, such as that quoted.[232] English churchmen had already faced the theological problem of why a Christian people should be overcome by less Christian enemies. In his *The Sermon of the Wolf to the English* 'when the Danes were greatly persecuting them', he insisted that peoples whose sins had 'infuriated God so excessively' were vulnerable to conquest and destruction by alien armies; the Danes were 'strong through the consent of God', 'entirely on account of our sins'. The Archbishop concluded with the exhortation to 'order our words and deeds rightly' and 'keep carefully oath and pledge', and 'consider the great Judgement to which we all must come'.[233] The archbishop's arguments of the military vulnerability consequent on moral decline had opened up a line of argument which the Normans, with or without direct knowledge of it, adapted with success. Whilst under Godwine and his sons England had self-evidently failed to measure up to the standards necessary for divine support, in 1085–6 the severe Danish threat raised its own moral questions about William's rule.

The crisis gave rise to frenetic activity; according to William of Malmesbury, 'the king was completely shaken and summoned a council and threw open discussion on what should be done'.[234] Unnamed Englishmen appealed to the Danish King Cnut (a great-nephew of Cnut the Great, king of England 1016–35), for aid against William's tyranny.[235] William was well aware that the affiliations of many, particularly in the north and east of his newly acquired kingdom, lay with the Danish claimant rather than with himself. After 1066, these people had 'repeatedly sent envoys to the Danes or some other people from whom they might hope for help';[236] and before 1084 there had been no fewer than three attempts by King Swegn and his sons to attack England, often in concert with English rebellion. William's own harsh reprisals, whilst militarily effective, were deleterious to revenues and disastrous in economic terms, making it difficult in the wasted counties to collect the gelds and rents he demanded; locally, they cannot but have turned defeat into hatred. Although by definition opposition views went unrecorded, the trail of physical destruction is more than evident in Domesday nearly twenty years later (it may indeed have been responsible for the long-term change in the economic balance between northern and southern England).[237] A deep-seated re-examination of

---

[232] D. Whitelock, 'Wulfstan's authorship of Cnut's laws', *EHR*, 70 (1955), 72–85. P. Wormald, *The Making of English Law: King Alfred to the Twelfth Century*, vol. 1, *Legislation and its Limits* (Oxford, 1999), considers Wulfstan's impact on legislation and its drafting.

[233] 'which was in the year 1014 after the Incarnation of our Lord Jesus Christ': EHD1, no. 240.

[234] *rex timore percitus*, WM, *Saints Lives*, 130–1; also 'the only person who shook his [William's] royal state was Cnut, king of the Danes', *GRA* I, 478–9; Maddicott, 'Responses to the threat of invasion, 1085', *EHR*, 122 (2007), 986–97.

[235] Life of Cnut, in *Vitae Sanctorum Danorum*, ed. M. C. Gertz (Copenhagen, 1908–12), 96–7.

[236] *WP*, 183.   [237] See n. 304 in this chapter.

policy was necessary, when William's Christmas Council of 1085 deliberated deeply 'about this country, how it was occupied and with what sort of people'.[238]

While essentially proactive by temperament, William nevertheless drew upon the legal expertise of the great ecclesiastics he had promoted and the experience of the officials and magnates he had created (who already seem to have addressed themselves in the autumn to the precariousness of their joint position and to finding solutions[239]). In what proved to be William's last two years, with a Danish invasion of great magnitude imminent, and an economy and taxation system already at full stretch, it was less an occasion to launch an encyclopaedia than for an urgent assessment of resources to deal with the current offensive. There remained, however, the deeper question of whether the Normans could hold the productive but unwilling territory by force alone indefinitely; and it concerned the magnates as much as the king: 'the stability' of 'William, king of the English, and his heirs' was amongst Roger de Builli's concerns in founding Blyth Priory in 1088.[240] William's clerical apologists had propounded the line that he was victorious at Hastings and afterwards because he had God's judgement behind him: God was with him and his cause—and his success proved it. But this circular argument was in danger of unravelling: what conclusion was to be drawn, now that his regime was put at hazard? What could be done to undermine popular support for the Danes?

In current cliché, was it now more than time to make a bid for 'hearts and minds'? To talk in such terms after emphasizing William's abilities as a ruthless strategist is perhaps not so incongruous; a policy of reconciliation was also a strategy—to be adopted when other tactics proved unproductive. There are enough small pointers within Domesday, and elsewhere, to raise the prospect that just such a revision of policy might have become William's strategy in England in his advancing years.

Whatever the participants' various intentions, the 'deep speech' between William and his magnates resulted in the launch of the Domesday Inquiry, bringing its returns within the year. William's magnates themselves made returns and at Salisbury in August 1086 they, and even their major tenants, the Anglo-Saxon chronicle insists, gave oaths of loyalty in person. This was an extraordinary assembly, with a wider lay element than those normal to the great councils. Even the summons to Old Sarum was both defensive and audacious. Had an element amongst the landholders resisted summons and whatever bargain or loyalty was demanded, the regime would have been gravely weakened. Now everything depended on the king's leadership—and on support from his ecclesiastics—now empowered by the data of the Domesday Survey. God's judgement on William's

---

[238] *ASC*, 1085.   [239] Maddicott, 'Responses to the threat of invasion, 1085', 986–91.
[240] *pro stabilitate regis Anglorum Willelmi, successorumque eius, Cartulary of Blyth Priory*, ed. Timson, Thoroton Society Records, 27, vol.1, no. 325.

kingship—and on the magnates' tenure of their remunerative landholdings—was in the balance.

The date chosen was an extraordinary threefold festival, one that can only have been selected with deliberation and some awareness of its symbolism. It was 1 August, Lammas, when the first fruits of the harvest were traditionally celebrated in England: however Domesday represented a Norman harvest, not an English one so, perhaps, a cruel irony. Yet it was also the feast of St Peter-ad-Vincula, celebrating the freedom of the imprisoned Peter and, given England's and King Edward's affinity with St Peter, perhaps a date of intended and reconciliatory symbolism.[241] In addition, it was the day when the western Church observed the Feast of the Holy Maccabees. One of the doctrinal philosophies attached to these ancient books was the value of suffering and martyrdom as means of expiation, and the Books of Maccabees themselves portray the successful struggle of the Jews against alien political and cultural domination:[242] again a choice of feast-day that seems to offer acknowledgement of English miseries, and reconciliation.

William had, of course, needed the support of the Church and churchmen throughout his career, a point underlined throughout this discussion of Domesday Book. Despite the violent aspects of his conquests and rule, William was overtly supportive of ecclesiastics in promulgating the movement called the Peace of God, developed in southern Gaul in the tenth century and designed to inculcate respect for the lives and property of clergy, widows, and the poor and for the livelihood of non-combatants in the course of military action. Indeed, as recently as 1080 in William's dukedom, under the First Canon of the Council of Lillebonne, *vicomtes* had been assigned to assist bishops in enforcing the Peace.[243] It was a concept to which rulers as well as bishops might feel obliged to subscribe, although its practical effect is questionable.[244] Even William's English obituarist said in 1087 that he 'was gentle to the good men who loved God',[245] and he was certainly reputed to be susceptible to thoughts of judgement. When, after suppressing the Ely rebellion in 1071, the victorious William entered the abbey church, he was said to have stood as far from the relics of the saint as possible, 'not daring to approach closer, for he feared to bring down on himself the judgement of God (*a Deo iudicium*) for the harm that his men had done in that place'.[246]

The commissioners sent on circuit in 1086 evidently had a mission to investigate officials—already notorious for their avidity in taking over the lands of the Church—and to expose the taking of excessive dues leading to the running down of peasant stock.[247] Carolingian kings, in need of the military and fiscal support of lesser freemen and cultivators, had given them some opportunity to air grievances

---

[241] *Vita Ædw*, 9, 44–5, 81, 86.
[242] Cross, *Oxford Dictionary of the Christian Church*, 839.   [243] OV 3.26–7.
[244] Recently, D. Bartholémy, 'The peace of God and bishops at war in the Gallic Lands from the late tenth to the early twelfth centuries', *ANS*, 32 (2009).
[245] *ASC*, 1087.   [246] *LE*, II, no. 11.
[247] e.g. LDB:283a (SUF:1,23; 1,26; 1,29–30); see Ch. 9 in this volume.

in royal courts about raised dues:[248] in 789, *missi* in Acquitaine were instructed to ask: 'Has any new customary obligation been imposed in the last twenty years?'[249] In 1086, on not a few occasions in eastern and south-eastern England, local men were permitted to oppose publicly the high sums obtained by the sheriff and his farmer with their lower estimated value.[250] More obviously censorious was the recording in Domesday of an action on the royal manor of Soham Toney, whose reeve 'sold' five freemen 'for a bridle' early in the reign—in practice this most probably meant their conversion into rent-paying villeins, although it was possible that they were indeed sold into slavery.[251] In 1086, the Checking of officials was doubly important: to ensure that more money entered the crown's coffers and to curtail discontent arising from the reeves' excessive exactions.

On occasion, even implied criticisms of the king were allowed to find their way into the Domesday record of proceedings, and to remain there during abbreviation. Land of Peterborough Abbey was subtenanted 'by order of the king, against the abbot's wishes';[252] the abbey, however, had long been in William's disfavour. Then there is the writ, just before Domesday, showing William's somewhat belated desire to make reparation to the monks of Fécamp for damage done at Hastings, which suggests some driven change of policy.[253] Nonetheless, Domesday retains hints of the king's iron hand behind the apparent legal ordering. At Barking, an Anglo-Saxon nunnery, its leadership possibly vacant, with its administration in the king's hands, Domesday records the plight of a number of freemen formerly affiliated to Barking: 'but now the king can do with them what he likes',[254] one of the most telling phrases in Domesday.

The Inquiry had an element of a publicity exercise. Whilst the numbers who attended the inquests in various capacities have been 'guesstimated' in different ways, undoubtedly the native men of the vills, hundreds, and shires would have constituted the majority, not the newcomers. Fleming originally suggested that 'as many as 7 or 8,000 people attended the inquests', but has since emphasized the range of meetings and courts that may have taken place and how easily the witnesses and magnates' own followers, let alone the onlookers, snowballed.[255] An alternative estimate based on the Domesday mention of some 6,500 vills, with eight representatives from each vill, plus twelve men from each hundred, plus some 3,000 landholders named in the text, proposes that 'in all, over 60,000 witnesses were probably heard in the court of the Domesday Inquiry'.[256] Much depends on whether the smaller vills and hamlets of the highland and western areas of the country were in fact each represented by six to eight men, as the larger settlements

---

[248] Nelson, 'Dispute settlement in Carolingian West Francia', 48–54.

[249] *MGH, Capitularia regum francorum* I, ed. A. Boretius (Hanover, 1883), no. 24, *Brevium Missorum Aquitanicum, cap.* 2, 5.

[250] See Ch. 7 in this volume, pp. 197–205.   [251] LDB:110b (NFK:1,7).

[252] GDB:222a (NTH:6a,27).   [253] *Acta*, no. 144.   [254] LDB:17b (ESS:9,5).

[255] R. Fleming, 'Oral testimony and the Domesday Inquest', *ANS*, 7 (1994), 105; *Law*, 15–17.

[256] Roffe, *Inquest*, 123.

of East Anglia evidently were.[257] It seems likely that at least 20,000 to 40,000 people contributed local knowledge at some stage, and as witnesses: and many more witnessed passively, for the spectacle; traditionally, assemblies for legal pleas might lead to witness by the county and 'a good thousand men' giving their oath.[258] In 1086, many men and women, hopeful of recovering some title to their father's land, some reduction in their rents, or some restoration of their families' fortunes, doubtless trudged across their counties to the traditional outdoor meeting-places of hundred and shire.

Although such hopes were largely shattered, it remains important that, on well over two hundred occasions, the abbreviated Domesday does record some of the revised estimates of value given by men of the locality in contradistinction to the inflated revenues raised by royal farmers and alien ecclesiastics—irrespective of whether or not such revisions were ever acted upon. The over 200 instances of contradictory estimates for the values from the two most productive circuits, eastern and south-eastern England, I and VII,[259] suggest some intention to curb the mounting rent demands, notwithstanding contrary pressure by officials and landholders. Similarly, the Checking gave burgesses a limited chance to protest at the distribution of taxation. There was a further unusual element in the data sought. Whilst surveys by medieval landlords usually divide each economic unit into two sectors—demesne and peasant holdings—rarely is the capital equipment of the peasant sector recorded; most surviving seigneurial documents detail only the holdings, rents, or services of the peasantry. Yet Domesday ascribes plough-teams—whose numbers are never in dispute—to peasant cultivators: their numbers were sought probably on fiscal as well as economic grounds, but, it could be seen as a reconciliatory gesture to confirm the peasants' possession of their main assets. Certainly, sheriffs were required to answer questions in public when the peasants' plough-teams on the lands in their charge had fallen in number.[260] Here, the interests of the king also coincided with those of some of the smallest English landholders. It was no support for the king to have the freeholders of East Anglia turned into 'poor bordars' like those of Norwich, unable to pay geld, at the same time as many baronial plots in boroughs were not paying any royal customary dues at all—a point central to an inquiry into the royal revenues.

Does this point to a 'hearts and minds' policy towards the English peasantry on whom William relied for his extensive defensive works and war expenditure? Richard fitzNigel said that the English could only retain their lands by earning them and the Suffolk Domesday hints of the time when only buying back or 'redeeming' lands was acceptable.[261] But it does seem that a pause had now been

---

[257] e.g. LDB:285b (SUF:1,76–77).
[258] All the men of West and East Kent, Charters, no. 41; also LE, II, no. 25.
[259] H. C. Darby, *Domesday England* (Cambridge, 1977), 211.   [260] LDB:1b–2a (ESS:1,2).
[261] *Dialogus*, 54; LDB:360b (SUF:14,39), 367b (SUF:14,101); in latter, Ingelric acts as king's commissioner or *baron*. William 'gave away every man's land', *ASC*, 1067, E (probably 1068).

called to this policy. Indeed, it has been adroitly observed that the conquerors appear 'strikingly preoccupied' with 'right' when they might have rested content with their own 'might'.[262] This is evident in Domesday, if only in order to render account for the Norman takeover and to gain some defensive support.

By 1085, William was nearly sixty and grossly fat;[263] long hours of fighting, and in the saddle, were no longer a welcome challenge. His astute and reliable wife—an effective commissioner of pleas and regent when required—had died in 1083, while his half-brother, Odo, younger than he, a source of moral support even in the thick of battle at Hastings, had proved untrustworthy and was now imprisoned. William was a superstitious as well as a ruthless warrior and, like fellow warriors counting on making amends before they died, showed the need for contact with Anselm, now prior of Bec—a great theologian and no mincer of words—with whom he struck a developing rapport.[264] William was visibly awed by Anselm's learning and holiness, and apparently calmed by his very presence; and it was Anselm whom the ailing king called for as he approached his end.[265]

At moments of crisis, bishops could and did exert their spiritual as well as their administrative influence. Princes were obliged to render account for their protection of the Church and bishops were the mediators of divine will and, as the king's consecrators, had divine accountability.[266] Leading ecclesiastics of Charlemagne's empire had seen over-aggressive rulers transgress the pale at close hand and counselled them accordingly; such precedents were well attested and several of William's bishops educated in Lorraine would have been aware of them. Bishop Hincmar's final argument to prevent Charlemagne's son, Louis the German, from invading the lands of his brother to the west, was that he would place his eternal soul in jeopardy: one day his power and wealth would disappear and, standing alone, without wife and children, councillors or vassals, he would 'come before the face of the eternal judge', with all his sins revealed. Hincmar had stressed that Louis' priority must be to choose officials who would not lay waste the harvest or meadows of the church, and to appoint judges and *missi* who would respect the property of the church and its people—a precept relevant to the context of the Domesday Inquiry. Otherwise, Louis was undoubtedly 'hell-bound'. Saint Eucher, bishop of Orleans, had seen a vision of Charles Martel tormented in fire, because 'this prince had stolen and divided [the Church's] properties and must surely receive sempiternal punishment for his sins. He must also pay for the sins of all those who had given the properties to the Lord and to his Saints in the hope of redeeming their souls'.[267] In 1085, William's bishops might well have pressed for the Inquiry to

[262] Wormald, 75.   [263] *GRA* 1.508–9.

[264] W. Fröhlich, 'St Anselm's special relationship with William the Conqueror', *ANS*, 10 (1987), 101–10; *Eadmer*, 24.

[265] *Eadmer*, 23–4.   [266] J. Nelson, 'Kingship, law and liturgy', *EHR*, 92 (1977), 246–8.

[267] P. E. Dutton, *The Politics of Dreaming in the Carolingian Empire* (Nebraska, 1994), 172–4.

restore the assets of the Church and to recognize those of the peasantry and, in order to enlist God's support for William's threatened regime, the king might well have acceded to these requests.

The logic of trial by battle in the victories of 1066–71 sat uneasily with the possibility of defeat. Could the new rulers always assume—as over fifty years later the Norman Walter Espec before the Battle of the Standard—that 'victory has been given to our race as if in fee by the Most High'.[268] Had the Normans been such good stewards in God's sight that they deserved to keep England?

Rulers, as others, needed to be seen as patrons of the Church to redeem their culpability. William was undoubtedly concerned for the Church. William of Poitiers praised his assiduity in holding Church Councils, and Orderic credited him with the founding of seventeen monasteries and six nunneries.[269] Yet, William's rule had seen the English church suffer, particularly from his ordering his core followers to take over the lands of freemen, whether they had been leased from the Church or not. But although he could be ruthless and vengeful, his rule was also characterized by dramatic acts of atonement.[270] Even his sceptical successor, Rufus, employed symbolism as well as piratical instincts, robbing Waltham of the valuable treasures—crosses, Gospel books, and even bells—to embellish his parents' own foundation of the monastery of St Stephen's at Caen, and provide some salvation for their souls.[271] Despite Ely's earlier association with rebellion, and at the expense of his own supporters at the margins, by the 1080s it was patently not William's will, nor in his interest, to trespass on the Church's legitimate holdings. A conflated, and possibly supplemented, Ely report of the king's orders to put to right the abbey's losses states that King William had 'neglected to protect the abbey over a period of fourteen years'.[272] While William himself did not formally admit 'neglect', a royal writ, 1081 × 1083, does concede to Ely that 'according to what he learns, the king will make an exchange or some other provision'.[273] We have seen that in 1085 he sought to make restitution to the abbey of Fécamp—a Norman monastery favoured by Edward the Confessor—for rents lost at Hastings. The action and timing are important.[274] William's belated attempts to reconcile his military takeover with the historic landholding rights of Churches hinted of his awareness of his own ultimate Judgement Day.

A gesture, mentioned earlier, by Eustace II of Boulogne, intermittently William's rival or ally—a central character in the Conquest drama since 1051—may have

---

[268] *cum victoria generi nostro quasi in feudum data sit ab Altissimo*, Ailred of Rievaulx, in *Relatio, Chronicles of the Reigns of Stephen, Henry I, and Richard I*, vol. 3, RS (London, 1886), 185.

[269] *WP*, 80–5, 87; OV 2.10–18.   [270] D. Bates, *William the Conqueror*, 205–25.

[271] *Waltham Chronicle*, 58–61; following the Norman conquest 'the Golden City [Peterborough] became a wretched city', *ASC*, 1066, E; C. R. Dodwell, *Anglo-Saxon Art* (Manchester, 1982), 216–30.

[272] *Acta*, no. 118, EHD2, no. 51.   [273] *Acta*, no. 119.

[274] *Acta*, nos 144, 146; discussed in Ch. 7 in this volume, p. 205.

given William food for thought. At some point between 1075 and 1085, maybe not long before his death—variously ascribed to between 1085 and 1088—Eustace II was 'led by the counsel of certain wise and just men [probably his baronial council], and by repentance', to restore certain lands to St Martin's, 'for the safety of my soul and that of my wife and of my sons Eustace and Geoffrey'.[275] Eustace's declaration of restitution even included an anathema directed at his own flesh and blood: 'If any of my sons or their parents by instigation of the Devil should wish to infringe the liberties of this church, may he be separated from God, St Martin and our friendship.' It was not uncommon for the most unscrupulous of leaders to conclude their careers with acts of repentance, and to enter religious houses in their final years to die in the habit of a monk, and to be buried and commemorated there. Robert of Flanders, who had supplanted the young son of his elder brother who had been William's ally, and had given his daughter in marriage and his ships for the invasion of England to Cnut the Holy, went to Jerusalem around 1090 'for the remission of all sins', renouncing the world on his return.[276] Shortly after William's own death, not a few of the most strident executors of the Norman landed settlement who have featured in these pages had similar intent: Richard fitzGilbert became a monk at the priory he had established at St Neot's by April 1088.[277] Hugh de Montfort, castigated in Domesday for his dubious acquisitions, became a monk of Bec in 1088.[278] Roger of Montgomery died in his abbey at Shrewsbury,[279] and the military Earl Hugh, similarly, at Chester.[280] Hugh de Port was inscribed in New Minster's Book of Life and became a monk at St Peter's, Gloucester, in 1096.[281] Others invested in foundations. Sheriff Picot seems to have founded what was to become Barnwell Priory.[282] Eudo Dapifer refounded the abbey at Colchester in 1096–7.[283] Sheriff Urse seems to have been instrumental in refounding Great Malvern as a Benedictine Priory.[284] His brother, Robert Dispenser, one of the core administrators of the regime, restored to Westminster land he had taken over wrongfully. With Robert probably still in harness in the late 1090s, this last-minute bequest was witnessed by his working colleagues, amongst them Walkelin of Winchester, Urse, Herbert the Chamberlain, Peter de Valognes, Ivo Taillebois, and Otto the Goldsmith.[285] Much later, in 1128, the month before he died,

---

[275] Taylor, 'Ingelric', *ANS*, 24 (2001), 215–37; charter, App. III. Near-contemporary debates about restitution of lands at the end of life are quoted in D. Crouch, *The Image of Aristocracy in Britain*, 215–16.

[276] *GRA* 1.474–7. Robert went on pilgrimage in late 1086, and renounced the world 3 years later, on his return, *GRA* 2.244.

[277] Keats-Rohan, 363.   [278] I. J. Sanders, *English Baronies* (Oxford, 1963), 120.

[279] OV 3.148, 1094.   [280] OV 5.314–15.

[281] *Regesta* 1, no. 379; *Liber Vitae*, 28v–29r.

[282] *English Episcopal Acta I, Lincoln 1067–1085*, ed. D. M. Smith (London, 1980) no. 2, 2–3, possibly *c*.1092–3, see editor's note; Abels, 'Sheriffs, lord-seeking and the Norman settlement of the south-east Midlands', *ANS*, 19 (1996), 36.

[283] Keats-Rohan, 194.

[284] E. Mason, 'Brothers at court: Urse de Abetot and Robert Dispenser', *ANS*, 31 (2008), 81–3.

[285] *Westminster Abbey Charters, 1066–c.1214*, ed. E. Mason, no. 488; Mason, 'Brothers at court', 77.

Rannulf Flambard ordered that he be carried into the church and, before many witnesses, 'by placing his ring upon the altar', restored the lands and liberties that he, 'seduced by greed', had taken away.[286] Yet the lands concerned are in fact thought to have been worth only £10. The nave of the great cathedral had demanded funding, and Rannulf's final reputation at Durham was as the great-hearted benefactor of Durham's golden age.[287]

Earlier rulers had repented fruitfully and their examples were widely proclaimed. Notwithstanding their conquests and treasure-seeking, King Cnut and Queen Emma sought to be depicted in the act of donating a great cross to the altar of New Minster, with attendant angels descending from Christ bringing a crown for Cnut and a veil for Emma.[288] The whole forms the frontispiece for a Book of Life wherein the names of friends and patrons, brethren and monks were inscribed, as its preface affirms, so that their commemoration be performed daily in holy mass and psalms, and that 'by making this record on earth in this written form, they may be inscribed on the page of the heavenly book'.[289] The royal couple's contemporary representation was not solely an imperial portrayal of powerful patrons. It represents Christ in Judgement as much as in Majesty: Mary and St Peter, with his key, intercede with Christ on the royal behalf.[290] Christ holds the heavenly Book of Life; a monk holds the earthly *Liber Vitae*. Confirming this theme, following overleaf, are line-drawings depicting the Last Judgement in three tiers: in the two first St Peter welcomes the saved, and uses his key to fend off the Devil (who brandishes an open book); in the lowest tier, an archangel locks the gates of Hell while a devil within forces men backwards into a monstrous mouth. The *Liber Vitae* continues with the names of kings, æthelings, bishops, ealdormen, bene-factors, and those in confraternity, including Rannulf Flambard and Hugh de Port. Other Anglo-Saxon depictions of Christ in a mandorla were similarly judgemental (see Figure 4).[291] Christ was the Just Judge and the King of Kings, and hence, the judge of kings.

Awareness of Judgement Day moved other great and unscrupulous men to penitential action. Earl Godwine, king-maker and assassin of princes, gave to Old Minster 'many gifts of ornaments and rents of land' for the redemption of his soul.[292] When in 1086 the Conqueror freed formally, with his great seal, eight hides of Westminster's manor of Pyrford from all customary dues and taxes, in the

---

[286] Symeon, 274–9; Offler, *Episcopal Charters*, nos 24, 25. Similarly Walkelin, *Ann Winton*, 39.

[287] Southern, *Humanism*, 202, 204.   [288] *Liber Vitae*, f.6r.

[289] *Liber Vitae*, 82–3, f.13, the corollary being that 'whosoever was not found written in the Book of Life was cast into the fire', *Revelation*, 20:15.

[290] J. Gerchow, 'Prayers for King Cnut: the liturgical commemoration of a conqueror', in C. Hicks (ed.), *England in the Eleventh Century*, Harlaxton Medieval Studies, vol. 2 (Stamford, 1992), 219–38, esp. 220–30.

[291] A Psalter miniature shows Christ holding a book and a scroll reading '*Ego sum Deus qui reddet uniquique juxta opus est*', facing Psalm 100, G. Henderson, 'The idiosyncrasy of late Anglo-Saxon religious imagery', in Hicks (ed.), *England in the Eleventh Century*, 241–2, plate 20. See Figure 4 from *Aelfric's Homilies*.

[292] *Vita Ædw*, 30.

writ issued just after the assembly of the Domesday information, it was done 'for the safety of my soul'.[293] Whilst the Conqueror had always held Westminster, founded by King Edward and the setting of William's own coronation, in esteem, we have seen that he had treated Harold's spiritual base at Waltham Holy Cross vindictively, handing over a large portion of its endowment to the bishop of Durham. Yet although Rufus further denuded Waltham of its treasures, he seems, according to the house tradition, to have later relented somewhat. Though no writ survives, its chronicle reported that William Rufus,

> to regain the favour of the Crucified One, whom we do not doubt he had greatly offended when he committed his acts of plunder, confirmed his endowment upon the church with his own charter. Under the proclamation of the above-mentioned anathema, and in the presence of the archbishops, bishops and clergy, he publicly confirmed it. Let his successors take warning . . . [294]

Nonetheless, the Waltham canons were compelled to pay annually towards works on Durham castle up until 1100–1101.[295] However, the canons still possessed their traditional powers: after Geoffrey de Mandeville had set fire to the great house he held in Waltham, burning the canons' houses also, the canons took down their famous cross in the hope that 'that wealthy man would be pinched with his conscience'. At that very hour, the earl received a mortal wound outside the castle of Burwell.[296] Even William II was mindful of God's anger, for a time at least: his seal became the first known to put 'by the grace of God' before the title 'king of the English'.

The presence of the shire and hundreds at the Domesday Inquiry outwardly conformed to due English process of conciliation and reconciliation. Disputes were ended when all had taken the oath, and the judgement had been carried out. Yet the Inquiry acted largely as a possessory assize and, in particular cases, brought merely temporary peace.[297] Domesday recounts the case of a priest and onetime freeholder whose tenure had been hawked from landholder to landholder during William's reign and whose ownership remained disputed. It concludes: 'the King's barons effected peace between Roger Bigod and Earl Hugh when they came into the County; and so he [the priest] shall be at peace until there is a judgement'.[298] The case shows how conflicting claims in the localities between newcomers arose from overlapping or conflicting royal instructions, and that final resolution had to wait for the king's court. But disclosure had been effected, the shires had been traversed—their men required to swear assent—and the Conqueror's peace asserted. The Inquiry had enabled the conquering elite to transform itself into the establishment.

[293] *Acta* no. 326; GDB:32b (SUR:6,5).   [294] *Waltham Chronicle*, 60–1.
[295] *Regesta* 2, no. 526.
[296] *Waltham Chronicle*, 78–9.   [297] Similarly, Roffe, 'Inquests in Medieval England', 18–24.
[298] LDB:377a (SUF:16,34).

The king might well have intended that his coinage should publicize his changed relationship with his taxpayers. Coinage projected the king's image at first hand: because old issues of coins had to be reminted, everyone needed to examine the design closely. In practical terms its weight and quality exemplified how his authority stretched to the smallest detail. And much symbolism was patent on the coins. On all types was the king's bust, with his name and title and a small cross on the surround; the reverse legend had a cross, the name of the moneyer, and of the mint. The issue most likely to be contemporaneous with the crisis of 1084–6 testifies to a tight uniform control of the weight of coins, and its lettering proclaimed a policy change with the insertion in the quarters of the cross on the reverse, the four letters *Paxs*. Its very spelling was significant: the presence of the 'S', like the insertion of the 'C' on Edward's issue, *Pacx*, was perhaps a variant of the Chrismon known from charters, representing the XPS or XPC, the standard Graeco-Latin abbreviation for 'Christus'. Thus these legends may be interpreted as 'a combined invocation of Christ and peace'.[299]

In earlier crises, William had successfully bought off previous Danish fleets led by Cnut, when prince, and his father, King Swein. Whereas these actions were a realistic recognition of his regime's instability, they were arguably not the best of signals to a rival. The particularly large coin issue of *Paxs* of the mid 1080s may well have been designed in order to have the silver ready to act quickly yet again. During the reign of their father, Cnut and his brother had arrived in 1069 with a fleet of 240 ships, which joined a rising of Edgar Ætheling and the earls Gospatric and Waltheof focused on York and Yorkshire, where the local population, many of whom had Danish affiliations, welcomed them. Their success had encouraged risings as far afield as Somerset, Shropshire, and Cheshire, supported in their turn by the Welsh princes. But by Christmas 1069, William had pacified Lincolnshire, crossed England to quell the rebellion in the western borderlands, and returned to York (which the Danes were attempting to reoccupy) to devastate its hinterland. The Danish princes and fleet, seeing the defeat of their English allies, accepted a bribe and left the region. Nevertheless, in the spring of 1070, King Swein of Denmark himself invaded, once more receiving local support, in particular from Hereward and his followers, who took Peterborough. William this time opened negotiations early, and was again successful.[300] Cnut fleet's reappeared in 1075, again in support of internal rebellion, but petered out after successful intervention by Lanfranc, presumably involving payment.[301] By 1085, however, William was an older man on whom over forty years of campaigning had taken its toll and, after

---

[299] S. Keynes, 'An interpretation of the *Pacx, Pax* and *Paxs* pennies', *ASE*, 7 (1978), 165–73, esp. 171–2; S.768; cf. the launch of the *Agnus Dei* penny of Athelred II discussed in the context of a great meeting of the witan and bishops at Pentecost, 1008, M. K. Lawson, 'Archbishop Wulfstan and the homiletic element in the laws of Æthelred II and Canute', in A. R. Rumble (ed.), *The Reign of Cnut: King of England, Denmark and Norway* (Leicester, 1994), 152–4.

[300] Douglas, *Conqueror*, 218–22.

[301] Lanfranc's Letters, no. 35; H. E. J. Cowdrey, *Lanfranc: Scholar, Monk, and Archbishop* (Oxford, 2003), 188–92; *ASC*, 1075, D, E.

high taxes and more confiscations, many men had even less affinity with his harsh and alien rule.

For the Danes, England offered the lure of a wealthy and well-organized country, tenuously held by a newly imposed class of landholders. In fact, the prospects for a Danish principality, certainly in the north and east of England, appeared high. In 1013, Northumbria, Lindsey, the Five Boroughs, and the eastern Danelaw had readily accepted an earlier King Svein of Denmark as king; and a separate northern kingdom for Cnut had been mooted in 1016.[302] William was known to be apprehensive that 'one of the Danes, Norwegians or Scots, who used to sail up to York in their attacks on the realm, might be made king, by the archbishop of York and the fickle and treacherous Yorkshiremen'.[303] (The Danelaw was both distinct and more advanced in some craft techniques and trading matters.[304]) The venture certainly offered an exciting prospect for his followers: at the very least, there was the lucrative prospect that they would be bought off again. But, in 1085, as the Danish king became preoccupied with relations with Schleswig, he became widely unpopular at home: to Cnut's taxation for the fleet and his serious debasement of the coinage—worse in western Denmark—was added his lack of action, the imprisonment of his brother, Olaf, who supported the English expedition, and finally, the disbanding of the fleet itself. In the following year Cnut experienced open revolt as he journeyed around Jutland.[305] Thus, Cnut was assassinated in July 1086 and his brother Olaf proclaimed king. It seems possible to me that William, always a schemer as well as a fighter, had taken pre-emptive action even earlier this time, by paying the dissidents to act: a speculation given some substance by the curious numismatic fact, otherwise unexplained, that there survives in Denmark and Scandinavia a larger quantity of the *Paxs* issue of English coin than any other type of William's reign.[306]

As, in this emergency, William had brought to this country 'a larger force of mounted men and soldiers than he had ever brought before' to meet the invasion, a large issue of coin was also needed to pay these mercenaries, who remained resident until it became clear that the invasion threat had ended.[307] But whatever desperate measures William might take in an emergency, he clearly could not sustain a forced rule indefinitely. He now sought to reinforce his land settlement with the oaths of English jurors and to obtain full information about the revenues in the possession of his own followers. The 1085 Christmas council consideration of 'how this

---

[302] *ASC*, 1013, 1016.   [303] *Hugh Chantor*, 3.

[304] e.g. pottery, D. H. Brown, 'Bound by tradition: A study of pottery in Anglo-Saxon England', *Anglo-Saxon Studies in Archaeology and History*, 12 (2003), 21–7, at 25. On trade, the prosperity of northern England is portrayed in P. Sawyer, *The Wealth of Anglo-Saxon England* (Oxford, 2013), 87–96.

[305] I thank Jonathan Grove for the point on coinage debasement and for navigating me through recent literature on Cnut's reign (1080–6); P. Gazzoli, 'Anglo-Danish connections and the Origins of the Cult of Knud', *Selected Papers from the Inaugural St. Magnus Conference 2011, Journal of the North Atlantic*, Special vol. 4, (2013): 69–76; *Vitae Sanctorum Danorum*, ed. Gertz, 102.

[306] On coins, Metcalf, *Atlas*, 188.   [307] *ASC*, 1085; *HistAbbend* 2, 16–17.

Figure 7. The Iron Age hill fort at Old Sarum, with Norman motte atop, engraved by David Lucas (1802–81), 1833, mezzotint engraving after John Constable. By permission of the Fitzwilliam Museum, University of Cambridge.

country was occupied or with what sort of people' could well have addressed the Scandinavian affiliations of eastern and north-eastern England and the long-term bases of his rule.[308] It was, arguably, adjudged time for a policy of 'PAXS'.

Old Sarum was a site to conjure apocalyptic expectations (see Figure 7). Only some twenty or so miles from Winchester, the major highway led past no less than five places of execution.[309] With inherited Iron Age defensive earthworks of a truly formidable scale, it remains today a dramatic fortified site. The steeply sided outer ramparts encircle one of the largest hill-forts of its kind in England, no less than seventy-two acres (twenty-nine hectares).[310] Newly strengthened by the Normans, it had historic attributes. The great earthwork had been a place of retreat and resort during previous Danish raids—a literal last-ditch protecting the local inhabitants—and had been the site of a mint in the difficult times after the 1003 Danish raids on Exeter and Wilton. Following William I's decision to build a royal castle there, more steep-sided earthworks were thrown up in the middle of the space enclosed by the Iron Age ramparts to create a large motte and inner bailey; within the hill-fort,

---

[308] *ASC*, 1085.

[309] A. Reynolds, 'Crime and punishment', in H. Hamerow, D. Hinton, and S. Crawford (eds), *The Oxford Handbook of Anglo-Saxon Archaeology* (Oxford, 2011), 902.

[310] For the following on Old Salisbury, see J. McNeill, *Old Sarum*, English Heritage Guidebooks (London, 2006), 1–40, at 23.

sub-ramparts divided off stables and ancillary buildings, probably topped by palisades, and with wooden structures to provide shelter to create an outer bailey. A cathedral was begun within the hill-fort in 1075 and, although not consecrated until 1092, it was already the focus for educated canons whose scribal skills were called upon to assist in creating the Exon Domesday, perhaps even to organize material for Great Domesday itself. The site lent itself to an element of coercion: once the gates to the single manifest entrance were swung shut,[311] it was claustrophobic indeed. As the site of an assembly it was not one from which contumacious persons could storm out or summon reinforcements from outside.

POST MORTEM

William's last injuries gave him the lingering chance to forgive some of his enemies and release them from captivity, and to reiterate the faults of others whom he could not forgive,[312] albeit the king lamented that events had given him insufficient time for reformation of life.[313] His obsequies epitomized his worst fears. Uncertainty over the succession meant that as soon as the king was dead, those surrounding him deserted immediately. Orderic recounts: 'the wealthier among them quickly mounted their horses and rode off as fast as they could to protect their properties. The lesser attendants, seeing that their superiors had absconded, seized the arms, vessels, clothing, linen, and all the royal furnishings, and hurried away leaving the king's body almost naked on the floor.' In Rouen, where he had died, the news caused chaos, and no provision was made for his body until a knight volunteered to shoulder the expense. When clerical authority was eventually established, his body was taken by boat to Caen for burial in the monastery that he had founded. But the great procession that the abbot of St Stephen's had assembled in Caen to meet the bier dispersed to deal with a raging fire, which caused great destruction, and only the monks remained to complete the half-finished office, and escort the body to the abbey church. Eventually, the great men of Normandy, including the newly released Odo, gathered formally for his funeral and the bishop of Évreux gave a long and eloquent valedictory—lauding the greatness, peace, and justice that William had brought to Normandy and his defence of churchmen and civilians, and calling on the congregation to intercede with the Almighty for the dead duke and for forgiveness of any wrongs he had done. At this, one man came forward and, asserting that the ground where William had built the abbey had been forcibly taken from his father, demanded its return, 'forbidding in God's name that the body of this robber be covered by earth that is mine or buried in my inheritance'.[314] After the bishops and magnates had pacified the man, verified his story, and offered him monetary compensation—£100 of silver was given at the request of Henry,

---

[311] McNeill, *Old Sarum*, 20–1.   [312] OV 4.90–101.
[313] *GRA* 1.510–11.   [314] OV 4.100–7, at 103 and 107.

'the only one of his children present'—the service continued. But the sarcophagus was too small for the swollen corpse that had been crammed into it and the corpse burst open.[315] Even incense could not conceal the stench, whereupon the service was hastily concluded, and everyone hurried from the church. Orderic, forever the monk, drew the sombre moral that oppression and robbery were in vain: for 'he who ruled over so many towns and villages lacked plot of free earth for his own burial'.[316] It was long known that anointing with myrrh and aloes gave the body considerable immunity from decay,[317] and the preservative qualities of honey have been traditionally recognized: William patently had not received this care for the revered.[318]

Some bishops who were key to Norman operations also suffered disturbing manifestations at the last. In 1091, Geoffrey, William's work-horse on tenure, saw his own lavishly embellished cathedral of Coutances struck by lightning and earthquake shortly after his retirement there: he died fifteen months later, still making efforts to expedite its restoration.[319] In 1092, Domesday commissioner Bishop Remigius of Lincoln died two days before the consecration of his new cathedral.[320] The cathedral at Salisbury, modelled somewhat on the lines of Queen Matilda's foundation, Holy Trinity, Caen, in particular its unusual cruciform piers, was consecrated in 1092 by two bishops who were integral to the whole Domesday operation—Osmund, its bishop and William I's former chancellor, and his treasurer, Walkelin of Winchester.[321] Four days after the ceremony, the cathedral was struck by lighting that badly damaged the walls and the tower roof.[322]

DOMESDAY'S AFTERMATH

William's ambition, vindictiveness, and arbitrary cruelty—extreme even by the standards of the time—had meant violent death, mutilation, or famine for many. The English inhabitants of 1085–6 knew from bitter experience, however, that two claimants meant war: and, whoever came out victor, little would redound to their personal benefit. The fate of those who had rebelled after Harold's death had demonstrated forcibly that it was the better course to acquiesce in the rule of the strong, albeit tyrannical, incumbent. The citizens of Exeter had rebelled early against William, but all their well-defended efforts had come to nothing except humiliation, with the result that, in the subsequent widespread rebellions of 1069–70, Exeter then supported the king.[323] However, despite William's actions

---

[315] *GRA* 1.512–13.   [316] OV 4.109.
[317] Rollason, *Saints and Relics in Anglo-Saxon England*, 38–9.
[318] Contrast, *Life of Ailred of Rievaulx*, ed. F. M. Powicke (London, 1950), 63.
[319] J. Le Patourel, 'Geoffrey of Montbray, bishop of Coutances', *EHR*, 69 (1944), 156–8.
[320] *GP*, 313; HH, 416–17.
[321] R. Gem, 'The first Romanesque cathedral at Salisbury', in E. Fernie and P. Crossley (eds), *Medieval Architecture and its Intellectual Context* (London, 1990), 9–18.
[322] *GRA* 1.568–9.   [323] OV 2.210–13; 228.

in the north of England, he was reputed to have been occasionally mindful that cultivators were the suppliers of the silver that he rated so highly. While he waited in Normandy for the right opportunity to launch his invasion of England, he, unsurprisingly, restrained his army: 'no one was permitted to seize anything; the cattle and flocks . . . grazed safely whether in the fields or on the waste. The crops waited unharmed for the scythe of the harvester . . . neither trampled by the proud stampede of horsemen, nor cut down by foragers'. And William of Poitiers insists that, on conquering England, William initially 'showed clemency to all, especially to the common people'.[324] The same eulogist attributes idealized sentiments to William on several occasions for which there is almost no other evidence; however, even the Anglo-Saxon Chronicler, who never flinched from describing William's avarice, records that, before he died, William asked that a hundred pounds of money be sent into each shire, 'to be distributed to poor men for his soul'.[325]

Through Domesday William surely went a considerable way in his last months towards redeeming his historical reputation. If William, in accord with the principle of the coin design *Paxs*, sought the backing of hearts and minds through sheer force of necessity, he was in part successful. The association between coinage and defensive security was strong and traditional.[326] Their hearts he never obtained; but he and two of his sons gained support enough amongst the lesser military classes and toleration enough amongst payers of dues and taxpayers, to ensure the survival of their regime for their lifetimes. With its foundation in Anglo-Saxon fiscal documents and in its role in the Checking of Officials, Domesday Book effectively reinforced the principle that he who held land was responsible for paying the tax, and the record resisted the formation of great immunities in taxation and justice to which feudal societies often succumbed.

Somehow or another, the later medieval image evolved of Domesday as a defence against unreasonable lordship. We have seen that from time to time in Domesday itself objections to the cupidity of the king's deputies were recorded, and that probing on this front was incorporated into the final Domesday; but was that sufficient to earn it this reputation?

Peasants in the thirteenth and fourteenth centuries obviously thought, mostly mistakenly, that the large sector Domesday describes as 'King's Land' afforded their inhabitants some protection: the puzzle is how this faith came about and persisted for some time until bitter experience proved it to be often ill-founded.[327] During the twelfth and thirteenth centuries, the royal fisc asserted the right to tax at will tenants on former royal demesne land, ring-fencing these lands from other taxation and services in order to render its own tallages more productive. On this 'ancient demesne' of the crown—lands once in royal hands—it was later argued that the

---

[324] *WP*, 102, 162.   [325] *ASC*, 1087.

[326] Cf. Æthelred's issue of *Agnus Dei* pennies amidst the crises of the beginning of the eleventh century.

[327] Elizabeth Hallam charts Domesday's complicated role in this intriguing topic, Hallam, 49–109. She also maps the ancient demesne at different periods, Hallam, 77–94.

peasantry were not 'villeins', but 'villein-sokemen', subject to royal tallage and to a higher level of aids, but protected from any increase in their services by intermediate lords.[328] Yet, inhabiting ancient demesne proved disadvantageous when the king wished to undertake military expeditions, as it could be tallaged at will.[329] Before the great revolt of 1381, villein tenants outside and inside the former royal demesne paid for official copies of extracts from Domesday to find out if their manor qualified for the protection from raised services: between 1376 and 1378 writs were issued on behalf of no fewer than forty villages hoping to obtain such exemptions, and landlordly fears of such actions formed part of a parliamentary petition of 1377.[330]

Since Domesday records almost nothing on manorial services, present or absent,[331] and it notes sokemen as a class in eastern England only, many investigations of ancient demesne produced nothing to assist the proof that such villeins were the heirs of villein sokemen: in the words of an official record of these cases, Domesday 'does nothing for them', *nil fac' pro eis*.[332] Yet tradition somehow insisted that on royal lands no unreasonable demands were sanctioned in that Book and that their work-force at one time had had acknowledged economic and legal standing. It is just possible that certain Domesday data provided some grounds for this trusted tradition: in the questioning of the 'renders' obtained from former free tenants that were particularly a feature in southern and eastern counties; and, also, and much more widespread, in the plough-teams it confirmed to the peasant population.

Domesday put a seal on William's new establishment and took away any hope of a reversal for the heirs of the greater Edwardian landholders and their thegnly compatriots and companions. But, unlike other rentals and landlordly documents, it at least enumerated and confirmed survivors in the peasant classes—and their newly down-graded recruits from the freeholders—in their possession of their ploughs and plough oxen, their valuable working capital. (Nevertheless, this division of these assets might also have had an ulterior fiscal motive: besides preventing the magnates from avoiding tax on their demesne and shifting their taxation onto the peasantry, their record would also have made the latter's fiscal responsibility inescapable.) Those who had survived this far as freeholders, farmers, or rent-payers of some sort were, moreover, more numerous than Great Domesday always shows.[333] Contemporary records from Rochester Cathedral, Evesham Abbey, and Yorkshire, and also Little Domesday, confirm what we suspect from Great Domesday, that those who acknowledged new lords and even 'bought

---

[328] By the fourteenth century, it appears that land in the king's hands in Domesday and ancient demesne were largely considered one and the same, Hoyt, *The Royal Demesne*, 171–207. References made to Domesday by peasant movements are discussed in Faith, 'Peasant Ideology', 43–72.

[329] Hallam, 97–9.   [330] Quoted in Faith, 'Peasant Ideology', 44, and discussed thereafter.

[331] It records the light ploughing services of *villani* of Leominster, GDB:180a (HEF:1,10a).

[332] Faith, 'Peasant Ideology', 50.

[333] J. F. R. Walmsley, 'The "censarii" of Burton Abbey and the Domesday population', *N. Staffordshire Journal of Field Studies*, 8 (1968), 73–80; Harvey 1988, discusses Domesday's 'missing' categories, 46–9.

back' or redeemed their lands were permitted to continue as tenants of manors or rent-payers.[334] Questions of legality apart, the newcomers, in their turn, were dependent upon the expertise of locals who knew and worked the land in order to obtain the large agricultural profits they coveted. Domesday's record indicates that the plough-teams attributed to the manorial peasants exceeded those owned directly by the demesnes of the great lords by more than 265 per cent.[335] Perhaps the upper echelons of the peasantry regarded its evidence as a source of inspiration because it became a possible way of taking on the power of their landlords by means that their lords had to recognize: the source of their own initial right in the land. Or perhaps the name alone, more than the contents, led men to trust Domesday Book, as invoking the day when all wrongs would be righted.[336]

EPITHET OR EPITAPH?

'To me belongs yesterday. I know tomorrow'
Ancient Egyptian Book of the Dead, from Spell 17,
first to second millennium BC

Domesday was essentially 'the king's charter' and 'the king's book of the treasury'. In the course of producing it, those responsible had checked and recorded tenure; they had checked and preserved data on taxation ratings, and produced other data for fiscal reassessment; and they had obtained, for the first time, the annual returns from landholding that the crown drew upon in vacancies, escheats, and exchanges. Furthermore, the Domesday Inquiry had made tenants-in-chief account for their lands and royal officials account for their actions. The final product existed as the foundation text for the new order in general and the Exchequer in particular. These three areas of competence—taxation, royal revenues, and a court of tenure—were thereby secured together, within the competence of the Exchequer. The Domesday Inquiry effectively assembled data for the three spheres intended—and much ancillary material on resources besides.

We should not be mesmerized by the data's due process through the shire and hundred courts. Aside from the centripetal forces that such surveys inevitably strengthened, legitimate order was exactly the impression the Conqueror sought. By citing approved 'antecessors', Domesday gave the impression of a changeover based upon some sort of principled order: precisely the intention when enlisting the

---

[334] Essential for this subject is Williams, *The English*, esp. ch. 5 'The Survivors'; also H. Tsurushima, 'The fraternity of Rochester Cathedral Priory *c*.1100', *ANS*, 14 (1991), 313–37.

[335] Domesday records 22,155 demesne ploughs, compared with 57,344 ploughs held by 'the men', with the AHRC project calculating 1,763 ploughs on small independent free-holdings—which are under-recorded in Domesday.

[336] G. R. Owst, *Literature and Pulpit in the Middle Ages* (London, 1961), 294–331, 540; Hallam, 104.

presence of 'Englishmen' from the hundreds and shires in the exercise. Yet wherever there is local evidence additional to the regular order of the record, a rather different story often unfurls.

We do not know when the record first started to be called 'Domesday' amongst the English. However, by the time the English name was picked up by the elite circle of bishops and their relatives who ran the Exchequer's affairs, the concept of a *iudicium dei* no longer favoured the Norman ruling house. William II, like his brother Richard much earlier, was shot and killed while hunting in the New Forest: retribution, in John of Worcester's eyes, for their father's action in reserving an additional 15,000–20,000 acres for the royal pursuit.[337] The three sons of the Conqueror who survived into maturity had persistently contested their inheritance amongst themselves, and the youngest, Henry, had imprisoned the eldest, Robert, for the rest of his long life and taken over his dukedom. Whilst Henry I's wise marriage to Matilda, daughter of Queen Margaret of Scotland—the exemplary sister of Edgar Ætheling—had temporarily papered over some of the cracks in the Norman takeover, Henry himself, having fathered no less than twenty illegitimate children, lost his sole legitimate son in the White Ship disaster, leaving only a daughter born in wedlock.[338] True, by that time, it was clear that the Norman landed settlement had become irreversible—not the case in 1085; but, after Henry's death, the Conqueror's heritage had been in dispute, and although the rival candidates were both direct descendants of the Conqueror, the direct male line no longer ruled in England or Normandy.[339] Only after years of conflict was the alien regime stabilized under Matilda's son, Henry II, who having some blood of the Anglo-Saxon royal house in his veins was greeted as 'the corner-stone which bound together the two walls of the English and Norman race',[340] and who felt it politic to permit the canonisation of King Edward in 1161.

But there was to be no question of this nod of acknowledgement to an English inheritance imposing practical constraints upon the tenure of land. Henry II soon banned Englishmen, but not others, from bringing claims of land based on seisin of an ancestor from any time before the death of Henry I.[341] Richard fitzNigel's authoritative verdict on Domesday's name was not offered without purpose. Whilst the Book's allocation of individual manors did, and still could, receive challenge, it was crucial for the Exchequer that he should give Domesday's designation the

---

[337] *JW* 3.92–3; *GRA* 1.502–5; F. H. Baring, 'The making of the New Forest', *EHR*, 16 (1901), 427–38.

[338] *GND* 2.249, n. 6.

[339] The Empress Matilda, daughter of Henry I was, through her mother, descended from Margaret, sister of Edgar Ætheling. Stephen was also a grandchild of the Conqueror, through his mother; his wife gave his sons descent from Margaret also.

[340] Aelred of Rievaulx, 'Vita Edwardi Regis et Confessoris', *Historiae Anglicanae Scriptores Decem*, ed. R. Twysden (London, 1652), col. 370.

[341] *statutum meum*, writ of Henry II addressed to his sheriffs and officials of England, 1155 × 1162; Galbraith, 'Royal charters to Winchester', *EHR*, 35 (1920), no. 43, 398–9; Van Caenegem, *Writs*, no. 169.

explicatory spin that the record was unchallengeable and its decisions 'unalterable': there must be no questioning the Norman invasion settlement.

Churchmen, like Orderic, continued to hope and trust that 'the judgement of God, who gives mighty protection to his Church everywhere', meant the downfall of unjust claims.[342] Domesday's English name probably remained unrecorded for so long because no contemporary senior official—all clerics, mostly bishops—would have adopted the name that designated the ruthless methods that gained Englishmen's endorsement of Domesday's authority, nor given official voice to the anathema that the name 'Domesday' willed upon the perpetrators and their heirs. It remained a deed without a name. Richard fitzNigel, educated amongst the historic archives of Ely, and conscious of the importance of his own dynasty and of his king's achievements, was surely aware of the name's English implications: his father Nigel, the treasurer of Henry I, and bishop of Ely, 1133–9, was nephew to the great chancellor, Roger of Salisbury; and Richard himself, as royal treasurer and arch-deacon of Ely, had administered the diocese of Ely from around 1165, becoming bishop of London in 1189.[343] As the author of the 'Dialogue of the Exchequer', he maintained that it was only 'metaphorically' that Domesday was so called by the English, because 'its decisions cannot be quashed or set aside without punishment' nor evaded by 'any skilful subterfuge'. He then made a second attempt at vindica-tion by identifying the name with the Exchequer rather than with Englishmen: 'we have called it the Book of Judgement, not because it contains decisions on difficult points, but because its decisions, like those of the Last Judgement, are unalter-able'.[344] Doubtless because his mother was English,[345] he was at pains to by-pass the conceptual link the English made between their loss in this world and its rightful consequences in the next. But, to Englishmen, the book's name signified the appointed time when the English had been compelled to give evidence on the tenures of 'the day on which King Edward was alive and dead' simply and solely to authenticate the authority of the current holder; with no restitution of their lands following. The awful record legitimated their losses, its name reflecting the dilem-mas and *iudicium dei* that witnesses had faced, and the finality of the land transfer to which they were solemnly and irrevocably sworn. Inherent, too, in the great land-book's English style was, as tradition demanded, the Judgement in the next world awaiting those who seized land illicitly.

---

[342] OV 2.120–2.   [343] *Dialogus*, xiv–xv, 27, 42.
[344] *Dialogus*, 63–4.   [345] *Dialogus*, xiv.

Index

Abels, Richard 254
Abingdon Abbey 20, 24, 26–7, 28, 67, 72–3, 74, 101–2, 165–6, 195, 231, 251–2, 273, 274, 275, 276, 277n, 279, 307–8
adoption by weapons 293–4
Ælfric, Abbot of Eynsham 11, 188, 208, 287, 290
Ælfric the reeve 189, 201, 253–4, 255, 263
Æthelwig, Abbot of Evesham 155–6, 307
Anselm, St, Abbot of Bec, archbishop of Canterbury 42, 46, 47–8, 58, 91, 112, 118, 120, 121, 275–6, 308, 314
   attitude to Conquest 275
   relations with Ranulf Flambard 118, 120–1
   relations with William I 46, 314
   on subtenancies 308
Æthelred, King 13, 143n, 149, 237, 273, 278, 288, 291, 298, 324n
   charters 18, 273
   coinage and weights 134–5, 138–9, 146, 154, 319n, 324n
   other legislation 38, 82, 149, 187–8
   taxation and tribute 28, 134, 211–12
antecessor 45, 78, 259, 264, 284–5, 305, 307, 326–7
arable 118, 130, 134, 176, 177, 180, 185, 187–8, 206–7, 223–5
articles of enquiry, see terms of reference
Arundel (Sussex) 59
assarting 220
Augustine, St 1, 95, 103

barones regis/king's barons 27, 63, 110–11, 220, 262, 265–6
Bartlett, Robert 277–8, 282–3, 286
Bates, David 22, 44
Bath Abbey 67, 126, 181, 195, 216n
Bath, borough 241
Battle Abbey 128, 137 (table), 187–8, 216n, 218, 220, 229–30, 297
Bayeux Tapestry (embroidery) 24, 108, 292, 293–7, 300, 303
Bayeux, cathedral 41, 111, 116, 150–1, 184
Bayeux, bishop, see Odo
Bec, Abbey of 41–2, 46, 316
Bede, Venerable 103, 271
Bedfordshire 51, 88, 255–6
Bisson, Thomas 147, 259, 268
Blair, John 60, 62n, 170, 224n
Book of Winchester 7–9
book-land 275–6; see also charters; land-grants
bordars xxi, 83
boroughs 63, 96–7, 125, 138, 143–5, 147–8, 150–2, 172, 212, 228, 230, 237, 239–50

borough courts 73, 144
customary dues 8, 71, 91, 144, 242–50, 261–2, 265, 313
customs 242, 245, 249–50
Domesday surveys of 242–50, 304, 313
farm 119, 242, 245, 250
Bosham 24, 159, 167, 294
Bristol 73–4, 241, 250, 260
Bridbury, A. R. 164–5
bridge-building and repair 122, 149, 227–30
Brooks, Nicholas 229–30, 287
burgesses and boroughs 73, 125, 132, 145, 149, 151, 228, 241–50, 258, 260, 284, 304, 313
   French burgesses and boroughs 237, 243, 248–9

Cambridge 135n, 243, 245, 248, 267
Canterbury, St Augustine's 57, 72–3, 80, 105, 116, 220, 263, 271n, 280, 282, 294
cartage 230–2, 245, 254
carrucate, see ploughland
chamberlains 20, 22–3, 97–8, 116, 127, 165–6, 173, 215, 223, 234, 250, 256, 261, 263, 265, 269, 316
chancellor 20–3, 33, 41–2, 47, 95, 110, 114–16, 127–8, 328
chancery, see writing office
charters 2, 12, 18–30, 43–4, 58, 85, 94n, 105–6, 110, 118, 120, 145, 157, 171, 187, 194, 205–6, 214, 272–7, 284, 293, 304, 316, 318–19, 327
   Domesday Book as the king's charter 236, 272–3, 276–7, 318, 326, 327
Cheshire 64, 84, 88–90, 93, 161n, 217, 319
Chester in Domesday 147, 170, 230
   diocese of Lichfield/Chester 38, 59, 72, 196, 226, 291, 316
Chibnall, M. 129
Chichester 72, 180
circuits 34, 40, 51, 53–4, 61, 84, 87–90, 96, 100–1, 112–13, 124–5, 204, 215, 236, 311, 313
   data varying by circuits 89, 161–3, 169–70, 182, 191, 207, 213, 218, 221, 224, 226, 249
Clarke, Howard B. 26n, 69, 245n
Clifford Castle, Herefs. 244
Cnut the Great, king of Denmark 1019–1035, king of Norway 1028–1035, king of all England 1016–1035: 6, 12–14, 15, 38, 71, 134–5, 208–9n, 211n, 211–12, 215, 237, 276, 292, 297, 299, 316–17
   charter 30
   legislation 63, 73n, 76, 82n, 134, 143n, 169n, 237–8, 276, 280n, 282n, 308